Family Law
in Africa

JCL Studies in Comparative Law: Second Series

Series Editors

Professor William E. Butler

Professor Michael Palmer

1. W. E. Butler and O. V. Kresin (eds.), *Discovering the Unexpected: Comparative Legal Studies in Eastern and Central Europe* (Clark, New Jersey, Talbot Publishing, 2021). ISBN 9781616196554

2. Simon Palmer and Zhai Xiaobo (eds.), *Bentham Around the World* (Clark, New Jersey, Talbot Publishing, 2021). ISBN 9781616196561

3. O. V. Kresin, *Comparative Law in Warsaw: 1800-1835*, transl. W. E. Butler (Clark, New Jersey, Talbot Publishing, 2022) ISBN 9781616196585

4. W. E. Butler and O. V. Kresin (eds.) *The Comparative Method in the Science of Law* by Lev Rebet (Clark, New Jersey, Talbot Publishing, 2022) ISBN 9781616196653

5. Horst Dippel, *Modern Constitutionalism*, 2 vols. (Clark, New Jersey, Talbot Publishing, 2022) ISBN 9781616196769

6. Stephan Meder, *Legal Machines* (Clark, New Jersey, Talbot Publishing, 2023) ISBN 9781616196813

7. Ama F. Hammond, Folashade Rose Adegbite, Maame Yaa A. Mensa-Bonsu, Prosper Batariwah (eds.), *Family Law in Africa: Perspectives on Selected Systems of Marriage* (Clark, New Jersey, Talbot Publishing, 2023) ISBN 9781616196844

STUDIES IN COMPARATIVE LAW
JCL
SECOND SERIES

Family Law *in* Africa

PERSPECTIVES ON SELECTED SYSTEMS OF MARRIAGE

EDITED BY
Ama F. Hammond, Folashade Rose Adegbite, Maame Yaa A. Mensa-Bonsu & Prosper Batariwah

TALBOT
PUBLISHING
Clark, New Jersey

ISBN: 978-1-61619-684-4

TALBOT PUBLISHING

AN IMPRINT OF
The Lawbook Exchange, Ltd.
33 Terminal Avenue
Clark, New Jersey 07066-1321

Please see our website for a selection of our other publications and fine facsimile reprints of classic works of legal history www.lawbookexchange.com

Library of Congress Cataloging-in-Publication Data

Names: Hammond, Ama Fowa, editor, author. | Adegbite, Folashade Rose, editor, author. | Mensa-Bonsu, Maame Yaa A., editor., author. | Batariwah, Prosper, editor, author.
Title: Family law in Africa : perspectives on selected systems of marriage / edited by Ama F. Hammond, Folashade Rose Adegbite, Maame Yaa A. Mensa-Bonsu, Prosper Batariwah.
Description: Clark, New Jersey : Talbot Publishing, an Imprint of The Lawbook Exchange, Ltd., 2023. | Series: JCL studies in comparative law ; second series, no. 7 | Includes bibliographical references and index.
Identifiers: LCCN 2023022498 | ISBN 9781616196844 (hardcover)
Subjects: LCSH: Marriage law--Africa. | Customary law--Africa. | Divorce--Law and legislation--Africa. | Marriage (Islamic law)--Africa. | Divorce (Islamic law)--Africa. | Domestic relations--Africa. | Marriage (Customary law)
Classification: LCC KQC160 .F36 2023 | DDC 346.6016 23/eng/20230--dc10
LC record available at https://lccn.loc.gov/2023022498

Printed in the United States of America on acid-free paper

Table of Contents

Series Introduction

WILLIAM E. BUTLER

The African continent constitutes a regional laboratory of comparative law – among the richest on the planet and, all the archaeological and anthropological evidence suggests, the probable place of origin of humankind. For the legal comparatist it has everything to offer: the earliest possible origins of law and legal systems; a remarkable plethora of ethnic identities and affiliations; an impressive history of customary and theological laws, the experience of being practitioners and subjects of colonial subjugation; the purveyors and recipients of alien and competitive laws and legal systems within Africa; objects of Christian and Islamic proselytizing; the legal impact of slavery; the challenges of decolonization and independence – to mention but some of the contextual and direct impacts upon legal development on the African continent.

The present volume brings together comparatists from eight African jurisdictions who explore legal traditions and change in that most fundamental domain of comparative jurisprudence – family law, with particular reference to marriage and divorce. Legal pluralism is predominant in most of the jurisdictions explored, although there is movement in some to reduce the role or importance of customary practices; in a few substantial pluralism is tolerated and some would argue, sanctioned. The pluralism extends to some countries assuming human rights obligations by treaty but continuing to permit practices that some regard as inconsistent with human rights obligations. "Cultural diversity" is sometimes deployed as an argument to defend policies or practices that derogate from human rights commitments or to justify delay in implementing human rights conventions.

Whatever balance will ultimately come to prevail, Africa once again in this volume gives evidence of rich comparative legal experience in the survival of traditional patterns of behavior, the selective acceptance of foreign transplants and influences, a receptiveness to and lively dialogue concerning legal change, and the cautious adaptation of new ideas – all factors that commended this volume for inclusion in the *Journal of Comparative Law* series of monographs.

Foreword

The existence of variety or difference in African legal systems is partly attributable to an indigenous (i.e., pre-colonial) origin, and partly to innovations which were imported or imposed by the colonial power – A. N. Allott[1]

The legal systems of most African countries are influenced by varied sources of law, foreign and domestic. These foreign laws may be of English, French, Portuguese, or German origin and may have been impacted by Christianity and Islam. These external influences have significantly affected how African legal systems are organized today. Yet, Africa's pre-colonial heterogenous customary laws, institutions, and religions persist. Africa, as Wole Soyinka put it, "… is an intimate part of the histories of others, both cause and consequence, a complex organism formed of its own internal pulsation and external interventions …".[2] Nevertheless, post-colonial African States continue to reconcile these external and internal influences and their accompanying systems of law to create legally pluralist frameworks which enhance the benefits of multiculturalism, contemporary notions of justice and fairness, and modernity.

One domain of exploration in this regard is marriage. African cultures, all pro-natalist, put a premium on marriage, however conceived in the particular culture. Throughout the continent, African States recognize and regulate marriages under different systems of law. On one hand, there are statutory or civil marriages with legal origins in the colonial enterprise. On the other hand, customary and religious marriages are governed primarily by customary and religious laws, which are sometimes incorporated into statute law. In some jurisdictions, the process for the celebration of Christian marriages is enmeshed with the statutory marriage process.

Family Law in Africa: Perspectives on Selected Systems of Marriage explores the legal dynamics of marriage on the African continent. There is little scholarship on comparative family law in Africa,

1 A. N. Allott, "Towards the Unification of Laws in Africa", *International and Comparative Law Quarterly*, XIV (1965), pp. 366, 369.

2 Wole Soyinka, Of Africa (2012).

especially with respect to contracting and dissolving marriages and related issues. This volume aims to fill this gap. The contributors from Ghana, Nigeria, Kenya, eSwatini, Zimbabwe, South Africa, Mauritius, and Côte d'Ivoire discuss the marital regimes of each domestic system of law; the necessary processes required to contract or dissolve marriages in these States; the tension between customary and Islamic marriages and State laws; and the need for reform.

This book will be a useful resource for researchers and scholars, especially those interested in comparative family law in Africa. It is hoped that they will identify informed similarities and differences between the marital regimes of African States and propose more clinical solutions to common issues which prevent aspects of these marital regimes from keeping up with contemporary developments. In particular, the systems that have unusual features, such as polyandry and other incidents outside the norm of mainstream marriages in Africa, would be better appreciated by receiving such academic visibility. It is anticipated that in the future more scholars will further develop this and related areas of law, such as property rights and child custody and adoption, to inform discourses on family law in Africa. This book is a ground-breaking effort to throw light on an otherwise shadowy, but critically-important area, of family law on the continent of Africa. I commend the authors and editors and encourage them to bring more light and clarity to such critically important areas of law which impinge on the personal well-being of the African, but which are poorly understood on and outside the continent.

Henrietta J. A. N. Mensa-Bonsu

Justice of the Supreme Court of Ghana

Professor of Law, formerly of the University of Ghana School of Law.

Deputy Special Representative, United Nations Secretary-General for the Rule of Law (DSRSG-RoL) at the United Nations Mission In Liberia (UNIMIL)

Acknowledgements

The editors are sincerely grateful to the authors and reviewers for their invaluable contributions and cooperation in making this publication possible. We also thank our editorial assistant, Mr. Stephen Menya-Amoako, who worked efficiently on this publication, and the University of Ghana School of Law for its support in producing this volume. Our sincere gratitude goes to Ms. Katherine Aglobitse, Dr Balica Braimah and Mr Kantier Pius Bito for translating from French to English the chapter from Côte d'Ivoire. Last but not least, we acknowledge Dr. Adegbite for creating the concept for this book. Editing this book has been an honor, and we hope that our readers will be constructively inspired by it.

Authors

Adegbite, Folashade Rose, LLB (Unilorin), LLM (UniLagos), PhD (UniLagos). Senior Lecturer, Department of Private and Property Law, Faculty of Law, University of Lagos, Nigeria

Bamba, Abdul Baasit Aziz, LLB (Ghana), LLM (Harvard), JSD (Harvard), Senior Lecturer, University of Ghana School of Law

Batariwah, Prosper, LLB (Ghana); Barrister-at-Law; Graduate Assistant, University of Ghana School of Law

Dlamini, Dumsani, LLB (Uneswa); LLM (UP); LLD (UJ); Lecturer, Department of Law, University of eSwatini

Dowuona-Hammond, Christine, LLB (Ghana), LLM (Michigan), Associate Professor of Law, University of Ghana School of Law

Gunputh, Rajendra Prasad, PhD in Private Law (Univ. la Réunion) with First Class Distinction, a PhD in Public Law (Univ. Paris V René Descartes, France) with First Class Distinction, a Post-Doct in Public Law (Univ. Paris X Nanterre, France), a P.G.C.E in Higher Education and Habilitation à Diriger de la Recherches (HDR) in all French universities; Personal Chair in International Comparative Law, Dean of Faculty of Law and Management (FLM), University of Mauritius

Hammond, Ama F., BA (Cape Coast); LLB (Ghana); LLM (Harvard); PhD (University of British Columbia); Barrister-at-Law; Senior Lecturer, University of Ghana School of Law

Imam-Tamim, Muhammed Kamaldeen, LLB (Unilorin, Nigeria); LLM (OAU, Nigeria); PhD (IIUM, Malaysia); Barrister-at-Law; Senior Lecturer, Faculty of Law, University of Ilorin

Jadeed, Moza, Lecturer, Faculty of Law, University of Nairobi (Kenya)

Kouassi, Alfred, PhD in Private Law; Assistant, Université des Lagunes (Abidjan-Côte d'Ivoire)

Mahamah, Mustapha Abdulai, BA (Social Work and Psychology), LLB (Ghana), Graduate Assistant, University of Ghana School of Law

Manyika, Lin Mary, LLB (Fort Hare, South Africa); LLM (UKZN, South Africa); LLD Candidate (UKZN); Legal Practitioner, Zimbabwe; Lecturer, Great Zimbabwe University

Mbogoh, Annette, LLB (UoN), LLM (SEARCWL-UZ), DPhilLaw (SEARCWL-UZ), CM (MTI); Advocate of the High Court of Kenya, Kituo cha Sheria; Lecturer, University of Nairobi

Mensa-Bonsu, Maame Yaa A., BA, LLB, QCL (Ghana), LLM (LSE); Barrister-at-Law; Lecturer, University of Ghana School of Law

Mokoena, Untalimile Crystal, LLB, LLM (Univen); LLD candidate, University of Pretoria; Lecturer, University of Venda

Mopai, Zama, LLB, LLM (Univen); PhD candidate, University of Cape Town; Lecturer, University of Venda

Ruombwa, Victor, LLB (University of Zimbabwe); LLM (University of Zimbabwe); Legal Practitioner, Zimbabwe; Lecturer, Great Zimbabwe University

Shilaho, Caroline Vicheti, LLB (Hons UON); Post Graduate Diploma in Law (KSL); Masters in Women's Law (UZ); LLD Candidate, UP; Lecturer, University of Nairobi

Chapter One
The Plurality of Forms of Marriage In Africa

This introductory chapter addresses the nature and implications of the plurality of systems of marriages in Côte d'Ivoire, eSwatini, Ghana, Kenya, Mauritius, Nigeria, South Africa, and Zimbabwe with an emphasis on the customary legal system. There is a dearth of literature on familial relationships in Africa, particularly comparative literature on marriages in Africa. Filling this gap is important as various law faculties in Africa strive to investigate the similarities and differences in the regulation of family relations in Africa. Most sovereign States in Africa experienced colonial rule and the concomitant transplanting of foreign laws onto local terrains that had their own indigenous laws.[1] Such legal diversity remains a hallmark of most legal systems in Africa. Accordingly, most African countries recognize more than one form of marriage, some regulated by customary law and some by statute law.

There has been some scholarly analysis of customary law and discourse. There are at least two strands: judicial customary law, or customary law as accepted by the courts, and customary law proper; that is to say, "the rules of law which by custom are applicable to particular communities".[2] It is herein not claimed that the African customary law, as it existed in the colonial era and even now, was pristine. Earlier civilizations may have influenced pre-colonial customary law. According to Lord Malcolm Hailey (1872-1969), "The law of the ancient Babylonians, Hebrews, Romans, and Saxons had close analogies to what we see among the primitive of the African peoples".[3] At present, it is greatly impacted by a

1 Abdulmumini Adebayo Oba, "The Future of Customary Law in Africa", in Jeanmarie Fenrich, Paolo Galizzi, and Tracy Higgins (eds.), *The Future of African Customary Law* (2011), p. 58.

2 Article 11, 1992 Constitution of Ghana.

3 Lord Hailey *The African Survey* (1938), p. 265.

host of influences, including "internally generated changes of social attitudes" and "external forces".[4] Numerous ethnic groups in Africa have their own customary laws, making it impossible to have *the* customary law of any particular country.[5]

There is a second level at which laws were assimilated into the various States: the influence of religion and religious laws. Within this level there may be two subdivisions: foreign laws, which are influenced by religion, mostly Christianity, and religious rules that are recognized as having their place within the legal system of the State, notably Islamic laws.[6]

Although religion and customary law have existed in Africa from time immemorial, the introduction of foreign law through colonization was the single defining event that altered the nature of law in Africa, imprinting colonized nations with distinct legal traditions, political institutions, and lawmaking processes. Whereas anglophone African countries regard themselves as belonging to the common law tradition, francophone African countries adhere firmly to the civil law tradition. Some countries, such as South Africa and Mauritius, contain an admixture of different legal traditions.

The foregoing systems of law and their subcategories have resulted in the fascinating and complex phenomenon of legal pluralism and led Brian Tamanaha to assert a "plurality of legal pluralisms".[7] The effect of legal pluralism, while felt in every sphere of law, is arguably most visible in marriages in Africa. The question of how marriages are

[4] Gordon Woodman, "A Survey of Customary Laws in Africa in Search of Lessons for the Future", in Fenrich, et al., note 1 above, p. 16.

[5] Oba, note 1 above, pp. 60, explains that there are over 800 ethnic or language groups in Africa, and each has its system of customary law. Akua Kuenyehia sets the number of ethnic groups at over a thousand and says that there are about as many cultures and related customary laws as there are ethnic groups. The customary laws vary from one ethnic group to another and sometimes from village to village. See Akua Kuenyehia, "Women, Marriage, and Intestate Succession in the Context of Legal Pluralism in Africa", *University of California Davis Law Review*, XL (2006), p. 388.

[6] Oba, note 1 above.

[7] Brian Tamanaha, "Understanding Legal Pluralism: Past to Present, Local to Global", *Sydney Law Review*, XXX (2008), p. 392.

validly contracted, dissolved, or otherwise terminated and the issues arising therefrom are enquiries to which there are not always definite answers due to the complex web of laws and the interplay between these systems of law, co-existing within a geographical space.

Such legal diversity in marriage arrangements is yet to be addressed in a single collection for the benefit of academics, students, and legal practitioners. The paucity of academic analysis and reflection on the myriad issues arising in this area is more problematic when one seeks a comparative perspective. There are many ways in which the experiences in marriage relations overlap across the continent due to a shared history of colonial rule and assimilation of foreign cultures. This common factor among most African States has led to different experiences and, therefore, potentially richer material for a study that presents a comparative lens through which the celebration and dissolution of marriages are explored. Thus, this book undertakes to fill the gaps in knowledge of marriage as a core feature of Family Law.

This introductory chapter briefly describes the approaches to legal pluralism described herein. This is followed by a thematic discussion of the contestations between the different legal systems in each country and the efforts to harmonize these legal regimes. Next is explored the impact of international legal instruments on domestic legal arrangements and the future of African customary law marriages in light of statutory arrangements in family relations. We then turn to an analytical summary of the chapters, focusing mainly on the recommendations made by the authors.

APPROACHES TO LEGAL PLURALISM

Most post-colonial societies are known to have plural legal systems by reason of their colonial past, Various legal regimes in these societies regulate the formation and dissolution of marriages. These regimes include State law, customary law, and religious law. In most cases, customary and religious laws co-exist with State law, and like the relationship between equity and common law, they sometimes "run in the same channel, ... side by side" and other times simply "do not mingle their waters".[8]

The term legal pluralism generally describes a situation where two or more legal systems exist within the confines of a given space.[9] The best-known and frequently cited definition is that of Sally Engle Merry, a Professor of Anthropology, who described it as "a situation in which two or more legal systems coexist in the same social field".[10] In essence, legal pluralism rejects the ideology of legal centralism, which asserts the supremacy of State law and maintains that "law is and should be the law of the state, uniform for all persons, exclusive ... and administered by a single set of state institutions".[11]

Early studies of legal pluralism focused on colonial and post-colonial societies, where foreign legal systems were imposed on the customary or indigenous legal systems of former colonies. This approach to legal pluralism is often called *classic* or *deep* legal pluralism[12] and may be described as "the coexistence of legal orders with different sources of authority".[13] Deep legal pluralism may result from the State acknowledging that it does not have exclusive authority to make laws and solely apply them.[14] Whereas this form of pluralism, in its entirety, may be uncommon, it may be practiced with respect to a specific area of law. For example, a State may recognize the sole jurisdiction of the customary legal system to determine the essentials of a customary law marriage. A variety of such pluralism may be presumed to

[8] Philip H. Petit, *Equity and the Law of Trust* (12th ed.; 2012).

[9] Jeremy Waldron, *No Barking: Legal Pluralism and the Contrast between Hart's Jurisprudence and Fuller's* (2008), p. 3 (Colloquium on The Hart-Fuller Debate 50 Years, Canberra, December 2008).

[10] Sally Engle Merry, "Legal Pluralism", *Law & Society Review*, XXII (1988), p. 870.

[11] John Griffiths "What is Legal Pluralism", *Journal of Legal Pluralism*, XXIV (1986), p. 3.

[12] Gordon R. Woodman, "Legal Pluralism and the Search for Justice", *Journal of African Law*, XL (1996), p. 157.

[13] Jennifer Corrin, "Exploring the Deep: Looking for Deep Legal Pluralism in the South Pacific", *Victoria University of Wellington Law Review*, XLVIII (2017), p. 306.

[14] Ibid.

exist in certain rural areas in Africa where the reach of the State is almost non-existent and traditional rulers appear to exercise exclusive legal authority. According to Tamanaha:

> Traditional leaders (custodians of customary law) exercise significant powers in many places across the Global South today, albeit with many variations. They have administrative authority in allocating land and benefits, legislative authority in declaring customary law and advising the legislature on the impact of proposed laws, and judicial authority in resolving local civil and criminal disputes. Their authority remains substantial in rural areas ... Traditional leaders defend their power and prerogatives against encroachments by the state, drawing on their support in the local community and ideological legitimation grounded in custom and tradition.[15]

Deep legal pluralism thrives in these rural areas because poor and probably neglectful governments are unable to invest in these local economies. Rural residents typically have less favorable living conditions than urban residents, as State resources do not sufficiently penetrate rural areas. There is a pervasive lack of access to high-quality education and necessary resources, including medical care:

> Many of these societies lack sufficient educational institutions and government revenues—lack social and economic capital—for state legal systems to efficiently function or to expand the reach of the state legal system to replace traditional authorities in rural area (sic) or at the village level. Nor is there a pressing need to undo the division of labor, particularly since state legal systems are struggling to handle their own tasks.[16]

Perhaps this is why it has been asserted that:

> Embedded in the concept of legal pluralism is not just the notion of multiple legalities, but also, an array

15 Tamanaha, *Legal Pluralism Explained: History, Theory, Consequences* (2021), p. 75.

16 Ibid., p. 94.

> of differing economic circumstances that need to be harmonized so that legal actors, especially those in the customary legal system, can participate in the economic life of the state.[17]

This form of pluralism is not without problems. The human rights abuses and social inequalities that accompany such pluralism are well documented.[18] The main argument is that deep legal pluralism is incompatible with the rule of law, which is an essential component of justice.[19]

State legal pluralism, on the other hand, may refer to "the coexistence of two or more bodies of norms that are recognized by the state, but with the proviso that the state is the source of authority for all laws".[20] It describes the recognition and incorporation of some norms of customary law into State claimed fields of jurisdiction.[21] Recognizing customary law may imply accepting it as fact, though doing so does not mean accepting its legal nature.[22] Analyzing an example of recognition, Morse and Woodman explain that in sentencing a convicted criminal, State law may consider customary law as part of the social setting and ideology of the offender.

However, this does not entail changing State law to reflect customary law.[23] State legal pluralism involves the State incorporating and enforcing customary rules into its norms, in whole or in part, thus giving them the same legal effect in State law as in customary law.[24] Nevertheless, Woodman contends that the incorporation of customary

[17] Ama F. Hammond, "Asserting an Embracive and Functional Concept of Legal Pluralism in Ghana", *University of Ghana Law Journal*, XXX (2017-2019), p. 14.

[18] Woodman, note 4 above, pp. 12-13.

[19] Woodman, note 12 above, p. 160.

[20] Corrin, note 13 above, p. 306.

[21] Woodman, note 12 above, p. 158.

[22] Bradford W. Morse and Gordon R. Woodman, "Introductory Essay: The State's Options", in Morse and Woodman (eds.), *Indigenous Law and the State* (1988).

[23] Ibid., pp. 10-11.

[24] Ibid., pp. 11-12.

norms typically results in their distortion, for the laws stated are not coterminous with the customary law norms.[25] Thus, although State law co-exists with the customary laws of the different communities and religious law, State law recognizes these non-State legal systems on its terms, telling them what they are.[26]

It is argued that incorporating customary law into State law privileges the State and ingrains legal centralism,[27] a proposition with which some scholars take issue. Campbell McLachlan, a legal scholar, argues that "the proper role of state law is not to appropriate or define customary law. It is rather to take account of its existence and adjust itself accordingly".[28] It must be pointed out that customary law is a component of both State pluralism and deep legal pluralism.[29] However, in the latter, customary law is applied by the State, which comprises various sources of law. State legal pluralism focuses on lawyers' or customary judicial law, as opposed to popular or living customary law, which is the subject of deep legal pluralism.[30] Nevertheless, the distinction between deep and State legal pluralism is artificial because the relationship between the State and non-State institutions is, in practice, dynamic, and "authority and control are often a question of degree".[31]

State legal pluralism is the dominant approach described herein. The contributions reveal interesting legal orderings, showing the interaction, competition, collaboration, and interdependence characterizing the relationships among various normative orders. We draw on examples from the jurisdictions under review in the ensuing discussions.

25 Ibid. This view is attributed to only Gordon Woodman.

26 Simon Roberts, "Against Legal Pluralism", *Journal of Legal Pluralism*, XLII (1998), p. 98.

27 Corrin, note 13 above, p. 307.

28 Campbell McLachlan, "The Recognition of Aboriginal Customary Law: Pluralism beyond the Colonial Paradigm: A Review Article", *International and Comparative Law Quarterly*, XXXVII (1988), p. 386.

29 Woodman, note 12 above, p. 159.

30 Ibid.

31 Corrin, note 13 above, p. 307.

CONTESTATIONS BETWEEN PLURALIST LEGAL SYSTEMS AND EFFORTS TO HARMONIZE THESE LEGAL REGIMES

A legally pluralist system contains areas of overlap and conflict. The general tenor of the contributions demonstrates a tendency for the State to claim authority to dominate the legal space, although there are spaces in which customary law has tenaciously retained legal control. We first discuss general themes, beginning with a discussion of the structure of the legal systems and how the ranking of sources of law in the different countries has led to the superiority of statutory marriages or statutory prescriptions and processes over religious and customary laws. The next section examines the nature and types of marriages discussed herein. Questions of legal capacity such as age, consent, and status will be considered, paying close attention to the areas of intra-jurisdictional conflict and inter-jurisdictional conflict. The latter is particularly important, as it brings out, despite a shared colonial inheritance, the fundamental differences in how the different jurisdictions have forced their respective colonial inheritance to adapt to their respective environments. Important issues of registration, publicity, and other procedural matters in marriage, divorce, and dissolution of marriage are considered.

State v. customary law

A common theme herein is the deliberate dominance by the State over the other legal players in the different countries. In all countries, the constitution is at the apex of the legal hierarchy, often seen in how the various national constitutions rank the different sources of law, whereas customary law is at the bottom. There is statutory superiority in the sense that State-made law is ranked superior to customary law. In these countries, the dominance is reinforced by the fact that all other laws and practices that conflict with or contravene the constitution are void to the extent of the conflict. The constitutions of Ghana and Zimbabwe exemplify this dominance.

Quite different is the Côte d'Ivoire, where customary law, particularly in the area of marriage, has been moved aside, as Alfred Kouassi observes.[32] There, the State, at least on paper, is supreme, legislating practically every sphere of life to the detriment of customary law. This is surprising, for it is frequently assumed that legal pluralism would be a shared feature of African legal systems due to the colonial history of a majority of the continent. Thus, contrary to the experience of Anglophone countries with legal pluralism, at least in marriage, the Ivorian example, and *a fortiori*, that of black francophone countries, leans towards legal centralism. However, given that customary law is generally created through the lived experiences of a people, the Ivorian example also demonstrates how the will of the people is manifest in their either circumventing State prohibitions, for example, on multiple spouses,[33] or completely disregarding them, as in the case of dowry.[34] Mauritius appears to have a different approach: although customary law does not appear to be listed in the hierarchy of laws properly so-called, it is left a limited space of operation, that is, in matters of marriage and divorce.

Despite being a heavily religious continent, religious law occupies a circumscribed domain in the countries herein considered. Nigeria appears to be the country with the widest recognition of the impact of Islamic law, as the Constitution specifically sets up Shariah Courts of Appeal. The Constitution of Kenya also provides some special recognition for Islamic law marriages, including legislating exceptions to rights that are generally considered universal and fundamental, such as the right to equality. This right, in particular, as noted by the Kenyan authors, is subject to Islamic law, for adherents of the faith.[35] This has had significant consequences discussed subsequently in this part. Thus, the power of Islam within the Nigerian and Kenyan legal systems is more strongly felt than in Ghana, where Christine Dowuona-Hammond *et al.* criticize judicial

32 Alfred Kouassi, "A Look at Marriage in Ivorian Law" (see below).

33 Ibid.

34 Ibid.

35 See Caroline Vicheti Shilaho, "Islamic Marriages in Kenya" (see below) and Annette Mbogoh, "My Marriage, My Choice: Kenya's Plural Marriage Law" (see below).

attitudes that have led to Islamic law being, at best, a type of customary law.[36] Indeed, they point out that there has been, consciously or unconsciously, (but more likely the former), an inexplicable tendency to even obliterate the mark of Islamic law on a marriage celebrated by Muslims under Islamic law by both statute and case law. Another country where religious law, particularly Islamic law, is disregarded, is Mauritius. The Mauritian legal system does not recognize religious marriages as valid at all. Also, it provides no legal exceptions to bigamy, despite Muslims being allowed to have multiple wives, and has ignored calls by Muslims for recognition of personal law.

Thus, in the battle of normative orders for legal dominance, one system becomes superimposed over the others, such that it attempts to force out aspects of the other that it regards as detracting from, or even endangering, principles to which the dominant order subscribes. The South African situation, pre-2000, is a vivid example of this, whereby customary law and practices, due to colonialism and apartheid, were, according to Crystal Mokoena and Zama Mopai, "regarded as repugnant to principles of natural justice mostly based on western law".[37] Thus, it was not until the year 2000 that marriages celebrated under customary law were recognized as valid.[38] With the effluxion of time, one system acquires more loyalty due to its appeal. A notable example is Côte d'Ivoire, where the Ivorian legislature, in the early post-independence phase, adopted a civil code based on the French Civil Code, which had the effect of "the abandonment of almost all of customary law."[39] This was justified, partly on the grounds that certain traditional practices were inimical to the harmonious development of the country.[40] Another justification offered for the State's

[36] Christine Dowuona-Hammond, Abdul Baasit Aziz Bamba and Mustapha Abdulai Mahamah, "The Regulation of Islamic Marriage and Divorce in Ghana: Legislative and Policy Roots of Discrimination" (see below).

[37] Zama Mopai and Untalimile Crystal Mokoena, "Analytical Overview of the Plurality of Marital Laws In South Africa" (see below).

[38] Ibid.

[39] Kouassi, note 32 above.

[40] Ibid.

incursions into areas that were governed by the personal law of the people is given by Moza Jadeed, writing that the Kenyan government had argued "the imperative of establishing a common law regime for all Kenyan residents, without any distinctions among groups".[41] This led to one statute dealing with all forms of marriage in Kenya, and, perhaps predictably, requiring all marriages to be registered.[42] Similarly, several authors herein have called for more State control over customary law, in the form of legislation, in order to provide proper records,[43] to define terms or words that are currently un- or ill-defined,[44] or to properly provide a framework for the rights of persons in de facto unions.[45] There is much force in Ama Hammond's observation that this tendency of a majority of people to be inclined more towards one system over another leads to the "othering of the other, usually, customary law".[46]

This superiority of statute is seen in different aspects of marriage; the rights attached to statutory marriages being better and offering more security to the spouses and children and in the mandatory hoops through which one must pass for a union to be recognized as a valid marriage.

Nature and types of marriages

A common thread running through the chapters is the heteronormative insistence in the definition of marriage. In all the countries discussed, marriage is limited to a man and woman, with some countries allowing for polygamy, in the form of polygyny. The key elements to be discussed relate

41 Moza Jadeed, "Islamic Marriages and Divorce in Kenya: Ethnocultural Diversity" (see below).

42 Mbogoh, note 35 above.

43 Folashade Rose Adegbite, "Examining Statutory and Customary Marriage In Nigeria" (see below).

44 Dumsani Dlamini, "The Marriage Law of eSwatini" (see below).

45 Maame Yaa A. Mensa-Bonsu, "Customary Marriage in Ghana" (see below).

46 Ama F. Hammond, "A Multi-Legal Perspective on Christian Marriages In Ghana" (see below).

to the sex of the parties and the number of spouses a man is permitted to have.

The definition of marriage, in terms of the sex of the parties, requires that men may marry only women. Considerable pressure has been brought to bear on different African governments to recognize non-heterosexual marriages and allow same-sex sexual relations.[47] Despite these pressures, some of which have been tied to foreign aid,[48] most governments in the countries covered herein have remained adamant, and in some cases, defiant,[49] that they will not permit same-sex sexual relations and unions in their respective jurisdictions. One African president declared that his country would turn down aid tied to LGBTQ rights.[50]

South Africa recognizes civil unions among the legal unions in the country. These unions, by definition, allow for parties of the same sex to participate. Although South Africa distinguishes between a civil marriage, (which is affected by the general heteronormative parameters discussed above) and civil unions, which is defined as, *inter alia,* "a union between two *persons* ...",[51] there does not appear to be any difference between the two types of unions at all, prompting the authors to question why they are regulated by different sets of legislation.[52] One therefore wonders about the requirement for the marriage officer to ask if the parties wish to be in a civil marriage or a civil partnership.[53] It may be that the word marriage is restricted, even in South Africa, which is hailed as progressive in its legislative human

47 Muhammad Kamaldeen Imam-Tamim, "The Islamic Marriage Contract in Nigeria" (see below).

48 *Ghana Refuses to Grant Gays' Rights Despite Aid Threat* (2011) (available online).

49 For example, Adegbite writes that Nigeria has introduced a prohibition on same-sex sexual unions in spite of considerable threats by America to cut aid to Nigeria; Mfonobong Nsehe, *Obama Fights Nigerian Anti-Gay Bill, Threatens to Cut Aid* (2011) (available online).

50 Ricci Shryock, *Gambian President Says No to Aid Money Tied to Gay Rights* (2022) (available online).

51 Mopai and Mokoena, note 37 above.

52 Ibid.

53 Ibid.

rights reforms, such that it cannot escape the inevitable heterosexual label the word entails.

One feature of the systems of marriage discussed is the existence of special same-sex marriages, despite the prohibition against same-sex marriages, which differ from those known in the West. These are woman-woman marriages. In Ghana, Nigeria, and South Africa, these marriages are not for the purpose of sexual relations between the two women, but to procure children and secure the bloodline.[54] Sexual relations, therefore, take place between the husband and the new wife, where the original couple is childless on account of the woman's infertility, or in the case of a woman, often one who is wealthy and childless, between her male relative and the new wife.[55]

Regarding the number of wives a man may marry, most jurisdictions discussed herein accept and recognize polygynous marriages as part of customary law marriages. All the countries maintain statutory marriages as strictly monogamous. Côte d'Ivoire strikes a unique pose by refusing to recognize polygamous unions as lawful.[56] The cosmopolitan and diverse island of Mauritius does not recognize polygamous unions, making all of them bigamous.

On the nature and types of marriage across Africa, one germane debate stems from the elevation of statutory marriage over customary and religious forms. The elevation is seen in those countries where registration, in particular, is not mandatory for all marriages. In those countries, there is greater protection afforded registered marriages over those given to customary marriages. In contrast, unregistered marriages are valid for limited purposes, usually relating to customary law on marriage, divorce, and custody and guardianship. In Zimbabwe, for example, registered customary law marriages are valid for all purposes. In contrast, unregistered marriages are valid for limited purposes, usually relating to customary law on marriage, divorce, and custody and guardianship. In South Africa, it

[54] Ibid.

[55] Mensa-Bonsu, note 45 above. Adegbite, note 43 above.

[56] Kouassi, note 32 above.

is reported that persons married under customary law often prefer to subsequently enter into a civil marriage for certainty of their marital status.[57] In Ghana, it is almost expected that after the customary marriage ceremony, the couple will undergo a second ceremony in which the statutory prescription will be complied with. This is particularly true of Christian families, hence Part Three of the Marriages Act, 1884-1985 being titled "Christian and Other Marriages." This is akin to what Folashade Rose Adegbite describes as "double-decker marriages"[58] in the Nigerian context. The ease of proving the existence of the marriage and the statutorily-imposed monogamy are among the perceived benefits that make couples marry multiple times. In Ghana, as in Nigeria, a couple cannot first have a civil marriage and then purport to marry each other again at custom, whereas the exact opposite is completely legal and, as noted above, frequently occurring.

In Côte d'Ivoire, there is no alternative if one wishes for their marriage to be valid. Kouassi explains that the only form of marriage that is legally recognized is one celebrated by a civil registrar.[59] He describes the situation as one in which parties often wish to comply with the dictates of custom, their religion and statute, and therefore engage in a "matrimonial triathlon."[60]

One interesting inter-jurisdictional difference in this regard is between Ghana and Nigeria. In Nigeria, Adegbite writes that it is unclear what the status of the marriages are relative to each other. She explains that it is not certain whether both marriages exist simultaneously or one takes precedence over the other, such that one is subsumed into the other.[61] In the Ghanaian context, there is no debate, as Maame Yaa A. Mensa-Bonsu discusses, that the customary marriage is converted into a statutory marriage when the

57 Mopai and Mokoena, note 37 above.

58 Adegbite, note 43 above.

59 Kouassi, note 32 above.

60 Ibid.

61 Adegbite, note 43 above.

parties undergo the full process as prescribed by law, such that the customary law marriage "dies".[62] The effect of this is that if the parties get divorced, the customary marriage also stands dissolved. On the contrary, if the statutory ceremony is held to be void because of some material defect in the process, the customary law marriage is revived, and any issues arising in respect of the marriage fall to be determined by recourse to the relevant customary law.[63]

The exception in this regard is eSwatini, where the Supreme Court has ruled that the marriages are of equal status, thus requiring parties must have two marriage certificates.[64] This implies that a party must procure two divorces to be fully divorced.[65] The challenge with the Supreme Court of eSwatini approach is that the parties can first enter into a civil marriage and remarry each other under eSwatini customary law.[66] This is challenging, as the philosophy of customary law marriages is fundamentally distinct from that of civil marriages, regarding the number of persons a man may marry. The former is permissive of multiple wives, whereas the latter is strictly monogamous. Thus, should the parties first undergo a civil marriage and then subsequently a customary one, is the man free to marry others then? Given that both marriages are equal, how does one reconcile the statutory monogamy of the one with the potential polygamy of the other?

Legal Capacity

Matters falling under the broad heading of legal capacity include age, consent, and status.

62 Mensa-Bonsu, note 45 above.

63 Ibid.

64 Dlamini, note 44 above.

65 Ibid.

66 Ibid.

Age

For most jurisdictions, the set minimum age for marriage is 18. The age of marriageability is often fixed either by the constitution (Nigeria) or by a statute dealing with either marriage, (Ghana) or with the rights and interests of children (eSwatini). Some countries have two ages of marriageability, as in the case of Ghana, where persons below the age of 21 but above the age of 18 may marry with the consent of their parents. This has been criticized as not having any proper justification, given that the age of suffrage and testamentary capacity is 18, and they do not require any parental supervision for those activities, both of which have significant legal consequences.[67] Others, such as South Africa, treat age as a relative incapacity, because a minor may contract a marriage with the consent of parents, guardians, or the State.[68]

A key issue is how religious law has impacted some jurisdictions, such that there are deviations from constitutional provisions. This is particularly true of Islam, which is said to both permit and encourage early marriage.[69] According to the authors writing on Islamic marriages, the age of marriageability in Islam is at puberty. Muhammad Imam-Tamim observes that although the range is often given as nine to eighteen years, it appears the most commonly accepted age is fifteen.[70] In spite of this, he also notes that in most of northern Nigeria, girls between the ages of nine and fifteen are often given away in marriage.[71] In the case of Nigeria, Adegbite argues that the Nigerian Constitution provides leeway for child marriages to exist, as it deems married persons as being of legal age to marry.[72] She is not alone in this criticism, as Imam-Tamim also notes that child

[67] Hammond, note 46 above.

[68] Mopai and Mokoena, note 37 above.

[69] Jadeed, note 41 above.

[70] Imam-Tamim, note 47 above.

[71] Ibid.

[72] Adegbite, note 43 above.

marriage is prevalent, particularly in Northern Nigeria.[73] That there appears to be some impunity with which this is done may be seen in the fact that no less a person than a senator, and former governor of one of the northern States, then 49 years old, is reported to have married a 13-year-old.[74] This is also likely to be the case in Ghana, hence the authors providing that the new draft Muslim Marriage and Divorce Bill, 2019, seeks to set the age of marriage at eighteen.[75]

Perhaps most controversial is the position taken by Moza Jadeed, who, contrary to international instruments and Kenyan law, advocates lowering the age limit to fourteen.[76] Her position is based on research showing that Kenyan children are engaging in sexual relations at fifteen, three years earlier than they can marry.[77] While the author explains the basis for her recommendation, one wonders whether an activity contrary to law should be permitted because it is commonplace.

Second, the evidence does not suggest that young teenage boys seek to marry these young girls. The reports show real potential for young girls to be married off to significantly older men, which may lead to abuse in that marriage, and for avaricious parents to use the girls to financial advantage. Given that Islam permits up to four wives, the teenage girl is likely to be the youngest wife and may be unable to hold her own against the older ones.

Finally, having sexual intercourse is only one event that occurs in a marriage. Marriage entails significant responsibilities to the spouse, in-laws, and children, among others, which such a young girl may struggle to manage. That young people are having sexual relations earlier appears not to justify lowering the age of marriage to fourteen.

[73] Imam-Tamim, note 47 above.

[74] Ibid.

[75] Dowuona-Hammond, Bamba, and Mahamah, note 36 above.

[76] Jadeed, note 41 above.

[77] Ibid.

Consent

All jurisdictions considered herein require that both parties give consent to the marriage. In some jurisdictions (Ghana, Nigeria, eSwatini), the families' consent is also required, especially under customary law.

Islamic religious law sometimes conflicts with this requirement. Imam-Tamim writes that although the practice is no longer as prevalent, forced marriage does happen. This is particularly where the bride's father, acting as her *waliyy*, gives her in marriage.[78] This may override her wishes. According to the author, some scholars believe that the power to compel marriage may be exercised by another person appointed to serve as guardian of the girl, under two conditions: where the father expressly authorized him to do so, and to a man specifically instructed by the father.[79] Another instance is where the girl is given to a person whom the parents believe cannot afford to marry, or is gifted to an Islamic scholar.[80]

Given that these practices do exist, albeit, on a lesser scale, it is not difficult to see why gender rights advocates and activists in Nigeria and Kenya criticize their respective constitutions for enabling these to remain in the legal system.[81]

Status

Generally, the parties must not be in a subsisting marriage, in the case of civil marriages, at the time of contracting the marriage. Marriages celebrated at custom are potentially polygamous, therefore, should the man already be in a customary marriage, this is no bar to him contracting another marriage at custom. However, a person married under customary law is not permitted to contract a civil marriage. The State, religion, and customary law each

[78] Imam-Tamim, note 47 above.

[79] Ibid.

[80] Ibid.

[81] Adegbite, note 43 above; Shilaho, note 35 above; Mbogoh, note 35 above.

establish prohibited degrees of consanguinity and affinity. The exception is Nigeria, where the Matrimonial Causes Act empowers a justice of the High Court to waive this prohibition and permit parties within the prohibited degree of consanguinity and affinity to marry.[82] The problem is, as noted by Hammond, where she cites the Ghanaian case of *Glah v. The Republic*,[83] that the State may create socio-moral conflict where it appears to sanction or disregard unions which the rest of that society would treat with opprobrium.[84]

Procedural matters

In all the jurisdictions, registration, where it is required, is supported by an elaborate framework, complete with the details necessary for registration, and timing of the registration, among other requirements. A major question arises: what is the legal effect of not registering a marriage? This is answered differently by different jurisdictions, depending on the type of marriage contracted. In some cases, registration is purely of evidentiary value, as non-registered marriages may be difficult to prove, particularly in rural areas where literacy is low. This is the case of customary marriages in Ghana, and Islamic marriages in Kenya. In such cases, the publicity attached to the ceremony is what enables the parties to prove the existence of the marriage. In eSwatini, although there is also a mandatory registration requirement, failure to do so does not render the marriage invalid, but merely difficult to prove.[85] The consequence of not complying with the mandatory registration requirement for customary law marriages in South Africa has a different flavor. This is because while the law provides no consequence for failing to register the marriage, a man can enter into a civil marriage without this being detected, as there is no record. Moreover, there is non-compliance with the mandatory judicial divorce. Thus, some couples, having divorced quietly, may find that their divorce is not legal

82 Ibid., Adegbite.

83 [1992] 2 GLR 15 (HC).

84 Hammond, note 46 above.

85 Dlamini, note 44 above.

and, therefore, remain married.[86] In other cases, registration is a tool for State-sponsored discrimination, providing some advantages not enjoyed by other unregistered marriages. In yet other cases, registration is a question of validity. In Ivorian and Kenyan marriages, except for Islamic marriages, this is the situation where regardless of the form of marriage one contracts, it must be registered to be valid.

Other issues

Divorce in the jurisdictions considered is largely fault-based. Only Côte d'Ivoire and Mauritius appear to have divorce by mutual consent.[87] eSwatini law provides the most obstacles to divorce. First, there are only two grounds for divorce: malicious desertion and adultery.[88] Second, there are stringent requirements, including, curiously, that the petitioner must also seek an order to restore conjugal rights where the petition is brought on the grounds of malicious desertion.[89] Should the petitioner be unwilling to resume conjugal relations, the petitioner is not granted the order of divorce.[90] It is difficult to see how an understandably hurt or angry petitioner is to compulsorily engage in sexual relations with the offending spouse instead of being granted a divorce. Even less clear is why the refusal of the petitioner to resume conjugal relations is not taken as proof that the marriage has broken down and the parties are better separated. Rather it becomes evidence of her desertion and wrong, such that she will not be permitted to "benefit" from her wrongdoing.[91] It is challenging to see why a person who seeks divorce on this ground must potentially be stuck in a loveless, sexless union.

Most often, where there is a clash between State and customary law, the State has worked to push customary

86 Mopai and Mokoena, note 37 above.

87 Kouassi, note 32 above.

88 Dlamini, note 44 above.

89 Ibid.

90 Ibid.

91 Ibid.

law to the side, even purporting, in some cases, to "vet" customary law. This is done not only by constitutional clauses, the effect of which is to serve as repugnancy clauses that enable the judiciary to "sift through" the customary law principles, but also by expressly allowing the judiciary to determine the content of customary law, regardless of the life experience of the people.[92] It is, therefore, no surprise that a Ghanaian court highlighted the role of customary law and its chances of survival as follows:

> Since the turn of the century, customary law has progressed and developed in accordance with the tempo of social, commercial and industrial progress ... customs which appear to be repugnant to natural justice, equity and good conscience have been gradually extinguished by judicial decisions ... If customary law is to retain its place as *the greatest adjunct to statutory law* and the common law, then it must not remain stagnant whilst other aspects of the law are in constant motion.[93]

This ousting of customary law from pride of place to the periphery has led to conflicts, particularly given the significant rural and illiterate population in the different jurisdictions who largely remain governed by customary law. These contestations create ripe opportunities for reform and modernization.

IMPACT OF INTERNATIONAL LEGAL INSTRUMENTS ON DOMESTIC LEGAL ARRANGEMENTS

Africa's legal systems, though sufficiently pluralistic to reflect the multicultural and multireligious ethos of the nation-State, are far from perfect. Whether State law, customary law, or religion-based systems of law, they reflect ingrained power imbalances and male hegemony, often to the detriment of vulnerable groups such as women and children. These imbalances are especially

[92] Mensa-Bonsu, note 45 above.

[93] *In Re Kofi Antubam, (dec'd) Quaico v. Fosu & Another* [2965] GLR p. 144 (emphasis added).

evident in family relationships, particularly marriages. The ensuing discussion explains how the received marital and customary laws discriminated against women, resulting in the introduction of international laws to ensure equal rights and opportunities for women.

Colonization itself was an imposition. Western European States, under the doctrine of discovery, appropriated African territories and imposed their systems of law on these territories. The received law was based on patriarchal values perpetuated for centuries in the corridors of Western States. While Robert Seidman argues that English law in the colonies "was a peculiar form of English Law that had excised from its corpus any of the democratic forms or economic protections ... claimed to be the brightest jewels in the English legal crown",[94] one need not go further than the words of Sir William Blackstone, writing in the eighteenth century on the doctrine of coverture. The doctrine of coverture in English law means "the very being or legal existence of the woman is suspended during the marriage, or at least is incorporated and consolidated into that of the husband: under whose wing, protection, and cover, she performs everything".[95]

The doctrine of coverture determined the legal rights, duties, and obligations of parties in a marriage.[96] Under this doctrine, there were limited circumstances under which women could sue and be sued without making their husbands plaintiffs or defendants.[97] A woman's ability to transfer or deal with property was severely restricted.[98] A husband was allowed to use "reasonable" violence to correct

[94] Robert Seidman, "The Reception of English Law in Colonial Africa Revisited", *East African Law Review*, II (1969), p. 78.

[95] William Blackstone, *Commentaries on the Laws of England* (1765), I, para. 430.

[96] Ibid., paras. 431-433ff.

[97] Ibid., para. 431; see also Emily Ireland, "Re-examining the Presumption: Coverture and 'Legal Impossibilities' in Early Modern English Criminal Law", *The Journal of Legal History*, XLIII, no. 2 (2022), p. 187.

[98] Joanne Bailey, "Favoured or Oppressed? Married Women, Property and 'Coverture' in England, 1660–1800", *Continuity and Change*, XVII, no. 3 (2002), p. 352.

his wife for gross misbehavior.[99] Women were treated as though they could not think for themselves and needed constant protection. Thus, Blackstone, while acknowledging these "disabilities." maintained that:

> These are the chief legal effects of marriage during the coverture; upon which we may observe, that even the disabilities, which the wife lies under, are for the most part intended for her protection and benefit. *So great a favorite is the female sex of the laws of England.*[100]

The doctrine of coverture was gradually rendered obsolete, beginning with the Married Women's Property Act of 1870, adopted in England to allow women to hold and deal with property in their own name. Even then, the concept of the "Victorian lady", whose duties were to care for the home and bear children, was pervasive.[101] When many anglophone African countries received English law into their jurisdictions, the doctrine of coverture had yet to meet its ultimate end. Hammond and Adegbite point out that under the received marriage laws in Ghana and Nigeria, respectively, parental consent to marry may only be obtained from a mother if the father is dead, is of unsound mind, or is absent from the country. This provision reinforces patriarchy and female subordination. It was only in the twentieth century that the doctrine of coverture fell out of use, and even then, not until the second half of the twentieth century.[102] The foregoing discussion provides the backdrop against which received marital laws discriminated against women, providing unequal rights to parties in marriages.

[99] Blackstone, note 95 above, I, para. 433.

[100] Ibid. (emphasis added).

[101] "Introduction: The Perfect Victorian Lady", in Martha Vicinus (ed.), *Suffer and be Still: Women in the Victorian Age* (2013).

[102] In England, sometime around the 1960s, the remains of the doctrine of coverture could be found primarily in three areas. First, a woman's domicile was tied to that of her husband. Second, spouses could not sue each other in tort. Third, a husband could sue his wife's co-adulterer for damages. All these incidents of the doctrine were swept away with the passage of the Domicile and Matrimonial Proceedings Act 1973, Law Reform (Husband and Wife) Act 1962, and the Law Reform (Miscellaneous Provisions) Act 1970 respectively.

On the customary law front, as shown by various contributors, customary marriages are not just unions of two persons, but unions of two families.[103] The consent of the parents or guardians of the parties must be sought.[104] Customary marriages are sealed with the payment of a bride price, which has been criticized for treating women like chattels.[105] Customary marriages are potentially polygamous. A man may marry additional wives, often resulting in a myriad of property rights issues.[106] Polygamy has been criticized intensely for subjugating women. On the death of one's husband, women are often required to go through certain widowhood rights, which may be dangerous to their health and mental well-being.[107] Women, at customary law, have little by way of property rights in customary unions. The concept of widow inheritance exists in many African societies. Women are either married off to surviving male members of the family or asked to return the bridewealth as a condition of leaving the deceased's extended family.[108] Customary law has no minimum marriageable age, meaning that children below eighteen years may be married off for cultural and economic reasons.[109]

[103] One Ghanaian jurist describes customary marriages as follows: "Now, one peculiar characteristic of our system of marriage which distinguishes it from the system of marriage in Europe and other places is that it is not just a union of 'this man' and 'this woman': it is a union of the family of 'this man' and the family of 'this woman'". *Yaotey v Quaye* [1961] GLR p. 579 (HC).

[104] Tshinetise David Raphalalani, "From the African Customary Marriages Law to the Recognition of Customary Marriages Act (Act 120 of 1998) (RCMA): A Descriptive Analysis", *Journal of Sociology and Social Anthropology*, VII, no. 4 (2016), p. 268.

[105] Sara Lowes and Nathan Nunn, "Bride Price and Well-Being of Women" in Siwan Anderson, Lori Beaman, and Jean-Philippe Platteau (eds.), *Towards Gender Equity in Development* (2018), p. 117.

[106] Lorraine Bowan, "Polygamy and Patriarchy: An Intimate Look at Marriage in Ghana through a Human Rights Lens", *Contemporary Journal of African Studies*, I, no. 2 (2013), p. 50.

[107] Lady Adaina Ajayi et al., "Gendered Violence and Human Rights: An Evaluation of Widowhood Rites in Nigeria", *Cogent Arts & Humanities*, VI (2019), p. 1.

[108] Lowes and Nunn, note 105 above.

[109] Adegbite, note 43 above; Dlamini, note 44 above.

In African countries which recognize Islamic marriages, the concern, as some authors show, is about the polygamous nature of Islamic marriages and the minimum marriageable age.[110] Islamic scholars, though divided about the exact minimum marriageable age, agree that it could be below eighteen years.[111] Islamic family law is said to encourage early, child, and forced marriages.[112] Other issues involve consent and divorce in Islamic law and how they undermine women's autonomy.

These identified issues intersect in the sense that they traverse intra-state legal systems and yet are multi-jurisdictional. As a result, the international community has recognized the need to leverage multilateralism to restore the power imbalances in matrimonial regimes worldwide and provide safe oases in the law to protect vulnerable groups, especially women and children. The authors herein have not shied away from recognizing how influential international treaties and conventions have been in reorganizing their marital laws. Even where these international efforts are not reflected in domestic legislation, States, when reporting on their treaty obligations to United Nations bodies, often admit that their laws are not consistent with their assumed international commitments. This admission of "misconduct" is in itself respectable and creates a culture of trust and accountability while galvanizing civil society to work harder to correct wrongs. We explore some areas where international treaties and obligations have had the greatest impact on domestic marital regimes.

Consent

Perhaps the most instructive international convention on consent is the Convention on Consent to Marriage, Minimum Age for Marriage and Registration of Marriages which was adopted by the United Nations on 7 November

[110] Musawah, *Report Written Pursuant to HRC Resolution A/HRC/RES/24/23 On Child, Early and Forced Marriage To UN High Commissioner for Human Rights* (2013) (available online).

[111] Ibid.

[112] Ibid.

1962 and entered into force on 9 December 1964. This treaty took cognizance of what it termed "customs, ancient laws and practices related to marriage" and how these were "inconsistent with the principles outlined in the Charter of the United Nations and the Universal Declaration of Human Rights".[113] The Convention establishes the basis of marriage as full and free consent by both parties.[114] The Convention applies to all forms of marriages in the territories of contracting States. In this volume, Zimbabwe is the only country which has ratified this treaty. In line with its treaty obligations, Zimbabwe, in its 2013 Constitution, inserted a provision which guarantees free and full consent. That is not to say other countries in this volume do not have similar provisions on consent; however, it is less clear whether the requirements of this Convention influence their provisions as compared to the Convention on the Elimination of All Forms of Discrimination Against Women (CEDAW). Kenya's Constitution, for example, guarantees the right of adult persons to marry on the basis of free consent.

Age of marriageability

Although the Convention on Consent to Marriage, Minimum Age for Marriage and Registration of Marriages encourages contracting States to pass legislation stating the minimum age of marriage, it fails to state an exact age.[115] This is probably its greatest shortfall. Curiously, the CEDAW also fails to provide an exact age.[116] However, the Convention on the Rights of the Child (CRC) defines a child as a person below eighteen years unless the domestic law applicable provides that the age of majority may be attained earlier.[117] In Ghana, the Children's Act of 1998, which was passed to domesticate the CRC, provides that the "minimum

113 Preamble, Convention on Consent to Marriage, Minimum Age of Marriage and Registration of Marriages.

114 Ibid., Article 1.

115 Article 2, Convention on Consent to Marriage, Minimum Age of Marriage and Registration of Marriage.

116 Article 16(2), CEDAW.

117 Article 1, Convention on the Rights of the Child.

age of marriage of whatever kind shall be eighteen years".[118] Ghana's Children's Act abolished betrothal, dowry transactions in respect of children, and child marriages.[119]

Kenya's Children's Act of 2022 abolished child and early marriages, and other harmful customary practices children may be forced to undergo.[120] Kenya's Marriages Act of 2014 also states that the minimum marriage age in Kenya is eighteen years.[121] Kenya's situation is intriguing. Caroline Shilaho argues that the marital laws of Kenya, while purporting to comply with international best practices regarding marriageable age, exempted Muslims from the requirements of the law, a circuitous process which re-introduces child and forced marriages and other undesirable consequences. The other contributor from Kenya, Jadeed, challenges the international normative structure, which puts the marriageable age at eighteen, arguing that it is inconsistent with global efforts to promote safe sex amongst adolescents. Côte d'Ivoire, the only civil law jurisdiction herein, has also stated eighteen in its new matrimonial law as the minimum marriageable age. Nigeria's Child's Right Act of 2003 set the minimum age of eighteen.

Equality during, before, and at the dissolution of marriages

Though the Universal Declaration of Human Rights, the International Covenant on Civil and Political Rights, and the International Covenant on Economic, Social and Cultural Rights are rich in provisions on the equality of sexes within the context of marriage,[122] the CEDAW stretches this equality to its most elastic limits.

118 Section 14(2), Ghana's Children's Act 1998.

119 Ibid., section 14(1).

120 Sections 14 and 119, Kenya's Children Act 2022.

121 Section 4, Kenya's Marriage Act 2014.

122 Article 16(1), Universal Declaration of Human Rights; Article 23(4), International Covenant on Civil and Political Rights; Article 10, International Covenant on Economic, Social and Cultural Rights.

Article 11 of CEDAW mandates States to remove all forms of discrimination faced by women and guarantee equality between the sexes. State parties are directed to take the necessary measures to prohibit the dismissal of women on the grounds of pregnancy, maternity leave, or marital status. They are further directed to encourage the provision of assistive social services to women so that they can combine family obligations and work requirements and provide special protection to women during pregnancy in types of work deemed harmful to pregnant women. Section 16 contains a list of general areas in which States must work to remove discrimination: It covers:

a) The same right to enter into marriage;

b) The same right to freely choose a spouse and to enter into marriage with their free and full consent;

c) The same rights and responsibilities during marriage and at its dissolution;

d) The same rights and responsibilities as parents, irrespective of their marital status, in matters relating to their children; in all cases, the interests of the children shall be paramount;

e) The same rights to decide freely and responsibly on the number and spacing of their children and to have access to the information, education and means to enable them to exercise these rights;

f) The same rights and responsibilities with regard to guardianship, wardship, trusteeship and adoption of children, or similar institutions where these concepts exist in national legislation; in all cases, the interests of the children shall be paramount;

g) The same personal rights as husband and wife, including the right to choose a family name, a profession and an occupation;

h) The same rights for both spouses in respect of the ownership, acquisition, management, administration, enjoyment and disposition of property, whether free of charge or for valuable consideration.

In light of these provisions, many States, even if their legal systems do not provide the kind of equality envisaged by CEDAW, have inserted provisions into their laws to affirm this principle of equality. The Constitutions of Zimbabwe and Kenya recognize the equal rights of parties during and at the dissolution of marriages.[123] Ghana, on the other hand, only recognizes equal access to marital property but says very little about equal rights of spouses in respect of other matters such as custody or access to children.[124]

Commenting on the principles of equality in CEDAW, the CEDAW Committee has on several occasions stated that polygamy and bridewealth are incompatible with the Convention.[125] On polygamy, the Committee states:

> Polygamous marriage contravenes a woman's right to equality with men and can have such serious emotional and financial consequences for her and her dependents that such marriages ought to be discouraged and prohibited. The Committee notes with concern that some States parties, whose constitutions guarantee equal rights, permit polygamous marriage in accordance with personal or customary law.[126]

On bridewealth, the Committee has noted:

> Other countries allow a woman's marriage to be arranged for payment or preferment...subject to reasonable restrictions based for example on a woman's youth or consanguinity with her partner, a woman's right to choose when, if, and whom she will marry must be protected and enforced at law.[127]

[123] Article 45(3), 2010 Constitution of Kenya.

[124] Article 22, 1992 Constitution of Ghana.

[125] Bridewealth may be defined as, "the transfer of substantial resources in the form of goods from the groom or his relatives to the family of the bride". See Menelaos Apostolou, "Bridewealth and Brideservice as Instruments of Parental Choice", *Journal of Social, Evolutionary, and Cultural Psychology*, II, no. 3 (2008), p. 91.

[126] UN Committee on the Elimination of All Forms of Discrimination Against Women, "General Recommendation No 21: Equality in marriage and family relations" in *Note by the Secretariat, Compilation of General Comments and General Recommendations Adopted by Human Treaty Bodies* (2006), para. 14.

[127] Ibid., para. 16.

> "Payment or preferment" refers to transactions in which cash, goods or livestock are given to the bride or her family by the groom or his family; or a similar payment is made by the bride or her family to the groom or his family. This practice should not be in any way required for a marriage to be valid, and such agreements should not be recognized by the State party as enforceable.[128]

Polygamy and bridewealth are important incidents of customary and Islamic marriages in Africa, as shown by the contributions herein. Contrary to the CEDAW Committee sharp criticisms of these concepts, customary and Islamic marriages have proved popular in Africa, outlasting any criticisms that characterize them as demeaning to women. The reaction of African States to this criticism, at least on a State level, has been different. Whereas Kenya routinely admits that polygamous marriages, as permitted by its marital laws, are contrary to its obligations under CEDAW, it appears to have found little need to amend its laws to realign them with its international obligations. Ghana's legislature has failed over the years to adopt a Property Rights of Spouses Bill intended to provide equal property rights to spouses. In the absence of such a law, Ghana's courts have had to rely on their judicial creativity to settle property rights on the dissolution of a marriage.[129] Though polygamy is ingrained in Nigeria's customary and Islamic culture, legislative inroads have been made to prevent the extortion of prospective grooms through bridewealth payments.[130] Curiously, Côte d'Ivoire and Mauritius have tried not to ascribe legal validity to all forms of polygamous unions and the associated bridewealth payments. Unfortunately,

[128] UN Committee on the Elimination of All Forms of Discrimination Against Women, "General Recommendation on article 16 of the Convention on the Elimination of All Forms of Discrimination against Women", *CEDAW/C/GC/29*, (2013), para 33.

[129] See Maame Yaa Mensa-Bonsu and Maame A. S. Mensa-Bonsu, "To Win Both the Battle and the War: Judicial Determination of Property Rights of Spouses in Ghana", in J. Jarpa Dawuni (ed.), *Gender, Judging and the Courts in Africa* (2021).

[130] For example, the Limitation of Dowry Law 1956 (Cap 76 Laws of Eastern Nigeria) applies to the States of Eastern Nigeria and limits the amount required as bridewealth.

these measures have largely failed. Ivorians and Mauritians continue to contract customary marriages regardless of the state of the law. Comparing the situation in Kenya, Zimbabwe, Ghana, and Nigeria to that of Côte d'Ivoire and Mauritius, it is disingenuous to conclude that States have failed to fulfil their obligations under CEDAW. Irrespective of the State's regulation of polygamous marriages, citizens will always contract such marriages regardless, and often out of their own free will. CEDAW takes a euro-centric view of women's rights and liberation and purports to universalize this view.

FUTURE OF AFRICAN CUSTOMARY LAW MARRIAGES IN LIGHT OF STATUTORY ARRANGEMENTS

An acknowledgement of a multiplicity of normative orders in the various countries leads to questions not just about how these different legal orders may interact meaningfully, but about the future of African customary law (being, theoretically, the weaker legal system) and customary marriages. Statutory reforms have altered customary law rules, including those on marriage. In some countries, these reforms outline the procedures for the application, ascertainment, recognition, assimilation, and declaration of customary law. Nevertheless, the dents made in the practice of customary law have not minimized its significance as the personal law of many Africans. Customary law influences decisions about important aspects of the lives of many Africans. Referring to its earlier decision in the South African case of *Alexkor v Richtersveld Community*,[131] Van Der Westhuizen J explained that "customary law must be recognized as 'an integral part of our law' and 'an independent source of norms within the legal system'. It is a body of law by which millions of South Africans regulate their lives and must be treated accordingly".[132] Indeed, "The social reality is that the customary laws existed first and have continued to be generally observed, whether or

[131] [2003] ZACC 18 (available online).

[132] [2008] ZACC 18, para. 43 (available online).

not they are in accord with state law".[133] Commenting on the continued significance of customary law, Abdulmumini Oba explains that,

> Customary law has proved very resilient in a number of ways.... customary law is still relevant in the lives of Africans. Many aspects of customary law have remained authoritative, and some others are making comebacks. Customary law thinking was very prominent in the transitional justice programs that addressed the genocide in Rwanda and other gross violations of human rights that occurred in parts of Africa, such as Sierra Leone, Uganda, and Kenya, within the last few decades.[134]

Customary marriages will continue to thrive despite regulatory attempts to change their nature. African customary law will survive because it is a way of life. Even in the face of modern ideals and westernization, customary law and marriages will persist. Like many other indigenous populations, the world over, "Aboriginal people did not perceive their customary law in isolation from its social and religious context".[135]

As people go about their daily lives, they are not thinking about whether their actions are consistent with customary law; they are just living out that which is deeply ingrained in them. Allott explained that, "as far as the Africans who are members of ...[a] tribe are concerned, their customary law is not an occasional variant from the general law applicable to them; it is their general law prima facie applicable in civil and criminal matters".[136]

Customary law attaches to the person. For example, the occurrence of customary law marriages between Ghanaians living abroad is a reality. Mensa-Bonsu, in her chapter, explains that customary marriages between persons living

[133] Woodman, note 4 above, pp. 9-30.

[134] Oba, note 1 above, p. 59.

[135] McLachlan, note 28 above, p. 372.

[136] A. N. Allott, "The Judicial Ascertainment of Customary Law in British Africa", *Modern Law Review*, XX, no. 3 (1957), p. 246.

abroad are celebrated in Ghana, where couples tune in through a virtual video conferencing platform to partake in the ceremony.[137] Adegbite also mentions that in Nigeria, customary marriages may be contracted by proxy, meaning the prospective couple need not be physically present in the jurisdiction to contract a valid marriage.[138] Even in States which have tried to invalidate customary marriages in favor of civil marriages, such efforts have been futile. Kouassi[139] from Côte d'Ivoire and Gunpath from Mauritius show how the recognition of only civil marriages in Côte d'Ivoire and Mauritius has not prevented citizens from incorporating the customary marriage process into the statutory marital regime. These examples prove that customary law fulfils deeper personal and collective needs and define how individuals order their lives irrespective of their physical location. Invariably, the recognition and legitimacy of customary marriages do not depend on the State but on the acceptance of customary law by the people who regard it as their primary or personal law.

Customary law marriages, with all their imperfections, have come to stay because customary law is flexible and versatile and will change consistently to meet emerging demands.[140] A great strength of customary law is its amenability to change. Existing definitions of customary law envisage constant change. In Ghana, customary law is described as "the rules of law which by custom are applicable to particular communities in Ghana".[141] Commenting on the conceptual basis of the constitutional definition of customary law in Ghana, Samuel Asante, a legal scholar, explains that "[t]his definition postulates an empirical reference for the content of the law, reaffirming the truism that customary law is grounded on the customs

137 Mensa-Bonsu, note 45 above.

138 Adegbite, note 43 above.

139 Kouassi, note 32 above.

140 Ibid.

141 Article 11(3), 1992 Constitution of Ghana.

actually prevailing in the community".[142] This definition excludes judicial endorsement. Admittedly this is different in other countries. In the South African case of *Shilubana and Others v Nwamitwa,*[143] Van Der Westhuizen J explained that:

> The status of customary law in South Africa is constitutionally entrenched. Section 211 of the Constitution provides that the institution, status and role of traditional leadership are recognized subject to the constitution. It further states that a traditional authority that observes a system of customary law may function subject to applicable legislation and customs, including amendments to or repeal of that legislation and those customs, and that courts must apply customary law where it is applicable, subject to the constitution and relevant legislation.[144]

In Kenya, section 3(2) of the Judicature Act limits the application of customary law, stating that it is to guide courts in civil matters so long as it meets a repugnancy test and is not inconsistent with any written law. It is bemoaned that section 3(2) of the Act gives the courts wide discretionary powers to declare rules of customary law repugnant because repugnancy is undefined in the law.[145]

Woodman insists that "[t]here is abundant empirical evidence that the content of the customary laws of Africa has changed significantly in the past century and continues to change today".[146] He describes how customary transactions are now in writing, the growth of the concept of individually owned property and corresponding methods of property disposition, and the significant changes in the customary laws on inheritance as examples of its flexibility

142 Samuel K. B. Asante, "Interests in Land in the Customary Law of Ghana-A New Appraisal", *Yale Law Journal*, LXXIV, no. 5 (1965), p. 848.

143 [2008] ZACC, paras. 1-94.

144 Ibid., para. 42.

145 Francis Kariuki, *Customary Law Jurisprudence from Kenyan Courts: Implications for Traditional Justice Systems*, p. 7 (available online).

146 Woodman, note 4 above, p. 15; see also: Oba, note 1 above, p. 59.

and development.[147] Describing the traditional items given to the woman and her family during the wedding ceremony, Mensa-Bonsu explains, "the fact that more and more women have careers outside the home has seen the grooms' families presenting items like computers, iPad".[148] Until recently, it was unheard of to include electronic gadgets in the traditional marriage list of items to be procured by the prospective groom.

These changes can be traced to "the monetarization and commoditization brought about by global commerce", as well as the autonomy that local communities exercise in deciding how to respond to these influences.[149] Admittedly though, in its flexibility lies one of its greatest flaws; being left open to exploitation by those in authority. Living customary law is not susceptible to every wind of change and may remain unyielding despite pressures for change. The distinction between practiced and judicial customary law is important because the crystalized principles of customary law applied by the courts on the grounds of *stare decisis* tend to stagnate the growth of aspects of customary law.[150] For example, based on the customary law practice at the time, it was judicially decided that on death intestate, female children from a patrilineal community only had a life interest in their deceased father's estate. In 2016, instead of advancing the customary law, the Supreme Court of Ghana followed existing legal authorities and held *obiter* that:

> In the appropriate case, this Court has to revisit the customary law and practice that restricts to a life interest, a female child's inheritance of her father's property, in patrilineal system of inheritance, in the

[147] Woodman, note 4 above, p. 16.

[148] Mensa-Bonsu, note 45 above.

[149] Ibid.

[150] Chuma Himonga "The Future of Living Customary Law in African Legal Systems in the Twenty-First Century and Beyond, with Special Reference to South Africa", in Jeanmarie Fenrich, Paolo Galizzi, and Tracy Higgins (eds.), *The Future of African Customary Law* (2011), p. 32.

> context of Article 17 of the Constitution and section 10 of PNDCL 111....[151]

This is an example of judicial customary law being behind practiced customary law. The Supreme Court of Ghana held in the case of *Amponsah and others v. Budu*[152] that children born to a woman from a patrilineal community could not succeed to intestate property that their mother inherited from her father. The decision was based on the fact that such children do not belong to their grandfather's family. Upon their mother's death intestate, the property she inherited from her father reverted to his patrilineal family. These instances represent an "unsafe reliance on a system of judicial precedent for determining a customary law".[153] The courts are cautioned to be mindful "that customary law, like any other law, regulates the lives of people. The need for flexibility and the imperative to facilitate development must be balanced against the value of legal certainty, respect for vested rights, and the protection of constitutional rights".[154] Some scholars have questioned the practicality of codifying customary law.[155]

African customary law and customary marriages will stand the test of time because some of the alternatives, such as ordinance marriages, are seen as western by sections of the population. According to Anselm Kludze, a legal academic:

> If you ... go to my village [in the Volta Region of Ghana] and ask the leaders or the chiefs what type of law they are administering, none of them is going to tell you that he is administering folk law and that the courts are administering state law. What is here being called state law they would call in a pejorative sense

151 *Odamtten v Wuta-Ofei* (SC, 12 December 2018).

152 *Amponsah And Others v Budu* [1989-90] 2 GLR pp. 291-314.

153 Woodman, note 4 above, p. 23.

154 *Shilubana and Others*, note 132 above.

155 Woodman, note 4 above, p. 23.

> – 'English law,' even though it may well have been enacted by the parliament of Ghana.[156]

Furthermore, because some rights granted under the "progressive" Tanzania Marriage Act were foreign to some citizens and did not align with their beliefs and values, they chose not to assert their rights under the Act.[157] Despite the flaws in the customary law of intestate succession in Ghana, some rural dwellers refuse to comply with the Intestate Succession Act because they are "unwilling to surrender their legal heritages" for the statute law.[158] A reaction against westernization and a desire to preserve African customary law will result in its endurance. Despite the disadvantages of marriage under customary law, parties will, among other reasons, prefer it. Adegbite explains that the Criminal Code of Nigeria creates rights and privileges for spouses of statutory marriages but not spouses of customary and Islamic law marriages. However, this does not prevent people from marrying under custom.[159]

African customary law is resilient. It may not have all the answers to possible legal and modern problems, but in its dictates and existence is a people's history, pain, victories, beliefs, and perceptions, however flawed they may be. For these reasons, customary law and marriages, despite modern needs and aspirations and international obligations, will remain an important source of law in the lives of most Africans. Oba, responding to the same question about the future of African customary law, says that:

> customary law is still very strong in the realm of family law.... Admittedly, modern living presents

[156] John Griffiths, "Introduction", in Antony Allott and Gordon Woodman (eds), *People's Law and State Law: The Bellagio Papers* (1985), p. 17.

[157] Barthazar A. Rwezaura and Ulrike Wanitzek, "Family Law Reform in Tanzania: A Socio-Legal Report", *International Journal of Law Policy and Family*, II, no. 1 (1998), p. 2.

[158] Victor Gedzi, *Principles and Practices of Dispute Resolution in Ghana: Ewe and Akan Procedures on Females Inheritance and Property Rights* (2009), p. 110 (PhD dissertation, Erasmus University).

[159] Adegbite, "Legal Pluralism and Marriage in Nigeria: A Structure for Denying Rights to Women", *University of Ghana Law Journal*, XXXI (2020-2021), pp. 140-141.

> many challenges to which customary law has no ready answers. Yet, some norms of customary law are positive, beneficial, and relevant even in modern times. These norms should be incorporated into modern laws.[160]

Marriage is an important institution that requires regulation. Nevertheless, such regulation must be cognizant of human rights considerations, life experience, and legitimate socio-cultural expectations, among other demands. These considerations may conflict, but such conflicts provide an opportunity for education, compromises, and reflection. Being focused on a desired legislative goal without due regard for other lived realities tends to leave behind rural populations, whose lives may be enriched by alternative legal systems. Customary law, and by extension, customary marriages, cannot be ignored. Accordingly, State law may extract from customary law that which is valuable, with a view to making State law relatable to ordinary citizens. State law should, as much as possible, reflect traditional understandings of law to ensure the enjoyment of modern forms of rights. Ultimately, the State must respond to the distinctiveness and popularity of customary law to promote the rule of law and protect fundamental rights.

We now examine the contributions in this volume, highlighting the recommendations made.

SUMMARY OF CHAPTERS

Ghana

Christine Dowuona-Hammond, Abdul Baasit Aziz Bamba, and Mustapha Abdulai Mahamah inquire into the legislative and policy roots of discrimination and differential treatment of parties to Muslim marriages in Ghana. The authors undertake a comparative analysis of all three types of marriages to establish provisions that discriminate against Islamic marriages. For example, they observe that whereas an ordinance marriage can be solemnized in three ways,

[160] Oba, note 1 above, p. 79.

Islamic marriages can only be solemnized in one. In the event of non-compliance with the procedures for solemnization of ordinance marriages, the Act allows parties to restart the process towards the valid celebration of the marriage but does not make the same provision for Islamic marriages. The authors, therefore, argue that the laws governing the celebration and dissolution of Muslim marriages are stricter than those governing customary and ordinance marriages. They explain that the failure of the law to recognize the validity of Islamic marriages which do not comply with the onerous statutory requirements undermines marital and property rights of Muslims.

Thus, they insist that the principles of equality, non-discrimination, and religious freedom in Ghana's Constitution are not reflected in current legislation governing marriage in Ghana. The authors note that a draft Muslim Marriages and Divorce Bill fails to address the legislative and policy gaps identified in their chapter. They suggest reworking the bill to address the concerns raised.

Ama F. Hammond examines the historical development of the rules governing Christian marriages to highlight the significant differences between the received law and the existing customary laws, and the diverse legal systems that inform Ghana's legislation governing marriages. Although Hammond admits that there is no satisfactory definition of marriage in Ghana, she describes an ordinance marriage as heteronormative, monogamous, and exclusive to the parties involved. She explains that an ordinance marriage, whether celebrated in a church or a marriage registrar's office, must strictly comply with the relevant statutory requirement to be valid. Against this background, she observes that some Ghanaians choose to have their customary marriage "blessed" at church under the misconception that doing so converts their union to a Christian marriage recognized by law, considering the similarities between the two rituals.

Hammond examines the procedures for the solemnization of an ordinance marriage in Ghana and examines other ancillary questions related to solemnization of marriages, including objections to marriages and void and voidable marriages. She observes that a marriage may be void in Ghana if it offends English principles on consanguinity and affinity. Hammond argues that this provision is a colonial relic that only perpetuates imported and incompatible English notions of marriage without recognizing the nuances of Ghana's socio-cultural context. Hammond provides a detailed account of the procedures for the dissolution of an ordinance marriage in Ghana. Though there is just one ground for divorce in Ghana, Hammond notes that as many as six facts may be proven to establish this ground. These include adultery, desertion, unreasonable behavior, and irreconcilable differences.

She concludes that although the current regulatory framework on Christian marriage and divorce is largely adequate, some laws need to be modified or repealed to meet current socio-economic and technological needs. She recommends that unclear expressions such as marriage, unreasonable behavior, and adultery be defined, while laws which discriminate against women should be repealed.

Maame Yaa A. Mensa-Bonsu presents a detailed discussion of the characteristics commonly accepted by Ghanaian courts as essential features of customary marriages, as well as the challenges and inconsistencies in the decisions and their implications on the development of customary law. She also provides insights into the lived customary law practices concerning marriage in different communities, their divorce processes, and how these might depart from the judicially accepted principles of customary law.

The chapter distinguishes between marriage and concubinage. The author criticizes some forms of cohabitation as being at odds with equitable principles. The author, in her recommendations, calls on Parliament to make laws that draw a clear distinction between marriage and loose unions, properly so-called.

Nigeria

Folashade Rose Adegbite discusses the legal regimes governing statutory and customary marriages in Nigeria. She thoroughly analyzes the two types of marriage, the conditions necessary for their formation and dissolution, the flaws and gaps in the existing marriage regimes, and makes suggestions for improving these regimes.

Adegbite contends that the failure of the marriage laws to provide a minimum age has led to many controversies. Though the constitution provides a legal age of eighteen, it also contains a presumption that a woman married is of legal age. This, the author argues, diminishes the autonomy and agency of young girls and promotes early marriages. She further argues that the legal provisions which predicate a mother's consent on the absence, death, or insanity of a father when one of the parties to a marriage is above eighteen years but below twenty-one years are discriminatory. The author also notes the problems surrounding "double-decker" marriages in Nigeria. These types of marriages occur when parties contract both customary and statutory marriages.

In her recommendations, Adegbite calls for the enactment of new marriage laws as the current ones, passed many generations ago, have outlived their purpose. She further recommends that the legislature be clear about its position on the legal ramifications of a "double-decker" marriage and the minimum age of marriage. Last, the author calls on the State to sensitize Nigerians to the legally recognized types of marriages, their legal implications and the processes for their celebration and dissolution.

Muhammad Kamaldeen Imam-Tamim, presents a detailed description of the principles of Islamic marriage held by the officially recognized school of Islamic Jurisprudence in Nigeria, that is, the Malikī school of thought. He demonstrates how Nigerian use of Islamic family law has been tainted by traditions and customs, which occasionally contradict Islamic law and attributes this to the Islamic legal system's lack of codification. He demonstrates that Shariah regards marriage as eternal and permits its dissolution (judicially or extrajudicially) for compelling reasons. However, one is not required to give reasons for the divorce.

In his recommendations, Imam-Tamim suggests the codification of Islamic family law to avoid imprecision in its application and to curtail the further commixture of Islamic laws with unacceptable customs. He contends that the codification of Islamic family law will lead to strict adherence to the laws, thereby preventing child marriages, marrying off children without their consent and withholding consent to marriage for ethnocentric reasons.

Kenya

Addressing Islamic marriages in Kenya, Caroline Vicheti Shilaho takes an entirely different view from Moza Jadeed. She posits that the liberties granted to Islamic marriages and divorces in Kenya are unjustified and significantly curtail the rights to non-discrimination and equality guaranteed under Kenyan law. As a result, she suggests a uniform set of laws applicable to all marriages and divorces and consistent with Kenya's fundamental human rights and the religious rights of Kenyan Muslims. Shilaho begins her arguments by highlighting some aspects of Islamic marriage that conflict with Kenya's Constitution and Marriage Act, such as its polygamous nature, the absence of a minimum age requirement for marriage, the husband's right to unilateral divorce, Muslims being allowed to marry their cousins and the performance of marriages without the consent of the spouses. The author then compares some Islamic marriage rules with the international conventions Kenya has ratified. The comparison shows that elements of Islamic marriages, such as the absence of equal rights for both spouses during and at the dissolution of the Islamic marriage, child marriage, forced marriage, polygamy, and unilateral divorce, are inconsistent with international conventions. Shilaho criticizes Kenyan courts for their reluctance to deal with these conflicts when such cases are brought before them. The author recommends codifying Islamic laws consistent with the constitution. Alternatively, she suggests that a specific clause should be included in both the constitution and the Marriage Act, placing constitutional rights above religious rights.

She argues that Islamic family law should reflect ratified international provisions by granting equal rights to married couples, granting equal divorce rights, criminalizing early marriages and discouraging polygamous marriages. Finally, the author urges the courts to reach a uniform interpretation of Islamic family laws by dealing with the contradictions in the law and reconciling them with the constitution.

In her chapter Moza Jadeed evaluates the degree to which Kenyan law, specifically the Marriage Act of 2014 and the 2010 Constitution, recognizes Islamic marriages and divorce. The chapter notes that while Kenyan law recognizes Islamic marriages and divorces, the law does not state the substantive rules governing Islamic marriages. This is perhaps an admission of Kenya's numerous strands and sub-strands of Islamic thought. This chapter argues that the recognition of Islamic family law by the State accords with the core tenets of multiculturalism, especially the requirement that the distinctive attributes of minority groups should, as much as possible, be preserved. Specifically, the author contends that arguments about Islamic family law being inconsistent with the equality provisions of Kenya's Constitution are exaggerated or patently untrue.

This chapter relies on Islamic legal sources and decisions of Kenya's specialized Islamic courts, the Kadhis' courts, to shed light on the polygamous and heterosexual nature of Islamic marriages, their contractual nature, and the crucial requirements for the validity of Islamic marriage. The chapter also reveals that although Islam frowns on divorce (both judicial and extrajudicial), it permits dissolution on grounds of adultery, cruelty, desertion, denial of conjugal rights, inadequate maintenance, and sheer dislike of the other party.

Jadeed recommends setting up a committee to codify the relevant Islamic laws to resolve the uncertainty surrounding Islamic family law. Alternatively, she recommends that the judiciary make available the recently published Kadhis' Court Bench Book, which offers a useful overview of Islamic family laws.

In her contribution Annette Mbogoh notes that there five different forms of marriage in Kenya. These are Christian, Islamic, civil, Hindu and customary marriages. Though different substantive principles govern these marriages, they are all addressed under Kenya's Marriage Act of 2014. The chapter addresses the common statutory essential requirements shared by all five types of marriages, the procedures, and the grounds for the dissolution of marriages. Mbogoh emphasizes that all five types of marriage have the same legal status but are only valid if registered per the procedures laid down by the Act.

However, Mbogoh posits that the accommodations given to Islamic marriages tend to do more harm than good as such accommodations lead to inequality in the status of spouses. She argues that the Act provides inadequate protection to women in customary marriages as there is no express prohibition of African customs and practices that threaten their right to equality. The author further contends that the presumption of marriage is undermined by the Marriage Act's recognition of only registered marriages, leaving the parties unprotected on the death of one's partner.

While applauding the harmonization of all forms of marriage in one Act, the author makes further recommendations for its improvement. She urges public education about the importance of registering customary marriages performed before the Act was promulgated to preserve their legality.

South Africa

In the chapter on South Africa, Zama Mopai and Untalimile Crystal Mokoena and demonstrate that in South Africa, different types of marriages are governed by various laws, a reflection of the diverse religious, social, and traditional beliefs in South Africa. Civil marriages are monogamous and heterosexual, governed by the Marriage Act of 1961, and can be dissolved by a court-issued divorce decree, the death of a spouse, or by the setting aside of a voidable marriage. The Recognition of Customary Marriages Act of 2000 (RMCA) governs traditional marriages, which can be monogamous or polygamous and are dissolved through a decree of divorce by the court. Civil unions are regulated by the Civil Unions Act of 2006; they are monogamous and homosexual or heterosexual, and are dissolved using the same legal channels available to civil marriages.

Although the RCMA acknowledges customary marriages, the authors argue that it only focuses on one type of customary marriage, excluding others like those entered into for bloodline progression and succession, such as woman-to-woman marriages. They also contend that Section 4(9) of the RCMA, which provides that failure to register a customary marriage does not invalidate the marriage, creates a huge loophole that often results in non-compliance with the process for the dissolution of customary marriages. The customary marriages are dissolved extrajudicially and, in many cases, lead to unequal distribution of wealth based on patriarchy. Finally, they argue that the Civil Unions Act's failure to include provisions for minors who might want to get married constitutes age discrimination and is, as a result, unconstitutional.

In their recommendations, Mokoena and Mopai suggest revisiting the discrepancy between the official and living customary law in customary marriages. To prevent the celebration of civil marriages after customary ones have been solemnized, they also advise raising public awareness on the equality of all marriages. Last, they suggest that Section 4(9) of the RCMA be revised to make registration of customary marriages a requirement for its validity.

eSwatini

The contribution by Dumsani Dlamini explores the two distinct types of eSwatini marriages, customary marriages and civil marriages, and the legal regimes that govern them. The author carefully presents the scope of both marriages and the requirements for their validity, juxtaposing the current eSwatini marriage legislation with the proposed Marriage bill, 2022. He extensively discusses the bill, stating its purpose and thoroughly noting the developments it seeks to bring to eSwatini marriage laws. He commends the proposed bill referring to some of its provisions as a "major legal development." This study is noteworthy because it demonstrates how difficult it is to dissolve an eSwatini customary marriage and how the laws governing such unions do not permit or even encourage such a step. The author observes that in eSwatini, there are only two fault-based grounds for divorce, adultery and malicious desertion.

Dlamini identifies the flaws in the rules governing these marriages. He suggests specific actions to fix them, most of which are addressed by the marriage bill before Parliament. The author tacitly appreciates the significance attributed to eSwatini marriages and proposes that, for the certainty of the law, the bill should adequately define the term marriage. He submits that the bill should expressly state the equal dominance of both legal regimes governing marriages. He further appeals for separate pieces of legislation for each type of eSwatini marriage.

Zimbabwe

Lin Mary Manyika and Victor Ruombwa discuss the three different types of marriages in Zimbabwe: civil marriages, registered customary marriages, and unregistered customary marriages. This is accomplished by examining the laws that govern these unions and their legal ramifications.

The authors argue that because unregistered customary marriages are governed by customary law, which upholds male superiority, there is an unequal distribution of assets upon the dissolution of the marriage. The authors critique the ingenuity of Zimbabwe's courts in using several legal devices to protect the property rights of women whose customary marriages are divided. The authors make the case that there is a hierarchy of marriages in Zimbabwe, with unregistered customary marriages receiving the least amount of protection and recognition compared to civil marriages.

The authors examine Zimbabwe's new marriage law. They note that the law establishes a legal minimum age for marriage; outlaws homosexual and child marriages; and promotes equal rights during and after marriage. The authors criticize the law for failing to address issues relating to inheritance, property rights, guardianship, and maintenance of spouses. They also fault the new law for failing to adequately protect parties in unregistered customary marriages in Zimbabwe.

Mauritius

Rajendra Parsad Gunputh analyzes the laws governing Mauritian marriages and divorces, as well as the extent to which legal pluralism has impacted these laws. Whereas the French Civil Code inspired the substantive laws, the procedural laws were inspired by English law.

The chapter looks at the requirements and processes for a valid civil marriage and the grounds for the nullity and dissolution of marriages. The author points out that although Mauritians contract civil, religious and customary marriages, the only legally recognized form of marriage is a civil marriage. Religious marriages have no legal effect unless preceded by a civil marriage. Consequently, children born in religious marriages are not legitimate but natural children.

In his recommendations, Gunputh urges a review of the laws to recognize customary and religious marriages to make the marriage laws consistent with individual rights.

Côte d'Ivoire

Alfred Kouassi examines the 2019 matrimonial law of Côte d'Ivoire, which abolished the legal validity of marriages other than civil marriages. Kouassi reveals that although the legal system recognizes only civil marriages as valid, the other forms of marriage (de facto unions) are recognized for limited purposes, such as guardianship and custody.

Kouassi begins by analyzing various forms of de facto unions in Côte d'Ivoire, such as religious marriages, concubinage, and customary marriages, and the legal ramifications of ending these unions. The chapter then outlines the fundamental conditions for celebrating civil marriages, such as the heterosexuality of the spouses, the attainment of a minimum age of eighteen, and the future spouses' free consent. This chapter considers the formal requirements for solemnizing a civil marriage, including pre-wedding and wedding day formalities. The chapter further outlines the conditions that may result in the annulment of marriages, including a defect in consent, marrying below the legal age, and lack of consent. The author assesses the requirements for the dissolution of a marriage. These include the death of one of the spouses, divorce, a judicial pronouncement on the absence of one of the spouses, among others. Kouassi notes that even though the Marriage Act recognizes only civil marriages as a valid form of matrimony, references to engagements (a de facto union) are made in the same Act as a basis for proving paternity. He, therefore, calls on Parliament to clarify its position on de facto and same-sex unions.

CONCLUSION

This book has been an enriching and worthwhile experience in understanding the nature, types, and legal marriage rules in Côte d'Ivoire, eSwatini, Ghana, Kenya, Mauritius, Nigeria, South Africa, and Zimbabwe. The diversity in the legal systems and arrangements in these countries is fascinating. Contrary to assumptions that the laws in African countries are similar, these chapters prove otherwise. To be sure, there are similarities not only in the laws but in the culture and beliefs that inform customary laws. There are similarities in the rules governing ordinance marriages in the common law countries. However, the striking differences present an opportunity for countries to learn and possibly adapt workable practices and laws from one another.

In all the chapters the need for legislative reform stands out, particularly in the State treatment of customary laws and marriages. While some countries assert the equality of all types of marriages, others subordinate customary marriages to those regulated by statute. Customary law and marriages may have shortcomings, but these should not preclude the State from constantly negotiating better outcomes for spouses, irrespective of the kind of marriage contracted. States need to make an effort to better understand customary law, and its importance in the lives of its people and guide it towards modification and regeneration.

Most authors demand clearer definitions of certain marriage-related expressions to promote legal certainty, without, of course, undermining the need for discretion to deal with differing circumstances. Others require clarity in ambiguous legal provisions. The importance of legal certainty in the administration of justice should not be underestimated. States must regulate conduct and processes with certainty to promote predictability and prevent arbitrariness.

Some insisted on well-defined administrative procedures for regulating and registering marriages and better administrative oversight to ensure compliance with laws. These demands require not only the political will of leadership to streamline administrative procedures to prevent multiple illegal marriages, but also an honest dedication to the goals of justice. States are encouraged to reexamine their laws and reconcile them with their international obligations.

States must exploit the benefits of information technology to accelerate the collection and dissemination of information, as manual processes can only go so far in detecting fraud and duplication in marriage arrangements.

Some marriage laws, by virtue of their historical origins, discriminate against women throughout the celebration and dissolution of the marriage. This must change. If Africa will realize its potential in all spheres of life, women must be respected and accorded all rights due them irrespective of the type of marriage they contract. The contribution of women to the stability, development, and wealth of their families and nations is key to the continent's growth. Africa should have a vested interest in building stronger families. But these families can only be strengthened if they are in regulatory spaces that engender equality, respect for fundamental human rights, and place value on women's contributions to society. States are enjoined to create and sustain a legal environment where women can thrive.

Last, States cannot take legal literacy for granted. A number of authors recommended that governments actively facilitate legal education on the nature and effect of marriages and their attendant rights and obligations. This is an important step towards equality in marriages. With education, parties, especially women, can make an informed choice among the various types of marriages and demand the one that best suits their interests and aspirations.

It is hoped that the next few years will witness rapid, informed, and well-intentioned changes in the laws regulating marriages in Africa.

Ghana

Chapter Two The Regulation of Islamic Marriage and Divorce in Ghana: Legislative and Policy Roots of Discrimination

Ghana's legal system is not dissimilar from other post-colonial systems in Africa to the extent that multiple systems of law operate within the same territorial space. This means that "[the] national legal system is based on the mixture of indigenous experiences, religious practices and received legal experiences from abroad".[1] Ghana's pluralist legal system means that the State recognizes, and its citizens are "subject to more than one system of law within a particular legal jurisdiction at one and the same time".[2] In other words, contemporary Ghanaian law reflects the received English law, customary law, and statutory law, which may be influenced from time to time by the country's religious ethos and cultural experiences. For the purpose of governance, most pluralistic legal systems must attempt to integrate and harmonize the different normative systems into a centralized legal framework. This involves unifying widely differing and heterogeneous normative systems with the ultimate aim of regulating the conduct of multiple groups often differentiated by ethnicity, geography, and religion.

Ghana's pluralistic legal system recognizes multiple forms of marriage and divorce, some regulated by customary law and others by statute law, and its experience in regulating

[1] Poku Adusei, "Towards a Transsystemic Study of the Ghana Legal System", *Global Journal of Comparative Law*, VI (2017), p. 33.

[2] Ibid.

the different kinds of marriage reveals the difficulties inherent in the State's mediatory role of reconciling and accommodating alternative normative systems for the purpose of governance. The impact of Ghana's pluralistic legal system is strongly manifested in its regulation of marriage, divorce, adoption, succession, and child custody and maintenance.

This chapter examines the inequities and imbalances embedded in regulating Islamic marriages and divorces within the context of its pluralistic legal system. The chapter critically assesses the laws regulating the different kinds of marriage in Ghana and draws attention to the comparative deficiencies in the current regulatory framework on Islamic marriages and divorces. Muslims in Ghana are faced with challenges presented by a severely deficient regulatory regime that undermines the validity and legitimacy of Islamic marriages and divorces. The factors which have influenced the design, scope, and focus of the existing regulatory infrastructure on Islamic marriages and divorces in Ghana are considered, paying attention to the areas of differentiation and discrimination, compared with the other kinds of marriages recognized under Ghana law. The chapter highlights how the existing legislative framework on Islamic marriages has nurtured practical impediments relating to succession and devolution of property, among other issues, for practicing Muslims in Ghana. We argue that the legislative and judicial approach to regulating Islamic marriages and divorces reveals systemic biases that arguably undermine the enjoyment of the right of Muslims to free religious expression as guaranteed in the 1992 Constitution.

The chapter is divided into four parts. An overview is presented of the key elements of legal pluralism in Ghana and the status discussed of Islamic family law in Ghana's legal system. This is followed by a brief review of Ghana's pluralistic regulatory framework on marriage and divorce and the constitutional right of free religious expression, accompanied by a comparative review of the statutory regulation of Islamic, Customary, and Ordinance Marriages and Divorces focusing on the distinctions in the formal requirements for validity, options for solemnization, and registration requirements. Next the impact is explored of the current regulatory framework for Islamic marriages and divorces on the right of Muslims to practice their religion and to manifest such practice. Proposals are made for improving the existing legal framework on Islamic marriages and divorces.

LEGAL PLURALISM AND THE STATUS OF ISLAMIC FAMILY LAW IN GHANA

Key elements of legal pluralism in Ghana

Ghana's pluralistic legal system reflects the legacy of political and legal developments that characterized the British presence in the country. Full-scale colonialism in Ghana was preceded by trade and missionary activities. Though the trade that occurred in the Gold Coast was initially confined to gold and ivory in the eighteenth century, slaves were the objects of trade during that century.[3] "Legitimate trade" in palm oil, cotton, rubber, gum copal, and others only took off after the abolition of the slave trade.[4] With respect to the flurry of missionary activities, different Christian missionary organizations started making incursions into the Gold Coast from about the 1830s. The mission was, for all intents and purposes, a civilizing mission. Motivated by a desire to obtain the necessary resources to feed their home populations and a diametrically contradictory objective of "saving the souls" of indigenous populations, the British set about colonizing the Gold Coast and, subsequently, other parts of present-day Ghana.

Although the implantation of English law is often dated to 1876, there is a widely held view that English jurisdiction was first introduced when some eight Fanti chiefs signed the Bond of 1844 with the British.[5] The Bond had a two-fold objective of ending harmful cultural practices, on one

[3] Robert Addo-Fening, "Ghana under Colonial Rule: An Outline of the Early Period and the Interwar Years", *Transactions of the Historical Society of Ghana*, XV (2013), pp. 39-40; William Burnett Harvey, *Law and Social Change in Ghana* (1966), p. 6.

[4] Ibid.

[5] Adusei, note 1 above, p. 31.

hand, and formalizing the introduction of English law over the native States that existed along the coast, on the other. In exchange, the British offered these States protection against the Ashanti further inland.[6] The context within which the Bond was signed and the nationalities of the parties are revealing in one respect: it confirmed that native States with established political and legal systems existed in parts of the territory today called Ghana.

The Bond of 1844 was followed by the Constitution of 1850, which had as one of its main pillars the promotion of Christianity among the natives.[7] Royal Instructions issued pursuant to the Royal Charter of 1850 that created the 1850 Constitution authorized the Governor "to promote religion and education among the native inhabitants ... and to take such measures as may appear ... to be necessary for their conversion to the Christian faith, and for their advancement in civilization".[8] Arguably, the privileging of Christianity in the 1850 Constitution together with the declared agenda of the Christian missionaries to "civilize" the African set in motion a legislative trajectory of differential treatment of various religious groups in modern-day Ghana.

Ghana's ethnic composition has remained diverse to this day. The Akans have occupied the southwestern part of Ghana for centuries. To the north are groups of the Mole-Dagbani stock. The southeastern areas of Ghana are peopled by Ewe-speaking communities, whereas the central plains of Ghana contain the Ga people.

The Constitution of 1874 took further steps in expanding British jurisdiction in Ghana and paved the way for the enactment of the Supreme Court Ordinance of 1876. This Ordinance established a legal system that reflected the incremental diversity of laws in the Gold Coast[9] and

[6] Ibid.

[7] F. A. R. Bennion, *Constitutional Law of Ghana* (1962), p. 11.

[8] Ibid., p. 11.

[9] See generally Atudiwe P Atupare, "Sarbah on Legal Pluralism and Sense of Legality in the Gold Coast: Some Insights for Ghana's Current legal System", *University of Ghana Law Journal*, XXVII (2014), pp. 100-124; Adusei, note 1 above, p. 25; Kofi Quashigah, "The Historical Development of the Legal System of Ghana:

formally introduced English law into the Gold Coast. Section 14 provided that, "the Common Law, the doctrines of Equity, and the statutes of general application which were in force in England at the date when the Colony obtained a local legislature, that is to say, on the 24th day of July 1874, shall be in force within the jurisdiction of the Court".[10] It is noteworthy to add that after 24 July 1874, laws passed in England had no automatic application in the Gold Coast. The umbilical cord was cut from that day, and English law would come to apply in the Gold Coast and take on a life of its own. This view is supported by section 17 of the Ordinance, which subjected the application of English law to "local circumstances" and "existing or future Ordinances" of the colonial legislature. Customary law was preserved under section 10, which mandated Courts to "respect Native Law as much as possible". The application of customary law depended on how well the law passed a "repugnancy test".[11] The law would only apply if it was not "repugnant to justice, equity and good conscience".[12]

To the extent the British in colonial Ghana were *colonialists* and *Christians*, it goes without saying that the legal structure established essentially reflected British political, social, and economic objectives as well as British notions of justice and fairness, which invariably would be deduced from the values of Christian Britain.

The germ of legal pluralism introduced in 1876 is still evident in Ghana's contemporary legal system. The 1992

An Example of the Coexistence of Two Systems of Law", *Fundamina*, XIV, no. 2 (2008), pp. 95-114.

10 Present-day Ghana is an amalgamation of several former British possessions: the Colony, the Ashanti Territories, the Northern Territories, and the Trans-Volta Togoland. The Colony initially did not include the Ashanti territories, the northern parts of Ghana, and the Tans-Volta Togoland. In 1901, after a series of wars with the Ashanti peoples, the Ashanti territories were annexed by the Crown through an Order-In-Council. Another Order-In-Council declared a British protectorate over the northern parts of Ghana. The Trans-Volta was a former German possession placed under British administration after the First World War. It subsequently joined the rest of the British possessions in the Gold Coast through a plebiscite held in 1956. See Bennion, note 7 above, pp. 23, 56-57.

11 Section 19, Supreme Court Ordinance 1876.

12 Ibid.

Constitution in Chapter 11 lists Ghana's diverse legal sources as the Constitution; enactments made by or under the authority of Parliament established by the Constitution; any Orders, Rules, and Regulations made by any person or authority under a power conferred by the Constitution; the existing law; and the common law.[13] The pluralism of Ghana's legal system is also reflected in its approaches to resolving conflicts within and between the various systems of law that constitute the legal system. Ghana's Courts Act 1994 (Act 459) contains elaborate "choice of law" rules.[14]

The common law of Ghana is defined to include the common law qua common law, rules of equity, and customary law.[15] Therefore, the common law of Ghana is not the same as the common law of England. Ghana's common law definition is more expansive though it embodies the substratum of that body of law developed in England from the practices of judges and referred to as the "common law".

Customary law itself is defined in Article 11(3) to mean "rules of law which by custom are applicable to particular communities in Ghana". This definition of customary law is quite unhelpful and raises more questions than it answers.[16] How might such rules be identified? Is there a way to identify polities that have these rules? How can one show that these rules are customarily applied to such polities? The Constitution provides no answers, although various laws related to chieftaincy and judicial decisions have provided some guidance on these matters. The imprecise nature of this definition notwithstanding, it is crucial to add that the Constitution has outlawed customary practices that are harmful.[17] Individuals and communities are free to practice their culture; indeed, it is a right. However, that right must

13 Article 11(1), 1992 Constitution of Ghana.

14 Section 54(1), Courts Act 1994.

15 Ibid., Article 11(2).

16 For a fuller discussion on problems of defining customary law in Ghana, see H. J. A. N. Mensa-Bonsu, "Of Nuts in the Ground Not Being Groundnuts – The Current State of Customary Law in Ghana", *University of Ghana Law Journal,* XXII (2002-2004), pp. 1-24.

17 Articles 26 and 39(2), 1992 Constitution of Ghana.

be exercised in a manner that does not cause harm to others. In line with this renewed thinking about harmful cultural practices, the Criminal Offences Act 1960 (Act 29) has taken steps to abolish harmful widowhood rights,[18] customary slavery,[19] and female genital mutilation[20] in Ghana.

Status of Islamic family law in Ghana's legal system

Islam has existed in Africa for centuries. Josiah Aryeh once described it thus:

> The religion claims a pedigree traceable from its early patriarchs, Abraham and Ishmael through Moses and Jesus Christ with links to the ancient lawgiver, Hammurabi of Babylon. The Sunni/Shiite division in Islam, so relevant elsewhere, has not been replicated in West Africa where Muslims are predominantly Sunnis of the Maliki School. Originally propagated by itinerant clerics and merchants, and long misrepresented in African historiography as militaristic, Islam has enjoyed widespread appeal and continues to attract adherents. The Islamic message found an easy conduit in the Hausa lingua franca of the northern parts of West Africa. In parts of Ghana, Islam is a vibrant socio-religious system providing succour and faith to adherents.[21]

A sizable number of Ghanaians are Muslims, emphasizing the need to properly understand how Islamic law fits into the legal architecture of the State.[22] Islam differs fundamentally from Christianity because the line that separates religion and the State is less clear. In Islam, the temporal and the spiritual aspects of life are enmeshed with each other. Islamic law, more appropriately called Sharia, pervades the entire life

[18] Section 88A, Criminal Offences Act 1960 as amended.

[19] Ibid., section 314A.

[20] Ibid., section 69A.

[21] N. A. Josiah-Aryeh, "A Basis for Islamic Law in Ghana", *University of Ghana Law Journal*, XXI (2000-2002), p. 92.

[22] Population and Housing Census 2021.

of an adherent. Sharia "serves as a guide and provides the means to resolve conflicts among individuals and between the individual and the State".[23] Sharia, therefore, transcends crime and punishment, a mischaracterization non-Muslims especially ascribe to it.[24]

The most important source of Islamic law is the Holy Quran, which is the word of Allah Himself.[25] The sayings of the Holy Prophet Mohammed, the Hadith, and the Sunna are next in the line of prominence.[26] These sayings and doings of the Holy Prophet help expound the general principles that the Holy Quran establishes. Other sources of Islamic law include the consensus of Islamic scholars on an issue (the Ijma), analogical deductions from Islamic principles (the Qiyas), and progressive reasoning by analogy (Ijtihad).[27]

The application of Islamic law is said to have been affected by the colonial policy, which made it applicable as a variation of customary law.[28] Early anthropological studies undertaken by colonial governments are said to be part of "efforts to dominate Muslim societies."[29] In order to achieve this objective, it was important for colonial officials to understand Islam and the milieu of political, social, and cultural structures within which Islam was situated.[30] Initially, some indigenous communities were identified as either Muslim or strongly influenced by Islam.[31] These

[23] Abdul Baasit Aziz-Bamba, "Accommodating Muslim Family Law in Ghana: Strategies and Challenges", in Henrietta J. A. N. Mensa-Bonsu, et al. (eds.), *Ghana Law Since Independence: History, Development and Prospects* (2007), p. 468.

[24] Ibid.

[25] Ibid.; See also Victor Essien, "Sources of Law in Ghana", *Journal of Black Studies*, XXIV, no. 3 (1994), p. 249.

[26] Ibid.

[27] Ibid.

[28] Ibid.

[29] John R. Bowen, "Anthropology and Islamic Law", in Anver M. Emon and Rumee Ahmed (eds.), *The Oxford Handbook of Islamic Law* (2015).

[30] Holger Weiss, *Between Accommodation and Revivalism: Muslims, the State and Society in Ghana from the Precolonial to the Postcolonial Era* (2008), p. 215.

[31] Ibid.

were the more centralized States of the Northern Territories. Others, especially the acephalous societies of the Northern Territories, were thought to view Islam with aversion.[32] However, George Ekum Ferguson's exploration into the Northern Territories showed that these territories' political, social, and cultural institutions had few traces of Islam. Nevertheless, Muslim communities in some societies held powerful and influential positions – including political ones – to the extent that the framework for Islamization had been laid in some communities.[33]

This observation is important because it lends credence to the view that Islamic law and culture are not synonymous with ethnic customary law and practices. Therefore, the relationship between Muslim and non-Muslim communities was one of negotiation and co-existence. The British abolished Islamic courts and instead pursued policies that gradually drove Muslim religious and political leaders out of the political sphere, to be replaced by non-Muslim rulers and British colonial officials.[34] In this way, the burgeoning legal system was weaned off Islamic law, leading to its extra-legal, intra-community application.

Though Islamic law is generally under-researched compared to other systems of law in Ghana, Islamic family law has received modest commentary. It should be noted that Islamic family law as applied in post-colonial Africa is invariably related to legal pluralism because "in several states in contemporary Africa, Islamic family law is applied simultaneously with other legal systems and each country has its own specific ways of applying laws, and different legal statuses accorded to it by law".[35] In Ghana, Islamic family law covers marriage, divorce, succession, custody of children, and maintenance.[36] Muslims have been applying

[32] Ibid.

[33] Ibid.

[34] Ibid., chapter 4.

[35] Fulera Issaka-Toure and Ousseina D. Alidou, "Introduction: Current Perspectives on Islamic Family law in Africa", *Islamic Africa*, XI (2020), p. 155.

[36] Aziz-Bamba, note 23 above, p. 468; Yushawu Abubakari, "Marriage under the Muhammadan Ordinance in Ghana: Knowledge and Perceptions of Muslims in

Islamic law to these matters even though the context of application excludes formal State and judicial structures. The result is that Islamic law has been "removed from the searching scrutiny of the courts and mainstream legal discourses".[37]

Commentary on Ghana's Islamic family law has often emanated from judicial and scholarly consideration of the Marriage of Mohammedans Ordinance, which now forms Part Two of the Marriages Act 1884-1985. This colonial-era legislation is perhaps the only express recognition of Islamic law in Ghana. The Ordinance contained provisions on the formal requirements relating to Muslim marriages and the procedures for registering these types of marriages. According to section 10 of the Marriage of Mohammedans Ordinance (CAP 129) (now repealed), where a Muslim marriage is registered in accordance with the Ordinance, succession to property on the death of one spouse falls to be decided according to the rules of Islamic law. However, many Muslims seem not to be aware of the existence of the Ordinance or the current Part Two of the Marriages Act. Those who are aware do not seem to accord any weight to its provisions. Currently, registration of Muslim marriages is rare.[38] Few Imams are registered under the provisions of the law, and worse still, few district assemblies keep registers of Muslim marriages.[39] The treatment Muslims accord to the provisions of the law emanates in part from its linguistic labeling. Many Muslims loathe the term "Mohammedan" and consider it derogatory. For these reasons, some scholars prefer not to address Muslim marriages when writing about marriages in Ghana.[40]

Regarding judicial attitudes to Muslim marriages and divorces, the Ghanaian courts have established a principle

Tamale in the Northern Region", *ADDRI Journal of Arts and Social Sciences Ghana,* XIX, no. 1(7) (2022), p. 175.

37 Aziz-Bamba, note 23 above, p. 467.

38 Gordon R. Woodman, "Family Law in Ghana under the Constitution 1992", in *International Survey of Family Law* (2003), p. 198.

39 Weiss, note 30 above, pp. 368-369.

40 Woodman, note 38 above.

of referring to unregistered Muslim marriages as customary marriages. In *Kwakye v Tuba*,[41] Ollennu J, as he then was, stated:

> [I]t is only a Muslim who married according to Mohammedan law, and had his said marriage registered under the Ordinance in the manner provided by the Ordinance whose succession shall be regulated by Mohammedan law. In the eyes of our law, a marriage by a Mohammedan, according to Mohammedan law, is at its very best a marriage by customary law and does not affect succession to his estate, unless the said marriage is registered under the Ordinance. Therefore, if a Mohammedan died not having married, or if married not having had his said marriage registered under the Marriage of Mohammedans Ordinance, the only law which can regulate succession to his estate is his personal law, i.e., the customary law of the tribe to which he belonged.[42]

The *Kwakye* case was followed by *Brimah and Cosbold v Asana*.[43] In this case, the deceased person was a Muslim. Before his death, he made a will and devised a house to the plaintiffs "upon trusts." The plaintiffs were granted probate to his will, but the widow, who occupied a portion of the house, refused to quit on the ground that she was entitled to a portion of the deceased's estate in Islamic law. Ollennu J, who had earlier decided the *Kwakye* case, noted that:

> It is wrongly assumed that because the deceased was a Muslim, his personal law as to succession must be regulated by Islamic law. That assumption is a grievous error. A Ghanaian can opt for any religious faith or creed, but that choice which he freely and voluntarily makes cannot operate to deprive him of rights and privileges under the law of the land, neither can it exempt him from his liabilities and duties under

[41] [1961] GLR 720-725 (H.C.).

[42] Ibid., p. 274.

[43] [1962] 1 GLR 118 – 120 (H.C.).

> it; whether a Christian or Muslim, pagan or atheist, a Ghanaian remains subject to the law of the land. And at his death, unless otherwise provided by law, devolution of his property upon testacy or intestacy would be regulated by his personal law as modified by statute or otherwise.[44]

Since the deceased was a Ga Mashie, it was the customary law of Ga Mashie that applied, the Court held. The requirement for compliance with the provisions of the Marriage of Mohammedans Ordinance was re-emphasized. In *Hausa v Haruna*,[45] the plaintiff, as the sole surviving wife, applied for letters of administration to administer the estate of her deceased husband, who died intestate without an issue. It was her claim that because she and her husband were Muslims, she was entitled to two-thirds of her husband's estate, for which reason she was the appropriate person entitled to the grant of letter of administration. The sister and paternal nephew of the deceased caveated. Lassey J, commenting on the issue, stated:

> There is no doubt that Muslims or Mohammedans form a large proportion of the population of present-day Ghana, but I know not of any special legislation which accords special recognition to Mohammedan law in respect of matters or causes between or exclusively affecting Mohammedans or Muslims, relating to their civil status, marriage, and succession or inheritance. Save for the provisions relating to the registration of marriages and divorces contained in the Marriage of Mohammedans Ordinance, Mohammedan or Muslim law in Ghana is treated as native law and custom and administered as such. [46]

These cases, it appears, seem to suggest that there are registered Muslim marriages under the Marriage of Mohammedans Ordinance and unregistered Muslim marriages that fall outside the ambit of the Ordinance.

[44] Ibid., p. 119.

[45] [1963] 2 GLR 212 – 219 (H.C.).

[46] Ibid., p. 212.

Interestingly, in referring to unregistered Muslim marriages as customary marriages, the judges have in mind the customary law of the party who contracted the Muslim marriage. For example, it could be Ga customary law, Akan customary law, or Dagomba customary law. In other words, describing an unregistered Muslim marriage in terms of customary law is just a circuitous way of declaring an unregistered Muslim marriage qua Muslim marriage as invalid.

Commenting on the status of Muslim marriages in 1965, Ollennu's justification for conceiving of Islamic law as customary law was that "in almost every community in Ghana where Islamic law is said to exist, it will be found that what prevails is Islamic customary law and not the pure Islamic law. The influence of Islamic law on customary law may be great or small but what is practiced is the customary law".[47] Yeboa suggests that most Muslim marriages are contracted according to customary law requirements with additional Islamic elements like the *Sadaki*.[48] It is this mingling of customary and religious practices that may have led jurists like Ollennu to conclude that Islamic law is not customary law properly so-called.[49]

This view cannot be correct, at least post-1992. The definition of customary law in Articles 11(2) and 11(3) of the 1992 Constitution is not based on ethnic or religious grounds. It refers to the rules of law that, by custom, are applicable to particular communities in Ghana. Thus, all that matters is whether a particular community has distinct customs. Neither is the definition of customary law tied to physical, geographic, or spatial considerations. Thus, the definition of "community" may be extended to a body of persons throughout the Republic, who by virtue of an essential characteristic, share the same customs. If this line of thinking is pursued, it may be argued that Islamic

[47] N. A. Ollennu, "Law of Succession in Ghana", *University of Ghana Law Journal*, II (1965), p. 13.

[48] Ken Y. Yeboa, "Bigamy and Islamic Marriages in the Law of Ghana: The Legislator's Dilemma or Studied Silence", *Review of Ghana Law*, XIX (1993-1995), p. 76.

[49] Ibid.

law could, under the right circumstances, be considered as customary law. In the case of detribalized areas such as the various "zongos", where different ethnic groups from within and outside Ghana have conglomerated and settled and formed a new culture, way of life, and indeed a new "customary" law based on the Islamic faith, that new culture based on the Islamic faith must qualify as their customary law. "Zongo" is a Hausa word used to refer to a camping place for caravan traders or a lodging place for travellers. [50] Historically, these areas were occupied largely by Muslim traders, who travelled from neighboring areas and regions, and are now religiously and ethnically pluralistic.[51]

Generally, the cases seem to take the view that Islamic law is not a system of law in its own right but is rather an overlay on customary law. On the contrary, the true and proper character of Islamic law is more complex. Ollennu's pronouncements reveal a lack of appreciation of the essence of Islamic law in failing to grasp the meaning of Islamic law and its status as a fully-fledged legal system in its own right. His characterization of Islamic law ignored the political factors that have contributed to the marginalization and near exclusion of Islamic law in official legal discourse. As explained earlier, the close connection between Muslim and non-Muslim communities does not lead to the irresistible conclusion that the customary law applied in each community mixes with the other. The fact that a person belongs to both communities does not mean such a person intends customary law to apply to them rather than Islamic law. It is rather a clash of customary laws to which the choice of law rules in Act 459 should apply.

It is particularly wrong to assume that a Muslim will always have a "residual customary law he/she can fall back on for some reason [when] he/she cannot have recourse

[50] Roy Clive Abraham, *Dictionary of the Hausa Language* (1962).

[51] Samuel Aniegye Ntewusu, "One Hundred Years of Muslim Community in Accra: A Historical Study of Tudu from 1900 to 2000", in Pade Badru and Brigid M. Sackey (eds.), *Islam in South of the Sahara: Essays in Gender Relations and Political Reforms* (2013), pp. 67-96; Stephen Owoahene-Acheampong and Charles Prempeh, "Contemporary Zongo Communities in Accra Interfaith Marriages: The Case of Muslims and Christians in Accra", *African Studies Quarterly*, XIX, no. 1 (2020), pp. 23-40.

to Islamic law as his/her personal law".[52] Muslims are encouraged to align their affairs with Islamic law, and some schools of Islamic jurisprudence only permit local customs and norms to the extent that they do not violate Islamic law.[53] Therefore, to a Muslim, Islamic law will most likely be the most prominent feature of his life and will be preferred over customary law, even trumping a Muslim's ethnic customary law. It is more conceivable that a Muslim would prefer to have his property devolve according to Islamic law than customary law. The judicial decisions examined here appear to undermine this nuance. If Islamic law is considered to be customary law, it only makes sense that when a marriage is not registered under the statutory provision, the provisions governing customary law marriages should apply.

It must be noted, however, that all these arguments may be academic because section 19(b) of the Intestate Succession Act has repealed section 10 of the Marriage of Mohammedans Ordinance, which made it possible for a married Muslim's estate to be governed by Islamic law upon his death intestate if his marriage was registered. Therefore, currently, irrespective of whether a Muslim marries under the Ordinance, his estate will devolve according to the rules of the Intestate Succession Act if he dies intestate. As Adinyira JSC stated in *Odamtten and Others v Wuta-Offei and Another*,[54] "PNDCL 111 introduced a unified system of intestate succession in Ghana, irrespective of the fact that the deceased came from a matrilineal or a patrilineal family, or was married under the Marriage Ordinance, Cap 127, or under the Marriage of Mohammedans Ordinance, Cap 129".[55] This new position further constricts the application of the provisions of the Marriage of Mohammedans Ordinance, which are now reproduced in Part Two of the Marriages Act. Thus, unless a Muslim makes a will choosing Islamic law as his personal law, it will be near impossible to apply Islamic law to their estate.

[52] Aziz-Bamba, note 23 above, p. 471.

[53] Ibid.

[54] (J4 20 of 2016) [2018] GHASC 63 (12 December 2018) (available online).

[55] Ibid.

It must be noted that the judicial approach championed by judges like Ollennu has not always been the case. There is evidence to suggest that local courts in Northern Ghana have, in the past, applied Islamic law to matters in which the parties were Muslim. Indeed, before independence, there was some evidence of the local court's recognition and application of Islamic law in disputes involving Muslim litigants.[56] This appeared to have been influenced by statutes that required local courts to apply native customary law within their areas of jurisdiction.[57] Nevertheless, in the judicial decisions examined, we grasp the colonial roots and the modern contexts that have contributed to the exclusion of Islamic law from mainstream law and the consequent relegation of Islamic law to extra-legal and judicial compartments of society.

KINDS OF MARRIAGES RECOGNIZED UNDER GHANA'S LEGAL SYSTEM

Turning to Ghana's pluralistic regulatory framework on marriage, divorce, and intestate succession and comments on the constitutional right of free religious expression, we undertake a comparative evaluation of the statutory regulation of Islamic, Customary, and Ordinance Marriages and Divorces. The distinctions are highlighted in the formal requirements for validity, options for solemnization, and registration requirements of the three kinds of marriage recognized in Ghana. The current regulatory regime on all three kinds of marriage in Ghana can be found in Parts One, Two, and Three of the Marriages Act, which was enacted to consolidate all the existing legislation on marriage in Ghana. The laws consolidated in the Act are the Customary Marriage and Divorce (Registration) Law 1985 (PNDCL 112) as amended; the Marriage of Mohammedans Ordinance

[56] J. N. D. Anderson, *Islamic Law in Africa* (1970), pp. 249-286; Yeboa, note 48 above, pp. 75-76.

[57] See Native Courts (Colony) Ordinance 1944; Native Courts (Ashanti) Ordinance 1935; Native Courts (Northern Territories) Ordinance 1935; and Native Courts (Southern Section of Togoland in the United Kingdom Trusteeship) Ordinance 1949, all as amended.

1907 (CAP 129); and the Marriage Ordinance 1884 (No. 14 of 1884) (CAP 127).[58]

Marriage recognized in Ghana

Ghanaian society places great value on the institution of marriage, which is seen as the penultimate, if not the final stage of transition to adulthood, with parenthood sometimes considered as the final stage.[59] In almost all communities in Ghana, married couples enjoy an elevated social status which carries with it a recognition of maturity, independence, and responsibility. A married woman is no longer considered the responsibility of her parents, but of her husband. A married man is considered a mature, independent, and responsible man who heads his nuclear family unit. The marriage system in Ghana is pluralistic, just like its legal system. Three kinds of marriage are legally recognized in Ghana: Customary, Islamic, and Ordinance marriages. In the case of *Appomasu v. Bremawuo,*[60] Apaloo CJ opined that two types of marriage are recognized in Ghana: purely customary polygamous unions and monogamous marriages. As a result of the pluralistic nature of marriage in Ghana, a standard definition of marriage has been elusive. Marriage has been defined as: "the act, ceremony or process by which the legal relationship of husband and wife is constituted. The legality of the union may be established by civil, religious or other means, as recognized by laws of each country".[61]

Customary marriage

Until the introduction of Christianity and Islam to Ghana, customary marriage was the only form of marriage recognized in Ghana and was exclusively regulated by customary law. Customary marriages were performed

[58] Marriages Act 1884-1985.

[59] A. A. Kyerematen, "Traditional Marriage in Ghana", *Africa: Rivista Trimestrale Di Studi E Documentazione Dell'istituto Italiano Per l'Africa E l'Oriente,* XXII, no 1 (1967), p. 95.

[60] (1980) GLR pp. 278 – 284 (C.A.).

[61] The Standard Operating Procedure for Civil Registration and Vital Statistics of Ghana.

according to the procedures developed over centuries by the various ethnic groups.[62] Although today customary marriages are no longer the only recognized form of marriage in Ghana, they continue to be practiced by a large proportion of the population.[63] They have also become a significant part of most modern marriages, having been so seamlessly integrated into the rituals of both Islamic and Christian marriages that they often appear to be one composite ritual or ceremony.[64]

Customary law marriages in Ghana are performed according to the requirements of the peculiar customs of each ethnic group or tribe. Even though the steps involved may vary even among different sub-groups within the same ethnic group or tribe, most customary marriages in Ghana share many common elements. As a result, there has come to be accepted, at least judicially, a set of essential elements which are applicable to most customary marriages in Ghana. In the case of *Yaotey v Quaye*,[65] the High Court laid down the following as essential elements for a valid customary marriage.

i. Agreement by the man and woman to live together as husband and wife.

ii. Consent of the man's family, which may be actual or constructive.

iii. Consent of the woman's family, which may be actual or constructive.

iv. Consummation by co-habitation.

However, in recent times, the courts have treated these essential elements as merely desirable and not a conclusive declaration of the true process of contracting a valid customary marriage. Therefore, where a man and woman agree to live together in the presence of the whole world, the courts are more willing to infer a valid customary marriage

62 Peter Qamaaru Kwame Amevor, *New Approaches to Marriage Preparation in the 1983 Code of Canon law: Challenges to the Particular Church in Ghana* (2010).

63 Ibid.

64 Ibid.

65 [1961] GLR pp. 573-584 (H.C.).

from their actions.[66] In other words, the courts appear to take the view that only the first requirement is essential. Though there is some debate about whether this is true, this chapter does not partake in this debate.

Customary marriages, as contradistinguished from Ordinance marriages, are not just a union of a man and woman, but also a union between their families.[67] Another incident of customary law marriages that is not necessarily present in Ordinance marriages is the man's obligation to "... provide maintenance and shelter for the wife."[68] This responsibility devolves upon his family in the event of his death.[69] The potentially polygamous nature of customary law marriages is another well-known distinguishing feature of this type of marriage.[70] In this regard, the customary marriage differs sharply from the Ordinance marriage, which is a purely monogamous marriage; in relation to Islamic marriages, it differs only in degree, since Islamic marriage limits the number of wives a man can have at any given time to four. The customary marriage, however, places no limit on the number of wives a man may have at any given time.[71]

Direct legislative regulation of customary marriages and divorces could be said to have begun with the enactment of the Customary Marriage and Divorce (Registration) Law 1985 (PNDCL 112), which was passed as a corollary

66 *Essilfie v Quarcoo* [1992] 2 GLR 180, p. 190 (H.C.); *Gorleku v Pobee and Another* [2012] 42 GMJ 53 (C.A.). The position taken by the courts is not of recent origin. Older case law demonstrates that customary marriages not contracted in the neat form laid down by Ollennu J can still be recognized as valid customary marriages. See the cases of *Quaye v Kuevi* [1934] D. Ct 31-37 and *Azumah v Khair* [1959] 1 GLR pp. 353-358 (C.A.).

67 Professor W. C. E. Daniels, a renowned Ghanaian scholar, observes that the African customary marriage consists of two inextricable elements: "The first is the individual aspect of the marriage, and is the true contractual element in the transaction. The second is the communal or collective aspect of the marriage transaction and relationship"; See William Cornelius Ekow Daniels, *The Law on Family Relations in Ghana* (2019), p. 76.

68 *Yaotey*, note 65 above.

69 Ibid.

70 *Appomasu*, note 60 above.

71 *Graham v Graham* [1965] GLR p. 410(H.C.).

to the Intestate Succession Act. Both laws came into force on 14 June 1985. PNDCL 112 was introduced to provide for the registration of customary law marriages and divorces. Additionally, the law stipulated a three-month timeframe for customary marriages to be registered.[72] The Act was subsequently amended in 1991 by the Customary Marriage and Divorce (Registration) (Amendment) Law 1991 (PNDCL 263) to make the registration of customary marriages optional.[73] The law still compels the registration of customary divorces.[74] PNDCL 112 and its amendment now form Part 1 of the Marriages Act.

Marriage under the Ordinance

Technically, the form of marriage described as marriage under the Ordinance is based on statute and is not exclusively a Christian marriage as it is commonly referred to. This kind of marriage was originally regulated by the Marriage Ordinance 1884 (CAP 105), which became CAP 127 in 1951 upon its revision pursuant to the Revised Edition of the Laws Ordinance 1951. The law was initially intended to apply only to the European expatriate community in the Gold Coast,[75] although it was later applied to the general population. Marriage under CAP 127 is exclusively monogamous and is the only form of marriage in Ghana which is not potentially polygamous. The Marriage Ordinance has now been consolidated in the Marriage Act as Part Three, which deals with *Christian and Other Marriages*.

Section 41 of the Marriages Act provides that a marriage may be solemnized under the authority of a Registrar's Certificate, a Marriage Officer's Certificate, or a Special License from the Registrar; each option comes with its own incidents and procedures for formal validity of the marriage.

72 Amevor, note 62 above.

73 Sections 1 and 2 of PNDCL 112, which now constitute sections 1 and 2 of the Marriages Act 1884-1985.

74 Section 6 of PNDCL 112, which now constitutes section 6 of the Marriages Act 1884-1985.

75 Enoch D. Kom, *Inheritance, Marriage and Divorce* (1999).

These three options for the solemnization of a valid marriage under the Marriages Act are briefly described as follows:

Marriage by a registrar of marriages

This option requires either party to the marriage to complete and submit a notice to the Registrar of the district where the marriage is to take place, setting out details such as their names, occupation, age, and dwelling place. A copy of the notice shall be affixed outside the door of the district assembly office for a minimum of twenty-one days and a maximum of three months. After twenty-one days, either party may swear and submit an affidavit to the effect that:

a. one party is resident within the district in which the marriage is to be celebrated at least 15 days prior to the grant of the certificate;
b. the requisite written consent has been given and is annexed to the affidavit, where a party to the marriage is not a widow(er) and is 21 years or below;
c. that no impediment of kindred or affinity, or any other lawful hindrance to the marriage exists;
d. that neither party is married under the applicable customary law to a person other than the person with whom the marriage is proposed to be contracted.

The Registrar may then, if he is satisfied, issue a Certificate of Notice to the couple, who may then proceed with the marriage. The marriage must occur within three months after the date of the initial notice submitted to the Registrar.

Marriage by a marriage officer

This option requires that at least four days before the first publication of banns of marriage, each party shall deliver to the marriage officer for the district a notice for banns. The marriage officer shall, after they receive the notice, personally publish the banns of marriage between the parties named in the notice: (a) at the place where the person giving the notice resides; (b) in the place of worship of the religious denomination to which the person belongs; or (c) shall cause the banns to be published by a person duly authorized for the purpose in writing by the marriage officer. The publication shall be audibly made before the congregation in English and the local language for at least three Sundays. Where the Marriage Officer is satisfied that the banns have been duly published, he shall, at any time within three months of the date of the last publication and, in the absence of a caveat, grant a marriage officer's certificate to one of the applicants. The marriage must be concluded within three months of the last publication of banns, otherwise, the publication and all proceedings consequent on the publication will be rendered void.

Marriage by special license

Under this option, the Registrar General's Office may waive certain conditions, such as the giving of notice, and the issue of a certificate of the Registrar or may permit a venue apart from the Registrar General's Office to be used for the performance of the marriage. The Registrar may issue the waiver if satisfied by an affidavit that no lawful impediment to the proposed marriage exists and the necessary consent to the marriage has been obtained. Under this option, the marriage must be conducted at the specific place and time granted under the Special License in order for it to be valid.

Islamic marriage

The introduction of Islam as a religion in Ghana in the early 1500s came with the recognition of marriages celebrated or contracted in accordance with the rites and prescriptions of the Islamic faith or religion, referred to in this chapter as Islamic or Muslim marriages. This kind of marriage is peculiar to persons who profess the Islamic faith. However, Islamic marriages were not governed by any legal regime at the time but remained within the domain of traditional authorities of particular communities. This kind of marriage is polygamous in that a Muslim man is allowed to contract a marriage with multiple women, but not exceeding four at a time.[76]

[76] Seymour Vesey-Fitzgerald, *Muhammedan Law: An Abridgment According to its*

For an Islamic marriage to be valid, there is essentially one core requirement: agreement. The agreement typically takes the form of a proposal and an acceptance of the said proposal, which must occur in one sitting or contemporaneously. There must be at least two witnesses (two adult male Muslims or one adult male Muslim and two adult female Muslims present to attest to this agreement and its voluntariness), one from each side.

Once these are met, generally, there is a valid Islamic marriage. Another key aspect of the marriage contract is the payment of the *mahr* or dowry. However, it must be noted that the *mahr* is an entitlement conferred on the woman, and it is her right to insist on receiving it. She may, however, choose to postpone the delivery of the *mahr* until after the consummation of the marriage or even waive it entirely.[77] There is no specific amount or formula for calculating a *mahr*. It is advised that it should be moderate and not exorbitant. It could even be given in kind or as a service and not necessarily money. In other words, it need not be adequate but merely sufficient.

Even though, generally, it is the man or his family who makes the marriage proposal, this is not a requirement. It is perfectly acceptable in Islam for a woman to propose marriage to a man. A proposal for an Islamic marriage may be verbal or written, even though it is typically verbal. Both the proposal and the acceptance must be freely given with no room for duress or undue influence. Forced marriages are prohibited in Islam.[78]

Various Schools (1931), p. 40.

[77] Quran 4:4 has been translated variously in English as: "Give women their bridal-due in good cheer (considering it a duty); but if they willingly remit any part of it, consume it with good pleasure." Or "And give the women (upon marriage) their bridal gifts graciously. But if they give up willingly to you anything of it, then take it in satisfaction".

[78] Quran 4:19 "O ye who believe! Ye are forbidden to inherit women against their will. Nor should ye treat them with harshness, that ye may Take away part of the dower ye have given them, except where they have been guilty of open lewdness; on the contrary live with them on a footing of kindness and equity. If ye take a dislike to them it may be that ye dislike a thing, and Allah brings about through it a great deal of good."

Under Muslim law, there are three types of divorce: the *khula* (mutual divorce initiated by the wife); the *talaq* (unilateral divorce initiated by the husband); and in countries with an Islamic legal and judicial system, the *tafriq* (a judicial divorce).

On 30 December 1907, the Marriage of Mohammedans Ordinance 1907 (CAP 129) was enacted and subsequently amended in 1931.[79] The Mohammedans Ordinance 1907 (CAP 107) was initially enacted only to apply to the southern part of the country. In 1931 it was extended to the northern territories through the promulgation of a Marriage of Mohammedans Ordinance for the Northern Territories (CAP 129) in the Gold Coast Gazette, No. 29 of May 2, 1931, and was subsequently amended in 1932. The statutory regulation of Islamic marriages in Ghana thus began with the enactment of the Marriage of Mohammedans Ordinance 1907, later known as CAP 129, which has now been consolidated into the Marriages Act as Part Two. Although the nomenclature employed to describe this form of marriage has for many centuries been "Mohammedan", it is a misnomer.

Islamic marriages and divorces in Ghana are currently governed by the regulatory provisions in Part Two of the Marriages Act. The Act prescribes the mandatory registration of an Islamic marriage or divorce after its celebration or performance and stipulates it as the sole determinant of its validity. Section 27(1) of the Marriages Act provides, "a marriage contracted, or divorce effected after the commencement of this Part by persons professing the Mohammedan faith is not valid unless registered under this Part". The Act prescribes that the bridegroom, the bride's *wali*, two witnesses to the marriage, and a Mohammedan priest licensed under section 21 shall, before the expiration of a week after the celebration of the marriage, attend the office of the District Chief Executive to register the marriage.[80] The marriage shall be recorded in the register and in the duplicate certificates, and the register and certificate shall

[79] Mervyn Hiskett, "Commissioner of Police v. Musa Kommanda and Aspects of the Working of the Gold Coast Marriage of Mohammedans Ordinance", *Journal of African Law*, XX, no. 2 (1976), pp. 127, 131-132.

[80] Section 24, Marriages Act 1884-1985.

then be signed by the bridegroom, the bride's *wali*, and the two witnesses who have attended for that purpose.

Where the stipulated period of one week elapses, or where any of the designated persons does not appear at the District Assembly, the parties must make an *ex parte* application to the High Court for the grant of an extension of time for the registration, or for an order dispensing with the signature of any of the persons referred to in section 24(1). The signature of the priest cannot be dispensed with in any circumstances. The provisions for the registration of divorces are virtually the same as those for marriage, except that the statutory time limit allowed for registration is one month after the divorce.

Non-Discrimination and religious freedom in Ghana

Ghana's 1992 Constitution guarantees the right and freedom of every person of full age and capacity to marry any man or woman of his or her choice, and by extension, to enter into any form of recognized marriage of his or her choice without any limitation or differentiation on grounds of "gender, race, color, ethnic origin, religion, creed or social or economic status".[81] The Constitution prohibits discrimination on any grounds, and defines discrimination as giving

> different treatment to different persons attributable only or mainly to their respective descriptions by race, place of origin, political opinions, color, gender, occupation, religion or creed, whereby persons of one description are subjected to disabilities or restrictions to which persons of another description are not made subject or are granted privileges or advantages which are not granted to persons of another description.[82]

The Constitution clarifies in Article 17(4) that the principle of equality before the law and non-discrimination does not prevent Parliament from enacting laws that are reasonably necessary to provide for matters relating to

81 Article 17, 1992 Constitution of Ghana.

82 Ibid., Article 17(3).

adoption, marriage, divorce, burial, devolution of property on death, or other matters of personal law. In the case of *Nartey v Gati*,[83] Date-Bah JSC (as he then was), explaining the import of the provision in Article 17(4), stated:

> The constitutional prescription in Article 17(1) that all persons shall be equal before the law should not, and does not, disable Parliament from enacting legislation that gives different rights to different classes of people, so long as the differentiation in rights bears a reasonable relationship to the legislative purpose that Parliament is seeking to achieve, and Parliament does not fall foul of any of the grounds set out in Article 17(2). Of course, one should also add the caveat that the legislative purpose sought to be achieved by Parliament must be constitutional. And one of the constitutional prescriptions that must be complied with, pursuant to Article 17(1), is that a law must operate equally on all persons similarly situated. The constitutional slogan has to be, equals must be treated equally by the law.[84]

The Constitution also guarantees the right of every citizen to practice any religion, manifest such practice, and enjoy, practice, profess, maintain and promote any tradition or religion subject to the provisions of the Constitution.[85] The provisions of Ghana's Constitution, 1992, on freedom of religion contain two interrelated rights: the right to hold a belief and the right to manifest that belief in practice.[86] The United Nations Human Rights Committee's General Comment No. 22 on Article 18 (Freedom of Thought, Conscience or Religion)[87] notes that the right to freedom of thought, conscience and religion (which includes the

[83] [2010] SCGLR 745 (SC).

[84] Ibid.

[85] Articles 21 and 26, 1992 Constitution of Ghana.

[86] Articles 21 (1) (b) and (c), 1992 Constitution of Ghana.

[87] Human Rights Committee, "General Comment No. 22: The Right to Freedom of Thought, Conscience", in *Note by the Secretariat, Compilation of General Comments and General Recommendations Adopted by Human Rights Treaty Bodies* (2006) (General Comment).

freedom to hold beliefs) is far-reaching and profound; it encompasses freedom of thought on all matters, personal conviction and the commitment to religion or belief, whether manifested individually or in community with others. Comment 22 further notes that:

> The observance and practice of religion or belief may include not only ceremonial acts but also such customs as the observance of dietary regulations, the wearing of distinctive clothing or head coverings, participation in rituals associated with certain stages of life, and the use of a particular language customarily spoken by a group. In addition, the practice and teaching of religion or belief includes acts integral to the conduct by religious groups of their basic affairs, such as the freedom to choose their religious leaders, priests and teachers, the freedom to establish seminaries or religious schools and the freedom to prepare and distribute religious texts or publications.[88]

The only limitation the Constitution allows to be imposed on the manifestation of a person's belief, religious or otherwise, is that stated in Article 21(4) (e), which bans the teaching or propagation of a doctrine that undermines respect for the State or fuels hatred of other members of the community. In *Bomfeh Jnr v Attorney General,*[89] the Supreme Court of Ghana acknowledged the important role religious groups perform in the nation's development. As stated by Adinyira JSC,

> There has been collaboration between the State and religion in Ghana by the establishment of educational institutions, medical facilities, and agricultural projects by all groups of Christian and other faiths in the country and thus contributing immensely to the socio-economic growth of the country. In some remote areas of Ghana, it is the religious bodies that pioneered the establishment of schools and health

[88] Ibid., paragraph 4.

[89] [(J1 14 of 2017) [2019] GHASC 2 (23 January 2019) (J1 14 of 2017) [2019] GHASC 2 (23 January 2019) (available online).

> facilities before the State recently ventured into those areas.[90]

The *Bomfeh Jnr* decision is important for two reasons: it outlines the institutional configurations necessary to safeguard religious freedom and articulates the test for determining whether or not religious freedom has been violated. Commenting on the institutional dimensions, or how the State should relate with religious groups, the Court held:

> The Constitution of the 4th Republic, while secular in nature, affirms and maintains the historical, cultural, and religious or atheist character of Ghanaian society. Obviously, secularism in the context of the Ghana Constitution must be understood to allow, and even encourage State *recognition* and *accommodation* of religion and religious identity. ...Constitution guarantees the equal right of all persons to subscribe to the religious belief and faith of their own choosing without interference or imposition by the State. The State is thus prohibited from discriminating against any person on grounds of religion or creed or the establishment of a state religion, and also preventing the free expression of religious orientations.[91]

As expressed by the Supreme Court, Ghana's Constitution emphasizes neutrality and non-discrimination and promotes the accommodation and recognition of the practices of the various religious groups that co-exist in the country. The *Bomfeh* decision provides the clearest articulation of the scope and meaning of freedom of religion in Ghana. The Supreme Court emphasized that to determine whether there has been a breach of this right, the Court must inquire into "whether the act or omission complained of, prevents any person resident in Ghana to practice any religion or belief of his choice, or *discriminates against any person with different religious persuasion*".[92]

[90] Ibid.

[91] Ibid.

[92] Ibid. (emphasis added).

Where general laws will impose an undue burden on a person's religious belief or practice, the courts have been accommodating, and in appropriate cases, have upheld conscientious objections made on religious grounds. In the case of *Nyameneba v The Republic,*[93] the plaintiffs who had used marijuana in their religious practices and denied ever having known that it was marijuana were acquitted on the ground of "mistake of fact". In the more apposite case of *Tyrone Marghuy (Suing by the Next Friend and Father Tereo Kwame Marghuy) v Board of Governors Achimota Senior High School and Attorney General,*[94] the Court held that the rule of the Achimota School which required students to keep their hair "short and neat" violated the plaintiff student's right to hold and manifest his religious belief in Rastafarianism. The Court stated that "the rules and regulations of the school should only be viewed in the lens of the provisions of the Constitution to ensure that they do not sin against the people's right to manifest and practice any religion they subscribe to except on reasonable justification for the public good".[95]

Comparative analysis of the statutory regulation of Islamic, customary, and ordinance marriages and divorces

We turn to a comparative analysis of the regulatory regime on Islamic marriages and divorces in Ghana and the regimes governing customary marriages and Ordinance marriages and discusses their implications on the right to free religious expression as guaranteed in the Constitution of Ghana 1992.

First, that the avenues by which Muslims in Ghana may contract a valid marriage are more constricted as compared to Ordinance marriages, even though both kinds of marriages are statutorily regulated. Whereas marriages under the Ordinance, which are governed by Part Three of the Marriages Act, may be solemnized using any of three possible means – a Registrar's Certificate; a Marriage

93 [1965] GLR pp. 723 – 729.

94 (HR/0055/2021) [2021] GHAHCHRD 1 (2 June 2021) (available online).

95 Ibid., p. 20.

Officers' Certificate; or a Special License from the Registrar – an Islamic marriage may only be solemnized in one way: by the authority of a Mohammedan priest licensed by the Minister of Interior.[96]

Regarding marriages solemnized under the Registrar's Certificate and the Marriage Officer's Certificate, the validity of the marriage is determined by compliance with certain conditions precedent to the issuance of a "Certificate of Notice" by either the Marriage Registrar or the Marriage Officer. Where the marriage does not occur within three months after the date of the notice, the notice and all proceedings consequent on the notice are void, and a fresh notice must be given before the parties can lawfully marry under a Registrar's Certificate. Where the marriage is not solemnized within three months of the last publication of banns, the publication and all proceedings consequent on the publication are void, and the banns shall be published anew before the parties can be married by banns.[97] Regarding marriage by Special License, the Marriages Act is silent as regards the effect of a failure to comply with the terms of the license. However, judging from the form of the license, which includes specific times and places for the celebration or solemnization of the marriage, which may only be varied by the Registrar of Marriages, it stands to reason that a failure to comply with the terms of the license would result in the license and all other proceedings consequent on the license being void like the other two forms of solemnization recognized by the Act.

It is significant to note that the prescribed procedures applicable to Ordinance marriages are to be complied with before the celebration of the marriage. Therefore, non-compliance prevents the marriage from taking place but does not nullify or invalidate a previously celebrated marriage. Also, in the event of non-compliance with these procedures, the Act allows parties to restart the process towards the valid celebration of the marriage. Regarding Islamic marriages, the requirement of registration is to be complied with after the marriage has been celebrated in

[96] Section 21, Marriages Act 1884-1985.

[97] Ibid., section 54.

accordance with the rites and prescriptions of the Islamic faith. It must be stressed that the registration validates the marriage. Failure to register an Islamic marriage within one week of its celebration results in the invalidation of the marriage, with dire consequences for the married persons; the process of salvaging an unregistered Islamic marriage from nullity is complicated, expensive, and burdensome.

The Marriage Act imposes a mandatory requirement of registration which serves as a pre-condition for the validity and recognition of Islamic marriages in the legal system. For a marriage under the Ordinance, there is no statutory requirement for registration of the marriage after it has been celebrated either under the Registrar's Certificate or the Marriage Officer's Certificate. The only validating requirement is that the marriage is celebrated within three months after the notice or after the publication of the banns. Significantly, the validity of a marriage under the Ordinance or customary marriage is in no way dependent on a post-facto registration of the marriage, as is the case with Islamic marriages under the Marriage Act. Thus, the Marriages Act, on the face of it, seems to subject Islamic marriages to additional layers of pre-conditions for validity which are not applicable to Ordinance or customary marriages. The significance of the mandatory requirements for registration of Islamic marriages is seen in the draconian consequences of non-compliance.

The Act creates a uniquely stringent set of rigid formal requirements for registering a marriage celebrated according to the prescriptions of the Islamic religion.[98] Compared to the other kinds of marriage, the requirements appear almost punitive. The registration must be done within one week, and the bridegroom, bride's *wali* or guardian, two witnesses to the marriage, and the priest must all go to the relevant District Assembly to have this done.[99] It is unclear what the rationale is for requiring as many as five persons to be physically present for the registration of an Islamic marriage.

98 Ibid., section 23.

99 Ibid., section 24.

The consequences of non-compliance with these timelines are burdensome. Where the prescribed statutory period of one week elapses, or where the attendance of any of the multiple persons required to be present for the registration at the District Assembly cannot be procured, an extension of time for registration can only be obtained by an ex parte application to the High Court, which must be supported by an affidavit stating the reason for the delay or non-attendance.[100] Only the High Court may dispense with the signature of any of the persons referred to, upon an ex parte application made to that Court. The signature of the priest cannot be dispensed with under any circumstances.[101] In contrast, persons who choose to enter into Ordinance marriages concluded under a Marriage Officer or Marriage Registrar's Certificate have a period of three months to perform their obligations under the law and the consequences of non-compliance within the period are relatively painless. The justifications for these distinctions are difficult to ascertain.

Furthermore, the High Court's mandate under the Marriages Act does not allow it to validate an unregistered Islamic marriage but merely empowers the court to grant an extension of time for registration or to issue a certificate to dispense with some of the required signatures for the registration. Consequently, the marriage registration requirement must be met even after the court has issued the certificate. The provisions relating to divorce are virtually the same as for marriage save that the time limit for registering a divorce is longer – one month – and this period can also only be extended by application to the High Court.

Under the current state of the law, instances where Islamic marriages or divorces will not be recognized as valid abound. First, if the Imam or Mohammedan priest who performs the marriage or divorce ceremony has not been registered as an Islamic priest, the marriage or divorce is invalid, no matter the extent to which they may be recognized in a particular

[100] Ibid., sections 24 (10) and (11).

[101] Ibid.

community or mosque.[102] Failure to register within seven days of the celebration of an Islamic marriage will result in it being void or invalid.[103] If the priest does not or is unable to sign, the marriage will be irredeemably invalid. If there is the slightest delay in registering a Muslim marriage, the parties to the marriage will have to engage the services of a lawyer to make an application, not to the district court or the circuit court, but to the High Court for an extension of time within which to register the marriage. If a person is unable to make the application within a reasonable time after the celebration of the marriage, the application is likely to be denied, and the marriage will not be recognized as an Islamic marriage. These onerous processes and the costs involved are a significant disincentive to Muslims who may wish to have their marriages registered under the Act.

Comparatively, Christians who get married under the Ordinance will normally have the Marriage Certificate issued immediately in the church where the marriage is celebrated. What remains to be done is to file a copy of the Certificate at the Assembly and/or the Registrar General's Office, and the parties have up to one month to do so. The filing of the copy does not determine the validity of the marriage celebrated under the Ordinance. In comparison with the relatively simple and easy procedures imposed on persons who marry under the Ordinance, it is also not clear why a Muslim who gets married has to travel to the District Assembly with the bridegroom or bride, two witnesses, and the Imam/priest who celebrated the marriage for purposes of the registration.

As noted, the requirement of post facto registration of the marriage as a condition for validity is exclusively applicable to Islamic marriages. No requirement of subsequent registration attaches to customary marriages or Ordinance marriages, nor is registration in any way linked to their validity. A marriage contracted under customary law is valid whether or not it is registered. There is no mandatory requirement of registration of customary marriages under the Marriages Act. Section 1 of the Act states that marriages

[102] Ibid., sections 21, 24 and 27.

[103] *Jebeille v. Ashkar* [1977], p. 459 (H.C)

contracted under customary law *may* be registered in accordance with the Act. The Act provides in section 16 that the Minister may prescribe the periods within which customary law marriages and divorces shall be registered. No regulations prescribing such timelines for registration of customary marriages have as yet been issued. Thus, a customary marriage may be registered any time after the celebration of the marriage, and the marriage remains valid while it is not registered.

Whereas the law makes room for alternative means of proving the existence of unregistered customary marriages,[104] no such alternative channels exist for Islamic marriages which are deemed invalid if not registered within one week. It is unclear why the same statutory privileges granted to customary marriages are not accorded to Islamic marriages. The Customary Marriages and Divorces Registration Law was amended for the same reason for which calls have constantly been made for the reform of the Marriage of Mohammedans Ordinance: that the law was unreasonably rigid and drastic in its impact.

Another notable area of unequal treatment between Muslim and Ordinance marriages rests on a statutory scheme that permits the conversion of customary marriages into Ordinance marriages, not vice-versa.[105] Under section 76 of the Marriages Act, a person who has contracted an Ordinance marriage "shall not during the continuance of that marriage contract a valid marriage under an applicable customary law".[106] As noted previously, an unregistered Muslim marriage is, at best, a customary marriage. This, in effect, means that an unregistered Muslim marriage as customary marriage can be converted into an Ordinance marriage, but an Ordinance marriage cannot be converted into a customary marriage in the form of an unregistered Muslim marriage. This is another instance of preferential

[104] Customary Marriage and Divorce (Registration) (Amendment) Law, 1991 (PNDCL 263).

[105] Section 46(2)(d), Marriages Act 1884-1985.

[106] Ibid., section 76.

treatment being accorded to Ordinance marriages as opposed to customary or Muslim marriages.

IMPLICATIONS AND CONSEQUENCES

The Ghanaian courts have strictly enforced the rigid consequences of non-registration and declared unregistered Islamic marriages invalid without any hesitation. In the *Brimah* case, Ollennu J held that a marriage not registered under CAP 129 was not a Muslim marriage properly so-called.[107] In *Jebeille v. Ashkar*,[108] the parties, who professed the Mohammedan faith, went through a Muslim marriage ceremony celebrated by a licensed Mohammedan Priest on 19 January 1976. The marriage was subsequently registered on the 13 February 1976, twenty-five days later. Griffiths Randolph J held that "to all appearances, the marriage ... between [the parties], who professed the Mohammedan faith, was a Muslim marriage ...",[109] and added that "The result [is] that under section 9 [of CAP 129], the marriage [is] not to be regarded as a valid Muslim Marriage [because it was not registered within one week] ... In the circumstances, I hereby declare the said marriage null and void, and of no effect".[110]

This rigid, mechanical, and almost dismissive approach to the recognition of a marriage appears to be reserved for Islamic marriages. The comparative review shows that the Marriage Act creates distinctions that result in married Muslims being subjected to disabilities that are not suffered by persons married under the Ordinance or customary law. These disabilities are created by the nature of the formal requirements for the validity of the marriage or divorce; the procedures for registration of Islamic marriages; the duration of timelines given for compliance with registration procedures; the opportunities granted for remedying non-compliance; and the options for solemnization of the marriage. No justifications can be discerned for the

107 *Brimah*, note 43 above.

108 [1977] GLR pp. 458-461 (H.C).

109 Ibid., p. 460.

110 Ibid., p. 461.

differential treatment of Islamic marriages within Ghana's regulatory regime.

The current regulatory framework on Islamic marriages and divorce affects Muslims in many critical ways and has deep implications for marital status; enjoyment of marital rights; child maintenance; inheritance; intestate succession; and the distribution of matrimonial property upon divorce. Compliance with the requirement of registration of Islamic marriages determines the mode of succession to the estate of Muslims. An unregistered Islamic marriage will be deemed as a customary law marriage at best, and issues relating to succession will be determined in accordance with the personal law of the deceased Muslim.[111] The Ghanaian courts have determined conclusively that where a Muslim dies not having registered his marriage, the only law that can regulate succession to his estate is customary law. In the *Kwakye case*, Ollennu J stated:

> In the eyes of the law, marriage by a Mohammedan according to Mohammedan Law is at its very best a marriage by customary law and does not affect succession to his estate unless the said marriage is registered under the Ordinance. Therefore, if a Mohammedan died not having married, or if married, not having had his said marriage registered under the Marriage of Mohammedan's Ordinance, the only law which can regulate succession to his estate is his personal law i.e., the customary law of the tribe to which he belonged.[112]

Thus, a Muslim who is unaware of the requirement of registration as a pre-condition for the validity of Islamic marriages (as most Muslims are), and assumes that his marriage is an Islamic marriage and orders his affairs accordingly, will, upon his death, have his property distributed in accordance with the Intestate Succession Act because the Ghanaian courts have declared that an unregistered marriage is not an Islamic marriage properly

[111] *Ayishetu Abdul-Kadiri v Abdulai Dwamena* [2020] DLCA 10013 (available online); *Kwakye*, note 41 above.

[112] *Kwakye*, note 41 above, p. 724.

so-called and is at best a customary marriage. Also, the courts have conclusively determined that Islamic law cannot be recognized as a Muslim's personal law. The Ghanaian courts have established in *Kwakye* and other cases that religious law cannot be the personal law of a Ghanaian unless the same was provided for by statute.[113] The only existing statute that contained such a provision was the Marriage of Mohammedans Ordinance, and its provisions could only apply to a person's affairs upon proof that he or she was married under that statute and the marriage was registered in accordance with the prescriptions of the Ordinance. Thus, prior to the enactment of the Intestate Succession Act, the only way a Muslim could ensure that Islamic law was applied as their personal law, in matters such as inheritance and succession, was to get married according to the prescriptions of the Marriage of Mohammedans Ordinance.

Thus, under the current legal framework, a person who is married under Islamic law, has properly registered the marriage under Part Two of the Marriages Act, and dies intestate cannot have his or her property devolved according to Islamic law. Moreover, even under the Intestate Succession Act, the residue of the property of an intestate who is Muslim cannot devolve in accordance with Islamic law because of the firm judicial position that Islamic law cannot be considered as the customary or personal law of a Ghanaian.[114] Thus, after 1985, the only way a Ghanaian Muslim can have Islamic law applied to the devolution of his estate upon death is by making a will to that effect. Considering that inheritance is perhaps the most significant reason for which a person would desire a particular system of law to apply to their affairs, one wonders what benefit is to be derived from complying with the rigid statutory requirements of registration of Islamic marriages beyond receiving a marriage certificate.

In other words, the practical utility or the purpose of registration has been significantly eroded by the repeal of

[113] See also *Acheampong v. Marshall in* A.K.P. Kludze, *Modern Law of Succession in Ghana* (1988), pp. 278-279.

[114] *Brimah*, note 43 above, pp. 119.

section 10 of the Marriage of Mohammedans Ordinance, which allowed intestate succession to be regulated by Islamic law. By repealing section 10, there is no applicable statute that would allow Islamic law to apply to succession. Without section 10, a Muslim marriage, even when registered, will be treated as a customary marriage for purposes of succession because of the universal application of the Intestate Succession Act. The benefits or the purpose of registering Islamic marriages are thus severely limited and do not include the application of Islamic law to the devolution of property. There is little incentive to register an Islamic marriage if it does not ensure security for the Muslim's family and property through the application of the Islamic law on succession.

Considering the state of the law and the position adopted by the Courts, few Islamic marriages qualify as valid Islamic marriages and are recognized by the law as such. The stark impact of the legislative requirement of registration is that thousands of marriages and divorces that have been celebrated/performed in Ghana in accordance with Islamic procedures and rites are not valid Islamic marriages or divorces in the eyes of the law. Considering that practicing Muslims are required by the dictates of their religion or faith, to order their affairs, including all matters relating to marriage, divorce, and succession, according to the prescriptions of Islamic law,[115] a legislative requirement that precludes Muslims from having their personal affairs governed by Islamic law, even when they so desire, undermines their right to practice their religion and manifest such practice. Further, the judicial position that unregistered Islamic marriages are deemed to be customary marriages presents enormous practical problems with regard to proving the existence of the marriage.[116] A married Muslim is faced with the challenge of producing oral or documentary evidence to prove the existence of a "customary" marriage that was actually celebrated according to the rites and prescriptions of the Islamic faith.

[115] Aziz-Bamba, note 23 above, p. 471.

[116] Section 15, Marriages Act 1884-1985.

In assessing the legislative regime on Islamic marriages in Ghana, it is important to ascertain whether the provisions of Part Two of the Marriages Act are so designed to motivate married Muslims to register their marriage to reap the benefits of recognition by the law. Experience has shown, uncontrovertibly, that the Marriage of Mohammedans Ordinance (now Part Two of the Marriages Act) has been totally emasculated with the repeal of section 10, and does not, in its current state, in any way incentivise Muslims in this country to register their marriages. Rather, the current regulatory framework on Islamic marriages ensures that the great majority of marriages celebrated according to Islamic rites and prescriptions are doomed to invalidity and bound to be recognized only as customary marriages.

Limited research has been conducted in Ghana on the level of compliance with or the impact of the regulatory laws on Islamic marriages and divorce. In 2003, the Legal Resources Centre (LRC), a local grassroots and human rights NGO, conducted research in five regions of Ghana (Greater Accra, Ashanti, Central, Upper East, and Northern region) to ascertain the different aspects of the impact of the Marriage of Mohammedans Ordinance (now consolidated in Part Two of the Marriages Act), from the perspective of those whose lives are regulated by the Marriage of Mohammedans Ordinance. The research sought to determine the preferences of Muslims in Ghana concerning issues such as the necessity for registering marriages; the form registration should take; whether Islamic law should be recognized as the personal law of Muslims; and what law should govern the devolution of estates upon death intestate.

The research showed that an overwhelming majority of Muslims are not aware of the requirement of registration, the process of registration, or the legal consequences of non-registration of Muslim marriages.[117] The research revealed that 96% of the respondents who were married under Islamic

[117] Raymond Atuguba, *The Registration of Islamic Marriages in Ghana's Plural Legal System. Challenges and Strategies for Improvement* (A Paper presented at a Workshop Organised by the Family Law Focal Area of the German Technical Cooperation GTZ 2003 on the Registration of Islamic Marriages in Ghana's Plural Legal System, Hohoe, Volta Region of Ghana, 20 May 2003) (available online).

law had not registered their marriages.[118] The survey showed that the majority of the respondents wanted Islamic law to be recognised as their personal law. Among the reasons offered for choosing Islamic law as their personal law was the fact that they were Muslims; Islamic law is the only customary law they practiced; the Quran teaches everything, and Western law contradicts Islamic practices; Islamic law keeps every Muslim on the right path; Islamic law is the only law they know because everything about the Muslim is in the Quran, it is from Allah; Muslims must follow and practice the teachings of Quran; and because Islam is their religion and way of life. Respondents indicated that the document given to them upon registration serves as evidence of the marriage; was needed in visa acquisition to travel; helpful in the event of divorce, death, and for devolution of property.

There is abundant empirical evidence that Muslims do not register their marriages because most are unaware of the legal requirement of registration.[119] This state of affairs is partly attributable to the severe lack of legal education in Ghanaian society. The research showed that the majority of Muslims are interested in registering especially for the purpose of succession and are of the view that the law should encourage registration by providing the incentive of applying Islamic law to their affairs.[120] A research study conducted in 2021 among married Muslims in the Tamale Metropolis of the Northern Region of Ghana, which investigated the level of knowledge and perceptions of Muslims in Ghana regarding the Marriage of Mohammedans Ordinance and its implications, largely confirmed the findings of the LRC 2003 research.[121]

The difficulties and deficiencies of the current regulatory regime emphasize the need for urgent law reform. We turn to the efforts made to reform the regulatory law on Islamic marriages and divorce and make specific proposals for such reform.

118 Ibid.

119 Ibid.

120 Ibid.

121 Abubakari, note 36 above.

DEVELOPING AN IMPROVED REGULATORY FRAMEWORK ON ISLAMIC MARRIAGES AND DIVORCE

Campaigning for Law Reform

According to the 2021 population census, Muslims constitute 19.9% of the population of Ghana. Studies show that majority of practising Muslims adhere to the prescriptions of the Quran regarding family law.[122] The fact that a significant proportion of Ghana's population is Muslim reinforces the need to better understand how Islamic law fits into the legal architecture of the State. An enhanced understanding of Islamic law will help in the purposeful drafting of laws to guarantee the protection of the rights and freedoms of Muslims in Ghana. The campaign for the reform of the law regulating Islamic marriages and divorce in Ghana has been a long-drawn-out one that began about two decades ago and has yielded no tangible results.

Based on the findings of its research and extensive community outreach activities in predominantly Muslim communities, the LRC developed a draft bill for the reform of the Marriage of Mohammedans Ordinance, which was submitted to the Ministry of Justice in 2007 for its consideration. The Draft bill and Research Report of the LRC remained under consideration until June 2020, when the Registrar-General's Department of the Ministry of Justice engaged the Muslim Lawyers Forum (MLF) to study and review the Draft Muslim Marriages and Divorce Bill 2019 (Draft bill) and make recommendations for its consideration towards the introduction of a new law on Muslim marriages and divorces. We review the major proposals made in the Draft bill and examine the extent to which they address the problems raised herein with regard to the regulation of Islamic marriages and divorce.

122 Atuguba, note 117 above.

Highlights of the draft Muslim Marriage and Divorce Bill 2019

The draft bill seeks to take into account the realities, concerns, and issues underlying the legislative regime on the registration of Muslim marriages and divorces. It attempts to achieve a careful balance between Ghana's secular Constitution and laws and to accommodate the interests of Muslims in applying Islamic law to marriage, divorce, and succession.[123] The draft bill would create a user-friendly institutional and regulatory framework for registering Islamic marriage and divorce. To this end, the draft bill proposes the establishment of a Muslim Marriage and Divorce Registry in each district of the country to register Islamic marriages and divorce. The production of an entry in the register or a certificate serves as conclusive proof of the fact of marriage or divorce. The bill proposes that to be licensed for the celebration of Muslim marriages, a mosque or place used for religious purposes must, among other requirements, have or be affiliated to a Muslim Family Law Arbitration or Counselling Unit (Unit). The Unit is charged with granting consent for contracting additional marriages and considering applications for divorce.

Licensing of imams and places for the celebration of Muslim marriages

Provision is made in the draft bill for the District Chief Executive to license places of Muslim public worship or any place used for Muslim religious purposes as places of marriage. The Draft bill also makes provision for the licensing of Imams by the Registrars of Marriages appointed for each district. The duties of an officiating Imam are to announce the celebration of an impending marriage; take the prospective couple through the necessary rites for a formal marriage in accordance with the dictates of the Islamic school of jurisprudence to which the parties belong; counsel the couple; issue certificates of marriage; and submit

[123] The Muslim Lawyers Forum (MLF), *Report of the Committee Established to Review the Draft Muslim Marriage and Divorce Bill* (2019).

monthly returns of registered marriages to the Registrar of Marriages within the district.

Requirements for valid Islamic marriages

The Draft bill stipulates the requirements of a valid Islamic marriage as the attainment of the age of eighteen years according to the Children's Act 1998 (Act 560); the consent of both parties to be married to each other; the celebration of the marriage under Islamic law; and the presence of witnesses as required by Islamic law at the time of the conclusion of the ceremony. The bill outlines the requirements for the celebration of Muslim marriages and stipulates specific conditions to be complied with when a Muslim man decides to contract successive marriages during the subsistence of a previous marriage or marriages.

Registration of Muslim marriages and divorces

The draft bill removes the requirement of registration and makes it optional. The bill, however, requires the bridegroom, bride, and witnesses, and a licensed Imam to go to the registry as soon as convenient to register the marriage. If possible, the registration should be done on the day of the marriage celebration to save cost. The procedure for the dissolution of Islamic marriage is outlined in the draft bill. Regarding the registration of divorce, the bill requires the man, woman, and two witnesses each of the parties to the divorce, to go to the office of the Registrar of Marriages to register the divorce within one month after the divorce. A party to the divorce may apply to the Unit to intervene in maintenance, custody, or settlement matters.

Succession

Regarding succession, the Draft bill stipulates in clause 23 that:

> On the death of a Muslim whose marriage has been duly registered under this Act, the succession to the property of that person shall be regulated by Islamic Law unless there is evidence to the contrary if

a. The person died intestate, and
b. Considering the circumstance of the marriage, the deceased is male, and other male members of the family fully observed their responsibilities in accordance with Islamic law towards the female members of the family.

The Draft bill proposes that where the Islamic marriage was not registered before the death of the person, the administrators of the estate shall register the marriage, and upon the posthumous registration of the marriage, the estate of the deceased married Muslim shall be regulated by Islamic law unless the deceased before death had indicated an unequivocal intention that his or her estate should not devolve according to Islamic law. Where a Muslim dies unmarried, with or without children, succession to their estate shall be regulated by Islamic law unless there are clear indications by the deceased to the contrary. The draft bill appears to maintain the requirement of registration of Islamic marriages as a condition for applying Islamic law to the estate of a deceased Muslim. It does not advocate for any change in the law regarding the possible application of Islamic law in the distribution of the estates of Muslim intestates whose marriages are unregistered.

Proposals for reform

We offer some fresh proposals for addressing the deficiencies highlighted in the current law and for the reform of Ghana's regulatory law on Islamic marriages generally.

Mode of registration of marriages and provision for celebration of marriage by special license

Clause 15 of the draft bill requires either or both parties to a marriage to apply to a licensed Imam or Registrar of Marriages within a month of the marriage, to register the marriage. The draft bill further provides that the licensed Imam, after satisfying himself that a marriage has been celebrated between the parties in accordance with Islamic principles, shall issue them with a marriage certificate. Under Clause 16, the proposed procedure for registration requires the bride, bridegroom, bride's *wali*, witnesses, and licensed Imam who officiated the marriage, to go to the office of the Registrar of Marriages of the district to have their marriage registered within a month of its celebration.

As noted by the Review Committee of the Muslim Lawyers Forum (MLF), the proposed registration process for Muslim marriages, particularly, the requirement that the bride, bridegroom, bride's *wali*, witnesses, and licensed Imam who officiated the marriage, should visit the office of the Registrar of Marriages of the district to have their marriage registered, is onerous, cumbersome, and impracticable.[124] The draft bill mysteriously repeats some deficiencies of Part Two of the Marriages Act, which made the observance of the provisions of the law unattractive to Muslims. In addition, the conditions and processes of registration proposed in the draft bill do not make room for the celebration of marriages in unlicensed places of worship, such as the homes of the celebrants, since not all marriages are celebrated in the mosque.

It is proposed that the new law be restructured to identify two modes of registration of a Muslim marriage: (a) before a licensed Imam who officiates the marriage at a mosque licensed as a place of marriage; and (b) before the Registrar of Marriages or through a Special License. To simplify the registration process, it is proposed that licensed Imams should conduct marriage ceremonies only at mosques licensed as places of marriage or under a Special License to be issued by the Registrar of Marriages, which would allow a marriage to be celebrated at an unlicensed place of marriage, for example, at the home of the couple, provided the marriage is celebrated by a licensed Imam. The licensed Imams should be able to issue marriage certificates at the time the marriage is contracted and do away with the cumbersome process of the bridegroom and the bride, among others, visiting a registry subsequently to have their marriage registered.

Registration by the Registrar can be two-fold. In the first place, the registration of marriages, which for one reason or

124 Ibid.

another were not celebrated at a licensed place of marriage, can be registered by the Registrar upon application by the bride, bride's *wali*, bridegroom, witnesses, and the licensed Imam. Second, the Registrar could, upon application, issue a special license to a licensed Imam to celebrate a marriage at an unlicensed place of marriage. The proposed solution will help simplify the registration process and also provide for the celebration of marriages at unlicensed places of marriage under a special license issued by the Registrar.

Recourse to the high court in respect of matters relating to registration of marriage and divorce

Clauses 16 and 21 of the Draft bill provide for recourse to the High Court in respect of applications for extension of time or dispensing with the signature of a person required for the registration of a Muslim marriage. Seeking an extension of time through the High Court and not the district courts, which are more readily available at the district level, would deter the belated registration of Muslim marriage and divorces. In addition, the costs associated with engaging the services of a lawyer and filing the application at the High Court, as opposed to the district courts, could be prohibitive for many couples. It is proposed by the MLF that, as a general rule, recourse should be made to the district court in respect of matters relating to the registration of a Muslim marriage or divorce instead of the High Court. District courts tend to be more readily available at the district level and have less complicated rules of procedure, making it easier for parties to conduct their own cases before such courts.

Mode of registration of divorces

Clause 19 envisages the dissolution of a Muslim marriage by a licensed Imam acting on the recommendation of the Muslim Family Law Arbitration and Counselling Unit attached to his licensed place of marriage. The Imam is expected to issue a certificate of divorce after the Unit has decreed the divorce and to file returns to the Registrar under Clause 20. The process of registration of divorce proposed in the draft bill requires the man, woman, two witnesses each, and a licensed Imam to visit a registration center to register the divorce. This process is too cumbersome and unrealistic and likely to deter registration. It must therefore be expunged from the bill. It is further suggested that all matters of divorce should be handled by the Unit and the divorce decrees issued by the licensed Imam in charge of that licensed place of marriage as and when the divorce is granted. Licensed Imams would then file the returns of divorces at the relevant Marriage and Divorce Registry. This will help simplify the process of registration of divorces and encourage compliance.

We turn to the vexsome question of which law should regulate intestate succession for Muslims. The law should be reformed to accommodate the interests of Ghanaian Muslims in having Islamic laws of succession apply to their estates as the default intestate succession law instead of the Intestate Succession Act.

Proposals for reform of the law on intestate succession of Muslims

The Intestate Succession Act, as noted, was enacted to establish a harmonized and universal legislative regime on intestate succession, irrespective of the ethnic group or religion to which a person belongs and the kind of marriage contracted by the intestate. If a person did not during his or her lifetime express any wishes in relation to how their estate should be distributed upon their demise in a manner recognized by the law, the provisions of the Intestate Succession Act would regulate the distribution of their estate. For Muslims, it could be argued that the Islamic law of succession is their default position regarding the mode of distribution of their estate upon intestacy because they believe in the sanctity and completeness of their faith. Muslims believe the Quran and Hadith have made provision for every facet of their lives from birth to death.[125]

One possible obstacle to accepting Islamic law as a means of distributing the Intestate Muslim's property is the criticism that some Islamic rules on succession are patently discriminatory in favor of male heirs. One such

[125] Abdul Aziz Bamba, note 23 above.

rule provides that where the deceased is survived by a son and a daughter, the Quran says, "Allah instructs you concerning your children, to the male, the equivalent portion of two females".[126] At first glance, this rule appears discriminatory, but a contextual interpretation reveals some justification which makes it equitable in its application. The primary justification for the differential or uneven distribution of the estate among children of the deceased is rooted in the different duties and obligations placed on them. For instance, the entitlement of a brother to a portion that is twice that allocated to a sister is justified based on the obligation of the brother by Islamic law to maintain and take care of his sister. No such obligation is imposed on women under Islamic law.[127]

As has been elucidated by the Supreme Court of Ghana in the case of *Nartey v Gati*,[128] "... mere differentiation does not *per se* amount to discrimination within the inhibition of the equal protection clause".[129] According to the Supreme Court, for a differential treatment to be considered truly discriminatory, it must be shown that the "differentiation is unreasonable or arbitrary", and "does not rest on any rational basis".[130] The Supreme Court, speaking through Dr Justice Date-Bah JSC (as he then was), noted that "Accordingly, it is widely recognized that equality before the law requires equal treatment of those similarly placed, implying different treatment in respect of those with different characteristics. In simple terms, equals must be treated equally, while the treatment of unequals must be different".[131] It is submitted, on this basis, that the formula for distribution of a Muslim intestate's estate is not necessarily discriminatory against women when interpreted within the proper context.

126 Quran, Chapter 4:11.

127 Abubakri Olakulehin Yekini, "Women and Intestate Succession in Islamic Law", *Islamic Law and Law of the Muslim World Research Paper Series at New York Law School*, no 08-49, (2008) (available online).

128 [2010] SCGLR pp. 745-761.

129 Ibid., p. 754.

130 Ibid., p. 755.

131 Ibid.

A further obstacle that must be overcome by the proposal to apply Islamic law by default to the estate of an intestate Muslim is found in the provisions of the Wills Act 1971 (Act 360). The Wills Act requires that any purported expression of wishes for the distribution of a deceased's estate must, among other demands, be in writing to be valid.[132] *Black's Law Dictionary*[133] defines a will as "A document by which a person directs his or her estate to be distributed upon death". This raises an interesting legal puzzle. On one hand, the Intestate Succession Act operates essentially on the premise that a person who dies without a will has failed to provide an objectively discernible indication of the desired mode of distribution of the person's estate. On the other hand, proponents of the "Islamic law default" seek to rebut this premise by arguing that this objectively discernible indication as to the desired mode of distribution of a person's estate can be identified in the case of Muslims to be the Islamic rules to succession.[134]

Mohammed Bin Salih states that Islam, through the injunctions of the Holy Quran, provides an explicit system for the distribution of the estate of a deceased Muslim among their relations and specifies definite fractional shares of the estate for the named heirs of a decedent, male and female.[135] He notes, in relation to the Muslim's obligation to adhere to the prescriptions on succession to property, that:

> As far as Islam is concerned, the share of every rightful heir has been explicitly defined by Allah as contained in the Holy Quran. The directive to make a will, does not infer that a testator has the prerogative of defining the fractional shares of the relations who are to be his heirs. It does not also give the testamentary freedom to determine who, from among our ascendants or descendants should inherit us. All these have been stipulated and spelt out in the Holy Quran by Allah. In effect, a Muslim cannot disown his/her biological

132 Section 2(1), Wills Act 1971.

133 B. Garner, *Black's Law Dictionary* (8th ed.; 2004), p. 1628.

134 Mohammed Bin Salih, *Law of Inheritance: An Islamic Perspective* (2010).

135 Ibid, p. 79.

> son or daughter, or for that matter any Quranic legal heir in favour of another. Shares can also not be reduced or increased arbitrarily for one heir to gain pecuniary or testamentary advantage. All shares, and a matter of fact, the quantum share entitlement of each heir of the deceased, have already been defined, and definite fractional shares fixed for the relations of a deceased.[136]

Jurisprudentially, it could be argued that the purpose behind the requirement for writing (of a will) is to ensure certainty with regard to the wishes of the testator in relation to the distribution of his estate. If this supposition is accepted, then judicial notice could be taken of the fact that every Muslim knows, or is presumed to know, the fixed rules of succession that apply to him or her according to Islam. It is reasonable, therefore, to presume that by accepting and identifying with the Islamic faith, every Muslim has *prima facie* also agreed to live by and be governed by the tenets of Islam to the extent permissible under the laws of Ghana. In that regard, Islamic law provides an objectively discernible and definite comprehensive set of instructions putatively adopted by every Muslim as applicable to their estate upon death. On this basis, the Islamic rules of succession should be accepted as the default regime for distributing a Muslim intestate's estate.

It is acknowledged, however, that this "discernible indication" may not, and is usually not presented in written form as required by the Wills Act 1971, a rather significant handicap. Within the existing legal and regulatory regime, no matter how clear and objective Islamic law is as a formula for the distribution of an estate, it falls short of the legal requirements of the Wills Act 1971 to be treated as a valid will. To address this, it could be proposed that the previously repealed section 10 of the Marriage of Mohammedans Ordinance, which provided that a Muslim intestate whose marriage had been validly registered under the Ordinance should have their estate distributed according to Islamic law, be reinstated.

[136] Ibid.

Section 10 of the Marriage of Mohammedans Ordinance provided in imperative terms that "on the death of a Mohammedan whose marriage has been duly registered under this Ordinance, the succession to his or her property *shall be* regulated by Mohammedan law" (emphasis added). This meant that even where a Muslim had executed a will prior to his demise, the provisions of the Marriage of Mohammedans Ordinance would be applied to his estate notwithstanding. This was the position taken by the court in the *Brimah* case by Ollennu J when he said,

> It will be noticed that while under section 48 of the Marriage Ordinance; a person married under the Ordinance must die intestate before the English law can be applied to part of his estate, under section 10 of the Marriage of Mohammedans Ordinance, all that is necessary for the application of Mohammedan law to the distribution of the estate of a person whose marriage was registered, is that he should die, not necessarily intestate. Whether this was the intention of the legislator or not, the effect of the provision of section 10 of the Marriage of Mohammedans Ordinance is to curtail the testamentary capacity of a Ghanaian Mohammedan who has registered his Mohammedan marriage under the Ordinance. For any will which he purports to make cannot oust or affect the manner of distribution of his estate as carefully provided by the Mohammedan law. In particular, Muslim law does not permit a disposal by will of more than one-third of the estate. Hence, where the Ordinance applies, a will which purports to dispose of more than one-third share is void pro tanto ...[137]

Section 10 of the Marriage of Mohammedans Ordinance, therefore, in its textual interpretation, operated to curtail the testamentary capacity of a Ghanaian Muslim who had registered his Muslim marriage under the Ordinance. Even though this position appears perplexing, it may possibly be explained on the basis that Muslims are, in any case,

137 *Brimah*, note 43 above, pp. 119-120.

not allowed by Islam to deviate from the fixed fractional entitlements prescribed by Islam in making testamentary dispositions. Thus, in effect, the specified entitlements prescribed by the Islamic rules of succession will apply whether the deceased Muslim died having made a will or not, since the will, to be valid under Islamic law, must comply with the specific fractional entitlements prescribed by the rules of Islam. As noted by Mohammed Bin Salih, "the directive to make a will, does not infer that a testator has the prerogative of defining the fractional shares of the relations who are to be his heirs. It does not also give the testamentary freedom to determine who, from among our ascendants or descendants, should inherit us".[138]

Commenting on this position of the law, Kludze JSC, in his article "Problems of Intestate Succession",[139] stated:

> Perhaps, to the Mohammedan, such denial or curtailment of testamentary capacity under our profane laws is hardly undesirable. Whether of the Sunni or Shia sect, and whether of the Maliki, Hanafi, Shafi, or Hanbali school of Muslim jurisprudence, the Muslim considers the prescriptions of the Mohammedan law of succession as an ordinance of Allah. They are to be found in the Holy Koran and are enjoined by Allah. Even as a Christian, one would consider that in this and some other respects, the Koran is not inferior to our Bible. For the Holy Koran sets out in great detail the entitlements of husbands, widows, parents, brothers, sisters, and children. It goes on even to prescribe that the male shall have double the share of the female! All this coming by way of divine ordinance, it is perfection itself, it is beyond question and it cannot be improved upon by human ingenuity. [140]

[138] Bin Salih, note 134 above, p. 79.

[139] A. K. P. Kludze, "Problems of Intestate Succession", *University of Ghana Law Journal*, IX (1972), pp. 89-122.

[140] Ibid., p. 96.

It is, however, recommended that, in seeking to reform the law to allow the application of Islamic rules of succession to the distribution of the estates of Muslims, any legislative provision introduced must be limited in its application so as not to disrupt the existing legal regime on succession. Moreover, any proposed reform to accommodate the interests of Muslims in having their estates governed by Islamic law must be evaluated within the context of the Intestate Succession Act and the Wills Act 1971. It is recognized, therefore, that the adoption of this proposal will require an amendment of the Intestate Succession Act to allow the intestate estates of Muslims to be regulated by the rules of succession of Islamic law or for the Wills Act 1971 to be amended to accommodate the concept of a statutory will. By this concept of a statutory will, a person whose personal law, in this case, Islamic law, recognizes a clear, certain, and specific formula for the distribution of their estate upon death could be presumed to have made a will on the basis of the said formula for the distribution of their estate unless there is a contrary intention. In the meantime, it appears that the only option available to Muslims to ensure that their estate is distributed according to the dictates of Islam is to make a valid will in accordance with the Wills Act prescribing the application of the Islamic rules of succession to the distribution of their estate upon death.

CONCLUSION

The bizarre state of the regulatory law on Islamic marriages and divorce clearly manifests the unequal treatment of Islamic law in Ghana's legal jurisprudence and the fact that Islamic family law has been consistently considered by the courts as an appendage, and perhaps, an inconvenience. Islamic marriages and divorce have not been accorded the same level of importance and dignity as Ordinance marriages and customary marriages in Ghana's pluralistic regulatory framework on marriage. Muslims have to grapple with rigid, inflexible, and impracticable statutory prescriptions and timelines on registration, with drastic consequences for non-compliance; and the distinctions in the regulatory procedures for Islamic marriages compared to ordinance and customary marriages cannot be rationalized on any discernible grounds.

In Ghana, the courts have consistently demonstrated a lukewarm, if not hostile and dismissive, attitude to the implementation of Islamic law. In cases where there are conflicts between Islamic Law and customary law, the courts have consistently opted to apply customary law on the grounds that Ghana is not a country "in which the great bulk of the population consists of adherents of Islam and in which Muslim law is recognised and to a large extent applied as being, in effect the *lex loci*".[141]

The invalidation and non-recognition of unregistered Islamic marriages as Islamic marriages create debilitating problems with regard to succession and devolution of property for Ghanaian Muslims. The difficult procedural requirements for registration and the consequences of non-compliance coupled with the judicial non-recognition of Islamic law as the personal law of a Muslim[142] lay the foundation for the insecurity of Muslim marriages and divorce. This chapter has demonstrated that Ghana's Marriages Act, in prescribing the requirement of post facto registration as a condition for the validity of Islamic marriages alone, and the courts' "conversion" of unregistered Islamic marriages into customary marriages, contribute to undermining and restricting the freedom of Muslims to practice their religion and manifest such practice as guaranteed in Article 21(b) of the Constitution, 1992.

The gaps and deficiencies in Ghana's regulatory regime on Islamic marriages and divorces have been identified and the implications explored of these shortcomings on intestate succession, marital rights, and child maintenance. Several proposals were advanced for establishing a more comprehensive and responsive legislative framework for regulating Islamic marriages and divorce in Ghana.

[141] Ekow Daniels, note 67 above, p. 70; Arthur Phillips and Henry F. Morris, *Marriage Laws in Africa* (1971), pp. 137, 140.

[142] Per Ollennu J (as he then was) in *Kwakye*, note 41 above.

Chapter Three
A Multi-Legal Perspective on Christian Marriages in Ghana

The present chapter analyzes the laws regulating Christian marriages and divorce in Ghana and makes suggestions for their improvement. Ghana, like most post-colonial societies, has a plural legal system. The various sources of law in Ghana are outlined in Article 11 of the 1992 Constitution; they include the common law, the doctrines of equity, and customary law.[1] In practice, such pluralism manifests itself in the co-existence of State law with judicial customary law, the living customary law of the various ethnic groups, and Islamic law.[2] Accordingly, the Marriages Act of Ghana (CAP 127) recognizes Christian, Mohammedan, and customary marriages. The legal rules governing these types of marriage differ, with those applicable to customary marriages varying according to ethnicity. It is demonstrated that the accepted and regulated legal diversity in familial relationships in Ghana exemplifies the interaction, competition, collaboration, and interdependence among plural legal orders in a given space.

The concentration herein is on Christian and other marriages regulated under Part Three of the Marriages Act 1884-1985 (CAP 127). A brief history of the Marriages Act, then an Ordinance, highlights the significant differences between the received law and the existing customary law. The original but repealed Marriage Ordinance 1884 (CAP 127) (1951 Rev) and the current Marriages Act 1884-1985 (CAP 127) are both called CAP 127. To distinguish the

[1] Article 11, 1992 Constitution of Ghana.

[2] It should be noted that a marriage celebrated according to Islamic law must be registered under Part 2 of the Marriages Act in order to be considered a Mohammedan marriage. If this criterion is not met, the marriage will be considered a customary law marriage. *Kwakye v Tuba* [1961] GLR pp. 720-725.

"original" from the current CAP 127, the former is referred to as the Marriage Ordinance and the latter, the Marriages Act.

Focusing primarily on the Marriages Act, the essential elements for the validity of Christian marriages in Ghana are examined. The Matrimonial Causes Act 1971 (Act 367) is then considered to provide a detailed description of the grounds for the dissolution of a marriage contracted under Part Three of the Marriages Act. Recommendations are made for improving the legal framework for Christian marriages in Ghana.

Emergence of the Marriage Ordinance (CAP 127) in a legally plural Gold Coast

Before 1884, customary marriage was the only legally recognized type of marriage in Ghana, then the Gold Coast.[3] In 1884 and 1901, respectively, the Marriage Ordinance (CAP 127) and the Marriage of Mohammedans Ordinance (CAP 129) were introduced. The genesis of the Marriage Ordinance is fascinating. It began in 1878 with a formal inquiry by the treasurer of the Basel mission at Christianborg, Mr. Buhl, on behalf of the Basel Mission, regarding the marriage of German nationals in the Gold Coast.[4] Assuming that English law regulated the marriages of Europeans in the Gold Coast, Mr. Buhl wrote to the then lieutenant-Governor, Captain C. C. Lees, asking for certification of marriages contracted by German nationals in the Gold Coast.[5]

It would seem that there was no law, as understood by the colonialists and missionaries, on marriages in the Gold Coast at the time. Lees set the ball rolling by writing to the Colonial Office to promulgate a marriage law after a discussion with the then-acting Chief Justice T. W. Jackson,

[3] Nii Amaa Ollennu, "Family Law in Ghana", in *Le Droit De La Famille En Afrique Noire et À Madagascar-Surveys made at the request of UNESCO* (1968), pp. 159-160.

[4] Shirley Zabel, "Legislative History of the Gold Coast and Lagos Marriage Ordinance: III", *Journal of African Law*, XXIII (1979), p. 10.

[5] Ibid., pp. 10-11.

who intimated the importance of such legislation.[6] Several drafts of the law were exchanged between Downing Street in London and the Gold Coast for over five years.[7] Finally, portions of the marriage law, initially made for the island of St Helena and modified for Hong Kong and Ceylon, were incorporated into a fresh draft prepared by Queen's Advocate, W. H. Quayle Jones, and adopted by the Legislative Council. The law included amendments from consultations in the Executive Council and with local religious leaders.[8]

Reconciling the apparently exotic Ordinance with African needs, beliefs, and customs was bound to create a "conflict of laws" situation; rival claims of authority by the different normative orders were inevitable. One significant problem was the effect of marriage under the Ordinance on native custom and succession. In this regard, they had to resolve:

> (i) The capacity or lack thereof of a person married under custom to another, to contract a valid marriage under the Ordinance. (2) The capacity or lack thereof of a person married under the Ordinance to contract a valid customary marriage with another, and the consequences thereof. (3) The effect of marriage under the Ordinance on choice of law governing succession.[9]

It was necessary to make definitive pronouncements on these questions because "without official foresight in this matter, Africans might have been left free to slide in and out of monogamy at will, thereby undermining the *Western* institution of marriage as we know it".[10] This concern of the colonialists presents insight into the unavoidable clash between different normative orders and the quest for dominance that sometimes typifies their relationship. Undoubtedly, as human sensibilities change, aspects of one legal system may become more appealing

6 Ibid.

7 Ibid., p. 11.

8 Ibid., pp. 10-13.

9 Ibid., pp. 16-17.

10 Ibid., p.17 (emphasis added).

to a greater number of people, resulting in the *othering* of the other, usually customary law. Yet, the fundamental values underlying the various systems may not be that far apart. The interpretation of these values may differ, for the customary law system, unlike the imported system, largely determines rights and responsibilities on the grounds of age, gender, kinship, and birth order.[11] The law took effect in the Gold Coast in 1885.[12]

Despite the efforts at reconciling the expectations of the different legal systems, some problems remained, which necessitated a further review of the law after adoption. An immediate impetus was the provision on succession to property upon death intestate. Under the Ordinance, intestate property devolved according to English rules, which left the property to *only* the spouse and children of the deceased.[13] The extended or traditional family of the deceased was excluded. Under matrilineal customary inheritance norms, a deceased person's property belongs to his extended family on death intestate.[14] This drastic change in legal ownership was bound to face resistance from the Africans. Not only did it reform the customary law, which the natives may have considered the colonialists unfit to change, it certainly undermined the capacity of the extended family to live up to its reputation as an effective system of social security. Indeed,

> the inability of the [received] law to make sense of other culturally embedded normative orders stems mainly from its eagerness to provide conclusive answers, which cannot accommodate all possible perspectives

[11] Gordon Woodman, "A Survey of Customary Laws in Africa in Search of Lessons for the Future", in Jeanmarie Fenrich, Paolo Galizzi, and Tracy Higgins (eds.), *The Future of African Customary Law* (2011), pp. 9-10.

[12] Zabel, note 4 above, p. 13.

[13] Ibid., p. 21.

[14] In matrilineal communities, spouses do not belong to each other's family; thus, the self-acquired property of a deceased intestate is family property. See, *In re Atta (Dec'd); Kwako v Tawiah* (2001-2002) SCGLR 461. It has been held that in patrilineal communities, children are entitled to succeed to their father's self-acquired property on death intestate since they belong to their father's family. See *Nartey v Others v. Koshi & Another* [1961] 2 GLR pp. 728 – 733.

> and also, crucially, drastically limit possibilities of change in the future. Therefore, there is indeed a need for regulation of conflict on the grounds of mutual recognition. Formulaic solutions to disputes cannot but generate disputes anew because they do not eliminate the reasons for dissent.[15]

It is reported that a commission of enquiry, including John Mensah Sarbah, a distinguished Gold Coast lawyer and nationalist, was established by the Governor of the Gold Coast in 1905 "to enquire into and report on the Marriage Ordinance 1884".[16] Among many recommendations, the committee suggested that two-thirds of the deceased's property should devolve according to English law and one-third by customary law.[17] This was a proposal toward a "separate but intertwined, autonomous but interdependent" relationship between the legal systems.[18]

In 1909 the Ordinance was amended to include the recommendation.[19] Specifically, section 48(1) of the Ordinance provided that where a person subject to native law or custom contracted a monogamous marriage under the Ordinance and died intestate, two-thirds of his or her property was to devolve on the surviving spouse and children according to the laws of England on the distribution of intestate property in force on 19 November 1884. The remaining one-third was to be distributed in line with the customary law of the intestate.[20]

[15] Emmanuel Melissaris, "Warwick Tie, Legal Pluralism: Towards A Multicultural Conception of Law", *Edinburgh Law Review*, IV (2000), p. 371.

[16] H. F. Morris, "Development of Statutory Marriage Law in Twentieth-Century British Colonial Africa", *Journal of African Law*, XXIII (1979), p. 40.

[17] Ibid.

[18] Gunther Teubner, "The Two Faces of Janus: Rethinking Legal Pluralism", *Cardozo Law Review*, XIII (1992), p. 1443.

[19] Nii Amaa Ollennu, *The Law of Testate and Intestate Succession in Ghana* (1966), pp. 243-244; Morris, note 16 above, p. 44.

[20] Interestingly, this law applied to children of such marriages even if they did not contract their marriages under the Ordinance. See *Vanderpuye v Golightly & Others* [1965] GLR pp. 453 – 461.

The mid-twentieth century saw a significant influx of English juristic, economic, and social ideas into the Gold Coast. This resulted in calls by the natives for changes in the laws of succession.[21] In May 1959 the Government appointed a Commission of Inquiry to study the existing forms of the customary law of inheritance and make recommendations. As a result, in May of 1961 the Government published a White Paper on Marriage, Divorce and Inheritance, which presented proposals and sought public opinion.[22] The White Paper, among many other recommendations, proposed the repeal of section 48 of the Marriage Ordinance, which gave the extended family a third of intestate property. Basically, it proposed that no property should devolve on the extended family if the deceased left behind a spouse, children, or descendants. It is reported that three bills were published pursuant to the proposals and the comments received, though none passed into law because of "opposition from various sections of the community".[23]

Section 48 of the Ordinance was eventually repealed in 1985 by the Intestate Succession Act 1985 (PNDC Law 111), a law justified on the basis that "[t]he growing importance of the nuclear family brings with it its own logic of moral justice"[24] and which gives the nuclear family a greater portion of the intestate estate.[25] In line with the competing demands of diverse legal orders, Roger Gocking, a historian, suggests that the "Conflict between the matrilineage and the nuclear family was an inevitable by-product of the success of Westernisation ...".[26] The dissension between transplanted

[21] Roger Gocking, "British Justice and the Native Tribunals of the Southern Gold Coast Colony", *Journal of African History*, XXXIV (1993), pp. 106-107.

[22] It is reported that the response was tremendous and that various proposals were submitted by traditional authorities, religious bodies, and individual citizens. W. C. Ekow Daniels, "Recent Reforms in Ghana's Family Law", *Journal of African Law (Essays in Honour of AN Allott)*, XXXI, nos. 1-2 (1987), p. 95; See also Ollennu, note 3 above, pp. 191-192.

[23] Ollennu, note 3 above, pp. 191-192.

[24] Memorandum to PNDC Law 111.

[25] See sections 3-7, Intestate Succession Act 1985 (PNDC Law 111).

[26] Roger Gocking, "Competing Systems of Inheritance before the British Courts of the Gold Coast Colony", *International Journal of African Historical Studies*, XXIII,

and indigenous law within the boundary of the nation-state describes *Classic or Deep* legal pluralism.[27] Scholars such as John Griffiths and Gordon Woodman articulated this approach to legal pluralism.[28] Griffiths explained that:

> Legal pluralism...has been a fixture of the colonial experience. Furthermore, it has generally persisted beyond the moment of formal "independence", proving one of the most enduring legacies of European expansion and characterising at the present day the larger part of all of the world's national legal systems.[29]

The struggles between the two systems have often resulted in the suppression of indigenous law. Imported law is often viewed as being more conducive to the goals of nation-building and economic development.[30]

It must be noted that despite its overwhelming significance in marital relations, the issue of succession to property will not be considered here because the focus is solely on the types of marriages recognized in Ghana.

Writing in 1968 about the reason for the promulgation of the Marriage Ordinance, Nii Amaa Ollennu explained that it was:

> (i) to create a system of marriage other than customary law marriage and to provide two modes - Church ceremony and civil ceremony - for contracting it, and to regulate the same; (ii) to legalize existing marriages celebrated by any Minister of any religious denomination or body according to the rites of such

no 4 (1990), p. 604.

[27] In respect of *Classic or Deep* legal pluralism, the transplanted law and indigenous law co-exist within the boundary of the nation-state. See, Gordon Woodman, "Legal Pluralism and the Search for Justice", *Journal of African Law Liber Amicorum for Professor James S. Read*, XL, no. 2 (1996), pp. 157-158.

[28] Ibid.; John Griffiths "What is Legal Pluralism", *Journal of Legal Pluralism and Unofficial Law*, XXIV, no. 1 (1986), p. 1.

[29] Griffiths, note 28 above, p. 6.

[30] Rina Verma Williams, *Postcolonial Politics and Personal Laws: Colonial Legal Legacies and the Indian State* (2006), p. 25.

religious denomination or body; and (iii) to provide for succession to the estate of parties to and issues of such marriage upon their death intestate.[31]

The different systems of marriage regulation introduced by the Ordinance were necessary to address the changing needs of some of the natives, needs developed through the spread of Christianity and education, among other attractions. It appears that before the promulgation of the Marriage Ordinance, the Basel mission had officiated several marriages between Africans, the status of which remained uncertain. In fact, the nineteenth century saw intense propagation of the gospel throughout the Gold Coast.[32] Missionaries established schools, and those who attended these schools developed notions of justice, fairness, and familial relationships that were essentially dissimilar from those sanctioned by African customary law.[33]

Having acquired different perspectives on certain customary law practices, some educated Africans and those who converted to Christianity were driven to sidestep traditional norms in favor of the received law.[34] As expected, the proselytized locals contracted marriages recognized by their churches, but mostly without the consent of their extended or customary families.[35] These marriages were neither legally enforceable nor recognized by the traditional families.[36]

The drawback of a marriage unrecognized by customary law was that on death intestate, the traditional family of the deceased refused to provide for the surviving spouse and

[31] Ollennu, note 3 above, p. 164.

[32] Paul Glen Grant, *Healing and Power in Ghana: Early Indigenous Expressions of Christianity* (2020), pp. 1-15.

[33] Kwabena Dei Ofori-Attah, "Urbanisation and Schooling in Africa: Trends, Issues, and Challenges from Ghana during the Colonial Era", in William T. Pink and George W. Noblit (eds.), *International Handbook on Urban Education* (2008), pp. 43-44.

[34] Jones Darkwa Amanor, "Pentecostalism in Ghana: An African Reformation", *Online: Cyber Journal for Pentecostal Charismatic Research* (undated; available online).

[35] Ollennu, note 19 above, pp. 239-240.

[36] Ibid.

children, even from the deceased's estate. The traditional families carried off most of a deceased relative's property, usually the husband, leaving widows and children destitute.[37] The Marriage Ordinance was thus passed, among a host of reasons, to salvage the situation created by these unions.[38] Unsurprisingly, the Ordinance legalized these "religious unions" and regulated succession to the intestate property of such persons and their children.[39]

It is clear that the Marriage Ordinance, based on prior English Marriage Acts, introduced in the Gold Coast English concepts of marriage and family, some of which were at variance with local prescriptions.[40] For instance, section 42 of the Ordinance provided that, "no marriage in the Gold Coast shall be valid, which if celebrated in England, would be null and void on the ground of kindred or affinity", a provision which curiously remains in the law of Ghana. Whatever the colonialists intended, Ordinance marriages are widely accepted in Ghana, though more people contract customary marriages; customary marriages precede almost all Ordinance marriages.[41] Undeniably, legal pluralism conceptualizes "a more complex and interactive relationship between official and unofficial forms of ordering" in the same social field.[42] In reality, the different legal orders may overlap, and each order may claim supremacy and legitimacy over the other in certain respects.[43]

37 Christine Dowuona-Hammond, "Women and Inheritance in Ghana", in A. Kuenyehia (ed.), *Women and Law in West Africa: Situational Analysis Of Some Key Issues Affecting Women* (1998), pp. 132-168; E. V. O. Dankwa, "Property Rights of Widows in their Deceased Husband's Estate", *University of Ghana Law Journal*, XVI (1982-85), pp. 1-24.

38 Ollennu, note 3 above, p. 164.

39 *Vanderpuye v Golightly & Others* [1965] GLR 453 – 461 (H.C.).

40 W. C. Ekow Daniels, "Development of Customary Law", *Review of Ghana Law*, XVIII (1991-92), p. 85.

41 Akua Kuenyehia, "Women, Marriage, and Intestate Succession in the Context of Legal Pluralism in Africa", *University of California Davis Law Review*, XL (2006), p. 391.

42 Sally Engle Merry, "Legal Pluralism", *Law & Society Review*, XXII (1988), p. 873.

43 Wibren van der Burg, "Conceptual Theories of Law and the Challenges of Global Legal Pluralism: A Legal Interactionist Approach", in Paul Schiff Berman

The original Marriages Ordinance regulated both Christian and civil marriages; the current Marriages Act consolidates the Customary Marriage and Divorce (Registration) Law 1985 (PNDCL 112) and its amendment, the Customary Marriage and Divorce (Registration) (Amendment) Law 1991 (PNDCL 263); the Marriage Ordinance 1884 (CAP 127) (1951 Rev.); and the Marriage of Mohammedan's Ordinance 1907 (CAP 129).

Understanding the concept of marriage in Ghana

The expression *marriage* is poorly defined in Ghana's primary laws on marriage.[44] The closest thing to a definition may be found in the Matrimonial Causes Act 1971, which defines marriage as "... a monogamous marriage".[45] This definition is consistent with a Christian marriage described by Lord Penzance in the nineteenth-century English case of *Hyde v. Hyde and Woodmansee*[46] as "the voluntary union for life of one man and one woman, to the exclusion of all others".[47] It is important to note that this definition is for the sole purpose of the Act in question. Evidently, the definition excludes customary and other potentially polygynous marriages, which are legally recognized in Ghana as marriages properly so-called.

The definition of marriage under the Domestic Violence Act 2007 (Act 732) is more inclusive. It states that marriage "includes marriage under any custom or religion",[48] thus recognizing all forms of marriage in Ghana. Despite the absence of a more educative and insightful definition of marriage, the various laws governing marriages largely set out the essentials of a valid marriage.

(ed.), *The Oxford Handbook of Global Legal Pluralism* (2020), p. 321.

44 The Marriages Act 1884-1985 (CAP 127) and the Matrimonial Causes Act 1971 (Act 367).

45 Section 43, Matrimonial Causes Act 1971 (on interpretations).

46 *Hyde* v. *Hyde and Woodmansee* (1866) LR 1 P. & D, p. 130.

47 Ibid., p. 133.

48 Section 42, Domestic Violence Act 2007.

The Marriages Act is not the only piece of legislation governing marriages in Ghana. Important provisions on marriage can be found in the Children's Act 1998 (Act 560), the Matrimonial Causes Act 1971, and the Domestic Violence Act 2007, among other laws.

MARRIAGE UNDER THE MARRIAGES ACT (CAP 127): CHRISTIAN AND OTHER MARRIAGES IN GHANA

Christian marriages and monogamy

As previously stated, unlike customary marriages, Christian marriages, regulated under Part Three of the Marriages Act and titled "Christian and Other Marriages", are strictly monogamous. Individuals married under this Part cannot contract any other type of marriage with another person while still married under the Act. In other words, a person who contracts a Christian marriage under the Marriages Act cannot marry another person, unless they dissolve the first marriage. Similarly, a person married under customary law cannot marry a different person under Part Three of the Marriages Act, while the customary marriage subsists. Both scenarios constitute bigamy.[49] Because customary marriages are legally polygynous, it is possible to be married to different women simultaneously under customary law; this is not bigamous.[50]

Bigamy is an offense under the Criminal and other Offences Act 1960 (Act 29).[51] The Marriages Act also states categorically that, "if either [party to a marriage] ...before the death of the other, shall contract another marriage while this remains undissolved, you will be thereby guilty of bigamy, and liable to the punishment inflicted for that

[49] Section 265(2), Criminal Offences Act 1960 as amended.

[50] Ibid., section 265(1).

[51] See section 265(2) of the Criminal Offences Act 1960, which states that: "A person may be guilty of bigamy or of an offence under section 264 if, having contracted a monogamous marriage with any person, he marries or purports to many any other person under customary law, or if, being married to any person by customary law, he goes through a monogamous ceremony of marriage with any other person".

offence".[52] Where a party in a subsisting marriage has attempted to contract a new one, the courts have been quick to reaffirm Ghana's legal position on such attempts. In the case of *Re Caveat by Clara Sackitey*[53] the Court held that, until a marriage contracted under customary law had been dissolved, one could not legally contract another marriage under the then Marriage Ordinance with another person.

In the case of *Ruth Arthur v. John Hector Ansah & Naomi Owusu*,[54] the plaintiff learned that the first defendant had married the second defendant under the Ordinance despite the subsisting customary marriage between her and the first defendant. The first defendant admitted being married to the plaintiff, with whom he had five surviving children, in 1973. However, the first defendant argued that the said customary marriage was dissolved sometime in 1988. The High Court found in favor of the plaintiff, holding that the customary marriage between the first defendant and the plaintiff subsisted, and declared the Ordinance marriage contracted between the first and second defendants illegal, null, and void.

Further explaining bigamous unions, it is common for a couple married under custom to convert their marriage into a Christian marriage under Part Three of the Marriages Act. This does not constitute bigamy, as the customary and Christian marriages are between the same persons. Some scholars see the idea of such conversion as depreciating customary law. According to Oti Adinkrah, "The Ordinance, in its demeaning attitude toward customary marriages, makes it impliedly possible for such lower forms of marriage to be 'converted' into the higher Ordinance marriage".[55] The incidence of a "double" marriage with the same person is arguably the result of western and Christian influences, which inexorably subjugate all things traditional or customary. The fact is that the first marriage,

[52] Section 68(3), Marriages Act, 1884-1985.

[53] *Caveat by Clara Sackitey* [1962] 1 GLR pp. 180 – 183 (H.C.).

[54] (C.A., 31 July 2003); See also *Genfi II v Genfi II* [1964] GLR pp. 548 – 551 (H.C.).

[55] Kofi Oti Adinkrah, "Ghana's Marriage Ordinance: An Inquiry into a Legal Transplant for Social Change", *African Law Studies*, XVIII (1980), p. 17.

which is usually the customary marriage, is termed an engagement, even though it is a marriage properly-so-called and regulated by law. While converting a customary marriage to a Christian marriage may arguably have some benefits,[56] such as making it monogamous, the designation of a customary marriage as an engagement seems to give the impression that until a marriage is converted into a Christian marriage, it is lacking in some respect. That it needs to be adorned with a "foreign" cloak to be respected and considered legitimate, thus emphasizing the competition and sometimes inequalities that characterize the relationship between different normative orders.

In questioning the supposed benefits of marriage under the Marriages Act, Adinkrah highlighted the effect of competition among diverse legal systems on the people. He asked, "The great question is whether the Ghanaian Ordinance spouse has changed his perceptions of marriage and family life in accordance with the intendment of the Ordinance".[57] He responds that such perceptions of marriage and family have not changed, but hastens to add that "there are perhaps too many variables to enable us to point to the Ordinance's independent effect ...".[58] Remarkably though, Hayfron-Benjamin JSC (as he then was) in *In re Asante (Decd); Owusu v Asante*[59] seemed to suggest that marriage under the Ordinance may not have changed traditional perceptions of marriage considering that men in such unions continue to contract similar unions with other women contrary to their vows. He referred to this phenomenon as "a social malaise which now afflicts our society":[60]

> The citizens, aided and in some cases, even abetted, by the Christian religious denominations, subscribe to marriage vows to live as man and wife to the exclusion of all others "till death do us part". This

[56] Ibid., p. 20.

[57] Ibid., p. 22.

[58] Ibid.

[59] [1993-94] 2 GLR pp. 271-323 (S.C.).

[60] Ibid., p. 315.

> serious undertaking is firmly supported by the Marriage Ordinance Cap 127, section 36 of which the parties to the marriage ceremony are warned of certain dire consequences to which they respond by giving their assent by pledging their troth. ... Yet in spite of the fact that countless numbers of our citizens marry under the Marriage Ordinance (Cap 127), they readily succumb to the primaeval instinct by compromising their vows and contract further marriages under our customary marriage laws which are potentially polygamous or form unrecognised liaisons commonly called concubinage.[61]

Whether or not Hayfron-Benjamin's observation answers the question asked by Adinkrah, we are reminded of the hybrid legal personality that some Ghanaians have come to inhabit perpetually at the crossroads of State law and customary law.[62]

After celebrating a customary marriage, some parties choose to have their marriages "blessed" by a Minister of their religious denomination at their place of worship. This is not a conversion of their marriage to one under Part Three of the Marriages Act, as some such spouses innocently believe. In the case of *Appomasu v. Bremawuo and another,*[63] the first respondent, and her deceased husband, first married under the customary law, and then went through a marriage ceremony at the Roman Catholic Church to have their marriage recognized by the church. There was no evidence that the ceremony complied with the imperative provisions of the then Marriage Ordinance. The only recorded evidence concerning the marriage was *an entry* in the official register of the church. The first respondent applied for letters of administration upon the death intestate of her husband, asserting that the ceremony which took

[61] Ibid., pp. 315-316.

[62] Ama F. Hammond, "Legal Reforms in Ghana and the Reality of a Hybrid Legal Personality", in R. F. Oppong and K. Agyebeng (eds.), *A Commitment to Law, Development and Public Policy: A Festschrift in Honour of Nana Dr. SKB Asante* (2016), pp. 637-652.

[63] [1980] GLR pp. 278 – 284 (C. A.).

place in the church converted their customary marriage into an Ordinance marriage. This claim was disputed by the appellant, the husband's customary successor, who argued that the church ceremony was merely a nuptial blessing of the customary marriage. The trial judge ruled in favor of the first respondent, stating that a valid monogamous marriage ought to be presumed given the evidence. On appeal, the court held that the church ceremony performed by a marriage officer between the first respondent and her deceased husband was not a marriage under the Marriage Ordinance, but simply a marriage blessed by the church. Thus, the procedures in Part Three of the Marriages Act must be strictly complied with for the law to recognize the existence of a marriage under the Act.

Be that as it may, Adinkrah explains that the "blessing ceremony" is not without problems:

> the practice of the churches in this case [blessing ceremony] greatly adds to the confusion. Under church rules, a customary law marriage can subsequently be "blessed" in order to receive full recognition in the church. But then the same priest who does the blessing may also celebrate an Ordinance marriage proper, using virtually the same procedures and rituals. To make confusion more confounded, the church issues its own certificate for the customary marriages it blesses for the parties! The average Ghanaian, therefore, sees no difference [between the two].[64]

In addition to constantly ensuring that their members are educated about marriage laws, marriage officers or priests must desist from replicating the processes in the Marriages Act when blessing customary marriages. Such replication appears disingenuous, considering Ghana's relatively low legal literacy rate.

64 Adinkrah, note 55 above, p. 20.

Capacity to marry

Parties forming a contractual union must have the legal capacity to do so. The Children's Act 1998 allows a man and woman aged 18 years and above to marry. Section 14(2) provides, "The minimum age of marriage of whatever kind shall be eighteen years". It is noteworthy that Article 16(1) of the 1948 Universal Declaration of Human Rights (UDHR) provides that parties who have attained the full age prescribed by the legal regime under which the marriage is contracted have the right to marry regardless of their race, nationality, or religion. It also recognizes that the consent of both parties to the union is required, and this must be freely and willingly given, rather than coerced.[65]

Oddly, section 59 of the Marriages Act provides that a father's written consent is required when either party to an intended marriage, who is not a widower or a widow, is under twenty-one years of age. Where the father is dead or is of unsound mind or is absent from the Republic, the mother's written consent is required. The guardian's written consent is required when the mother is dead or of unsound mind or absent from the Republic. However, in respect of the issue of consent, section 61 provides that, where a parent or guardian of a party to an impending marriage does not reside in the Republic and accordingly is incapable of consenting to the marriage, either a Justice of the High Court, the Attorney-General, or a Magistrate, can issue the required consent after ascertaining the propriety of the impending marriage.

Is it not perplexing that an eighteen-year-old has the legal capacity to marry, but needs parental consent to marry if under twenty years of age? Admittedly, the State is responsible for protecting children from their inexperience, but if a person can vote at eighteen,[66] write a will at eighteen,[67] and consent to sexual intercourse at sixteen,[68]

65 Article 16(2), Universal Declaration of Human Rights (UDHR).

66 Article 42, 1992 Constitution of Ghana.

67 Section 1, Wills Act 1971.

68 Section 1, Criminal Offences Act 1960 implies that a sixteen-year-old can

why should a person above eighteen years of age but below twenty-one require consent to marry? There appears to be no justification for this provision, and accordingly, it must be revised. Furthermore, it is discriminatory that a mother is second in line in consenting to the marriage of a person below the age of twenty-one. Similarly, the law gives no reason for this distinction between sexes. Therefore, this old-fashioned patriarchy-induced provision is inconsistent with Article 17(2) of the Constitution of Ghana, which prohibits discrimination on grounds of gender.

On the issue of the legal capacity of parties to a union, the law requires that the parties not be closely related by blood. Under section 105 of the Criminal Offences Act 1960 as amended, the offense of incest is committed where a male or female, 16 years old or over, has sex with a person whom he or she knows to be his or her grand-daughter or grand-son; daughter or son; sister or brother; mother or father, and finally, grandmother or grandfather. By extension, marriage by a male or female to another within the preceding classes of relations is prohibited. Despite the prescriptions of State law, the acceptable degrees of consanguinity under customary law differ, and from one ethnic group to another. Thus, section 105 may offend some rules of customary law. Addressing this difference is important because it is inconceivable how one can enjoy a union that is frowned upon as morally opprobrious by everyone in a given locale, apart from the State, as seen in the case of *Glah* v. *The Republic*.[69]

In *Glah*, the first appellant had an affair with his mother-in-law and sister-in-law. They were found guilty of "conduct conducive to a breach of the peace", contrary to section 207 of Act 29, and were given custodial sentences. On appeal, they argued that their affairs did not constitute criminal offenses. In support of their convictions, the State argued that the chief and elders of the village had warned the appellants to refrain from such immoral associations. The court allowed the appeal explaining that, "There is no doubt that customary law frowns upon such a conduct, but it is not

consent to sexual intercourse.

69 [1992] 2 GLR pp. 15 – 18.

caught by any section of Act 29 and the family cannot take an easy line of things by pursuing their criminal action".[70] This was a pyrrhic victory for the appellants and also for the State, which has limited permitted domestic relationships, thus slighting deeply held convictions about what is morally right and wrong under customary law.

It is suggested that the Criminal Offences Act be modified to state that, in determining whether the crime of incest has been committed, the court shall also consider the personal law of the accused. It is unclear, though, how this recommendation can be reconciled with Article 19(11) of the constitution, which states, "No one shall be convicted of a criminal offence unless the offence is defined and the penalty for it is prescribed in a *written law*" (emphasis added). This issue is worth pondering.

A controversial issue concerning the capacity to marry relates to the sex of the parties. Perhaps it is accurate to state that in Ghana, any marriage under the Marriages Act must be between a man and a woman. This assumption is based on the description of the parties to the union as a man and a woman throughout the Act. Although it is uncertain if Ghana has a clear statutory provision prohibiting same-sex unions, it is widely asserted that section 104 of the Criminal Offences Act 1960 prohibits sexual intercourse between persons of the same sex, and inferably, marriage between such persons. Section 104 provides that:

1. Whoever has unnatural carnal knowledge –
    a. of any person of the age of 16 years or over without his consent shall be guilty of a first-degree felony and shall be liable on summary conviction to imprisonment of a term of not less than five years and not more than 25 years;
    b. or of any person of 16 years or over with his consent is guilty of a misdemeanour; or
    c. of any animal is guilty of a misdemeanour.

[70] Ibid., p. 17.

2. Unnatural carnal knowledge is sexual intercourse with a person in an unnatural manner or with an animal.

The expression "unnatural carnal knowledge" is not defined satisfactorily, thereby undermining the intention of the lawmaker. If the foregoing provision has the meaning widely attributed to it by the legal fraternity, then it appears that intercourse between persons of the same sex, and by extension, same-sex marriages, are legally prohibited in Ghana. Same-sex marriages continue to enjoy legal acceptance in several western societies. A consistent argument for their recognition and acceptance is based on human rights considerations. Regarding the Ghanaian position on the matter, it must be noted that the sociocultural dimensions of laws and their role in promoting deference to law cannot be overstated: "Law is not an abstract concept, neutrally poised above political, social and cultural realities of a given community, but a normative framework that regulates the society's constitutive processes".[71] Thus, to ensure respect for the law, laws must satisfy legitimate sociocultural expectations. In deciding the path to take, Ghana must consider its social, political, and even economic circumstances to guide its people toward what they need and should aspire to. We turn to marriages that are deemed voidable under the Marriages Act.

Voidable marriages under the Matrimonial Causes Act

A marriage may be void even if the courts have not so determined, and this paves the way for it to be annulled. A divorce, on the other hand, terminates a valid marriage. A voidable marriage becomes void after a court has annulled it. In the case of *De Reneville v De Reneville*,[72] Lord Greene MR explained the distinction between void and voidable marriages as follows:

> A void marriage is one that will be regarded by every court in any case in which the existence of

[71] Francis Deng, "The Crossfire of Sudan's War of Identities", in Deborah Isser (ed.), *Customary Justice and the Rule of Law in War-torn Societies* (2011), p. 293.

[72] [1948] 1 AER pp. 56 – 100 (C. A).

> the marriage is in issue as never having taken place and can be so treated by both parties to it without the necessity of any decree annulling it; a voidable marriage is one that will be regarded by every court as a valid subsisting marriage until a decree annulling it has been pronounced by a court of competent jurisdiction.[73]

According to section 13 of the Matrimonial Causes Act 1971, a marriage is voidable (a) if it has not been consummated because the respondent willfully refuses to; (b) if either party to the marriage was of unsound mind or subject to recurrent attacks of insanity at the time of the marriage; or (c) if at the time of the marriage the respondent was pregnant with the child of another person; or (d) if, at the time of the marriage, the respondent had an incurable infectious venereal disease. These grounds are in addition to others on which a marriage is, by law, void or voidable. Including this omnibus provision to cover circumstances not explicitly mentioned in the law is commendable as it guarantees legal protection for partners.

The courts will only annul the marriage if the petitioner is able to prove ignorance of the facts making the marriage voidable at the time of the marriage,[74] and the annulment proceedings must also be instituted within a year from the date of the marriage.[75] In addition, the petitioner must establish that there has been no sexual intercourse with his or her consent since the discovery of the facts making the marriage voidable.[76] Though conscious of human frailties, this provision on sexual intercourse is fair since annulments are intended to protect parties from fraud, among other problems, and parties should not be seen to be ratifying the very fraud which forms the basis of the annulment. Arguably, while fraud vitiates consent, consent should also vitiate fraud.

[73] Ibid., p. 60, per Lord Greene MR.

[74] Section 13(3)(a), Matrimonial Causes Act 1971.

[75] Ibid., section 13(3)(b).

[76] Ibid., section 13(3)(c).

Section 14 of the Matrimonial Causes Act 1971 states that where the marriage is annulled, a child of the parties is deemed to have the same status and rights as if the marriage of the parents had been dissolved rather than annulled. This provision ensures that children are not denied any rights that could impair their social, emotional, and educational development.

Invalid marriages under the Marriages Act

Under the Marriages Act, some unions are invalid. For instance, even though a man is permitted to marry his deceased wife's sister or niece, he is not permitted to celebrate a marriage that would be void on the ground of kindred or affinity if it was celebrated in England.[77] Unless it can be inferred that this provision also permits a woman to marry her deceased husband's brother or nephew, it is discriminatory and must be amended. Moreover, why is Ghana still reliant on England when independence was obtained over sixty years ago? What about the grounds of kindred and affinity acceptable to Ghanaians? As the saying goes, this provision has outlived its usefulness.

Furthermore, a marriage is invalid if one party has a prior subsisting marriage with another person under customary law.[78] The subsequent marriage under Part Three of the Marriages Act is invalid and constitutes bigamy.

Next, marriages must be celebrated in the locations designated by law. Where the parties knowingly celebrate their marriage in an undesignated place, the resulting union is invalid, unless the requisite permission was sought.[79] In addition, where the parties marry using false names or without the prescribed certificates and licenses, or by a legally designated person, the marriage is invalid.[80]

This section aims at averting fictitious marriages and claims that may be made subsequently based on such

[77] Ibid., section 74(1)(a).

[78] Ibid., section 74(1)(b).

[79] Ibid., section 74(2).

[80] Ibid.

marriages. Marriage forms the basis upon which several rights are sought, including property rights. It also gives spouses the right to make significant decisions for each other, especially in times of sickness. Thus, the State is responsible for ensuring that fake unions are easily detected and invalidated. We turn to the authorities and procedures for solemnizing Christian Marriages in Ghana.

AUTHORITIES AND PROCEDURES FOR THE SOLEMNIZATION OF CHRISTIAN MARRIAGES

Under section 41 of the Marriages Act, a marriage may be solemnized under the authority of either a Registrar's certificate, a Marriage Officer's certificate, or a special license from the Registrar of Marriages. We consider the procedures for the validity of each certificate.

Marriage under a registrar's certificate

Individuals seeking to marry under a registrar's certificate are required to file a notice of marriage with the registrar of marriages in the Registrar General's office or at one's local Municipal or District Assembly. This may be done by any party to the intended marriage. The notice of marriage provides information about the couple. For instance, it includes the name and occupation of the prospective spouses, whether the bridegroom is a bachelor or widower, or whether the bride is a spinster or widow.[81] The notice must also state the age of the prospective spouses. This document must be signed by the party giving the notice.[82] The information obtained is then recorded in the marriage notice book by the registrar, after which official notice of the intended marriage is displayed publicly for three months.[83]

[81] Ibid., section 42.

[82] Where the applicant is unable to write or is insufficiently acquainted with the English language, the applicant shall place a mark or cross to the relevant document in the presence of a literate person who shall attest the notice (see ibid., section 43); The Registrar is required to supply forms of notice gratuitously to persons applying for the forms (see ibid., section 44).

[83] Ibid., section 45; Normally, this is done by posting the notice on noticeboards at the registry or on the outer door of the office for a maximum period of 3 months or until the grant of the marriage certificate.

The purpose for publicly displaying this information and for a reasonable period is to allow any member of the public who intends to oppose the marriage the opportunity and time to do so.[84] A registrar's certificate to marry is issued to the parties to the proposed marriage after twenty-one days of filing a notice of marriage, but before a three-month period, provided that a number of conditions are fulfilled.[85] Where the marriage does not occur within three months after the date of the notice, the notice and all proceedings consequent on the notice are void. A fresh notice will have to be published before the parties can lawfully marry under a registrar's certificate. In other words, after the notice is filed, the couple has three months to get married. After this period, the registrar's certificate expires, necessitating the filing of a new notice if they still intend to get married. Also, the marriage must be celebrated between the hours of 08:00 and 16:00 in the registrar's office.[86] The registrar's certificate is issued after the parties have met all legal requirements. The registrar must be satisfied that there are no lawful impediments to the marriage.[87] As earlier indicated, such impediments may relate to the parties' age and the degree of consanguinity between the parties.

It is important that the State establishes verifiable procedures for the solemnization of marriages, because it is a foundation upon which important entitlements and privileges are demanded. Thus, the procedures are intended to protect parties and to fill potential loopholes, rather than frustrate them. It is submitted, though, that the law should employ the use of information technology to make some of the procedures, such as the giving of notices, easier and simpler.

84 The marriage notice book may be inspected during office hours without the payment of a fee (see ibid., section 45(2)).

85 Ibid., section 46.

86 Ibid., section 68.

87 Ibid., section 46.

Marriage under the certificate of the marriage officer

A person who intends to marry under the authority of a marriage officer's certificate must, at least four days before the time required for the first publication of the banns of marriage, submit to a marriage officer for the district in which that person resides a notice indicating the names of the parties and their places of residence, among other relevant pieces of information.[88] Under section 48(2) of the Act, a single notice can be given by either party. Where both persons have for fifteen days before giving the notice resided in the same town or village and are members of the same religious denomination, a single notice is sufficient, and the banns will be published only in the place of worship. One marriage officer's certificate is sufficient to solemnize the marriage.

Where separate notices of an intended marriage are required to be given, the banns must be published separately in respect of each notice.[89] Upon receipt of the notice of the intended marriage, the marriage officer must publish the banns between the parties at their location of residence or their place of worship.[90] The officer may also cause the banns to be published by a duly authorized person.[91] At the place of worship, the banns must be published in English and in the requisite local language[92] during public service on three consecutive Sundays.[93]

A clergyman or a marriage officer is not authorized to act as a marriage officer in a marriage that contravenes the

[88] Ibid., section 48(1).

[89] Ibid., section 49(2).

[90] Ibid., section 49(1)(a).

[91] Ibid., section 49.

[92] Where the person authorized to publish the banns is not familiar with the requisite local language, that person may deputize another person to publish the banns in the local language, and the banns shall be so published immediately after their publication in English (see ibid., section 50(30)).

[93] The person publishing the banns shall endorse the dates of the publications on the notice, in the Form H set out in the Fifth Schedule and where that person is not the marriage officer, that person shall return the notice duly endorsed to the marriage officer (see ibid., section 51).

rules of their religious denomination.[94] If the marriage is not solemnized within three months of the last publication of banns, the publication and all proceedings consequent on the publication are void, and the banns will have to be republished before the parties can solemnize their marriage.[95] The marriage must be celebrated between 08:00 and 18:00 hours in a licensed place of worship.[96]

Like a marriage under a registrar's certificate, the procedures and timelines are strict, but as already stated, marriages are important to societies, and for this reason, they seek to ensure that they are properly celebrated. We turn to the important role that special licenses issued by the registrar of marriages play in the marriage process in Ghana.

Marriage under a special license

Under Section 55 of the Marriages Act, a person can apply for and obtain a special license from the registrar of marriages for the solemnization of their marriage, provided they provide an affidavit that there is no lawful impediment to the intended marriage and that written consent has been obtained in the case of a person below twenty-one years of age.[97] Once the registrar is satisfied that these conditions have been met, the registrar may dispense with some of the formalities for celebrating a marriage.[98] For instance, the marriage may also be held somewhere other than a permitted place of worship or a registrar's office.[99]

The special license may allow a registrar or a recognized minister of a religious denomination, who may not be a marriage officer, to perform the marriage ceremony between the couple. The registrar of the marriage district is required to provide the parties with a blank certificate of marriage in

94 Ibid., section 38(3).

95 Ibid., section 54.

96 Ibid., section 62.

97 See ibid., section 59, on consent to marriage of minors.

98 Ibid., section 55(1).

99 Ibid., section 55(2).

duplicate, which must be filled in by a minister or registrar who is required to follow all prescribed formalities in respect of marriages celebrated in a licensed place of worship or the registrar's office.[100]

The special license is significant because it gives parties a measure of flexibility in making decisions about their marriage. For instance, obtaining a special license gives parties greater choice over where to marry, especially since the covid-19 pandemic has proven that traditional venues may not always be feasible. For an event that is significant to the parties, it is important that they make some substantive and procedural choices backed by law.

It is clear from the above discussion that the procedures for solemnizing Christian marriages are complex, perhaps justifiably. However, to ease the pressures of the procedures on the parties, the law must take advantage of modern technology to simplify the various processes.

We turn to how a marriage intended to be celebrated under the certificate of a registrar or a marriage officer may be forbidden.

Forbidding a marriage

A person with just cause or who knows of a just cause why the impending marriage should be disallowed may file a caveat to prevent solemnization. A caveat is a legal objection to a marriage that must state the reasons why a marriage should be disallowed.

Where the marriage is to be solemnized under the Registrar's Certificate, a caveat may be entered at any time before the issue of the certificate by writing the word "Forbidden" opposite to the entry of the notice in the Marriage Notice Book, and_appending to the notice the name and place of residence of the caveator, and the grounds for caveating.[101] A caveat in relation to marriage under a Registrar's Certificate must be filed within twenty-one days of publication of the notice. A popular case on

[100] Ibid., section 70.

[101] Ibid., section 56(1)(a).

forbidding a marriage is *Re caveat By Clara Sackitey.* In this case, Clara Sackitey, a caveatrix, filed a caveat against the issuing of a registrar's certificate in respect of an ordinance marriage intended between the respondent and another. The caveatrix contended that she remained validly married to the respondent under customary law and insisted that the respondent was barred from marrying under the provisions of the Marriage Ordinance to a different woman besides herself. The court sought to determine whether the parties had a valid customary marriage. And if yes, whether the customary marriage subsisted to bar a future Ordinance marriage to a different wife by the respondent. The High Court held that the customary rites performed, coupled with cohabitation between the caveatrix and respondent, constituted a valid marriage under customary law and accordingly barred the respondent from marrying a different woman under the Ordinance, except the caveatrix.

Ruth Arthur suggests that where a person entitled to caveat by law was not and could not have been aware of the intended marriage, despite the publication of the notice for twenty-one days and accordingly does not file a caveat, the omission is irrelevant if one of the parties to the intended marriage is married to the caveatrix.[102] The Court of Appeal, per Owusu-Ansah J.A., held that since the plaintiff had no idea of the publication of the intended marriage, the publication was inconsequential.

The Marriages Act sets out a procedure for entering a caveat regarding a marriage to be solemnized under the Certificate of a Marriage Officer. Section 56 (1) (b) empowers a person whose consent to a marriage is required, or who may know of a just cause why the marriage should not take place, to enter a caveat against the issue of a Marriage Officer's Certificate. A caveat is entered by:

i. by giving notice in writing to the person publishing the banns to forbid the marriage,

ii. by appending the name and place of abode of that person to the notice, and

[102] *Ruth Arthur,* note 54 above.

iii. by specifying in the notice, the grounds for forbidding the marriage.

The person publishing the banns, if not the marriage officer, must forward the notice without delay to the marriage officer. Unless the notice of the intending marriage has been returned to the marriage officer, this person must also record on the notice the fact and date of receipt of the notice forbidding the marriage. It should be noted that a registrar or marriage officer shall not issue the certificate until the caveat is removed.[103]

If the marriage officer is satisfied that the banns have been appropriately published and a caveat has not been entered, or the caveat has been duly removed, the marriage officer shall grant a marriage officer's certificate.[104]

Although the right to enter a caveat is fair, the requirement that the word "forbidden" be written opposite the entry of the notice in the marriage notice book, and the various manual processes that hinder the extensive reach of information are outmoded and must be modified to reflect current modes of communication.

Cohabitation and concubinage as marriage?

There is no presumption of marriage in Ghana. The existence of a marriage will not be presumed in favor of a couple, no matter how long they have lived together and held themselves out as husband and wife. In the case of *Gym* v. *Insaidoo,*[105] the Ghanaian court clarified that the presumption arose if the couple cohabited after a legally recognizable marriage ceremony had been celebrated. In that case, Koranteng Addow J. said:

> I was invited by learned counsel for the defendant in his submissions to presume marriage from the fact of cohabitation ... Since the cohabitation did not begin with a marriage ceremony it is my view that

[103] Section 56, Marriages Act 1884-1985.

[104] Ibid., section 53.

[105] *Gym* v. *Insaidoo* [1965] GLR pp. 574 – 588 (H.C.).

> the presumption of marriage would not arise and that the defendant has to prove affirmatively his contention that he performed the customary marriage ceremony.[106]

She emphasized in *Re Blankson-Hemans* that "when the fact of marriage is in dispute ... it has to be proved strictly and affirmatively like any other disputed fact. It does not have to be inferred".[107]

The closest that any proposed law has come to recognizing persons in such unions as spouses is section 3(2) of the stalled Property Rights of Spouses Bill 2013:

> A man and a woman who hold themselves out together to the public as husband and wife for a reasonable period of time, which period of time shall in any case not be less than two years shall be deemed to be spouses and have the rights of spouses for the purpose of this Act.

Possibly, the legitimate concern to protect the property rights of parties to informal unions does not provide a compelling justification to confer marital status on unmarried persons. The provision is understandably traceable to international and local efforts to eradicate the "feminization of poverty".[108]

Under the Domestic Violence Act 2007, however, a domestic relationship includes a "relationship akin to a family relationship".[109] In other words, the law recognizes relationships "in the nature of a marriage even if they [the parties] are not...married to each other".[110] While the law appreciates that such relationships are functionally similar

[106] Ibid., pp. 582-583.

[107] *In re Blankson-Hemans (decd.); Blankson-Hemans v. Monney and Another* [1973] 1 GLR p. 467 (H.C.).

[108] Ministry of Gender, Children and Social Protection, *National Gender Policy, Mainstreaming Gender Equality and Women's Empowerment into Ghana's Development Efforts* (2015).

[109] Section 2(1), Domestic Violence Act 2007.

[110] Ibid., section 2(1) b.

to marriage, they are not regarded as marriages, and parties in such unions do not get the legal protections specifically for married couples.

A number of questions need to be answered in making a decision about the presumption of marriage in Ghana. Should the law presume for people what they either do not want or are not courageous enough to demand for themselves? Will the presumption extend to people the benefit of being "single" when it works for them and being "married" when it inures to their benefit? Are there no avenues for such persons to enforce the rights being demanded? Is marriage the only legal space in which justice is guaranteed? On the other hand, should a union's lack of "formality" impede the protection of rights and obstruct justice? Finding the requisite balance among competing interests should satisfy social considerations and legal aspirations.

Child marriages

Child marriages are prohibited in Ghana.[111] The Children's Act allows only persons who are 18 years and above to marry.[112] Ghana nonetheless has yet to rid itself of the phenomenon of child marriages. A paper by Richard de Groot and colleagues suggests that the prevalence of child marriage in Ghana remains high and that one in five girls marries before her eighteenth birthday.[113] This is a result of deeply rooted beliefs about gender inequalities and economic insecurity, among other factors, and must be eradicated.[114]

Ghana has a National Strategic Framework on Ending Child Marriage in Ghana (2017-2026). The Framework seeks to empower girls and boys to prevent and respond to child marriage; ensure changes in the beliefs, attitudes, and social

[111] Section 14(1), Children's Act 1998.

[112] Ibid., section 14(2).

[113] Richard de Groot, Maxwell Yiryele Kuunyem, and Tia Palermo "Child Marriage and Associated Outcomes in Northern Ghana: A Cross-Sectional Study", *BMC Public Health*, XVIII (2018), p. 2.

[114] Ministry of Gender, Children and Social Protection, *National Strategic Framework on Ending Child Marriage in Ghana 2017-2026* (2016), p. 7.

norms of communities involved in child marriage, and provide education on sexual and reproductive health and related services. It also seeks to ensure that applicable laws are effectively enforced and implemented.[115] It is hoped that child marriages will soon be extinct with improved education and more economic opportunities for families.

DISSOLUTION OF MARRIAGES CONTRACTED UNDER PART THREE OF THE MARRIAGES ACT

The Matrimonial Causes Act 1971 was enacted to provide for matrimonial causes, such as divorce, child custody, financial provision, and other related matters. It primarily regulates the dissolution of monogamous marriages.[116] However, its provisions could apply to other types of marriages.[117] For instance, a customary marriage can be dissolved under Act 367.

Either spouse may present a petition to the court for a divorce.[118] The petitioner must be a citizen of Ghana, domiciled in Ghana, or resident in Ghana for three years.[119] According to Act 367, the sole ground for granting a petition for divorce must be that the marriage has broken down beyond reconciliation.[120] To prove that the marriage has broken down beyond reconciliation, a petitioner must establish one or more of the following facts:

a. That the respondent has committed adultery.

b. That the respondent's behavior is unreasonable

c. That the Respondent has deserted the petitioner for at least two years.

d. That the parties have not lived together as husband and wife for a continuous period of at least two years.

[115] Ibid., p. 15.

[116] Section 41(1), Matrimonial Causes Act 1971.

[117] Ibid., sections 41(2) - (4).

[118] Ibid., sections 1(1).

[119] Ibid., section 31.

[120] Ibid., section 1(2).

e. That the parties have not lived together as husband and wife for a continuous period of at least five years and that

f. The parties are unable to reconcile their differences.[121]

The succeeding subheadings will examine these facts supporting them with judicial decisions, but before then, it should be noted that the petitioner is under a legal obligation to prove the foregoing applicable facts and not just plead them.[122] The court, on the other hand, is "under a statutory and positive duty to inquire so far as it reasonably can, into the charges and counter-charges alleged" to determine whether the marriage has broken down beyond reconciliation.[123] This is always a question of fact.[124] A court may refuse to grant a divorce even if one or more of the facts is established if it is unconvinced that the marriage has broken down beyond reconciliation.[125] If the court fails to conduct this enquiry, its judgment may be set aside on appeal.[126] It should be noted that the Act seems to mandate the court to play "an inquisitorial role" in all circumstances.[127] It has been held that an inquest may only be held where necessary because procedural and practical difficulties, such as the cost of litigation, would increase if an inquiry had to be held in all cases, even when the evidence presented was uncontroverted.[128]

Adultery by the respondent

As indicated, the petitioner must prove that the respondent has committed adultery and that by reason of the adultery, the petitioner finds it intolerable to live with

121 Ibid., section 2(1) (a-f).

122 *Danquah v. Danquah* [1979] GLR 371 (H.C.).

123 *Donkor v Donkor* [1982-1983] GLR p. 1159 (H.C.).

124 *Mensah v Mensah* [1972] 2 GLR 198, p. 203 (H.C.).

125 *Adjetey and Another v Adjetey* [1973] 1 GLR p. 220 (H.C.).

126 Sections 1 (2) and (3), Matrimonial Causes Act 1971.

127 *Mensah*, note 124 above, p. 209.

128 Ibid., pp. 208-209.

the respondent.[129] It must be emphasized that apart from the fact of adultery, the petitioner must also prove that they cannot, as a result, live with the respondent.

The case of *Quartey v Quartey*[130] held that the party who alleges adultery must prove the allegation beyond reasonable doubt and with evidence that is not "tainted, indifferent, suspicious or uncertain".[131] It further held that the court was at liberty to accept the evidence supporting the allegation of adultery if it was deemed trustworthy and a "clear, distinct and unequivocal admission of adultery", yet uncorroborated.[132] Admitting to the rarity of direct evidence of adultery, the court in *Adjetey v Adjetey*[133] held that the evidence need not reach the level of certainty required in criminal proceedings but must carry a high degree of probability. As is usually the case, adultery can be proven by circumstantial evidence; the evidence must satisfy the court.[134] In Ghana, while there must be proof of a "disposition" or a "strong inclination" and "evidence of opportunity" to commit adultery, these factors alone do not lead to an irrebuttable presumption that adultery had been committed.[135] Similarly, the court is not bound to infer adultery solely from evidence of opportunity.

In respect of adultery, where the parties live together as husband and wife for more than six months after the discovery of adultery, intending to reconcile, the petitioner cannot rely on the fact of adultery to establish that the petitioner finds it intolerable to live with the respondent. However, if the parties lived together as husband and wife

129 Section 2(1)(a), Matrimonial Causes Act 1971.

130 [1972] 1 GLR pp. 6 – 21 (H.C.).

131 Ibid., p. 13.

132 Ibid.

133 *Adjetey*, note 125 above.

134 Ibid., p. 219.

135 Ibid., p. 218, citing *Halsbury's Laws of England* (3d ed.), XII, pp. 237-238, para. 446.

less than six months after discovering the indiscretion, the petitioner can rely on the fact of adultery.[136]

It is argued that proof that the parties were living together as husband and wife with a view to reconciliation does not establish condonation, and a party must be allowed to rely on the said adultery. The circumstances of how they lived together should prevail as opposed to the length of time they lived together.

Act 367 defines adultery as "the voluntary sexual intercourse of a married person with one of the opposite sex other than his or her spouse".[137] This means that sexual intercourse with someone of the same sex is not considered adultery. It is submitted that sexual intercourse with any person should be classified as adultery, and adultery should cover all types of sexual behavior.

Unreasonable behavior of the respondent

To prove that a marriage has broken down beyond reconciliation, the petitioner must prove that the respondent behaved in a way that the petitioner cannot reasonably be expected to live with.[138]

The case of *Knudsen v Knudsen*[139] provides a good example of the meaning of unreasonable behavior. In this case, the respondent destroyed the petitioner's property, some of which was inherited, on suspicion that the petitioner was cheating, among other claims. She shamed him publicly, especially by calling his place of employment to accuse coworkers of flirting with the petitioner. Basically, the aggressive acts made it almost impossible for the petitioner to practice his profession, on which the whole family relied financially. Eventually, he lost his job. It is also alleged that she struck him with a machete and had him arrested on false charges, humiliating him and depriving him of personal liberty. The court determined that the petitioner could not

[136] Section 3, Matrimonial Causes Act 1971.

[137] Ibid., section 43.

[138] Ibid., section 2(1)(b).

[139] [1976] 1 GLR pp. 204 – 216 (C.A.).

reasonably be expected to live with the respondent because of her unreasonable behavior. The court held that the test for determining whether the petitioner can reasonably be expected to live with the respondent is objective.

In *Hughes v Hughes,*[140] the court held that one could not point to isolated infuriating acts by a spouse as constituting unreasonable behavior. To succeed, a petitioner had to show that the respondent's conduct had reached a certain degree of severity that no reasonable person would tolerate.[141] Similarly, Hayfron-Benjamin J (as he then was) explained in *Mensah* that the conduct complained about "must be grave and weighty" and that "mere trivialities will not suffice, for Act 367 is not a Cassanova's Charter".[142]

Section 4 of the Matrimonial Causes Act 1971 provides that in determining whether the petitioner can reasonably be expected to live with the respondent, the court shall disregard any period not exceeding six months during which the parties lived as husband and wife after the occurrence of the final incident relied on by the petitioner. If the parties live together for more than six months after the decisive event, it is possible to infer condonation.[143] The couple in *Knudsen* lived in Ghana from May to September after a defining incident. Relying on this period of cohabitation and the lack of attempts at reconciliation, the trial judge held that the marriage had not broken down beyond reconciliation. This was in spite of the serious allegations made against the wife. The Court of Appeal overturned the judgment of the High court.[144]

Not only does Act 367 not define unreasonable behavior, it also mandates the court to consider if the parties lived together for six months after the incident in question. An inference of condonation could be made from this arrangement. These limitations must be addressed.

140 [1973] 2 GLR 342 – 348 (H.C.).

141 Ibid., p. 346.

142 *Mensah,* note 124 above, p. 204.

143 *Knudsen,* note 139 above.

144 Ibid.

Desertion by respondent

The petitioner must prove that the respondent has deserted the petitioner for a continuous period of at least two years immediately before the presentation of the petition.[145] In *Hughes,* the petitioner husband sought to dissolve his marriage to the respondent, arguing that the marriage had broken down beyond reconciliation. Among other arguments, he contended that the respondent had deserted him. Explaining why it found no evidence of desertion, the court noted that where a husband and wife did not have decent accommodation, the wife was not guilty of desertion if she chose a job that required her to stay away from the matrimonial home with the approval of her husband. The court held that for the respondent's conduct to amount to desertion, the court had to satisfy itself that there was "an unjustifiable withdrawal from cohabitation without the consent of the petitioner".[146] It held further that mere separation was not enough and that the respondent, to be guilty of desertion, should have the intention of remaining separated permanently from the petitioner.[147] Thus, to establish desertion, the petitioner must prove a withdrawal from cohabitation by the spouse, who intends to end cohabitation permanently. The petitioner must also prove that he does not consent to the other spouse's desertion. Last, the desertion must be unjustifiable and must be for a continuous period of more than two years.

The case of *Arku v Arku and Abraham*[148] is one of constructive desertion. Explaining the concept of constructive desertion, Djabanor J quoted *Halsbury's Laws of England*:

> Desertion is not to be tested by merely ascertaining which party left the matrimonial home first. If one spouse is forced by the conduct of the other to leave home, it may be that the spouse responsible for the driving out is guilty of desertion. There is no

[145] Section 2(1)(c), Matrimonial Causes Act 1971.

[146] *Hughes,* note 140 above, p. 344.

[147] Ibid.

[148] [1965] GLR pp. 269 – 278 (H.C.).

> substantial difference between the case of a man who intends to cease cohabitation and leaves his wife, and the case of a man who compels his wife by his conduct, with the same intention, to leave him.[149]

In this case, the petitioner claimed that the respondent left the matrimonial home and has never returned; the court found that the attempt at reconciliation had failed and that the respondent left with the consent of the petitioner. The court determined that it was actually the petitioner who asked for the respondent's belongings to be removed from their matrimonial home. Accordingly, the judge found that the respondent did not desert the petitioner without reasonable cause or without his consent.

The court will disregard periods of not more than six months in total during which the parties resumed living as husband and wife in evaluating whether the period of desertion was continuous.[150] The court may treat a period of desertion as having lasted, though the deserting party is incapable of continuing with the requisite intention; this is if the evidence before the court is such that, had that party not been thus incapable, the court would have inferred that the desertion persisted at the time. [151]

Even though the cases have been indispensable in understanding the term *desertion*, Act 367 should have defined the expression. The six-month "limitation period" is arguably unscientific and should be modified to reflect the realities of life and of unions.

Separation for a period of two years

To establish that a marriage has broken down beyond reconciliation, the parties must not have lived as husband and wife for a continuous period of at least two years immediately preceding the presentation of the petition, and the respondent must consent to the grant of divorce. The

149 Ibid, p. 275.

150 Section 5, Matrimonial Causes Act 1971.

151 Ibid.

respondent's consent must not be unreasonably withheld in such circumstances; if consent is so withheld, the court may still grant a divorce petition.[152]

Once the respondent has been given the information necessary to appreciate the implications of consenting, the court shall be satisfied that the respondent has consented to the divorce. If the petitioner misled the respondent intentionally or unintentionally, concerning a factor that the respondent considered in deciding to consent to the divorce, the court may dismiss the proceedings any time before the divorce is granted.[153]

Still on the issue of consent, in *Addo v Addo*,[154] the petitioner sought to dissolve his marriage, explaining that it had broken down beyond reconciliation. He stated specifically that he and the respondent had not lived as man and wife for a continuous period of over two years. The problems in the marriage had affected the respondent to the point where she was seeking medical treatment. The respondent did not want to consent to the divorce despite this fact. The court explained that even though some people were good at enduring hardship, the court was obliged to objectively assess what a reasonable person in the respondent's position would do. Accordingly, the court held that the respondent had unreasonably withheld consent and dissolved the marriage. This provision is fair; it is also appropriate that the courts use an objective test, instead of focusing on individuals' uniqueness in determining whether consent is reasonably withheld.

Separation for a continuous period of five years

The courts are likely to dissolve the marriage if the petitioner proves that the parties to the marriage have not lived as husband and wife for a continuous period of at least five years immediately preceding the presentation of

[152] Ibid., section 2(1)(d).

[153] Ibid., section 6.

[154] [1973] 2 GLR pp. 103 – 107 (H.C.).

the petition.[155] In *Kotei v Kotei,*[156] the couple married in 1962 and separated in 1968. They had not lived as man and wife for six years. Sarkodie J explained that despite the years of separation, there must be proof that the parties have not *lived as man and wife* for at least five years immediately preceding the presentation of the petition. He explained further, "There must be a total breakdown of the consortium vitae. Mere physical separation is not sufficient; a petitioner has to prove not only the factum of separation but also that they have ceased to recognize the marriage as subsisting and intended never to return to the other spouse".[157] This case is interesting because it shows that a couple may be physically separated, yet may still be deemed to have lived as husband and wife, thus emphasizing the legal meaning of living as man and wife.

Inability to reconcile differences

It is important to the courts that the parties should have taken steps to reconcile their differences. Where this has not been done, the courts may order the parties to fulfill this requirement before the marriage is ended, if need be. Section 8 of the Matrimonial Causes Act 1971 gives the court power to adjourn the proceedings for a reasonable time to enable attempts at reconciliation. It states specifically that:

> If at any stage of the proceedings for divorce it appears to the court that there is a reasonable possibility of reconciliation, the court may adjourn the proceedings for a reasonable time to enable attempts to be made to effect a reconciliation, and may direct that the parties to the marriage, together with representatives of their families or any conciliator appointed by the court and mutually agreeable to the parties, attempt to effect a reconciliation.

Where the court exercises this discretion, it shall require a report indicating the success or otherwise of the

155 Ibid., section 2(1)(e).

156 [1974] 2 GLR pp. 172 – 176 (H.C.).

157 Ibid., pp. 175-176.

reconciliation efforts, or whether more time is needed for such.[158]

In *Knudsen,* Amissah JA indicated that the absence of reconciliation efforts does not bar the courts from ending the marriage when the evidence suggests that attempts at reconciliation are hopeless. He added that "In such cases, I think that the law does not require that the useless exercise be gone through just for the sake of form".[159]

Hayfron-Benjamin J (as he then was) explained in *Mensah* that the court's power of adjournment to order reconciliation is exercisable only where there appears to be a reasonable possibility of reconciliation.[160] He explained: "It seems to me that even where the parties say categorically and insistently that they shall never cohabit as husband and wife again, the court is not precluded from exercising its powers under this section".[161] He suggested that in exercising its discretion to end the marriage despite the absence of reconciliation efforts, the court should consider the ages, temperaments, and dispositions of the parties and the age and condition of the children, among other factors. He refused to exercise powers under section 8 of the Matrimonial Causes Act 1971 because it did not appear that there was any reasonable possibility of reconciliation.[162] Although the provisions on reconciliation are fair and satisfactory, it is also reasonable that the courts can disregard this requirement when it is obvious that reconciliation efforts will be futile. The discretion given to the courts is commended, especially as the courts deal with issues as sensitive as those involved in marital relations.

Other matters

Even though section 9 of the Matrimonial Causes Act 1971 stipulates that a divorce petition shall not be presented

158 Section 8(3), Matrimonial Causes Act 1971.

159 *Knudsen,* note 139 above, p. 216.

160 *Mensah,* note 124 above, p. 208.

161 Ibid.

162 Ibid.

to the court within two years from the marriage date, there are exceptions to this rule. A court may allow such a petition for divorce within the first two years of the marriage, if the petitioner has suffered substantial hardship or if the respondent is depraved. According to section 9 (4), though, if leave to file the petition of divorce is granted by the court on an application brought within the first two years of the marriage, but such leave was obtained by misrepresentation or concealment of the nature of the case, the court may dismiss the petition. However, the court may hear any petition presented after the first two years of the marriage on the same or substantially the same facts as those proved in support of the dismissed petition.[163] This provision is reasonable because it encourages parties to adjust to the early years of marriage, which arguably can be challenging. But, at the same time, it leaves room for genuine problems to be addressed by the courts within the first two years of marriage.

RECOMMENDATIONS

It is clear from the above that the legal framework for regulating marriages is satisfactory; it adequately addresses a host of needs and requirements. Nevertheless, some aspects of the framework need to be modified or repealed to meet current socioeconomic needs.

Definitions

Defining marriage and a spouse

The laws on marriage do not adequately define some expressions that are crucial to understanding the institution, its scope, and permitted relationships. The term *marriage* falls into this category. Perhaps, if the term *spouse* were adequately defined in the law, it would compensate for the omission. It is recommended that the terms be properly defined to make the law certain, an attribute upon which justice thrives.

[163] Section 9(5), Matrimonial Causes Act 1971.

Defining adultery

The Matrimonial Causes Act 1971 defines adultery as "the voluntary sexual intercourse of a married person with one of the opposite sex other than his or her spouse".[164] Could this mean that sexual intercourse with someone of the same sex is not considered adultery? What is the meaning of sexual intercourse in the context of adultery? Should its meaning be limited to the penetration of the vagina during a sexual act? Will a limited definition of sexual intercourse not absolve from liability parties whose actions stop short of actual penetration? Arguably, a more expansive definition, which covers a range of sexual behavior, may reinforce the sanctity of marriage by holding married couples to expected moral standards. Moreover, within the context of adultery, the expression "opposite sex" should be defined to include persons of both sexes so that sexual acts by a married person with a man or woman would constitute adultery.

Other key expressions

Other expressions like *unreasonable behavior* and *desertion,* which are grounds for divorce, have not been defined in Act 367. An appreciation of the expressions is derived primarily from Ghanaian case law, which in turn relies heavily on English cases. It is recommended that these expressions are defined to guide the courts in determining related cases.

Same-sex marriages

As earlier indicated, it is unclear whether the Criminal Offences Act 1960 (Act 29) categorically prohibits same-sex marriages.[165] It would seem that what Act 29 criminalizes is sexual intercourse between persons of the same sex. By criminalizing such intercourse, one can infer that marriage between persons of the same sex is prohibited. Without this inference, it would mean that same-sex marriages can never be consummated, a most unlikely expectation. Next, as the law stands, unnatural carnal knowledge may prohibit more

[164] Ibid., section 43.

[165] See section 104, Criminal Offences Act 1960, as discussed above.

sexual activities than just sex between a same-sex couple. Describing what qualifies as *natural* carnal knowledge in *Banousin v The Republic,*[166] Dotse JSC explained that "It is the female sex organs called the vulva and vagina that are normally penetrated into during any sexual act which can qualify to be carnal knowledge under sections 98 and 99 of Act 29".[167] Could this interpretation mean that penetration of other parts of the body during sexual intercourse between a heterosexual couple is unnatural carnal knowledge? More importantly, what would this interpretation imply for legally married couples? For the avoidance of doubt, Act 29 might be modified to reflect the lawmakers' intention regarding same-sex marriages in Ghana, as well as natural and unnatural carnal knowledge in the context of marriage.

Invalid marriages

Section 74(1) provides:

> A marriage may be lawfully celebrated under this Part between a man and the sister or niece of the deceased wife, but a marriage is not valid, (a) *which if celebrated in England, would be void on the ground of kindred or affinity …*

It is unclear if this provision applies to a woman whose husband is deceased. If not, the provision should be amended to be more gender-sensitive. It is unsettling that accepted degrees of affinity and consanguinity in England are still applicable in Ghana. What about the prohibited grounds of consanguinity stated in section 105 of Act 29? With the passage of the same-sex (Marriage) Act in England in 2013, which makes a marriage of same-sex couples in England and Wales lawful, will a person be in breach of the law in Ghana if she marries her late husband's sister since such a union is within the acceptable relationships in England? This question is legitimate, considering that the law purportedly criminalizing same-sex unions in

[166] *Banousin v The Republic* (J3 2 of 2014) [2014] GHASC 10 (18 March 2014) (available online).

[167] Ibid.

Ghana is unclear. The provision must be amended to reflect permissible relationships in Ghana.

Condonation

If a spouse discovers that his or her partner has committed adultery but still lives with the adulterer as husband and wife for more than six months thereafter, with a view to reconciliation, the spouse cannot rely on the said adultery as the ground for divorce. When determining whether a party has acted unreasonably or deserted a spouse, the courts consider periods exceeding six months during which the parties lived as husband and wife. There seems to be no scientific basis for the six-month limitation period. It is submitted that emphasis should rather be placed on the quality of the time spent together as opposed to the length of time spent together. In determining the quality of time spent together, the courts should seek to determine whether the time spent together was focused on strengthening the relationship or simply undermining it.

Parental consent

It was noted above that a person aged eighteen years and above has the legal capacity to marry. However, if such a person is not a widower or a widow, and is under twenty-one years of age, parental consent is required for the person to marry. It was argued that because the State entrusts a host of responsibilities to eighteen-year-olds, it was unjustifiable to demand parental consent. The provision requiring such consent should be repealed.

Discrimination against women

Related to the preceding recommendation is the fact that parental consent may only be obtained from a mother if the father is dead, is of unsound mind, or is absent from the Republic. This provision is a relic of patriarchy; it perpetuates and reinforces a system of female subordination and male domination and should be repealed. If there is any justification for obtaining parental consent, the provision must be modified to place both parents on equal footing.

Legal requirements under Part Three of the Marriages Act and information technology

Marriage under Part Three of the Marriages Act is characterized by the submission and provision of a host of notices and licenses, all of which must be done manually. For example, under section 48(1) of the Marriages Act, a person who intends to marry under the authority of a Marriage Officer's Certificate is required to physically submit to a marriage officer a notice indicating the names of the parties, and their places of residence, among other relevant pieces of information. It is time for the State and its institutions to embrace the advantages of information technology by including web-based or similar applications to automate and expedite most of these manual processes. This should simplify the marriage process.

In addition, the Covid-19 pandemic has exposed several omissions in our laws, especially concerning processes requiring one's physical presence. For instance, the requirement that the word "forbidden" must actually be written opposite the entry in the Marriage Notice book to object to a marriage is obsolete. Likewise, the caveating process requires other manual processes which limit the reasonable dissemination of information. Since these defects could inhibit the enjoyment of the right to caveat, the adoption of user-friendly online applications to facilitate the various processes would be timely.

The Marriages Act requires the publication of banns, which in practice are usually posted on public notice boards. Perhaps the laws should explicitly allow for the online publication of banns. Similarly, the requirement that banns be published in places of worship must explicitly include "online places of worship". The COVID-19 pandemic saw many churches move online and develop valuable practices to facilitate their activities. Some of these practices should be legalized.

Whatever applications or processes are employed should be accessible to end users. Admittedly web-based applications may be inaccessible to a significant number of Ghanaians; a hybrid system of technology-based solutions and manual processes should be synchronized to consolidate data, prevent duplication, and maintain consistency in information regarding marriages.

CONCLUSION

The history of the Marriages Act shows that, like most colonial initiatives, it was meant, first, to further European interests. In fact, "It was not unprecedented for the Europeans to take their own law with themselves to the colonies, for themselves…".[168] Second, it was meant to civilize the natives who, according to the colonialists, did not realize the seriousness of marriages and accordingly contracted them "lightly".[169] Thus, some provisions were, and still are, inconsistent with existing customary law rules. But the truth remains that "It is not easy to decide what ought to be the true morality in a particular colony's conditions. A constant judicial [and legislative] dilemma is to strike a nice balance between what is reasonably tolerable and what is essentially below the minimum standard of civilized values in the contemporary world."[170]

For plural legal orders to thrive in a given space, there must be mutual respect. Legal actors in the various systems must be able to embrace aspects of each system with no repercussions. In respect of marriages, this should ensure stronger families, willing and able to contribute positively to the community and country. Despite the contentious beginnings of the Marriages Act and what it stands for, marriages contracted under it remain suitable to the needs of some Ghanaians, especially those who seek monogamous unions and probably desire a marriage ordained by God. The Act offers an alternative to customary marriages, which may appeal less to those whose sensibilities have somewhat outgrown customary law dictates. Its strength lies in clearly outlined procedures for contracting legitimate unions.

Its complementary Act, the Matrimonial Causes Act 1971, shares the same advantage, though to a lesser degree.

[168] Rina Verma Williams, note 30 above, p. 42.

[169] See Adinkrah, note 55 above, p. 9, quoting one John Samuel Ellenberger, then Superintendent of Aburi Circuit of the Presbyterian Church, Ghana.

[170] A. N. Allott, *The Limits of Law* (1980), p. 99.

While both Acts are satisfactory, they are not adequate, especially when considered in light of modern technological advancements. The Marriages Act would benefit significantly from incorporating modern means of communication into its procedures and repealing obsolete provisions. On the other hand, the Matrimonial Causes Act 1971 will better serve societal needs by defining and clarifying key terms that are fundamental to the Act, thereby ensuring legal certainty. Ghana has come a long way in its quest to build a better society, but this can only be fully achieved by strengthening family units through more equitable and progressive laws.

Chapter Four Customary Marriage in Ghana

As custom is neither static nor homogeneous, customary marriage practices differ from one area to another. The heterogeneity of customary law and practices leads to a complex legal space as it translates into different cultural methodologies about all the important aspects of group life, marriage being no exception. The legal landscape of customary law comprises not only rules of custom, but also those rules that are pronounced by the superior courts of Ghana to be valid customary law.[1] Thus, the customary law of Ghana is a unique combination of what pertains in the community, that is, the lived customary law and judicially determined customary law.

The regime of marriage in Ghana is two-tiered: it comprises statutory (Christian and other marriages), and customary marriages, the latter comprising Islamic marriage and marriages contracted under customary law. The statutory regime, though imperfect, is comparatively straightforward, whereas the customary regime, by its nature, is practically labyrinthic. As aforementioned, customary practices and rules of custom relating to marriage are as diverse as the Ghanaian ethnic landscape. Sometimes, even within one ethnic group, there are multiple forms of marriage and unions loosely referred to as marriage. For example, Rattray purportedly identified no less than six forms of marriage or similar unions among the Ashanti.[2] Among the Ga[3], there is more than one form of marriage, including the prestigious

[1] Article 11, 1992 Constitution of Ghana.

[2] Robert Sutherland Rattray, *Ashanti Law and Constitution* (1956), p. 23. The Ashanti (Asante) are part of the larger group of tribes referred to as Akan, which is predominant in southern Ghana and parts of Ivory Coast.

[3] The Ga is a tribe in Ghana, occupying the Greater Accra Region.

six-cloth marriage.[4] Similarly, Ahortor wrote of the Mafi people, discussing three types of marriage.[5]

Aside from the potential multiplicity of forms of marriage at custom, the ways in which a marriage is validly contracted depend on the practices that pertain to the particular customary area. Whereas in some groups or communities, the dowry consists of cash or cows or other items, in others, such as the Bimoba, it has been held that the only form of dowry known to that community is an exchange of unmarried women from the families.[6] To further complicate an already substantially complicated arena, judicial pronouncements on the accepted "essentials" of customary law marriages have not been consistent. The parameters by which a marriage celebrated at custom is judged to be valid, have sometimes differed depending on the judge determining that question. Accordingly, it is virtually impossible to give an account of every different system of marriage as practiced within the many communities in Ghana.

This article first provides an overview of the legal framework for assessing and recognizing a marriage as validly celebrated under particular rules of customary law. As it is nigh impossible to discuss every rule or practice of customary law relating to marriage, judicial outcomes are examined, highlighting inconsistencies between the cases, in terms of what has been held to be *sine qua non* to a valid customary marriage, accompanied by a critical analysis of the judicial approach to determining the validity of customary marriages. Where appropriate and available, use is made of anthropological and sociological studies on marriage customs among various ethnic groups in Ghana. Other requirements are considered for the validity of a customary marriage, the incidents of marriage at custom, and

[4] The six-cloth marriage is said to be prestigious because it conveys several benefits and rights on both the wife and the issue of the union, compared to other forms of customary marriage among the Ga. See D. A. Nii-Aponsah, "The Scope of the Right of Testation and Incidents of the Ga Six-Cloth Marriage", *Review of Ghana Law*, XIX (1993-95), pp. 140-158.

[5] Godson Ahortor, "Marriage, Sexuality and Moral Responsibility among the Tongu Mafi People of Ghana", *Legon Journal of the Humanities*, XXVII (2016), pp. 77-78.

[6] See for example, *Kombat v Lambim* [1989-90] 1 GLR pp. 324 – 339 (HC).

a distinction is drawn between marriage and concubinage. This distinction, it is argued, is in danger of being effaced due to the modern judicial stance in determining the validity of marriages. In conclusion, there is a brief discussion of the dissolution of marriages at custom and recommendations for providing more clarity in the area of customary law marriages.

LEGAL FRAMEWORK

In Ghana, the statutory law, the common law and doctrines of equity, customary law – both judicially determined and as practiced by the various communities in Ghana, as well as Islamic customary law co-exist and regulate marriage and other areas of law concurrently. How these multiple orders interact can cause dilution of some practices and rules, particularly of customary law. The presence of multiple normative orders within the same territory sometimes leads to collisions. For example, there are cases where a customary practice was not evaluated from the perspective of the relevant community but was discarded by the courts because the practice or norm was inconsistent with doctrines of equity and good conscience. At other times, the multiple interactions have led to a peaceful, albeit sometimes awkward co-existence, and yet others, like the incursion of Christianity into customary law in the form of a Bible and ring at customary marriages,[7] to a kind of hybrid – a normative centaur – within the legal system. This complexity has led scholars to describe Ghana as a "comparative law laboratory".[8]

The legal framework for the recognition of marriages celebrated at custom begins with the 1992 Constitution of Ghana. In Article 11, customary law is subsumed under the common law, which is defined to comprise the rules of law generally known as the common law, doctrines of equity and the rules of customary law, including judicially determined customary law. It is important to note that customary law

[7] *Mariam Obeng Mintah v Francis Ampenyin* [2010] DLCA 228; *Afrifa v Class-Peter* [1975] 1 GLR pp. 359-366 (CA).

[8] Anthony Nicholas Allott, "Marriage and Internal Conflict of Laws in Ghana", *Journal of African Law,* II, no. 3 (1958), p. 164.

is defined in the Constitution as "the rules of law, which by custom are applicable to particular communities in Ghana".[9] This accounts for the complexity of this area of law, because the Constitution recognizes not just the non-homogeneity of customary law but also allows the superior courts to say what customary law is. This creates the two-layered nature of customary law, which can create conflict between what is actually practiced and what the courts say the practice is.[10]

The Marriages Act 1885-1985 (Cap 127) provides the statutory framework for all marriages in Ghana, including customary law marriages, which are captured under Part I. However, it should be noted that the provisions center on the registration of customary marriages and divorces.

The Courts Act 1993 (Act 459) is the third piece in the statutory framework on customary law generally which is applicable to customary marriages. It establishes guidelines for inquiring into and assessing a rule or practice of customary law. In determining whether a customary marriage has been validly celebrated, the court must look to the customary law under which the marriage was celebrated to determine if it fulfilled the requirements of the community governed by those rules. Thus, the court must test the marriage against the relevant rules to resolve issues relating to the validity of the marriage. If there are doubts about the content or existence of a rule of customary law that the court is unable to resolve after consulting credible sources, the court may adjourn the case to enable an inquiry to be made.[11] As the judge(s) are not likely to come from the customary area, they may not be equipped with the information necessary to dispose of the matter. The court may thus request a House of Chiefs, Divisional or Traditional Council, or other body

[9] Article 11(3), 1992 Constitution of Ghana.

[10] See, for example, Gordon Woodman, "Essentials of an Akan Customary Marriage; McCabe v Mc Cabe", *Journal of African Law*, XXXVII, no. 2 (1993), pp. 199-205; Ama Fowa Hammond, *Towards an Inclusive Vision of Law Reform and Legal Pluralism in Ghana* (2016) (Ph.D. dissertation; University of British Columbia).

[11] Section 55, Courts Act 1993.

with knowledge of the customary law in question to provide a written opinion on the matter.[12]

These provisions may be argued as necessary to prevent judges from relying on their knowledge of their own customary rules and practices as the standard for assessing a phenomenon, the particulars of which may be unfamiliar to such judges. However, the question of the existence of a customary law is one of law, not of fact.[13] This means that a court need not follow what the experts on that customary rule or practice is, and could decide for itself whether that rule or practice should be upheld.[14] Thus such practices as compelling an unwilling wife to return to cohabit with her husband have been held not to be part of customary law, in spite of evidence provided that it was a feature of the actual customary law of the area.[15] This demonstrates the conflict that may occur between judicial customary law and the practiced customary law.

Another challenge is that the courts use different measures of what modernity is, and what is acceptable at the relevant time. This has the effect of creating inconsistent positions where customary rules and practices come into question.[16] Furthermore, scholars have criticized judges for extrapolating principles from one case on a practice or rule of customary law of one ethnic group (usually, the Akan) and applying them as general principles in other cases which involved different ethnic groups.[17] This has been referred to as the "Akanization" of customary law,[18] which has led to

[12] Ibid.

[13] Ibid.

[14] *Abangana v Akologo* [1976] GLR pp. 382-388 (H.C).

[15] See *Ibrahim v Amalibini* [1978] GLR pp. 368-403 (H.C).

[16] Henrietta Mensa-Bonsu, "Of Nuts in the Ground not being Groundnuts – The Current State of Customary Law in Ghana", *University of Ghana Law Journal,* XXII (2002-2004), p. 1.

[17] Nii-Aponsah, note 4 above, criticizes some judicial pronouncements that treated succession among the Ga-Mashi as a matrilineal rather than a patrilineal matter.

[18] Mensa-Bonsu, note 16 above.

persons whose personal law is not Akan being subject to standards set by cases in which the parties were Akan.

ESSENTIAL FEATURES OF A CUSTOMARY MARRIAGE

As explained above, when a marriage at custom is alleged or challenged, the relevant rules of customary law to which the marriage is subject are applied in assessing whether the purported marriage can be upheld as validly celebrated at custom. Several elements have been identified in judicial decisions as "essential" to the validity of a customary marriage. These include publicity of the ceremony, consent of the two families, the nature of the ceremony itself, consent of the parties to be married, and consummation. The "essential" nature of some of these elements has been challenged by Adinkrah, who points out that an element is essential where its absence would invalidate the marriage, yet there are several judicial decisions recognizing marriages as valid, in spite of the absence of some of the so-called essentials.[19] In spite of the criticisms, these elements are still referred to as the essentials, and while there have been substantial modifications, they remain largely relevant today. The discussion focuses on the essentials as originally established, and considers criticisms proffered by scholars on the essential nature of these features. Other key elements that have not received as much judicial attention are also discussed.

The *locus classicus* in this area is the celebrated case of *Yaotey v Quaye*.[20] In spite of being an older case, it continues to be cited in modern judicial decisions, even where the judges have departed or made substantial modifications to the requirements for validity of customary marriages. In that case the court was invited to determine the existence of a marriage between the defendant and the deceased. The

[19] Kofi Oti Adinkrah, "Essentials of a Customary Law Marriage: A New Approach", *Review of Ghana Law*, XII (1980), p. 40.

[20] [1961] GLR pp. 573-584.

court set out the following as essentials of a valid customary marriage:[21]

- agreement by the parties to live together,
- consent from the family of the man that he should have the woman as his wife (either expressly or tacitly, by the man's family acknowledging the woman as wife of the man),
- consent of the family of the woman that she should be married to the man, which could be indicated by acceptance of drink from the man or his family, or the family of the woman acknowledging the man as the husband of the woman; and
- consummation of the marriage, that is, the man and the woman living together in the sight of all the world as husband and wife.

Applying these elements, the court found that the defendant lived openly with the deceased in the same house until his death. Upon the death of the deceased's father and aunt subsequently, members of his family asked the defendant to perform some customary rites like holding the feet of the deceased, and the provision of items for the bathing of the corpse, which are traditionally the obligation of a wife to perform. There was evidence to show that the deceased had provided drinks and money in performance of a customary marriage ceremony. Examining these and other facts, the court held that the defendant was validly married at custom to the deceased.

The courts have, however, not maintained a uniform stance in respect of the validity of a marriage that does not satisfy all the above so-called "essentials" and, in so doing, have created a disturbing opacity which presents a challenge to persons intending to submit the question of the validity of a marriage to a court. In what follows, the essentials are examined seriatim and the relevant case law on the essentials evaluated. This provides relevant context to the discussion and enables readers to follow the trajectory of the evolution of the legal principles on customary law

[21] Ibid., pp. 578-579.

marriages as determined by the courts, as well as providing a basis to recommend changes in this area.

Agreement by the parties

The first essential, that is, agreement by the parties, is unexceptional and does not call for much comment, as it is unlikely to be a source of contention except in the case of forced marriages. However, not only are forced marriages void *ab initio*, they are also subject to the criminal law.[22] In *Ibrahim v Amalibini*,[23] the court was faced with the issue of whether the husband was entitled as a matter of law, where the marriage was still subsisting, to obtain a court order for the return of his wife. The court held that this amounted to treating her as a chattel, and that "custom that a particular wife who no more wants to cohabit with her husband must nevertheless be compelled to do so violates demonstrably fundamental concepts of our law and cannot exist in the legal system".[24] Similarly, the court in *Kombat v Lambim*,[25] refused to order the return of a woman to her husband, stating unequivocally that "[i]t would be repugnant to public policy in this age of women's liberation for a court to uphold a customary practice which encourages forcible marriage; it is reminiscent of slavery".[26] The ability to freely enter into the marriage contract is (and rightly so), fiercely protected by the courts, as a crucial element in contracting a valid marriage at custom.

22 See section 100, Criminal Offences Act 1960 which provides: "If a female is compelled to marry another person by duress as to make the marriage void or voidable, the marriage is of no effect for the purpose of Part I of this Code with respect to consent"; See also, section 109 which provides: "Whoever by duress causes a person to marry against his or her will, shall be guilty of a misdemeanour".

23 *Ibrahim*, note 15 above.

24 Ibid., p. 381.

25 *Kombat*, note 6 above.

26 Ibid., p. 338.

Consent by the families of the parties

It is important to start with a brief outline of what family means under Ghanaian law. The family system in Ghana, broadly described, may be either patrilineal, that is, the line of descent is traced through the male (father's) line, or matrilineal, where the line of descent is traced through the female (mother's) line.[27] The family of the parties who are being joined, therefore, comprises more than just the nuclear families of the couple; it includes the larger family to which they belong.

Marriage in Ghana is more than a union between two persons; it is an institution which unites two families. In *Yaotey*, Ollennu J. (as he then was) stated the issue as follows: "Now one peculiar characteristic of our system of marriage which distinguishes it from the system of marriage in Europe and other places is that it is not just a union of this man and this woman: it is a union of the family of "this man" and "this woman".[28]

Similarly, marriage has been explained as an alliance not just between the two individuals, it is an alliance between two families or even kin groups.[29] For this reason, the consent of the families to being so joined has been held to be an essential element of the customary law marriage. Typically, consent by the families is manifested in the presentation of drink(s) by the man's family, and acceptance of those drinks by the woman's family.

In the case of *Asumah v Khair*,[30] the Court of Appeal, speaking through Ollennu J (as he then was), reiterated the importance of the family's consent as an essential element of a customary marriage. The court, basing its decision largely

[27] For a discussion on the family systems and their impact on Ghanaian marriages, see Baffour K. Takyi and Stephen Obeng Gyimah, "Matrilineal Family Ties and Marital Dissolution in Ghana", *Journal of Family Issues*, XXVIII (2007), pp. 682 -705.

[28] *Yaotey*, note 20 above (emphasis added).

[29] Roger Klomegah, "Socio-economic Characteristics of Ghanaian Women in Polygynous Marriages", *Journal of Comparative Family Studies*, XXVIII (1997), p. 73.

[30] [1959] GLR pp. 353-358 (C.A).

on Sarbah's *Fante Customary Laws,*[31] outlined the four ways in which, in the opinion of the court, the consent of the families could be sought and given, and therefore a valid marriage contracted. The first is the commonest form of marriage whereupon the man expressing an intent to marry presents drinks and gifts to the woman's family, often at a ceremony organized for that purpose. The acceptance of the drinks and gifts by the woman's family constitutes their consent to the marriage.[32] The second way occurs where the man accepts responsibility for the pregnancy of an unmarried woman with whom he is intimately associated. The putative father then sends a drink to acknowledge paternity, and then subsequently, a second set of drinks and gifts. The acceptance of the second drink and gifts by the woman's family amounts to an acceptance of the man's request to marry the woman, which is symbolized by the presentation of the said drinks.

In *Essilfie v Quarcoo,*[33] however, this insistence on two presentations of drink was criticized as not reflecting the true position of the law. According to Lutterodt J (as she then was), the parties' consent and that of their families, for them to live together in the eyes of the world as husband and wife, and actually living together as such, sufficed to establish a valid marriage. They did not need to have gone through all the marital rites before the consent could be said to have been given. The family accepted the first drinks, and thereafter the couple lived together as a married couple with no objection from the family. Additionally, during the woman's father's funeral, the man performed rites of a son-in-law, and when she herself passed away, the man provided the shroud and grave for the deceased in the capacity of the husband. Thus, the consent was tacitly given, and therefore, a marriage had been validly contracted. This was also the process by which the marriage was contracted in *Quaye v Kuevi.*[34]

31 John Mensah Sarbah, *Fante Customary Law* (1968).

32 *Beatrice Ziga v. John Kwaku Zigah Caveator* [2016] DLHC 399 (H.C).

33 [1992] 2 GLR pp. 180-194 (H.C).

34 (1934) DCt 31-37.

The third way in which the consent of the family is sought and obtained as identified by the court is where the man is involved in a sexual relationship with another man's wife. The husband, on discovering the adultery, may elect to have the marriage dissolved, and have the customary drinks and/or fees and gifts returned to him by his wife's family. The family then may claim these refunded items from the new man, and if he presents the requested items, and they are accepted by the woman's family, it entitles him to be recognized as the new husband of the woman.

The fourth process by which the consent is expressed is similar to the third, in that here too the effect of the consent is that the man steps into the shoes of the previous husband. In this one, the couple does not cohabit together, and the new suitor induces the woman to break the marriage. The woman's family then obtains the absent husband's consent to break the union, returns all gifts, and refunds all expenses to the husband. The new suitor then pays the same amount to the woman's family, the acceptance of which entitles him to be recognized as the woman's husband.

Three years after *Asumah*, Ollennu J (as he then was) provided further parameters for this element, when he stated that the consent of the families could be express, as in a formal request for the hand of the woman by the man's family and the acceptance of drinks by the woman's family, or constructive, whereby the families recognized and acknowledged the status of the parties as husband or wife, by their permitting them to perform customary rites such as those reserved for widows, widowers, or in-laws.[35]

Kofi Adinkrah, in his seminal piece on the essentials of customary law marriage, argues that this element is not an essential as the absence of consent is hardly ever pleaded as a ground for invalidating a marriage, even in those cases where the court put forward consent as an essential element.[36] Although this may be so, the fact that parties hardly plead lack of consent as a ground for invalidating a

[35] *Re Caveat by Clara Sackitey: Re Marriage Ordinance, Cap 127* [1962] 1 GLR pp. 180-183 (H.C).

[36] Adinkrah, note 19 above.

marriage, does not mean that no unions have been declared invalid on grounds relating to the lack of evidence of the family's consent.[37] Or that a groom and his friends can, with a bride and her friends, validly contract a customary law marriage. This position finds support in the case of *Quaye,* where Dean CJ stated that the only prerequisites for a valid marriage were the consent of the parties to be so joined, and consent of the woman's family, together with the giving of the woman to the man. He then added that, although proof of this consent signified by the giving and acceptance of drink was desirable, failure to establish this was not fatal to a case, if there was other evidence to establish the existence of the marriage, coupled with the couple living *"together in the sight of the world as man and wife"* (emphasis added).

However, it is submitted that even in this latter case, the requirement that the couple should have lived together in the sight of the world as man and wife implies some consent by the families, who should surely object in a culturally-relevant manner if they have not consented to such a union. "Living together in the sight of the world as man and wife" in Ghana implies the families' consent, and that is always a provable or deducible fact, being a thing that must be communicated tangibly. It is therefore argued that this requirement does not mean merely living together without any objection from the families, but that the families should treat the couple as married, the evidence of this treatment would then be proof of consent given tacitly by the families. For example, where after the death of a person, the head of his family wrote to the plaintiffs referring to them as the wives of the deceased and inviting them to a meeting to discuss the care and maintenance of themselves and their children, the court found that there was clearly consent by the families, demonstrated by the deceased's family conduct.[38] Thus, where a person performed rites reserved for in-laws, or the surviving spouse, with the consent of or at the family's request, it would be held to be proof of

[37] See for example *Owusu v Nyarko* [1980] GLR pp. 428-430 where the High Court found that the union was not a customary marriage because there was no evidence of the consent of the families.

[38] *Grace Adu and Dzigbordi Egbenya v. Martin Anaglate & Ors* (2019) JELR 64573 (H.C). Cases with "JELR' can be obtained from: www.judy.legal.

consent to be married, as happened in the case of *Yaotey* and *Essilfie*. This would then distinguish cohabitation and concubinage to which the families have turned a blind eye, from a marriage that has united two families, as happened where the defendant was held not to be validly married to the deceased because there was no formal marriage ceremony, nor was she able to establish the consent of the families.[39]

Adinkrah further argues that not only is consent not an essential, but it is also outmoded in light of changing social trends.[40] However, this was not true in 1977, nor is it true today. Family consent has not been rendered obsolete in contemporary times by reason of changing social trends. Social trends actually point in the opposite direction anecdotally. Even in the absence of the parties, often due to immigration, the marriage ceremony and the presentation of drinks to the woman's family is done. It is common to see at a traditional marriage ceremony pictures of the couple propped up in seats, representing where they would have sat had they been attending in person. The advent of technology has been instrumental in such ceremonies as the couple living abroad can now tune in for the woman to give consent to the family's accepting the drinks and gifts presented.

Further, it is instructive that although a statutory marriage does not, in fact, require a preceding traditional marriage, the practice continues to be that it is done before the statutory ceremony. Even at Christian weddings, it is often asked if the groom has sought the consent of the woman's family to be married, through the performance of the necessary customary rites. Thus, the general sociocultural norms have developed new aspects to the customary marriage rather than eroded its essentials. For example, it is now common to see a ring and the Bible presented to the bride by her groom where the parties and the families are Christian, because it appears on the list given by the bride's family to the groom's family of things to be presented. Similarly, technology, and the fact that more and more women have careers outside the

39 *Richard Bentum & anor v Eunice Pappoe* (2016) JELR 107134 (H.C).

40 Adinkrah, note 19 above.

home have seen the grooms' families presenting items like computers, iPads, and the like. The consent of the families remains as relevant now as it ever was. This is because the acceptance of the union by both families carries with it some rights and obligations at custom. For example, the right to maintenance at custom does not exist for a concubine, but a wife may assert this right against the customary successor of her deceased husband, as happened in *Manu v Kuma,*[41] the widow was allowed her claim against the customary successor for expenses incurred in maintaining and providing medical treatment for herself and her children.[42]

Likewise, there are certain rites which by custom, are the exclusive province of an in-law or widow (or widower) to perform. For example, in Akan custom, the daughter-in-law provides the "adwaredeɛ" which are the things that are used to wash and dress the corpse of the deceased mother-in-law or father-in-law. In *Yaotey*, the defendant provided a sponge, soap, and other customary things for the bathing of the corpse, and she was given to the paternal brother of the deceased as a customary wife. These were established as acts that cannot be performed by a concubine; hence the courts have held that where a person was allowed to perform such rites, the family was estopped from denying the existence of the marriage.[43]

Judicial decisions appear to have moved away from a strict requirement of the *Yaotey* essentials, preferring the position adopted by Lutterodt J (as she then was), in the above-mentioned *Essilfie*[44] (hereinafter the EvQ formulation) and have held marriages to be valid, even in the absence of a presentation of drinks or payment of bride price. In *Irene Gorleku v Justice Pobee & Anor.*[45] Appau JA held that,

> non-interference by family members in the long cohabitation of any of their members with another

41 [1963] 1 GLR pp. 464-471 (S.C).

42 This was also held in *Hayford v. Moses* [1980] GLR pp. 757-764 (H.C).

43 *Essilfie,* note 33 above.

44 Ibid.

45 [2012] 42 GMJ 53 ff (C.A).

> person of the opposite sex as man and wife in the eye of the public constitutes implied consent. In my view therefore, the agreement of the man and wife and the fact that they lived as such is more paramount than the consent of their families; either express or implied when it comes to the determination as to whether or not they were legally married in a situation like the one before us . . . and particularly where the issues involved property sharing. In fact, it is the deciding factor.[46]

The Court of Appeal in *Buckman v Ankomayi,*[47] preferred the EvQ formulation, as did the High Court in *Francis Ayeh v Mary Agyemang.*[48] The court in *Grace Adu and Dzigbordi Egbenya v. Martin Anaglate & Ors*[49] refused to recognize Ollenu J's (as he then was) essentials as a rigidly upheld principle of customary law, and stated categorically that "the absence of any of the proposed essentials by Ollennu J will not invalidate a marriage".[50]

In sum, the prevailing position of the law, with respect to consent in customary law marriages, is that one can either go through the formalities of presenting drinks and other gifts to the woman's family, the acceptance of which signifies their consent, or the consent of the families that the couple should be recognized as married is constructively determined by their non-interference by family members in the long cohabitation of the couple as husband and wife before the whole world.

Consummation of the marriage

This is the most debatable of the so-called "essentials" of a customary law marriage in various respects. First, what

46 Ibid, p. 76.

47 [2012] 47 GMJ pp. 170-171 (S.C).

48 (2016) JELR 64579 (H.C).

49 *Adu,* note 38 above.

50 Ibid.

is meant by consummation is controversial.[51] As Woodman points out, tongue-in-cheek, it is to be hoped that it does not mean sexual intercourse, as consummation does in western family law, for this would be rather scandalous, seeing that the consummation must be done in the sight of the world.[52] A more serious issue is raised by Adinkrah, when he questions how, if sexual intercourse is what is meant by consummation, this is to be proved, or if this is to be presumed from the fact of cohabitation.

If sexual intercourse does not take place immediately, is the marriage valid only after it finally does take place (if ever)? If this is the case, then what is the legal status of the customary marriage in the time between when it is celebrated and when sexual intercourse takes place? Will the least degree of penetration suffice as proof of sexual intercourse? These and other questions arise when one holds up consummation as an "essential" characteristic of customary law marriage to scrutiny.

In the case of *Sowa v Sowa*,[53] the marriage was celebrated by proxy, yet there was no suggestion that proxy marriage was not valid by reason of non-consummation. The question of whether this so-called essential refers to cohabitation or to sexual intercourse has not been satisfactorily answered. It appears from a reading of *Yaotey*, that the latter is implied by evidence of the former. However, Offei argues that they can be mutually exclusive, as cohabitation can occur without copulation, and copulation can happen without cohabitation.[54]

Whichever is meant, this element is no longer a problem because the courts no longer add this to the restatement of the essentials. This exclusion does not present any issues as it is arguably reflected in the requirement that the couple should be living as married in the sight of the whole world.

51 See Adinkrah, note 19 above; Woodman, note 10 above.

52 Woodman, note 10 above.

53 [1961] EWCA Civ J0210-1 (C.A).

54 William Offei, *Family Law in Ghana (2014).*

Challenges with the contemporary judicial stance on the essentials

The challenge with the more flexible position adopted by the courts is that it blurs the lines between cohabitation (concubinage) and marriage. This is no semantic problem because there are incidents that attach to the institution of marriage that do not exist for concubinage. It has implications, for example, in intestate succession and in testate succession where the testator (trix) omits the partner's name from the will. Under the Wills Act 1971 (Act 360), a spouse, mother, father, or child below eighteen years can apply to the High Court, within a stated period, for reasonable provision out of the deceased's estate.[55] In such instances, the first question to be determined by the courts is whether the testator and the applicant were married at the time of the testator's death. If there was no valid marriage subsisting at the relevant time, the application for reasonable provision out of the deceased's estate will be dismissed, and the concubine who believed herself a spouse is sent away empty-handed.[56]

The emphasis on "long-term cohabitation" as an important factor in determining whether a union is a marriage may disadvantage the partner who is unfortunate enough to lose the other to an untimely demise. Particularly now, in the time of COVID-19 with its devastating effects on all age groups, a couple is not assured of "long-term cohabitation", so if a couple were to cohabit as husband and wife in the eyes of the whole world, for six months before one tragically dies, is it marriage? What length of time suffices for "long-term" is unclear, which would lead to uncertainty in this area of family law. The mere fact of long-term cohabitation does not make the union morph into what it never was, and to hold otherwise is to turn the proverbial log into a crocodile.[57]

55 Section 13, Wills Act 1971.

56 *Humphrey-Bonsu v Quaynor* [1999-2000] 2 GLR p. 781 ff, *Agyeiwaa v Marfoa* (J4 42 of 2012) [2016] GHASC 84 (9 November 2016) (available online).

57 Refers to an African saying that however long a log lays in water, it will not become a crocodile. This is often said of foreigners with long term residence in a particular locality who due to the length of time, forget that they are strangers to

Blurring the distinction will create rights for persons who ought not to have any, at the expense of those who do. More importantly, it has the potential to deprive some persons of the rights that other similarly-situated persons have enjoyed, only because they were unlucky enough not to have had a long-term cohabitation. It is therefore important that there is clarity regarding distinctions between customary marriage and concubinage, unless the law is developed to include all forms of intimate relationships, as has been proposed by some scholars.[58]

Other features of a customary marriage

Other matters may provide evidence in support of or opposition to a claim of the existence of a customary marriage. We turn to features which have been held by the courts to be germane to the issue of proof of a customary marriage in the sense that they invalidate an otherwise validly celebrated marriage.

No pre-existing statutory "Ordinance" marriage

The first is that there should be no pre-existing marriage celebrated under Part 3 of the Marriages Act. As noted above, there are different forms of marriage in Ghana: customary, Christian, statutory, and Islamic marriages. Of these, the first and the last are potentially polygamous. Thus, a man who marries at custom may marry other women under customary law. All these marriages are valid. However, where a party is already married under Part 3 of the Marriages Act, then a purported marriage at custom is invalid[59] by reason of the fact that Part 3 (Ordinance) marriages, as noted above, are monogamous, regardless of the religion of the parties.[60] Similarly, where a customary marriage exists, in the absence

the land and therefore not entitled to the same rights as the indigenes.

[58] See Ama Fowa Hammond, "What Man Has Put Together: Recognizing the Rights of 'Spouses' *in De Facto Unions*", *University of Ghana Law Journal*, XXIV (2008-2010), pp. 231-271.

[59] Section 76, Marriages Act.

[60] *Beatrice Asomani v Darteh-Adjei* (2016) JELR 107591(H.C); *Barake v. Barake* (1993-94) 1 GLR 635-668 (H.C).

of proof of its dissolution, the parties are precluded from contracting another marriage under Part 3 of the Marriages Act.[61] It has been held that in the absence of evidence in rebuttal, there is a strong presumption of the continuance of the customary marriage, and this would render any marriage purportedly celebrated under the Marriages Act null and void.[62] A marriage celebrated in contravention of this is a bigamous marriage; it is not only subject to annulment, but may entail criminal sanctions, as bigamy is an offense.[63]

Publicity

It may be argued that publicity was required implicitly under the earlier-formulated principles because the consent of the families implies knowledge of the existence of the marriage by persons who witnessed the exchange of drinks or other token and can therefore testify to this effect. Woodman mentions for example, that although not provided as an "essential" in *Yaotey*, it can be inferred that publicity was essential given that the couple was to live in the sight of the world, as husband and wife.[64] It was stated explicitly in the case of *Gym v Insaidoo*[65] that in the absence of writing, publicity was not only an essential feature, but also a requirement of customary transactions, including marriages contracted at custom. The learned judge based her decision on Danquah's *Akan Laws and Customs*, wherein the author described the process of contracting marriage under Akan customary law in which some of the money presented to the woman's parents is given to the witnesses present. The absence of witnesses to the alleged marriage in the case led the judge to prefer the testimony of the plaintiff, that the parties had been living together in concubinage, and no ceremony was performed to transform this into a marriage.

61 *Ruth Arthur v. John Hector Ansah & Naomi Owusu* [2003] DLCA 6941 (C.A).

62 *Genfi II v. Genfi II* [1964] GLR 548-551 (H.C).

63 See section 262-264, Criminal Offences Act, 1960.

64 Woodman, note 10 above.

65 [1965] GLR pp. 574-588 (H.C).

CUSTOMARY MARRIAGE DISTINGUISHED FROM OTHER TYPES OF MARRIAGE

Several forms of marriage are encapsulated under Parts 1, 2 and 3 of the Marriages Act. Part 1 deals with customary marriages, whereas 2 and 3 govern Islamic marriages and Christian and other marriages, respectively. Although they are all captured under the Act, there are major differences between them, including how they are celebrated, the conditions for validity, as well as the key features of each system of marriage. Thus, a Ghanaian married under customary law, and one married in church or by the registrar may describe themselves as married, but although they both use the same word, they are speaking of completely different phenomena in terms of incidents, manifestations, processes, and the like.

The first distinction between customary marriages and the other marriages is the absence of an institutionally backed person to celebrate the marriage. Customary marriages are celebrated by the families, and usually recognized by the presentation of gifts, drinks and other items to the bride and members of her family. There is no central figure who is responsible for the marriage ceremony, unlike in the other forms of marriage where there is such a key figure for example, the Imam, priest, the registrar of marriages etc. Additionally, the person officiating the other forms of marriage must equally be licensed, or otherwise recognized by law as a competent person to celebrate the marriage. Failure to ensure this will result in the marriage being declared void.

Second, customary marriages may be celebrated anywhere the families decide to meet for that purpose. The other forms of marriage must be celebrated in a specific place that is licensed or recognized by law as a place where a marriage may be validly celebrated.

Third, customary law marriages are potentially polygamous, whereas the marriages under Part 3 are strictly monogamous. The form of polygamy practiced in Ghana is polygyny, and there is no limit to how many wives a man may have. This is another area where customary law differs from Mohammedan marriages because, although these marriages are also potentially polygamous, there is a limit as the man may not marry more than four wives.

Customary law marriages need not be registered to be valid, but the other forms of marriage, if not registered are invalidated by this failure.

Finally, a customary law marriage, typically, does not involve the provision of key items pertaining to a specific religion, nor are there symbols like rings given or exchanged as visual evidence of the subsistence of the marriage, unlike Christian and other marriages in Part 3. *Afrifa v. Class-Peter,*[66] decided in 1975, was an action for breach of promise to marry. The defendant-appellant's evidence included that he had sent to the family of the plaintiff-respondent, gifts of money, drinks, a ring and a Bible, which he relied on as proof that the parties had undergone a customary law marriage. The court observed correctly that the Bible and ring were not known in customary law, and therefore demonstrated an intention to marry the plaintiff in a Christian monogamic marriage. However, an interesting development has slowly but steadily crept into customary law marriages celebrated by Christians before converting the marriage to a Part 3 one. In the case of *Mariam Obeng Mintah v Francis Ampenyin,*[67] the Court of Appeal, speaking through Ofoe JA, took judicial notice of the fact that customary law marriages had so developed that there was hardly any customary marriage without the presentation of a Bible and ring. The learned judge was of the view that:

> the Bible and the ring has [sic] now taken a firm position as one of the gifts presented at our customary marriage rites they can't be ignored or considered unknown in our customary marriages. Their addition to the rites however can't mean anything more than conclusion of a customary marriage.[68]

This epitomizes the interaction between customary law and the common law relating to marriage because the latter

[66] [1975] 1 GLR 359-366 (C.A).

[67] *Mintah,* note 7 above.

[68] Ibid., p. 5 (emphasis added).

is heavily influenced by Christian values. The Bible and ring, previously unknown under customary law, have become part of the evidence offered as proof that the marriage was validly celebrated at custom and are no longer the exclusive province of monogamous marriages by couples who adhere to the tenets of Christianity.

This demonstrates the phenomenon discussed above – legal pluralism – which refers to the co-existence of multiple legal systems in the same jurisdiction.[69] In the area of customary law marriages, the operation of multiple normative structures has infused customary marriage with different religious flavors that hitherto were unknown, as well as technological advancements, as has been discussed above.

Failure to convert customary marriage to Part 3 marriage

A unique feature of Ghanaian marriages is that the majority of couples, to the eyes of a stranger to the legal system, are married twice: first under customary law, and then in accordance with Part 3. However, the correct position of the law is that by undergoing a Part 3 marriage process, the couple has converted their customary law marriage into a Part 3 marriage. The import of this is that if the conversion fails due to the failure of the couple to adhere to the rules under Part 3, the Part 3 marriage is held to be null and void. The union reverts to a customary marriage, and issues arising under the marriage are determined by recourse to customary law.[70]

Mohammedan Marriages are judicially treated as customary law marriages,[71] where the customary laws are not those that govern an ethnic group, but rather a religious group. Such marriages are deemed as celebrated under Islamic customary law. Part 2 of the Marriages Act provides for the registration of Islamic marriages in Ghana. This

[69] For a thorough discussion on legal pluralism in Ghana, see Hammond, note 10 above.

[70] See *Appomasu v. Bremawuo* [1980] GLR pp. 278-283 (C.A); *Setse v. Setse* [1959] GLR pp. 155-157 (H.C).

[71] *Kwakye v Tuba* [1961] GLR pp.720-725 (C.A).

form of marriage is dealt with below in detail. It suffices to mention that where a marriage is celebrated in accordance with Islamic rites, it must be registered in accordance with Part 2 of the Marriages Act for it to be deemed an Islamic marriage. Failure to comply with this requirement means the marriage will be deemed to be a customary law marriage at best, and issues pertaining to matters like succession will not be determined in accordance with Islamic law, but with the personal law of the relevant party.[72]

MARRIAGE AS DISTINCT FROM CONCUBINAGE

We turn to key differences between customary marriages and concubinage at custom. This is an important discussion, for the rights and privileges, as well as the burdens of a wife at custom, differ significantly from those of a concubine.

Regardless of how much like a wife the concubine conducts herself, giving of her time, labor, bearing children, and so forth, the relationship never attains the respectability associated with marriage. Therefore the assumption of the burdens of a wife by a concubine do not yield the benefits associated with that status. According to Sarbah, "[a] woman living with a man as concubine, mistress, or friend, is not encouraged in the eyes of the Customary Law, which stamps the relationship as immoral, to be remedied as quickly as possible".[73] With this in mind, it is important to highlight the distinguishing features, and attendant consequences, because these are always called into question when the courts must determine whether the evidence presented supports the claim that the parties were or had been married at the material time.

Given the inconsistencies in judicial reasoning as to how a customary marriage may validly come about, and also an arguably excessive fidelity to the formalities, it is no surprise that some unfortunate person (usually a woman) who has cohabited with their partners, with or without some presentation of items to the woman's parents, thinks herself

[72] *Ayishetu Abdul-Kadiri v Abdulai Dwamena* [2020] DLCA 10013.

[73] Sarbah, note 31 above, p. 51.

married, and, on the termination of the marriage through either death or dissolution, has the rug pulled out from under her when she is held to be merely a concubine rather than occupying the hallowed position of wife.[74]

The importance of the distinction lies in the incidents of marriage, particularly in terms of inheritance and claims for maintenance for herself and/or for their children. In the case of *Owusu v Nyarko*,[75] the father of the woman gave his daughter to the defendant to live with him as his wife, but there was no formal meeting of the families. The court found that there was no evidence of the conditions for validity of Akan marriages having been satisfied and held that the plaintiff was not the wife of the defendant, even though they had lived together for seven years prior to his death and had had three children. The court found that the defendant had not been in a position to perform the customary rites. The report is silent as to why the court reached this understanding, but it was likely due to the man's indigence at the time.

This was rather fortunate for the plaintiff because the position of Akan customary law, per the court, was that it was the responsibility of the wife and children to assist the man in whatever work he did in his station of life, and such assistance did not thereby entitle the woman or children to an interest in any property acquired with the proceeds of such labor. However, this position does not apply to concubines, for there is no obligation on a concubine to assist her lover with her labor. Having found that their union was one of concubinage, rather than marriage, the court dismissed the appeal and affirmed the right of the plaintiff to one-third of the cocoa farms she had helped the defendant to farm.

The other side of the coin is that the concubine is not entitled to sue for maintenance, as in the absence of a duty to assist him, there is no corresponding obligation to maintain a concubine, as there is for a wife. A concubine may only

[74] Prof. Mensa-Bonsu discusses the importance of marriage, in particular, the status and economic safety net it presents for many. See Henrietta Joy Abena Nyarko Mensa-Bonsu, "The Action for Breach of Promise to Marry in Ghana: New Life to an Old Rule", *Review of Ghana Law*, XIX (1993-1995), pp. 41-68.

[75] *Owusu*, note 37 above.

sue for maintenance of any children of the union, as the duty to maintain one's child exists regardless of the nature of the union from which the child was gotten. The case of *Badu v. Boakye*[76] is instructive on this point. In that case, the woman, the plaintiff, sued *inter alia* for breach of promise to marry. She, however, alleged that she had been married to the defendant after she had become pregnant by him. The defendant's explanation was that after securing plaintiff's acceptance of his love proposal, they cohabited, to see if he would approve of her character and therefore marry her. The defendant claimed that the drinks he had presented to the plaintiff's father and uncle were presented pursuant to the customary practice of *akotoagyan* which literally means *"bought for nothing"*. The opinion of the Regional House of Chiefs of Ghana's Brong-Ahafo region (RHC) indicated that this practice was a way of introducing the man to the girl's parents to avoid offending them by consorting with the girl without the parents' knowledge. The court accepted the opinion of the RHC and found that the practice of *akotoagyan* did not create any legal relations between the parties, nor was the drink refundable by the woman's family if she terminated the union. Additionally, the woman could not sue for breach of promise to marry, as the drinks so presented did not amount to a token promise to marry. Essentially, per the court's finding, the man could engage in this form of relationship, in which he had no liabilities if he decided against entering into a more formal process with her, but which afforded him all the potential benefits of marriage, including consortium, and domestic services of the woman. The woman, in this case, was not entitled to maintenance as she was a concubine.

This case demonstrates the not-so-hidden protection of the "boys club", which among others,[77] protects men against any liability while ensuring that they enjoy benefits of the woman's expectations and hopes that she would be

[76] [1975] 1 GLR pp. 283-291.

[77] The bias in favor of men in judicial reasoning is often seen in cases involving the distribution of property on the termination of marriage. For further discussion, see Maame Yaa Akyiaa Barnes, "Equality is Equity…or Is it? A Critical Examination of the 'Equality Principle' in the Distribution of Marital Property", in Christine Dowuona-Hammond, Ama F. Hammond and Raymond A. Atuguba (eds.), *Ghana @60: Mobilising the Law for Ghana's Future* (2020).

upgraded to wife status on account of her conduct. It is unlikely that a woman seeking marriage would invest less than her best efforts to ensure that she is in the best position to be a wife one day. This would mean that while the woman was motivated (or perhaps induced) to conduct herself as a wife, performing all the roles traditionally associated with wives, the male beneficiary could terminate this at will and have no further obligations towards her beyond ensuring that he returned her to her parents in good health, much like one is expected to return in good condition a car that one had taken on a test drive. This cannot be in consonance with equity, good conscience, and public policy that the courts have used in refusing to recognize a customary practice as valid. The court in *Badu v Boakye* was rightly criticized by Edward Wiredu J (as he then was), for failing to treat the practice of *akotoagyan* with the opprobrium it deserves.[78]

In terms of inheritance, the now abandoned judicially accepted customary law principle was that the wife and/or child were not entitled to proprietary rights to the deceased husband's estate. They were entitled only to maintenance. The farthest the courts were willing to go, before the 1992 Constitution came into force,[79] was to give her a life estate in the property,[80] unless she could demonstrate that she had contributed money or in money's worth to the acquisition of the properties[81] because the duty of a wife at custom, to assist her husband in his chosen work, did not extend to her making financial contributions.[82] Wives were afforded better protection under the Intestate Succession Act 1985 (PNDCL 111),[83] which recognizes only marriage

[78] See *Abangana*, note 14 above.

[79] For the impact of the 1992 Constitution on distribution of marital property on death or dissolution of the marriage, see Maame Yaa Akyiaa Mensa-Bonsu and Maame Abena Siem Mensa-Bonsu, "To Win Both the Battle and the War: Judicial Determination of Property Rights of Spouses in Ghana", in Josephine Jarpa Dawuni, *Gender, Judging and the Courts in Africa* (2021).

[80] *In Re Kofi Antubam (Decd.), Quaico v. Fosu* and Another [1965] GLR pp. 138- 145 (H.C).

[81] *Achiampong v Achiampong* [1982-83] GLR pp. 1017-1039 (C.A).

[82] *Abebreseh v. Kaah* [1976] 2 GLR pp. 46-62 (H.C.).

[83] The challenges with this Act are important but fall outside the scope of this

as the union that entitles the surviving party to property of the estate. Therefore, a concubine would not be able to claim provision under the Act.[84] Similarly, to be able to get reasonable provision out of a deceased testator's estate, the woman would have to prove first that she was a wife.[85]

Prohibited unions

Consanguinity

The scope of prohibited degrees of consanguinity at customary law depends on where one hails from. Some ethnic groups treat consanguinity as an excluding factor, others treat it as a preference-creating factor. Among the Akans, for example, the scope appears to be wider than that under the common law. In the case of *Ababio v. Karikari,*[86] evidence was given of a case on which the Okyehene ruled in 1959, in respect of a prohibited marriage at custom. Though there was no clear indication of the degree of consanguinity between the offending couple, there was evidence to suggest that members of the three royal families of Akyem Abuakwa, like the couple, could not marry from among themselves, as it was considered taboo. They were three different sections of the ruling Asona family, but as each family was entitled to present candidates for the throne, they were deemed in the customary law of the area as being too closely related, and therefore unions between members of those families were incestuous.

Both the couple and the heads of their respective families were subjected to customary sanctions for this offence. Similarly, Kwadwo Mensah-Brown writes of the Sefwi-Akan, who are Akan, that marriage between members of the same totemic clan, is prohibited.[87] The exception to the

chapter. See H. J. A. N. Mensa-Bonsu, "The Intestate Succession Law of Ghana: Practical Problems in Application", *Yearbook of African Law,* VIII (1994), p. 105.

[84] *Prempeh v Agyapong* [1989-90] 2 GLR pp. 407- 419 (C.A.).

[85] *Humphrey-Bonsu,* note 56 above.

[86] [2002] DLSC 1069.

[87] Kodwo Mensah-Brown, "Marriage in Sefwi-Akan Customary Law: A

Akan rules on consanguinity is cross-cousin marriage, where a man may marry his maternal uncle's daughter.[88] This is because Akans are matrilineal, and therefore the parties belong to different matrilineages. An Akan, according to the writer, may also marry his father's sister's daughter, but marriage between a father's brother's daughter is strictly prohibited, as they are considered as descending from the same father.[89]

The venerable Sarbah wrote of the Fante that a man was not allowed to marry his uterine sister, his father or mother's sister, or brother's daughter, or mother's sister's daughter but he could marry his father's sister's child, though this was not encouraged.[90] In other words, a man could not marry his sister, or aunt, or niece or maternal cousin. According to Sarbah, this rule also applied to an adopted son or daughter in both their adoptive and natural families.[91]

Among the Tongu Ewe on the other hand, it has been found that marriage between closely-related members of the clan is not only allowed, but even preferred.[92]Among the Tongu-Mafi, however, marriage between parents and children, including adopted children and step children, siblings, both uterine, adopted and step, between a person and their aunt or uncle, and marriage among in-laws is prohibited. Additionally, a person cannot marry two sisters, unless they are twins, and a person cannot marry their brother's wife or ex-wife.[93]

Among the many tribes in northern Ghana there is no uniform position on cross-cousin marriages. Among the Gonja, for example, cross-cousin marriage is permitted,

Comparative Study in Ethno-Jurisprudence", *Présence Africaine,* LXVIII (1968), p. 66.

88 Ibid.

89 Ibid., p. 65.

90 Sarbah, note 31 above, p. 46.

91 Ibid.

92 Godwin Kwaku Nukunya, *Tradition and change in Ghana: An Introduction to Sociology* (2003), p. 12.

93 Ahortor, note 5 above, pp. 74-75.

while this is considered incestuous and taboo and is therefore prohibited among the Tallensi and the Konkomba.[94]

Same-sex marriages

There is little evidence of same-sex unions at customary law. Of those that do exist, these appear not to be sexual in nature, but may be an expression of a deep friendship[95] or for the purpose of ensuring continuity of lineage. In the case of the latter, it has been written of the Nankani that woman-woman marriages are practiced where the male dies without issue. It is said of the Nankani that dying without descendants means one cannot be an ancestor. Thus dying without issue excludes a person automatically from fundamental beliefs and practices in the religio-cultural infrastructure of the Nankani. Thus, where the male stock is almost depleted and there is no other option, a woman may be allowed to marry another woman. In this situation, a woman of the deceased husband's family marries the widow. The widow is expected to have discreet liaisons with members of the matrimonial extended family. Children born of such unions are culturally the children of the deceased; the biological fathers have no claims to the children.[96] It is unlikely that same-sex sexual unions are permitted at customary law.

INCIDENTS OF MARRIAGE AT CUSTOM

At custom, marriage entitles a man to sue another for the seduction of his wife.[97] Sarbah writes that the fine imposed was to pacify the injured husband and was the equivalent in value to the dowry and all marriage expenses, unless the conduct of the wife was brought about by the husband's

[94] Jack Goody and Esther Goody, "Cross-Cousin Marriage in Northern Ghana", *Man*, I (1966), p. 343.

[95] Italo Signorini, "Agɔnwole Agyalɛ: The Marriage Between Two Persons of the Same Sex among the Nzema of Southwestern Ghana", *Journal de la Société des Africanistes*, XLIII, no. 2 (1973), p. 221.

[96] For the full discussion on this uncommon form of marriage, see Rose Mary Amenga-Etego, "Marriage Without Sex? Same-Sex Marriages and Female Identity Among the Nankani of Northern Ghana", *Ghana Journal of Religion and Theology*, IV (2012), pp. 14-37.

[97] See, for example, *Kombat*, note 6 above.

treatment, in which case the fine was only nominal.[98] Thus, a plaintiff husband is entitled to claim damages from the defendant for the latter's interference with the husband's conjugal rights and for the "injury done to his feelings, honour and pride".[99] This is regardless of the wife's wishes. These seduction actions, it is argued, treats women as merely objects; the "competition" is between the men, whereby the "ownership" of one is challenged by the actions of the other. How the woman feels, the fact that she is an adult of sound mind, competent, and capable of making choices, even if per the norms of the land they are wrongful moral choices, is disregarded. The customary law recognizes the proprietary interest of the husband, which is injured by the defendant's conduct.

Second, customary law recognizes the husband's right to consortium of his wife and entitles him to sue, again, another man, for enticement of the wife. Enticement of one's wife is not the same as a seduction action, in that in the former action, there is no requirement that the defendant be proved to have committed adultery with the wife. The aggrieved husband was required to prove that his wife was persuaded or induced by the defendant to depart from the matrimonial home and that the husband lost her consortium.[100] It has been held that the action for enticement is "wholly independent of sexually immoral factors".[101]

Among the Ga, it has been written that contracting marriage through the six-cloth marriage process, provided "unrivalled security" for the wife and the issue of that marriage. Such a wife enjoyed privilege and status, and a man who committed adultery with such a wife could be subject to banishment or even to death by decapitation or drowning. This punishment has been commuted to heavy fines.[102]

[98] Sarbah, note 31 above, p. 48.

[99] *Avuugi v Abugri* [1987-88] 2 GLR pp. 515-520 (H.C).

[100] *Attah v Annan* [1975] 1 GLR pp. 366-373 (H.C).

[101] *Mate v. Amanor* [1973] 1 GLR pp. 469-482 (H.C).

[102] Nii-Aponsah, note 4 above.

Moreover, the husband has a right to his wife's labor and the fruits of that labor. Per the court in *Quartey* which position prevailed with some modification until the coming into force of the 1992 Constitution,[103] the fruits of her joint labor with the husband did not entitle her to any proprietary interest in properties acquired therefrom.

In the case of the woman, marriage entitles the wife to maintenance for herself and her children.[104] On the death of her husband, she is entitled to maintenance from the customary successor of her husband, and on some authorities, to reside in any house built by him.[105] However, the latter view appears to have been challenged in the case of *Adjei v Foriwaa,*[106] where the court held that "[c]ustomary law knew no personal right of occupation by a customary wife".[107] The rights of a wife in respect of inheritance however, falls outside the purview of this chapter.

DISSOLUTION OF CUSTOMARY LAW MARRIAGE

Process of customary law divorce

It appears that the customary law, is not in favor of divorce. If the marriage falls on the rocks, the families must make every effort to investigate the source of the unhappy circumstances and salvage the marriage. It has been held that dissolution or divorce is resorted to as a last measure, where it is clear that there is a total breakdown of the marriage, or the circumstances warrant the divorce.[108]

[103] Barnes, note 77 above.

[104] *Manu,* note 41 above; *Tengey & Mary Doe v George Doe* [1962] 1 GLR pp. 361-363 (H.C).

[105] *Abebreseh,* note 82 above.

[106] [1981] 1 GLR 378-387 (H.C).

[107] Ibid., p. 385.

[108] *Attah,* note 100 above.

In the case of *Ruth Ansah v John Hector Ansah & Naomi Owusu,*[109] the court held in respect of the formalities to effect a divorce on the basis of Akan custom:

> It is well settled customary law that when there is a declaration of intention to seek divorce, both families of the couple meet together for the dissolution of the marriage. They try to reconcile the couple. When reconciliation fails, they find out if either party owes the other. Then libation is poured, and Kaolin is smeared on the body of the woman in the presence of both families and other neutral and responsible persons. Where it is the wife who seeks the divorce she is requested to return the dowry paid. Where it is the husband who seeks the divorce he is normally to give some lump sum to the wife as some kind of alimony or compensation.[110]

This process was outlined in the earlier case of *Attah v. Annan,*[111] where the court held that a marriage could not be unilaterally and capriciously terminated by the act of one relation of either party. There had to be first an arbitration, at which members of the family of each spouse and neutral persons were present. The arbitrators had to try their utmost to effect reconciliation between the spouses to resuscitate the marriage, especially if the couple had children. If, however, in the opinion of the arbitrators, the marriage should be dissolved, the spouses had to settle all legitimate accounts between them. The husband would then release the wife from the union either by chalking her or saying so in the presence of the persons therein gathered.[112]

Thus, for a divorce in Akan custom to be valid, the minimum requirements are the knowledge of the families of the intention of the parties to dissolve the union, the declaration by the one seeking the divorce to that effect, the

109 *Ansah,* note 61 above.

110 Ibid.

111 *Attah,* note 100 above.

112 This decision was based on the description by Sarbah of the process for divorce in Akan custom. See Sarbah, note 31 above, p. 52.

payment of some money, either as compensation and/or alimony, or return of the dowry paid, and a release of the wife from the union.

However, when the marriage has turned particularly acrimonious, it is said that one need only return the drinks, and the marriage is thus terminated. The families may be at such loggerheads, perhaps based on the treatment meted out to their member by the spouse, that they are unable to calmly discuss and dissolve the union. There is anecdotal evidence of families simply leaving the drinks at the gate of the other family and walking away, thereby indicating that they have terminated the marriage.

Other cases have illuminated practices in other ethnic groups. For example, In *Ginbuuro & Another v. Kaba,*[113] the court found that, under Frafra custom, the return of the calabash constituted dissolution. The calabash symbolized the woman given in marriage to the man, and its return is the privilege of the husband's family. However, the wife's family could also request the return of the calabash where the wife was initiating the divorce. The husband could refuse to return the calabash, indicating that he did not consent to the divorce, but in doing so, he ran the risk, as happened in that case, of the wife's family unilaterally considering the marriage as terminated.

Grounds for customary divorce

Adultery by the wife appears to be ground for divorce at custom in different parts of Ghana. Sarbah writes of the grounds for divorce in Akan custom to include adultery and witchcraft on the part of the wife. In *Billa v. Salifu,*[114] there was evidence to suggest that the only grounds for divorce in Dagomba custom is adultery of the wife. More interesting is the evidence suggesting that there are four different forms of adultery, depending on the time and circumstance.[115] In that case, the court held, denying the husband's claim to

[113] [1971] 2 GLR pp. 416-420 (H.C).

[114] [1971] 2 GLR pp. 87-107 (H.C).

[115] The four categories of adultery in Dagomba custom as stated in *Billa v Salifu* are:

damages against the defendant for adulterous association with his wife, that there was no such right under Dagomba customary law. Adultery, in the Dagomba custom, was punished as a quasi-criminal act. Monetary compensation was due to the husband only when the husband was divorcing his wife on the grounds of adultery.

Adultery cannot be committed by the husband, and therefore infidelity of the man is no ground for divorce,[116] given that customary marriages are potentially polygamous. The grounds for divorcing one's husband in Akan custom include the man's impotence, neglect or flagrant ill-treatment, and abandonment for a lengthy period of time.[117]

An area which bears more investigation is divorce after one spouse has died. This is interesting because divorce proceedings in respect of Part 3 marriages automatically terminate on the death of a spouse, and therefore there can be no further divorce issues where one party dies. However, there is the suggestion in *Hayford v. Moses*[118] that where one spouse in a customary law marriage dies, the family of the deceased may divorce her formally and give her a send-off, or the surviving spouse could, at custom, take a formal divorce from the family. Although the court does not

(a) pag-faa (confiscation of wife): an adulterer takes away somebody's wife and has been asked to pay a sum by the chief and also refund the cost of marrying the woman to the former husband or returning the woman to the husband and paying a fine to the chief.

(b) pag-pulli pahibu: this is where a woman who has been pregnant is found carnally known by an adulterer. The husband goes to the chief of the village to swear an oath for the adulterer to be summoned before the chief and asked to pay an amount to and a sheep to the husband, plus a fine.

(c) pag-bikoba wobbu: here, a woman has given birth and the child eventually dies and she goes home for some four or five months before she can get back to the husband and has sexual relations with another. The adulterer is charged in the same manner under the Dagomba custom as under (b).

(d) bia-zugu yagbu: here, the woman has had a child with the legitimate husband and gone home to her parents for the child to be fully grown, and before she can get back to the husband she engages in an adulterous affair.

116 Ibid; For more on the unequal ground for men and women in customary divorce, see Ekow Daniels, "The Legal Position of Women Under Our Marriage Laws", *University of Ghana Law Journal*, IX, no. 1 (1972), p. 39-63.

117 Ibid., p. 53.

118 *Hayford*, note 42 above, p. 76.

explain what this means, it is likely referencing the practice of some communities to give the widow in marriage to the deceased's brother or successor in a levirate marriage. The court held in that case that this form of divorce would be unfair to the widow, observing that the widow was an old woman in deteriorating health and had no chance of remarrying. This suggests that if a divorce of this nature occurs, the wife is no longer entitled to maintenance by the deceased's successor.

Dissolution under the Matrimonial Causes Act

Until the passage of the Matrimonial Causes Act, 1971 (Act 367), the courts lacked jurisdiction over petitions for dissolution of a customary marriage.[119] The grounds for a divorce of a customary law marriage under Act 367 include, subject to justice, equity, and good conscience:

- willful neglect to maintain a wife or child;
- impotence;
- barrenness or sterility;
- intercourse prohibited under that personal law on account of consanguinity, affinity, or other relationship and
- persistent false allegations of infidelity by one spouse against another.[120]

The Matrimonial Causes Act does not specifically provide for adultery as a ground for a dissolution of a customary law marriage under the statutory regime. It, therefore, raises the question of whether a wife married under customary law can petition for a divorce from her husband on account of his adultery, which, as noted above, would not be possible if the marriage is dissolved under customary law. There is little case law on dissolution of customary marriages, probably because customary law regulates customary marriages firmly and completely. Parties who end up in court usually do so with respect to distribution of marital property.

[119] *Adjei*, note 106 above.

[120] Section 41(3), Matrimonial Causes Act 1971.

REGISTRATION OF CUSTOMARY MARRIAGES AND DIVORCES

As noted earlier, Part 1 of the Marriages Act provides for the registration on customary marriages and divorces. Parties intending to register their customary marriages are required to furnish the Registrar of Marriages with information on a marriage registration form. This includes the names and residences of the parties, as well as the date of the marriage, among other pertinent details.[121] In addition, the parties must attach a statutory declaration with this information and a statement to the effect that the marriage satisfied the conditions for validity in accordance with the applicable customary law. To ensure that the families consented, the statutory declaration must be supported by either the parents of the spouses or the persons standing in loco parentis to them.[122]

Publicity is a core feature of the requirements under Part 1. Here, the Registrar of Marriages is mandated to register the marriage and, within twenty-eight days of receiving the application, give notice to the public of the registration of the marriage.[123] A person who desires to object to the registration of the marriage, having received notice of same, may do so in the District Court of the district where the marriage was registered.[124] If the court is satisfied that there are legal grounds for the objection, it shall order the registrar to expunge from the register, the entry so affected.[125]

It is unclear from the Act whether expunging the entry from the register would have invalidated the marriage in question, or whether the act of registration is merely a formality, the value of which is probative. In either case, it is difficult to see how, in the absence of false or fraudulent statements by the spouses, and the specified witnesses, an objection will be made out. It is submitted that registration

121 Schedule 1, Marriages Act.

122 Ibid., section 3 (2).

123 Ibid., section 4.

124 Ibid., section 5.

125 Ibid., section 5(3).

of a customary marriage is only a formality, the absence of which does not invalidate a marriage.[126] In the case of *Adade v Dade,*[127] the question as to the import of registration under the Act was answered when the court held that failure to register a customary marriage did not disentitle a spouse from benefitting under the Intestate Succession Act 1985 (PNDCL 111). More importantly, the court, speaking through Ampiah JA, stated that the registration of the customary marriage, in the absence of fraud, would serve as conclusive evidence of the marriage, whereas a non-registered customary marriage, depending upon the circumstances, would have to be proved. This position is further affirmed by Cap 127 itself, which provides that in the absence of registration, oral and documentary evidence may be adduced to prove the existence of a marriage.[128] In other words, the value of registration is purely evidentiary.

Dissolution of a customary marriage in accordance with custom may be registered in the same way as customary marriages. The relevant details about the dissolution of the marriage must be provided, including the statutory declaration to the effect that the marriage was dissolved in accordance with the applicable customary laws.[129] The requirement of registration does not apply to marriages dissolved under the Matrimonial Causes Act, 1971 (Act 367).[130] Because the marriage dissolved under Act 367 could only have been done judicially, there will be a record in writing of this fact, thereby obviating the need to register the divorce.

RECOMMENDATIONS

The first recommendation relates to a major grey area that needs more examination and legislative action: the distinction between marriages and other loose unions,

126 *In Re Pratt's Caveat; Bentil v Pratt* [1989-90] 2 GLR pp. 476-489 (H.C).

127 [1991] 1 GLR pp. 267-273 (C.A).

128 Section 15(2), Marriages Act.

129 Customary Marriage (Divorce and Registration) Act 1985 (PNDCL 112) as amended.

130 Section 6(2), Marriages Act.

often lumped into the category of concubinage, and their respective incidents. While it is admirable that the courts have been less inclined towards rigid adherence to form, this has the disadvantage of blurring the lines between marriages and these other unions. Some judicial pronouncements have been so liberal as to practically efface the distinction between marriage and unions that would previously have been considered non-marriages. The law has also created grey areas regarding the incidents of the unions, especially the distribution of property upon the dissolution of the union through death or divorce.

All rights to property are decided on whether a marriage exists. Perhaps this is why the courts moved in this direction, to do justice for the surviving spouse, most often the wife. Thus, if a party is unable to establish that he or she had been married to the other party, or to the deceased, she has very little protection for her interests. She would have to prove that financially she had contributed to the acquisition of the properties, as there is no expectation or obligation on a concubine to lend her labor to the man's. For this reason there is no counter obligation on the male party to maintain the concubine that can attach to his estate. Nor can he be compelled to make financial provision and maintenance for her in the event that the union goes sour, which he could do if it were a marriage and she sued for maintenance under the Matrimonial Causes Act. Similarly, if a deceased testator (or testatrix) were to disinherit the applicant, the applicant would not be entitled to any provision from the estate unless she could prove that she had been married to the testator at the time of his death. A concubine would not get any provision, regardless of the length of time they had remained in that union.

Thus, the modern judicial decisions, which have given what would otherwise have been deemed concubinage a cloak of respectability, have created more shadows regarding the rights of the parties in the unions. Parliament should address the rights of persons in intimate unions and clarify these and other issues. Either lines are drawn between marital and non-marital unions, with their respective identifiable and distinguishable rights, or adequate and equitable provision is made for all parties in an intimate relationship, howsoever described.

The second option would likewise generate its own problems; for example, that it would be unfair to treat both concubines and wives the same; or similarly, when the obligations and social expectations of each are distinct; or in the case of concubines, arguably non-existent. If marriage is such an invaluable institution in many, if not all, customary areas, then treating wives and concubines equally in terms of rights to property and maintenance, for example, could be seen as elevating the latter and less desirable union to the same position as the traditionally exalted one. This would obviate the need to incur the expense or to live under the pressures and expectations associated with being a wife. It would create further problems for determining entitlement to property in intestate succession, including exacerbating the existing challenge with sharing the house(s) of the deceased, where there are multiple wives with their children and children of the intestate born out of other intimate non-marital alliances.[131]

These are not easy questions, nor should they be hastily or casually treated. Parliament should provide the lacking, but sorely needed, clarity.

CONCLUSION

This chapter has examined the customary law framework for the celebration and dissolution of marriage by considering the interplay between custom, statute, and practices borrowed from the colonial past and how this interplay has diluted or imported things that were hitherto unknown, like the Bible and ring, into customary law practices. The essentials have been discussed together with the trajectory of judicial decisions determining the existence or otherwise of a customary marriage. The courts appear to be moving away from *Yaotey*, preferring to be less formalistic in the evaluation of the evidence presented to support the existence of a customary marriage.

131 See Mensa-Bonsu, note 79 above.

This departure from the rigid requirements of *Yaotey* has been critiqued, highlighting the challenges this poses for other areas of family law, including the distribution of marital property, and application for relief when a person who thought herself a spouse is disinherited by the deceased testator husband. Attention has been drawn to the need for legislative clarity on what makes a marriage valid and the rights that pertain to different intimate unions. As things stand, the rights of persons in unions not under the statutory regime often depend on the beneficence of the judicial mind tasked with resolving the matter. It is hoped that whether a marriage exists or was validly celebrated at custom, the rights and responsibilities pertaining to intimate unions will not continue to present a quandary.

Nigeria

Chapter Five
Examining Statutory and Customary Marriage in Nigeria

In Nigeria, as is common in most African jurisdictions, the types, incidents, and processes of marriages differ owing to the effect of colonial history whereby a foreign system of law was introduced to blend with existing customary systems, thus leading to more legal pluralism.[1] The three types of marriages legally recognized in Nigeria are statutory, customary, and Islamic. The formation, incidents, and rights accruing from these three types differ: they have different legal and regulatory frameworks as well as different essential requirements that affect their celebration, dissolution, and property rights. Various legal regimes regulate the three types of marriages concurrently.

The present chapter examines the various types of marriages in Nigeria. The processes for their formation, essential requirements, and legal framework are analyzed and discussed, together with the laws governing each form, the efficacy of the laws, and the impact of legal pluralism on marriages. Gaps and challenges arising from the regulatory framework are identified. Recommendations are made to potentially enhance the effective formation, operation, and dissolution of statutory and customary marriages in Nigeria.

MARRIAGE IN NIGERIA

Defining marriage in today's world can be challenging given the evolution of the marriage institution. For example, the incidence of same-sex marriage, cohabitation, and civil partnership is a departure from the traditional concept that

[1] Folashade Rose Adegbite, "Legal Pluralism and Marriage in Nigeria: A Structure for Denying Rights to Women", *University of Ghana Law Journal*, XXXI (2020-2021), p. 110.

had prevailed before the twenty-first century.[2] Globally, various jurisdictions have notions of marriage that reflect their social reality. Nonetheless, marriage is a hallowed institution recognized and respected universally. Marriage may be defined in neutral terms as a "legally recognized social contract between two people, traditionally based on a sexual relationship and implying a permanence of the union".[3] The term "marriage" can be viewed from three perspectives: agreement to marry, the act of marrying, and the state of being married.

In Nigeria, there are two forms of marriage: monogamous and polygamous. The monogamous marriage is between one man and one woman to the exclusion of all others. According to Section 18 of the Interpretation Act, monogamous marriage is one which is recognized by the law of the place where it is contracted as a voluntary union of one man and the woman to the exclusion of all others during the continuance of the marriage.[4] This is known as a statutory marriage. A polygamous marriage consists of a man and one or several women. The main characteristic of a polygamous marriage that distinguishes it from the monogamous one is a man's capacity to marry more than one wife. Customary and Islamic marriages are polygamous marriages. While a man may marry an unlimited number of women under the former, he is restricted to four women under the latter.

Under the Same Sex (Prohibition) Act, only marriages contracted between parties of the opposite sex shall be recognized as valid in Nigeria.[5] Accordingly, this chapter will describe marriage in the Nigerian context as a voluntary

[2] Gemma Margaret Anne Barriteau, *Marriage in the 21st Century: From a State of Confusion to a State of Being* (2016) (Ph.D. dissertation; Duquesne University) (available online).

[3] William Little and Ron McGivern, *Introduction to Sociology* (2016).

[4] Section 18, Interpretation Act 2004, Laws of the Federation.

[5] See section 3, Same Sex (Prohibition) Act 2013 which provides that anyone who enters into a same-sex marriage or a civil union shall be liable to imprisonment for fourteen years. Further, s 5 adds that any person or group of persons who administers, witnesses, aids, or abets the celebration of a same-sex marriage or civil union shall also be liable on conviction to imprisonment for ten years.

lifelong union between a man and a woman or women. The fact that a marital union starts with just one man and one woman in a polygamous marriage does not automatically mean it is a monogamous one; there is always the potential for another woman to join the union.

STATUTORY MARRIAGE

Statutory marriages are regulated by the Matrimonial Causes Act[6] and the Marriage Act of 1914. Historically, the Matrimonial Causes Act evolved from the Marriage Ordinance of 1914, which became applicable throughout the entity referred to as Nigeria in 1914 when the Northern Protectorate and the Southern Protectorate were merged.[7] The Marriage Ordinance of 1914 itself repealed the Marriage Ordinance of 1908, the Marriage Proclamation of 1907, and the Foreign Marriage Ordinance of 1913, which applied to parts of Nigeria.

A statutory marriage is a monogamous marriage contracted under the Act. It is described as a voluntary union of a man and a woman for life to the exclusion of all others during the continuance of such marriage.[8] This form of marriage has legal and social duties and responsibilities that the parties to the union cannot vary by agreement. The terms and conditions are imperative provisions of legislation that may not be altered by mutual agreement.[9] Statutory marriages enjoy certain rights and privileges over customary and Islamic marriages in Nigeria.[10] Various requirements precede the celebration of a statutory marriage, which requirements must be adhered to before parties can celebrate a statutory marriage. The essential requirements for a valid statutory marriage, steps for their celebration,

6 The Matrimonial Causes Act 1970, Cap M7, Laws of the Federation, 2004.

7 Marriage Ordinance No. 18 of 1914.

8 *Hyde* v *Hyde* [1866] LR 1 PD 130.

9 Olabanjo Ayenakin and Itunu Kolade-Faseyi, "Procedural and Legal Complexities in Matrimonial Proceedings before Trial Courts in Nigeria", *International Review of Law and Jurisprudence,* III, no. 3 (2021), p. 60.

10 In aspects such as property rights, succession, and maintenance.

and methods of dissolution and annulment processes are considered below.

Essential requirements of statutory marriage in Nigeria

The essential requirements for celebrating a statutory marriage center around the following: age, marital status, consent of the parties, consanguinity and affinity, parental consent, and capacity.

Age

Section 3(1) (e) of the Matrimonial Causes Act makes any marriage celebrated by parties who are not of "marriageable age" void. However, both the Matrimonial Causes Act and the Marriage Act do not define "marriageable age". This omission has generated considerable confusion over the acceptable age for a statutory marriage.

However, a number of provisions in laws indicate the minimum age for marriage in Nigeria. Foremost is section 29(4)(a) of Nigeria's Constitution, which describes "full age" as eighteen (18) years and above. Although, there is a rider in 29(4)(b) to the effect that "any woman who is married shall be deemed to be of full age". This claw-back to section 29(4) has the potential to ratify early and child marriages in Nigeria because parents and relations who marry off their children might argue that the Constitution sanctions their actions because the child is deemed to be of full age. Curiously, only underaged girls are deemed to fall within the provision; it does not apply to boys. This difference in treatment is discriminatory. Section 29(4) is designed to unduly deprive young girls of their personal agency and individual autonomy because attribution of full age to these girls means that marriages contracted on their behalf, with or without their consent, could be deemed valid.[11]

However, in practice, twenty-one years has been adopted as the "marriageable age" for celebrating a statutory

[11] Another provision worth mentioning is section 21 of the Child's Right Act 2003, which provides that "No person under the age of 18 is capable of contracting a valid marriage, and accordingly, a marriage so contracted is null and void and of no effect whatsoever".

marriage. This is based on the combined reading of sections 11(1)(b), 18, 19, and 20 of the Marriage Act, which provides that when parties are under the age of twenty-one, and not previously a widow or widower, the written consent of parents or guardian is required. Therefore, parties to a statutory marriage (neither a widow nor a widower and below twenty-one years) must be twenty-one years of age or shall obtain the written consent of parents or guardian before contracting a valid statutory marriage.

None of the parties should be in a pre-existing marriage with a third party

Parties to a subsisting marriage cannot contract a statutory marriage with another person.[12] It is irrelevant that the subsisting marriage is either a customary or Islamic marriage. Non-compliance with this provision automatically vitiates the statutory marriage. It is also a criminal offense.[13] However, the same parties to a subsisting customary or Islamic marriage can contract a valid statutory marriage. In situations where there are other wives in the subsisting customary or Islamic law marriage, neither the husband nor his wife (wives) can contract a statutory marriage. This particular provision is only applicable to statutory marriages; under customary and Islamic marriages, the potential groom may already be married before marrying an additional wife.

Consent of the parties

Section 3(1)(d) of the Matrimonial Causes Act provides that the parties to a statutory marriage must consent to the marriage; such consent must be freely given and genuine, meaning a party's consent must be true and real. A party's consent must represent the true intention to enter a statutory marriage with the other person. The question may arise that since the parties presented themselves physically

[12] *Obele v Obele* [1973] 1 NMLR 155.

[13] Sections 33(1), 35, 47 and 48, Marriage Act; Section 370, Criminal Code Act, Cap C38, Laws of the Federation of Nigeria (LFN) 2004. See also *R v Princewill* [1963] NNLR 54.

at the place of celebration, they apparently gave consent. However, there could be some vitiating factors that may invalidate consent in certain circumstances. These include duress, fraud, misrepresentation, or deceit.

Fraud exists when there is dishonest misrepresentation by one party to the marriage to induce the consent of the other.[14] Duress is when one party to the marriage is compelled, coerced, or forced into the marriage. The other party to the marriage only consents out of fear. The fear must be reasonably entertained and sufficient to vitiate consent.[15] Further, mistake vitiates consent when a party is mistaken about the identity of the other party or the nature of the marriage performed. However, not every type of mistake invalidates a marriage. For example, when a party voluntarily marries the other party believing that the party they are marrying is materially wealthy and it turns out not to be true, the mistaken assumption will not invalidate the marriage. It is only a mistake that goes to the root of the marriage that can render it void for lack of consent.[16]

Fatai-Williams JSC in *Osamwonyi v Osamwonyi,* commenting on the importance of consent, stated, "In my view, consent is not only basic but fundamental to either a potentially polygamous union such as a customary marriage or a monogamous union as marriage under the Act. Special provisions for obtaining consent are inserted in the Marriage Act".[17]

Prohibited degree of affinity and consanguinity

Parties desiring to contract a statutory marriage must not be within the prohibited degree of affinity or consanguinity. Section 3(1)(b) of the Matrimonial Causes Act makes such marriages void. A marriage will fall within this prohibition if the woman is or has been the man's ancestress, descendant, father's sister, mother's sister, brother's daughter, sister's

[14] Nasiru Tijani, *Matrimonial Causes in Nigeria: Law and Practice* (2007), p. 105.

[15] Ibid., p. 104

[16] *Osamwonyoi* v *Osamwonyi [1972] 10 SC 1.*

[17] Ibid.

daughter, daughter. The list of such prohibitions is enumerated in the Schedule to Matrimonial Causes Act.[18]

However, an exception to this rule is found in Section 4 of the Matrimonial Causes Act, which enables parties within the prohibited degree of affinity and consanguinity to apply in writing to a High Court Judge for permission to marry. The judge may grant the parties such permission if the judge is satisfied that exceptional circumstances justify the marriage.[19] When such permission is granted, the marriage will be valid even though the parties are within the prohibited degree of affinity and consanguinity. However, the Act does not identify circumstances that can justify the granting of such permission by a High Court judge; this gap in the Act requires legislative attention.

An illustration of what can constitute exceptional circumstances was given by Nwogugu, a Nigerian legal scholar. To him, if a cohabiting couple from the same village and within the prohibited degree have a child together, the cohabitation may be converted into a statutory marriage if the parties so wish.[20] Although it can be contended that this provision softens section 3(1)(b) of the Matrimonial Causes Act, there are lingering concerns arising from the proviso in section 4. First, it is an open-ended provision which may challenge social morality as it permits blood relations to enter into marital and sexual relationships. Further, this provision is open to abuse as parties may intentionally create such exceptional circumstances.

Capacity

Capacity implies that the parties must possess a sound mind to understand the nature of the marriage contract. A statutory marriage will be voidable if, at the time it was contracted, one (or both) of the parties was "mentally defective" and lacked the requisite capacity. A mentally defective person is defined thus:

18 1st schedule, Matrimonial Causes Act.

19 Ibid., sections 4(1) and 4(2).

20 Edwin Ifeanyinchukwu Nwogugu, *Family Law in Nigeria* (2011), p. 25.

> [A] person, who owing to an arrested or incomplete development of mind whether arising from inherent causes or induced by disease or injury, requires oversight, care of control for his own protection or for the protection of others and is, by reason of that fact, unfitted for the responsibility of marriage.[21]

The defective mind may be from birth or might have arisen later. What matters most is that the "mentally defective" party lacks the ability to retain, process, and evaluate information on the reasonable consequences of marriage. Such a person is incapable of carrying on a normal marital relationship. Likewise, if, at the time of the marriage, a spouse is subject to recurrent bouts of insanity, then such marriage is voidable.

Parental consent

Parental consent is necessary when an intending party to a marriage is under the age of twenty-one. The written consent of the father is required.[22] However, where the father is deceased or of unsound mind or absent from Nigeria, the mother can give consent. When both parents are unable to give consent, the guardian can give consent.[23] If any of these persons is unable or unavailable to give consent, then the following persons may consent to such marriage in writing upon being satisfied after due inquiry that the marriage is a proper one: (a) the Governor of the State, (b) a Judge of the High Court of the State or the Federal Capital Territory; or (c) any officer of or above the grade of assistant secretary.[24]

The mother of a party is given the opportunity to grant consent only when the father is dead, absent, or of unsound mind. This provision accentuates the gender disparity that exists in Nigerian laws. This law emphasizes male superiority and gender discrimination.

21 Section 5(2), Matrimonial Causes Act.

22 Section 18, Marriage Act.

23 Ibid.

24 Since the first two on this list are the public servants, it can be inferred that the assistant secretary should be in public service. Section 20, Marriage Act.

Celebration of statutory marriage in Nigeria

Celebration is the solemnization or formalization that occurs after the parties have taken the steps stated in the Act. The process is broken down into three stages as follows:

First stage (the preliminary stage)

One party to the intended marriage will sign and give to the registrar of the district in which the marriage is to take place a notice "Form A".[25] An illiterate applicant takes Form B, which allows the applicant to place his mark in the presence of some literate person who shall attest to the same Form B.[26] Upon receiving this notice, the registrar shall enter the notice into the Marriage Notice Book and thereafter display a copy of the notice on the registrar's outer door until the registrar grants the registrar's certificate, or after three months have elapsed.[27] The Marriage Notice Book is open to the general public for inspection without a fee during working hours.[28]

At this stage, a caveat can be entered by any person whose consent to a marriage is required or who may know of any just cause why the parties should not be legally married. This is done by writing the word "Forbidden" opposite the entry of notice in the Marriage Notice Book any time before the issuance of the registrar's certificate.[29] The registrar shall not issue his certificate until the caveat is removed.[30] When a caveat is entered, the matter is referred to a Judge of the High Court, who shall summarily determine the case subject to a right of appeal. If there is no merit in the caveat entered,

[25] Section 7, Marriage Act.

[26] 1st schedule and section 8, Marriage Act.

[27] Ibid., section 10.

[28] Ibid.

[29] Ibid., section 14(1); if the person who wants to enter caveat is illiterate, such caveat shall be entered on his behalf in the marriage notice book by the registrar on the verbal notice of that illiterate. See section 14(2).

[30] Ibid., section 14(1).

the judge shall cancel the word "Forbidden" entered in the Marriage Notice Book.[31]

Second stage (obtaining the Registrar's Certificate)

Subsequently, the registrar shall issue his certificate as prescribed in Form C at any time after the expiration of twenty-one days and before the end of three months from the notice.[32] This will only be done if he is satisfied by affidavit that:[33]

- One party to the intended marriage is resident in the district where the marriage is to take place at least fifteen days before granting the certificate.
- That either party to the proposed marriage is twenty-one years old. If a party is younger, they must have obtained the written consent of a parent or guardian as required by section 18 of the Matrimonial Causes Act, unless the underage party is a widow or a widower.
- There is no impediment of affinity and consanguinity between the parties or any other lawful hindrance.
- There is no previous customary marriage to third parties by either of the intending couple.[34]

The marriage shall occur within three months after the date of the notice.[35] Failure to celebrate the marriage within this period shall make all prior proceedings void. A fresh notice must then be given before the parties can lawfully marry.[36]

In some instances, the procedure described above may be dispensed with. The Minister of Internal Affairs

[31] ibid., sections 15 and 16.

[32] 1st schedule, Marriage Act.

[33] The affidavit may be sworn to before a registrar, or before an administrative officer or a recognized minister of religion, see ibid., section 11(2).

[34] Ibid., section 11(1)(a) - (d).

[35] Ibid., section 12.

[36] Ibid.

is empowered to issue a special license in accordance with Form D in the First Schedule. This special license is issued when the Minister is satisfied that, considering the circumstances of a particular case, he can dispense with the above procedure and grant a special license.[37] He needs to be satisfied that there is no lawful impediment to the intended marriage and that the necessary consent has been obtained. This special license authorizes the celebration of the marriage between the parties named in the license by a registrar, or by a recognized minister of some religious denomination or body.[38] This power to grant a special license by the Minister of Internal Affairs has been delegated to the Permanent Secretary of the Federal Ministry of Internal Affairs and the Permanent Secretaries of any State ministry that has been given the responsibility for marriage; or any officer in these ministries not below the rank of an Administrative Officer Class II.[39]

Third stage (solemnization of the marriage)

The marriage ceremony can take place in either of the ways explained below:

Licensed place of worship. The marriage must be officiated by a recognized minister of a church, denomination or body.[40] Regarding a "licensed place of worship", the Governor of a State is authorized to license any place within his State for the celebration of marriages.[41] The ceremony must take place with open doors between 08:00 and 18:00 hours in the presence of at least two witnesses aside from the officiating

[37] Section 13, Marriage Act.

[38] Ibid.

[39] Marriage Act (Delegation of Powers) Notice L.N. 44 of 1973.

[40] Section 21, Marriage Act; Often this form of ceremony is referred to as "white wedding" by a large population in Nigeria, a phrase that originated from the traditional outfit brides are adorned with at statutory marriages, particularly the ones celebrated at licensed places of worship. The bride's outfit is usually a long white flowing attire. A couple that has contracted a customary marriage may subsequently contract a statutory marriage.

[41] Ibid.

priest[42] and must be according to the denomination or church's rites and usage.[43]

There are other ceremonies, often referred to as a "church marriage" and "church blessings" that resemble statutory marriages but are not legally recognized. These ceremonies do not comply with procedures prescribed by statute and are often mistaken for statutory marriages.

"Church marriages" are Christian intra-denominational ceremonies that usually have spiritual benefits for the parties involved. Some denominations have denominational processes and rites that members must adhere to for their marriage to be recognized. However, where these processes and rites do not comply with the procedure under the Marriage Act, the religious ceremony is not a valid statutory marriage. For instance, the Roman Catholic may celebrate a church marriage by publishing the marriage banns after an assurance that the parties are in or intend a monogamous union. Last, the ceremony must be officiated by a priest with two lay witnesses. When this procedure is complied with, the marriage is regarded as valid by the Roman Catholic Church even though it does not comply with the provisions of the Marriage Act. The Roman Catholic Church equally issues a "certificate of marriage" that differs from the certificate under Form E of the First Schedule of the Marriage Act.[44]

Various denominations have their versions of a church marriage and their own marriage certificate issued to a couple after observing the marriage procedures. However, many denominations have found a way of harmonizing their religious system with the statutory marriage procedure. These churches give two certificates on the day of celebration, the marriage certificate in form E and their own church certificate, thereby making the marriage both legally valid and holy by the religious dictates of the denomination. Nonetheless, section 22 of the Marriages Act states that a minister should not celebrate a marriage if he is aware of any impediment to such marriage; the minister shall also

[42] Ibid.

[43] Ibid.

[44] *Akuwudike v Akuwudike* [1963] 7 ENLR 5.

not celebrate such a marriage until the parties deliver to him the registrar's certificate or the special license under section 13. Failure by the minister to comply with these statutory requirements constitutes an offense in law punishable by five years' imprisonment.[45]

On the other hand, there is the "church blessing". In some denominations, before a marriage is accepted as valid and holy, the couple must submit to a "church blessing", particularly if the couple contracted a customary marriage or a statutory marriage celebrated at the Registrar's Office. In this regard, a "church blessing" does not constitute a valid statutory marriage if the procedure under the Marriage Act for contracting a valid statutory marriage is not complied with.[46]

The Registrar's office. After issuance of the certificate under section 11 or a license under section 13 of the Marriage Act, parties may decide to celebrate the marriage at the Registrar's Office between 10:00 and 16:00 hours in the presence of two witnesses before the Marriage Registrar.[47]A Marriage celebrated at the Registrar's Office is a valid statutory marriage not needing any further civil or religious rites or legal celebrations. The registrar must complete the Marriage Certificate in duplicate, and the parties and the witnesses, must sign each certificate. A copy of the certificate is given to the parties, and another is filed in the Registrar's Office. The registrar also fills in and signs the counterfoil.[48] In social parlance, the phrase "Court Wedding" is often used loosely to describe a marriage celebrated at the Registrar's Office. The misconception arose from time past when there was a paucity of civil servants to handle the various desks in the civil service. Consequently, judicial officers also took on the role of registrars of marriages.

Nigerian diplomatic mission. Celebration of a statutory marriage can also occur at a Nigerian diplomatic mission or

45 Section 42, Marriage Act.

46 Nwogugu, note 20 above, p. 36.

47 Section 27, Marriage Act.

48 Section 28, Marriage Act.

a consulate before a Nigerian diplomat or consular officer of the rank of secretary or above.[49] However, this celebration is only permitted if one of the parties to the intended marriage is a Nigerian citizen.[50]

Marriage celebrated under special license. Whenever a special license is obtained under section 13 of the Marriage Act, the marriage celebration can occur at a place other than the registrar's office or a licensed place of worship.[51] However, it must be celebrated by either the Marriage Registrar or a minister of a religious denomination.[52] Even when a special license is issued, there must be strict adherence to all the formalities of celebrations prescribed as to marriages in a licensed place of worship or registrar's office.[53]

Dissolution of statutory marriage

The High Court of each State and that of the Federal Capital Territory have jurisdiction to dissolve statutory marriages.[54] Before an action can commence for the dissolution of a marriage, the "two-year rule" has to be observed. This rule simply states that no proceedings for divorce may be brought within two years of marriage without leave of court, except where the divorce proceeding is based on the facts of willful and persistent refusal of one party to consummate the marriage, adultery, rape, sodomy, or bestiality.[55] On the other hand, the Matrimonial Causes Act provides circumstances where a leave of the court precedes the presentation of a petition for the dissolution of a marriage. Leave may only be granted if the court is satisfied that a refusal to grant such leave would impose exceptional hardship on the applicant or the case is one

49 The Marriage Act (Amendment) Decree No 14 of 1971.

50 Ibid.

51 Section 29, Marriage Act.

52 Ibid.

53 Ibid.

54 Section 2(1), Matrimonial Causes Act.

55 Ibid., section 30(1).

involving exceptional depravity on the part of the other party to the marriage.[56] Either party to a statutory marriage can present a petition for divorce on the ground that the marriage has broken down irretrievably.[57]

According to section 15(1) of the Matrimonial Causes Act, the only ground for dissolution of marriage in Nigeria is that the marriage has broken down irretrievably. However, there are eight facts, one or more of which parties can establish to prove conclusively that their marriage has broken down irretrievably.[58] A court cannot declare that a statutory marriage has broken down irretrievably even if it appears that this is so, unless at least one of the facts listed in section 15 of the Matrimonial Causes Act is established by the petitioner. The petitioner must state the specific grounds for the dissolution as listed in section 15(2) Matrimonial Causes Act.

Section 15 itemizes these facts as follows upon which the court can hold a marriage to have broken down irretrievably.

Willful refusal of the respondent to consummate the marriage

The Act does not specify what constitutes willful or persistent refusal, but the courts will examine several issues to conclude that there is indeed willful or persistent refusal to consummate the marriage. The facts of each case will determine what constitutes a "willful or persistent refusal to consummate the marriage".[59] However, there must have been several direct and implied requests for consummation made by the petitioner, and the respondent must have flatly refused all these requests.[60] For a court to hold that there is a willful and consistent refusal to consummate, the marriage must not have been consummated until the divorce petition

56 Ibid., section 30(3).

57 *Anioke v Anioke* [2013] All FWLR (Pt 658) 975.

58 *Ibrahim v. Ibrahim* [2007] 1 NWLR (Pt 1015) 383.

59 Section 15(2)(a), Matrimonial Causes Act.

60 *Horton v Horton* [1947] 2 All ER p. 874.

is brought before the court.[61] All the relevant facts giving rise to the petition must be set out to enable the court to make an informed decision.

Adultery

The petitioner must establish that "the respondent has committed adultery and the petitioner finds it intolerable to live with the respondent".[62] It should be emphasized that under this fact, the commission of adultery alone is not sufficient; the second leg of the section must follow; that is, that the petitioner cannot live with the act of adultery by the respondent. Therefore, the petitioner has to prove that they find the commission of adultery by the respondent intolerable to live with.[63] The adultery in question must have occurred after the celebration of the marriage.

Unreasonable behavior

When the respondent conducts himself or herself in such a way that the petitioner can neither bear nor reasonably be expected to bear, this can form a fact upon which the petitioner can bring a petition for dissolution.[64] Such conduct must have occurred after the celebration of the marriage. The conduct complained of should affect or have an impact on the marriage.[65]

There are two major strands to this fact. The first is the presence of conduct or behavior that is deleterious, relevant, and impacts the marriage negatively. The second is that the conduct must be of a nature that the petitioner is reasonably expected not to be able to bear. Section 16 of the Matrimonial Causes Act further explains the requirements for unreasonable behavior by highlighting certain forms of

[61] Section 21, Matrimonial Causes Act.

[62] Ibid., section 15(2)(b).

[63] *Agu v Agu* [1972] 2 ECSLR 452.

[64] Section 15(2)(c), Matrimonial Causes Act.

[65] Nwogugu, note 20 above, p. 168.

conduct that the petitioner, *prima facie,* cannot reasonably be expected to bear. These are as follows:[66]

a. Respondent has, since the marriage, committed rape, sodomy or bestiality.

b. For a period of not less than two years since the marriage, the respondent has been habitually intoxicated by using excessive sedative narcotic or stimulating drugs or preparation; or has been a habitual drunkard.

c. After the celebration of the marriage, the respondent has, within a period not exceeding five years, suffered frequent convictions for crimes and has been sentenced to an aggregate term of imprisonment of not less than three years, thereby leaving the petitioner with no reasonable means of support.

d. After the celebration of the marriage, the respondent, has spent not less than three years in prison pursuant to a conviction for an offence punishable with death, life imprisonment, or incarceration for a period of five years or more, and the respondent is still in prison at the date of the petition.

e. The respondent has, within one year immediately preceding the petition, been convicted of an attempt to murder or unlawfully kill the petitioner or that the respondent has, within the time stated, been convicted of an offence of inflicting grievous bodily harm on the petitioner.

f. The respondent has habitually and willfully refused to pay maintenance to the petitioner even though there is a court order to that effect or a separation agreement.

g. It can be established that the respondent, as at the time of the petition, has an unsound mind, and there is no likelihood of the respondent recovering. It must be proved that since the celebration of the marriage, or within a period of six years immediately preceding the petition, the respondent has been confined in

[66] Sections 16(1)(a) – (g), Matrimonial Causes Act.

an institution for persons of unsound mind within or outside Nigeria. The petitioner must satisfy the court that the respondent is not likely to recover and be restored to a state whereby the respondent can manage his or her affairs.

The forms of unreasonable behavior listed in section 16 are not exhaustive. Any other conduct which is of equal gravity to the ones provided under section 16(1) may properly be considered.

There is a provision for reconciliation. Section 17 of the Matrimonial Causes Act provides possible reconciliation between the parties. If the parties have lived together for a period or periods not exceeding six months after the occurrence of the final incident used to support the petition, that period should be disregarded in deciding whether the fact is established. This provision aims to preserve the sanctity of marriage by encouraging reconciliation between parties who bring applications based on section 15(2)(c), for the section states that the fact of cohabitation for six months or less from the date of latest incident will not work against the petitioner. This provision allows parties to accommodate each other's misdeeds and the possibility of a change of conduct without the fear that they would be barred from petitioning.[67]

Desertion for continuous period of at least one year immediately preceding the submission of the petition

Desertion implies that the respondent intends to bring the marriage to an end. According to Nwogugu, four elements must be present jointly to prove desertion: the *de facto* separation of the respondent and petitioner; *animus deserendi,* that is, the intention to bring the cohabitation to an end permanently; lack of just cause for withdrawal from cohabitation; and lack of consent from the deserted party.[68] The desertion must have been for a continuous period of

[67] Mary Oluwakemi Adekile, "Legal Framework For Settling Marital Disputes Through Reconciliation in Nigeria", University of Lagos Student Paper (2009) (available online).

[68] Nwogugu, note 20 above, pp. 178-191.

one year immediately preceding the petition for dissolution in court. Desertion may be terminated before the end of the statutory period if one of the four elements constituting desertion ceases to exist during the period prescribed.

Separation for continuous period of at least two years immediately preceding the petition

Parties who have lived apart for a continuous period of at least two years immediately preceding the presentation of the divorce petition to the court may bring their petition under the above.[69] To fall under this category, the parties should have intended that their living apart constitutes an end to the marriage because mere physical separation does not constitute living apart. There must also be a termination of consortium and a clear intention that the parties are ending the marriage. Section 15(3) of the Matrimonial Causes Act further states that the parties will be deemed to be living apart unless they live in the same household. It should be noted, however, that if there are exigencies of life such as professional calling, education, or war compel the parties to live apart, these scenarios will not be treated as "living apart" under this section. A vital second element to this provision is that the respondent should not object to the petition for dissolution of marriage. In other words, both parties must consent to the dissolution of the marriage. Under this rule, the court does not concern itself with fault within the marriage, that is, who caused the living apart; this can only arise in financial matters.

Separation for continuous period of three years immediately preceding the submission of the petition.

The parties to the marriage have lived apart for a continuous period of three years or more immediately preceding the presentation of the petition for dissolution of the marriage.[70] Unlike the provision in section 15(2)(e) above, the second element on consent by both parties to the dissolution of the marriage is not applicable.

[69] Section 15(2)(f), Matrimonial Causes Act.

[70] Ibid., section 15 (2)(f).

Failure by the other party to comply with the court decree of restitution of conjugal rights for a period of no less than one year

This provision will be activated when the other party fails to comply with the court decree for the restitution of conjugal rights for no less than one year.[71] When the court makes an order for the restitution of conjugal rights, the court's primary objective is to preserve the marriage, but the question is whether this order violates an individual's right to privacy and autonomy.

Nigerian courts may draw inspiration from decisions of the courts in India in determining whether intimacy, a conjugal right, is within the scope of the right to privacy. In *Gobind* v *State of Madhya*,[72] the Indian Supreme Court explained that personal intimacies and marriages fall within an individual's right to privacy, with which the law should not interfere. However, in *Harvinder Kaur* v *Harmander Singh Chaudhary*,[73] the court adopted a different approach by distinguishing between sexual relations from consortium or cohabitation, thus concluding that it was not ordering a sexual relationship between the parties but reinstating consortium. *Therefore, the order to resume conjugal rights may be regarded as an infringement on fundamental rights and personal liberties.*

Nonetheless, the final decision to comply with this order lies with the parties, and there are no punitive consequences arising from non-compliance; rather, a party's failure to obey can only be a fact on which the petitioner can bring an action for the dissolution of that marriage.

Presumption of death

A divorce petition can be brought when there is a presumption that the other party to the marriage is dead. In doing so, the petitioner must establish that the other party has been absent for a period such that it can be inferred

[71] Section 15(2)(g), Matrimonial Causes Act.

[72] AIR 1975 SC 1378, para. 24.

[73] AIR 1984 Delhi 66, paras. 9, 10,11 and 12.

reasonably that the party is dead.[74] The inferred time of absence has been provided for in the Evidence Act of 2011:

> A person shown not to have been heard of for seven years by those, if any, who if he had been alive would naturally have heard of him, is presumed to be dead unless such as to account for his not being heard of without assuming his death; but there is no presumption as to the time when he died, and the burden of proving his death at any particular time is upon the person who asserts it.[75]

If a decree of dissolution is granted based on this fact, but before it becomes a decree absolute, it is found that the respondent is alive, such decree *nisi* shall be rescinded by the court.

Annulment of statutory marriage

Aside from the dissolution of marriage in Nigeria, a statutory marriage can equally come to an end by a decree of annulment. A statutory marriage can be nullified on the basis that it is void or voidable under the provisions of section 3(1) (a) of the Matrimonial Causes Act and section 33(1)(a)- (d) of the Marriage Act. A marriage is void when in the eyes of the law it never existed, whereas a voidable marriage is good while subsisting but may be annulled by either party based on a defect.[76]

Section 3 of the Matrimonial Causes Act lays down the grounds on which a statutory marriage will be void *ab initio,* among them:

- Cases in which one party is already married to a third party.
- When the parties fall within the prohibited degree of consanguinity and affinity.
- The marriage is invalidated by the *lex loci celebrationis*.

[74] Section 15(1)(2)(h), Matrimonial Causes Act.

[75] Section 164 (1), Evidence Act 2011.

[76] Nwogugu, note 20 above, p. 122.

- When there is no real consent by either party or such consent is obtained under duress or by fraud.
- Where there is a mistake as to the identity of the party the other intends to marry or a mistake as to the nature of the marriage performed.
- When either party is not of marriageable age.

A statutory marriage can also be annulled if it is voidable, and the grounds for which it can be declared voidable are as follows:[77]

- When either party is incapable of consummating the marriage.
- If one party to the marriage is of unsound mind, has a mental disorder or epilepsy.
- When either party is suffering from a venereal disease that is communicable at the time of the marriage.
- If the wife is pregnant with the child of another person at the time of the marriage.

There are further restrictions imposed on granting a decree of nullity in respect of a voidable marriage when it is based on insanity, venereal disease, or pregnancy at the time of the marriage.[78] One is that the petitioner must have been ignorant of the fact constituting the ground for annulment at the time of the marriage celebration. It must be shown that the petitioner filed the petition no later than twelve months from the date of the marriage. Marital intercourse should not have occurred with the petitioner's consent after the petitioner discovered the facts constituting the ground for annulment.[79]

CUSTOMARY MARRIAGE IN NIGERIA

As its name implies, a customary marriage is one contracted in line with the native laws and customs of a

[77] Section 5(a) – (d), Matrimonial Causes Act.

[78] Ibid., section 37.

[79] Ibid., section 37(c).

particular ethnic group.[80] Custom, according to the Evidence Act, is a rule in a particular district that has obtained the force of law from long usage.[81] Customs differ across Nigeria. Therefore the customary law applicable to marriage equally differs. However, some customs are similar.

Customary marriage is a voluntary union of one man with one or several wives.[82] It is a potentially polygamous marriage, meaning the husband is at liberty to marry as many wives as he desires. Under customary marriage, generally there is no limit to the number of wives a man can marry simultaneously. Unlike statutory marriages, customary marriages transcend the parties involved, as it encompasses the families of both the bride and the groom.[83] Therefore, at times, death does not necessarily terminate a customary marriage, particularly for the woman, who may choose to remain in the late husband's family and marry one of his siblings or kinsmen.[84]

Essential requirements for a valid customary marriage

For a valid customary marriage to exist, certain essential and formal requirements must be adhered to in its formation:

Age

Most customs only prescribe that the right age for marriage is the age of "puberty". What is meant by the age of puberty is uncertain and may be rather subjective. The uncertainty in the age of marriage under customary

[80] Harinder Boparai, "The Customary and Statutory Law of Marriage in Nigeria", *The Rabel Journal of Comparative and International Private Law,* XLVI (1982), p. 530 (available online).

[81] Section 258(1), Evidence Act 2011; See also *Agbai v. Okagbue* (1991) NWLR (Pt. 204), p. 416 per Nwokedi JSC.

[82] Nwogugu, note 20 above, p. xxxi.

[83] Takim Asu Ojua, Felicia Ekwok Lukpata, and Chiemezie Atama, "Exploring the Neglect of African Family Value Systems and its Effects on Sustainable Development", *American Journal of Human Ecology,* III, no. 3 (2014), p. 43 (available online).

[84] Yinka Olomojobi, *Marriage in Nigeria Across Ages: Problems and Prospects* (2016) (available online).

law is mostly responsible for the high incidence of child marriage in the country. The erudite scholar, Sagay, puts the age of puberty at fourteen for girls and seventeen for boys amongst the Yorubas.[85] However, over time certain pieces of legislation, especially at the State level, have made incursions into the age of marriage under customary marriage. These include the following: Section 3 of the Age of Marriage Law 1956, applicable in the Eastern Region, specifies sixteen as the minimum; Cross River State's Girl Child Marriage and Female Circumcision (Prohibition) Law 200 puts it as eighteen; Bayelsa State also has provision for a minimum age in section 2 of its Age of Customary Marriage Law. [86]

However, the Child's Right Act of 2003, in its bid to protect children and prevent child marriage, places the age of marriage at eighteen years.[87] According to section 21 of the Child's Right Act, no one under eighteen years can contract a valid marriage; if such is contracted, it is null and void and of no effect. This provision should certainly extend to customary marriages.

There are contentions around the constitutional provisions on the use of the term "full age" as discussed earlier in this chapter. The Constitution appears to ratify the marriages of minor girls who were incapable of contracting marriages at the time of the marriage. This provision discriminates against young girls and encourages child marriages in Nigeria.[88]

Consent

Consent to customary marriage is in two phases, the first being the consent of the parties to the marriage. It is

[85] Itse Sagay, *Nigeria Family Law* (1999), p. 825.

[86] Cap A5, Laws of Bayelsa State, 2006.

[87] Section 18, Child's Right Act.

[88] Enyinna Sodienye Nwauche, "Child marriage in Nigeria: (Il) legal and (un) constitutional", *African Human Rights Law Journal,* XV (2015), pp. 421-432; See also, Kayode Olatunbosun Fayokun "Legality of Child Marriage in Nigeria and Inhibitions Against Realisation of Education Rights", *US-CHINA Law Review,* XII (2015), p. 812.

important that parties to a customary marriage consent to the marriage. Where a party does not consent to the marriage, they may refuse to go through with the ceremony. The Criminal Code Act provides that anyone who with the intention of marrying or having carnal knowledge of a female of any age, takes her away or detains her against her will is guilty of a felony, which is punishable by imprisonment for seven years.[89] This provision is to prevent abduction and forced marriage of young girls without their consent. This is buttressed in *Osamwonyin v Osamwonyin*,[90] where the court held that a girl cannot be married off to any man without her consent under Benin customary law.

The second form of consent is from the parents of the parties. The consent of parents is necessary before the celebration of any customary marriage since customary marriage is generally regarded as a union between two families.[91] Parents in this context means the father or guardian or anyone standing *in loco parentis* to the parties. For the bride, parental consent would be regarded as mandatory because without it, the exchange of bride price cannot take place since there will be no one to accept or receive the bride price, which is a vital component of customary marriage. However, there are also statutory incursions in this regard, with several statutes made over the years to override parental consent.[92] By Section 5 of the Marriage, Divorce and Custody of Children Adoptive By-Laws of 1958, when a parent or guardian withholds consent, the parties may bring an action against the parent or guardian to show cause why they are refusing to consent or accept the bride price. If in the court's opinion, sufficient has not been shown, it can order the parties to proceed with the marriage without the consent of the parent or guardian.

89 Section 361, Criminal Code Act.

90 [1972] 10 SC 1.

91 Nwogugu, note 20 above, p. 46.

92 An example is The Marriage, Divorce and Custody of Children Adoptive By-Laws 1958 WRLN 456 of 1958.

Status

Anyone married validly under the Marriage Act is incapable of contracting a customary marriage with a third person. Section 35 of the Marriage Act provides that anyone who is married under the Act cannot contract a valid marriage under customary law during the continuance of such statutory marriage. However, the same parties who have contracted a valid customary marriage can subsequently contract a valid marriage under the Act.

Prohibited degree of consanguinity and affinity

Generally, marriage is forbidden between persons related by blood. The prohibitions vary from one ethnic group to another.[93] Among the Ijaw, Itsekiri, Yoruba, and Igbo peoples, marriage between persons related by blood is forbidden, irrespective of how remote the parties are.[94] Among some ethnic groups, when people remotely related by blood marry, certain sacrifices or appeasements must be made to cleanse the land, presumably desecrated by the marriage.[95] Similarly, marriage between persons related by marriage is prohibited among many ethnic groups in Nigeria. The degree of prohibition of relationships through affinity depends on each ethnic group.

Bride price

The bride price is any payment, gifts, or consideration furnished either in money, natural produce, brass rods, cowries or any form of property to the parents or guardians of the bride on account of a marriage of that bride.[96] It is "a payment from the groom to the bride's family at the time of

[93] Sagay, note 85 above, p. 825.

[94] Nwogugu, note 20 above, p. 48.

[95] Linus Onyekaozurule Nwauzi "The Rules of Marriages under Customary Law", in Linus Onyekaozurule Nwauzi and Grace O. Akolokwu (eds.), *General Principles of Nigerian Customary Law* (2019), pp. 84-85.

[96] Section 2, Limitation of Dowry Law 1956, Cap 76, Laws of Eastern Nigeria [1963].

marriage".[97] Quite often, the expressions bride "price" and "dowry" are used interchangeably, but strictly speaking, they do not describe the same thing. The bride price means the price paid to the bride's family by the husband in respect of an intended marriage, while the dowry is "money, goods, or estate that a woman brings to her husband in marriage".[98]

There is no uniformity in the quantum, nature, or form of the bride price; it depends on each ethnic group and, at times, on the negotiations between the two families and the status of the bride involved. A "most improved" bride, on account of her educational qualifications or vocational training, will attract a higher bride price. As with other aspects of customary marriage, the amount of money to be paid as bride price has experienced legislative incursion over the years. These legislative interventions are necessary because some ethnic groups charge exorbitant amounts of money as bride price. An example of this is the Limitation of Dowry Law 1956 which regulates the quantum of the bride price to be paid in four Eastern States- Imo, Cross River, Anambra and River States.

The payment of a bride price is essential under customary marriage because it validates and legitimizes a marriage; it not only makes a customary marriage legal, but establishes the legitimacy of the children ensuing from the marriage.[99] The bride price can be in the form of rendering services to the bride by the husband and his family. Such services include farming, making yam heaps,[100] harvesting farm produce for the bride's family, and other forms of manual labor .[101]

97 Sara Lowes and Nathan Nunn, "Bride Price and the Well-Being of Women", in Siwan Anderson, Lori Beaman, and Jean-Philippe Platteau (eds.), *Towards Gender Equity in Development* (2018).

98 *Merriam Webster Dictionary* (available online).

99 Ngutor Sambe, Moses Yandev Avanger, and Solomon Arumun Agba, "The Effects of High Bride Price on Marital Stability", *IOSR Journal of Humanities and Social Science,* XVII (2013), p. 65.

100 These are mounds or heaped up soil where yams are planted.

101 Solomon Olusola Ademiluka, "Bride Price and Christian Marriage in Nigeria", *HTS Theologies Studies/Theological Studies,* LXXVII (2021), p. 6533; Bolanle Oluwakemi Eniola and Joseph I. Aremo, "Bride Price and Sexual and Reproductive; Rights of Women: A Case Study of South Africa and Nigeria", *Journal of Law, Policy*

Usually, the bride's father receives the bride price; however, in the absence of the bride's father, the male head of his immediate family receives it. In instances where neither the father nor the male head is available to collect the bride price, the bride's guardian or the person standing in loco parentis has the right to take the bride price from the husband's family. It is pertinent to note that payment of the bride price does not complete a valid customary marriage; it constitutes a betrothal.[102]

In today's world, given the infiltration of western culture into Nigerian culture, there have been instances whereby the bride price was waived. The question then arises as to whether waiving the bride price invalidates customary law marriage. Often, the waiver has to do with just the monetary payment or some part of the total bride price; in such a case, there is no serious consequence since some form of consideration has been furnished.[103] However, what is the validity of a customary law marriage when the totality of the bride price is waived? Scholars are correct who argue that the validity of customary law marriage is anchored on payment of the bride price. According to Scheidler, a theologian and bible scholar, the bride price in traditional African society confirms that the groom is sincere and serious about his intention.[104] It also represents a symbol of commitment and faithfulness to the marriage, as it gives assurance and confidence to the bride.[105]

Celebration of customary marriage in Nigeria

After fulfilling the essential requirements for the celebration of a valid customary marriage, what comes next

and Globalization, XCVI (2020), p. 26; Jane C. Diala, "In The Name of Tradition: Reflections on Bride Wealth Negotiation in Southern Nigeria", *Journal of the Oxford Centre for Socio-Legal Studies,* I (2018), p. 46.

102 *Ogunremi v Ogunremi* [1972] 2 UILR 466.

103 *Nickaf v Nickaf* (Court of Appeal, Kaduna Division, 1984).

104 Bill Scheidler, "What the Bible Says about *Lobola*", (2010) (available online).

105 Titi Chrisitianah Falana, "Bride Price Syndrome and Dominance in Marriage: An Expository Analysis", *International Journal of Humanities Social Sciences and Education,* VI, no. 8 (2019), p. 132.

for the couple is the celebration. The court held in *Agbeja* v *Agbeja* that for a valid customary marriage, there must be a ceremony and the handing over of the bride to the man's family.[106] Cohabitation and having children do not necessarily create customary marriage.[107]

There is no uniformity as to what constitutes a valid celebration; this is dependent on the customary practices of each ethnic group. In some cultures, payment of the bride price is done openly and in the presence of witnesses during the marriage celebration, whereas in others the payment must have been received before setting a date for the final celebration. Whichever it is, traditionally, in most cultures, the customary marriage is accompanied by funfair, music, and consumption of food and drinks. It should also be noted that customary marriage can be contracted by proxy.[108]

Where a customary marriage is alleged to exist, the essential ingredients, such as payment of the bride price and handing over of the bride, must be proved. Sufficient evidence must be produced to establish these ingredients.[109]

Other forms of marriages under customary law

Other forms of marriage exist under the customary laws in Nigeria, although they tend to occur in certain jurisdictions and ethnic groupings.[110] The first is referred to as "levirate marriage" or widow inheritance. This occurs when the widow is married off to the deceased husband's younger brother or kinsman. The marriage is a continuation of the existing one with the deceased, since there is no fresh negotiation of the bride price and other incidences leading to customary marriage. The widow is often given the right

[106] *Agbeja v Agbeja* [1985] 3 NWLR (Pt 11) 11.

[107] Babatunde Adetunji Oni, "Dissolution of Marriage Contracted under Customary Law in Nigeria: Comments on Ezeaku v. Okonkwo", *US-China Law Review*, XII (2015), p. 624. See also *Lawal Osula v. Lawal Osula* [1993] 2 NWLR (Pt 274) 158.

[108] *Ogunremi*, note 102 above.

[109] *Osamyonyi*, note 16 above.

[110] Particularly among the Ibos of the Eastern Nigeria and the Yoruba of the Western Nigeria.

to choose whether to remarry within her late husband's household or to leave and remarry another person unrelated to her late husband. She is also often given the right to choose who to marry amongst the late husband's brothers or kinsmen. This is habitually practiced when the widow is young and still of childbearing age.

The flip side to this type of arrangement is what is referred to as "sororate or replacement marriage". Under this arrangement, the younger sister or younger relative of the deceased wife is presented as a substitute to the deceased wife's husband to continue the marriage without fresh customary marriage procedures. Presently though, this type of customary marriage is fast becoming obsolete.[111]

The third form of marriage under customary law is the "woman-to-woman" marriage. Some situations, such as barrenness, may present themselves in a married woman's life, necessitate her acquiring a younger woman as a co-wife for her husband. However, the first wife pays the bride price and performs other marital requirements, so the new wife is attached to her and regarded as her wife. But unlike western same-sex marriage, this relationship does not involve woman-to-woman sexual relations; the sexual aspect of the union is between the husband and the co-wife. Another scenario is when a wealthy but barren woman wishes to have children and so marries a woman as her own wife but gets a male relative to do the consummation.[112] The Supreme Court in *Meribe* v *Egwu* differentiated this customary marriage from present-day same-sex marriage. The Court found that the old wife did not marry the new wife for herself but for her husband. The arrangement was not, therefore, immoral or contrary to public policy.[113]

Dissolution of customary marriage in Nigeria

Dissolving a customary marriage is not as complex as a statutory marriage. Generally, there are no homogeneous

[111] Mary Aderibigbe, *Family Law, A Friendly Guide to Rights and Obligations in Marriage and the Family* (2006), p. 25.

[112] *Meribe v Egwe* [1976] 1 ALL NLR 266.

[113] Ibid.

or particular sets of grounds for which customary marriage can be dissolved; these vary based on customs and the facts of each marriage. The focus is usually on the fact that the marriage has failed and is beyond redemption.

Unlike the philosophical bases of statutory marriage, which have eliminated fault-based grounds, the fault of a party often has a place in concluding that the marriage has broken down beyond repair. However, there are generally accepted factors that can trigger dissolution. These include bad behavior or character, maltreatment, adultery (particularly on the wife's part), cruelty, harmful diseases, witchcraft, desertion, impotence, and crime. A customary marriage may be dissolved without judicial intervention. Adultery by the wife is greatly abhorred under customary marriage and may be treated as a sin against the "gods" and the ancestors; certain rituals are performed to appease the gods and ancestors and to cleanse the women. Therefore, adultery by the woman is vital for the dissolution of customary marriage.[114] In fact, the customary society believes that condonation of adultery by the husband may result in the death of either the husband or the children of the marriage. In *Loye v Loye*,[115] the marriage was dissolved on the ground of adultery. Conversely, because customary law marriage permits men to have multiple wives, adultery on the part of the husband attracts little or no penance and draws little or no revulsion as that of the wife.

Further, while the husband's impotence can be a ground for dissolution, the wife's barrenness often does not constitute grounds for divorce. The husband does not have to divorce a wife who cannot have a child; instead, the husband may marry more wives who can produce the number of children he desires. Under a customary law marriage, the husband is expected to provide for the wife's needs and take care of her; not to treat her cruelly or maltreat her. However, when a woman suffers any of these, she can seek dissolution of her marriage.

114 Eunice Nkuru Uzodike, "Judicial Concepts of Adultery, Intolerability and Damages in Nigeria", *Journal of African Law*, XXXIV, no. 2 (1990), pp. 93-103.

115 (1981) O.Y.S.H.C.L.R. 140.

There are two ways in which a customary marriage can be dissolved: through non-judicial or judicial procedure. Both procedures are discussed below:

Non-judicial means of dissolution

Customary marriage can be dissolved without recourse to the court or any judicial process.[116] The process can be activated by the mutual agreement of the parties or by a unilateral decision of one of the parties to the marriage. Mutual agreement to bring the marriage to an end can arise when the parties have fallen out and reconciliation attempts have failed. The parties can jointly agree to bring the marriage to an end. When this arises, the families agree to the quantum of the bride price to be repaid.[117] However, if the families cannot agree on the returnable bride price, the aggrieved party can proceed to the court to determine the issue. Secondly, customary marriage can end by the unilateral decision of one of the parties when the husband, intending to end the marriage, drives his wife out permanently, or when the wife, with the intent of ending the marriage, leaves her matrimonial home.[118]

In either instance, the bride price will be demanded and refunded. Although this is the general position under the dissolution of customary marriage, there are certain differences across cultures.[119] However, there must be a formal act on the part of the spouse unwilling to continue with the marriage.[120] Usually, the two families are involved

[116] Maurice Okechukwu Christian Izunwa, "Divorce in Nigerian Statutory and Customary Marriage: A Comparative Critique of Grounds, Procedure and relief Attaching thereto", *Peak Journal of Social Sciences and Humanities*, III, no. 6 (2015), p. 77.

[117] *Nwangwa v. Ubani* [1997] 10 NWLR (Pt 526) 559.

[118] Izunwa, note 116, above.

[119] For instance, under the Biu native law, only the husband has the right to send the wife packing, See section 8, The Biu Native Authority (Declaration of Biu Native Marriage Law and Custom) Order NRLR 9 1964. Although it is not so certain what the position of the court will be it such is brought before the court in contemporary times, it may be regarded as a repugnant law since it suppresses the right and liberty of women.

[120] Oni, note 107 above.

in the dissolution, with intermediaries who try to mediate and reconcile the parties when necessary. The actual return of the bride price is a decisive indicator that the marriage is dissolved. Mere separation of the parties without the return of the bride price is not a final indication of dissolution. Likewise, the lapse of time without the return of the bride price does not amount to the dissolution of a customary marriage.[121]

Judicial Means

A customary court can dissolve a customary marriage. This method of dissolution is gaining prominence because of its clarity and the presence of records. However, the drawback of the judicial means of dissolution could be the long delay in the administration of justice often experienced in Nigeria. If the court refuses to grant a dissolution, parties can resort to non-judicial means. However, in certain instances, the magistrate's court may possess jurisdiction to determine matrimonial causes between parties married under customary law.[122]

THE ISSUE OF DOUBLE-DECKER MARRIAGES

It is a common practice in Nigeria that parties first contract a customary marriage before entering into a statutory marriage, a process referred to as "double-decker marriage".[123] In fact, some parties simultaneously contract the three forms of marriage in Nigeria: customary, Islamic, and statutory. The Marriage Act validates this practice and has enabled parties married under customary law to contract a valid statutory marriage.[124] Parties may contract a double-decker marriage if they are insecure about their customary marriage, since customary and Islamic marriages appear to have no statutory backing when it comes to some

121 Ibid., 630; Nwogugu, note 20 above, pp. 218-219.

122 Especially when there are no customary courts in the locality. See *Okpakap* v *Okor and Anor* (High Court, Lagos, 22 May 1970)

123 Margaret Chinyere Onokah, *Family Law* (2003), p. 143.

124 Section 33(1), Marriage Act.

issues of rights and privileges, such as inheritance and succession. Moreover, whenever parties need to interact with the international community, there is no documentary evidence to establish their married status under customary law. Contracting a statutory marriage after a customary marriage helps preclude polygyny, which most women are presumed to deem unacceptable. Moreover, the statutory marriage is preferred by many religious sects since it is celebrated openly and ceremoniously by the priests or headship of such religious groups. Nevertheless, people are still attached to their cultural background and desire to enjoy the advantages of a customary marriage, including extended and communal family security. The law has not attempted to harmonize these discrepancies in rights and privileges. Therefore, parties contract a double-decker marriage to "super-lock" their wedlock.

A number of legal issues flow from the practice of double-decker marriages: whether the statutory marriage supersedes or subsumes the customary marriage, whether they co-exist,[125] and whether the dissolution of one (particularly the statutory marriage) adequately dissolves the customary marriage. Another issue arising from this arrangement is what becomes of the customary marriage when the statutory marriage is void *ab initio*. Does the customary marriage subsist, or does the void statutory marriage automatically annul the customary marriage, particularly if the ground for annulment under statutory marriage does not constitute a ground under customary marriage? In finding answers to the legal questions on double-decker marriage, it should be noted that there are three possible outlooks on this issue.

The first is the conversion theory, which posits that a statutory marriage subsumes the customary marriage, since the latter automatically merges with or converts its legality to a statutory one, implying a loss of its characteristics, legal incidents and consequences. According to Sagay, a statutory marriage assimilates the customary marriage and eliminates all its incidents and substitutes its own incidents.[126] Thus, the

125 *Asiata v. Goncalo* [1900] 1 NLR.41; *Ohochucku v. Ohochuku* [1960] 1 All E.R. 253.

126 Sagay, note 85 above.

dissolution of a statutory marriage automatically dissolves the customary marriage.[127]

The second position is that of co-existence, which posits that both marriages co-exist and that despite the dissolution of the statutory marriage, the customary marriage subsists and remains undissolved. Therefore, the dissolution of the statutory marriage will not automatically dissolve the customary marriage.[128] This means that the customary marriage is just in abeyance and automatically revives when the statutory marriage is dissolved.

The third possible theory is that if customary marriage is first in time, the subsequent statutory marriage is of no legal effect. However, in Nigeria, this third theory has no definite case law. Even though the following cases give some information about the application of the third theory, it is doubtful if the courts will apply the same principles to a case before it. A few of these cases are discussed.

The first is *Asiata v Goncalo.*[129] In this case, a Yoruba man named Alli Elese, who was taken as a slave to Brazil, married Selia, an African free woman. The two had first married according to Muslim rites and then another according to Christian rites in Brazil. The parties had two daughters together. Later Alli Elese returned to Nigeria with Selia. However, Alli Elese married another woman Asatu under Muslim rites after the passing of the Marriage Ordinance 1884. The marriage between Alli Elese and Asatu was blessed with a child, Asiatu. On Alli Elese's death, issues arose as to which of the children was entitled to his estate and whether Alli Elese's marriage to Asatu was legal. The Divisional Court held that based on the Christian marriage contracted by Alli Elese, the second marriage to Asatu was invalid.

127 Ibid.

128 Emmanuel Folayan Ijalana and Julius Olaseinde Agbana, "A Critical Appraisal of the Concept of Double-Decker Marriage under the Nigerian Family Law", *Beijing Law Review*, XII (2021), p. 1163 citing *Akparanta v Akparanta* [1972] 2 ECSLR 779.

129 *Asiata,* note 125 above.

However, on appeal, the full court held that the Christian marriage contracted with Selia was merely a formality with no attendant legal effects. By virtue of this, Asatu's marriage was legal, and her children were entitled to share in the estate of Alli. There were several reasons the court adduced for reaching this decision. First, the court held that the parties were taken against their will to Brazil, a Christian country, as slaves. Further, the court pointed out that Nigeria is not a Christian country and that the customary law (Islamic Law inclusive) allows a man to marry more than a wife. The third reason for this decision is that the parties lived and died as Muslims; it was merely by the accident of them being in Brazil, a Christian State, that they had to comply with the form of marriage in Brazil. Last, the court held that Selia did not object to the second Muslim marriage to Asatu. For these reasons this case cannot be an authority because of all these special circumstances of the case.

Another case is *Ohochuku v Ohochuku*.[130] The English court granted a divorce for the marriage celebrated in England, stating that it has no jurisdiction to dissolve a polygamous marriage. The Nigerian court, faced with a similar situation, will undoubtedly not adopt the same position. The parties had a customary law marriage in Nigeria, after which the husband proceeded to study in England. The wife later joined him, and they went through a second ceremony at St. Pancras Register Office in London. The second ceremony was to enable the wife to produce a marriage certificate in England. Later, the wife brought a divorce petition, and Wrangham J. granted a divorce *nisi* for the dissolution of the London marriage and not that of the Nigerian marriage. He held that English courts have no jurisdiction to dissolve polygamous marriages.

This case cannot be regarded as good authority for the view that a divorce granted in respect of a subsequent statutory marriage does not dissolve an earlier customary law marriage. This is so because of the concomitant conflict of laws. By the English rules, English courts do not have jurisdiction to dissolve polygamous marriages though such marriages can be recognized to determine status and

130 *Ohochuku*, note 125 above.

other ancillary matters. If a similar case were brought to a Nigerian court, the decision would certainly be different since the court is not bound by the same principle. The Nigerian decree nisi would have dissolved both marriages.

REGISTRATION OF MARRIAGES

Statutory marriages

The President is empowered to divide Nigeria into marriage districts,[131] and appoint persons considered fit and proper to the principal registrars of marriages, registrar of marriages. The President may also appoint a deputy registrar of marriages for any district to act in the absence, illness, or incapacitation of a registrar.[132] The implication of this is that various marriage districts and registrars of marriage are spread across the nation authorized by Section 11 of the Marriage Act to issue marriage certificates in their respective jurisdictions. Meanwhile, there are no coordinated central means of collating and keeping in a single system marriages celebrated or dissolved in each district. It has become possible for dubious people to generate fake or forged marriage or divorce certificates.

According to Ehuria, a Nigerian public servant,[133] the lack of a central record system wherein a statutory marriage can be verified instantly has created gaps that allows the proliferation of marriage certificates.[134] She also observed that the Federal Government receives calls from organizations and embassies seeking clarification for marriage certificates that parties submit as documents. The present writer has met several married women with two statutory certificates: one from a marriage celebrated at the Registrar's Office and the other from a celebration at a licensed place of worship. There should be a central record system to identify the status of persons approaching any marriage registrar for a

131 Section 2, Marriage Act.

132 Ibid., section 4(1)(2).

133 *Fed Govt to Tackle Proliferation of Marriage Certificates* (2019) (available online).

134 Ibid.

license. Further, security features should be introduced into the marriage certificates to curtail forgery and corruption.

Customary marriages

Not all customary marriages are registered. Registration depends on the laws of each Local Government Area. This is contrary to some international conventions, especially the Protocol to the African Charter on Human and Peoples' Rights on the Rights of Women in Africa. Article 6 provides that "every marriage shall be recorded in writing and registered in accordance with national laws, in order to be legally recognized". Registration of marriages, of whatever type, is essential. The existence and authenticity of a statutory marriage can be verified for official use where certificates are issued.

There have been various nationwide efforts at documenting and registering customary marriages, although there is no uniform, standardized process or system for the documentation or registration of customary marriage. The Constitution makes provision for the Local Government Councils to register marriages.[135] The Local Governments in most States have made bylaws for registering customary marriage in their jurisdictions, with some making it compulsory and others making it optional.

SHORTCOMINGS IN THE LAWS REGULATING MARRIAGE IN NIGERIA AND RECOMMENDATIONS

The laws regulating marriages in Nigeria are not fully developed, particularly in terms of concepts and realities reflecting contemporary family life. There are insufficient legal provisions for a number of areas, for example, division of property and surrogacy, although case law attempts to fill these gaps. Also, multiple legal systems regulating marriage in Nigeria create discrepancies in rights, duties, and status. There are gaps in operation of the laws regulating marriages.

[135] Section 1 (i) and schedule IV, 1999 Constitution of the Federal Republic of Nigeria: Functions of a Local Government Council.

Statutory and customary marriages

Double-decker marriages

Many marriages in Nigeria are double-decker, and there is no precise judicial or legislative pronouncement on the consequences. There is a need for legislative intervention, particularly to clarify the status of customary marriages celebrated before statutory marriages, the relationship between the two, and the effect of the dissolution of one on the other. There should be legislation on the legal effect of double-decker marriages.

Unequal rights in respect of different forms of marriages

Nigeria's legal system draws heavily from the English legal system based on its colonial past. However, some existing customary marriage laws dating from before colonial rule still apply in parts of Nigeria. Nonetheless, all laws in force derive their legitimacy from the Constitution. Every type of marriage in Nigeria comes with its own privileges and rights. The issue with legal pluralism in Nigeria is that the rights and privileges enjoyed by each form of marriage are different and, in some cases, unequal. The legal system discriminates against customary and Islamic law marriages. Unequal rights and privileges exist in certain statutory provisions relating to property rights, proof of marriage, maintenance, inheritance and succession, evidence and even dissolution of marriage.[136] As things stand, a statutory marriage enjoys more rights, privileges, and protections than the other forms of marriage, even though the three types of marriage are recognized legally. It is therefore submitted that since all three types of marriage are legally recognized, the law should grant them equal rights and privileges. All right accruing to statutory marriages should be extended to all other forms of marriages in Nigeria. The necessary amendments should be made to the relevant laws to reflect this recommendation.

136 Adegbite, note 1 above.

Statutory marriages

The age of marriageability

Under statutory marriage, mention is made of "marriageable age" for prospective spouses without specifying the required age. It is only through inferences that the age of twenty-one has been arrived at. [137] This is a major omission in both the Matrimonial Causes Act and the Marriage Act. The Constitution does not help the situation when it states that "full age" is eighteen and above but provides at the same time that any married woman is deemed to be of "full age". The proviso to the Constitution appears to encourage child marriage, particularly for the girl child, since the provision does not apply to boys or men.[138]

Ignorance about various processes of contracting statutory marriage

There is considerable ignorance in the public sphere about what constitutes a statutory marriage. Many intending parties do not understand the various forms of marriage and the position of the law regarding them. Parties fail to see a marriage celebrated in a licensed place of worship (that is, the church) as a valid legal marriage that enjoys the rights, duties, and privileges of the marriage celebrated at the Registrar's Office, hence the multiplicity of statutory marriages by parties. After celebrating a valid statutory marriage in the church or licensed place of worship, parties still proceed to activate a duplicate process to celebrate another statutory marriage at the Registrar's Office but under the label "court marriage".

[137] Sections 11(1)(b), 18, 19 and 20, Marriage Act.

[138] Azubike Onuora-Ouguna, *Constitutionalizing the Violation of the Rights of the Girl Child in Nigeria: Exploring Constitutional Safeguards and Pitfalls* (2013) (available online).

The imprecise philosophical basis for dissolution of statutory marriages

Under the modern "no-fault principle" in the dissolution of marriages, a party seeking to establish that their marriage is irretrievably broken down must prove irreconcilable difference, incompatibility, or having lived apart for a period of time or a combination of some of these.[139] The fault of parties leading to the breakdown should not be in contention before the court. The Matrimonial Causes Act tries to move beyond this age-old fault-based principle in the dissolution of marriage by stating that the only ground for which statutory marriage can be dissolved is that it has broken down irretrievably. However, it still goes ahead in section 15(2) to itemize facts which can be used to establish that the marriage has indeed broken down irretrievably. This set of facts portrays fault and contradicts the modern no-fault principle.[140] This contradictory philosophical basis tends to exacerbate the conflicts and tension that dissolution brings between parties, while also impacting the children from the marriage and post-dissolution relations.[141] A fault-based approach in divorce cases, especially in an adversarial, time-consuming court system, is stressful to the parties concerned. A no-fault approach to divorce is simpler, less rancorous and affords the parties the environment to peacefully settle ancillary issues such as maintenance, custody and property rights. The law needs to move completely towards a "no-fault" approach in the dissolution of marriage, particularly statutory marriages.

139 Michael Attah and Linda Osagie, "Reforming The Irretrievable Breakdown Rule – Historical Perspectives From Common Law Jurisdictions And Lessons For Nigeria", *Nnamdi Azikiwe University Journal of International Law and Jurisprudence* XI, no. 1 (2020), p. 29. See also, Lynn D. Wardle, "No-Fault Divorce and the Divorce Conundrum", *Brigham Young University Law Review* (1991), p. 79.

140 Ibid.

141 Ibid.

Absence of centralized records for marriages celebrated, dissolved, or annulled

A statutory marriage presumably has records, even though this is not entirely correct. There is no centralized record system for statutory marriages celebrated, dissolved, or annulled in all the thirty-six States of the Federation and the Federal Capital Territory. Therefore, there is a need for a centralized system to verify the marital status of intending couples before a marriage registrar issues a license. Given the current record-keeping system for statutory marriages in Nigeria, persons can celebrate several marriages, including statutory marriages, with different persons concomitantly without dissolving previous ones since there is no centralized method of detecting this anomaly.

Customary marriages

Extra-judicial dissolution of customary marriages

As observed above, customary marriages can be dissolved non-judicially; however, the implication is that there are no written documents to record this event. The absence of records regarding the time of dissolution leaves too much to discretion. When ancillary issues such as property rights and the paternity of children (particularly children conceived but not yet born at the time of dissolution) arise, the time of dissolution may become an issue of contention since there is no document to this effect. Other issues that may arise on the occasion of non-judicial dissolution is proof of the status of parties when either needs to perform certain legal functions requiring a single status, an example being remarriage. Consequently, it is suggested that there should be centralized and harmonized documentation and registration of customary marriages across the nation, including at State and Local Government levels. This will aid registration and verification of customary marriage divorce as well.

Having examined the various gaps in the marriage structure and law in Nigeria, it is recommended that there should be a total overhaul of family law statutes in Nigeria.

The Marriage Act came into existence in December 1914, over a century ago. Similarly, the Matrimonial Causes Act is an old legislation that came into being in 1970, reflecting old ideologies, realities, and challenges. Much has happened since the adoption of those laws requiring a total revamp, update, and repositioning to incorporate contemporary issues and challenges reflective of modern perspectives. There is reason to acknowledge certain technological and scientific incursions into daily living that need legislative regulation. For example, the traditional understanding of the nuclear family is that it comprises only the father, the mother, and the children. However, with the arrival of assisted reproductive techniques, the concept of the nuclear family appears to be challenged by the expansion of the meaning of motherhood and fatherhood. Such issues need to have provisions in the new modern family law legislation.

CONCLUSION

In Nigeria, three types of marriages are legally recognized: statutory, customary, and Islamic law marriages. This chapter examined two types of marriage: statutory and customary together with the essential and formal requirements to be complied with in contracting a valid statutory or customary marriage. Parties contracting a statutory marriage must comply with both the Marriage Act and the Matrimonial Causes Act. The customary laws of each locality and ethnic group form the bases for contracting a valid customary marriage, although, over time, there has been a point of convergence in the various customary laws regarding marriage. Similarly, there are legal procedures for the dissolution and annulment of marriages in Nigeria.

The gaps and challenges in the different pieces of legislation, customary laws, and practices are identified and examined in discussing the various essential and formal requirements. Some laws need to be revised. Some problems are more systemic and require fundamental changes to the legal system. Generally, there is a need to strengthen the regulatory and administrative framework for marriages in Nigeria.

Chapter Six
The Islamic Marriage Contract in Nigeria

Before the introduction of statutory marriage laws in Nigeria, Islamic marriage was the other system of marriage, other than customary law, recognized and practiced by communities. Islamic marriages in Nigeria are primarily celebrated according to the jurisprudential principles of the Maliki school of thought, the prevalent Islamic jurisprudential school whose principles are widely applied by Muslim scholars in Nigeria. Herein we examine the rules governing marriages contracted under Islamic law from the Maliki jurisprudential viewpoint and how Nigerian Muslims strive to comply with these rules. Views of other orthodox Islamic schools of thought – *Hanafī, Hanbalī, and Shāfi'ī* – will be referred to when necessary and relevant. Significant reliance is placed on the jurisprudential treatises of Maliki scholars, among other works on Islamic family law.

We begin by observing that Islamic law in Nigeria is not codified, and any determination of how it regulates Islamic marriages starts from authoritative expositions of Islamic law. We then turn to preliminary legal marriage requirements, concentrating on the legal capacity of parties to enter into a marriage. Next to be examined are the essential elements that must be complied with to contract a valid Islamic marriage in Nigeria followed by an explanation of the various ways by which an Islamic marriage can be dissolved. Recommendations on how to improve the legal regime governing Islamic marriages in Nigeria are made.

MARRIAGE UNDER ISLAMIC LAW IN NIGERIA

Until recently, no part of Islamic law (Shariah) was codified in Nigeria. Even the attempts by some northern states to codify certain principles of Shariah were directed at Islamic criminal law.[1] Although the application of Shariah is recognized in the Nigerian Constitution through the establishment of the Shariah Courts of Appeal,[2] their jurisdiction is restricted to adjudicating matters within the purview of Islamic personal law.[3] The Constitution technically defers the power to legislate on Islamic marriage to the respective federated states. It provides that "the formation, annulment and dissolution of marriages other than marriages under Islamic law and customary law, including matrimonial causes relating thereto"[4] are preserved under the exclusive legislative lists[5]. This means that any matter relating to the formation, annulment and dissolution of Islamic law marriage falls under the residual legislative list within the sole purview of the state legislature. However, no state in Nigeria has adopted a law regarding the celebration of marriage or the administration of Islamic family law.

State legislatures are unable to enact family law codes for customary law and Islamic law mainly because of the high heterogeneity of customs in Nigeria.[6] Islamic law was, for a long time, treated as a variant of customary law in the

1 Some states in northern Nigeria attempted to codify certain principles of Islamic criminal law through the enactment of Shariah Penal Codes. The states include Zamfara, Bauchi, Borno, Gombe, Jigawa, Kaduna, Kano, Katsina, Kebbi, Niger, Sokoto and Yobe. For a full discussion, see generally Philip Ostien (ed.), *Sharia Implementation in Northern Nigeria 1999-2006: A Sourcebook* (2007), pp. 575-577; See also Philip Ostien and Albert Dekker, "Sharia and National Law in Nigeria", in Jan Michiel Otto (ed.), *Sharia Incorporated: A Comparative Overview of Twelve Islamic Countries in Past and Present* (2010), pp. 555-560.

2 Sections 260 and 275, 1999 Constitution of the Federal Republic of Nigeria.

3 Ibid., sections 262 and 275; See also Abdur Rahman I. Doi, *Islam in a Multi-Religious Society Nigeria: A Case Study* (1992), p. 212.

4 Item 61 of Part 1 of the First Schedule, 1999 Constitution of the Federal Republic of Nigeria.

5 Exclusive legislative lists comprise the list of matters for which only the National Assembly has exclusive power to legislate.

6 Interview with Abiodun Dada, Legal Practitioner and Principal Partner, Abiodun Dada and Co., (Isolo Opin, Kwara State, 5 September 2013); Interview with John Olusola Baiyeshea, Senior Pastor and Legal Practitioner, Testimony Chambers, Ilorin (Lokoja, Kogi State, 6 September 2013); Interview with Akin Akintoye, Legal Practitioner, Principal Partner, D. A. Akintoye & Co, Ilorin, (Ilorin, Kwara State, 26 September 2013).

country[7] and is still so treated by some legal stakeholders. The position, therefore, is that Islamic family law in Nigeria is not codified. The Nigerian Islamic law courts (where available) apply the rules of Islamic family law as contained in the classical books of Islamic jurisprudence, especially as espoused by the Maliki school of Islamic jurisprudence (*madhhab Maliki*).[8] Although the application of the Malik school of Islamic jurisprudence as the Islamic doctrinal school in Nigeria is a result of the historical path through which Islam was introduced in Nigeria, it has been institutionalized in the northern Nigeria states through the instrumentality of the Shariah Court of Appeal Law of the Northern Region.[9] No such law operates in southern Nigeria, mainly because none of these states has established a Shariah Court of Appeal, despite agitation by Muslims to do so.[10]

Muslims in Nigeria usually celebrate their marriages according to Islamic law principles as interpreted through the jurisprudence of the Maliki school. However, the general procedures for Islamic marriages differ from one part of the country to another. There is no homogenous way of celebrating an Islamic law marriage in Nigeria. The

[7] Umar A. Oseni, "Towards the Effective Legal Regulation of Waqf in Nigeria: Problems and Prospects", in Syed Khalid Rashid and Arif Hasan (eds.), *Waqf Laws and Management With Special Reference to Malaysia* (2012); see also A. A. Oba, "Islamic Law as Customary Law: The Changing Perspective in Nigeria", *International and Comparative Law Quarterly*, LI, (2002), p. 817; Y. K. Saadu, "Islamic Law is NOT Customary Law", *Kwara Law Review*, VI (1997), p. 136; L. A. Kelani, "Islamic Law and the Customary Law/Native Law: A Line of Distinction", *Unilorin Sharia Journal*, I (2000), p. 43.

[8] Titles include *Bidāyah al-Mujtahid wa Nihāyah al-Muqtaṣid, Bulūgh al-Marām, al-Murshid al-Mu'īn, Mudawwanah, Al-Qawaninu al-Fiqhiyyah, Al-Risala: A Treatise on Maliki Fiqh, Muwāṭṭa' Imām Mālik.* For details about the common books consulted by the Nigerian *Sharī'ah* judges, see Ahmed S. Garba and Philip Ostien, "Sixty Authoritative Islamic Texts in Use in Northern Nigeria", in Philip Ostien (ed.), *Sharia Implementation in Northern Nigeria 1999-2006: A Sourcebook* (2007), V, pp. 108-121.

[9] See sections 2 and 11, Shariah Court of Appeal Law (Cap 122 Laws of Northern Nigeria 1963), now adopted as part of the laws of the states forming the former northern Nigeria.

[10] Abikan Ibrahim Abdulqadir, "The Application of Islamic Law in Civil Causes in Nigerian Courts", *Journal of International and Comparative Law* (2002), p. 95; Doi, note 3 above, p. 213.

differences in procedures are as varied as the tribes and sub-tribes in the country. Shariah accommodates the continuous application of any custom or local tradition that is not contrary to express rulings and tenets of Shariah.[11] The Muslims in Nigeria use this as an opportunity to syncretize their customary practices with Islamic marriage procedures.

PRELIMINARY LEGAL REQUIREMENTS FOR MARRIAGE UNDER ISLAMIC LAW

The preliminary legal requirements of an Islamic marriage under the Maliki School include legal capacity and betrothal. The legal capacity to marry is with respect to age, marital status, gender, prohibited degrees of affinity and consanguinity, and religion. In marriage contracts, consent is usually treated as one salient aspect of capacity, but under Islamic law, it is embedded in the essentials of the marriage contract, hence, its absence from the above list.

Age of marriage

Regarding the age of the parties to marry under Islamic law, the Maliki School's position, which aligns with the other schools, is that marriage must be contracted between persons who have reached the age of puberty.[12] That is, they must be adults.[13] Upon reaching puberty, a Muslim male may enter into a marriage contract for the first time without requiring the consent of his parents or guardians.[14] A woman can also enter into a valid marriage contract that can be consummated immediately, but she requires her parent's or guardian's consent.[15] The Quran and Hadith are both silent on what constitutes the age of puberty; thus, certain

11 Abdur Rahman I. Doi, *Sharī'ah: The Islamic Law* (1984), p. 84.

12 Ibn Juzaiyy, *Al-Qawanīnu al-Fiqihiyyah* (2005), p. 161; see also Ala'eddin Kharofa, *Islamic Family Law: A Comparative Study with Other Religions* (2004), p. 62.

13 Kanam Yunus, "The Islamic Law of Marriage and Rights of Children under such Marriage", in Akinola Aguda and Isabella E. Adi (eds.), *The Marriage Laws of Nigeria* (1981), p. 11.

14 Ibn Juzaiyy, note 12 above, p. 161; see also Kanam, note 13 above, pp. 59, 62.

15 Ibn Juzaiyy note 12 above, pp. 162-163. See also Ibn Ashir, *Al-murshid al-Mu'in, Guiding Helper: Main Texts and Explanatory Notes* (2001-2002), p. 254, note 2272.

Maliki scholars posit that the couple could be of any age.[16] The majority of scholars suggest that the parties must attain puberty before they marry.[17] The Maliki scholars agree that puberty should be determined by certain anatomical and hormonal changes, such as when a male starts to experience wet dreams, develops a hoarse voice, and can impregnate a female.[18]

A female is deemed to have attained puberty when she menstruates or becomes pregnant.[19] The signs of puberty usually include the development of breasts in girls, the growth of a beard in boys, and the growth of pubic hair in either sex. Scholars, including the Maliki scholars, unanimously agree that where these signs fail to manifest, the determinant will be the age of the persons involved.[20] The scholars, however, diverge on the minimum age of puberty.[21] Imam Malik stipulated eighteen years as the age of puberty for both sexes, whereas scholars of other schools recommended between nine and eighteen years as the minimum age of marriage.[22] An examination of the opinions of the scholars of the Islamic orthodox schools shows that although scholars generally stipulate ages ranging from nine to eighteen,[23] the age of fifteen appears to be the most widely adopted among scholars and thus is the *ijmāʿ*.[24] This

16 Ibn Ashir, note 15 above.

17 Ibn Juzaiyy, note 12 above, pp. 161-162.

18 Kanam, note 13 above, pp. 56-58; Mahfuth Khamis Amafua, *Legal Capacity (al-Ahliyyah) between the Sharīʿah and Developmental Psychology* (2008), p. 14.

19 Kanam, note 13 above; Amafua, note 18 above.

20 Kharofa, note 12 above, p. 57.

21 Al-Imām ai-Juwainī, ʿAbd al-Malik, ibn ʿAbd Allāh, *al-Burhan fi Uṣūl al-Fiqh* (n.d), II, p. 716; see also Amafua, note 18 above.

22 Al-Qurṭubī, Abū ʿAbd Allāh Muḥammad bin Aḥmad, Al-Anṣārī, *al-Jāmiʿu li Aḥkam al-Qurʾān* (2002), III, p. 36.

23 See generally, Kharofa, note 12 above, pp. 57-58; David Pearl, *A Textbook on Muslim Law* (1979), p. 42-45.

24 Muhammad Zayd Al-Abyani, *Sharḥ al-Aḥkām al-Sharʿiyya fi al-ahwāl al-Shakhsiyya* (1992), II, pp. 225-226. See also Amafua, note 18 above, p. 14; In Islamic jurisprudence, *ijmāʿ* refers to "the unanimous consensus of the Muslim Ummah on a given issue, usually as represented by the agreement of the jurists". See New

shows that the Maliki School's view on the minimum age of marriage is in the minority.

Subject to certain conditions, the Maliki School permits a marriage contract between parties who have not attained puberty or where one has not yet attained puberty.[25] Thus, a minor can enter into a marriage, albeit with conditions. According to Imam Malik, with the consensus of other scholars, the first condition is the consent of the parents or guardian.[26] The second condition is that the parent or guardian must be the father[27] or one of the *aṣaba,* a male relation from the father's family.[28] The scholars place justification for allowing the marriage of a minor child on the verse of the Quran that states:

> And those of your women who have passed the age of monthly courses, for them the *'iddah* (prescribed period) if you have doubt (about their period) is three months; and for those who have no courses[29] (i.e., if they are still immature) their *'iddah* (waiting period) is three months likewise, (except in case of death) ...[30]

Ibn Kathīr and Zamakhshari, among other exegetes of the Quran, interpreted the underlined words as referring to young, immature females who have not menstruated.[31]

World Encyclopedia, *Ijma* (available online).

25 Ibn Juzaiyy, note 12 above, p. 161. See also Alhaji Umar Alkali, "An X-ray of the Conflicts between the Child's Right Act 2003 and Islamic Law on Child Marriage and Legitimacy", in Yusuf Dankofa (ed.), *Human Rights Review* (2012), p. 73; Kharofa, note 12 above, pp. 59-62.

26 Ibn Juzaiyy, note 12 above, pp. 161-162; Alkali, note 25 above, p. 73. See also Kharofa, note 12 above, p. 59; Baillie Neil Benjamin Edmonstone, *A Digest of Moohummudan Law* (1975), p. 7.

27 Al-Qayrawānī, 'Abdullah ibn Abi Zayd, *Matn Nazm al-Risala li Abi Zayd al-Qayrawani* (n.d.) (available online).

28 Doi, note 11 above, p. 142; Baillie, note 26 above, p. 7.

29 Emphasis added.

30 Q.65: 4 (Suratul Talaq). See Muhammad Taqi al-Din al-Hilali and Muhammad Muhsin Khan, *The Noble Qur'an in the English Language: A Summarized Version of At-Tabari, Al-Qurtubi, and Ibn Kathir with Comments from Sahih al-Bukhari* (1996), pp. 770-771.

31 See Ibn Kathir, *Tafsir Ibn Kathir* (2003), IV, p. 121; Abu Al-Qasim Muhammad

Although most Islamic scholars adopt this interpretation, a few view it differently. For instance, Shams Pirzada cannot fathom how the verse justifies contracting a marriage with a minor. He suggests that the phrase "Those who have not menstruated" should be understood to refer to women who do not menstruate due to illness or physiological challenges even though they have reached puberty.[32] In his view the verse is better understood when read together with Surah al-Ahzab verse 49, where Allah ruled that if a man marries a Muslim woman and divorces her before consummation of the marriage, the woman need not observe the usual waiting period required of widows and divorcees. This waiting period is known as *iddah*. Pirzada thus argues that naturally, a man who marries a minor cannot have sex with her as it is against Shariah and human nature.[33]

The preceding authorities suggest that only a female minor requires the consent of a parent to marry. This consent guarantees that the young girl's interest is protected and prevents her from being harmed and abused by her husband due to her vulnerability.[34] It is similarly argued that "the practice of child marriage was also fortified by the desire of Muslims to ensure that a girl was protected by marriage as soon as possible from being tempted into any immorality ...".[35] These female-centered opinions are discriminatory and do not reflect the general Islamic law position. The authorities mentioned above show that the minority view is not gender-based. The Maliki scholars rarely segregate the sexes when discussing the marriage of minors.[36] For instance, while commenting on the verse on

bin Umar al-Zamakhshari al-Khawarizmi, *Tafsir al-Kashaf An Haqa'iq al-Tanzil Wa Uyun Al-Aqawil Fi Wojuh Al-Ta'wil* (n.d.), IV, p. 1116.

32 Shams Pirzada, *Dawat ul Quran* (1991), p. 749.

33 Ibid.

34 Alkali, note 25 above, p. 73. See also Doi, note 11 above, p. 142.

35 Jamila Hussain, *Islam: Its Law and Society* (2011), p. 94.

36 See, for example, Ibn Juzaiyy, note 12 above, p. 161. For the position of scholars see Alkali, note 25 above, pp. 73-74; Kharofa, note 12 above; Baillie, note 26 above, p. 7.

marriage guardianship in *al-Murshid al-Mu'īn*, al-Hasani said:

> ... it is not necessary for the adult male groom to have a guardian for him (at the marriage ceremony) or to get permission for marriage from his parents; rather, adult males (those past puberty) may always marry at their own accord (however, adult males may still opt to have a representative speak on their behalf at the marriage ceremony).[37]

According to this commentary, only when a male becomes an adult does he not require the consent of a guardian; all minors require consent to marry. Furthermore, legal capacity (*al-Ahliyyah*) under the Shariah is generally divided into two; that is, the capacity for acquiring and inheriting rights and obligations (*Ahliyyah al-Wujūb*) and the capacity for executing one's rights against others and the establishment of other's rights against oneself (*al-Ahliyyah al-Ādā*). Each category is further subdivided into two, that is, complete legal capacity[38] and deficient or incomplete legal capacity.[39] These sub-categories are used to determine the level of obligation and liability a person can acquire at a particular period in their lifetime.[40] However, according to most Islamic jurists, including the Maliki scholars, a child, irrespective of gender, who has attained the age of discernment or discretion but not the age of puberty cannot contract a marriage without the permission of their guardian.[41] This is because such a child has not acquired full legal capacity.[42]

37 Ibn Ashir, note 15 above, p. 255.

38 Known in Arabic as *al-Ahliyyah al-Kāmila*.

39 Known in Arabic as *al-Ahliyyah al-Nāqiṣa*.

40 Imran Aḥsan Khan Nyazee, *Islamic Jurisprudence* (2000), p. 112; Imām Bukhārī Alaudīn Aḥmad, *Kashf al-Asrār an Uṣūl Fakhr al-Islām al-Bazdawī* (1994), IV, p. 411; Zuḥailī, Wahbah, *al-Fiqh al-Islāmī wa Adillatuhu* (1984), p. 121; Al-Mu'tazilī, Abū al-Ḥasan, Muḥammad, bin 'Ali bin al-Tayyib, Al-Basarī, *Al-Mu'tamad fi al-Uṣūl al-Fiqh* (n. d), II, p. 273.

41 Ibn Juzaiyy, note 12 above, p. 161; Ibn Qudāmah, Al-Maqdisī, 'Abd Allāh, bin Aḥmad, *Rawḍah al-Naẓir wa Jannah al-Munāẓir* (n. d), II, p. 48.

42 Amafua, note 18 above, pp. 12-17.

However, children who have attained the age of discernment are only allowed to enter into contracts that confer benefits on them. In other words, they cannot enter into any transaction that requires them to pay money or establishes a benefit in favor of another person and against the child.[43] A marriage contract falls within the kind of transaction that establishes rights and obligations both in favor and against the parties involved. This position is justified because a child at that stage lacks the intellectual ability to properly comprehend their rights and obligations in a marriage contract.[44] From the foregoing, the requirement of a guardian's permission for a child who has not reached the age of discernment or discretion to marry is not limited to only the girl child. It applies to both males and females.

According to the majority of scholars, including the Maliki school, if the *waliyy* (guardian for the purpose of marriage) contracts a marriage on behalf of a minor, the marriage will be binding on the minor even after the attainment of puberty and discretion.[45] However, when a girl reaches puberty, she is entitled to dissolve the marriage, especially where it was originally contracted on her behalf by a guardian other than her father and without her consent.[46] Similarly, a *waliyy*, other than the father, is not allowed to arrange the marriage of a minor girl until she reaches the age of puberty and gives her consent.[47] The author of *al-Risālah* cited *Mudawwanah* and *Mukhtasar* and the opinion of Ibn Nājī to show that Maliki scholars are of the opinion that a guardian can, however, arrange the marriage of a female minor when her father

[43] Al-Zarkashi, Badr al-Din, bin Muḥammad bin Bahawīr bin 'Abd Allāh, *Al-Bahr al-Muḥīṭ* (1992), V, p. 111. See also Amafua, note 18 above, pp. 13, 16.

[44] Ibn Qudāmah, note 41 above, p. 48; Muhammad bin Rushd, *Bidāyah al-Mujtahid wa Nihāyah al-Muqtaṣid* (1424/2003), II, p. 36.

[45] Imam Malik Bn Anas, *Al-Muwāṭṭa'* (2012), p. 540; Hadith No. 28.2.5 and Hadith No. 28.2.7. See also Baillie, note 26 above, pp. 7, 10; Alkali, note 25 above, pp. 73-74; and Doi, note 11 above, p. 123.

[46] An-Nasā'i, Ahmad bin Shu'aib bin 'Ali, *Sunan An-Nasā'i* (2007), IV, p. 118. See the case of *Bida v Bida* (June 1980) Shariah Law Reports 38 ff. See also Doi, note 11 above, p. 142 citing *Sunan Abu Dā'ud*, 12:25. See also James Norman Dalrymple Anderson, *Islamic Law in Africa* (1955), p. 192.

[47] Al-Qayrawānī, note 28 above, para 32.2b.

appoints him as the girl's marriage guardian in his will and also identifies the proposed husband in that will.[48]

In Nigeria, however, the marriage of minors is common, especially in northern Nigeria, where Muslims are in the majority.[49] The practice disproportionately affects young girls.[50] Thus, while boys are allowed to grow to full maturity before marrying, girls are often married off as soon as they show outward signs of puberty. In northern Nigeria, girls between the ages of nine and fifteen are married off, and in most cases, to elderly persons.[51] The parents who give away their minor children often claim that child and early marriages are permitted by Shariah and point to the example of the Prophet's (s.a.w.) marriage to A'isha (r.a.).The prevalence of this practice, especially in northern Nigeria, has resulted in various socio-medical implications for the girl child.[52] Recent surveys in Western and Eastern Nigeria show that the practice is drastically reducing among Muslims because more parents are sending their female children to school.[53]

48 Ibid.

49 UNFPA Nigeria, *Early Marriage in Nigeria* (available online); Udoka Okafor, *The Practice of Child Marriage in Nigeria* (2014) (available online); Girls Not Brides, *Maimuna's Story, Nigeria* (2013) (available online).

50 Iyabode Ogunniran, "Child Bride and Child Sex: Combating Child Marriages in Nigeria", *Nnamdi Azikiwe University Journal of International Law and Jurisprudence,* II (2011), p. 85.

51 For instance, in 2011, the Nigeria media was awash with the news of a 49-year-old Senator (also a former Governor of a state in northern Nigeria) who married a 13-year-old girl. See Al Jazeera, *Nigerian Senator Marries Girl of 13* (2010) (available online). See also Carol Ajie, "Overcoming Challenges of Senator Yerima's Child Marriage in Nigeria (2)", *International Bar Association Annual Conference Dublin* (2012).

52 Ogunniran, note 50 above, pp. 89-91; Gimba Victor Kyari and Joseph Ayodele, "The Socio-Economic Effect of Early Marriage in North Western Nigeria", *Mediterranean Journal of Social Sciences,* V, no 14 (2014), p. 582.

53 Canada: Immigration and Refugee Board of Canada, *Nigeria: Forced marriage among the Yoruba, Igbo, and Hausa-Fulani; Prevalence, Consequences for a Woman or Minor Who Refuses to Participate in the Marriage; Availability of State Protection* (2006)" (available online).

Gender of parties

Islamic law also requires that marriage must be contracted only between persons of the opposite sex, that is, a male and a female.[54] The basis for this is found in the Quran where Allah says, "And that He createth the two spouses, the male and the female; From a sperm drop when it is ejaculated ..."[55]

These verses point to the fact that the existence of humanity is naturally a result of intercourse between a man and woman. One primary purpose of marriage in Islamic law, aside from providing company and love,[56] is procreation. The Quran says that, "And Allah has made for you your mates of your own nature and made for you, out of them sons and daughters, and grandchildren, and provide for you sustenance of the best".[57] The Prophet Muhammad (s.a.w.), in a hadith, enjoined Muslim males to marry loving and fertile women so that their union would produce more children to increase the size of the Muslim population as compared to other nations.[58] To elucidate this position, Ibn Ashir explained in *Al-Murshid Al-Mu'īn* that:

> *Companionship* with (i.e. having a friend/companion of) the opposite gender *is a real* physical and psychological *need,* just like food and water *for almost* all *people.* This is because Allah has created the male and female as complements of each other from the time of 'Adam and Hawa'. As our din does not allow intimate friendships with unrelated people of the opposite gender, marriage is the offered alternative. Marriage provides a stable environment for raising a new generation of humans. Thus through marriage (lawful or unlawful) of a male and female, humans

[54] Hussain, note 35 above, p. 93; Muhammed Sodipo, "Virtues of Marriage in Islam", *Al-Maslaha,* I (1998), p. 73; Abdulkadir Orire, "Marriage in Shari'ah", in Aguda and Adi, note 13 above, p. 85.

[55] Quran 53:45-46 (Surah An-Najm).

[56] Quran 30:21 (Surah al-Rum).

[57] Quran 16:72 (Surah an-Nahl).

[58] Reported in *Musnad Ahmad, Sunan Abu Dā'ud* and others.

> will continue to have offspring until the Last Hour (by Allah's decree). Other methods of producing human offspring (e.g., laboratory-simulated conception, implanting embryos in women, cloning humans in a synthetic environment, simulating a woman's womb with a machine and letting the embryo/fetus fully grow in this machine, etc.) are not mandated by our din, and the safer position is that they should not be practiced.[59]

The above authorities show that sexual relations, and thus marriage between persons of the same sex, are considered unnatural, unlawful, and void under Islamic law.[60] The calls for recognition of the rights of lesbians, gays, bisexuals, and transgender persons are not supported by Islamic law.

Generally, Nigerians of all religious affiliations do not accept or recognize same-sex marriages. This rejection is based on their religious and cultural values,[61]and explains why most Nigerians applauded the law on the prohibition of same-sex marriage despite international condemnation.[62]

Marital status

Another preliminary requirement by Shariah is that the woman must not be in any other valid marriage[63] or within *'iddah* period[64] at the time of celebrating the marriage. Thus,

[59] Ibn 'Ashir, note 15 above, p. 252.

[60] See generally Jim Wafer, "Muhammad and Male Homosexuality", in Will Roscoe and Stephen O. Murray (eds.), *Islamic Homosexualities: Culture, History and Literature* (1997), p. 88; Scott Siraj Al-Haqq Kugle, *Homosexuality in Islam: Critical Reflections on Gay, Lesbian and Transgender Muslims* (2010), pp. 42-49.

[61] On the attitude of Nigerian Muslims and Christians to same-sex marriage, see Monday Ateboh, *Nigeria: Anti-Gay Law – Islamic Group Warns U.S., E.U Others to Leave Nigeria Alone* (2014) (available online); News Agency of Nigeria, *Nigeria: Bishop – Jonathan's Assent to Same-Sex Marriage Popular among Nigerians* (2014) (available online).

[62] See generally Rasheed Abubakar, *The World Reacts to Same Sex Prohibition Act ... as Nigerians Rejoice over End to Immorality* (2014) (available online); Yemi Adebowale, *The Storm Over Same Sex Marriage Prohibition* (2014) (available online).

[63] See Quran 4: 23 (suratun Nisa').

[64] See Mutalib Ahmad Ambali, *The Practice of Muslim Family Law in Nigeria*

the prospective wife must not be married at the time of the marriage proposal. This requirement is in line with the Quranic injunction that: "... do not make a secret contract with them except in terms honorable, nor resolve on the tie of marriage till the term prescribed is fulfilled".[65]

This verse prohibits a man from proposing marriage to a woman in *'iddah.*[66] A man must not be married to four wives when he proposes.[67] The difference in the treatment of the sexes is because whereas polyandry is not allowed under Islamic law, polygyny is permitted, but on condition that a man's wives must not exceed four at a time.[68] There is no divergence of opinion between the scholars of Maliki school and other orthodox schools regarding this issue. A few Muslims in Nigeria disregard this requirement and marry more than four. This phenomenon is common among wealthy Muslims and Muslim scholars. There are reports of Nigerian Muslims who marry between thirteen and eighty-six women.[69]

Prohibited degrees

Parties to a marriage under Islamic law cannot marry those related to them either by kinship or marriage. This legal proscription establishes the prohibited degrees of marriage under Islamic law. There are two types of prohibited marriage relationships under Islamic law: permanent and temporary prohibitions.[70] The basis for the permanent prohibition is found in the Quran, which stipulates that a person is forbidden from marrying his mother, daughter,

(1998), pp. 157-158.

65 Quran 2:235 (Surah al-Baqarah).

66 The *iddah* refers to a statutorily prescribed period that a divorced or widowed woman must wait before going into another marriage.

67 Ambali, note 64 above, p. 155.

68 Doi, note 11 above, pp. 144-153; Hammudah 'Abd al-Ati, *The Family Structure in Islam* (2008), pp. 109-127.

69 See for example, Claire Soares, *Man Condemned for Having 86 Wives Vows to Marry Yet More* (2008) (available online).

70 Doi, note 11 above, p. 124; Ambali, note 64 above, p. 158.

sister, father's sister (paternal aunt), mother's sister (maternal aunt), brother's or sister's daughter (niece), foster mother, foster sister, mother-in-law, step-daughter whose mother's marriage has been consummated, and daughter-in-law.[71] Although the prohibitions appear to be directed at males, they are of general application; they apply with equal force to females.[72]

On the other hand, a Muslim is temporarily prohibited from marrying his wife's sister, aunt, or niece while the marriage subsists. He may marry anyone in the preceding categories if the marriage collapses or his wife dies.[73] He is temporarily barred from marrying a married woman until she divorces her husband and exhausts her *'iddah* period.[74] Imam Malik and the other orthodox scholars are unanimous regarding this issue because it is a direct prohibitory injunction from Allah (s.w.t.).[75]

This Islamic principle is consistent with the existing customary marital practices in Nigeria. It is rare to find a Nigerian Muslim whose marriage falls within the Shariah-prescribed prohibited degrees. The customary laws in Nigeria prohibit marriage between persons who share either consanguineous or affinal relationships, however remote.[76] However, just as Islamic law, customary law permits a person to marry a partner's blood relations on the partner's death.

Once the parties are free from all the impediments highlighted, they are deemed to possess the legal capacity to marry. Either party can make the marriage proposal.

[71] Quran 4:23 (Surah al-Nisa').

[72] Muhammad Iqbal Siddiqui, *The Family Laws of Islam* (1994), p. 61.

[73] Ambali, note 64 above, p. 158; Siddiqui, note 72 above, p. 65; Doi, note 11 above, p. 125.

[74] Doi, note 11 above, p. 125; Ambali, note 64 above, p. 158; Siddiqui, note 72 above, p. 65-66.

[75] Ibn Rushd, note 44 above, pp. 61-75; Hasan Ayyoub, *Fiqh al-Usrah al-Muslimah* (1999), p. 86.

[76] See generally Margaret Chinyere Onokah, *Family Law* (2003), pp. 74-78; Itsejuwa Esanjumi Sagay, *Nigerian Family Law: Principles, Cases, Statutes and Commentaries* (1999), p. 825.

Betrothal

After the parties have satisfied the preliminary requirements, they may enter into the marriage contract. But where the parties are not ready for marriage, the Maliki school, with the consensus of other schools, allows them to be engaged to one another.[77] This is known as betrothal (*khiṭbah*).[78] Betrothal is recognized under Islamic law, although not in the form recognized by customary and common law. Under Islamic law, the parties to a marriage contract are required to have full knowledge and understanding of each other.[79] Therefore, the parties are allowed to examine one another, although the extent of the examination is subject to debate.[80] According to Imam Malik, supported by Imams Hanbal and Shafii, the parties are only allowed to examine the areas of the opposite sex's body that do not form part of their private parts with their consent.[81] Imam Malik ruled that a man can only look at the girl's face and hands.[82] Imam Abu Hanifa also ruled that he may also look at her feet.[83] Imam Malik's position is, however, endorsed by the majority of Scholars, including Ibn ʿAbbas and Imam Shāfiʿī.[84]

The Maliki school allows the parties to hold brief conversations to learn more about each other's culture, opinions, manners, and other qualities.[85] They prohibit

77 Ibn Juzaiyy, note 12 above, p. 159; Ibn Rushd, note 44 above, p. 23.

78 Ibid.

79 Siddiqui, note 72 above, p. 67; Dawoud Sudqi El Alami, *The Marriage Contract in Islamic Law* (1992) p. 12.

80 Hasan Ayyoub, note 75 above, p. 9.

81 Ibid., p. 10.

82 Ibid; Ibn Juzaiyy, note 12 above, p. 159; Ibn Rushd, note 44 above, p. 24; Al-Khurashī, Imām Muḥammad bin ʿAbd Allah bin ʿAlī al-Mālikī, *Hāshiyah al-Khurashī ʿalā Mukhtasar Sīdī al-Khalīl* (1998), IV, p. 122.

83 Ibid.

84 Hasan Ayyoub, note 75 above, p. 11.

85 Ibn Juzaiyy, note 12 above, p. 159; Hasan Ayyoub, note 75 above, p. 10.

the parties from having constant and repeated meetings[86] or from having these meetings without the presence of a third party, preferably a member of the girl's family.[87] The prohibition is based on the hadith of the Prophet (s.a.w.) that "never let a man be alone with a (strange) woman, for Satan will be their third (companion)".[88]

Betrothal in Islamic law marriage is recognized as a promise to marry in the future.[89] It is not a valid marriage, irrespective of whatever is exchanged between the parties.[90] Betrothal has no legal consequence, and either party may end the engagement.[91] An engagement is merely an informal agreement between the parties to marry upon fulfilment of the legal elements of marriage as stipulated by Shariah.[92] Therefore, unlike a statutory marriage, a breach of a promise to marry is not actionable.[93] By and large, the betrothal only prevents another man from proposing marriage to the girl except where the proposed marriage contract fails. This is based on the hadith narrated by Ibn Umar that the Prophet (s.a.w.) said: "A believer is a brother of a believer; hence it is not lawful for him to bargain upon the bargain of a brother, nor propose (the hand of a girl) on the marriage proposal of his brother until the latter (voluntarily) withdraws the proposal".[94] Thus, either party (including the girl's guardian) has the right to withdraw from the betrothal.[95] A

86 Ibid.

87 Hasan Ayyoub, note 75 above, p. 10; Muhammad Abdul-Rauf, *Marriage in Islam* (1989), p. 24.

88 Abu Amina Elias, *Hadith on Mahram: Men and Women Should Not Mix in Private* (available online).

89 Kharofa, note 12 above, p. 32; Kanam, note 13 above, p. 9.

90 Kanam, note 13 above, pp. 32-33.

91 Hussain, note 35 above, pp. 92-93; Kanam, note 13 above, p. 9.

92 Abdul-Rauf, note 87 above, pp. 23-24.

93 Kanam, note 13 above p. 9; El Alami, note 79 above, pp. 15-16.

94 Reported in Al-Shawkany, Muhammad Ali ibn Muhammad, *Nayl al-Awtar* (1983), part 6, Hadith No 1, p. 107; Abu Dawud, Sulayman Ibn al-Ash'ath al-Sajistani (Al-Azadi), *Sunan Abu Dawud*, part 2, hadith no. 2080, p. 228.

95 Hasan Ayyoub, note 75 above, p. 76.

man cannot make a marriage offer to a girl whose hand has been sought in marriage by another Muslim.[96] He should wait until the girl decides whether to accept or reject the existing offer before he makes his offer. This position claims authority from the hadith narrated above and another one narrated by Abū Hurairah where the Prophet (s.a.w.) said: "A man is not to propose to a girl already sought by another man till the latter either gets married to another girl or gives up his claim".[97]

The Maliki scholars are, however, divided on the legal implications of a marriage contracted with a betrothed woman while an existing betrothal subsists. Some argue that the marriage is not invalidated; others suggest that the marriage could be invalidated before consummation but once consummated, it becomes valid.[98] However, according to the majority of scholars, the marriage is valid since the ruling only affects *khiṭbah*, which is not a condition for the validity of the marriage.[99]

Betrothal courtship is common among prospective Muslim couples in Nigeria. However, there is a difference in the manner of the courtship in the northern and western parts of Nigeria. The marriage procedure generally begins among Muslims in the north with the selection of spouses. Whereas it is allowed for the boy to look for a suitable bride to marry, the prevalent practice is for parents to arrange marriages for their children.[100] This is done with the parties' consent because, in many cases, the boy is required to visit the girl to decide if he likes her.

[96] Ibid., p. 75; Ibn Juzaiyy, note 12 above, p. 159; Ibn Rushd, note 44 above, p. 24.

[97] Saheeh Bukhari, Hadith Nos. 4746, 5142 and Saheeh Muslim, Hadith No. 1412 (available online).

[98] Hasan Ayyoub, note 75 above, p. 76; Ibn Rushd, note 44 above, p. 24.

[99] Hasan Ayyoub, note 75 above, pp. 75-76; Ibn Rushd, note 44 above, p. 24.

[100] Interview with Falalu Abba, Legal Researcher, Umar Musa Yaradua University, Katsina, Nigeria (Kuala Lumpur, Malaysia, 10 August 2014); Interview with Alhaji Umar Alkali, Legal Researcher and Islamic Law Lecturer, University of Maiduguri, Maiduguri, Nigeria (Kuala Lumpur, Malaysia, 11 August 2014); Interview with Magaji Chiroma, Legal Researcher and Lecturer, University of Maiduguri, Maiduguri, Nigeria (Kuala Lumpur, Malaysia, 21 August 2014).

The girl's parents will also ensure that she approves of the boy. Once they approve of each other, the fiancé–fiancée relationship is formally established, enabling them to get to know each other better.[101] In this relationship, only the boy is allowed to visit the girl in her house. The girl is hardly allowed to visit the boy at all or alone.[102] In line with the requirement of Shariah to have a *maḥram* (chaperone or unmarriageable kin) around in such situations, anytime the parties have to meet, a young boy or girl will accompany the girl.[103] This practice is in line with the Shariah principle that a man and a woman should not be allowed to stay together in a lonely place lest Satan accompanies them.[104]

Among the Yoruba Muslims in western Nigeria, the process for contracting a marriage starts with the proposal, courtship, and betrothal stages. However, unlike before, where the selection of spouses was traditionally the prerogative of parents or the elderly in the family, parties can find suitable spouses for themselves.[105] Although parents may find suitable prospective spouses for their wards, the Yoruba Muslims tend to allow their male wards to find wives for themselves. This is to ensure that the proposed spouses are in love.[106] Until recently, pre-marriage intimate relationships were not allowed by the Yoruba people, both Muslims and non-Muslims. This was due to the importance attached to virginity.[107] The change in attitudes, especially with the increase in western education and values, has significantly reduced the value attached to virginity.[108]

101 Doi, note 3 above, p. 98.

102 Ibid.

103 Ibid.

104 Hasan Ayyoub, note 75 above, pp. 18-19.

105 Omobola C. Odejobi, "Influence of Socio-Economic Change on Marriage Norms in the Yoruba Society in Southwest Nigeria", *Academic Journal of Interdisciplinary Studies*, II, no. 3 (2013), p. 142.

106 Interview with Anifowoshe Mutalib, Chartered Accountant and Married (Gombak, Selangor, 22 August 2014); Interview with Sekoni Adeola Mutalib, Married (Gombak, Selangor, 22 August 2014).

107 Nathanie Akinremi Fadipe, *The Sociology of the Yoruba* (1970), pp. 81-84.

108 Alaba Olugboyega, *Understanding Sexuality in the Yoruba Culture* (2004).

Courtship is now common among Yoruba Muslims, and prospective couples can visit each other. It is common to find the girl visiting the boy's house and, in most cases, without being escorted by a male relative as required by Shariah. This is contrary to the prescription of the Prophet (s.a.w.) that a male and a female should not stay together in a secluded place, for Satan will always be their third party and may misguide them to commit acts prohibited by Islam.[109] The implication is apparent as many marriages are now arranged due to premarital pregnancy, and Muslim scholars condone this.[110]

Whereas the Hausa-Fulani tribes in northern Nigeria opposed western modernization to ensure that prospective couples keep within the confines of Shariah regarding pre-marriage courtship, the Yoruba Muslims in western Nigeria have embraced modernity and conduct marriages accordingly. This has encouraged pre-marital intimacy between couples.

FORMS AND ESSENTIAL ELEMENTS OF MARRIAGE CONTRACT UNDER ISLAMIC LAW

Notwithstanding performance of the preliminary legal requirements of marriage, a marriage will not be recognized as valid unless certain procedures are followed. A Muslim marriage must have contracting parties (*Al-Mahal*), who must exchange formal statements of an offer and a corresponding acceptance (*al-ijāb wa al-qubūl*). It must include a guardian (*waliyy*), a marriage gift (*mahr* or *ṣadāq*), and witnesses (*shuhūd*).

Contracting parties (*al-Mahal*)

First, to contract a marriage, the man and woman must have the capacity to enter into a legitimate marital union[111]

[109] Narrated by Ahmad and Tirmidhi, as cited in Hasan Ayyoub, note 75 above, p. 18.

[110] Olugboyega, note 108 above.

[111] Ambali, note 64 above, p. 142.

and desire to marry each other.[112] As the contracting parties,[113] they must be free from any legal impediment that may prevent them from marrying each other.[114] Neither party must suffer from a death-threatening sickness. The general position in the Maliki school is that a marriage celebrated by a sick person will be nullified by divorce before it is consummated, and the woman will not be entitled to anything.[115] However, where the marriage has been consummated, most Maliki scholars, including Ibn Najī, state that the woman will be entitled to her stipulated dowry.[116] In contrast, a few scholars, including Ibn al-Qāsim, state that she would only be entitled to a suitable dowry.[117] The parties must not be drunk or unconscious when performing the marriage contract.[118]

The parties to the marriage must be Muslims;[119] otherwise, the prospective husband will be asked to accept Islam before he can marry a Muslim woman.[120] According to Maliki scholars, a marriage between a Muslim woman and a non-Muslim man is invalid.[121] It is not forbidden for a Muslim man to marry a non-Muslim woman provided she belongs to one of the recognized scriptural religions like Christianity or Judaism (*kitābiyyah*).[122] If she does not belong

112 Ibn Ashir, note 15 above, p. 254.

113 Orire, note 54 above, p. 85.

114 Al-Shādhilī, Abu Hasān Al-Malikī, *Muqaddimah al-'Izziyyah* (1990), pp. 134-135.

115 Al-Qayrawani, note 27 above, ch 31.13a.

116 Ibid.

117 Ibid.

118 Ibn Ashir, note 15 above, p. 254.

119 Ibid.

120 Ibid.

121 Al-Shādhilī, note 114 above, p. 134; See also Ibn Juzaiyy, note 12 above, pp. 160-161.

122 Ibn Ashir, note 15 above, p. 254.

to any of these, she will be asked to accept one of these religions or Islam, before marrying a Muslim.[123]

It is unlawful for a Muslim male to have sexual intercourse with a *kāfir* woman (that is, someone who is not from the people of the book[124]).[125] The basis for this prohibition is the injunction in the Quran that, "do not marry idolatrous women until they believe".[126] Al-Qayrawānī identified the idolaters to include the Magians and the Sabeans, who deviated from Judaism and Christianity and worshipped angels, idols, the sun, and the moon.[127] However, Imam Malik ruled that one is not permitted to marry the *kitābiyyah*.[128] This position is supported by Ibn Umar, Ibn Abbas, and some contemporary scholars.[129]

Muslims in the northern and western parts of Nigeria have different attitudes toward fulfilling the requirements of Shariah regarding the parties to a marriage.[130] The Muslims in northern Nigeria do not always allow their wards to marry a non-Muslim, whether *kitābiyyah* or not.[131] For instance, a researcher maintained that the practice is so entrenched in his society that one cannot find any Kanuri person who marries a non-Muslim.[132] The northern Muslims

123 Ibid.

124 Referred to in Arabic as *ahl al-Kitāb.*

125 Ibn Juzaiyy, note 12 above, p. 161.

126 Quran 2:221 (Surah al-Baqarah).

127 Al-Qayrawanī, note 27 above.

128 Al-Jaziri, Abd al-Rahman Ibn Muhammad Awad, *Kitāb al-Fiqh 'alā al-Madhāhib al-Arba'* (al-Maktaba al-Assrya, n.d.), IV, p. 76.

129 Ibn Juzaiyy, note 12 above, p. 161; Yusuf Al-Qarḍawī, *al-Ḥalāl wa al-Harām fi al-Islām* (1977), p. 245.

130 The Northern part of Nigeria comprises three major tribes (Hausas, Fulanis, and Kanuris) and minor tribes. While the Hausa-Fulanis are found in all parts of northern Nigeria, the Kanuris are primarily found in the North-Eastern part of the country, especially Borno, Yobe, Gombe, Bauchi, and Adamawa states; The western part of Nigeria is primarily inhabited by the Yoruba people with different dialects such as ijebu, ijesha, ekiti, egba, oyo, ibolo, among others.

131 Interview with Magashi Awwal, Associate Professor, Bayero University Kano, Nigeria, (Kuala Lumpur, 20 August 2014).

132 Interview with Alhaji Umar Alkali, note 100 above.

are so strict in upholding this principle that they would not even allow their wards to marry a Muslim whose parents include a non-Muslim.[133]

Many Muslims among the Yoruba in western Nigeria are liberal with this principle; they allow their wards to marry non-Muslims provided they love each other.[134] The different attitudes are the result of the differentiated attitudes of both societies toward Islam and Christianity. While the Hausa-Fulani of the north adopted Islam and largely assimilated its principles and tenets into their cultures,[135] the Yoruba of western Nigeria separate religion from culture.[136] Similarly, whereas the Hausa-Fulani Muslims will ostracize any member of their families who converts out of Islam, the Yoruba believe all religions are from the same God, only that the people worship differently.[137] The Igbo Muslims of eastern Nigeria take a middle-course attitude toward the religious affiliation of their wards' prospective spouses. Like the Hausa-Fulani of the north, the Ibo Muslims in Eastern Nigeria do not give their daughters in marriage to non-Muslims, but their males marry non-Muslim girls.[138] The male Ibo Muslim marries the non-Muslim intending to convert her to Islam after the marriage.[139]

A related issue concerns how some Nigerians, including Muslims, prohibit their wards from marrying prospective husbands or wives because they come from a different tribe, ethnicity, region, or state. The Yoruba people, including the Muslims, are particular about the place of origin of their wards' proposed spouses. For instance, when the

133 Interview with Magashi Awwal, note 131 above.

134 Doi, note 3 above, p. 143.

135 Oluwole Agbede, "The Different Systems of Law: Nature and Basis of Conflict of Law", in Yemi Osinbajo and Awa U. Kalu (eds.), *Towards a Restatement of Nigerian Customary Law* (1991), p. 45.

136 Muhsin Adekunle Balogun, *Syncretic Beliefs and Practices amongst Muslims in Lagos State Nigeria: With Special Reference to the Yoruba Speaking People of Epe* (2011), p. 306 (PhD Thesis, University of Birmingham).

137 Ibid., p. 306.

138 Doi, note 3 above, p. 180.

139 Ibid.

prospective couple introduce each other to their biological parents or guardians, the latter will conduct background checks to ascertain the tribe, dialect, region, or state of the other.[140] This is because certain sub-tribes of the Yoruba people commonly oppose allowing their wards to marry from certain other sub-tribes, mainly due to historical prejudices.[141] For instance, an Ijebu man may not be allowed to marry an Egba woman or Ibadan lady, just as an Ondo man may not be permitted to marry a girl from Ogbomosho despite being from the same Yoruba tribe.[142] There are similar reports about the Hausas and the Kanuris.[143]

These marriage prohibitions are common to a majority of societies in Nigeria, although their practice is gradually declining. The attitude is not based on religious principles but cultural and historical prejudices.[144] It is known as *nasabiyyah* (tribalism or segregation based on ethnicity), which is not encouraged in Islam and is not one of the qualifying factors for marriage under the Maliki school.[145] Shariah allows inter-cultural marriage, especially where the prospective spouse is a Muslim. The Prophet (s.a.w.) was reported to have said: "If there comes to you a man whose religious commitment and character you approve of, then give your daughter's hand to him in marriage, and if you don't there will be tribulations in the land and great corruption".[146] Thus, according to the rules of Islam, a Muslim can choose a suitor from any part of the world.

140 Balogun, note 136 above, p. 306.

141 Ibid.

142 Ibid.

143 Interview with Magashi Awwal, note 131 above; Discussion with Garba Umaru, Senior Lecturer, University of Maiduguri, (Kuala Lumpur, Malaysia 17 October 2014).

144 Balogun, note 136 above, p. 306.

145 See the Quran 49:10 (Sūrah al-Ḥujurāt); See also Khurshid Ahmad, *Islām: Its Meaning and Message* (1977) p. 69; Akram Ḍiyā' Al-'Umarī, *Madīnan Society at the Time of the Prophet* (1995), pp. 233-234.

146 *Sunan Al-Tirmidhi, Hadith Nos. 1090-1091.*

Offer and acceptance (*Ijāb* and *Qabūl*)

The second requirement for a valid Muslim marriage is an express pronouncement of the intention to marry.[147] The marriage offer is to be made orally, and its acceptance must be expressed at the same venue where the offer was made.[148] Therefore, the groom, bride, and the bride's guardian must be at the same location during the marriage. According to Maliki scholars, it is not permissible to contract marriage over a long distance, with the parties communicating through indirect communication devices, such as telephones.[149] Online marriages are not permitted, according to the Maliki school. It is a common practice for Nigerians, including Muslims, to make marriage proposals in writing. The proposal letter is usually written to the head of the bride's family, who, in most cases, is not her biological parent.

Writing proposal letters is a contemporary customary practice and not necessarily a prescription of Shariah. However, some Maliki scholars consider it permissible to support the verbal marriage contract with a written marriage contract signed by the couple and their guardians. The contract contains the lawful marriage conditions stipulated by the couple and their guardians on both sides.[150] According to the Maliki school, the required verbal marriage contract must be customarily recognized as connoting marriage.[151] Thus, the party making the offer of marriage must state directly that they want to marry the other party. The party accepting the marriage offer must also respond similarly.[152] However, where the proposed party or the guardian is a person with a hearing disability, the Maliki school allows

147 Ibn Ashir, note 15 above, p. 254; Hammudah 'Abd al-'Ati, note 68 above, p. 60.

148 Ibn Ashir, note 15 above, p. 254, Ambali, note 64 above, pp. 143-144; Pearl, note 23 above, p. 41; Mahmud, Abubakar, "Marriage under Islamic Law", in Aguda and Adi, note 13 above, p. 100.

149 Ibn Ashir, note 15 above, p. 254.

150 Ibid., p. 256.

151 Al-Shādhilī, note 114 above, p. 136.

152 Ibn Ashir, note 15 above, p. 256.

them to write their intentions in legible form or make explicit motions with their hands.[153]

A female can make an offer of marriage. This is in line with the Sunnah of the Prophet (s.a.w.). Anas ibn Malik reported in a hadith that "A woman came to the Messenger of Allah and offered herself in marriage to him. She said: O Messenger of Allah, do you want to marry me?"[154] In another hadith,

> Sahl bin Sa'd said: 'I was among the people with the Prophet (s.a.w.) when a woman stood up and said: "O Messenger of Allah, she has offered herself in marriage to you, so see what you think of her." He remained silent and the Prophet (s.a.w.) did not give any answer. Then she stood up (again) and said: 'O Messenger of Allah, she has offered herself in marriage to you, so see what you think of her.' A man stood up and said: 'Marry her to me, O Messenger of Allah!' He said: 'Do you have anything?' He said: 'No.' He said: 'Go and look, even if it is just an iron ring.' So he went and looked then he came and said: 'I could not find anything, not even an iron ring.' He said: 'Have you memorised anything of the Quran?' He said: 'Yes, Sūrah such-and-such and Sūrah such-and-such.' He said: 'I marry you to her on the basis of what you have memorised of the Quran'.[155]

These hadiths indicate that a woman can offer herself in marriage to whomever she likes since this happened during the Prophet's (s.a.w.) lifetime, and he did not object. It has become a *sunnah al-Taqririyyah* (*sunnah* by tacit approval). But Nigerians, including Nigerian Muslims, believe it is an aberration for a woman to propose marriage to a man. The offer usually comes from the would-be husband.[156] A woman can enlist the support of a member of her family or a friend to help create a mutual connection between herself and a

[153] Ibid.

[154] An-Nasā'i, note 50 above, Hadith 3251, p. 113.

[155] An-Nasā'i, *Sunan*, note 46 above, Hadith 3282, p. 129-130.

[156] Kanam, note 13 above, p. 18.

man she likes; from there, the relationship may eventually ripen into marriage.

The express declaration of the offer and acceptance ensures that the consent of the parties, especially the woman, is obtained. Before the *waliyy* of the bride can make a declaration of acceptance of the marriage offer, he must ask the girl whether she desires to marry the man who seeks her hand in marriage. If the girl has never been married and does not answer the question, her silence is deemed to be an acceptance of the man as her husband. However, if the girl has been married before, she must respond because Shariah considers her experienced in marital affairs. In either case, if the girl does not approve of the suitor, she must explicitly state her rejection to the guardian, who may relay it to the man.[157] If the consent of either party, especially the girl, is not obtained and a marriage is contracted on their behalf, either party may repudiate the contract.[158] This is because, first, a sane adult Muslim male does not require the consent of his parents or guardian to marry.[159] Equally, a previously-married female who has passed the age of puberty does not need the permission of her father to remarry.[160] This is based on the hadith reported by Ibn ʿAbbās that the Prophet (s.a.w.) said:

> A previously married woman has more right to decide about herself (with regard to marriage) than her guardian, and a virgin should be asked for permission with regard to marriage, and her permission is her silence.[161]

Second, the Prophet (s.a.w.) annulled several marriages on the ground that the girls did not consent to the marriages. For example, in a hadith, a female companion, Khansāʾ bint Khidhām, narrated that her father married her off despite being previously married and unwilling. She went

157 Ibn Ashir, note 15 above, p. 254.

158 Uthman bn Uthayn, *Siraj al-Salik Sharh As-hal al-Masalik,* II, p. 43.

159 See Ibn Ashir, note 15 above, p. 255.

160 Ibid.

161 Reported in Al-Qayrawānī, note 27 above, ch 32.2c.

to the Messenger of Allah, and he annulled the marriage.[162] Similarly, the Prophet annulled the marriage of a virgin girl who was not previously married. It was narrated from 'Āishah that:

> A girl came to her and said: 'My father married me to his brother's son so that he might raise his own status thereby, and I was unwilling.' She said: 'Sit here until the Prophet (s.a.w.) comes.' Then the Messenger of Allah came, and I told him (what she had said). He sent word to her father, calling him, and he left the matter up to her. She said: 'O Messenger of Allah, I accept what my father did, but I wanted to know whether women have any say in the matter.[163]

The import of this narration is that the Prophet (s.a.w.) indicated that a father may not arrange the marriage of a virgin girl without her consent. If he does this, the marriage may be annulled.[164]

Traditionally in Nigeria, making an offer and accepting a marriage offer are primarily the responsibilities of the parents and families of the prospective couple. In the past, parents used to arrange marriages for their children.[165] This practice cuts across the different cultures in the country.[166] With the accommodation of acceptable customs by Shariah, this practice is retained by the Muslims in Nigeria, although with modification. Due to the changes in cultural norms resulting from urbanization, increasing education, and enlightenment, parents no longer play prominent roles in selecting partners for their children, especially in southwestern Nigeria. The parties can choose their partners and make offers and acceptances of marriage directly to each other. In Nigeria, the offer and acceptance of marriage

[162] An-Nasā'ī, note 46 above, Hadith 3270, p. 124; *Ṣahīh al-Bukhārī*, Book 43, Hadith 5138.

[163] An-Nasā'ī, note 46 above, Hadith 3271, pp. 124-125.

[164] Ibid., p. 125; Imām Ibn Hajār al-'Asqalānī, *Bulūgh al-Marām min 'Adillat al-'Ahkām* (2003); Hadith Nos 1017.

[165] A. K. Ajisafe, *The Law and Customs of the Yoruba People* (1924), p. 48.

[166] Ibid.

occur twice in almost all types of marriage, first between the prospective couple and then between the parents or families of the couple.

The offer and acceptance of marriage by the families is considered an essential element of marriage and is made publicly. For instance, in northern Nigeria, the offer for marriage is usually made by the boy's parents to the girl's parents or guardians. To make the offer, a delegation of men (generally excluding the boy's father) is sent to the parents of the girl to communicate their intention to marry their daughter for their son.[167] In some parts of northern Nigeria, the delegation is expected to present gifts of clothes, cosmetics, and shoes, among other items, to the bride as a symbol of the boy's interest in the girl.[168] This is called *kayan na gani ina so* (literally, "Gift for permitting me to see what I like")[169] or *kayan zance* (literally, "Gift for opening marriage conversation")[170] and is usually taken to the girl's house by women amidst singing and dancing.[171] Without these items, the girl's family will not receive the boy's delegation.[172]

After the marriage proposal is accepted, the boy's delegation is expected to pay the girl's parents a *kudin gaisuwa* (greeting or homage fee).[173] This payment is solely for the bride's parents and symbolizes the boy's parents' appreciation of the acceptance, opening the door for formal

[167] Interview with Falalu Abba, note 100 above; Interview with Alhaji Umar Alkali, note 100 above; Interview with Magaji Chiroma, note 100 above.

[168] Hafsat Sulaiman, "The Impact of the Hausa Customary Practices and/ or Payments on the Quantum of Consideration for Khul", *Journal of Islamic and Comparative Law*, XXVII (2006), p. 146.

[169] Ibid.

[170] Doi, note 3 above, p. 97.

[171] Interview with Alhaji Umar Alkali, note 100 above; Interview with Magaji Chiroma, note 100 above.

[172] Interview with Falalu Abba, note 100 above; Interview with Alhaji Umar Alkali, note 100 above. According to one respondent, it is impossible to even initiate a marriage process without having those materials available. The respondent noted that he had not witnessed any marriage where provision of these materials was waived.

[173] Doi, note 3 above; Sulaiman, note 168 above, p. 146.

discussions by both families.[174] In practice, the girl's parents are usually informed of the impending visit. Accordingly, they form a group to receive the boy's delegation.[175] The group of people constituted by the girl's family comprises male members of the girl's family, her father's friend, and a Muslim cleric from the girl's community.[176] The bride's parents' delegates do not act as the official *waliyy* of the girl. They only act as the *wakil* (agent) of the girl's father or guardian, who is the official *waliyy*.[177] This is permissible in Shariah and approved by Imams Malik, Hanbalī, Hammad, and al-Hasan.[178]

For the Muslims in the Yoruba land, the boy's parents approach the girl's parents to officially seek her hand in marriage.[179] A date is fixed for bringing both families together to make the official offer and acceptance and to formally betroth the boy and the girl; this is popularly referred to as "engagement". During the ceremony, the boy's family is required to produce certain customary items to solemnize the marriage. Such customary items include tubers of yam, bags of salt, fruits of all kinds, kola nuts, bitter kola, alligator pepper, bottles of honey, catfish, and electric fish, among other things.[180] Some Muslim families require that a bottle of alcohol, mostly *schnapps*, be provided alongside the other items.[181] This is contrary to the provision of Shariah that items used for solemnizing a marriage should not include unlawful things.

Traditionally, the items collected are used symbolically to pray for the couple and invoke blessings on the marriage.

174 Ibid.

175 Interview with Falalu Abba, note 100 above.

176 Ibid.

177 Ibid.; Interview with Alhaji Umar Alkali, note 100 above.

178 Hasan Ayyoub, note 75 above, pp. 33-34.

179 Interview with Anifowoshe Mutalib, note 106 above; Interview with Sekoni Adeola Mutalib, note 106 above. See also Doi, note 3 above, p. 141.

180 Interview with Anifowoshe Mutalib, note 106 above; See also Balogun, note 135 above, p. 306.

181 Balogun, note 136 above, p. 306.

Some Yoruba Muslims substitute these items with other items with Islamic connotations, such as a kettle, praying mat, rosary, and a copy of the Quran, which the officiating cleric uses to explain the significance of worshipping Allah to the couple, especially the bride.[182] The boy's family will be required to provide specified sums of money in order to be accepted by different groups of the bride's family.[183] The items prescribed must be delivered, otherwise, the offer will not be accepted, and the marriage will not be solemnized.[184] The collection of these items is customary without any direct support in Islamic family law, especially from the Maliki school's perspective, but Yoruba Muslims have made them a part of the primary requirements for marriage for two reasons. First, Yoruba Muslims are largely syncretists who mix Islamic principles with cultural principles because Islam accommodates certain established customs that align with Islamic rulings.[185] It is a common saying among the Yoruba Muslims that "*esin o pe k'ama s'oro*" (religion does not prevent us from performing our traditional rites). Second, the Muslim scholars encourage some of these practices for selfish economic reasons.[186]

Marriage guardian *(Waliyy)*

The third essential requirement of a valid Islamic law marriage is the presence of a *waliyy* for the woman.[187] According to the majority of Islamic jurists, including Màliki scholars, a woman cannot enter into a valid marriage contract without the permission of her *waliyy*.[188] If she

[182] Ibid., p. 313.

[183] Ibid., p. 306; Odejobi, note 105 above, pp. 140-141.

[184] Odejobi, note 105 above, p. 144. See also Interview with Anifowoshe Mutalib, note 106 above; See also Balogun, note 136 above, p. 306.

[185] Ismail Ayinla Babatunde Balogun, "Religion and Cultural Identity in Nigeria", in Adelumo Dopamu and Ade Odumuyiwa (eds.), *Religion, Science and Culture*, (2001), p. 141. See also Balogun, note 136 above, p. 306.

[186] Doi, note 3 above, p. 253.

[187] Ambali, note 64 above, p. 136.

[188] Imam Malik Bn Anas, *Al-Muwāṭṭa'*, note 49 above, p. 540, Book 28, Hadith Nos. 28.2.5, 28.2.6 and 28.2.7; Ibn Ashir, note 15 above, p. 254; Al-Qayrawani, note

does, the marriage will be void, notwithstanding that the marriage has been celebrated or the woman has given birth to several children.[189] The Maliki school bases its position on the principle of marriage narrated in *Sunan Ibn Majah thus*: "*Any* woman whose marriage is not arranged by her guardian, her marriage is invalid, her marriage *is* invalid, her marriage is invalid".[190] A similar principle narrated in the *Ṣahīh Bukhārī* states that: "No woman should arrange the marriage of another woman, and no woman should arrange her own marriage".[191]

However, according to Hanafī jurists, the role of a *waliyy* in a marriage is not compulsory for an adult woman who is sane, mature, and who appreciates the distinction between right and wrong.[192] The Shariah courts in Nigeria apply the Maliki School's position.[193] It should be noted that the according to the Maliki School, under no circumstance can a woman contract a marriage without the permission of her *waliyy*, whether she is a virgin or a matron, intelligent or stupid, freeborn or slave.[194] The *waliyy* must be a male adult Muslim who is free and sane.[195] The right of *waliyy* primarily resides in the father of the woman except where he is dead

27 above, ch 32.1a; Al-Shādhilī, note 114 above, pp. 132-133; Imām Ibn Hajār, note 164 above, Hadith Nos 1010 and 1011; Kanam, note 13 above, p. 20.

189 Al-Qayrawānī, note 27 above, ch 32.1a; Ibn Juzaiyy, note 12 above, p. 162; Ibn Ashir, note 15 above, p. 254; Al-Shādhilī, note 114 above, pp. 132-133; Imām Ibn Hajār, note 164 above, Hadith No. 1012; Doi, note 11 above, pp. 140-141; Doi, *Women in Sharī'ah*, (1990), pp. 34-35. See also the case of *Fatimo Igboo & Anor v. Baba Ogun* (1997) Sharia Court of Appeal Annual Report, pp. 136-137.

190 Imam Muhammad Bin Yazeed Ibn Majah Al-Qazwini, *English Translation of Sunan Ibn Majah* (2007) p. 78, Hadith 1879.

191 Ibid., p. 79, Hadith 1882. See also Imām Ibn Hajār, note 164 above, Hadith No. 1015.

192 Ibn Juzaiyy, note 12 above, p. 162; Doi, *Shari'ah: The Islamic Law*, note 11 above, p. 140; Jamal J Nasir, *The Islamic Law of Personal Status* (1990), p. 50.

193 See the cases of *Jimoh Adigun v. Awawu Ajika & Oba Owolabi* (1995) Sharia Court of Appeal Kwara State Annual Report, p. 25; *Fatimo Igboo & Anor v. Baba Ogun* (1997) Sharia Court of Appeal Annual Report, pp. 136-137. Ibn Juzaiyy, note 12 above, p. 162.

194 Ibid.

195 Al-Qayrawānī, note 27 above, ch 32.1a; Ibn Ashir, note 15 above, p. 254; Al-Shādhilī, note 114 above, pp. 132-133.

or permanently incapable of performing his duty in this regard.[196] Where this is the case, his duty may fall upon any of his male relatives, failing which it falls on the State through the judge.[197]

According to most Maliki scholars, the girl's father has the power of compulsion (*ijbār*)[198] to marry his daughter, whether virgin or previously married, to whoever he wishes without consulting her.[199] This view is based on the hadiths in *Muwāṭṭa*ʾ that:

> Yahya related to me from Malik that he had heard that al-Qasim ibn Muhammad and Salim ibn Abdullah were marrying off their daughters and they did not consult them. Malik said, "That is what is done among us about the marriage of virgins." Malik said, "A virgin has no right to her property until she enters her house and her state (competence, maturity etc.) is known for sure.[200]

Another hadith reported that:

> Yahya related to me from Malik that he had heard that al-Qasim ibn Muhammad and Salim ibn Abdullah and Sulayman ibn Yasar said about the virgin given by her father in marriage without her permission, "That is binding on her."[201]

A few Maliki scholars, however, opine that it is recommended (*mustaḥab*) that he seeks his daughter's consent.[202] The Shariah courts in Nigeria appear to align

[196] Ibn Ashir, note 15 above, p. 254.

[197] See Assayid 'Uthman Al-Ju'aliy Al-Malikiy, *Sirajus Salik, Sharhu As-halul Masalik* (1982), II, p. 38.

[198] This is the power given by Shariah to only a father (or in some cases paternal grandfather) to marry out a girl without necessarily seeking her consent before doing so.

[199] Al-Qayrawānī, note 27 above, ch 32.2a.

[200] Imam Malik Bn Anas, note 45 above, p. 540, Book 28.2.6.

[201] Ibid., Book 28.2.7.

[202] Ibn Juzaiyy, note 12 above, p. 163; Al-Qayrawānī, note 27 above, ch 32.2a.

with the latter position, as demonstrated in the cases of *Karimatu Yakubu & Anor v Alhaji Yakubu Tafida Paiko & Anor*[203] and *Idrisu Ibrahim v Ndamakun Mama Jiya.*[204] In *Karimatu Yakubu,* the first appellant (Karimatu), a nineteen-year-old girl, was married to the second respondent by her father (first respondent) without her consent. She objected to the marriage, ran away, and moved into the house of second appellant whom she wanted to marry. She filed an action in court to nullify her marriage with the second respondent. Both the trial court and the Upper Area Court granted her claim, but the Shari'ah Court of Appeal reversed the decision. She appealed to the Court of Appeal, which relied on the authorities in *Bahjah* and *Risalah* to hold that, although the majority opinion of Maliki scholars is that the father has the power to compel his virgin daughter to marry without her consent, if she has attained puberty (at least fourteen years), it is desirable that he consults her to confirm if she agrees to the marriage.[205] The court thus overruled the two earlier decisions and nullified the marriage between Karimatu and the second respondent.

In *Idrisu Ibrahim,* the appellant's daughter was raised by the respondent. After her primary school education, the girl expressed her wish to marry. One Adamu proposed to her, and she agreed to marry him. He then sought the consent of the appellant, which was denied. After all efforts to get the appellant's consent failed, the matter was referred to the Etsu of Patigi (the traditional ruler of their community), who ordered that the marriage should be celebrated with the respondent acting as the representative of the guardian. The appellant sued for the nullification of the marriage. The trial court dismissed his claim, so he appealed to the Shariah Court of Appeal. The Shariah Court of Appeal held that because the girl had consented to the marriage, the appellant should not unreasonably withhold his consent. And since

[203] Court of Appeal, Kaduna Judicial Division, (11 December 1985).

[204] (2011) Kwara State Shariah Court of Appeal Annual Reports, pp. 284-299; See also *Ramatu Baba v Alh. Mustafa Alamu* (1994) Kwara State Sharia Court of Appeal Annual Report, pp. 39-41.

[205] See also *Alhaji Isa Bida vs. Baiwa the daughter of Alhaji Isa Bida,* Northwestern State Shariah Court of Appeal (19 March 1971).

his consent was unreasonably withheld, the marriage was valid.

Apart from the father, other categories of persons that are eligible to act as *waliyy* for a bride include her son, grandson, full brother, paternal half-brother, full brother's son, paternal half-brother's son, paternal grandfather, paternal uncle, paternal uncle's son, an upright Muslim adult male in the community, an imam, a scholar, religious leader, or a judge.[206] The suitability of the *waliyy* depends on his closeness to the bride.[207] Apart from the father, however, all other categories of *waliyy* do not have the power to marry the girl to anyone until she reaches puberty and her consent is sought.[208] Some Maliki scholars argue that a *waliyy* appointed by the father can exercise the power of compulsion (*ijbār*) on the girl, subject to two conditions. First, the father must have expressly authorized him to do so and second, the father must have specified the proposed husband.[209]

In practice, Muslims in Nigeria, like other non-Muslims, consider the permission of the father of the prospective couple, especially the woman's, as an essential element of marriage. Without permission, the marriage will not be considered valid. The principle of Shariah corresponds with customary practices in this regard. Due to the paternalistic nature of Nigerian societies in general, where the father is not available to perform the role of the *waliyy*, the responsibility automatically falls on other male members of the family based on kinship proximity.

206 Ibn Juzaiyy, note 12 above, pp. 162-163; Imam Malik Bn Anas, *Al-Muwāṭṭa'* (2012) 540 Book 28.2.5; Ibn Ashir, note 15 above, p. 254; Al-Qayrawānī, note 27 above, ch 32.1a.

207 Abu al-Hasan Ali ibn Abd al-Salam al-Tassuli, *Al-Bahjah fi Sharh al-Tuhfah ala al-Urjuzah al-Musamah bi Tuhfat al-Hukkam* (1951), p. 79; Muḥammad bn Aḥmad Dah al-Shinqītī, *Fatḥ al-Raḥīm 'ala Fiqh al-Imām Mālik bi al-Adillah* (1969), p. 35. See the case of *Adama Gidado v. Musa Mohammed Yola*, CA/J/21s/91, Court of Appeal, Jos Judicial Division delivered by the Sharī'ah panel of the Court of Appeal, Jos Division, per Uthman Mohammed, PJ (as he then was), pp. 33-34.

208 Al-Qayrawānī, note 27 above, ch 32.2b; Ibn Juzaiyy, note 12 above, p. 163.

209 Ibid.

This is also in accordance with the principle of Shariah. For example, under the Hausa-Fulani and the Yoruba marriage practices, the parents or the prospective groom's family must visit the prospective bride's parents or family to seek their permission to marry the girl. This is notwithstanding any previous agreement between the prospective couple themselves. The exercise of absolute power of *ijbār*, waning among the Yoruba people, is still applied by the Hausa-Fulani tribes, especially those who live in rural communities. This is evident in the prevalence of early and child marriages in northern Nigeria. Moreover, in some tribes in Nigeria, permission to marry the girl is often not given directly by the biological parent of the girl. In many instances, the biological father delegates the right to give permission to marry to other male members of his family, especially the family heads.[210] Such a person, however, cannot be regarded as the official *waliyy* of the girl. He only acts as the agent (*wakīl*) of the girl's father or guardian, who is the official *waliyy*.[211] This is permissible in Shariah and approved by Imams Malik, Hanbalī, Hammad and al-Hasan.[212]

Dower (mahr or ṣaddāq)

The fourth requirement is the husband's presentation of a dower to the wife.[213] The dower is any lawful property given or promised to be given by the husband to the wife as a sign of his commitment to their marriage and to make the consummation of the marriage lawful.[214] The Maliki School, along with other orthodox schools, unanimously agrees that payment of dowry is an obligatory step in celebrating

[210] Interview with Falalu Abba, note 100 above; Interview with Alhaji Umar Alkali, note 100 above; Interview with Magaji Chiroma, note 100 above.

[211] See Doi, note 3 above, p. 141. See also Interview with Anifowoshe Mutalib, note 106 above; Interview with Sekoni Adeola Mutalib, note 106 above; Interview with Falalu Abba, note 100 above; Interview with Alhaji Umar Alkali, note 100 above.

[212] Hasan Ayyoub, note 75 above, pp. 33-34.

[213] Ambali, note 64 above, p. 136.

[214] Ibn Juzaiyy, note 12 above, p. 165; Doi, *Sharī'ah: The Islamic Law*, note 11 above, p. 159.

a marriage.[215] The various express injunctions in the Quran regarding the payment of dowry justify this position. Allah (s.w.t.) said in the Quran that, "O Prophet! We have made lawful to thee thy wives when thou have paid their dowries "*'ujur*"..."[216] Allah (s.w.t.) also said:

> ... And lawful to you are [all others] beyond these, [provided] that you seek them [in marriage] with [gifts from] your property, desiring chastity, not unlawful sexual intercourse. So for whatever you enjoy [of marriage] from them, give them their due compensation as an obligation ...[217]

Allah (s.w.t.) further said that:

> And give to the women (whom you marry) their Mahr (obligatory bridal money given by the husband to his wife at the time of marriage) with a good heart ...[218]

In addition to the Quran injunctions, there are several hadiths of the Prophet (s.a.w.) stressing the importance of the presentation of the dower in an Islamic marriage.[219] Based on all these authorities, the scholars unanimously agree that the dower must be agreed before the marriage is consummated,[220] specified by the two parties, and handed over to the wife, who keeps it as her property.[221] Any marriage where the parties agree to non-payment of dower will be invalid if discovered before consummation.[222]

215 Ibn Rushd, note 44 above, p. 43.

216 Quran Chapter 33:50 (Suratul al-Ahzāb)

217 Quran Chapter 4:24 (Suratul an-Nisā ').

218 Quran Chapter 4:4 (Suratul an-Nisā '); See also Quran Chapter 4:25 (Suratul an-Nisā ').

219 A1-Bukhari, Muhamrned Ibn Ismaiel, *Sahih Al-Bukhari* (Muhammad Muhsin Khan (Tr.) (1997), VII, pp. 64-66, Hadiths 5148-5150. See also Imam Malik Bn Anas, *Al-Muwāṭṭa'*, note 45 above, pp. 540-544, Book 28, Section 3.

220 Ibn Rushd, note 44 above, p. 43; Al-Qayrawānī, note 28 above, ch 32.10b; Doi, note 11 above, p. 159.

221 See Quran Chapter 4:4 (Suratul an-Nisa'); See also Ibn Juzaiyy, note 12 above, p. 165 and Hussain, note 35 above, p. 98.

222 Al-Shādhilī, note 114 above, p. 134.

However, if the marriage has been consummated, it will be made valid by mandating the husband to give the wife the dower equivalent to that given to women of her social status.[223] This is known as *Ṣaddāq mithl* and is calculated based on the dower given to her sisters, paternal aunts, and uncle's daughters, according to her family's social position.[224] Therefore, according to the Maliki School, the payment of the dower is not to validate the marriage; it is required to legalize the consummation of the marriage.[225] According to the Maliki School, the dower is expected to be determined and paid when the marriage contract is concluded, otherwise, it must be paid afterwards.[226]

The dower, however, must be paid out of lawful objects capable of being possessed or bought.[227] Any marriage conducted upon the dower of unlawful objects such as pigs, dead animals, stolen goods, and intoxicants is null and void.[228] The dower may be tangible or intangible property or a mixture of both.[229] The dower should be in the form of valuable objects;[230] it could be given in the form of cash, liquid assets, material possessions (for example, a ring, a necklace, a vehicle of transportation, books, clothes, and so on), or may be a combination of these.[231] Neither the Quran nor hadith specifies the amount or the value of the dower.[232] However, Imam Malik stipulates that the minimum dower should be equivalent to three dirhams of silver or a quarter

[223] Abu Bakr Jabir Al-Jaza'iri, *Minhaj al-Muslim* (2001), p. 327. See also Al-Qayrawānī, note 27 above, ch 32.10b.

[224] Doi, note 11 above, pp. 160-161.

[225] Ibn Juzaiyy, note 12 above, p. 165; Al-Shādhilī, note 114 above, p. 134; Al-Qurṭubī, note 22 above, p. 43.

[226] Ibn Juzaiyy, note 12 above, p. 165; Doi, note 11 above, pp. 160-161.

[227] Ibn Juzaiyy, note 12 above, p. 165.

[228] Ibid.; Doi, note 11 above, p. 165.

[229] Ibn Juzaiyy, note 12 above, p. 165.

[230] Ibid.; Doi, note 11 above, p. 164.

[231] Ibn Ashir, note 15 above, p. 255; Ibn Juzaiyy, note 12 above, p. 165.

[232] Doi, note 3 above, p. 163.

of a dinar of gold.[233] This was calculated to be equivalent to 1.06 grams of gold.[234] But a majority of scholars, including Imam Shāfiʿī, Imam Hanbalī, and Isḥaq insist that there is no minimum amount in respect of what can be given as dower. The latter opinion notwithstanding, the scholars unanimously agree that one need not request an exorbitant dowry, especially when the man cannot afford it.[235]

Nonetheless, Muslims in northern Nigeria collect exorbitant dowry from the groom and his family. Customarily, on the date fixed for the marriage, the bridegroom is required to provide three main items: the dower, bride price,[236] and *kayan lefe*.[237] The dower is usually given in money.[238] Most Hausas use the minimum dowry allowed in Shariah, which is currently about thirty thousand Naira, to determine how much should be paid.[239] However, the Kanuri people do not always collect money for the dower.[240] They collect gold jewelry, which, if converted into money, usually costs more than one hundred thousand Nigerian Naira.[241] The dower is given to the wife together with another gift called *kayan lefe*.[242] This gift usually consists of clothes, cosmetics, shoes, bags, jewelry, and other accessories, and is larger in

233 Ibn Juzaiyy, note 12 above, p. 165.

234 Ibn Ashir, note 15 above, p. 255.

235 Hasan Ayyoub, note 75 above, p. 40. See also Jade Mohammed, "Women and Islam in Southern Nigeria: Between Shariah and Culture", in Wole Abbas and Jade Mohammed (eds.), *Women, Islam and Current Issues in Development,* (2009), p. 43.

236 Locally known as "*dukiyan aure*" and translated as "marriage property"; Doi, note 3 above, p. 97; Sulaiman, note 168 above, p. 146.

237 Interview with Falalu Abba, note 100 above; Interview with Alhaji Umar Alkali, note 100 above; Interview with Magaji Chiroma, note 100 above. See also Doi, note 3 above, p. 98; Sulaiman, note 168 above, p. 146.

238 Interview with Falalu Abba, note 100 above; Interview with Magaji Chiroma, note 100 above.

239 Interview with Falalu Abba, note 100 above.

240 Interview with Alhaji Umar Alkali, note 100 above.

241 Ibid.

242 Sulaiman, note 168 above, p. 146; See also Interview with Falalu Abba, note 100 above.

quantity than the *kayan na gani ina so*.[243] This gift usually costs hundreds of thousands of Nigerian Naira. The bride price comprises another sum of money that must be given to the bride's parents and other items like kola nuts and sweet candies.[244] Although the items collected as part of the bride price vary from locality to locality, money must be paid.[245] In some cases, the money is used to help the couple to furnish their residence and purchase foodstuffs.[246]

Although the collection of these items may be justified based on custom and as part of the betrothal process, most Muslim families in northern Nigeria accepted these items as requirements for marriage, without which the marriage contract is not allowed.[247] This practice is supported by Shariah on a principle that marriage conditions must be based on what is customary to the parties. Any customary practice in a marriage contract that does not contravene the Shariah must be complied with.[248] Although there is a divergence of opinion among Islamic scholars on whether betrothal gifts are recoverable, some scholars of the Maliki School support the return of such gifts, especially where they form part of the customary requirements of marriage.[249] This particular view is stated in *As-hal al-madārik sharḥ Irshād al-Sālik*, where it is opined that all the items collected form part of the dower:

> Whatever the man offers in addition to the dower in the form of gifts before or during the solemnisation

243 Sulaiman, note 168 above, p. 146; See also Interview with Falalu Abba, note 100 above; Interview with Alhaji Umar Alkali, note 100 above.

244 Doi, note 3 above, p. 97; Sulaiman, note 168 above, p. 146.

245 Doi, note 3 above, p. 97

246 Sulaiman, note 168 above, p. 146.

247 Ibid., p. 154; See also Interview with Falalu Abba, note 100 above; Interview with Alhaji Umar Alkali, note 100 above; Interview with Magaji Chiroma, note 100 above.

248 Islam's Women, *The Marriage Contract* (available online).

249 See (2011) *Medinat & Alamoyo v Jamiu Adam* Kwara State Shariah Court of Appeal Annual Reports, p. 260.

> of the marriage shall be treated as *sadāq* and so is whatever is taken by custom of the people.[250]

Similar provisions are found in Islamic texts such as *Iḥkām al-Aḥkām*[251] and *Taysīr al-'allām*[252] that the validity of dower is founded upon both the Shariah prescriptions and acceptable customs of the parties.

Other scholars of the Maliki School argue that such items, once given, are collateral gifts and can no longer be recovered. In *Iḥkām al-Aḥkām 'ala sharḥ al-Ḥukām*, the view is expressed that:

> Whatever a man gives to his wife in form of ornaments, cloths (consumable and perishable) which were referred to as gifts shall not be retrieved except where the marriage is terminated before consummation.[253]

Shariah courts in Nigeria have applied the two positions. The first was applied in the case of *Medinat & Alamoyo v Jamiu Adam*,[254] where the respondent, as plaintiff, sued the appellants for the recovery of the sum of thirty-one thousand Naira, being the expenses incurred during the period of betrothal between him and the first appellant. The trial Shariah court ruled that the defendants should refund the sum of five thousand Naira to the plaintiff, hence the appeal. Although the Shariah Court of Appeal overturned the trial court's decision on a procedural irregularity, it nevertheless agreed with the view expressed in *As-hal al-madārik sharḥ Irshād al-Sālik* that the betrothal gifts are reclaimable.

250 Emphasis added. See Abubakr bn Hassan al-Katsinawiy, *Ashalul Madārik Sharḥ Irshād al-Sālik* (1995), II, p. 110.

251 Taqiyuddin Ibn Daqiq al-'Id, *Ihkam al-Ahkam Sharh Umdat al-Ahkam* (1995), cited in Ahmad Muhammad Shakir and Hamid al-Faqi, *Shuruh Umdat al-Ahkam* (2009), p. 417.

252 Abdullah Ibn Salih Aal Bassam, *Taysir al-Allam Sharh Umdat al-Ahkam* (Maktabat al-Tabi'een, Cairo 2006), cited in Ahmad Muhammad Shakir and Hamid al-Faqi, note 251 above, p. 419.

253 Attasuli, Ali bn Abdussalam Abul Hasan, *Al-Bahjah Fi Sharh Al-Tuhfah* (1991) 107, cited (though wrongly as *Ihkam al-Ahkam 'ala Sharh al-Hukkam*) in *Halima Tswayan v Tsawayan Mamudu* (2012) Kwara State Shariah Court of Appeal Annual Reports, pp. 10-11.

254 *Medinat & Alamoyo*, note 249 above, p. 261.

The second position was applied in the case of *Halima Tswayan v Tsawayan Mamudu,*[255] where the appellant sought khulʿ.[256] The respondent agreed to it, but claimed the return of ninety-six thousand and two hundred Naira as the money he expended in marrying the appellant. The trial court ordered the plaintiff/appellant to refund the sum of seventy thousand and two hundred Naira. The plaintiff was dissatisfied and appealed to the Shariah Court of Appeal. According to Maliki school jurisprudence, the appellate court held that the money expended during the marriage is generally divided into two: claimable and unclaimable.[257] The claimable fund must, however, not exceed the amount agreed to by the parties as dowry.[258] Any other amount given to the wife, her parents or family, other than the dowry, is not recoverable because it was given to win the woman's love or strengthen the marital relationship.

The first position is dominant in northern Nigeria because among the Hausa-Fulani tribes, when a woman seeks divorce by *khulʿ*, the husband usually claims a refund of the extra payments as part of the dowry, and the courts often grant such claims.[259] For instance, in the case of *Indo Alhaji Ibrahim v Danladi Ali,*[260] the husband paid forty Naira as dowry along with the other customarily required properties. The marriage produced one child. When the wife sought divorce by *khulʿ*, the husband claimed a refund of two hundred and forty-eight Naira and fifty-three Kobo being the expenses he incurred during the marriage ceremony. The trial court ordered the wife to refund the

255 *Halima Tswayan,* note 253 above.

256 This is the term used to describe the process of divorce initiated by the wife against her husband.

257 *Halima Tswayan,* note 253 above, pp. 9-10.

258 Ibid. The court relied on the authority of the opinion in Abi Abdullahi Muhammad ibn Ahmad al-Mayyara al-Fasi al-Malikiyy, *Sharh al-Mayyarat al-Fasi ala Tuhfat al-Hukkam fi Nukt al-Uqud wa al-Ahkam* (n.d.), I, p. 224, where Imam Malikī is reported to have said that "I have not seen any woman being demanded to pay more than her dowry to get release (khul'u Divorce)".

259 Sulaiman, note 168 above, pp. 153-154.

260 (1970) The Shariah Court of Appeal of Plateau/Borno State Law Report, p. 13ff.

sum of eighty Naira only. The husband appealed to the Upper Area Court and subsequently to the Shariah Court of Appeal in Jos. Although both courts held that expenses incurred on gifts are not refundable, they ordered the woman to refund the sum of one hundred and twenty Naira to the husband. Furthermore, it is reported that the courts are more amenable to the first position.[261]

Notwithstanding the positions of the Maliki scholars, the Prophet (s.a.w.) disapproves of the husband claiming more than what was agreed as the dower.[262] However, some companions such as Ibn ʿAbbās and Ibn ʿUmar, as well as a majority of scholars, including Imam Malik, Shāfiʿī, Ḥanafī, and Ḥanbalī, agree that if the woman chooses to give more than her dower, the husband is permitted to accept it.[263]

The mode of giving the dower is different among the Yoruba. Until recently, the dower was usually fixed by the bride's parents.[264] Presently, the prospective bride is allowed to request what she would like to receive as her dowry from her prospective husband.[265] Commonly, the bride considers her proposed husband's capability before asking for the dowry. There are cases where some brides request a copy of the Quran, *Bulūgh al-Marām* or even ask their prospective husbands to memorize some parts of the Quran.[266] This is common among the enlightened contemporary Muslim youths who strive to follow the deeds of the Prophet (s.a.w.). A majority of Yoruba Muslim youth who are not very enlightened in the religion usually request money, whereas others request items like a sewing machine or even

261 Sulaiman Hafsat spoke to several divorced women and personally observed judicial proceedings. She found that the courts always ruled that the wives should refund every amount expended by the husband, including the value of the properties he gave as *kayan lefe*; See Sulaiman, note 168 above, pp. 153-154.

262 Hasan Ayyoub, note 75 above, p. 283; Sulaiman, note 168 above, p. 155-156; *Halima Tswayan*, note 253 above.

263 Hasan Ayyoub, note 75 above, p. 282; Sulaiman, note 168 above, p. 156.

264 Doi, note 3 above, p. 141.

265 Interview with Anifowoshe Mutalib, note 106 above; Interview with Sekoni Adeola Mutalib, note 106 above.

266 Ibid.

a car, depending on the financial resources of the husband and his family.[267]

Although the Yoruba Muslims know that giving the dower can be postponed, this is rarely done because the Yoruba (including the Muslims) frown upon a marriage where nothing is given. Yoruba Muslims, just as the entire Yoruba people, consider the dower payment as the seal that makes the husband the legitimate father of any child born during the marriage.[268] Although this was the established traditional philosophy for collecting dowry during the pre-Islamic era, it corresponds with the views of Maliki scholars (including those of other schools), that intercourse will only be legitimate in a marriage when the dower has been fixed or paid.[269] Yoruba Muslims consider the payment of the dower significant to the legitimacy of marriage so much that even if parties originally contracted a marriage without the permission of the parents, but the dower was later paid and accepted, the marriage is valid. This is not in accordance with the ruling of the Maliki school, which invalidates a marriage without the permission of the bride's guardian. There are, however, few instances where some Muslims gratuitously give their daughters in marriage to a Muslim man whom they believe cannot afford to marry or as a gift to a scholar. In such instances, the girl's consent is not sought as she is "taken" without prior notice and handed over to the putative husband. All marriage conditions, including receipt of dowry, are forgone by the father.

Witnesses (Shahādah)

The last requirement is the presence of witnesses. Islamic jurisprudence unanimously requires that at least two credible witnesses bear testimony to the marital union between the parties.[270] This requirement is based on the

[267] Ibid.

[268] Doi, note 3 above, p. 141.

[269] Ibn Juzaiyy, note 12 above, p. 165; Al-Shādhilī, note 114 above, p. 134; Doi, note 11 above, p. 160-161.

[270] Al-Khurashī, note 82, p.126; Hasan Ayyoub, note 75, p. 38; Kanam, note 13, pp. 27-28; Doi, note 3 above, p. 138.

injunction contained in the narration of ʿĀʾisha (r.a.) that the Prophet (s.a.w.) said, "marriage is invalid without a guardian and two upright witnesses".[271] It is also narrated by Ibn Abbas (r.a.) that the Prophet (s.a.w.) said: "whores are those who conduct their own marriage without proof".[272] The proof mentioned in this ḥadith refers to either the two witnesses or the guardian.[273]

Imam Malik and the other three Orthodox schools agree that witnessing is a condition of marriage under Shariah.[274] Although the imams differ on whether its conditionality is for the legitimation of consummation of the marriage or whether it relates to the validity of the marriage, they are unanimous that a secret marriage is not allowed under the Shariah.[275] In fact, Imam Malik ruled that if the witnesses know of a marriage, but keep it a secret, the marriage will be considered a secret marriage and accordingly invalid.[276] But according to Hanafī and Shafiʿī, it does not amount to a secret marriage and is thus valid.[277] According to the Maliki school, the requirement of the witnesses is a condition for the legitimization of the consummation of the marriage and not for the validity of the marriage contract.[278] The witnesses must bear testimony to the celebration of the marriage at the same time. However, the Maliki scholars opined that if the witnesses are not present at the place of the marriage contract, it is sufficient if they are informed thereafter by the

271 Narrated by Ad-Daraqutni and Al-Bayhaqi, quoted in Hasan Ayyoub, note 75 above, p. 37. Note that this hadith was also traced to Ibn 'Abbas in Ibn Rushd, note 44 above, p. 42.

272 Narrated by Tirmidhi.

273 Hasan Ayyoub, note 75 above, p. 37.

274 Ibn Rushd, note 44 above, p. 42.

275 Ibid.

276 Ibid. See also Orire, note 54 above, 86.

277 Ibid.

278 Ibn Juzaiyy, note 12 above, p. 160; Al-Shādhilī, note 114 above, p. 134; Al-Qayrawānī, note 27 above, ch 32.1c; Ibn Ashir, note 15 above, p. 256. See also Mahmud, note 148 above, p. 66.

parties or their guardians, but until that happens, the party must not consummate the marriage.[279]

Based on the requirement of the hadith, the Maliki School ruled that the witnesses must be upright.[280] Imam Shafi'ī and other schools supported the position, but Imam Hanafī disagreed and argued that a marriage could be validly concluded based on the testimony of unrighteous and dishonorable witnesses[281] because the objective of Shariah in requiring witnesses is only for a declaratory purpose.[282] The witnesses are also required to be adult males and sane.[283] Imam Malik ruled that it is not allowed for a marriage to be witnessed by a man and two women.[284] The Maliki scholars, however, opined that where legally acceptable witnesses are not available, the marriage should be celebrated in the presence of a lot of witnesses, at least between thirty and forty people.[285] To comply with the requirement of witnesses, either party shall organize a marriage feast, though it is more incumbent upon the husband. This is considered a *Sunnah al-Mu'akkadah* (imperative Sunnah),[286] and is also a form of publicizing the marriage[287] based on the instruction of the Prophet that "make the marriage publicly known, and perform it in the mosque, and beat at it with duff".[288]

Generally, in Nigeria, a marriage ceremony is witnessed by many people invited by both families. This applies to all

[279] Hasan Ayyoub, note 75 above, p. 38; Al-Qayrawānī, note 28 above, ch 32.1d; Ibn Ashir, note 15 above, p. 256.

[280] Ibn Juzaiyy, note 12 above, p. 160; Ibn Rushd, note 44 above, p. 42; Hasan Ayyoub, note 75 above, p. 38.

[281] Ibid.; Ibn Juzaiyy, note 12 above, p. 160; Ibn Rushd, note 44 above, p. 42.

[282] Ibid.

[283] Ibn Ashir, note 15 above, p. 256.

[284] Ibn Juzaiyy, note 12 above, p. 160.

[285] Al-Qayrawānī, note 27 above, ch 32.1c.

[286] Ibn Juzaiyy, note 12 above, p. 160; Hasan Ayyoub, note 75 above, p. 53. See also Doi, note 3 above, p. 140.

[287] Al-Khurashī, note 82 above, p. 126.

[288] Narrated by Tirmidhī, Hadith No. 1089.

cultural groups in the country. Although Shariah requires the presence of at least two witnesses, the Muslims in Nigeria, like other members of their society, prefer to involve many people in the marriage for two reasons. First, marriage is a family affair; all members of the extended family, paternal and maternal, and friends are invited to grace the occasion.[289] Second, it is difficult to determine who is present just for the purpose of witnessing a marriage.[290]

DISSOLUTION OF MARRIAGES UNDER ISLAMIC LAW IN NIGERIA

The Shariah legal system operates on the basis of human idiosyncrasies; it recognizes human frailties and, accordingly, the need to dissolve a marriage. Although the Shariah envisages marriage as a permanent contract, it recognizes instances where the continuation of the marriage is not in the interest of the parties and indeed would contravene the objectives of Shariah. Under Shariah, both parties have the right to dissolve the marriage. However, the marriage must be dissolved for a compelling reason,[291] though revealing the grounds for the divorce is not obligatory.[292] Under the Shariah there are different modes of dissolution; some are judicially dissolved, while others are dissolved extra-judicially.[293] The different modes of dissolution of marriage under Shariah include (1) *Talaq* (the divorce activated at the instance of the husband), (2) *Khul'* (divorce instituted by the wife), (3) *li'an* (divorce by mutual recrimination and imprecation, that is, after a husband denies the paternity of a child or accuses the wife of marital infidelity), (4) *'ila* (divorce activated by husband's vow of continence, that is, vow to abstain from sexual relations with the wife for a period beyond four months), and (5) *Zihar* (divorce occasioned by the husband

289 Muhib O. Opeloye, "The Yorùbá Muslims' Cultural Identity Question", *Ilorin Journal of Religious Studies*, I, no. 2 (2011), p. 1.

290 Interview with Magaji Chiroma, note 100 above.

291 Abd al-Ati, note 68 above, p. 224.

292 Ibid.

293 Ambali, note 64 above, p. 268.

deliberately comparing his wife's sexuality with that of any women whom he is permanently prohibited to marry).[294]

In Nigeria, only the *talaq* and *khul'* modes of dissolution are common. Sociologically, the practice of *Zihar* does not seem to be prevalent among Nigerian communities. Although the practices culminating in *'ila* and *li'an* are recurrent, parties do not consider them as constituting the dissolution of their marriages. Therefore, there are couples whose marriages have been legally dissolved but who consider themselves married. This reflects ignorance on one part and syncretization of religious rules with customary values on the other.[295] A majority of the divorce processes and proceedings among Muslim couples occur outside of court, though the volume of divorce cases presented before the Shariah/Area courts in the northern region and the Shariah Arbitration Panels in the southern region, particularly south-west is high. According to Shariah, either party is allowed to initiate the divorce process.

For the *talaq*, the husband has the right to unilaterally repudiate the marriage, whereas for the *khul'*, the wife must request that the husband frees her from the marriage bond.[296] Where the husband activates the *talaq*, he cannot collect anything already given to the wife as a symbol of his love, particularly the dower.[297] On the other hand, a wife who requests *khul'* would ordinarily be required to return the dower given by the husband;[298] but the need to return the dower by the wife is not absolute. This requirement would be dispensed with where the wife's request was

294 F. H. Ruxton, *Maliki Law: Summary of Mukhtasar of Sidi Khalil* (2004), p. 131.

295 Balogun, note 136 above, pp. 306, 313.

296 Ruxton, note 294 above, p. 131.

297 In the Quran, Chapter 4:20, Allah warned the husbands not to collect anything from their divorced wives even if they had given them "a heap of gold" (*al-Qintar*) as marital gifts.

298 The requirement is legally founded upon the injunction of Allah in the Quran Chapter 2:229 and the Prophet's sunnah in the hadith of Thabit bn Qays and Habibah bint Sahl reported by Imams Malik, Ahmad, Bukhari, and others. See Ayyoub, note 75 above, pp. 279-280.

borne out of established acts of domestic violence.[299] After a *talaq* is pronounced, the wife must remain with the husband for a period of three menstrual cycles.[300] During this period, she is not obliged to perform any uxorial role, yet the husband must maintain her during the period. The objective of the waiting period is primarily to foster reconciliation, which is easier when the parties see themselves from a new perspective but at close quarters.[301] Except in certain circumstances, the process of reconciliation and revocation of the divorce is not strictly formal but must be activated before the expiration of the *'iddah*.[302]

RECOMMENDATIONS

In view of the nature of Islamic law (which itself is more or less a written law), it is recommended that to avoid the imprecision involved in the process of applying Islamic family law and curtail the commixture of the rules of Shariah with unacceptable customary norms, there is need for codification of the Islamic family law. The codification would contribute to the proper regulation of Muslim family law in the country.

Because the rules and conditions of the marriage contract have been expressed in the Quran, the recorded Sunnah of the Prophet, and the numerous books of Islamic legal scholars, some believe that further codification would be superfluous.[303] But the patriarchal and paternalistic attitude of Nigerians, which is more pronounced by syncretization of culture with Islamic values,[304] have pushed the Muslims to

[299] Ruxton, note 294 above, p. 123; Asaf Ali Asghar Fyzee, "Family Law", in Majid Khadduri, Herbert J. Liebesny, and Robert H. Jackson (eds.), *Law in the Middle East* (1955), p. 147.

[300] This is called *'iddah* (waiting period) in Shari'*ah*.

[301] Abd al-Ati, note 68 above, p. 246.

[302] Ambali, note 64 above, pp. 276-277.

[303] Zanariah Noor, "Gender Justice and Islamic Family Law Reform in Malaysia", *Kajian Malaysia, Jld*, XXV, no. 2 (2007), p. 125.

[304] See generally Abdul-Fattah Kola Makinde, *The Institution of Sharī'ah in Oyo and Osun States, Nigeria, 1890 – 2005* (2007), pp. 173-174 (PhD Thesis, University of Ibadan); Balogun, note 136 above, pp. 243-318.

disregard many of the principles of Islamic family law. For instance, some parents still collect the dower and distribute it among their family members. Some parents still attempt to marry off their daughters without their consent, while others unreasonably withhold consent for personal reasons. Most divorces are made extra-judicially without due regard to the legal processes stipulated by Shariah.

The problem with these practices is not the absence of Islamic rules regarding each matter highlighted, but the fact that the enforcement of these rules is seen more from a moral than a legal perspective.[305] In view of these abuses and misapplication of the principles of Islamic family law, it would be desirable to have, by way of reform, a code embodying those rules.[306] This position is supported by the views of many contemporary jurists of Shariah.[307]

CONCLUSION

Marriage is an aspect of culture. In Nigeria, each of the three systems of law has rules regulating marriages contracted according to its tenets. The laws and practice of Islamic marriage in Nigeria have been described by introducing the substantive rules of Islamic family law while analyzing how those rules are applied in practice by Nigerian Muslims, particularly the Yoruba and Hausa.

The legal basis for the operation of the Islamic family law in Nigeria is the 1999 Constitution of the Federal Republic of Nigeria, which recognizes the establishment of Shariah Courts of Appeal and gives the federating states the legislative power to enact laws on both Islamic and customary marriages. Unfortunately, no state has seized this opportunity. As a result, Nigeria has no codified state

[305] Noor, note 303 above, p. 125.

[306] Anandamoy Bhattacharjee, *The Muslim Women (Protection of Rights on Divorce) Act,* (1986), pp. 33-34; Noor, note 303 above, p. 135.

[307] Noor, note 303, p. 121; Isa Mohammed Dodo, "Judicial Administration of Customary Law – A Sharia View Point", in Yemi Osinbajo and Awa U Kalu (eds.), *Towards a Restatement of Nigerian Customary Law* (1991), p. 251; Bhattacharjee, note 306 above, pp. 33-34; James Norman Dalrymple Anderson, "Modern Trends in Islam: Legal Reform and Modernisation in the Middle East", *International and Comparative Law Quarterly*, XX (1971), p. 15.

law on Islamic marriage. Muslims and Shariah judges rely on the principles of Islamic family law buried in the various and numerous books of Islamic jurisprudence.

The Islamic principles have been set out that regulate Muslim marriages in Nigeria. This chapter does so by critically analyzing and synthesizing Islamic sources often referred to by Islamic scholars in Nigeria, particularly Maliki Islamic scholars whom a greater number of Nigerian Muslims follow. At its root, a Muslim marriage is a contract constituted by an offer and an acceptance, with accompanying consideration in the nature of gifts exchanged between the parties. Therefore, the preliminaries that give the parties the capacity to contract an Islamic marriage were first examined. Issues of consent and the heteronormativity of Islamic marriages were considered and some attention given to the acts that constitute an offer and an acceptance of marriage, which, whether made orally or in writing, must be unequivocal. Using instantaneous means of communication to convey either is discouraged.

The discussion of dower concludes that the dower and bride price have been heavily influenced by cultural attitudes and practices, especially among Yoruba Muslims. For the actual solemnization of Islamic marriages, the necessity is stressed of having witnesses present. Whereas Islamic scholars generally agree that witnesses should be upright persons, the debate is unsettled regarding the effect of having unrighteous persons present. However, this debate is academic as many Islamic marriages, which are usually family affairs, are celebrated before numerous family members and friends.

As with any contract, the dissolution of a marriage cannot be ruled out. The modes of divorce available to Muslims in Nigeria are considered, including the *talaq*, *khul*, *ila*, and *lian*. Each mode of divorce can only be initiated under specific conditions by specific parties. Attention is drawn to the effects of the absence of a codified law on Islamic family law in Nigeria. That the lacuna has resulted in many Muslims violating the rules of Islamic family law and replacing them with distorted cultural notions that are not in tune with the principles of Islam. In any case, finding out what the rules are is as tedious as it is impossible because one will have to burrow through many Islamic sources that might even conflict in some detail. The various states in the Federation must make honest attempts to cure the unsatisfactory state of affairs through the codification of the salient principles of Islamic family law. Not only will a legislative intervention compel Muslims to obey the principles to which they have subscribed, the law will also have to be accessible and useful, especially for Shariah judges who adjudicate disputes pertaining to Islamic marriages.

Kenya

Chapter Seven
Islamic Marriages in Kenya

The Marriage Act 2014 (Marriage Act) is Kenya's primary codified law governing marriage and family relations.[1] The Act recognizes five types of marriages: civil, customary, Christian, Hindu, and Islamic.[2] Whereas Christian, Hindu, and civil marriages are monogamous, the Islamic and customary marriages are potentially polygamous.[3] The five types of marriages enjoy the same legal status under the Act,[4] and are all required to be registered.[5] Although the Marriages Act recognizes these different types of marriages, it only provides the general principles governing them. The actual solemnization of each type of marriage is regulated by the distinct legal system under which it is celebrated. Effectively, legal pluralism exists in Kenya, with State laws and customary and religious laws existing side by side.[6]

Islamic marriages do not specify the minimum age of marriage, are potentially polygamous, and allow unilateral divorce (*talaq*) by the husband, with the wife entitled to seek divorce only on specific grounds. In certain instances, marriages take place without the consent of the bride and groom as long as a male guardian, especially the father and grandfather, approves the marriage.[7] The main contours of Islamic marriages outlined above are at odds with the prescriptions of the Constitution, which provides for

1 Act No. 4, 2014 Laws of Kenya.

2 Section 6(1), Marriage Act.

3 Ibid., section 6(2) and (3).

4 Ibid., section 3(3).

5 Ibid., section 12.

6 Kevin Odimbe Wanyonyi, "The Kadhis' Courts in Kenya Towards Enhancing Access to Justice for Muslim Women", University of Lund Student Paper (2016), p. 8.

7 Musawah, *Comparative Legal Review of Impact of Muslim Family Laws on Women across Commonwealth Asia and Africa* (2019), pp. 114-116.

equality, non-discrimination, eighteen years as the minimum age of marriage, and voluntary marriage and divorce. The Marriage Act and international human rights conventions to which Kenya subscribes echo similar sentiments as the Constitution.[8]

However, despite the Marriage Act regulating all marriages in Kenya, it is significant that Muslims enjoy specific accommodations both in the Constitution and the Act. These accommodations, explored in detail herein, exempt Muslims from some provisions of the general law on marriages and divorces. It may be argued that these exemptions protect a minority Muslim population whose practices regarding marriages and divorces are not widely shared by the rest of the population. Some Christian leaders and scholars argue that Islamic marriages and divorce are favored over other religious marriages and divorces, thereby violating fundamental constitutional and human rights norms on equality and religious freedom.

The present chapter assesses the principles of Islamic family law in Kenya vis-à-vis the general legal framework regulating marriages and divorces in Kenya. Though religious accommodation is necessary to guarantee the practice of religion, it is contended that the accommodations granted to Muslims, apart from being unjustified, undermine fundamental constitutional and human rights principles on equality and non-discrimination, especially before, during, and at the dissolution of marriages.

First examined are the relevant provisions of the Kenya Constitution, the Marriage Act, and other laws on marriage and divorce. This is followed by a consideration of the rights and obligations of parties in Islamic marriages. The Islamic practices on marriage and divorce are reviewed in relation to national and international human rights

[8] Such legislation includes the Children's Act 2022 and the Sexual Offences Act 2006. International human rights treaties ratified by Kenya include the Convention on the Elimination of Violence against Women (CEDAW), International Covenant on Civil and Political Rights (ICCPR), International Covenant on Social and Economic Rights (ICESCR), Convention on the Rights of the Child, and the Protocol to the African Charter on Human and People's Rights on the Rights of Women in Africa (Maputo Protocol), and the African Charter on the Rights and Welfare of the Child (ACRWC).

instruments, focusing primarily on the accommodations given to Muslims by the Constitution and the Marriage Act. Last, recommendations on balancing the rights of Muslims to practice their religion, on one hand, and the requirements of other Kenyan laws and international human rights conventions, on the other hand, are proposed.

BACKGROUND

Kenya does not have a specific codified law guiding Islamic marriages and family relations.[9] The 2009 Census on Population and Housing revealed that Muslims in Kenya constitute 11.1% of the population,[10] with some Muslim groups placing the percentage at about 30%.[11] There are different Islamic sects in Kenya. About 73% of Kenyan Muslims belong to the *Sunni* sect and adhere to the *Shafi'i madhab* school of Islamic jurisprudence, with a smaller percentage belonging to the *Hanafi* and *Shi'a* communities that follow the *Ja'fari, Zaydi,* and *Ahmadi* jurisprudence.[12] The result is that there is no universally accepted Muslim jurisprudence governing marriage, divorce, and inheritance in Kenya. These areas are governed by the *Shari'ah* and other schools of jurisprudence, as interpreted according to the individual Kadhis courts' understanding of the relevant issues.[13] The reliance on different schools sometimes results in different and unpredictable decisions and judicial precedents.

Article 170(5) of the Kenya Constitution states that questions of Muslim law relating to marriage, divorce, or

[9] Musawah and Advocacy for Women in Peace and Security Africa (AWAPSA), *Joint Report on Article 16, Muslim Family Law and Muslim Women's Rights in Kenya* (2017), p. 5 (available online).

[10] Kenyan National Bureau of Statistics - Ministry of Planning, National Development and Vision 2030, *2009 Kenya Population and Housing Census, Population and Housing Census* (available online).

[11] United States Department of State, B*ureau of Democracy, Human Rights, and Labor, Kenya: International Freedom Report* (2007) (available online).

[12] Ngala Chome, "From Islamic Reform to Muslim Activism: the Evolution of an Islamist Ideology in Kenya", *African Affairs*, CXVIII, (2019), pp. 535–536; Musawah – AWAPSA, note 9 above, pp. 4 and 6.

[13] Wanyonyi, note 6 above, pp. 20-24.

inheritance are determined by the Kadhis courts when all the parties profess the Muslim religion and submit to the Kadhis court's jurisdiction. Section 5 of the Kadhis' Courts Act[14] echoes the same. Article 165 of the Constitution gives the High courts original and appellate jurisdiction in civil matters. These courts have jurisdiction over issues pertaining to Muslim law.

The inclusion of Kadhis courts in the Constitution and the accommodations given to Muslims were highly contentious during the talks before the final drafting of the 2010 Constitution. Opposition was mainly voiced by Christian and other religious leaders who argued that Kenya was a secular State with a secular constitution and lacked room for religious structures.[15] On the other hand, Muslims were determined to have specific rights included in the Constitution.[16] Among the questions in issue in the constitutional referendum of 2010 were the exemptions given to Islamic practice and the inclusion of the Kadhis courts in the court structure; these questions were approved by Kenyan voters in the referendum.[17]

LEGAL FRAMEWORK FOR MARRIAGES AND DIVORCES IN KENYA

General provisions applicable to all marriages in Kenya

The Marriage Act, the primary Act governing marriages in Kenya, sets specific requirements for the different types of marriages. These requirements are aligned with the provisions in the Kenyan Constitution.

Regarding the marriage age, Section 4 of the Act specifies that a person shall not marry unless they are eighteen years. This section is based on Article 45(2) of the Constitution,

14 Cap 11, Laws of Kenya.

15 Anne Cussac, "Muslims and Politics in Kenya: The Issue of the Kadhis' Courts in the Constitution Review Process", *Journal of Muslim Minority Affairs*, XXVIII (2008), p. 297.

16 Ibid., p. 300.

17 Alan Masakhalia Wanga, *The Kenyan Constitutional Referendum of 4th August 2010: A Case Study* (2011).

which states that a marriage must be between adults. The Constitution, the Marriage Act, and the Children's Act uniformly define a child as a person below eighteen years.

The union must be voluntary. Section 3(1) of the Act defines marriage as the voluntary union of a man and a woman, whether in a monogamous or polygamous union and registered under the Act. The Act reiterates Article 45(2) of the Constitution, which states that every adult has the right to marry a person of the opposite sex based on their free consent.

Another relevant requirement is the equality of rights for both spouses. Section 3(2) of the Act stipulates that parties to a marriage have equal rights and obligations at the time of the marriage, during, and at the dissolution of the marriage. This section echoes Article 45(3) of the Constitution, which provides for equal rights during and at the dissolution of the marriage.

With respect to religion and directly relevant to Christian and Islamic marriages, Articles 32(1) and 32(2) of the Constitution, respectively, provide for every person's right to freedom of religion and the right to manifest that religion respectively. Similarly, the Constitution recognizes marriages conducted under any religion, tradition, personal, or family law as long as the marriage is not inconsistent with Article 45(3) of the Constitution. Article 32(4) of the Constitution prohibits acts which compel any person to act contrary to the person's belief or religion. This provision may be interpreted as permitting Muslims to contravene the legal provisions on the minimum age of marriage, equal rights in marriage, and non-unilateral divorce provisions.

Provisions specific to Islamic marriages and practice

Section 6(1)(e) of the Marriage Act lists Islamic marriages among the marriages to be registered under the Act. Islamic marriages are recognized alongside customary marriages as potentially polygamous under section 6(3) of the Act. Section 48 of the Act adds that Islamic marriages apply only to those who profess the Islamic faith. Sections 49 and 57 of the Act require the Registrar of Marriages to register Islamic marriages.

Furthermore, section 3(2) of the Act gives parties to a marriage equal rights and obligations in marriage. However, Section 3 (4) of the Act qualifies section 3(2) by stating that 3(4) is subject to 3(2), meaning that the parties to an Islamic marriage shall only have the rights granted under Islamic law. Although the Constitution contains equality provisions, Article 24(4) exempts Muslims litigating before the Khadis' courts from these provisions.

The exemptions given to Muslims appear to directly impact Article 45(3) of the Constitution, which stipulates that parties shall enjoy equal rights at the time of the marriage, during, and at the dissolution of the marriage. Section 49(3) of the Act explicitly provides that any provision of the Act inconsistent with Islamic law and practices does not apply to persons who profess the Islamic faith. One interpretation of these exemptions by the Marriage Act and the constitutional provisions is that Islamic marriages are prioritized over other forms of marriage. Stating that provisions inconsistent with Islamic law do not apply to Muslims could be interpreted to mean that the requirements regarding the minimum marriage age, equality, consent to marry, divorce and polygamy, *inter alia*, do not apply to Muslims if they are contrary to Islamic practice.

The exemptions appear to permit Islamic practices that deviate from the known rights on the equality of men and women as identified in the Constitution and other international instruments. Consequently, some have argued that Islamic marriages have been given precedence over other marriages, thus calling into question the Act's stipulation that all marriages have the same legal status.[18]

NATURE OF ISLAMIC MARRIAGES AND DIVORCES

Requirements of a valid Islamic marriage

The starting point when it comes to the requirements of a Muslim marriage is the Quran.[19] Neither the Marriage Act

[18] Section 3(3), Marriage Act.

[19] Jamil Ddamulira Mujuzi, "The Islamic Law of Marriage and Inheritance in

nor the Kadhis' Courts Act fully stipulates the conditions or requirements for a valid Muslim marriage. There are no substantive provisions on the rights of parties in Islamic marriages.[20] The requirements are determined mainly from Islamic scholarly teachings and case law with reference to the practices of the specific Islamic sect of the parties.[21] For instance, in the *RWK v AMA*, the Kadhi's court referred to an Islamic law textbook to determine the conditions of a valid Islamic marriage.[22] The court found that the conditions included being of sound mind, having reached the age of marriage, and the parties' consent to the marriage.[23]

A Muslim marriage is considered a contract with accompanying legal rights and obligations between the prospective wife and husband or between those entering into the marriage contract on their behalf.[24] While the marriage may be constituted without any particular formalities, certain minimum requirements must be met. These include a clear offer and acceptance made by the parties to the marriage. The parties making and accepting the marriage offer should not be within the prohibited degrees of affinity or consanguinity.[25] In Kenya, the prohibited relationships are listed under section 10 of the Act. Unlike other marriages, the Act permits Muslims to marry their cousins.

Only competent parties are allowed to make the offer and acceptance.[26] Where the parties are legally incompetent on account of age or unsoundness of mind, the guardians

Kenya", *Journal of African Law,* LXV (2021), p. 381.

20 *NUFR v MSC* [2015] eKLR, para. 27 (all cases from the electronic Kenyan Law Report (eKLR).

21 Ibid.

22 *RWK v AMA* [2015] eKLR.

23 Ibid.

24 Kecia Ali, *Muslim Sexual Ethics: Marriage Contracts in Islamic Jurisprudence* (2003) (available online).

25 Syeda Shajia Sharmin and Mir Mohammad Azad, "Laws of Muslim Marriage from the Concept of the Holy Qur'an", *International Journal of Engineering and Applied Sciences,* V, no. 7 (2018), p. 30.

26 Ibid., p. 30.

may enter into a valid marriage contract on their behalf.[27] The contracting parties to the marriage should be adults or have reached the age of puberty, as there appears to be no specified minimum age of marriage.[28] The absence of a minimum marriage age is contrary to the Constitution, the Marriage Act, and the Children's Act which are categorical that the parties must be eighteen years and above.

Additionally, two male witnesses must be present where the parties subscribe to the *Hanafi* law, with no witness required where the parties adhere to the *Shia* law.[29] For the marriage to be deemed valid, the words used to make the offer and acceptance while contracting the marriage must be "clear and unambiguous".[30]

The dower or *mahr* is a vital part of a valid Islamic marriage. Based on the Quran, a "...dower is either a sum of money or other form of property to which the wife becomes entitled by marriage.... It is an obligation imposed by law on the husband as a mark of respect for the wife...".[31] *Mahr* differs from a dowry or gift since it is mandatory for a Muslim marriage and is paid by the groom to the bride, usually at the time of marriage, for her exclusive use. The exception is where the two mutually agree to delay part of the payment.[32]

The Kadhi's court in the Kenyan case of *SMK v RHH*[33] reiterated the above requirements for a valid marriage, referring to the *Hanafi* school:

> The validity of a marriage contract depends on the parties or their guardian being of sound mind and mature and on the proposal and acceptance being made by the consenting parties in one meeting. In

27 Ibid.

28 Ibid.

29 Ibid.

30 Ibid.

31 Abdur Rahim, *The Principles of Muhammad and Jurisprudence* (1911), p. 334.

32 GK Today, *Types of Muslim Marriages and Divorce* (2016) (available online).

33 [2015] eKLR.

the presence and hearing of two or more mature and prudent witnesses, provided there is no legal disability on the person of any contracting party or parties of a nature that it may prove to be an impediment to the marriage contract.[34]

Types of Islamic marriages

Islamic marriages fall into three categories; these are valid (*sahih*) marriages, void (*batil*) marriages, and irregular (*fasid*) marriages.[35]

Sahih (valid) marriages

Sahih marriages are valid marriages that have fulfilled all the legal requirements with no impediments affecting the parties.[36] When the marriage is valid, the children are considered legitimate, while the wife is entitled to a dower or *mahr* and maintenance.[37] The children and the parties are entitled to an inheritance as well.

Batil (void) marriages

On the other hand, void or *batil* marriages are unlawful under Islamic law. For instance, where the parties marrying are within prohibited degrees of affinity and consanguinity or where a man marries another man's wife without following due procedure.[38] A void marriage gives no rights or obligations to the parties. The children from the union are deemed illegitimate.[39] An illegitimate child under Islamic

[34] Ibid.

[35] Sharmin and Azad, note 25 above, p. 32.

[36] GK Today, note 32 above.

[37] Ibid.

[38] Ibid.

[39] Sharmin and Azad, note 25 above, p. 32.

law does not inherit any property from their father, but they can inherit from their mother.[40]

Fasid (irregular) marriages

An irregular or *fasid* marriage is a marriage that is not necessarily unlawful but is disadvantaged by a temporary obstacle or a procedural irregularity or failure. For instance, marrying a fifth wife, or marrying without a guardian's consent where necessary, or failing to have the requisite number of witnesses to a marriage.[41] Under an irregular marriage, the children born are legitimate. However, no mutual rights of inheritance can arise between the parties.[42]

Rights acquired after marriage

Besides the requirement for both spouses to give "mutual good treatment", which is not legally defined, their rights and obligations are classed according to gender.[43] The rights and duties acquired after marriage are interdependent, whereby the failure of a spouse to perform a specific duty may disentitle that spouse from asserting a particular right.[44] An Islamic marriage gives duties to both spouses, with some obligations being reciprocal, others complementary, and others handled individually by each party.[45]

The husband has an obligation to pay the agreed dower, and the woman must receive it. The dower may be a token sum of money or a significant amount, jewels, or other

[40] Mzee Mustafa Mzee, "Islamic Law of Inheritance: The Case of Illegitimate Child and Possibility of Having an Assets of Deceased Father: A Tanzanian Case Study", *Journal of Law, Policy and Globalization*, XLV (2016), p. 57.

[41] GK Today, note 32 above.

[42] Sharmin and Azad note 25 above, p. 32.

[43] Ali, note 24 above.

[44] Ibid.

[45] Lawal Mohammed Bani and Hamza A. Pate, "The Role of Spouses under Islamic Family Law", *International Affairs and Global Strategy*, XXXVII (2015), p. 104.

items the wife can save, invest, or spend as she prefers.[46] The dower should be paid before the marriage contract is considered complete and may be paid in installments, or part of the payment may be postponed.[47] The man must treat the wife with compassion and love.

Men also have the obligation as "*Qawwamun*", meaning that they have a duty to protect and maintain their wives based on the responsibility imposed on them by the Quran.[48] This includes providing lodging, clothing, and support to the wife.[49] In return for the dower and providing for the wife and children, the husband gets the "*milk al-nikah*" or "ownership or control" of the marriage.[50] On the other hand, the wife is expected to be totally obedient or submissive to the husband.[51]

Where a man has more than one wife, they are entitled to an equal share of her husband's time. On the other hand, the husband enjoys the right to restrict the wife's movements and to expect her availability for sexual intimacy.[52] Should the wife reject the husband's sexual advances or leave the marital home without permission, she loses her right to her husband's support and a claim to his time.[53]

Islamic family law fails to set eighteen years as the minimum marriage age, thereby arguably allowing child marriages. Consent to the marriage by the parties is not mandatory since a guardian or parent can arrange the marriage on behalf of the child. There is also the control of the wife by the husband and the restriction of the wife's movements. These issues arguably contravene the

[46] Ali, note 24 above.

[47] Bani and Pate, note 45 above, p. 104.

[48] Ibid; Quran 4:34 (Sura-An Nisa): "Men are the caretakers of women, as men have been provisioned by Allah over women and tasked with supporting them financially".

[49] Ali, note 24 above.

[50] Ibid.

[51] Bani and Pate, note 45 above, p. 110.

[52] Ali, note 24 above.

[53] Ibid.

Constitution and the Marriage Act provision on equal rights for both men and women in marriage, consent to marry, and the prohibition of child marriages. Neither do they conform to relevant international human rights provisions on these issues.

Divorce under Islamic law

The Quran considers divorce permissible though it is not encouraged since it is reported that the Prophet Muhammad said, "that of all things permitted, divorce is the most hated by God".[54] Reconciliation is encouraged between spouses, who may use mediators from their families, with divorce being the last option.[55] A divorce under Islamic law may be initiated by the parties (extra-judicial divorce) or through a decree of a court of law (judicial divorce).

The grounds for divorce vary according to different schools. Under the Hanafi School, the wife has almost no grounds for divorce if the marriage has been consummated.[56] Under the Hanafi School, whether the husband abuses his wife, is imprisoned for life, or fails to support her, the wife is not entitled to a divorce. Where the husband is declared missing, the marriage can only be dissolved on presumed widowhood grounds when the husband would have turned ninety years of age.[57] In contrast, under the Maliki school, the wife is allowed to seek divorce for lack of support, abandonment, and all injuries (*darar*), physical or otherwise.[58]

The Marriage Act lays out the different grounds for divorce and the procedures for Hindu, Christian, and customary marriages. An exemption is, however, made for Islamic divorces in the Act, which leaves it to the rules of Islamic family law to determine the procedure for Islamic

[54] Kecia Ali, *Muslim Sexual Ethics: Divorce The Feminist Sexual Ethics Project* (2003) (available online).

[55] Ibid.

[56] Ibid.

[57] Ibid.

[58] Ibid.

divorces.[59] The Kadhi's Court in Kenya determined the grounds for divorce in the case of *HAA v JOG*.[60] The grounds for divorce include dispossessing a wife of her property and her rights over it and forcing the wife to lead an immoral life. Other grounds are where the husband keeps the company of women of ill repute and obstructs the wife in observing her religious practice. Additional grounds acknowledged in the case include the husband's failure to treat his wives equitably, as required by the Qur'an. Last, physical or psychological assault or mistreatment is a ground for divorce.

Under Islamic law, there are six common types of divorce, with the man and woman both entitled to seek divorce.[61] However, the right of women to initiate divorce, compared to a man's, is limited.[62]

Talaq

Talaq is the most common type of divorce. *Talaq* comes from the Arabic word "*Talaaq,*" which means to "release".[63] *Talaq* is the husband's unilateral repudiation of the wife and does not require the wife's consent.[64] It signifies the absolute power which the husband possesses to divorce his wife.[65] Because the husband maintains control of the marriage, only he can unilaterally end the marriage at any time by a pronouncement of repudiation (*talaq*).[66] Where it is an irrevocable divorce, the husband declares to his wife three times that he is divorcing her, either on one occasion or three separate occasions depending on the school of Islamic

59 Sections 65, 70 and 71, Marriage Act.

60 [2018] eKLR.

61 GK Today, note 32 above.

62 Bani and Pate, note 45 above, p. 142.

63 Ali, note 54 above.

64 Ibid.

65 Bani and Pate, note 45 above, p. 138.

66 Ali, note 54 above.

jurisprudence.[67] *Talaq* is recognized by all the schools, including the Sunnis and the Shias.[68] The absolute power of a Muslim husband to unilaterally divorce his wife "without assigning any reason, literally at his whim, even in jest or in a state of intoxication, and without recourse to the court, and even in the absence of the wife, is recognized in Islam".[69] Consequently, how, when, and why the husband gives the talaq is inconsequential as long as he pronounces *talaq*.[70] The first and second *talaq* constitute repudiatory divorces. Therefore, a husband who has divorced his wife using the first or second *talaq* may take her back. However, the third repudiation of *talaq* constitutes a final and irrevocable divorce.[71] After the final, irrevocable *talaq*, the wife keeps her dower, and if there is any unpaid dower by the husband, it becomes immediately payable upon divorce.[72] Immediately after the *talaq*, the wife must observe a waiting period of approximately three months *(iddat)* to ensure she is not pregnant, after which she is free to remarry.

Khul / Kula

Khul is a divorce initiated by the wife, also referred to as divorce for compensation.[73] Under this divorce, the wife returns her dower or pays some other sum to her husband to obtain his agreement to divorce. The Kadhis court reiterated this position in the case of *HAA v JOG*,[74] where it held that a wife has a right to seek a *khul* divorce but has to pay compensation to the husband to secure the divorce. However, if she has grounds for divorce, she may seek a

[67] Ruth Levush, *Religious Matrimonial Laws in Selected Middle East and African Countries* (2017) (available online).

[68] Bani and Pate, note 45 above, p. 138.

[69] Ibid.

[70] Ibid.

[71] Ali, note 54 above.

[72] Ibid.

[73] Ibid.

[74] [2018] eKLR.

judicial divorce, depending on the school of legal thought to which she belongs.[75]

This right of a wife has been equated to buying her release from the marriage from her husband.[76] Most Islamic jurists and national laws deem the husband's agreement essential to the *khul'* divorce. However, a few countries such as Egypt have permitted wives the right to obtain a *khul'* divorce without the husband's consent.[77] *Khul'*, once obtained, is irrevocable, and the husband cannot take the wife back, although they may remarry subsequently by mutual consent. The wife must observe a waiting period of three months (*iddat*) before remarriage.[78] Significantly, although men can divorce their wives easily, because it is not easy for women to deal with legal and financial obstacles such as the repayment of her dower and marriage expenses.[79]

Mubarat

This type of divorce occurs through the mutual agreement of the husband and wife, where both desire a divorce.[80] Either party may initiate the divorce. However, the wife loses her dower, whereas the husband remains liable to maintain his children.

Ila

Ila is a type of constructive divorce. In *Ila,* the husband takes an oath not to have sexual relations with his wife, following which there is no consummation for four months.[81] The marriage dissolves irrevocably at the end of this period. However, if the husband resumes cohabitation

75 Ali, note 24 above.

76 GK Today, note 32 above.

77 Ali, note 54 above.

78 Ibid.

79 Bani and Pate, note 45 above, p. 141.

80 GK Today, note 32 above.

81 Bani and Pate, note 45 above, p. 141.

within the four-month period, *Ila* is cancelled, and the marriage continues.[82] The Shi'a school does not recognize *Ila* as a divorce unless a court order is issued.[83] Upon the end of the four-month period, the wife becomes entitled to a judicial divorce, or she may file a suit for restitution of conjugal rights against the husband.[84]

Zihar

Zihar, similar to *Lian* and *Ila*, is a constructive divorce by the husband.[85] Under this type of divorce, the husband deliberately compares his wife with his mother, sister, or any other female within the prohibited degrees of relationships with a view to ending the marriage.[86] Following the comparison, the husband abstains from cohabiting with his wife for four months.[87] Upon the expiry of the said period, *Zihar* is complete, and the wife becomes entitled to go to court for a divorce decree or seek the court's restitution of conjugal rights.[88] If the husband desires to revoke the *Zihar* by the resumption of cohabitation within the said period, the wife loses the right to seek judicial divorce.[89]

Lian

In this case, the wife is entitled to ask for a divorce if the husband falsely accuses her of unchastity or adultery, thereby defaming her character.[90] Only a deliberate false charge of adultery by the husband entitles the wife to a

[82] Ibid.

[83] Ibid.

[84] Ibid.

[85] Ibid.

[86] GK Today, note 32 above.

[87] Bani and Pate, note 45 above, p. 141.

[88] Ibid.

[89] Ibid., p. 142.

[90] Ibid.

divorce decree on the ground of *Lian*.[91] For a *Lian* divorce to apply, certain conditions must exist. First, the marriage must subsist, and second, the marriage contract must be valid. Third, the husband must be capable of being called as a witness to the adultery allegations against his wife if his accusations are true (*Gazf*).[92]

NATIONAL AND INTERNATIONAL HUMAN RIGHTS PERSPECTIVES

Specific issues arise regarding Islamic marriages as juxtaposed against the Kenya Constitution, Marriage Act, Children's Act, other laws, and international and regional human rights instruments. These issues include the lack of provision for equal rights generally, and specifically, the rights of both spouses at the time of, during, and at the dissolution of the Islamic marriage. Other issues are child marriage, forced marriage, polygamy, and unilateral divorce. The ratified international instruments take on more meaning in the Kenyan context considering that Articles 2(5) and 2(6) of the Constitution state that general rules of international law and ratified treaties form part of Kenyan laws. Articles 2(5) and 2(6) arguably pave the way for ratified treaties such as the International Covenant on Civil and Political Rights (ICCPR), Convention on the Elimination of all Forms of Discrimination Against Women (CEDAW), International Covenant on Economic, Social and Cultural Rights (ICESCR), and the Protocol to the African Charter on Human and People's Rights on the Rights of Women in Africa (Maputo Protocol), to be directly incorporated by the judiciary and other State organs.

Equal rights regarding marriages and divorces

In Islamic marriages spouses do not have equal rights. The husband is the head of the family, the primary provider, and the protector of his wives and children. In return, the wife or wives are expected to submit to the husband, and

91 Ibid.

92 Ibid.

sometimes cede parental authority.[93] The different roles have occasionally been used to justify the differentiated treatment of men and women in a marriage. For example, the United Arab Emirates reported to the CEDAW Committee that "Sharia honors women and makes the man responsible for the financial support of the woman, whether his wife, daughter, mother or sister, not requiring the wife to support either herself or her family even if she is wealthy".[94] However, some Muslim-practicing countries such as Bahrain and Saudi Arabia have reiterated that Islam provides for equal rights of men and women.[95]

Human rights standards require the equality of men and women in all spheres, including the "same rights and responsibilities during marriage and at its dissolution". The Universal Declaration of Human Rights (UDHR) guarantees both men and women the right to marry and the entitlement to equal rights during marriage and at its dissolution.[96] Equal rights during marriage have been echoed in different international and regional human instruments, including the ICCPR[97] and CEDAW[98]. The CEDAW further provides for the same rights and responsibilities during marriage and at its dissolution.[99] The Maputo Protocol reiterates this

[93] Musawah -AWAPSA, note 9 above, pp. 17-18.

[94] CEDAW Committee, "Consideration of Reports Submitted by States Parties under Article 18 of the Convention on the Elimination of All Forms of Discrimination against Women: Initial Periodic Report of State Parties, United Arab Emirates", *U.N. Doc. CEDAW/C/ARE/1*, (2008), para. 58.

[95] CEDAW Committee, "Consideration of Reports Submitted by States Parties under Article 18 of the Convention on the Elimination of All Forms of Discrimination against Women: Combined Initial and Second Periodic Reports of State Parties, Bahrain", *U.N. Doc. CEDAW/ C/BHR/2*, (2007), para. 32; CEDAW Committee, "Consideration of Reports Submitted by States Parties under Article 18 of the Convention on the Elimination of All Forms of Discrimination against Women: Combined Initial and Second Periodic Reports of State Parties, Saudi Arabia" *CEDAW/C/SAU/2*, (2007).

[96] Article 16(1), UDHR.

[97] Article 23(4), ICCPR.

[98] Article 16(1)(a), CEDAW.

[99] Ibid., Article 16(1) (c) and (d).

when it states that "women and men enjoy equal rights and are regarded as equal partners in marriage".[100]

The Constitution provides for equal political, cultural, economic, and social rights for men and women and equality before the law in Articles 27(3) and 27(1), respectively. Article 27(4) expressly forbids discrimination against any person, whether by individuals or State organs based on sex, marital status, and religion, among other grounds.

The CEDAW Committee emphasizes the equal rights of women and men in marriage.[101] The Committee considers that principles of justice and equality in Articles 2, 5, 16, and 24 of the CEDAW are violated when women are not given *de jure* equality status in marriage with equal responsibility. The CEDAW Committee has recommended that:

> State parties should adopt written family codes or personal status laws that provide for equality between spouses or partners irrespective of their religious or ethnic identity ... Personal laws should embody the fundamental principle of equality between women and men ... so as to eliminate all discrimination against women in all matters relating to marriage and family.[102]

Specific to marriage, Article 45(3) of the Constitution, in line with the human rights instruments, guarantees equal rights at the time of, during, and at the dissolution of the marriage. This guarantee is duplicated in section 3(2) of the Marriage Act. However, as previously discussed, there is a qualification to the equality rights under Article 24(4) regarding Muslims. By implication, Article 24(4) of the

[100] Article 6, Maputo Protocol.

[101] CEDAW Committee, "General Recommendation No 21: Equality in Marriage and Family Relations", in *Note by the Secretariat, Compilation of General Comments and General Recommendations Adopted by Human Rights Treaty Bodies* (2006), comment on article 16, paras. 12 and 13; CEDAW Committee, "General Recommendation No 19: Violence against Women" in *Note by the Secretariat, Compilation of General Comments and General Recommendations Adopted by Human Rights Treaty Bodies* (2006), general comment para. 7(f).

[102] CEDAW Committee, "General Recommendation on Article 16 of the Convention on the Elimination of All Forms of Discrimination against Women", *CEDAW/C/GC/29*, (2013), para. 15.

Constitution removes the requirement for Muslims to adhere to the equality provisions, including those concerning marriage, divorce, and inheritance. As earlier indicated, one interpretation of the exemptions is that the provisions on non-discrimination under Article 27 and those in Article 45 on equal rights during and after marriage do not apply to persons professing the Muslim faith.

On the basis of the international instruments mentioned above on equal rights, it can be argued that the qualification under Article 24(4) of the Constitution exempting persons adhering to the Islamic faith from equal rights in marriage and divorce is contrary to the human rights treaties.

Minimum marriage age

As previously noted, the Quran does not specify the age of marriage, the general requirement being that one must attain puberty and be of sound mind before marriage. Imam Abu Hanifah, the founder of the Hanafi School, is said to have noted that, barring other evidence, a boy is regarded as having reached the age of majority at eighteen years and a girl at sixteen.[103]

The Marriage Act specifies that a person shall not marry unless they have attained eighteen years.[104] The Children's Act 2022 defines "early marriage" as marriage or cohabitation with a child or any arrangement made for such marriage or cohabitation.[105] In the same vein, the Constitution defines a *"child"* as an individual who has not attained eighteen years.[106] The Constitution in Article 45(2) recognizes the right to marriage only between heterosexual "adults".

Consequently, a union is considered void under the Marriage Act if either party is below eighteen years at the

[103] Musawah, *CEDAW and Muslim Family Laws in Search of Common Ground* (2011), p. 30 (available online).

[104] Section 4, Marriage Act.

[105] Section 2, Children's Act 2022.

[106] Article 260, 2010 Constitution; This definition is echoed in section 2 of the Marriage Act, and section 2 of the Children's Act 2022.

time of the marriage.[107] It an offence for any person to marry a person below eighteen years of age[108] or to celebrate or witness a union purporting to be a marriage where the person knows or should know that at least one party is below eighteen years.[109]

In the same vein, the Children's Act 2022 provides for the child's best interests as the first consideration in any legal action, reiterating Article 53 of the Kenya Constitution.[110] The Children's Act prohibits subjecting any child to early marriage, other cultural rites, customs, or traditional practices that may negatively affect the child's life, health, and social welfare.[111] Besides the Marriage Act, the Children's Act and the Constitution, the Sexual Offences Act 2006 makes it a punishable offence of defilement for any male or female to have sexual relations with a child below eighteen years.[112]

Several international and regional human rights instruments define *a child* as an individual below eighteen years and discourage child marriages. The Convention on the Rights of the Child defines *a child* as a person below the age of eighteen years unless majority is attained earlier under the law applicable to the child. International human rights monitoring Committees such as the Committee on the Rights of the Child, the Human Rights Committee,[113] and the Committee on the Elimination of Discrimination against Women have all emphasized that the minimum marriage age for both boys and girls should be eighteen years. They recommend

107 Section 11(1)(a), Marriage Act.

108 Ibid., section 87.

109 Ibid., section 92(1)(a).

110 Section 8, Children's Act 2022.

111 Ibid., section 23.

112 Section 8, Sexual Offences Act 2006.

113 The Committee requires States to ensure that the minimum marriage age complies with international standards and that active measures to prevent early marriage of girls are adopted; See for example, United Nations Human Rights Committee, "Concluding Observations on the Fifth Periodic Report of Uruguay", CCPR/C/URY/CO/5, (2013); United Nations Human Rights Committee, "Concluding observations of the Human Rights Committee United Republic of Tanzania", *CCPR/C/TZA/CO/4/*, (2009), para. 9(a).

abolishing the difference in the marriage ages between boys and girls.[114]

The African Charter on the Rights and Welfare of the Child (ACRWC) is more unequivocal in defining a *"child"* as a person below eighteen years.[115] The Maputo Protocol is categorical that a woman's minimum age for marriage shall be eighteen years.[116] Likewise, the CEDAW and ACRWC prohibit child marriages and the betrothal of girls and boys and demand legislative measures to specify the minimum marriage age as eighteen.[117]

The Kenya government, in its 2016 State party report to the CEDAW Committee, submitted that the adoption of the Marriage Act 2014 was a significant victory for women in Kenya as "it champions equality in marriage as well as reiterates the minimum age of marriage for all women across religious and cultural divides as outlined in Section 4 of the Act".[118] The CEDAW Committee, in its concluding observations to Kenya in 2017 on the eighth report,[119] remained concerned about "harmful practices, such as child and forced marriage, female genital mutilation, polygamy, bride price and widowhood rites such as widow inheritance".[120] Despite Kenya's assurance on the minimum age for marriage, the exemption given to Islamic marriages under section 49(3) of the Marriage Act is inconsistent with Kenya's international obligations. It leaves room for doubt about Kenya's commitment to the CEDAW and other instruments. This position is especially so since Islamic marriages do not specify the age of marriage, meaning it may be lower than eighteen years.

[114] CEDAW Committee, "General Recommendation No 21: Equality in Marriage and Family Relations" note 100 above, comment on article 16, para. 36.

[115] Article 2, ACRWC.

[116] Article 6(b), Maputo Protocol.

[117] Article 16(2), CEDAW; Article 21(2), ACRWC.

[118] CEDAW Committee, "Consideration of Reports Submitted by States Parties under Article 18 of the Convention", CEDAW/C/KEN/8, (2016), para. 195.

[119] CEDAW Committee, "Concluding Observations on the Eighth Periodic Report of Kenya" *CEDAW/C/KEN/CO/8*, (2017).

[120] Ibid., para. 18.

Consent of parties to a marriage

The issue of consent in marriage relates to whether the two parties consent to be married and, second, whether anyone else must consent to the marriage.[121] Consent must be freely given. It encompasses the right to choose if, whom, and when to marry.[122]

Different schools of jurisprudence determine consent in Islamic marriages.[123] Under the *Shafi'i* school, a prospective bride requires the consent of a marital guardian (*wali*) to enter into a marriage contract regardless of age.[124] Guardianship (*wilaya*) for marriage is considered a critical element in Islamic marriage procedures.[125] In Kenya, the common Muslim practice is that a father is deemed to have the right to conclude a marriage on behalf of a virgin daughter of any age, even against her will, with the consequence that a forced marriage (*ijbar*) may occur.[126] However, where the prospective bride is an adult who has been married before, her consent and not that of her guardian, is considered mandatory. The need for male authority (*qiwamah*) and male guardianship (*wilayah*) is seen as removing free consent.[127] The guardian must be a sane adult male Muslim relative of the prospective bride, usually her father and, under special circumstances, the paternal grandfather, closest brother, or uncle.[128] Where the father is absent, another guardian takes his place to validate the marriage, but the other guardian cannot compel his ward to marry.[129]

121 Musawah, note 102 above, p. 32.

122 Ibid., p. 32.

123 Musawah, note 7 above, p. 18.

124 'Musawah - AWAPSA, note 9 above, p. 10.

125 Kecia Ali, *Muslim Sexual Ethics: Consent and Forced Marriage* (2003) (available online).

126 Musawah, note 7 above, p. 18.

127 Musawah – AWAPSA, note 9 above, p. 11.

128 Musawah, note 7 above, p. 19.

129 Ali, note 124 above.

All four *Sunni* schools recognize the power of a father to contract binding marriages for his sons and daughters who are minors, usually at age nine or the start of menstruation for girls and up to fifteen years for boys, with the children having no say in the matter.[130] A boy married against his wishes may nevertheless choose to divorce his wife unilaterally upon maturity. The father or the grandfather also has the right to marry off their virgin daughter or granddaughter against her will, hence the reference to them as *"wali mudjbir"* or "*wali* with power to coerce".[131] This practice is common under the *Maliki* and *Shafi'i* schools of legal thought, and to some extent, the *Hanbali* school. On the other hand, the *Hanafi* regard an adult woman as legally capable of consenting to marriage, as opposed to the Malikis, the Shafi'is, and the Hanbalis, who require that a guardian (*wali)* must contract a marriage on behalf of the woman even if she is an adult.[132] The Kadhis court in the Kenyan case of *SMK v RHH*[133] referred to the Hanafi School and held that a marriage contracted without the valid consent of the parties is invalid. The court further held that a woman's consent is necessary whether she is a virgin or was previously married, and her guardian, according to Hanafi lawyers, cannot compel her to enter into a marriage contract.

The Constitution, in Article 45(2), provides that "every adult has the right to marry a person of the opposite sex, based on *the free consent* of the parties". This requirement is repeated in section 3(1) of the Marriage Act, which states that a marriage is the *voluntary* union of a man and a woman. Under section 11(e) of the Marriage Act, a union is void if the consent of either party is not freely given. A party may also seek an annulment of the marriage under section 73(1)(d) of the Act, where the petitioner's consent to the marriage was not freely given.

130 Ibid.

131 Clifford Edmund Bosworth, Emeri Johannes Van Donzel, Wolfart Peter Heinrichs, and Gerard Lecomte (eds.), *Encyclopedia of Islam* (1995), VIII, p. 27.

132 Ali, note 124 above.

133 [2015] eKLR.

Section 11(2) of the Marriage Act provides that consent is not considered freely given where the party purporting to consent is influenced by coercion or fraud or is mistaken as to the nature or purport of the ceremony. Moreover, it is not free consent where the party is suffering from any mental condition, whether permanent or temporary, is intoxicated, or under the influence of drugs, and consequently is unable to appreciate the nature or purport of the ceremony. It is a punishable offence to be a party to a ceremony purported to be a marriage, knowing that the other party's consent was induced by coercion, fraud, or by mistake.[134]

All the principal international human rights treaties, among them the UDHR, CEDAW, ICCPR, ICESCR, and Maputo Protocol, guarantee the rights of all persons to consent to a marriage and to enter into it of their free will.[135] The CEDAW Committee has stated that "A woman's right to choose a spouse and enter freely into marriage is central to her life and her dignity and equality as a human being".[136]The Human Rights Committee has also reiterated the right to enter into marriage only with the free and full consent of the parties.[137] The Committee further points out factors that may prevent women from making an informed and uncoerced decision to marry.[138] The factors include being below the minimum age of marriage and where a guardian, generally a male, consents to the marriage instead of the woman herself, preventing her from exercising a free choice. The Human Committee requires States to provide information on the measures taken to abolish the laws and eradicate the practices which undermine women's rights

134 Section 89, Marriage Act.

135 Article 16, UDHR; Article 16, CEDAW; Article 23(3), ICCPR; Article 10(1), ICESCR; Article 6(a), Maputo Protocol.

136 CEDAW Committee, "General Recommendation No 21: Equality in Marriage and Family Relations", note 100 above, comment on Article 16(1) (a) and (b), para. 16.

137 UN Human Rights Committee, "General Comment 28, Equality of rights between men and women", in *Note by the Secretariat, Compilation of General Comments and General Recommendations Adopted by Human Rights Treaty Bodies* (2006), para. 23.

138 Ibid., para 23ff.

to marry with their free and full consent.[139] The Committee stresses that polygamy is incompatible with the principle of free consent.[140]

The practice supported by the Maliki, the Shafi'i, and the Hanbali Muslim sects, whereby guardians consent to the marriage and do not seek the consent of the prospective parties, is contrary to the human rights instruments that Kenya has ratified. It is also a violation of the constitutional provisions and the Marriage Act. The exemptions given to Islamic marriages raise questions about double standards because non-Muslim Kenyans are required to adhere to the relevant provisions. These arguably depict a lack of will to implement international human rights and even the bill of rights in the Constitution. Further, the requirement for a guardian to grant his consent to the marriage of an adult woman appears to make women "perpetual minors".[141]

Polygamy

In Kenya, a Muslim man may marry up to four wives with no legal requirement for him to seek the court's permission or his existing wife's permission.[142] The failure to seek the wives' consent contributes to unequal power relations between men and women.[143] One position is that polygamy is provided for in the Qur'an or the *Shari'ah*. For instance, Libya had reservations about CEDAW discouragement of polygamy because polygamy is incontrovertibly provided for under Sharia law.[144] A contrasting view by Egypt suggests that while some Islamic jurists interpret Koranic verses as permitting polygamy, other groups interpret

139 Ibid., para 24.

140 Ibid.

141 Musawah, note 102 above, p. 32.

142 'Musawah – AWAPSA, *Joint Thematic Report on Kenya; Article 16 Muslim Family Law and Muslim Women's Rights in Kenya,* (68th CEDAW Session Geneva, Switzerland, October 2017) p. 14 (available online); Musawah, note 7 above, p. 19.

143 Musawah, note 7 above, p. 19.

144 CEDAW Committee, "Summary Record of the 879th Meeting" UN Doc CEDAW/C/SR.879, (2009), para. 38.

polygamy as conditional and not generally applicable.[145] Islamic marriages are recognized under Kenyan law as being polygamous or potentially polygamous according to section 6(3) of the Marriage Act.

The CEDAW Committee states that a "polygamous marriage contravenes a woman's right to equality with men and can have such serious emotional and financial consequences for her and her dependents that such marriages ought to be discouraged and prohibited".[146] The Committee noted that some "States parties whose constitutions guarantee equal rights also permit polygamous marriage based on personal or customary law. This violates women's constitutional rights and breaches the provisions of Article 5(a) of the Convention". Kenya falls into the said category. On one hand, it advocates equal rights in marriage in Article 45(3); on the other, it permits polygamy under Islamic and customary marriages, giving men superior rights. In paragraph 39 of the CEDAW Committee's General Comment number 21, States parties are urged to comply with the Convention by establishing equality between partners and prohibiting polygamy. The Kenyan State party report submitted to the CEDAW Committee in 2016 acknowledged that "polygamy has onerous implications on women. It serves to reinforce male dominance and subjugation of women in the private sphere of marriage ... Polygamy also runs counter to the very Constitution that outlaws discrimination and inequality of sexes".[147] Despite Kenya's acknowledgement, polygamy has been retained in Kenyan laws for Islamic and customary marriages, thereby contradicting its own laws and the human rights instruments it has ratified.

The CEDAW Committee, in its concluding observations on Kenya's eighth periodic report, expressed concern that the legal framework in Kenya, including exemptions

[145] CEDAW Committee, "Concluding observations of the Committee on the Elimination of Discrimination against Women: Egypt State Party Report", UN/Doc/CEDAW/C/EGY/7, (2010), para. 48.

[146] CEDAW Committee, "General Recommendation No 21: Equality in Marriage and Family Relations", note 100 above, comment on Article 16, para. 14.

[147] CEDAW Committee, note 117 above, para. 206.

under Article 45 of the Constitution and Article 49(3) of the Marriage Act, discriminates against Muslim women and women in customary marriages.[148] The Committee pointed out that:

> the explicit exemption of the Kadhi courts from constitutional equality provisions and the fact that women cannot serve as Kadhis, as well as the legalisation of polygamy, in violation of the non-discrimination provisions of the Constitution and the Convention, run counter to general recommendations No. 21 (1994) on equality in marriage and family relations and No. 29.[149]

The CEDAW Committee recommended that Kenya should repeal or amend discriminatory religious and customary laws and harmonize them with Article 16 of the CEDAW.[150] The Committee required Kenya to codify Muslim family law in a manner compatible with Article 27 of the Kenya Constitution and Articles 1, 2, and 16 of the Convention (9 b).

The Human Rights Committee, just as the CEDAW Committee, stated that polygamy violates the dignity of women and discriminates against them.[151] The Committee urged States to abolish polygamy where it continues to exist. The Maputo Protocol in Article 6(c) stipulates that monogamy is encouraged as the preferred form of marriage.[152] Polygamy is seen as incompatible with the fundamental human rights principle of equality of men and women articulated in several human rights instruments, including CEDAW Article 1, which defines discrimination and a woman's right to dignity. The fact that women can be coerced into polygamous relationships violates the "free and full consent to marriage" provisions of various human

[148] CEDAW Committee, note 118 above, para. 8.

[149] Ibid.

[150] Ibid., para. 9.

[151] UN Human Rights Committee, note 136 above, para. 24.

[152] Article 6(c), Maputo Protocol.

rights instruments.[153] Justice Mumbi Ngugi reiterated this fact in the case of *Mary W Muiga v Attorney General & another*,[154] holding that "polygamy cannot, therefore, be said to promote equality between men and women, and if measured against the clear provisions of the Constitution and international conventions to which Kenya is a party, is clearly unconstitutional and a form of discrimination against women".[155] Nevertheless, the judge noted that polygamy was entrenched in the society and therefore added that where it must happen, polygamy "without the consent of the previous wife or wives is inconsistent with the equality provisions of the Constitution".[156] In effect, where polygamy was unavoidable, the consent of the first or previous wives was necessary.

Unilateral divorce initiation

As noted above, divorce rights are unequal between women and men under Muslim family laws, with clear differences regarding the grounds for divorce and the conditions and procedures applicable to wives and husbands in initiating and pursuing a divorce.[157] In most countries, including Kenya, husbands have the legal right to divorce their wives unilaterally. However, Muslim wives are permitted to seek divorce from their husbands in limited instances and on specific grounds.[158] Where a Muslim wife seeks divorce, the burden of proving that she is entitled to the divorce lies with the woman, with the man required to consent, and if he refuses, the divorce is not granted.[159] A

153 Musawah, note 102 above, p. 34.

154 [2015] eKLR.

155 Ibid., para. 75.

156 Ibid., paras. 75 and 78 (ii).

157 Musawah, note 7 above, p. 7.

158 Ibid.

159 Ibid., p. 22.

woman can only get a *khul* divorce in exchange for a mutually agreed compensation payment made to the husband.[160]

The Maputo Protocol provides in Article 7(a) that a judicial order should give effect to the separation, divorce, or annulment of marriage. In addition, women and men shall have the same rights to seek separation, divorce, or marriage annulment (7b). It is argued that a system that does not give equal rights to both spouses to seek separation or divorce is against the Protocol. The Human Rights Committee likewise requires that the grounds for divorce and annulment be the same for men and women.[161] The Human Rights Committee has reiterated spouses' equal rights and responsibilities during and at the dissolution of marriage in General Comment 19.[162] Consequently, the Comment requires that any discriminatory treatment regarding the grounds and procedures for separation or divorce be prohibited.

In its concluding observations on Kenya's eighth periodic report in 2017, the CEDAW Committee observed that there was "discrimination against women married under Islamic law, including the right of men to divorce their wives unilaterally, and reports of abusive behavior, including the withholding of divorce certificates and forced concessions in return for the divorce certificate".[163] The CEDAW Committee recommended that Kenya should ensure equality of women and men in Muslim marriages and, upon divorce, abolish the practice of a husband divorcing his wife unilaterally and ensure the compulsory registration of all divorces.[164]

Kenya has yet to implement these recommendations on equality and unilateral divorce. This failure means that Kenya is in violation of its own constitutional provisions in Article 27 on non-discrimination and equality and those in the human rights instruments.

[160] Ibid.

[161] UN Human Rights Committee, note 136 above, para. 26.

[162] UN Human Rights Committee, "General Comment 19, Article 23", in *Note by the Secretariat, Compilation of General Comments and General Recommendations Adopted by Human Rights Treaty Bodies* (2006)

[163] CEDAW Committee, note 118 above, para. 50(e).

[164] Ibid., para. 51(d), (e).

CASE LAW

The leading case that has dealt with the conflict between the constitutional provisions, the Marriage Act, and Islamic marriage practices is *Council of Imams and Preachers of Kenya, Malindi & 4 others v Attorney General & 5 others.*[165] The main contentious issue was that the third and fourth petitioners, together with one other person, were charged with the offence of subjecting a child to harmful cultural rites contrary to section 14 as read with section 20 of the Children's Act of 2001 by subjecting her to early marriage (below eighteen years). The petitioners sought to have the charges against them dropped, seeking a declaration that the provisions of Sections 2, 4, 8(1), (2), 14, and 20 of the Children's Act do not apply to marriages conducted under Islamic Law. The petitioners further sought a restraining order against all the respondents who sought to prevent the second to fifth petitioners from exercising their religious rights and beliefs by entering into a marriage relationship as provided under the Constitution. The petitioners admitted to marrying off the minor while she was below eighteen years old. However, they argued that their religious rights and freedoms in Articles 32(1), (2), and (4) of the Constitution were breached because they were exercising their religious rights and freedoms. The petitioners contended that their arrest by the respondents was illegal since the petitioner was a Muslim of seventeen years of age, of sound mind, and good health at the material time, capable of entering into a marriage contract with the consent of the third petitioner, her father; a right recognized under Articles 45 and 170(5) of the Constitution. They argued that the fifth and sixth respondents misapprehended, misrepresented, or misinterpreted the relevant provisions of the Children Act read together with Articles 2(4), 32, 45, and 170(5) of the Constitution.

The petitioners further submitted that the Constitution authorizes the practice of Islam under Article 32(1). The Petitioners argued that if the Constitution intended to limit the age of marriage where Muslims are concerned, it

165 [2015] eKLR.

would have clearly expressed this under Article 24. They submitted that the marriage practice involving a Muslim below eighteen years of age was an Islamic practice founded in the Holy Quran and *Sunnah*, which dictate the capacity to marry. The petitioners cited section 49(3) of the Marriage Act, which states that any provision of the Act inconsistent with the Islamic faith shall not apply to those who profess Islam. Based on section 49(3), they argued that the second petitioner's age was not an issue since she was seventeen years at the material time; she also consented to the marriage and expressed her wish to get married and not return to school. The issues, therefore, involved the provisions of the Constitution, the Children Act, and the Marriage Act versus Islamic law. The respondents, on the other hand,_contended that, on the contrary, Articles 32(2) and (4) of the Constitution could not be read in isolation or in disregard of Articles 45(1), 53, and 260 of the Constitution.

In determining the issue of the age of marriage, the court held that Article 45(2) and 45(4) of the Constitution provide that marriages or personal law systems should be consistent with the Constitution. In essence, therefore, any marriage, whether conducted under any tradition, system of religion, or family law, should be in line with the requirements of the Constitution. The court further considered the context of Article 32 of the Constitution, which guarantees religious freedoms and expression as read together with Article 45 (4), which recognizes marriages under religious laws, and found that Article 24 of the Constitution acknowledges that not all rights and fundamental freedoms in the Bill of Rights are absolute.

The court further noted that unless a right or fundamental freedom is considered under Article 25 of the Constitution as a right that cannot be limited, it is not an absolute right. Islamic marriages, therefore, fell among the rights which can be limited under Article 25. The court concluded that Article 32 could not be read in isolation but rather in "wholesome and in context", with Article 53(1) Constitution, which provides the right to free compulsory education, and Article 53(2) of the Constitution, which provides that a child's best interests are paramount in every matter concerning the child. The court further acknowledged the petitioners' argument that under Muslim religious practice, girls can be married off before they reach the age of majority. However, the court disagreed with the view that the Kenya Constitution, in protecting the child's best interest, allows children to be married before they reach the age of majority as an expression of their religious freedom. The court referred to Article 53(1)(d) of the Constitution, which provides that every child has the right to be protected from abuse, neglect, harmful cultural practices, all forms of violence, inhuman treatment and punishment. The court found that the third, fourth, and fifth petitioners, in "allowing" or organizing the marriage of a minor, perpetrated a crime. The Constitution could not be interpreted to further the commission of a crime. Judge Chitembwe, on 29 October 2015, held that:

> The bottom line is that the Kenyan Law does not permit marriages of people below the age of 18 years. The 2nd respondent was a child under the provisions of article 260 of the Constitution. The right to marry under Article 45 (2) of the Constitution is only available to adults. Article 260 defines an adult as someone who has attained the age of 18 years. The Constitution grants the freedom to exercise one's religion. However, that freedom has to be carried out in line with the other Constitutional provisions. If each religion is given a free hand to exercise its belief without a common ground, then the end result will be disharmony in the Kenyan society… In the same line, the Constitution outlaws marriages of people below 18 years. This is irrespective of one's religious belief.

The court, therefore, refused to prioritize child marriages contracted under Islamic law despite the exemptions in the Constitution and the Marriage Act. However, some courts have been reluctant to deal directly with any conflict between Islamic law and the equality provisions under the Constitution and other Kenyan laws. For instance, while dealing with a succession matter which involved Article 24(4) and 27 of the Constitution, the Court of Appeal avoided making any finding on the "alleged unconstitutionality of the implicated principles of succession under Islamic law" as argued by the appellants.[166] The Court of Appeal also declined to get into the issue of the consistency of international human rights instruments with the exemptive constitutional provisions of Articles 24(4) and 27, among other laws. Instead, the court found that even if the strict conditions allowing derogation from the Bill of Rights provisions were fulfilled, "the Constitution allows application of Islamic law even though it may be perceived as discriminatory".[167]

The seeming lack of clarity on Article 24(4) was also evident in the High Court decision in the same case, which was the subject of the appeal.[168] The High Court acknowledged that referring to any child as illegitimate was "outrageous", but held that "as long as the estate herein belongs to a deceased Muslim and as long as article 24(4) remains in our Constitution … the court's hands are tied".[169] The Court justified the decision on the basis that the right to equality and freedom from discrimination guaranteed by Article 27 of the Constitution was not absolute because it was qualified by Article 24(4) and was instead limited to matters of personal status, marriage, divorce, and inheritance for persons professing the Islamic faith.[170] The High Court consequently found that the failure to use Sharia law in matters relating to a Muslim's personal status, marriage, divorce, and inheritance conflicted with the Muslims' freedom of religion guaranteed by the Constitution.[171]

The different interpretations by the courts in the cases of *Council of Imams*, *Mary W Muigai*, and *CKC* above regarding the exemption clauses in Article 24(4) of the Constitution and those in the Marriage Act, among others, capture the

166 *CKC and Another (Suing through their mother and next friend JWN) v ANC* [2019] eKLR.

167 Ibid.

168 *In re Estate of CCBH (Deceased)* [2017] eKLR.

169 Ibid., paras. 27.

170 Ibid., paras. 20.

171 Ibid., para. 21.

unclear and sometimes conflicting position of Islamic law marriages and divorce in Kenya.

RECOMMENDATIONS

There is evident tension based on the accommodations made for Muslims in the Constitution, the Marriage Act, other national laws, and international treaty obligations. Kenya, therefore, seems to have different standards for different groups regarding international human rights and the bill of rights in the Constitution. The Constitution and the Marriage Act provide for non-discrimination and equal rights, consent to marry, and the prohibition of child marriages. Yet, blanket provisions exempt Muslims from adhering to the same obligations. This position creates the impression that Islamic law marriage and divorce practice holds a higher position than the Constitution and other types of marriages. The exemptions further confuse the judicial institutions, which interpret the same issues differently.

The ambiguity is especially notable when provisions of the Constitution seem to conflict. On one hand, there is the freedom to practice one's religion to which all Muslims are entitled; on the other, Muslims are exempt from the equality provisions, and by extension, the non-discrimination provisions which underscore the bill of rights in the Constitution. It is contradictory for Kenya to ratify and accept to be bound by human rights provisions yet exempt Islamic law from obligations contained in the said instruments. The relevant Committees, such as CEDAW, and the Human Rights Committee among others, have pointed out these contradictions and violations. It is necessary to find some middle ground that allows the practice of Islamic marriages and divorce without it appearing to contradict the Constitution, the Marriage Act, other relevant legislation and international human rights instruments by which Kenya is bound. To deal with the seeming conflict in the laws, the following is proposed:

Codification of Islamic family law

With the participation of all Islamic stakeholders, Kenya should codify a Muslim family law or code that fully complies with the relevant provisions in the Constitution and the Marriage Act, particularly the provisions on equality, free consent to marry, and the prohibition of child marriages, without any exemptions. In effect, Kenya should implement the CEDAW and the human rights Committee recommendations to codify Muslim family law in a manner compatible with Article 27 of the Constitution. In the alternative, a specific clause should be included in the Constitution and the Marriage Act, explicitly stating that the right to religion should not affect the enjoyment of other constitutional rights and freedoms. This approach can be borrowed from the Parliamentary Assembly of the Council of Europe, which stipulates that the right to manifest one's religion is limited and should "not aim at the destruction of other Convention rights and freedoms".[172] Such a clause will balance Muslims' right to religious freedom but also protect other rights.

Equal rights during and after marriage

Having ratified CEDAW, Maputo Protocol ICCPR, and ICESCR CEDAW, among others, Kenya has an obligation to ensure that, in line with the CEDAW Committee recommendation, it adopts a written family law that provides for equality of spouses irrespective of their religion. The Kenyan laws that exempt Islamic marriages without codifying any mandatory standards should be amended or repealed. The law should disallow any unequal and discriminatory laws and practices irrespective of religion and avoid different human rights standards for other groups within the country.

Consent to marry

Kenya should implement the Human Rights Committee recommendation that laws permitting marriage without consent should be amended or repealed. In this case, the exemptions given to Islamic marriages under the Constitution and the Marriage Act should be repealed. This

[172] Council of Europe, Parliamentary Assembly, "Sharia, the Cairo Declaration and the European Convention on Human Rights", Resolution 2253 (2019).

should be done with the active participation of Muslim leaders, clerics, and other stakeholders.

Divorce rights

The Marriage Act should be amended to emphasize equal divorce rights, with unilateral divorce prohibited, and judicial divorce encouraged. Kenya should strive to implement the CEDAW Committee and the Human Rights Committee recommendations on the prohibition of unilateral divorces and institute the same grounds for divorce for both men and women, for Kenya entered no reservations.

Polygamy

In conformity with its international obligations, Kenya legislation should reflect the position of the CEDAW Committee observations and the Maputo Protocol that polygamous marriages should neither be encouraged nor legitimized. Having admitted that polygamy subjugates women, Kenya should amend the Marriage Act and the Constitution, which place polygamous marriages on the same level as monogamous ones. In the alternative, the requirement for consent by the previous wife or wives should be included in the Act. This provision was initially in the Marriage bill 2013 but was removed by Parliament. It can be reintroduced as an amendment.

Case law

Courts need to reach a uniform interpretation regarding Islamic law practices relating to the consent to marry, child marriages, mutual consent to a divorce, equal rights in marriage, and polygamy which are in line with the bill of rights in the Constitution and in adherence to human rights instruments. The courts should not shy away from dealing with the contradictions in the law and should strive to reconcile certain Islamic practices relating to marriage and divorce with other constitutional provisions, relevant legislation, and human rights provisions. Decisions, such as *Council of Imams and Preachers of Kenya*, which acknowledged the limitations of religious freedom, should be encouraged.

CONCLUSION

Islamic marriages enjoy recognition under Kenyan laws equal to the other four types of marriage. Nonetheless, Muslims are exempt from adhering to the Marriage Act where its provisions are inconsistent with Islamic practice. Article 24(4) of the Constitution exempts Islamic law from the equality provisions. These exemptions permit the violation of equal rights in marriage, free consent in marriage, the minimum marriage age, and equal divorce rights in the Constitution, the Marriage Act, and other legislation. Some Islamic marriage and divorce practices are not consistent with Kenya's international human rights obligations. These conflicts are reflected in court decisions. Kenya cannot have double standards. The amendment and repeal of the exemption clauses have been proposed to align relevant Islamic practices with the constitutional provisions, the Marriage Act, and international human rights treaties. A balance must be achieved without denying Muslims the right to freedom of religion and ensuring no violation of other relevant rights. This is a conversation that all relevant stakeholders must have, including the Muslim representatives, the judiciary, and the legislature.

Chapter Eight
Islamic Marriages and Divorce in Kenya: Ethnocultural Diversity

In Kenya, Muslims constitute a significant minority, estimated in the latest population census to be 11%.[1] Previously concentrated along the coastal and northeastern regions, this Muslim populace is now spread across the country. Successive laws, both before and after independence, have recognized Islamic marriages and divorces.

The 2010 Constitution of Kenya recognizes different forms of marriage and divorce, including those contracted under Islamic law. The Constitution has created specialized judicial institutions called the Kadhis' courts, whose competence includes marital and divorce cases involving Muslims.[2] The Marriage Act of 2014,[3] in particular, recognizes Islamic marriages alongside four others: civil, customary, Christian, and Hindu.[4]

The continued recognition of Islamic marriages and divorces alongside the four others reflects Kenya's ethnocultural diversity. As a multicultural society, the State must enshrine individual and group human rights in its normative structures. Constituted minorities, like religious minorities, deserve special attention, and rights that recognize their distinctive way of life ought to be safeguarded to prevent the law from being used as a tool

1 Kenya National Bureau of Statistics, *2019 Kenya Population and Housing Census Volume IV: Distribution of Population by Socio-Economic Characteristics* (2019), p. 422 (available online).

2 Article 170(5), 2010 Constitution of Kenya.

3 No. 4 of 2014.

4 See section 6(1), Marriages Act 2014.

that essentializes dominant groups.[5] In other words, the incorporation of Islamic family law into the Kenyan legal system protects the right of Muslims to profess their religion and enjoy appurtenant rights thereon, including those governing marriage, divorce and succession.

Because Islam is also transnational,[6] Kenya's Islamic law on marriage and divorce is similar to that of many other jurisdictions.[7] This explains why the Marriage Act simply prescribes that Islamic marriages shall be "celebrated according to Islamic law".[8] The dissolution of such marriages shall also be "governed by Islamic law".[9] However, the application of Islamic law differs, sometimes because of the juristic thought (that is, the understanding of the elemental sources of Islamic law: the Quran[10] and the *Sunnah*)[11] to which a particular country or community subscribes.[12] Intra-community disparities also exist in solemnizing and terminating marriages, primarily because of cultural idiosyncrasies.[13]

This article discusses the law on Islamic marriages and divorce from the perspective of Islamic family law and

[5] Sandra Fredman, "Substantive Equality Revisited", *International Journal of Constitutional Law*, XIV (2016), p. 719.

[6] Miriam Cooke, "Multiple Critique: Islamic Feminist Rhetorical Strategies", *Nepantla: Views from South*, I (2000), pp. 96-98.

[7] See, for example, *MEM v AD* [2015] eKLR, where the Kadhi's court made reference to Egypt and Lebanon to explain the grounds on which a woman may demand judicial separation.

[8] Section 49(1), Marriages Act 2014.

[9] Ibid., section 71.

[10] This is the Muslim Holy Book. The transliteration of the Arabic words and phrases herein is the author's own because she is a Swahili speaker. Like the Arabic language, the Swahili language is rich and offers a more precise pronunciation of the former language than its English counterpart. In fact, some Swahili words derive from the Arabic language.

[11] This is the Muslim Prophet's Tradition. It means his sayings, deeds, and tacit approval of the statements and actions of others.

[12] Abdullahi A. An-Na'im (ed.), *Islamic Family Law in A Changing World: A Global Resource Book* (2002), p. 7.

[13] Anita M Weiss, "Interpreting Islam and Women's Rights: Implementing CEDAW in Pakistan", *International Sociology*, XVIII (2003), pp. 581, 593.

assesses the extent to which the Kenyan legal system, as a pluralistic post-colonial legal system, recognizes such marriages and divorces. Based on a review of the law and relevant scholarly works, the application of Islamic family law in Kenya is contextualized. Points of tension between the Kenyan legal system and the rules of Islamic family law are identified and addressed, especially on polygyny and child marriages. Apart from the constitutional and statutory provisions that regulate family law in Kenya, several cases from the Kenyan courts, including the Kadhis' courts, are considered.

Furthermore, the argument made herein is reinforced by insights from thematic readings of the Quran as supported by prophetic sayings that explain Islamic family law. A thematic or intratextual reading of the Quran means using one verse (or more) to explicate another (or others), provided that the additional prescription(s) address a similar or related situation. To be clear, the analysis is confined to prophetic sayings declared authentic (*swahiih*) by their compilers and later eminent scholars.[14] Some sayings are contained in the *Kadhis' Court Bench Book*.[15]

This is followed by an overview of Islamic law and its application to Islamic marriages and divorces in Kenya. The inclusion of Islamic law in the Kenyan legal system is justified through the epistemology of multiculturalism. The celebration and registration of Islamic marriage in the country is examined by discussing the nature and essentials comprising this institution from the vantage point of justice as plural. The innumerable ways of ending an Islamic marriage are considered. Responding to criticism of the

[14] The compilation of the Prophetic sayings increased immediately after his demise. In the third century of the Islamic Calendar (c. ninth century AD), however, a group of scholars studied critically the preceding compilations. These scholars developed treatises which identified the earlier compiled sayings as authentic, reliable, or weak. About six such works remain seminal: Sahîh Muslim, Sahih Bukhari, Sunan Abu Dawud, Jāmil at-Tirmidhi, Sunan An-Nasâ'i, and Sunan ibn Mâjah – all identified by their compilers' names. The computation of the Islamic calendar commences from the migration of the Prophet and early Muslims from *Makkah* to *Madinah* to flee persecution from the pagan Arabs. It is identified as 'After *Hijrah*' (abbreviated as AH). *Hijrah* is Arabic word for migration. It is 1444 AH today. Both *Madinah* and *Makkah* are in Saudi Arabia.

[15] Judiciary of Kenya, *Kadhis' Court Bench Book* (2020).

discordant ways in which men and women dissolve their marriage, these differences, it is suggested, are predicated on gendered religious duties. Ways are proposed of improving the application of the law on Islamic marriage and divorce in the country.

ISLAMIC FAMILY LAW IN KENYA

Multiplicity of Islamic strands and inconsistent jurisprudence

Muslims began living in parts of present-day Kenya as early as the seventh century.[16] Archaeological discoveries and historical writings suggest that Islamic communities and kingdoms occupied Mombasa, Malindi, and the Lamu archipelago, which are part of the contemporary Kenyan littoral zone.[17] For example, the Moroccan explorer, Hajj Ibn Battuta, reported that when he visited the East African Coast in 1331, Mombasa was an island inhabited by religious, trustworthy, and righteous people who followed the *Shafi'i* school of jurisprudence.[18] *Shafi'i* juristic thought is one of the remaining *Sunni* Muslim schools in the world,[19] alongside *Hanafi, Maliki,* and *Hanbali* – all named after the *imaam*[20] who led the respective explication of the *Quran* and the Prophetic

[16] Pravin Bowry, "Looking for Way Forward on Muslim Law", *The Standard* (Nairobi, 21 May 2014) p. 15; Abdulkadir Hashim Abdulkadir, *Reforming and Retreating: British Policies on Transforming the Administration of Islamic Law and Its Institutions in the Busa'idi Sultanate 1890-1963* (2010) (DPhil Thesis, University of the Western Cape) pp. 5, 7, 10 (available online).

[17] See, for example, Ahmed Idha Salim, "The Impact of Colonialism upon Muslim Life in Kenya", *Institute of Muslim Minority Affairs Journal,* I (1979), p. 60; Marc J. Swartz, "Religious Courts, Community, and Ethnicity among the Swahili of Mombasa: An Historical Study of Social Boundaries", *Africa: Journal of the International African Institute,* XLIX (1979), p. 32.

[18] Said Hamdun (ed.), *Ibn Battuta in Black Africa* (2003), pp. 22-23.

[19] *Sunni* are the traditionalists or orthodox Muslims.

[20] Arabic word for a Muslim leader especially in religious matters, including Islamic prayers. All the meanings of Arabic words in this chapter, unless contained in a quote, are derived from Rohi Baalbaki, *Al-Mawrid: A Modern Arabic-English Dictionary* (1995). Where necessary, however, definitions of terminologies in Islamic jurisprudence are taken from Muhammad Rawwas Qal' ajy, *Encyclopedia of Fiqh Scholars' Jargon: Arabic - English* (1988).

Tradition. Today, a majority of Kenyan Muslims follow the *Sunni* or *Shafi'i schools of* jurisprudence,[21] estimated to constitute 73% of the country's 5,193,461 Muslims.[22] A sizeable following of other understandings of Islam, including the *Sunni* (for example, Hanafi) and *Shia* (for example, Ja'fari, Zaydi, Ahmadi, and Ithna-Asheri), exist.[23]

Given this faith representation, most users of the Kadhis' courts are *Sunni* Muslims of *Shafi'i* persuasion,[24] a strand of jurisprudence that dominates the courts' decisions. During the validation of the draft Kadhis' Court Bench Book in Mombasa, for instance, a section of the *Shia* leadership demanded the inclusion of the *Shia* understanding of Islamic family law in the Book.[25] While ordinarily *Shia* Muslims resolve their grievances using their community dispute resolution mechanisms,[26] some members take their cases to the Kadhi's court.[27]

Critics contest the existence of pluralism within Islamic law, arguing that the existence of numerous schools of thought on the interpretation of the Quran and the *Sunnah* exposes women to different dispute-resolution processes and possible outcomes,[28] hence the unpredictability of

21 An-Na'im, note 12 above, p. 55.

22 Musawah and Advocacy for Women in Peace and Security, Africa, (AWAPSA), *Joint Report on Article 16, Muslim Family Law and Muslim Women's Rights in Kenya* (2017) p. 4; the total population of Muslims in Kenya. This figure corresponds to the 2019 Population Census.

23 An-Na'im, note 12 above, p. 55; Rule 5(b) of The Marriage (Muslim Marriage) Rules 2017 (Legal Notice 288) names some Muslim sects in the country.

24 Swartz, note 17 above, p. 35.

25 The author attended this validation workshop on 27 March 2019 at the Castle Hotel in Mombasa.

26 "Memorandum Presented to the Constitution of Kenya Review Commission by the Shia Ithna-Asheri Muslim Community", *Report of the Constitution of Kenya Review Commission: Technical Appendices*, V(2) (2003), p. 524.

27 For example, *Fazleabbas Mohammed Chandoo v AI Hussein & 4 others* [2015] eKLR is a constitutional petition that arose from such a case.

28 Kevin Wanyonyi, *The Kadhis' Courts in Kenya. Towards Enhancing Access to Justice for Muslim Women* (2016), pp. 20-24 (MS Thesis, Lund University).

decisions relating to Islamic marriages and divorce.[29] These critics further identify the absence of a codified law on Islamic marriage and divorce as contributing to the different outcomes from different benches (or courts) and different dispute resolution mechanisms.[30] Moreover, both Muslim and non-Muslim lawyers appear in the Kadhi's court to prosecute cases relating to Islamic marriages and divorces. Sometimes, the mainstream courts try these cases or hear their appeals.[31] Most lawyers, magistrates, and judges in the country are non-Muslim and ignorant of Islamic law.[32] Consequently, there have been fervent calls since the year 2000 by Muslim lawyers,[33] Kadhis,[34] and scholars[35] following the initiation of the constitutional review process to codify Islamic personal law. While the Attorney General is yet to act, the office of the Chief Kadhi has drafted a bench book that summarizes the applicable Islamic personal law in Kenya.

In establishing the Kadhi's court, the Constitution opened these courts to various strands of Islamic thought. Article 170(2)(b) provides that a Kadhi shall be any Muslim who "possesses such knowledge of the Muslim law applicable to *any sects* of Muslims and deemed so fit by the Judicial Service Commission" (emphasis added). Thus, a Kadhi is within his mandate if he decides two similar cases differently because he has applied two different scholarly

29 Ibid.

30 Musawah and AWAPSA, note 22 above, p. 5.

31 Article 165(3)(a), 2010 Constitution of Kenya, gives the High Court unlimited original jurisdiction in criminal and civil matters; also see, section 5, Kadhi's Court Act (CAP 11) which extends the Kadhis' courts' jurisdiction to the High Court.

32 Moza Ally Jadeed, *The Inheritance Rights of Muslim Women in Kenya: Reality or Rhetoric?* (2020), p. 212 (DPhil Thesis, University of Nairobi).

33 John Chesworth, "Kadhi's Courts in Kenya: Reaction and Responses", in Abdulkader Tayob and Joseph Wandera (eds.), *Constitutional Review in Kenya and Kadhis Courts: Selected Papers presented at the Workshop, 20 March 2010, St. Paul's University, Limuru, Kenya* (2011), p. 8 (available online).

34 *SMK v RHH* [2015] eKLR. (all cases from the electronic Kenyan Law Report (eKLR) can be obtained online).

Ibid.

35 See. for example, Jadeed, note 32 above. pp. 214, 283.

understandings of Islamic law according to the sectoral persuasions of the parties before him. The *Shia* Muslims' preference for alternative dispute resolution (ADR) processes *in lieu* of the Kadhis's courts is similarly safeguarded by the Constitution. Articles 48 and 159(2)(c) of the Kenyan Constitution guarantee access to justice through the ADR mechanisms, among other dispute resolution processes. Article 159(3) enjoins the employment of traditional dispute resolution systems provided that they do not contravene the Bill of Rights, are not repugnant to justice and morality, and do not violate the Constitution or other written laws. In line with these provisions, the judiciary launched an Alternative Justice Systems (AJS) Policy in 2020 as part of celebrations commemorating the tenth anniversary of the Kenyan Constitution.[36] Furthermore, the National Steering Committee on the Implementation of the AJS Policy is training AJS champions across the country to activate AJS mechanisms in the champions' localities.[37] There is also a pending Bill on ADR mechanisms in the Senate.[38]

Application of Islamic law on marriage and divorce: law and supporting theory

The Marriage Act is the primary legislation governing marriage and divorce in Kenya. As mentioned above, this Act recognizes both Islamic marriage and divorce. However, just like its predecessors – the Mohammedan Marriage Divorce and Succession Act (CAP 156) and the Mohammedan Marriage and Divorce Registration Act (CAP 155) - the Marriage Act does not detail the form and content of Islamic law that should govern the celebration and dissolution of Islamic marriages. Thus, where a court is faced with a matter dealing with a question on either Islamic marriage or divorce, recourse is to the sources of

[36] See generally The Judiciary of Kenya, *Alternative Justice Systems Framework Policy* (2020).

[37] The author had previously been selected as an AJS champion for Mombasa County.

[38] See The Alternative Dispute Resolution Bill, 2021 *Kenya Gazette Supplement No 97* (Senate Bills No. 34).

Islamic law.[39] In *NUFR v MSC*,[40] the High Court affirmed this position. The Marriage Act, however, describes Islamic marriages as polygynous or potentially polygynous.[41] Consequently, the Act grants them the same legal status as monogamous marriages under the Hindu, Christian, and civil systems.[42]

The Marriage Act is the culmination of a protracted journey of legal reform to develop uniform, comprehensive family laws in Kenya. Immediately after independence in 1963, Kenya sought to replace all the country's four extant marriage, divorce, and succession legal regimes, including their attendant pieces of legislation.[43] These plural laws were British law, (African) customary law, Islamic law, and Hindu law. A Marriage and Divorce Commission established in the 1960s to harmonize and consolidate the various pieces of legislation met heavy resistance from the Muslim community.[44] Where the Commission succeeded in laying a bill before the National Assembly, the male-dominated Assembly refused to adopt the bill because it was too Western and deprecatory of customary practices.[45] Later attempts in the 1980s and 1990s achieved little result despite the optimism expressed by scholars such as Eugene Cotran.[46]

No further attempt to consolidate marriage and divorce laws occurred until 2007. Following initial rejection by religious leaders, including Muslim leaders, the 2007

39 These are the Quran, the Prophetic Tradition (through his sayings), jurists' consensus (*ijmaa'i*), and personal reasoned analogy (*qiyaas*) in that order. See Mohammad Hashim Kamali, *Shari'ah Law: An Introduction* (2008), p. 19.

40 *NUFR v MSC* [2015] eKLR, para. 27.

41 Section 6(3), Marriages Act 2014.

42 Ibid., section 3(3).

43 Eugene Cotran, "The Development and Reform of the Law in Kenya", *Journal of African Law*, XXVII (1983), p. 56.

44 Eugene Cotran, "Marriage, Divorce and Succession Laws in Kenya: Is Integration or Unification Possible?", *Journal of African Law*, XL (1996), p. 202.

45 Ibid.

46 Ibid., pp. 202-203.

Marriage bill underwent several revisions,[47] culminating in the Marriage Act of 2014. Although it repealed the seven pieces of legislation governing the five systems of marriage and divorce, the Act retained these systems.[48] This outcome, however, did not match the post-independence reasons for the Act. Then, the government argued the imperative of establishing a common law regime for all Kenyan residents, without any distinctions among groups.[49]

Consequently, critics contest the status quo because it treats women differently, some women, especially Muslim women, being unfavorably treated.[50] Examples of "reprehensible" practices foisted on women in the name of legal pluralism include polygamy and child marriage.[51] On the face of it, legal pluralism may seem problematic because of the inconsistencies it creates in a territory. However, "legal differentiation by itself is (...) a common and expected feature of the law",[52] dictated by the composition of the society it serves. The Kenyan society is heterogeneous, consisting of multiple ethnic, cultural, and religious communities, as noted in the preamble to the country's Constitution. In a bid "to live in peace and unity as one indivisible sovereign nation" amid this diversity – as the preamble dictates – "some forms of cultural [and religious]

[47] Peter Leftie, "Proposed Marriage Laws Raise Storm", *Daily Nation* (Nairobi, 30 September 2009), p. 10.

[48] See Part III (Christian marriages); Part IV (Civil marriages); Part V (Customary marriages); Part VI (Hindu marriages); Part VII (Islamic marriages); and Part X (different provisions for divorce and settlement of marital disputes in the five systems of marriage).

[49] Cotran, note 44 above, p. 196, reproducing Attorney General Charles Njonjo's speech at the inauguration of the Law Commissions.

[50] Convention on the Elimination of All Forms of Discrimination against Women; Committee on the Elimination of Discrimination against Women (CEDAW Committee), "Consideration of Reports Submitted by State Parties under Article 18 of the Convention: Kenya", *UN Doc CEDAW/C/KEN/8* (2016), para. 206.

[51] Susan Moller Okin, "Is Multiculturalism Bad for Women?", in Joshua Cohen, Mathew Howard, and Martha C Nussbaum (eds.), *Is Multiculturalism Bad for Women? Susan Moller Okin with Respondents* (1999), p. 16.

[52] Anver M Emon, "The Paradox of Equality and the Politics of Difference: Gender Equality, Islamic Law and the Modern Muslim State", in Ziba Mir-Hosseini, and others (eds.), *Gender and Equality in Muslim Family Law: Justice and Ethics in the Islamic Legal Process* (2013), p. 238.

difference" must be accommodated "through special legal or constitutional measures".[53] It would therefore be unfair to expect Muslims to forgo their religion's prescriptions and assimilate into the dominant secular law.

This chapter, therefore, adopts multiculturalist theory to justify the inclusion of Islamic family law in the Kenyan legal system. Multiculturalism demands that the unique interests of each significant group in a society should reflect in that society's laws and institutions, including special legal provisions for minority groups.[54] Enacting such provisions enables minority groups to enjoy "the same treatment in law and in fact as other nationals".[55] It allows these minorities to participate in their distinct characteristics without fearing domination by the majority.[56] It further allows them to participate in their country's socio-economic and political affairs without anticipating exclusion.[57] As they celebrate their national identity, minorities also retain their uniqueness.[58] In the case of Kenyan Muslims, therefore, these special provisions encompass, at the least, their family laws, which are of exceptional importance to them. As a former *liwali*[59] for the country's coastal region once advised the British colonial government, "any interference as to the applicability of the Sheria[60] in such questions renders the parties concerned non-Muslim".[61]

53 Will Kymlicka, *Multicultural Citizenship: A Liberal Theory of Minority Rights* (1996), p. 26.

54 Robert McCorquodale, "Self-Determination: A Human Rights Approach", *The International and Comparative Law Quarterly*, XLIII (1994), p. 859.

55 Patrick Thornberry, "Self-Determination, Minorities, Human Rights: A Review of International Instruments", *The International and Comparative Law Quarterly*, XXXVIII (1989), p. 870.

56 McCorquodale, note 55 above.

57 Ibid.

58 *Minority Schools in Albania* [1935] PCIJ Series A/B No 64 17.

59 This is a Swahili word which stems from the Arabic word '*al-wali*' meaning a governor. Abdulkadir, note 16 above 44.

60 This is a Swahili word for the Arabic word *Sharii'ah* which means Islamic law.

61 Abdulkadir, note 16 above, pp. 199-200.

ISLAMIC MARRIAGE: NATURE AND ESSENTIALS

Polygynous and heterosexual relationships

Islamic marriages are heterosexual and polygynous. Both the Quran and the Prophetic Tradition are unequivocal about this fact.[62] In his Farewell Sermon, for instance, Prophet Muhammad (Peace Be upon Him),[63] while advising men on how to treat their wives, proclaimed, "People, fear Allah concerning your women. Verily you have taken them on security of Allah and have *made them lawful for you* by the words of Allah".[64] This important sermon, which summarized the Prophet's Message to the world, reiterated that Islamic marriage is between a man and a woman. Thus, a Muslim man can marry up to a maximum of four women at any given time. Quran 4:3 commences by instructing men to wed "two, or three, or four"[65] women of their choice. However, it enjoins these males to take only one wife if they cannot deal justly with multiple wives.[66]

While Quran 4:3 emerged following a discussion on the property rights of females orphaned during one of the early battles involving nascent Muslims, its instruction transcends this context.[67] During the Battle of *Uhud*, about seventy Muslim male soldiers died.[68] This loss created

62 See Quran 30:21; and 49:13. The first number in Quranic citations refers to a *surah* (Arabic word for a chapter of the Holy Quran), and the second relates to an *ayah* (plural *ayaat*), which means a verse.

63 Abbreviated PBUH, refers to the salutations of peace (or prayers) that Muslims send to their Prophet whenever he is mentioned. The salutations are a form of worship.

64 See also Safi-ur-Rahman Al-Mubarakpuri, *The Sealed Nectar: The Biography of the Noble Prophet (SAW)* (2011), p. 611 (emphasis added); The Farewell Sermon, also known as the Last Sermon, is that which the Prophet delivered during his only pilgrimage. He died a few months later.

65 Abdullah Yusuf Ali, *The Meaning of the Holy Qur'an* (2001), p. 184. All translations of the *Quran* in this chapter are derived from this source.

66 Ibid.

67 Ibid.

68 This was the second battle that Muslims (living in *Madinah*) fought against the

numerous orphans and widows. Quran 4:3, therefore, begins by warning men, hitherto property managers, who desired to marry these orphans but were not keen to give them a fair dowry because of their inherited property.[69] It instructs these property managers to keep off such orphans and marry other women because, after all, God has allowed them to marry up to four women.[70] Indeed, an intratextual reading of Quran 4:3 and Quran 4:129 shows that the ruling on polygyny outlives the context of the protection of the property of female orphans. *Quran* 4:129, which verse offers marital counselling, determines that men in polygynous relationships cannot exude perfect justice between their wives in every respect.[71] While they may divide material things between their wives equally, they may exhibit varying levels of love towards these women. Thus *Quran* 4:129 calls on men to treat all their wives honorably even when these differences exist. While this prescription recognizes that some husbands may be inclined towards some of their wives, it rebukes them for deserting the remaining wives and calls on them to observe the rights due to all their wives. Polygyny is legitimate in Islam, but is an optional practice subject to precise conditions.[72]

Both the polygynous and heterosexual nature of Islamic marriage accords with mainstream Kenyan law. As mentioned earlier, the Marriage Act describes Islamic marriage as polygynous or potentially polygynous. The Act also provides that a marriage is a voluntary union between

pagan Arabs of *Makkah*. Fought in 3 AH (624 AD), it marked the heaviest defeat of early Muslim history. See Quran 3:152-155, 166.

[69] Hadiith 2068 in Sulaiman bin Ash'ath Abu Dawud, *English Translation of Sunan Abu Dawud* (2008), pp. 511-513.

[70] Ibid.

[71] Hafiz Ibn Kathir, *Tafsir Ibn Kathir (Abridged)* (2003), p. 601.the correct understanding for the Qur'an is necessary for every Muslim. The Tafsir of Ibn Kathir is the most renowned and accepted explanation of the Qur'an in the entire world. In it one finds the best presentation of Ahadith, history, and scholarly commentary. Tafsir Al-Qur'an Al-Azim, which is famous by the title *Tafsir Ibn Kathir*, by Al-Hafiz. Abu Al-Fida' 'Imad Ad-Din Isma'il bin 'Umar bin Kathir Al-Qurashi Al-Busrawi (d. 774 H.

[72] Asma Barlas, "Believing Women", in *Islam Unreading Patriarchal Interpretations of the Qur'an* (2002) pp. 192, 198 (available online).

a man and a woman, whether it be "monogamous or polygamous", provided it is registered.[73] This recognition of Kenyan marriages as heterosexual emanates from the Constitution. Article 45(2) is emphatic that marriage is between persons of the opposite sex. Article 45(4), on the other hand, calls for the enactment of a law which recognizes, *inter alia*, religious marriages. But such marriages must remain consistent with the Constitution. The Marriage Act is a response to the call in Article 45(4), with its recognition of marriages under Islamic law also fitting this call.

As noted, critics consider the Marriage Act unconstitutional because it permits polygynous marriages.[74] Both the Committee on the Convention on the Elimination of All forms of Discrimination against Women (CEDAW Committee) and the Kenyan delegation to the Committee shared this perspective in Kenya's periodic reports.

However, the view that polygyny violates women's rights is incorrect, at least in the case of Islamic marriages. Muslim males can only marry two, three, or four women if they can guarantee justice between the said wives. Justice here includes substantive equality in provision, spending time, and sexual relations.[75] Otherwise, a Muslim man can only marry one woman. These guidelines are a win for women.[76] They afford justice to women generally and give widows and female orphans an opportunity to enter lawful relationships, helping them keep within the law against adultery. For a long time and because of many factors such as wars, the population of women in the world has exceeded that of men. The limitation to four wives also ended a pre-Islamic practice where men could marry as many as a hundred wives.[77]

[73] Section 3(1), Marriages Act 2014.

[74] See for example, CEDAW Committee, "Concluding Observations of the Committee on the Eighth Periodic Report of Kenya", *UN Doc CEDAW/C/KEN/CO/8*, (2017), para. 50(a); CEDAW Committee, note 50 above, para. 206.

[75] Amina Wadud, *Qur'an and Woman: Rereading the Sacred Text from a Woman's Perspective* (1999), p. 83.

[76] Barlas, note 72 above, p. 157.

[77] Azizah al-Hibri, "A Study of Islamic Herstory: Or How Did We Ever Get

The view that the recognition of polygyny erodes constitutional rights or perpetuates sexual inequality is also incorrect. The principle of equality has long been misunderstood.[78] The Constitution refers to substantive equality in Articles 27(4) and (5), and 24(4). This approach does not isolate Kenya from other open and democratic societies, as many national and international legal documents have done the same, through either an explicit proscription of direct and indirect forms of discrimination[79] or the construction of the principle of equality as substantive.[80] Both freedom from indirect discrimination (under the principle of equality) and freedom of religion thus safeguard polygyny. Indeed, in its General Comment 19, the Human Rights Committee acknowledged that the right to religion embodies the right to religious marriages.[81]

The CEDAW Committee also endorsed substantive equality for all women's rights, save for the rights in a family. In its observations about Benin, Slovakia, and Brazil, for example, the Committee recommended to these Member States (and others in a similar position) "to adopt laws and practices that embody a substantive equality approach".[82]

into This Mess?", *Women's Studies International Forum*, V (1982), p. 209; Nazīrah Zein Ed-Dīn, "Removing the Veil and Veiling: Lectures and Reflections towards Women's Liberation and Social Reform in the Islamic World", *Women's Studies International Forum*, V (1982), p. 222.

78 Jadeed, note 32 above, pp. 96-100 demonstrates the admission of this strand globally.

79 See for example, Article 1, CEDAW ('effect or purpose'); Article 56(4), 2013 Constitution of Zimbabwe; Articles 9(3) and (4), 1996 Constitution of the Republic of South Africa; Article 15, 1982 Constitution Act of Canada.

80 CEDAW Committee, "General Recommendation 28", *UN Doc CEDAW/C/GC/28*, (2010), paras. 9 and 16; UN Committee on the Elimination of All Forms of Discrimination Against Women, "General Recommendation No 25", in *Note by the Secretariat, Compilation of General Comments and General Recommendations Adopted by Human Treaty Bodies* (2008), paras. 6-8; UN Human Rights Committee, "General Comment 18", *Note by the Secretariat, Compilation of General Comments and General Recommendations Adopted by Human Treaty Bodies* (2008), paras. 8 and 13.

81 See UN Human Rights Committee, "General Comment 19", *Note by the Secretariat, Compilation of General Comments and General Recommendations Adopted by Human Treaty Bodies* (2008), para. 4.

82 CEDAW Committee, "Concluding Comments: Benin", *UN Doc CEDAW/C/BEN/CO/1-3*, (2005), para. 20; CEDAW Committee, "Draft Concluding Observations

The insistence of the Committee and other critics on identical rights between the genders in the realm of family law seems to stem from article 16(1) (c) of the Convention. This provision calls on States to guarantee women and men the "*same* rights" (emphasis added) during and at the dissolution of a marriage. In essence, this provision expounds explicitly, the phraseology "on a basis of equality of men and women" in the chapeau to Article 16(1) as sameness of treatment or what is known as formal equality. While this phrase also means substantive equality, it does not portend so in relation to marriage, divorce, and inheritance by a plain reading of Article 16(1) (c).

However, in recognition of the diversity of her people, Kenya, just as other countries with minority communities, has extended the application of substantive equality to the realm of family law. This conclusion is compelling, at least in the instance of Islamic marriage and divorce, especially when one reads Article 24(4) of the Constitution. Therein the Constitution subjects the meaning of equality in the Bill of Rights to the Islamic understanding of equality when a case (relating to succession, divorce, or marriage) is before the Kadhi's court. This means, for example, that when a litigant demands equal treatment and equal socio-economic opportunities[83] or equal rights before, during, and after marriage[84] at the Kadhi's court, the court will interpret the demanded equality substantively.

The introduction of Article 24(4) into the Kenyan Constitution was not achieved by the Muslim community but by a coalition of Kenyan women's rights activists[85]

of the Committee on the Elimination of Discrimination against Women: Slovakia", *UN Doc CEDAW/C/SVK/CO/4*, (2008), para. 8; CEDAW Committee, "Report of the Committee on the Elimination of Discrimination against Women (Twenty-Eighth and Twenty-Nineth Sessions)", *GAOR 58th Session Supp No 38 UN Doc (A/58/38)*, (2003), para. 98; see also Andrew Byrnes, "Article 1", in Marsha A. Freeman, Christine Chinkin, and Beate Rudolf (eds.), *The UN Convention on the Elimination of All Forms of Discrimination Against Women: A Commentary* (2012), p. 65.

83 Article 27(3), 2010 Constitution of Kenya.

84 Ibid., Article 45(3).

85 These were Federation of Women Lawyers – Kenya, Institute for Education in Democracy, Kenya Human Rights Commission, and the League of Kenya Women Voters. See Athena D. Mutua, "Gender Equality and Women's Solidarity across

during the first constitutional review process in 2003.[86] To this women's alliance, which had anchored its campaign for gender equality and women's empowerment on the principle of equality, substantive equality regarded all women as stakeholders in "policy formation" and respected their different views.[87] Thus, as it related to the Kadhi's court, the coalition respected Muslim women's conception of rights, despite its divergence from the majority of non-Muslim women's predilections.[88] The inclusion of this provision in the Constitution was, however, unnecessary.[89] Even without it, the understanding of equality as substantive in any court or institution in the country is evident in Articles 27(4) and (5) of the Constitution. But Kenya, perhaps, wanted to eliminate any doubt about the application of this principle to its Muslim populace, especially when they are before the Kadhi's court. Therefore, the Marriage Act's recognition of Islamic marriages as polygynous or potentially polygynous is constitutional because it aligns with Article 45(3) when read together with Article 24(4). It is also consistent with Articles 27(4) and (5).

Contractual relationship

Whether an Islamic marriage turns out to be polygynous, it is a contract between an individual man and an individual woman.[90] Thus, just as any other contract, mutual rights and obligations ensue for the husband and the wife. Quran 4:1 recognizes these rights and obligations between spouses.[91] Spouses have identical conjugal rights.[92] However, the man

Religious, Ethnic, and Class Differences in the Kenyan Constitutional Review Process", *William and Mary Journal of Women and the Law*, XIII (2006-2007), p. 4.

86 Ibid., pp. 4, 92. See also section 34(4), 2005 Proposed Constitution of Kenya.

87 Ibid., p. 91.

88 Ibid.

89 Jadeed, note 32, p. 104.

90 George S Batcheller, "Mohammedan Marriage, Divorce and Domestic Relation", *The North American Review*, CLXXXV (1997), p. 767.

91 See Ali, note 65 above, p. 183.

92 See Quran 2:187 and 30:21.

bears solely the "religious duty" of maintaining his wife and children (that is, providing food, shelter, clothing, and other incidentals to the woman's or family living) according to his economic means.[93] In the Farewell Sermon, the Prophet elucidated this duty thus: "It is incumbent upon them to honor their conjugal rights and not to commit any acts of impropriety (...). If your wives refrain from impropriety and are faithful to you, clothe and feed them suitably".[94] Thus, a wife is duty-bound to be obedient and respectful to her husband while guarding her chastity, her husband's property, and children (if any).[95] However, such obedience does not include anything impermissible in Islam.[96]

An Islamic marriage is a form of worship. The parties' obligations to each other constitute part of their *mu'aammalat*[97] duties, observing the rights of God's creations.[98] Indeed, because of the presumed tranquility a marriage affords the spouses (through comfort, love, and satisfaction of sexual needs)[99] to engage in their daily pursuits, the Prophet described it as a fulfilment of half of the religion.[100] The Prophet also declared marriage his tradition and distanced himself from those who abstain from it.[101] Thus, the growing tendency among some Kenyan Muslims (both men and women) to refuse to marry can be

93 Ḥammūdah'Abd al-'Āṭī, *The Family Structure in Islam* (1977), p. 269; Riffat Hassan, "An Islamic Perspective", in Karen Lebacqz and David Sinacore-Guinn (eds.), *Sexuality: A Reader* (1999), p. 354; See also *Quran* 2:233; 4:34; 65:1, and 6-7.

94 See Al-Mubarakpuri, note 64 above, p. 611.

95 See Quran 4:34. See also *Hadiith* 1829 in Muslim ibn al-Ḥajjāj al-Qushayrī, *Ṣaḥīḥ Muslim: English Translation of Sahîh Muslim* (2007), p. 155.

96 Muḥammad'Alī Hāshimī, *The Ideal Muslimah: The True Islamic Personality of the Muslim Woman as Defined in the Qur'an and Sunnah* (2005), p, 188.

97 Arabic word for dealings, transactions, behavior, or conduct.

98 See Jadeed, note 32 above, p. 67, where these duties as called social-communal. The other duty of humans is *'ibadah*, meaning to worship God.

99 Mohamed Mraja, "The Reform Ideas of Shaykh 'AbdallāhSālih al-Farsī and the Transformation of Marital Practices among Digo Muslims of Kenya", *Islamic Law and Society* XVII (2010), p. 245.

100 Kadhis' Court Bench Book, note 15 above, p. 82.

101 Said Abdullah Seif Hatimy, *Woman in Islam: A Comparative Study* (1979), p. 24.

termed un-Islamic,[102] given that marriage is the only lawful institution where the satisfaction of instinctive sexual desires can be fulfilled legitimately.[103] Unless a person suffers from an incurable infectious disease, has a physical impediment which prevents them from engaging in sexual acts, and cannot discharge the remaining obligations attendant to the union, celibacy may not be an option for them.[104] In this regard, Kenyan Muslim clerics exhort Muslims to embrace marriage.[105] They also advise parents against inflating the dowry due their daughters,[106] which has made many young men hesitate to marry.

The High Court had occasion to describe marriage as a contract. In *RMM v M aka JKM*,[107] the court observed that "a valid marriage is a legally binding contract". In an earlier case, while equating Islamic marriage to an English marriage, the court described it as a special contract involving a "strong interpersonal relationship between the bride and the bridegroom".[108] As such, it is generally accepted in Kenya that an Islamic marriage is contractual. The Kadhis' courts have made innumerable references to the accompanying civil rights and obligations of the parties.[109]

Essentials

Before parties enter into an Islamic marriage, however, several conditions must be met to make it valid, including

102 Mraja, note 99 above, p. 276.

103 Meraj Ahmad Meraj, "The Importance of Marriage in Islam", *International Journal of Research Granthaalayah*, VI (2018), p. 2.

104 Ibid; See also Haruna Abdulrauf, *Early Marriage Is an Antidote to Illegal Relationship among the Youths: A Case Study in Ilorin South Local Government* (2016), pp. 22-24, which mentions instances when a marriage is obligatory, recommended, permissible, detested, and prohibited.

105 Mraja, note 99 above, p. 275.

106 Ibid.

107 *RMM v M aka JKM* [2019] eKLR, para. 46.

108 *Farhana d/o Zafarullah Kahn and Another v Mohammed Shafiq Qureshi* [1997] eKLR.

109 See for example, *RDJ v AHW* [2016] eKLR; *DNG v AOP* [2016] eKLR.

paying the bride's dowry, obtaining the consent of both the bride and her guardian, and finding two male witnesses.[110] Similarly, the intended bride and groom, as well as the guardian and the witnesses, must have the capacity to contract or discharge their respective roles. This means that they must have attained the age of majority and be of sound mind. The marriage between the intended bride and groom must be within the permissible degree of affinity and consanguinity.

The dowry

It is a man's duty to pay a dowry (*mahr*) to the woman he intends to marry.[111] This instruction appears at least six times in the Quran.[112] Whether the intending bride agrees to receive the dowry in whole or in installments, or before or during the solemnization of the marriage, the dowry remains mandatory.[113] This explains why Muslims objected to the initial draft of the Marriage Bill, which sought to regulate dowry payment. The 2007 bill operated on the assumption that paying a dowry is purchasing women just like property and provided that a marriage cannot be invalidated by the failure to pay a dowry. The bill also curbed the commercialization of dowry and instructed that agreements to pay a dowry were not enforceable in court. A suit could not be filed for the return of a dowry, wholly or partially. These positions contravened Islamic law. Apparently, the drafters of the bill had conflated dowry with bride price.

But section 2 of the Marriage Act recognizes dowry payment; that is, any "token of stock, goods, money or other property given or promised in consideration of an intended marriage". In an appeal from the Kadhi's court, the High

110 See generally Abdul-Azeem Badawi, *The Concise Presentation of the Fiqh of the Sunnah and the Noble Book* (2007), pp. 372-373.

111 Alamin Mazrui, "The Equality Bill 2000: An Alternative Islamic Perspective", *Human Rights as Politics* (2003), p. 317 (available online). See also *MEM*, note 7 above, para. 4.

112 See Quran 4:4, 24; 5:5; 33:50 and 60:10-11.

113 *HSA v AAL* [2020] eKLR, para. 18.

Court distinguished a dowry from a bride price.[114] The court observed that whereas the latter is "a gift or payment made to the bride's parents at marriage," the former is "a gift given to the woman in a marriage, which becomes her sole property".[115] The court noted that the promise to pay dowry is enforceable.[116] These last two views of the High Court conform with Islamic law. Although some Muslim communities on the Kenyan coast, such as the Swahili and the Digo, usually demand additional financial payments for the bride's father (known as *kilemba*)[117] and mother (known as *maziwa*[118] or *ukaja*)[119] to recognize the parents' efforts in raising the bride;[120] these practices are purely cultural.

The essence of a dowry payment in Islam is to compensate a woman for relinquishing her modesty to a man. Quran 4:24 and Quran 4:20-21 are explicit on this point. Thus, contrary to the practice of some Muslim families, the dowry belongs to the bride-to-be,[121] and the power to decide its nature and size lies with her. Neither her family (including her parents) nor the groom-to-be can dictate the nature and size of the dowry. Not even a Muslim priest can decide on the nature of the dowry.[122] The gift can be anything permissible in Islam (visible or invisible, tangible or intangible) and of whatever size (large or small), depending on the woman's choice. The bride elects how she appropriates the gift, which remains the woman's property during and after marriage (whether due to divorce or death of either party), whether or not the

114 See *FBI v BG* [2018] eKLR, para. 40.

115 Ibid.

116 Ibid.

117 Swahili word for a head turban.

118 Swahili word for milk. Contextually, it means breastfeeding.

119 Swahili word for a cloth used to strap babies on their mothers' back.

120 Mraja, note 99 above, p. 273.

121 *MEM*, note 7 above, para. 4.

122 Hafiz Ibn Kathir, *Tafsir Ibn Kathir (Abridged)* (2003), pp. 410-411 narrates how Umar ibn al-Khattab, the second Caliph, refrained from putting a ceiling on the dower after a woman reminded her of Quran 4:20. Caliph (Arabic *Khaliifah*) means the successors of the Prophet in leading the Muslim community.

marriage is consummated.[123] If the parties divorce before the consummation of the marriage, the woman takes half of the dowry. But Quran 2:237 enjoins the man to give her the remaining half because doing so is "nearest to righteousness". In fact, Quran 4:19-21 admonishes husbands against taking back the dowry, even constructively, for example, by mistreating a wife so badly that she sues for divorce and thereby loses the dowry.

Debts are the second charge to a deceased's estate after fulfilling legacies. Thus, where the dowry remains unpaid until the husband's death, the unpaid dowry, whether whole or in part, becomes a debt to his estate. [124] Similarly, where no specific amount is fixed and the two divorce before the consummation of the marriage, the husband must give the woman a reasonable gift nonetheless. This is what is referred to as *mut'-'atultwwalaaq,*[125] commonly written as *mut'ah* gift or compensation.[126] The Kadhis' courts have repeatedly awarded this one-off compensation to divorced women to comfort them[127] and to enable them "re-start, reorganize and continue"[128] with their lives without struggling. Moreover, both the High Court and Court of Appeal have upheld these awards, provided that the Kadhis' courts factored in the erstwhile husband's financial abilities as instructed by *Quran* 2:236 and 241.[129] In *MAAA v FSS*[130] the Court of Appeal remitted the case to the Kadhi's court for the latter to reach "a fair award of (...) compensation"[131] after assessing the financial ability of the deceased's estate. The

123 *MEM,* note 7 above, para. 5.

124 See Quran 4:11 and 12.

125 Arabic phrase for compensation given to a divorced woman.

126 See Quran 2:236.

127 *MI v AA* [2018] eKLR, para. 13.

128 *AA v HSS* [2021] eKLR, para. 44.

129 See for example, ibid; *HM v SK* [2020] eKLR; *MAAA (suing in his capacity as the administrator of the Estate of Abubaker Mohamed Al Amin (Deceased) v FSS* [2022] KECA 166.

130 [2022] KECA 166.

131 Ibid., para. 47.

Court of Appeal had faulted the Kadhi's court for arriving at a compensatory figure without assessing the deceased husband's ability to pay.[132]

Bride's consent

Next to the dowry is the vital condition of the consent of the intended bride. A bride's consent stands whether it is her first or a subsequent marriage. A woman cannot be married off without her consent, even if her father or guardian consents to the union. [133] While a father or guardian of a minor may enter into a marriage on behalf of a minor without the minor's consent, the minor has the option to consummate the marriage or rescind it upon attaining the age of majority.[134] A marriage is invalid if the woman is forced into it, hence the freedom of the courts to annul it.[135] This Islamic position aligns with the Constitution and the Marriage Act. Article 45(2) of the Constitution and section 3(1) of the Marriage Act identify marriage as a consensual relationship. Thus, section 11(1) (e) of the Act makes such a marriage void if the consent of either party is forced. On its part, section 89 of the Act further criminalizes participation in a marriage ceremony in which there is knowledge or reason to believe that the consent of the other party was coerced or obtained fraudulently or by mistake as to the nature of the ceremony.

Consent of bride's guardian

The consent of the bride's guardian is equally an important condition, next to the bride's consent. According to a Prophetic saying, a woman cannot marry off another woman, nor marry herself off, for if she does so, it will amount to adultery.[136] The resulting marriage would be

132 Ibid., para. 40.

133 Hāshimī, note 96 above, p. 25.

134 Ibid.

135 Kadhis' Court Bench Book, note 15 above, p. 86.

136 Kathir, note 122 above, p. 426.

void.[137] The guardian is the bride's male relative who bears the religious duty of maintaining her. Because Islam is patrilineal,[138] this duty is placed on husbands (or fathers), sons, and the full or consanguine (that is, paternal) brothers.[139] Thus, the responsible male may differ depending on the woman's status (whether she is a daughter, sister, or mother). As noted above, Islam places the duty of family maintenance on the husband. These husbands are fathers where children are present. In the father's absence, this duty of provision falls on the father's father (that is, the children's grandfather), whom Islamic law treats as a father in the absence of the children's father.[140] In the absence of the grandfather, the sons or the full or paternal brothers (as the case may be) will assume this responsibility. This chain of duty-bearing extends to the possible existing male agnate relative.[141] In the absence of such a person, the Muslim ruler takes over. In the Kenyan situation, this ruler would be a Kadhi.[142] A woman may lack a male agnate relative because these relatives are either dead or non-Muslim.

The males' religious duty to provide for or maintain their families extends to safeguarding their daughters', sisters', and mothers' interests and moral integrity during their marriage. Such safeguard is secured by these males' consenting to a proposed union or seeking a suitable suitor for her. Ideally, in the former instance, the guardian is supposed to enquire about the intended groom and his family to establish if he is fit for the woman, especially spiritually and character-wise. The Prophet said, "If someone whose religion and

137 See Abdul-Azeem Badawi, note 110 above, p. 372.

138 Quran 33:5 derives this deduction.

139 A broader interpretation of Quran 4:34 renders this outcome.

140 Abid Hussain, *The Islamic Law of Succession* (2005), p. 183.

141 Kadhis' Court Bench Book, note 15 above, p. 87. Agnates or the Residuaries (*'aswabah*) are consanguine relations; that is, those heirs whose "relation to the deceased is traced without the intervention of female links". Hamid Khan, *Islamic Law of Inheritance: A Comparative Study with Emphasis on Contemporary Problems* (1980), p. 44. There is a relationship between the law on inheritance, male duty to provide, and guardianship roles.

142 Kadhis' Court Bench Book, note 15 above, p. 87. See also *RWK v AMA* [2015] eKLR.

character you are pleased with comes to you (to marry your daughter or ward), then marry (her off) to him (...)".[143] Thus if the guardian is pleased with the man, he should consent to the union. Where a guardian withholds his consent without a valid reason, the intended bride can report the matter to the Kadhi's court, which would then summon the guardian to state his reasons for the objection. If the reasons are untenable under Islamic law or the guardian willfully disobeys the Kadhi's court summons, the Kadhi would assume guardianship and marry off the woman. Many marriages have been so performed. However, this approach is exercised only as a last resort to ensure continued amiable relations between the woman and her guardian.

Because a father bears the foremost responsibility for providing for and protecting his daughters, he is the first guardian to offer consent for his daughters' marriages. The father may elect someone else to assume this responsibility in his absence. Where the father is deceased, the order of guardianship is determined by the grandfather and transcends to the remaining male agnates in their degree of proximity to the bride. If the bride is a mother entering a subsequent marriage, her son (of majority age) becomes her guardian if both her father and grandfather are dead.[144]

However, critics fault this condition. First, they argue that the power exercised by the guardian condones forced marriages, since the guardian can conclude the marriage of a virgin daughter against her will. Accordingly, forced or coerced marriages are common in rural and urban Kenya, especially out of the view of the authorities.[145] Those who refuse arranged marriages mostly suffer exclusion from their families.[146] Second, critics find the insistence on the guardian's consent as conditioning women to accept

143 Abdul-Azeem Badawi, note 110 above, p. 369.

144 Kadhis' Court Bench Book, note 15 above, p. 87 provides a full chronological list of the guardians.

145 Musawah and AWAPSA, note 22 above, p. 10.

146 The author knows of a female graduate who succumbed to pressure to marry a relative who had only reached secondary education.

perpetual minority.[147] Third, critics argue that women from nomadic families tend to experience difficulties when they want to marry owing to the absence of their male relatives, who would have travelled to distant lands in search of pasture.[148] Therefore, such commentators recommend the removal of the requirement of a guardian's consent, since it emanates from a classical patriarchal understanding of the Quran and the Prophetic Tradition.[149] Critics cite other Muslim countries, such as Pakistan and Sri Lanka, where the guardian's consent is dispensed with for women who subscribe to the Hanafi jurist school.[150]

While it is true that forced marriages of either young adolescents or adult women occur in the country, such idiosyncrasies are far removed from the law on Islamic marriages, as bridal consent remains pivotal to the contracting of marriage. While a guardian can enter a marriage contract on behalf of a minor, the minor has a right to repudiate the contract if she disagrees with it upon attaining the age of majority. In both cases, however, the guardian's consent is part of his duty to safeguard the interests of his family, especially the females. This consent is equivalent to the conventional practice of giving away one's daughter, sister, or mother to her intended spouse – just before exchanging vows. Scenes of males accompanying their female relatives as the latter walk down the aisle abound at many mainstream weddings. Meanwhile, the physical absence of a male guardian is not a legal impediment to a woman's marriage. A father can always appoint a representative. Similarly, it is still possible to reach the guardian and seek their consent via the telephone in this technological age. In many cases, consent has, in fact, been given under such circumstances. However, it is untrue that the condition for a male guardian's consent emanates from jurisprudence. Its source, instead, is a Prophetic saying. It is reported that the Prophet repeated

147 Sisters in Islam, *CEDAW and Muslim Family Laws: In Search of Common Ground* (2011), p. 33 (available online).

148 Musawah and AWAPSA, note 22 above, p. 10.

149 Ibid., p. 11.

150 Ibid.

three times the implication of a woman's marrying without her guardian's permission: "her marriage is void".[151]

Capacity to enter marriage contract

Both parties to a marriage must have attained the age of majority and be of sound mind to conclude a valid contract. The age of majority in Islam, however, commences at puberty, that is, is, when a girl starts menstruating and a boy's voice breaks, among other changed bodily features. Unlike the mainstream numerical premises of defining childhood,[152] the Islamic premise is based on physiological features. Once a child (both male and female) witnesses defining bodily changes, experiences a child has never had since the formative years, such a child transitions to adulthood. The child, subsequently, becomes accountable in their relations with God in the observance of both worship and social-communal activities. Islam also recognizes that sexual feelings commence at puberty.[153] Because it identifies marriage as the only lawful institution to satiate such instinctive urges, Islam permits marriage from the outset of puberty. Other factors to be considered include the parties' mental maturity in relation to the nature of and responsibilities in a marriage and the man's financial means.[154]

Islamic law has been heavily criticized on the issue of marriageable age. Critics argue that early marriages violate section 8 of the Sexual Offences Act,[155] section 4 of the Marriage Act, and section 2 of the Children Act,[156] which identify a child as a person below 18 years of age. Article 45(2) of the Constitution also prescribes that a

[151] Hadith 2083 in Abu Dawud, note 70 above, p. 520.

[152] Mercy Deche, Sarah Kinyanjui, and Kiarie Mwaura, "The Double Standards of Childhood in the Kenyan Legal Framework: The Minimum Age of Criminal Responsibility versus Age of Consent", *East African Law Journal* (2019), p. 5.

[153] Abdulrauf, note 104 above, p. 31.

[154] Ibid., p. 32.

[155] No. 3 of 2006.

[156] No. 8 of 2001.

marriage can be celebrated only between adults. According to Article 260, an adult is a person aged 18 and above. Thus, in *Council of Imams and Preachers of Kenya, Malindi & 4 others v Attorney General & 5 others,*[157] the Constitutional Court found a marriage involving a seventeen-year-old girl unconstitutional because it violated Articles 45(2) and 53 (rights of children). While recognizing that the freedom of religion encapsulated the observance of religious marriages, the court argued that the same Constitution disallowed early marriages – both as a harmful cultural practice and a derogation of the best interests of a child.[158]

Islam permits and encourages early marriages.[159] It is reported that the Prophet urged Muslim youths who are "capable"[160] of marrying to do so. Here, capability refers to having the required mental and physical (health and financial) wherewithal; thus, the Prophet's position in the same saying was that "whoever cannot do so should fast, for it will act as a *Wijā* [161] for him".[162] This saying is explicit that the permission and encouragement of early marriages aim to guide Muslims against sex outside of wedlock. Islam advocates sexual purity, frowning vehemently upon *zinaa* (adultery or fornication), whether between teenagers of relatively similar ages or persons of disproportionate maturity. The Quran equates such premarital or extramarital relations to the sin of murder.[163] Thus, Quran 17:32 admonishes Muslims not to go near adultery, "for it is a shameful deed and an evil, opening the road [to other evils]".[164] In any case, while marriage at puberty is

157 [2015] eKLR.

158 Ibid.

159 Abdulrauf, note 104 above, p. 32.

160 Hadith 2046 in Abu Dawud, note 69 above, p. 499.

161 Arabic word for a shield or protection. Contextually, it means protection against sexual lusts.

162 Hadith 2046 in Abu Dawud, note 69 above, p. 406.

163 See Quran 25:68.

164 Ali, see note 83 above, pp. 682-683.

permissible, it does not mean every Muslim must marry at puberty.

In Kenya, the prohibition of early marriages appears hypocritical. Basically, one common activity in a marriage is sex. Continued recognition that some Kenyan adolescents engage in sex as early as 15,[165] as well as calls to provide contraceptives to those who cannot abstain, is an admission that sex is a human right which cannot easily be denied upon puberty.[166] Most policy documents on sexual and reproductive health rights advocate the provision of condoms to this latter group.[167] In essence, the government and development partners, both local and international, apparently endorse sex between unmarried teenagers, provided it is protected.[168] The end goal here is to prevent the girl from conceiving or both parties from contracting sexually transmitted diseases rather than preventing copulation.[169] It seems that society has more or less accepted that adolescents cannot easily abstain from sex upon attaining puberty.

It also appears that consensual premarital sex between adolescents is an acceptable exception to the law against sexual abuse, as both parties are treated as children in need of protection and therefore referred for counselling or put on probation.[170] But when the age difference between the teenagers is huge or when one party is eighteen or above,

[165] Ministry of Health, *National Adolescent Sexual and Reproductive Health Policy* (2015), p. 9; Kenya National Bureau of Statistics, *Kenya Demographic and Health Survey KDHS 2014*(2014), p. 60.

[166] *Eliud Waweru Wambui v Republic* [2019] eKLR.

[167] See, for example, Ministry of Health, see note 165 above, p. 18; *Adolescent, Young People Sexual Reproductive Health & Rights, HIV Strategic Response for Kilifi County 2019 – 2022* (2019), p. 9.

[168] See for example, United Nations Population Fund, *Harmonization of Minimum Ages and Adolescent Sexual and Reproductive Health Rights: Consent to Sex, Marriage, and Access to Sexual and Reproductive Health Rights in East and Southern Africa* (2020), p. 1.

[169] Ministry of Health, see note 165 above, p. 18.

[170] See for example *GO v Republic* [2017] eKLR, para. 12; *POO (A Minor) v Director of Public Prosecutions & another* [2017] eKLR, para. 31.

this act is deemed criminal.[171] Thus, in 2016, when the High Court set aside the conviction of a 24-year-old man because the girl he was accused of defiling had behaved like an adult,[172] the judge stood condemned at home and abroad.[173] In that case, the court found that the evidence showed no signs of defilement, as the fourteen-year-old girl had visited the appellant for sex and returned to her parent's home several times.[174] To the court, it was unfair to jail the appellant for twenty years when the complainant had, in fact, enjoyed the relationship.[175]

However, such an arrangement is penalized if it happens in a marriage. That is why in *Council of Imams,* the court ordered the prosecution of the third, fourth, and fifth petitioners for subjecting a seventeen-year-old girl to the harmful cultural practice of early marriage, even when the court acknowledged that there was no evidence that the marriage had been consummated. The court noted that under the Sexual Offences Act, a child could not consent to sex. The judge who decided this case was the same who determined *Martin Charo* six months later, by which time, he seems to have experienced a shift in jurisprudence.[176] But it may well be an application of the law based on double standards.

Nonetheless, the increasing engagement of adolescents in premarital sex has forced Kenyan society to consider lowering the age of consent, with the Court of Appeal making this suggestion in 2019.[177] While setting aside the appellant's conviction for defilement, the court observed that it was time Kenya reexamined the Sexual Offences

171 See generally *SNN v Republic* [2019] eKLR.

172 *Martin Charo v Republic* [2016] eKLR.

173 Willis Oketch, "Outrage as Judge Sets Free Defiler Because Girl Was Willing" (2016) (available online); "Kenyan Judge Shoots to Global Infamy for Shameful Verdict", *The East African* (Nairobi, 9 June 2017) (available online).

174 *Martin Charo,* note 172 above, para. 3.

175 Ibid, para. 4.

176 The case of *Council of Imams* was decided on 29 October 2015; the case of *Martin Charo* was decided on 25 April 2016.

177 See *Eliud Waweru Wambui,* note 166 above.

Act. The court faulted the Act for assuming that teenagers often engage in sex ignorantly. Rather, the court opined, these adolescents have a full sense of agency "and can make intelligent and informed decisions about their lives and bodies".[178] The court thus lamented the innumerable number of young men jailed for having sex with adolescent girls whose consent was ignored because they were below eighteen.[179] The court's suggestion led to an uproar, with some supporting and others opposing it. In the end, the government stuck to the status quo.[180] Given the realities on the ground, the court's proposal appears to have some merit.

Permissible degree of marriage

Once the capacity of the parties to a marriage is settled, it must be established that their proposed marriage is within the permissible degree of consanguinity and affinity. The Quran has demarcated between women within this category and those within the prohibited group. Quran 4:22-24 sets out the list of women that men are prohibited from marrying either permanently or temporarily. Therefore, any woman outside these two prohibited groups is permitted to marry.

The permanent prohibition concerns women related to the man in three ways: by blood, affinity, and fosterage.[181] A man cannot marry a woman who is his close blood relation, such as (1) his mother or grandmother;[182] (2) daughters (and granddaughters, daughters of granddaughters of any degree); (3) sisters (full, paternal, or maternal); (4) sisters' daughters (their sons' or daughters' daughters of any degree); (5) brothers' daughters (their sons' or daughters' daughters of any degree); and (6) both paternal and

[178] Ibid.

[179] Ibid.

[180] Kevin Cheruiyot, "There Will Be No Lowering of Consent Age - Matiang'I" (2019) (available online); Akello Odenyo, "Ministry Launches Report on Minimum Age of Consent" (2021) (available online).

[181] Abdulrauf, note 104 above, p. 25.

[182] Just as the meaning of a father extends to a grandfather, so does the meaning of a mother.

maternal aunts. A man cannot also marry any of his female relatives by affinity, such as (1) the wives of his father (or grandfathers);[183] or (2) daughters (and granddaughters of any degree) of his wives if the man has consummated his marriage with the wife (or wives); (3) the wives of his sons (or grandsons of any degree); and (4) the mother (or grandmother) of his wife (or wives). Finally, a man can never marry a woman who wet-nursed him five times or more in the first two years of his life.[184] Similarly, such a man cannot marry his wet nurse's mother, mother-in-law, sisters, daughters (and granddaughters), husband's sister, and other women who were also wet-nursed by the same woman.[185]

On the other hand, temporary prohibited marriages exist because a specific situation pertains. Until this situation expires, a man cannot marry certain women.[186] Thus, a man cannot marry two sisters or a woman and her aunt simultaneously. Similarly, a man cannot also take a fifth wife. Only after the death or divorce of one of his four existing wives can the man add another wife. A man cannot also marry a woman in her *iddah*.[187] While a man can marry a Jew or a Christian, he cannot marry an atheist or a polytheist until she worships Allah and only Him.

On the other hand, a woman cannot marry any of such persons. Thus, in *Sakina Sote Kaitanny & another v Mary Wamaitha,*[188] the Court of Appeal held that if a Muslim man changes his religion, his marriage to a Muslim woman becomes void.[189] A man cannot further marry a fornicator

183 This means another wife of the father (or grandfather) who is not the man's mother (or grandmother).

184 The specificity of the period and number of wet nursing is laid down by the Quran and Hadith. Quran 2:233 is discussed below in the section of divorce.

185 See *ahaadiith* 2055 and 2056 in Abu Dawud, note 69 above, pp. 504-505.

186 Abdulrauf, note 104 above, p. 24.

187 A woman's prescribed waiting period after divorce or death of her husband. See Quran 2:235. See also *Abdirahman Mohamed Abdi & Another v Adan Yusuf* [2013] eKLR.

188 [1995] eKLR.

189 Ibid.

(or adulteress), and a woman cannot marry a fornicator or an adulterer until they have repented.[190]

In addition to a woman being in a permissible degree of marriage, she must not be in a marital relationship. Quran 24:32 enjoins men to "Marry those among you who are single (...)".[191]

Presence of two male witnesses

The final condition is that there must be two males to witness the marriage. The Prophet stated: "There is no marriage except with a guardian and two reputable witnesses".[192] Thus, during the solemnization of the marriage, two males must be present to witness both the celebration of the marriage and the signing of the marriage certificate.

Solemnization and registration of marriage

Once all the conditions above have been established or obtained, the intended bride and groom are ready to enter into the marriage contract. Section 49(1) and (2) of the Marriage Act provides that an Islamic marriage "shall be officiated by a Kadhi, sheikh or imam" who is so authorized by the Registrar of Marriages. Jurisprudentially, *sheikh* (leader) means a Muslim scholar. Section 49(3) further stipulates that the celebration of an Islamic marriage shall be done according to Islamic law. A marriage contract is formed with an offer, an acceptance, and the presence of two male witnesses.[193] The offer and acceptance must be exchanged in one meeting and in the presence of the two witnesses and possibly the bride's guardian. While the bride's guardian's consent is mandatory, he need not be present physically during the *nikaa-h* (marriage) ceremony.

190 Quran 24:3.

191 Ali, note 64 above, p. 874.

192 Abdul-Azeem Badawi, note 110 above, p. 372.

193 *In re estate of Mohamed Kismala* [2017] eKLR, para. 10.

Ideally, the bride's guardian verbally makes the offer to the intended groom thus: "ABC, I marry you XYZ". However, the Kadhi, *sheikh* or *imaam* can do it on behalf of the guardian. Whether it is the bride's guardian or the official who makes the offer to the intended groom, he must make plain the identities of both the bride and the groom. He must pronounce the full names of both parties to eliminate any possible ambiguity about who is entering into that contract.[194] Conversely, the intended groom must accept the offer by uttering, "I marry her" or "I agree to marry XYZ", or "I accept her marriage". At this point, the parties become husband and wife. If the groom has a speech or hearing disability, the offer should be made to him in writing or sign language, and he should respond similarly.

Under Islamic law, it is not required that either the bride or the groom be present at the solemnization ceremony. The bride's attendance can be dispensed with, especially when she is decorated and wearing perfume. If she appears at the ceremony in that state, the bride will offend the prescriptions on *hijaab*[195] as laid down in *Quran* 24:31. Thus, the bride's guardian often represents her in such a public ceremony. The word "public" in Islam refers to the presence of strange (that is, unrelated) members of the opposite sex (*ajnabiyy*). The term "strange" refers to men "within the permissible degree of marriage".[196] The groom may also send a proxy to the ceremony to marry on his behalf. The practice in Kenya has been that the groom prepares a power of attorney authorizing an identified person to enter the marriage contract on his behalf. The attested power of attorney and the groom's identification documents are then presented to the bride's guardian and/or the official solemnizing the union. The officials also recognize a letter written or an affidavit sworn to by the intended groom.

Under the Marriage Act, however, the absence of either the bride or the groom at the solemnization ceremony is

194 Kadhis' Court Bench Book, note 15 above, p. 86.

195 An Arabic word which means a veil, a curtain, a screen, a mantle, or a drape. Jurisprudentially, it refers to observing modesty.

196 Any male who can possibly marry a particular woman, including her cousins, is regarded as a stranger to that woman under Islamic law.

fatal. Section 11(1)(f) nullifies a marriage if "either party is absent from the ceremony". The Muslim Marriage Rules, which are drawn from the Act, also require the presence of at least one party to the marriage.[197] However, the negative consequence of both provisions is muted by section 49(3) of the Act, which voids any provision of the Act that is inconsistent with Islamic law and practices and prevents its application to Muslims.

Be that as it may, the Marriage Act requires that once the marriage is solemnized, the authorized official should record the details of the marriage in a prescribed form and issue the parties with a marriage certificate.[198] The official should then present the form and the certificate to the Registrar of Marriages within two weeks of the marriage to facilitate its registration.[199] It is important to note that although the Marriage Act requires registration of an Islamic marriage, Islamic law does not.[200] However, complying with the statutory requirement does not exempt a Muslim from Islamic law. Instead, such a requirement finds accommodation in Islamic law because it does not "mandate an act which is forbidden".[201] This requirement also does not require a Muslim to abandon what is obligatory.[202] Section 59(1) of the Act identifies the purpose of the certificate as proof of the marriage, a point earlier underscored by the High Court.[203]

Notwithstanding this mandate, the Act is realistic in noting that sometimes the marriage celebration can happen at a place where such formal registers are non-existent; for example, in remote settings. In such circumstances, the celebration of a marriage in a public place of worship is

197 Rule 14(2), Muslim Marriage Rules.

198 Sections 49(2) and 57, Marriage Act 2014.

199 Rule 10(3), Muslim Marriage Rules.

200 *Re Kismala,* note 193 above, para. 10.

201 Mraja, note 99 above, p. 270.

202 Ibid.

203 See *NNS v SAM* [2002] eKLR.

sufficient proof of the marriage.[204] It is important for the official who solemnized the marriage to produce notes and for the two witnesses to testify that the marriage took place. Before the Marriage Act, this is how many marriages were proved.

DISSOLUTION OF AN ISLAMIC MARRIAGE

The Islamic perspective is that an Islamic marriage can be terminated just as any other contract.[205] Section 71 of the Marriage Act recognizes that Islamic marriages will be dissolved according to Islamic law. Ordinarily, such dissolution can happen at the instance of either party through the pronouncement of divorce by the husband, or where the wife discharges herself from the union at will, or via a judicial separation. Dissolution can also occur by operation of law (that is, automatically), when either party renounces Islam, a man equates his wife to his mother, or a stipulated condition occurs. Whereas the law recognizes three avenues for terminating the marriage, the Kadhi's court in *AGC v SSS* erroneously identified two grounds for dissolving an Islamic marriage: judicial and extrajudicial.[206]

Though Islam frowns on divorce,[207] it makes dissolution available where the continued cohabitation of the two becomes untenable.[208] The grounds for dissolution depend on a couple's specific situation or an instance that triggers the operation of the law.[209] The Kenyan courts have affirmed some of these grounds as adultery,[210] cruelty,[211]

204 Section 59(2), Marriage Act 2014.

205 *Farhana d/o Zafarullah,* note 108 above, para. 4.

206 *AGC v SSS* [2019] eKLR.

207 *FAO v MB* [2011] eKLR, para. 9.

208 *FBI,* note 114 above, para 38.

209 *NHA v MMMSA* [2015] eKLR.

210 See *Abdirahman Mohamed,* note 187 above.

211 See *NK v AL* [2020] eKLR.

desertion,[212] denial of conjugal rights,[213] inadequate maintenance,[214] and sheer dislike of the other party[215]. Most of these grounds are similar to those identified by the Marriage Act for the Christian,[216] civil,[217] customary,[218] and Hindu[219] marriages. The courts must be convinced that the marriage has broken down irretrievably and that the objects of love, affection, tranquility, and mercy, as identified in the Quran 30:21, have faded.[220] In *MI v AA*, the High Court faulted the Kadhi's court for failing to dissolve a marriage despite acknowledging that the parties were no longer interested in fostering the union.[221] The High Court referred the matter to another Kadhi's court for issuance of a certificate of divorce.[222]

An Islamic marriage will only be dissolved where all attempts at reconciliation have failed.[223] This court's standing derives from the spirit of Quran 4:34-35, which lists four steps preceding divorce, including family arbitration. During the celebration of the marriage, the man is reminded of Quran 2:229 and 231, which enjoin men to live with their wives harmoniously and to part with them amicably if the need arises.[224]

212 *STM v RMD* [2016] eKLR.

213 *UAM v MOA* [2021] eKLR.

214 *FAO,* note 207 above.

215 *STM,* note 212 above.

216 Section 65, Marriage Act 2014.

217 Ibid., section 66(2).

218 Ibid., section 69(1).

219 Ibid., section 70.

220 *FBM v MS* [2015] eKLR.

221 *MI,* note 127 above, para. 11.

222 See ibid., para. 27.

223 See for example, *HHA v IMI* [2021] eKLR, para. 13; *STM,* note 214 above, para. 2; *AAAN v MJK aka SJK* [2015] eKLR.

224 Susan F. Hirsch, *Pronouncing and Persevering: Gender and the Discourses of Disputing in an African Islamic Court* (1998), p. 17.

Divorce

The commonly known mode of ending an Islamic marriage is *a-twwalaaq*,[225] a measure that can be exercised only by the husband.[226] Because a man bears the religious duty of maintaining his wife (and children) and the entire guardianship role over his family (he heads the household), he has the first right to end a marriage.[227] Quran 2:237 describes the man as the one "in whose hands is the marriage tie". Therefore, in *RWK*, the High Court observed that if there is a dispute about whether a divorce has been pronounced or not, the husband's testimony prevails in the absence of opposing evidence.[228] But the Quran enjoins the man to pronounce divorce as a last resort after exhausting a sequence of reconciliatory efforts. The Quran also offers the parties two chances of separation (repudiatory divorce) akin to the conventional decree *nisi* before making their parting irrevocable.[229]

The reconciliation efforts are fourfold and sequential. The first three are between the couple, and the last involves the families of both the husband and the wife. These steps are admonishing the wife, suspending sexual relations, beating the wife lightly, and appointing arbitrators.[230] If the wife becomes obedient to the husband after any of the first three steps, the husband is dissuaded from nagging the wife or reminding her of past faults. He is also estopped from taking any further steps towards divorce. To be sure, the aspect of beating the wife lightly would raise eyebrows, but its discussion is beyond the scope of this chapter. Suffice it to say, however, that it is a "symbolic beating that does not involve inflicting any physical harm or injury" on the wife.[231]

225 Arabic word for divorce.

226 *RWK*, note 142 above, para. 39; *STM*, note 212 above, para. 2.

227 Barlas, note 72 above, p. 196.

228 *RWK*, note 142 above, para. 39.

229 See Quran 2:229.

230 See Quran 4:34-35.

231 Kadhis' Court Bench Book, note 15 above, p. 116.

It is supposed to signify the husband's utmost disgust with his wife's conduct, and the beating should not touch the face.[232] When asked about the responsibilities of a husband toward his wife, Prophet responded: "To feed her when you eat, clothe her when you buy clothes for yourself, refrain from striking her face or cursing her, and to not abandon her, except in the house".[233]

When none of the four reconciliatory efforts resolves the discord between the couple, the husband exercises the option of divorce.[234] Contrary to what is commonly believed, this pronouncement is not uttered as '*twwalaaq, twwalaaq, twwalaaq*'. While a man can divorce his wife three times, these divorces are spread out in his lifetime with the wife. Thus, when he exhausts the last, the man cannot get back to this woman until she remarries, consummates the next marriage, and gets divorced without the influence of her previous husband. This third divorce is irrevocable. The first two divorces are revocable (that is, *a-twwalaaqraj'i*). They give the man a chance to reunite with his wife[235] either under the first contract (during the woman's waiting period) or a subsequent one (after the woman's waiting period).

According to Quran 2:229, "A divorce is only permissible twice: after that, the parties should either hold together on equitable terms or separate with kindness".[236] Thus, ideally, a man is supposed to pronounce the first divorce. When he does so, the woman enters a waiting period, which is three menstrual cycles for menstruating women, three months for post-menopausal women, and the end of a pregnancy for an expecting woman.[237] The waiting period serves three purposes. First, it is a form of worship. The woman is expected to observe it without question, just as any of God's commandments. Second, it seeks to establish

232 *HSA*, note 113 above, paras. 13-15.

233 Kathir, note 122 above, p. 446.

234 *KNM v MHM* [2019] eKLR, para. 33.

235 *Abdirahman Mohamed*, note 187 above, para 3.

236 Ali, note 65 above, p. 92.

237 See Quran 2:228 and 65:4.

if the woman is pregnant and deters the mixing of kinship (should a woman remarry) if the result is positive.[238] As noted earlier, the law on marriage and divorce aligns with the law on inheritance.[239] The property of a Muslim can only be inherited by his relatives by blood or marriage.[240] Third, it affords the parties an opportunity to reunite. By living together in the same house, the husband may reconsider his decision and get back with his wife.[241] Quran 65:1 instructs that the divorced woman should observe her waiting period in her matrimonial home.

During this waiting period, the maintenance of the woman (food, clothes, and other essentials) remains the man's responsibility. This maintenance should be of the same living standards as the man's.[242] If the man fails to so provide, then the woman can reclaim this alimony in a court of law. Over the years, the courts, both the Kadhis' and mainstream courts, have upheld the divorced woman's rights.[243] In *MAAA*, for instance, after the Court of Appeal found that the respondent was entitled to *'iddah* maintenance, the court remitted the file to the Kadhis' court for assessment of the deceased husband's estate's financial ability in order to arrive at a fair figure. The Court of Appeal faulted the Kadhi's court for reaching an earlier amount without such a determination.[244] The Court of Appeal also criticized the High Court for upholding the Kadhi's court's assessment on the mere basis that the deceased husband was not a pauper.[245]

[238] Abdul-Azeem Badawi, note 110 above, p. 453.

[239] Cotran, note 44 above, p. 195, reproducing former Attorney General Charles Njonjo's speech when setting up the Commission on the Law of Marriage and Divorce in 1967.

[240] Siraj Sait and Hilary Lim, *Land, Law and Islam: Property and Human Rights in the Muslim World* (2006), p. 109.

[241] Abdul-Azeem Badawi, note 110 above, pp. 436-437.

[242] See Quran 65:6.

[243] See, for example, *AAAN*, note 223 above; *OSM v MMO* [2019] eKLR; *AA v HSS*, note 128 above; *MAAA*, note 130 above.

[244] *MAAA*, note 130 above, para 40.

[245] Ibid., para 39.

The Court of Appeal approach is correct and heeds the guidance in Quran 65:6: "Let the women live (in *'iddah*) in the same style as ye live, *according to your means*".[246] Thus, the calculation must be based on the husband's present financial ability, not his wherewithal of the past or future. In the foregoing, therefore, the High Court in *AA v HSS* was wrong to set the *"iddah* maintenance according to the living condition of the woman before the divorce".[247]

Be that as it may, the first divorce (or the first of the dual decree *nisi*) permits the man to resume marital relations with his wife. He can do so during the woman's waiting period without marrying her again. But upon the expiry of the waiting period, the man can only reunite with the woman after entering another contract with her – freshly negotiated. Even in the case of this second scenario, one divorce is counted as having passed between the couple. Thus, the man has one more chance of a repudiatory divorce. If some other discord arises between the couple and the four-step reconciliatory steps yield no result, the man may pronounce the second divorce. Then the same process (as in the first divorce) ensues, that is, the woman enters a waiting period, the man provides for her (and the children, if any), and the man can resume cohabitation with her during her waiting period or marry her after the expiry of the waiting period. Thus, in *RWK v AMA*, the High Court correctly found that the sexual relations undertaken by the parties after the expiry of the *'iddah* were wrongful.[248]

When a man decides to take back his wife, he should treat her kindly. The Quran prohibits men from reuniting with their wives to get even with them or misusing this right.[249] It also recommends that two male witnesses should confirm the reunion. Quran 65:2, reiterating the terms of reunion and separation, stipulates: "And take for witness two persons from among you, *endued with justice, and establish the evidence*

246 Ali, note 65 above, p. 1486 (emphasis added).

247 *AA*, note 128 above, para. 57.

248 *RWK*, note 142 above, paras. 30-32.

249 See Quran 2:231.

(as) before Allah".[250] In *UAM*, the Kadhi's court dissolved the marriage despite the respondent's repeated claim of loving his wife.[251] The court noted that the statements and interactions of the parties before and during the hearing indicated dislike and hatred between the two, demonstrating that the respondent wanted to retain the relationship "not for love and compassion, but just to enslave the petitioner for reasons known to himself alone".[252] However, if a man chooses not to get back with his wife, the marriage ends. Quran 2:231 enjoins Muslims to ensure that such a marriage ends amicably. The woman's maintenance stops at the expiry of her waiting period, and neither party can inherit from the other.[253]

Where, after the second revocable divorce, a subsequent instance of discord leads to divorce (after exhaustion of reconciliatory steps), this divorce becomes irrevocable. While the woman will observe her waiting period, she is not to stay in her matrimonial home. This is because the goal of the waiting period is to ascertain whether or not she is pregnant. There is no chance of the man reuniting with her. And if he really wants to, he has to wait for the woman to remarry, consummate her new marriage, get divorced, and exhaust her waiting period.[254] All these are expected to happen naturally or at the instance of the woman. It is sinful for the erstwhile husband to plan these events. In *RWK*, the High Court reiterated these points succinctly.[255]

In any case, however, divorce can be pronounced orally, in writing, or in sign language.[256] But at all times, it must be in the language understood by the woman.[257] It is sufficient

250 Ali, note 65 above, p. 1484 (emphasis added).

251 *UAM*, note 213 above.

252 Ibid.

253 Cassandra Balchin, *Women, Law, and Society: An Action Manual for NGOs* (1996), p. 158.

254 See Quran 2:230.

255 *RWK*, note 142 above, para. 37.

256 *AAAN*, note 223 above, para 2.

257 Kadhis' Court Bench Book, note 15 above, p. 137.

for the man to say, "I divorce you". When in writing, the divorce must be dated and signed and should identify both the husband and the wife by name. A written divorce takes effect from the date of signature.[258] A divorce can be expressed or implied.[259] The former means that the words are unequivocal that they mean so. In the latter case, the husband employs ambiguous words which may signify divorce or something else.[260] In such a case, the husband's actual intention must be established. If he meant the divorce, then it ensues. Because Islam treats divorce seriously, men are warned against mentioning words which impute it, even as a joke.[261] The High Court in *FBI*, after acknowledging that divorce in Islam is either expressed or implied, held that "the action of the respondent handing over the appellant to elders to take her to her parents' home did not amount to divorce".[262]

Depending on its timing, a divorce can be in the approved mode (*a-twwalaaq al-Sunnah*) or the disapproved mode (*a-twwalaaqbid'a*). The former divorce is done according to the *Quran* and the Prophetic Tradition. In this case, the woman is divorced in the manner prescribed above (the three divorces sequentially, if at all). It must be during her purity (not menstruating), and the two must not had sexual intercourse during this period (the time between the woman's last menses and the pronunciation of the divorce). A divorce is disapproved if it contradicts the Quran and the Prophetic Tradition. This happens when the husband pronounces the three divorces at once or divorces the wife (even if once) during her menses or during her purity but after the two have had sexual intercourse. A man who divorces his wife in a disapproved manner is considered sinful.[263] However, in all three instances, the divorce stands

258 Ibid.

259 Abdul-Azeem Badawi, note 110 above, p. 437.

260 Ibid., p. 438 gives examples of this case.

261 Kadhis' Court Bench Book, note 15 above, p. 136.

262 *FBI*, note 114 above, para. 33.

263 Abdul-Azeem Badawi, note 110 above, p. 440.

except that the three instant pronouncements are treated as one.[264]

Wife's self-release from marriage through compensation

Despite divorce being the husband's right, the wife may release herself from the union by paying the husband. This form of dissolving a marriage is known as *khul'*,[265] which literally means "extracting oneself".[266] The basis for this mode of divorce is Quran 2:229, which reads partly thus: "If ye (judges) do indeed fear that they would be unable to keep the limits ordained by Allah, *there is no blame on either of them if she gives something for her freedom* (...)".[267] This payment seeks to compensate the man for the loss he will suffer because of the separation.[268] In any case, the dowry returned should not exceed the dowry paid according to both Quran 2:29 and 4:19. Thus, in *NK*, the High Court noted that while a woman is entitled to request a divorce, "she forfeits any financial rights due to her *and further returns any dowry* or gifts given to her by her husband".[269] The court, therefore, upheld the Kadhi's court's decision of refusing *mut'ah* compensation to the appellant.[270]

As with a divorce, the ground for the dissolution of marriage under the *khul'* mode is the untenability of the parties' continued cohabitation.[271] This position may result from several factors, including the husband's cruelty or a

264 Ibid., pp. 440-441.

265 Arabic word for divorce (in return for monetary compensation to be paid by the wife to the husband).

266 Muhammad Ifzaal Mehmood, "Judicial Separation at the Wife's Initiative: A Study of Redemption (Khul) in Islamic Law and Contemporary Legislation in Pakistan and Malaysia", *Journal of Islamic Legal Studies* II (2016), pp. 1, 3. The High Court in *MI*, note 127 above, para 15, considered this definition.

267 Ali, note 65 above, p. 93 (emphasis added).

268 Abdul-Azeem Badawi, note 110 above, p. 444.

269 *NK*, note 213 above, para. 20 (emphasis added).

270 Ibid., para. 49.

271 Ibid., para. 18.

sheer dislike of him.[272] At all times, the wife must prove to the court that her continued living with the husband equates to "forcing her into a hateful union".[273] In *FAO*, for example, the court granted the plaintiff divorce after it noted that she had "suffered severe psychological treatment and was denied her fundamental rights of marriage under Islamic law to the extent that she was afraid of her own life". [274] In *STM*, on the other hand, the court granted the defendant/applicant divorce even after it noted that the plaintiff still loved the wife but the wife "clearly" did not love the plaintiff.[275]

Once the court orders that the woman is discharged from her marriage or orders the husband to divorce her, the marriage terminates. If the woman cannot pay the compensation immediately, the husband can demand it from her later. Unlike in a divorce, however, the man has no right to get back with his wife unless she consents. When she consents, a fresh *nikaah* must be performed. The wife also observes a waiting period for one menstrual cycle or one month or until the end of her pregnancy, as the case may be.[276] Here, the purport of the '*iddah* is to follow God's command and establish whether the woman is pregnant, in the case of a woman within menstruating age. The High Court rightly affirmed this position in *NK*. The court observed that the *iddah* period is one month after the woman initiates the divorce.[277]

[272] See for example, *FAO*, note 209 above; *STM*, note 212 above.

[273] Kadhis' Court Bench Book, note 15 above, p. 146.

[274] *FAO*, note 207 above, para. 10.

[275] *STM*, note 212 above.

[276] Abdul-Azeem Badawi, note 110 above, p. 447.

[277] *NK*, note 211 above, para. 31.

Judicial decree

In addition to exercising her right of *khul'*, a wife can seek to rescind her marriage by petitioning the court when the prevailing circumstances make the marriage untenable, but the husband refuses to divorce her. This form of termination is known as *faskhu a-nikaah*. Factors actuating its operation differ; they include the husband's prolonged absence due to travel or desertion and the wife's inability to tolerate the absence of her conjugal rights. Another factor is the husband's failure or inability to maintain the wife, the husband's long imprisonment, impotence, and insanity for a period of two years. Furthermore, the husband's leprosy or venereal disease, husband's cruelty, and a wife repudiating a marriage contracted on her behalf when she was a minor are also factors for the termination of a marriage. When the court is satisfied that these situations pertain, it will issue the divorce whether or not the husband agrees. Thus, in *MAAA*, the High Court upheld the Kadhi's court's decision to dissolve the marriage because the respondent's "marital rights, security, and peace' were violated by the husband".[278] In *HSA*, on the other hand, the Kadhi's court granted the plaintiff divorce after it was satisfied that she had been patient for a long time, yet the defendant had offended the objectives of marriage.[279]

The difference between divorce through judicial decree and *khul'* is that the former is a constructive divorce, where the husband precipitates the divorce by failing or being unable to discharge his obligations in the marriage. It may be that the wife ends the union because her husband mistreats her, contrary to Quran 4:19. Thus, while a wife is not entitled to *mut'ah* compensation in the case of *khul'*, she actually receives it in the case of a divorce through judicial decree.[280] The woman also gets other befitting awards such as *'iddah* maintenance and past unfulfilled maintenance (as

[278] *MAAA*, note 130 above, para. 30.

[279] *HSA*, note 113 above, paras. 10 and 16.

[280] John R Bowen, "Gender, Islam, and Law", in Siwan Anderson, Lori A Beaman, and J. P. Platteau (eds.), *Towards Gender Equity in Development* (2018), p. 284.

the case may be).[281] In *FBM*, the plaintiff sought divorce because the defendant had deserted her for three years and cut communication with her. Furthermore, the defendant failed to maintain her and deprived her of conjugal rights. The court noted that under Islamic law, a wife is entitled to seek divorce if four months have lapsed without sexual intimacy.[282] However, it found the husband's failure to maintain his wife a stronger reason. The Kadhi's court dissolved the marriage and awarded the plaintiff thirty-one months of past-due maintenance.

Some Muslims and the mainstream court conflate separation through judicial decree and *khul'*. Where a woman sues for divorce and the court awards her *mut'ah* compensation, the husband may complain about the misapplication of the law, if he believes that the application for separation made by the woman is *khul'* only. Yet, in this instance, it is *faskhu a-nikaah*. Similarly, mainstream courts sometimes mix up the law of one instance with the other. In *MI v AA*, for instance, while the High Court found that the appellant had exercised her right of *khul'*, it nonetheless indicated that the evidence suggested that the fault was the respondent. The court concluded that the respondent was "forbidden in Islam" to receive any compensation from the appellant.[283] The court, however, upheld the Kadhi's court decision and declined to grant *mut'ah* compensation to the wife. While the appellant may have filed her case through *khul'*, it behooved the courts – both the trial court and the High Court (as a first appellate court) – to read the claim as *faskhu a-nikaah*, given that the evidence pointed to the second scenario.

Sometimes, litigants make mistakes regarding the prayers they seek before the court or the provisions of the law that they employ to seek the court's audience. However, because courts are clothed with inherent powers which they must invoke "if circumstances so demand, to do

281 Ibid. See, for example, *SM v JHA* [2017] eKLR.

282 *FBM*, note 220 above.

283 *MI*, note 127 above, para. 19.

justice",[284] the courts entertain these parties nonetheless. In *Outa*, for example, despite the Supreme Court noting that the application before it deserved dismissal because it was filed out of time, it nonetheless adjudicated it because the questions it raised were "not only novel, but weighty".[285]

Vow of continence

A woman can further petition the court to order her husband to divorce her if the man, potent and of sound mind, swears in the name of God not to have sexual intercourse with her for four months or more and actually fulfills the oath.[286] This form of oath (*alay*) is mentioned in Quran 2:226-227. If the court so orders and the husband declines to divorce the wife, the court will dissolve the marriage.[287] However, if the husband resumes conjugal relations with the wife within the four-month period, the marriage subsists. The computation of time commences even if the vow was made when the wife was in her menses.[288]

Allegation of adultery sworn against one's wife

Where a man falsely accuses his wife of adultery, the wife can petition the court for divorce. During the hearing, the husband is required to substantiate this allegation. Since an allegation of adultery can only be proved by four male witnesses of reputable character,[289] an often-difficult condition to meet, the man is obligated to testify four times in the name of God that he is truthful and the fifth time to invoke God's wrath on himself if he is lying. On her part, the wife would also make four oaths in God's name that the husband is lying and subsequently invoke God's wrath on herself if the husband is telling the truth. After these

[284] *Fredrick Otieno Outa v Jared Odoyo Okello & 3 others* [2017] eKLR, para. 1.

[285] Ibid., para. 55.

[286] See Quran 2:226-227.

[287] Kadhis' Court Bench Book, note 15 above, p. 148.

[288] Ibid., p. 149.

[289] See Quran 24:4.

oaths, the marriage dissolves irrevocably.[290] In addition to ending the marriage, these sworn testimonies (*li'aan*) relieve both parties from punishment. The husband is absolved of the punishment of false accusers against chaste women contained in Quran 24:4, and the wife is absolved of the punishment for adultery. The husband also loses paternity of the child in the woman's womb, even if he later claims that the child is his.[291]

While in Kenya no married spouse is punished for engaging in adultery or falsely accusing their partner of committing adultery, the law nonetheless recognizes divorce through *li'aan*. In *Abdirahman,* the High Court ordered the case for retrial because the Kadhi's court failed to exhaust the Islamic law on evidence relating to a man's suspicion of adultery by wife.[292] The court noted that under that the law, the man is required to bring four eyewitnesses, failing which both he and his wife take an oath.[293] Similarly, in *FBI,* the High Court found that the respondent failed to prove the charge of adultery because he did not take the oath at the Kadhi's court.[294]

Man equating his wife to his mother

Where a man likens his wife (sexually) to his mother or such other woman in a prohibited degree of marriage, the wife has a right to deny him sexual intercourse until the husband offers expiation (*kaffara*). In default, the woman has a right to apply for divorce by a judicial decree.[295] This comparison (*dhihaar*), which stems from a pre-Islamic Arabic custom of equating a wife to one's mother, frustrates sex between the two, although the woman is not divorced.

[290] See Quran 6-9.

[291] Kadhis' Court Bench Book, note 15 above, p. 154.

[292] *Abdirahman Mohamed,* note 187 above, para 17.

[293] Ibid., para. 15.

[294] *FBI,* note 114 above, para. 34.

[295] Kadhis' Court Bench Book, note 15 above, p. 151.

Quran 58:2 adjudges it an abominable practice and terms such an equation "*iniquitous and false* (...)".[296]

To purge the iniquity, a man is required to free a slave or fast for two consecutive months, or feed sixty indigent people — in that order. Because of the absence of slavery today, the man is required to fast for fifty-eight or sixty consecutive days[297] unless his fasting is interrupted by an obligatory fast or a genuine legal reason such as sickness.[298] If he cannot fast, he can, alternatively, feed sixty poor people one meal.[299]

Occurrence of stipulated condition

Where a husband intends that upon the occurrence of a certain fact or set of facts the marriage dissolves, the marriage will so dissolve upon the satisfaction of that fact.[300] Thus, if the man tells his wife that "if you do ABC, you are divorced" and he means it, the wife is automatically divorced if she does the prohibited act. If the husband uttered this statement to discourage his wife from doing ABC, then the statement is interpreted as an oath, not an intention to divorce. Since no divorce occurs in such circumstances, the husband must offer expiation for breaking the oath.[301]

Apostasy

Where either of the parties to a marriage renounces Islam (*riddah*), the other party is discharged from the marriage automatically. The other party to the marriage can petition the court to certify this fact with evidence. The court would then issue an order recognizing the termination

296 Ali, note 67 above, p. 1432.

297 The Islamic calendar follows a lunar month – which lasts 29 or 30 days.

298 The Islamic position on slavery is beyond the scope of this chapter. However, Islam enjoined the freedom of slaves in numerous expiations as a way of ending the practice over time.

299 See Quran 58: 3-4.

300 Kadhis' Court Bench Book, note 15 above, p. 143.

301 Abdul-Azeem Badawi, note 110 above, p. 439.

of their marriage. Thus, in *Sakina Sote Kaitanny & another v Mary Wamaitha,*[302] the Court of Appeal found that it was hypocritical of the first appellant to claim that she had no knowledge of the deceased's apostasy when she lived in the locality of her in-laws.[303] The court noted that since the deceased's parents and brother attended his marriage to the respondent, whereupon he declared his religion as Christianity, the first appellant must have known of his changed religion.[304] The majority bench ruled that the first appellant's marriage to the deceased became void when the deceased was baptized and confirmed as a member of the St. Andrew's PCEA Church on 30 June 1976.[305]

These different modes of ending an Islamic marriage notwithstanding, critics argue that divorce rights between the sexes remain unequal. While the man enjoys the unilateral right to divorce, the wife may seek divorce only on specific grounds.[306] Even then, a woman must compensate her husband by returning her dowry, a specified amount determined by the court, or both. These divergent practices, observers argue, infringe international law, including Article 7(a) of the Protocol to the African Charter on Human and Peoples' Rights on the Rights of Women in Africa. This provision requires the dissolution of a marriage through the courts only. Critics also contend that divorced women are abandoned without maintenance and become their children's sole carers.[307] As a consequence, abandoned children from poor families risk joining extremist groups.[308]

The husband and wife, indeed, have different rights in ending the marriage. It is also accurate that the man

302 [1995] eKLR.

303 Ibid.

304 Ibid.

305 Ibid.

306 Muhammad Zubair Abbasi, "From Faskh to Khula: Transformation of Muslim Women's Right to Divorce in Pakistan (1947-2017)", in Javaid Rehman (ed.), *Asian Yearbook of Human Rights and Humanitarian Law* (2019), p. 332.

307 Musawah and AWAPSA, note 22 above, p. 17.

308 Ibid.

bears the right to pronounce divorce and that the woman compensates the man when she seeks release from the marriage. However, these different rights do not ensue because of the sex of the parties. Rather, they are predicated on the husband's religious duty towards maintaining his family. In Islamic law, only the man is required to head a family — a situation that gives him the first right to decide whether the union continues or not.[309] The Quran is explicit about this differentiation in divorce matters: "And women shall have rights similar to the rights against them, according to what is equitable; *but men have a degree (of advantage) over them*".[310]

Other than a man's right to terminate the union first, both parties enjoy compensation when the marriage ends at the instance of either party. In cases where the marriage terminates at the husband's initiative and without good cause,[311] the courts have been known to award the divorced wives compensation to comfort them for "the loss, pain and suffering the divorce may cause" them.[312] The courts have been sympathetic towards stay-at-home mums and granted them alimony to enable them to live more decently after the marriage.[313] Often, such a compensation order is accompanied by *'iddah* maintenance and child support.[314] In rare cases, the courts have requested mothers to contribute to the maintenance of their children.[315] On the other hand, where the divorce is at the instance of the wife (*khul'*), the courts have ordered the wives to compensate the man. But the courts have been reluctant to order the women to make such reimbursement in cases of a constructive divorce.[316]

309 Abbasi, note 306 above, p. 332.

310 Ali, note 65 above, p. 92, translating Quran 2:228 (emphasis added).

311 *MI*, note 127 above, para. 12.

312 *HM*, note 129 above, para. 12.

313 Ibid., para. 13.

314 See, for example, *RWK*, note 142 above, para. 41; *HSA*, note 113 above, para. 28.

315 See, for example, *SMK*, note 36 above; *MEM*, note 12 above.

316 See, for example, *MI*, note 127 above.

In the foregoing, both forms of compensation are intended to check the spouses against arbitrarily ending a marriage.[317] In the case of a woman, she cannot retain the dowry if she removes herself from the marriage through *khul'*, whereas the man cannot reclaim it if he initiates the divorce.[318]

Registration of dissolution of marriage

Islamic law does not require the registration of a marriage or divorce, a fact acknowledged by the High Court in *RWK*. The court noted that "once the divorce is pronounced, it becomes effective".[319] The Marriage Act, however, requires a Kadhi, a *sheikh*, an *imam*, or such other authorized person who dissolves an Islamic marriage to issue a copy of his decree to the Registrar of Marriages for registration.[320] Such a document is vital in proving the woman's singlehood when she chooses to remarry.

THE WAY FORWARD

Having described the elements of Islamic family law generally and the rules governing Islamic marriages and divorce in particular, it is contended that the Kenyan Constitution and the Marriage Act acknowledge Islamic family law and have therefore provided specific rules that incorporate the rules of Islamic family law into the legal system. The mainstream courts work collaboratively with special-purpose courts, such as the Kadhis' courts, to enforce the rules of Islamic family law that apply to the celebration or termination of marriages contracted under Islamic law. Most Muslims have positively embraced the recognition of this law in the country. Both the High Court and the Kadhi's courts are busy with cases initiated by Muslims to determine their marriages' legitimacy or terminate them. About 68.67% of the 8,954 cases filed at the Kadhi's courts

[317] *NK*, note 211 above, para. 21.

[318] Ibid.

[319] *RWK*, note 142 above, para. 36.

[320] Section 72, Marriage Act 2014.

in the fiscal year 2020/2021, for example, concerned marital and divorce issues.[321]

Advocates of women's rights have decried the legality of early marriages, polygyny, and the different treatment of men and women during a divorce. The suggestions herein seek to enhance the application of the law in the country.

First, the Attorney General should commission a task force to codify Islamic family rules on marriages and divorces to make the rules accessible to legal practitioners, both at the bench and bar, and other stakeholders. Because the Constitution and the Marriage Act recognize the different Muslim sects in the country, the code should embody these different understandings of the law as practically as possible. Ideally, the code could commence with the jurisprudence of *Sunni* juristic school to which the majority of Kenyan Muslims subscribe and which has been employed extensively by the courts.

Second, and in the alternative, the judiciary should publicize the Kadhis' Court Bench Book, which provides a decent summary of the Islamic rules applicable to marriages and divorces and is readily available. Because it was developed locally with the engagement of Kadhis, magistrates, judges, Muslim scholars, Muslim lawyers, and civil society organizations (CSOs) dealing with the law, the Bench Book better addresses Kenyan idiosyncrasies as compared to the global Islamic Family Charter that is presently employed by the courts.

Third, law enforcement agents should strictly observe the provisions against forced marriages in the Marriage Act. Regardless of the ages of the parties involved, village elders and area chiefs must sensitize their communities to the need to report such cases to the police and disregard the stigma of being labeled "nosy neighbors".

Fourth, women's rights organizations and Muslim lawyers should conduct civic education to train Muslim females on their rights in an Islamic marriage and upon

[321] The Judiciary of Kenya, *State of the Judiciary and the Administration of Justice: Annual Report 2020/2021* (2021), pp. 62-63.

divorce. This guidance will assist these females in presenting the requisite petitions to the courts when needed.

Fifth, the Kadhis', the Magistrates', and the High Courts must employ their inherent powers to exercise justice whenever a party before them is mistaken regarding the accurate redress for their grievance. The courts should avoid adjudicating such cases regardless of the incongruity in the evidence. As other courts have done before, these courts should point out the mistake and reframe the issue brought before them before deciding the case.

Sixth, Parliament should amend the Sexual Offences Act and lower the age of consent to at least fourteen. This proposal is well within the environs of popular law (nationally and internationally). For example, the Convention on the Rights of the Child envisages that the age of majority can be below eighteen.[322] Moreover, the constitutions of democratic countries such as the United States and South Africa, on which the present Kenyan Constitution is modeled, have the average age of consent at sixteen.[323] Such a change will eliminate the present double-standard application of the law proscribing early marriages, on one hand, and allowing protected consensual sex among sexually active adolescents as young as twelve years old, on the other.

CONCLUSION

This chapter has explained that the recognition of Islamic marriages and divorce in Kenya reflects the country's ethnocultural diversity. Kenya is populated by a citizenry that observes divergent family laws, including Islamic laws. Although Kenyan Muslims are a diverse population, a majority follow the *Sunni Shafi'te* jurisprudence, and a majority of decisions emanating from the Kadhi and mainstream courts embody this juristic thought.

An Islamic marriage is both polygynous and heterosexual; the Constitution and the Marriage Act stipulate this. Criticisms

[322] Article 1, Convention on the Rights of the Child.

[323] United Nations Population Fund, note 168 above, p. 4. See also *Martin Charo,* note 172 above, enlisting a number of Western democracies where the marriageable age is 15 with parental consent.

that label polygynous relationships as unconstitutional or discriminatory against women are incorrect. An Islamic marriage is a contract between an individual man and an individual woman despite its polygynous nature. Such a contract must fulfill six pre-requisites to be valid: dowry payable to the bride-to-be; the bride's consent; the consent of the bride's guardian; requisite marriageable age for the bride and groom; two male witnesses; and the permissible degree of relationship between the intended couple. Only when these conditions are met can the bride's guardian, or a Kadhi, or an authorized sheikh or imam solemnize the union and have it registered by the Registrar of Marriages.

There are three main ways of ending an Islamic marriage reiterated by the Kadhi's courts and the High Court. These are through the will of either party, judicial separation, and by the operation of law. In the first instance, the husband can separate from his wife twice before the divorce becomes absolute; and the wife can also remove herself from the union by approaching the court and returning her dowry. In the second instance, a woman can apply to the court to dissolve her marriage if the man is cruel or deserts her; vows to, and indeed, does not have sexual relations with her for four months or more; falsely accuses her of adultery; or likens her to his mother. Finally, a marriage terminates automatically when a stipulated condition happens or one of the parties renounces Islam. Regardless of which ground ends an Islamic marriage, the Marriage Act requires that the Registrar of Marriages register such dissolution.

Attention was drawn to some incongruities between mainstream and Islamic family law. One notable difference between these two systems of law is the proscription of early marriages. While both the Constitution and various statutes prohibit child marriages, Islamic family law permits them provided that the child has attained puberty, understands and is capable of discharging the responsibilities in a marriage. Given that the Government and development partners have permitted consensual protected sex between sexually active adolescents, the prohibition of early marriage is hypocritical. The age of consent should be lowered to fourteen years because, in either instance, sex happens, and in the case of Islamic marriages, such sex is consensual.

Chapter Nine
My Marriage, My Choice: Kenya's Plural Marriage Law

Kenya's Marriage Act came into force on 24 May 2014. The Act is a comprehensive consolidation of the five different family law regimes recognized in Kenya: Christian, civil, Islamic, customary, and Hindu. A valid marriage can only be contracted in these recognized forms. Prior to the Act, there were specific statutes for the formalization of different forms of marriage and their dissolution.[1] These statutes were all repealed to pave the way for a harmonized Marriage Act.

The entrenchment of legal pluralism in Kenya's legal system and its influence on the development of marriage laws in the colonial and post-colonial eras is first examined. Next the general requirements for entering into a marriage under the Marriage Act 2014, the forms of marriage, and the emerging issues relating to the presumption of marriage and registration of marriages are considered, followed by recommendations on the way forward.

LEGAL PLURALISM IN KENYA

Kenya's contemporary legal history can be traced to British colonial rule. During the colonial period, the country adopted English laws through reception clauses in various reception statutes.[2] The colonial laws were applied

[1] Marriage Act (as last amended in 1975), African Christian Marriage and Divorce Act (as last amended in 1975), Matrimonial Causes Act (as last amended in 1975), Subordinate Courts (Separation and Maintenance Act) (as last amended in 1972), Mohammedan Marriage and Divorce Registration Act (as last amended in 1972), Mohammedan Marriage, Divorce and Succession Act, and the Hindu Marriage and Divorce Act (as last amended in 1962)

[2] These are Kenya Colony Order-in-Council 1921, the Kenyan (Constitution) Order-in-Council 1958, and the East African Order-in-Council 1897.

alongside existing African customary laws. The reception clauses resulted in a dual system of law in Kenya.

Although both customary and colonial law were applicable within the same territory, these laws applied to different persons. The "imported law" was applied to Europeans and Indians and administered in English courts. African customary law was for the indigenous communities and enforced in Native courts.[3] The development of legal pluralism in Kenya was directly linked to the evolution of Kenya's plural marriage laws.

Historical perspective

In the colonial era, the State sought to find effective forms of interventions to consolidate power and control over the indigenous communities. The interventions included introducing State laws informed by Anglo-Saxon law and tradition and adopting a limited range of African customs, practices, and traditions.

Three major phases underlie the development of marriage law in Kenya. In the first phase, British colonial rule introduced foreign statutes in their colonial territory as general or basic law. The foreign statutes were a version of English law. As a result, the European colonial community was governed by English law, and the indigenous population was governed by African customary law. However, certain areas of law were under the purview of the English legal system, irrespective of the parties involved. These included criminal law, contract law, law of tort, tax law, traffic law, and administrative law, among other areas. Areas primarily governed by African customary law were marriage, divorce, succession, land tenure, and guardianship.

House-Bidamba describes the second phase of development as characterized by the colonial efforts to expand the coverage of foreign laws across the indigenous populations.[4] This heightened the conflicts between the

[3] Kenya Courts Ordinance (Cap 3) of the Laws of Kenya and the African Courts Ordinance 1951.

[4] Bessie House-Midamba, "Legal Pluralism and Attendant Internal Conflicts in Marital and Inheritance Laws in Kenya", *Africa: Quarterly Journal of Studies and*

two systems of law, especially in areas where individuals married across ethnic lines. Two systems of law applied in such instances, yet the court could only use one system of law. The trend was then to accord colonial law a superior status to African customary law. The terms "repugnant to justice and morality" and "inconsistent with written law" were coined to assess and delegitimize African customary laws antithetical to British colonial culture, tradition, or law. For example, the African customary law practice of paying a dowry to seal a marriage was viewed as "wife purchase" and repugnant to justice and morality and unlawful. Statutory law, which was written, was given preference over African customary law.

In addition, colonial courts faced challenges in adjudicating disputes arising from customary marriages because it was unwritten. The courts relied on customs, norms, and practices as detailed by elders. An ambitious attempt was made to reduce customary law to writing through the 1970s Restatement of African Law Project. Due to the diversity and dynamism of culture, practices, and customs, the codification of customary law is yet to be adequately achieved.

Finally, the last development phase involved the codification of marriage laws by the Government. In Kenya, the initial attempt was made through the development of several legislative acts to codify the rules of the different normative orders, such as civil, Islamic, Hindu, and Christian. Initially, African customary law was exempted from this exercise and remained un-codified and unwritten. Later, the Kenya government sought to record customary laws. In 1967, two commissions were established: the Law of Marriage and Divorce and the Law of Succession commissions. The terms of reference of the former included reviewing the existing laws relating to marriage and divorce and recommending a new, harmonized marriage and divorce law applicable to all Kenyans. The Commission was required to pay particular attention to the status of women within the context of marriage and divorce in a free and democratic society.

When the Commission on Law of Marriage and Divorce was established, the existing legislation on marriage was scattered in several statute books targeting different types of marriages. For instance, marriages under the Marriage Act were regarded as civil marriages open to all persons irrespective of religion and race. The African Christian Marriage and Divorce Act included procedures for marriage involving African Christians and the conversion of customary marriages, which were potentially polygamous, into monogamous statutory marriages. The Hindu Marriage and Divorce Act governed Hindu marriages and divorce, while the Mohammedan Marriage, Divorce and Succession Act governed Muslims.

The Commission on Law of Marriage and Divorce made recommendations to the Kenya Government in line with its terms of reference. The Commission recommended that all the forms of marriage should be retained, accorded equal status, and registered. General prerequisites for a valid marriage were applicable to all forms of marriage. These preconditions included free and full consent, meeting the minimum age of marriage, and having the capacity to marry. Both polygamous and monogamous marriages were proposed to be recognized by law. In polygamous marriages, a wife was given a right to object to a subsequent wife on particular grounds that would be heard and determined by a Marriage Tribunal. The Commission proposed the prohibition of harmful cultural practices such as widow inheritance. It was recommended that only a court of law could dissolve a marriage on the grounds that it had irretrievably broken down. Divorces were to be preceded by conciliation or arbitration before a Marriage Tribunal.

Three attempts were made to pass the draft bill in Parliament. The last attempt was made in 1979. All attempts failed, with legislators expressing concerns that the draft bill conferred too much power on women and was too westernized. They accused the Government of "throwing our customs to the dogs".[5] A few changes were made to the draft bill to incorporate the views of the legislators. However,

[5] "The Rejection of the Marriage Bill in Kenya", *Journal of African Law*, XXIII, no. 2 (1979), p. 109.

the revised draft bill was never reintroduced in Parliament. In 1982, the Government established a permanent Law Reform Commission "to review all the law of Kenya so as to ensure its systematic development and reform and in particular the integration, unification and codification of the law, repeal of the obsolete and unnecessary enactments and generally its simplification and modernization".[6] Not until 1993 did the Law Reform Commission review the draft marriage bill. The Attorney-General appointed a Task Force to review laws relating to women in Kenya. The law relating to marriage and divorce was among the laws that the Task Force was mandated to review.

Post-2010 constitutional dispensation era

Kenya's legal system, being pluralistic, incorporates numerous sources of law that spell out the rights and duties of citizens.[7] The sources of law in Kenya include Acts of Parliament, doctrines of equity, and common law formulated by the British and enforceable in Kenya through the interpretation of a reception clause, African customary law, which derives its legitimacy from practices of various ethnic groups and finally, religious laws.[8]

The 2010 Constitution of Kenya has been described as progressive and modelled after its South African counterpart. The Bill of Rights renders first, second and third-generation rights justiciable and enforceable. Under Article 2(5) and (6) of the Constitution, general rules of international law and treaties and conventions ratified by Kenya are part of the laws of Kenya.[9] Any law, including customary law, which

[6] Law Reform Commission Act No. 2 of 1982.

[7] See House-Midamba, note 4 above.

[8] Smokin Wanjala, "Conflict of Laws and Burial", in Jackton Ojwang and Jesse Kanyua Mugambi (eds.), *The SM Otieno Case, Death and Burial in Modern Kenya* (1989), p. 103.

[9] As a result, the following international instruments are part of Kenya's laws: Universal Declaration of Human Rights, International Covenant on Civil and Political Rights, International Covenant on Economic, Social and Cultural Rights, UN Convention on the Elimination of All Forms of Discrimination against Women, African Charter on Human and Peoples Rights, and African Charter on Human and People's Rights on the Rights of Women. As a State party to these

is inconsistent with the Constitution is null and void to the extent of its inconsistency with the Constitution.[10]

The Constitution recognizes the right of every person to participate in the cultural life of their choice. However, any act that seeks to compel another's participation in harmful cultural practices contravenes the Constitution.[11] Harmful cultural practices such as early, forced, or arranged marriages are not specifically prohibited; they are impliedly prohibited. However, specific statutes have criminalized early and forced marriages.[12]

The Constitution specifically guarantees equality in marriage and the family. In addition to a general equality provision,[13] the Constitution provides that "women and men have the right to equal treatment, including the right to equal opportunities in political, economic, cultural and social spheres".[14] More specifically, the Constitution provides that "parties to a marriage are entitled to equal rights at the time of the marriage, during the marriage and at the dissolution of the marriage".[15] The Constitution improves women's legal status by guaranteeing them equal treatment as men in all spheres of life. However, this position is not reflected in statutes and their lived realities.

Under the Constitution, the State is prohibited from discriminating against persons on the basis of race, sex, pregnancy, marital status, health status, ethnic or social origin, color, age, disability, religion, conscience, belief, culture, dress, language or birth.[16] The grounds for discrimination are wider than those outlined in international

international instruments, Kenya has a legal obligation to respect and realize their provisions.

10 Article 2(4), 2010 Constitution of Kenya.

11 Ibid., Article 44.

12 For example, section 14, Children Act 2022.

13 Article 27(1) of the 2010 Constitution of Kenya states, "every person is equal before the law and has the right to equal protection and equal benefit of the law".

14 Ibid., Article 27(3).

15 Ibid., Article 45(3).

16 Ibid., Article 27(4).

and regional instruments in that constitutional protection against discrimination arising from marital status is specifically provided.

However, the right to non-discrimination has a clawback clause limiting its application. Article 24(4) of the Constitution stipulates that the provision on equality shall be qualified when the Kadhi's Courts apply Islamic law to persons who profess the Muslim faith in matters relating to personal status, marriage, divorce, and inheritance. The effect of the clawback clause is the absence of a legal obligation to ensure equality at the time, during, and upon dissolution of an Islamic marriage. In other words, the law permits differential and discriminatory treatment of a husband and wife in respect of a marriage contracted under Islamic law. The application of Islamic law in marriages embodies the interaction between State and religious law within a plural legal system. The interface between State law and religious law gives rise to different lived realities in the experience of the law.

Just as the international legal framework, the Constitution provides that every person has inherent dignity, freedom, and security of the person that must be respected and protected.[17] Article 45 of the Constitution anchors marriage within the context of the family. The Constitution views the "family" as the natural and fundamental unit of society and the necessary basis of social order; it enjoys the recognition and protection of the State. The right to marry is only available to adults of the opposite sex who, on the basis of their free consent, decide to marry.[18] Thus, the Constitution expressly prohibits same-sex marriages, and the minimum age of marriage for both women and men is eighteen. Forced or arranged and early marriages are unconstitutional; the parties must give their free consent and be of the age of majority. The Constitution also authorizes Parliament to enact legislation that recognizes:[19]

17 Ibid., Articles 28 and 29.

18 Ibid., Article 45, which stipulates that "every adult has the right to marry a person of the opposite sex, based on the free consent of the parties".

19 Ibid., Article 45(4).

(a) marriages conducted under any tradition or system of religious, personal or family law; and

(b) any system of personal and family law under any tradition or adhered to by persons professing a particular religion.

In line with Parliament's constitutional obligation, it was essential for the legislature to harmonize and recognize marriages conducted under any custom, tradition, religion, or personal law. In other words, the Constitution mandated the legal recognition by State law of marriages conducted in semi-autonomous social fields of religion or custom. While doing so, it was necessary for the marriage systems to comply fully with the Constitution, which espouses free consent, heteronormativity, provides for the age of majority at marriage, and equality before, during and upon dissolution of marriage.

In 2013, the marriage bill, which largely incorporated the recommendations of the 1967 Commission on the law of marriage and divorce, was discussed in Parliament. The provisions on polygamy and cohabitation elicited contention during the parliamentary debates, which demonstrated the patriarchal perceptions about the right to equality within the institution of marriage. [20] Parliament subsequently enacted the Marriage Act 2014.

The plural nature of the legal system extends to marriage laws. The framework for marriages demonstrates the delicate balance and interplay between State law and other normative systems such as religion and custom. At the same time, the Kenyan experience is marked by State capture of normative regulatory frameworks through their incorporation into State law. The incorporation into State law of other non-state regulatory systems, such as religion and custom, upgrades them to the status of statutory law, which is higher up the hierarchy of sources of law.[21]

[20] *President Uhuru Kenyatta Signs Kenya Polygamy Law* (2014) (available online).

[21] Section 3, Judicature Act provides that: (1) The jurisdiction of the High Court, the Court of Appeal and of all subordinate courts shall be exercised in conformity with:

(a) the Constitution;

The English case of *Hyde v. Hyde*[22] provides the classic definition of marriage, which is also applicable in Kenya. Lord Penzance asserted, "Marriage as understood in Christendom, may be defined as the voluntary union for life of one man and one woman to the exclusion of all others".[23] This *obiter dictum* has become the accepted definition of the traditional Christian marriage. The Act varies this definition to accommodate other forms of marriage. The Marriage Act 2014 recognizes five forms of marriage.[24] Section 3(1) of the Act defines marriage as "the voluntary union of a man and a woman whether in a monogamous or polygamous union and registered in accordance with the Act".[25] Marriage must therefore be a consensual social contract between heterosexual parties with legal capacity to contract. Registration of the marriage in accordance with the provisions of the Act is an essential requirement for its validity. Following the Con-

(b) subject thereto, all other written laws, including Acts of Parliament of the United Kingdom cited in Part I of the Schedule to this Act, modified in accordance with Part II of that Schedule;

(c) subject thereto and so far as those written laws do not extend or apply, the substance of common law, the doctrines of equity and that statutes of general application in force in England on the 12th August 1897, and the procedure and practice observed in courts of justice in England at that date: provided that the said common law, doctrines of equity and statutes of general application shall apply so far only as circumstances of Kenya and its inhabitants permit and subject to such qualifications as those circumstances may render necessary.

(2) The High Court, the Court of Appeal and all subordinate courts shall be guided by African customary law in civil cases in which one or more of the parties is subject to it or affected by it, so far as it is applicable and is not repugnant to justice and morality or inconsistent with any written law, and shall decide all such cases according to substantial justice without undue regard to technicalities of procedure and without undue delay.

22 (1866) L.R. 1 P&D 130.

23 Ibid.

24 Section 6(1), Marriage Act 2014, which enumerates the following forms: customary law marriages, Islamic law marriages, Hindu law marriages, civil marriages, and Christian marriages.

25 Ibid., section 4.

stitution of Kenya, the Act sets the minimum age of marriage at eighteen years for both parties.[26]

In the interpretation section, the Act defines a monogamous marriage and a polygamous marriage. A monogamous marriage is "a marriage whose character has been converted to a monogamous marriage by declaration including an originally polygamous or potentially polygamous marriage".[27] On the other hand, polygamy means "the practice or state of a man having more than one wife simultaneously".[28]

A potentially polygamous marriage may be converted into a monogamous marriage if each spouse voluntarily agrees to such a conversion and the man only has one wife at the time. The underlying reason for this restriction is the need to protect women in polygamous unions from losing their legal status through conversions to monogamous unions. In addition, the Act does not allow the conversion of monogamous marriages into polygamous ones.[29] Once a monogamous marriage is contracted, the parties lose their legal capacity to contract another marriage.[30] A person who attempts to celebrate a marriage during the subsistence of a monogamous marriage commits the criminal offence of bigamy, punishable by five years imprisonment.[31]

Section 3(3) of the Act states that all marriages have the same legal status; none is superior to the other. Potentially polygamous marriages (customary and Islamic) and monogamous marriages (Christian, Hindu, and civil) are equal and valid if registered under the Act. Prior to the Act, statutory marriages were viewed as legally superior to customary marriages because the last operated outside the purview of written law. Considering the low ranking of customary law in the hierarchy of laws under the Judicature

26 Ibid.

27 Ibid., section 2.

28 Ibid.

29 Ibid., section 8.

30 Ibid., sections 9 and 11(1)(c).

31 Section 171, Penal Code.

Act,[32] any marriage emanating from the system was considered inferior to a statutory marriage. It was common for parties contracting a marriage under customary law to convert it into a statutory marriage through a civil or Christian wedding celebration after performing customary rites.

Section 3(2) affords parties to any form of marriage equal rights at the time of, during, and upon dissolution of the marriage. However, it should be noted that Islamic marriages are not subject to the equality provisions of the Marriages Act because of the constitutional provision in Article 24(4) discussed above.[33]

General requirements for contracting marriages

The Act stipulates core requirements for marriages under the five systems. The failure to comply with these general provisions renders any marriage invalid and illegal.

First, the person who celebrates the marriage must be licensed and recognized by the Registrar of Marriages. The marriage ceremony must be witnessed by two competent persons who must be of the age of majority; mentally sane; understand the language used during the ceremony; and are not parties to the marriage. [34]

The Act proscribes marriage between persons in certain relationships. Section 10 provides that a person shall not marry a grandparent, parent, child, grandchild, sister, brother, cousin, great aunt, great uncle, aunt, uncle, niece, nephew, great niece or great nephew and any half-blood relationship. Nor shall a person marry the grandparent, parent, child, or grandchild of a spouse or former spouse. The provision further prohibits marriage by a person to someone they have adopted or by whom they have been adopted. Marriages prohibited under customary law are captured under the Act. However, the Act exempts Muslims

[32] Section 3, Judicature Act Cap 8 of the Laws of Kenya.

[33] Article 24(4), Constitution of Kenya.

[34] Section 5, Marriage Act 2014.

from observing the prohibited degrees of consanguinity and allows marriage between cousins.[35]

The legislation provides substantive and procedural requirements applicable to all forms of marriage, which, if violated, would render a marriage contract void.[36] For instance, the parties must have attained the minimum age of marriage.[37] Previously, the repealed Marriage Act allowed children aged sixteen years to marry with the consent of their parents or guardians. Section 87 of the Marriage Act criminalizes any person who attempts to marry a person below the minimum age of eighteen years. They are liable to imprisonment for a term not exceeding five years or a fine not exceeding US$10,000 or both. The Children Act 2022 prohibits early marriages and endorses the position of the Marriage Act 2014.[38] The Sexual Offences Act 2006 provides that anyone under eighteen years is incapable of consenting to sexual relations and criminalizes any form of penetrative sexual acts with a minor.[39]

Likewise, the absence of either party to the marriage during the ceremony (contracting a marriage by proxy); mistaken identity; fraud; or lack of consent is unlawful and will render the marriage null and void.[40] Both parties must be present at the marriage ceremony.[41]

Failure to register a marriage contract renders it voidable.[42] The marriage contract would also be rendered voidable if the officiating person lacked proper authorization,[43] if either

35 Ibid., section 10(4).

36 Ibid., section 11.

37 Ibid., section 11(1)(a).

38 Section 23, Children Act 2022.

39 Section 8, Sexual Offences Act 2006.

40 Section 11(1)(f), (g), (h), (i), Marriage Act 2014.

41 Ibid., section 73.

42 Ibid., section 12(e).

43 Ibid., section 12(c).

party lacked the ability to consummate the marriage,[44] or suffered from a recurring mental issue.[45] A marriage is voidable if the parties violated an essential procedural requirement, such as failing to give notice of their intention to marry or not withdrawing a notice of objection to the intended marriage.[46]

The Act states that a spouse shall not be responsible for the torts of the other spouse by virtue of marriage; each spouse bears liability for their wrongs.[47] Similarly, marriage does not preclude the tortious liability of a spouse towards a fellow spouse. The Sexual Offences Act does not recognize marital rape.

Section 15 of the Act confers an express right to widows and widowers to elect whether to re-marry. A marriage will subsist until the death of a spouse. A decree declaring the presumption of death of a spouse, and a decree of annulment or divorce obtained in or outside Kenya may suffice to bring a marriage to an end.[48] In civil marriages, the parties may agree to live separately for one year. Such an agreement is enforceable by the court. The court may vary or set aside the agreement if satisfied that there is a material change of circumstances. [49] Upon the expiry of a year, a party to a civil marriage may seek the determination of their status by the court.

After contracting a marriage, parties are required by law to register their marriages.[50] Kenyans who celebrate marriages outside the country may apply to the Registrar to register such a marriage in Kenya.[51] Once the Registrar is satisfied that the provisions of the Act are fulfilled, the

44 Ibid., section 12(a)(i).

45 Ibid., section 12(a)(ii).

46 Ibid., section 12(b)(c).

47 Ibid., section 13.

48 Ibid., section 16.

49 Ibid., section 14.

50 Ibid., part ix.

51 Ibid., section 58(1).

marriage will be registered. The Registrar may also consider a marriage certificate issued in the other country or some other proof before registering the marriage. Where the marriage certificate is not in the official languages of Kenya, it must be accompanied by a certified translation.[52]

Christian marriages

Christian marriages are classified as statutory marriages. One begins with a promise to marry. Under the initial marriage bill of 2013, a breach of a promise to marry was worth compensation, but this was deleted before the adoption of the Act. Under section 76 of the Marriage Act, a promise to marry is not binding; therefore, no legal claim may arise from its breach. However, section 170 of the Penal Code protects agreements to marry: any person who willfully and fraudulently causes any woman who is not lawfully married to him to believe she is lawfully married to him and to cohabit or have sexual intercourse with him in that belief shall be guilty of a felony punishable by imprisonment for ten years.

Christian marriages are officiated by a licensed church minister who is appointed by the Registrar. Any person aware of an impediment to an intended marriage may give written notice of their objection to the minister in charge of the place of worship where the notice of the intended marriage is posted.[53] A notice of objection shall include the objector's name, the objector's relationship to either of the intended parties to the marriage, and the reasons for the objection.[54] The notice to objection may be withdrawn in writing at any time by the objector.[55] Section 20 of the Act requires that the person in charge of the place of worship should hear the objection immediately. If there is a need, the minister in charge may postpone the marriage until a full hearing and determination of the objection according to the church's

[52] Ibid., section 58(2).

[53] Ibid., section 19(1).

[54] Ibid., section 19(2).

[55] Ibid., section 19(3).

regulations.[56] That notwithstanding, the objection must be determined within a reasonable period of not more than seven (7) days after its hearing.[57] A report shall be prepared in a prescribed form and submitted to the Registrar on how the objection was determined.[58] The report must be served within seven days of the determination of the objection.[59] An aggrieved party may appeal to the court within fourteen (14) days of the decision.[60]

The Act criminalizes the making of frivolous, malicious, or fraudulent objections. Any person convicted of the offence is liable to imprisonment for a term not exceeding five years or a fine not exceeding one-million Kenya shillings or both.[61] Anyone who makes a false statement in the notice of intention to marry or the notice of objection to marry commits an offence and is liable to imprisonment for a term not exceeding two years or a fine not exceeding two million shillings or to both.[62]

Once a Christian marriage is celebrated, the person officiating the ceremony must complete and sign a marriage certificate in the prescribed form.[63] The parties and witnesses must also sign the marriage certificate. The person officiating the marriage ceremony issues three certificates. One is given to the parties, another is retained by the minister, and the third is delivered to the Registrar of Marriages.[64]

Finally, the Act recognizes a marriage celebrated outside the Kenyan jurisdiction so long as:

56 Ibid., section 20(1).

57 Ibid., section 20(2).

58 Ibid., section 20(3).

59 Ibid.

60 Ibid., section 20(4).

61 Ibid., section 29(4).

62 Ibid., section 86.

63 Ibid., section 21(1).

64 Ibid., section 21(2).

- it is contracted in accordance with the law of the country where it was celebrated and is consistent with the requirements for a Christian marriage under the Act;
- the parties to the marriage had the legal capacity to marry at the time of celebration under the laws of the country of the marriage; or
- the parties to the marriage are domiciled in Kenya and had the capacity to marry under the Act.[65]

A marriage celebrated in the embassy, high commission, or consulate of a foreign country in Kenya is a Christian marriage if:

- it is contracted according to the law on Christian marriages of the foreign country,
- at the time of the marriage, the parties had the capacity to marry under the law of the foreign country and the Act; or
- at the time of the marriage, either party was domiciled in Kenya.[66]

Civil marriages

A civil marriage is celebrated by the Registrar in the place so determined by the Registrar. The parties must give the Registrar and the person in charge of the marriage venue a written notice of their intention to marry.[67] The notice period is for a minimum of twenty-one days and no more than three months.[68] The information to be provided in the written notice is standardized across all marriage systems. Under section 33 of the Act, the Registrar may by license in the prescribed form dispense with the requirement for notice where there is sufficient reason to do so. Before dispensing with the notice, the Registrar must confirm that neither

[65] Ibid., section 38.

[66] Ibid., section 24.

[67] Ibid., section 25.

[68] Ibid.

party intending to marry is in a prohibited relationship.[69] The power to dispense with notice can only be exercised by the Registrar if there is no notice of objection or where the said objection has been withdrawn.[70]

The Registrar has an obligation to publish the notice in the place where the marriage is to be celebrated. A notice of objection may be lodged with the Registrar or the person in charge of the place of the intended marriage.[71] Where there is no objection to the marriage celebration, the Registrar shall issue a certificate of no impediment to the parties.[72] In addition, the certificate of no impediment can be issued on application by a Kenyan who wishes to celebrate a marriage outside Kenya if there is no objection to the intended marriage.[73]

After the marriage has been celebrated in the presence of the Registrar, they complete and sign a marriage certificate of the prescribed form. Three certificates are signed by the parties and the witnesses to the marriage. Two duly executed marriage certificates are given to the parties, and the Registrar retains one.

Civil marriages can be celebrated in a foreign country if:

- contracted in accordance with the law of the foreign country and consistent with the laws of Kenya;
- the parties had the capacity to marry under the law of that country, and it is consistent with Kenyan law;
- either party is domiciled in Kenya and has the capacity to marry under the Act;
- the Registrar is satisfied that the parties obtained a certificate of no impediment if required in the country of the marriage.[74]

69 Ibid, section 33.

70 Ibid., sections 27(3) and 33.

71 Ibid., s 27.

72 Ibid., section 32(1).

73 Ibid., section 32(2).

74 Ibid., section 38.

The requirements to validate civil marriages celebrated out of the Kenyan jurisdiction are similar to those provided for Christian marriages. A Kenyan may celebrate a civil marriage in a Kenyan embassy, high commission, or consulate, if it is in accordance with the law of the foreign country or both parties have the capacity to marry under the said law. [75]

As in the other forms of marriages, the Registrar must register a civil marriage contracted under the Act. The register includes marriages celebrated outside the country. A person who celebrates or officiates a marriage is expected to deliver a copy of the marriage certificate to the Registrar, who then enters the details in a register of marriages.[76] A person who fails to register a marriage commits an offence and, upon conviction, will be liable to a fine not exceeding five-thousand Kenya shillings or community service order or both. [77]

Islamic marriages

Islamic marriages may be contracted by persons who profess the Muslim faith. The Act limits its application in instances where its provisions are inconsistent with Islamic law.[78] Therefore, general provisions that may offend Islamic law, for example, the equality of spouses during marriage, do not apply to parties in an Islamic marriage.

Agreements to marry are entered into between the parents of the intended spouses. Until the actual marriage, no contractual obligations arise between the intended spouses, and a breach of promise to marry is not actionable. However, where gifts or ornaments have been exchanged between the two families, they are to be returned if the agreement to marry is breached.

[75] Ibid., section 39(1).

[76] Ibid., section 42(1).

[77] Ibid., section 42(3).

[78] Ibid., section 49(3) provides: "Any provision of this Act which is inconsistent with Islamic law and practices shall not apply to persons who profess the Islamic faith".

A relevant case is *Fazaldin Satardin v Din Mohamed and Hajra Begum*,[79] where the bride's father agreed to betroth her without her consent. The intended bride declined to marry the prospective suitor. The latter brought an action claiming damages for breach of the agreement to marry and an injunction to restrain the intended bride from marrying any other person until he was compensated. The court held that the prospective suitor could only recover gifts and ornaments that he had given but not damages.

An Islamic marriage is officiated by a Kadhi, Sheikh, or Imam as authorized by the Registrar and celebrated according Islamic law.[80] Section 57(1)(b) of the Marriage Act confers on the person officiating the Islamic marriage the power to issue a marriage certificate. He records the details of the marriage in a prescribed form and delivers it to the Registrar for registration. Prior to registration, the Registrar will ensure that all the requirements under the Act have been met so long as they do not contravene Islamic law.

Hindu marriages

The Hindu marriage may be celebrated by parties who profess the Hindu faith. Under Hindu law, agreements to marry, just as in Islamic marriages, are made between the parents of respective spouses. A betrothal in respect of a boy and a girl can be done when they are infants. Consequently, damages in the event of breach are not recoverable. However, gifts are expected to be returned.[81]

A person authorized by the Registrar may officiate a Hindu marriage. The marriage will be conducted according to the Hindu religious rites of the parties to the marriage.

Once the marriage is celebrated, the person officiating will record the details in the prescribed form and deliver

[79] (1928) 11 KLR.41.

[80] Section 49, Marriage Act 2014.

[81] See *Vishram Dhanji v Lalji Ruda* (1957) 1 EA 110, where the court held that a marriage contract made against someone's will is contrary to morality. Damages were not recoverable. However, the parents could recover their gifts.

the record to the Registrar. The Registrar ensures that the requirements under the Act have been fulfilled and then registers the marriage.[82]

Customary marriages

Under customary law, agreements to marry normally take the form of betrothals; the nature of the betrothal will differ between communities. Some communities conduct an elaborate formal ceremony, whereas others have a simple family affair with a few witnesses. The agreement under customary law occurs between the parties' families and not the intended spouses. The effect of a betrothal under customary law is the prohibition of sexual relations of the intended bride with any other man. It is the obligation of the family of the intended bride to maintain her sexual purity and chastity. On the other hand, the intended groom and his family are obliged to pay a dowry to his spouse's family. A breach of promise to marry is not actionable under Kenyan customary law. That notwithstanding, there are other remedies in the Magistrates Act, which include actions for damages for seduction and pregnancy.

The Marriage Act introduces reforms to how customary marriages are contracted and dissolved. First, the general laws concerning marriage must be followed for a customary marriage to be considered valid. For example, there must be free and full consent, the parties must have attained the minimum age of eighteen, and the relationship should not be within the prohibited degrees of consanguinity. One divergence from the repealed customary marriage system is the mandatory registration requirement. Before the 2014 Act, customary marriages were fluid and largely excluded from formal regulation. The prerequisites for this form of marriage lay within customary practices that were not codified but instead passed down from one generation to the next through oral literature.

The Act recognizes polygamy as part of customary marriages. In this case, polygamy means the legal right of the husband to marry additional wives and not vice versa.

[82] Section 56, Marriage Act 2014.

While the Act stresses the need for consent to contract any form of marriage, it does not specifically prohibit the entrenched customary practices of widow inheritance or levirate unions. A levirate union involves a widow being married to the brother or male relative of her deceased husband with the intention that any children of that marriage be named after the deceased.[83] A widow may be pressured into the arrangement with the threat of being disinherited or dispossessed of her deceased husband's property.[84]

Despite the legal provisions stipulating that parties to a marriage have equal rights at the time of, during, and after the dissolution of the marriage, there is no express prohibition of African customs and practices that threaten this right. The implied acceptance of such practices as levirate unions without the express provision of a right to re-marry, places women in customary marriage in a precarious and disempowered legal position. Therefore, the Act provides inadequate protection to women in customary marriages. Women are unable to fully enjoy their agency and equality within the context of the family, especially after the death of their spouses.

The legislation does not reduce the importance of dowry in contracting customary marriages. Payment of dowry by the intended bridegroom to the family of the intended bridge is a precondition for the validity of a marriage.

A customary marriage is celebrated in accordance with the customs of the communities of one or both parties to the intended marriage. Should payment of dowry be required to prove a marriage under customary law, paying a token amount in dowry is sufficient to prove a customary marriage. The application of section 43(2) of the Act prohibits invalidation of customary marriages where dowry payment is not made in full. Due to the commercialization

[83] Eugene Cotran, *Law Of Marriage And Divorce: Kenya (Restatement of African Law)* (1968), pp. 13, 50, 128, and 159.

[84] The International Women's Human Rights Clinic, Georgetown University Law Center and The Federation of Women Lawyers: Kenya, "Empowering Women with Rights to Inheritance — A Report on Amendments to the Law of Succession Act Necessary to Ensure Women's Human Rights: A Human Rights Report and Proposed Legislation", *Georgetown Journal of International Law*, XL (2009), p. 140.

of dowry, families may overprice it to the detriment of the prospective husband, as he may be rendered incapable of making payment, thus threatening the validity of the intended customary marriage.

As regards customary marriages, parties are required to notify the Registrar of the marriage within three months after its celebration.[85] The notification of marriage must:

a) specify the customary law applicable to the marriage of the parties;

b) contain a written declaration by the parties that the customary requirements to prove marriage have been undertaken;

c) contain the signatures or personal marks of two adult witnesses; the witnesses shall have played a cultural role in the marriage celebration;

d) confirm that the parties to the marriage were eighteen years and above at the time of the celebration;

e) state that the marriage is not between parties who are within a prohibited marriage relationship; and

f) confirm that the parties freely consented to the marriage.[86]

Under section 55(1) of the Act, customary marriages must be registered like other forms of marriage. The parties apply to the Registrar for a certificate within six months of their marriage.[87] For the issuance of the certificate, both spouses must appear in person before the Registrar.[88] Once the Registrar is satisfied that all the general provisions of the Act have been complied with and the customary rites have been completed, the marriage is registered and the parties presented with the marriage certificate.[89]

85 Section 45, Marriage Act 2014.

86 Ibid.

87 Ibid., section 55(1).

88 Ibid., section 55(2).

89 Ibid., section 55(3).

EMERGING CONCERNS ABOUT THE 2014 ACT

Before the Marriage Act 2014, the court insisted upon prolonged cohabitation between a man and a woman to establish a presumption of marriage. In the case of *Hortensiah Wanjiku Yaweh v Public Trustee,*[90] the court stated: "The presumption does not depend on the law or a system of marriage. The presumption is just an assumption based on a very long cohabitation and repute that the parties are husband and wife". Later, in the case of *Joseph Gitau Githongo v Victoria Mwihaki,*[91] the court asserted:

> It [the presumption of marriage] is a concept born from an appreciation of the needs of the realities of life. A presumption of marriage arises when a man and woman cohabit for a long period without solemnizing that union by going through a recognized form of marriage. If the woman is left stranded either because she was cast away by the "husband", or because he dies, the law, subject to the requisite proof, bestows the status of "wife" upon the woman to enable her to qualify for maintenance or a share in the estate of her deceased "husband".

The presumption of marriage is a matter of fact and must be established by evidence before a court of law.[92] The presumption of marriage does not create a marriage. A marriage can only be created by complying with the provisions of the Marriage Act 2014. Therefore, any relationship between a man and a woman, even where there is cohabitation, is not considered a marriage unless it is registered under the Marriage Act. Section 2 of the Act defines "cohabit" as "an arrangement in which an

[90] Civil Appeal No. 13 of 1976.

[91] (2014) eKLR.

[92] The Evidence Act clarifies the manner of evidentiary use of presumptions in Section 119: "The court may presume the existence of any fact which it thinks likely to have happened, regard being had to the common course of natural events, human conduct and public and private business, in their relation to the facts of the particular case." Consequently, the presumption of marriage is not evidence of marriage but may continue to be used by the court to determine collateral questions; for example, the right of succession.

unmarried couple lives together in a long-term relationship that resembles a marriage". Therefore, the objective of a presumption is to allow the court to determine a connected question.

Following the enactment of the Marriage Act, the presumption of marriage will not create or prove a marriage. In fact, section 59(1) of the Act provides specific documents as the only evidence of marriage in Kenya. These are either a certificate of marriage under the Act or written law, a certified copy of a certificate of marriage under the Act or other written law, an entry in a register of marriages, a certified copy of the entry in a register of marriages, or an entry in a register of marriages maintained by the proper religious authority of the Khoja Shia, Ith'nasheri, Shia imam, Ismaili or Bohra' communities. The presumption of marriage can only enable the person relying on it to make a claim on matters relating to inheritance.[93]

The other emerging concern relates to the registration of marriages. The Act has made registration of marriages a compulsory prerequisite for its validity. Section 96(2) of the Act provides a reprieve of three years for persons married under customary, Islamic or Hindu law before the commencement of the Act to register their marriages under the new law. That notwithstanding, section 98 of the Act asserts that marriages that were valid before the commencement of the Act will remain valid under the new dispensation. The two provisions of the law seem contradictory in that one requires registration of previous marriages for validity while the other acknowledges the validity of the same marriages. The three-year reprieve for persons yet to register their marriages has since expired and was not widely publicized to educate the public. Consequently, a number of couples failed to register their marriages under the new Act due to a lack of awareness. The legal status of such unions remains unknown and precarious. Judicial interpretation of sections 96 and 98 is required to provide direction on the legal position in such situations.

[93] Elvis Abenga, *Presumption of Marriage Under Kenyan Law* (2020) (available online).

CONCLUDING OBSERVATIONS AND RECOMMENDATIONS

The harmonization and consolidation of all forms of marriage, including the general and overarching requirements, was a constructive step towards clarity on marriage procedures under the different family law regimes. However, the transitional provisions of the Marriage Act 2014 are confusing and impractical, especially regarding the requirement of registration of customary marriages contracted before the enactment of the Act. Due to the limited public awareness around the need to register previous marriages, it is anticipated that many couples may not have complied with the provision. As such, the legality of their marital status may be in question.

The Marriage Act also impliedly acknowledges that codifying African customary law is difficult, if not impossible, within the Kenyan society, which has forty-two ethnic communities with distinct practices and marriage rites. In addition, African culture is dynamic and continues to evolve. Proof by the parties that the essential requirements for a valid customary marriage have been met is sufficient evidence for the issuance of a marriage certificate. The fact that the law recognizes that the payment of dowry need not have been fully remitted is a positive step towards wider recognition of customary marriages.

The Act weakens the status, if any, of parties within a cohabitation arrangement. The Act takes away the freedom to choose not to marry and yet enjoy the appurtenant "legal" rights that accrue within a legally recognized marriage, for example, conjugal, maintenance, and consortium rights. Most youths prefer to establish long-term relationships without formalization through marriage. However, the Act impliedly and explicitly views such arrangements as extra-legal and unrecognizable in law. It is imperative to enhance public awareness and education, especially amongst persons of marriageable age, on the dangers and pitfalls of entering into permanent, long-term relationships without solemnization under the Act. In the same vein, it may be essential to reflect on the importance of legal recognition of specific forms of marriage to the exclusion of other evolving forms of domestic partnerships.

South Africa

Chapter Ten
Analytical Overview of the Plurality of Marital Laws in South Africa

Marriages in South Africa are regulated by different legislative acts, which allow people to exercise their freedom of choice in identifying their suitable spouse and marriage type. Three types of marriage are recognized in South Africa: civil marriages, civil unions, and customary marriages. South Africa is a multicultural society, where people of different cultures, ethnicity, races, and socialization co-exist. Whereas the Constitution is supreme, the other primary sources of law are common law (Roman-Dutch law with English law), customary law, legislation, and judicial precedents. Accordingly, when it comes to marriage, South Africa currently has three legal instruments regulating the different types of marriages.

An overview of South African marital law shows how each type of union is recognized and regulated by examining the requirements for the celebration and dissolution of all marriage types. This chapter first looks at civil marriages, the oldest recognized marital system of the three. Then we explore customary marriages and conclude with civil unions. Some positive developments in respect of marriages are noted, together with possible solutions to challenges emanating from the three different marital regimes.

CIVIL MARRIAGES

Nature and concept of civil marriages in South Africa

A civil marriage is a "legally recognized life-long voluntary union between one man and one woman to the exclusion of all other persons".[1] Essentially based on common law, these are marriages regulated by the Marriage Act.[2] The definition suggests that this type of marriage has stringent requirements: it is strictly for couples of opposite sexes and can only accommodate two persons, compared to its customary counterpart, which permits polygamy.[3] Furthermore, it is individualistic as it focuses on the parties in the purported marriage and does not cater to any arranged unions, either through the agency of family, religion, or any third party. This is the classic type of marriage recognized globally and accepted at common law.[4] It is also the most prevalent type of marriage in South Africa, probably because it has existed longer than all other types of unions. South Africans are more acquainted with civil marriages to the extent that even those who enter into customary marriages prefer to enter into civil marriages for certainty of marital status.[5] The concept of a civil marriage is mainly due to it being entirely sanctioned by the State through legislative provisions.

Although the Marriage Act has been in operation since January 1962, it has undergone several amendments to suit and comply with the evolving legal systems, needs, and human rights philosophy over the decades.

Requirements for valid civil marriage

There are generally three main requirements for a valid civil marriage in South Africa. The prospective spouses

[1] Jacqueline Heaton and Hanneretha Kruger, *South African Family Law* (2015), p. 13. The Marriages Act did not define a marriage until the Appellate Division did in *Ismail v Ismail* 1983 (1) SA p. 1006 ff (A), where this definition was given by the court in giving guidelines on why marriages solemnized according to Islamic rite cannot be regarded as marriages in terms of the Act.

[2] Marriage Act (No. 25 of 1961).

[3] Polygamy is the type of marriage where a man marries more than one wife.

[4] South African common law is Eurocentric, being based on Roman-Dutch law mixed with English law.

[5] Aubrey Manthwa, "Towards an Afrikan Approach in Resolving the Conundrum Between a Civil and Customary Marriage", *Southern African Public Law* (2009), p. 9.

must have the capacity to marry, consent to the marriage, and comply with the prescribed formalities.

No person lacking the legal capacity to marry can contract a valid civil marriage. The incapacity to marry may be absolute or relative. An absolute incapacity arises where one or both parties are prohibited from entering into a civil marriage. For instance, persons already married,[6] below the permissible marriageable age, [7] or mentally incapacitated[8] cannot enter into a valid marriage. Relative incapacity is when a person cannot enter into a civil marriage because of what or who they are. For example, unlike civil unions, persons in civil marriages of the same sex cannot marry each other. Age is a relative incapacity because minors require the consent of the parents, guardians, or even the Minister of Home Affairs, where necessary, to enter into a marriage; otherwise, the marriage is voidable.[9] Persons within prohibited degrees of relationship cannot marry one another.[10] Those declared prodigals lack the capacity to marry. This is because a person declared or interdicted as prodigal under South African common law must be placed under a curator who must consent to their legal activities due to their inability to manage their affairs.[11] Guardians

[6] Either according to the Marriage Act, customary marriage, or even civil unions. See *Netshituka v Netshituka* 2011 (5) SA 453 (SCA), where the Court held that a person who was already in a customary marriage is not eligible or lacks the capacity to enter into a civil marriage with another during the subsistence of the said customary marriage. See also the Marriage and Matrimonial Property Amendment Act (No. 3 of 1988).

[7] *De Greeff v De Greeff* 1982 (1) SA 882 (O).

[8] Ann Skelton, et al., *Family Law in South Africa* (2014), chapter 3.

[9] A void marriage is a marriage that has no legal consequences because it does not adhere to the requirements. Whereas a voidable marriage is a marriage that came into existence, but may be annulled in the future due to a material defect at the formation of the marriage.

[10] See Articles 5, 6, and 7, Political Ordinance 1580; D. S. P. Cronje and Jacqueline Heaton, *South African Family Law* (2004).

[11] However, in *Pienaar v Piennar's curator* 1930 OPD 171, the court held that should a prodigal enter into a civil marriage, such marriage will be deemed to be out of community of property. This led to a debate whether this means that a prodigal can still enter into a valid civil marriage without the consent of his/her curator, but the marriage will be out of community of property. Courts exercise their discretion in this case.

and wards cannot marry one another, except with the court's permission.[12] Thus, one's capacity to enter into a civil marriage must be ascertained before the marriage is entered into; otherwise, the said marriage could be void or voidable.

Parties to a union must be willing to marry each other. This consent must be declared during the solemnization of the marriage by a competent marriage officer.[13] Consent to marry is vitiated if it can be proven that there was a material mistake in the mind of either party about the marriage, or that a material misrepresentation was made by either of the parties which induced the other. Consent is further vitiated if it is proven that a party was unduly influenced or was under duress to consent to marriage.[14]

Prospective spouses must comply with the prescribed marriage formalities. A civil marriage must be solemnized by a competent marriage officer,[15] and there must not be an objection to the marriage by any party of interest. The marriage may be solemnized in a public or private building with open doors, and in the presence of at least two competent witnesses. Last, the marriage must be registered and parties presented with a marriage certificate serving as *prima facie* proof of the validity of the marriage.

Legal consequences of a civil marriage

A civil marriage has personal and patrimonial consequences for the parties to the union. The consequences are often referred to as invariable consequences, because they give rise to a moral duty on spouses towards one another, whether they agree to it or not. This is also known as *consortium omnis vitae*, where parties in the marriage have a physical, moral, and spiritual community of life.[16] Marriage

[12] Herman Robert Hahlo and Ellison Kahn, *The Union of South Africa: The Development of its Laws and Constitution* (1960).

[13] Sections 2 and 3, Marriage Act.

[14] Ibid.

[15] A judicial officer, special justice of the peace, dedicated commissioners, public servants at the Department of Home Affairs, and religious leaders.

[16] Herman Robert Hahlo and Ellison Kahn, *The South African Law of Husband and*

gives rise to a reciprocal duty of support, meaning spouses have the right to demand and provide maintenance towards one another from the date of the marriage.[17] Even though this right may be subject to a means test of the parties, it can be enforceable through courts.[18] Another invariable consequence of civil marriages is that it creates new legally binding relationships, and children for whom both parents are equally responsible and have rights over. This is not peculiar to civil marriages; it applies to civil unions and customary marriages to a certain extent, if not similarly.

The patrimonial consequences, on the other hand, pertain to the financial consequences of marriage. These are often referred to as variable consequences because parties choose a matrimonial property system by which to govern their marriage. These consequences not only determine the financial relationship between the spouses, but also with their creditors, and are regulated by the Matrimonial Property Act (No. 88 of 1984).[19] The spouses may choose between the following matrimonial property systems:

- In community of property, with profit and loss,
- Out of community of property with the accrual system, and
- Out of community of property without the accrual system (excluding profit and loss).[20]

In South Africa, the default matrimonial property system applicable to all monogamous marriages, including civil marriages, is in community of property.[21] However, this default system can be excluded before the marriage

Wife (1985), p. 130.

17 *Reyneke v Reyneke* 1990 (3) SA 927.

18 *Wiese v Moolman* 2009 (3) SA 122 (T).

19 Later amended by the Matrimonial Property Amendment Act (No. 3 of 1988).

20 Ibid.

21 Under common law, the husband's law of domicile (*lex domicilii*) dictates the default matrimonial property system. Where the law of domicile dictates that the default system is out of community of property, then the marriage will adopt the same unless such effect is excluded by an antenuptial contract.

is entered into, by an antenuptial contract where the prospective spouses specify which system they prefer.[22]

Dissolution of civil marriages

A civil marriage can be dissolved on the death of one of the spouses, by a court decree, or by setting aside a voidable marriage.[23] Only the dissolution of marriages by divorce is discussed herein because a court order is required, unlike the other types of dissolution.

Grounds for divorce

Dissolution of marriage by divorce in South Africa is regulated by the Divorce Act (No. 70 of 1979).[24] Such dissolution requires a decree of divorce by a competent court. A decree of divorce may be granted on grounds that the marriage has irretrievably broken down with no prospect of a restoration,[25] because of mental illness, or on account of continuous unconsciousness of one of the parties.[26] This method of dissolving a marriage is more focused on the realistic and desirable state of the marriage relationship between the parties. On the first ground, the court needs first to satisfy itself that the marriage has reached a state of disintegration where there is no reasonable prospect of restoring it; that is, the *consortium omnis vitae* of the marriage is totally broken down.[27] The court may consider several factors in making that determination, including that the parties have not lived together for a continuous

[22] An antenuptial contract must be notarially executed and registered pursuant to section 87 of the Deeds Registries Act (No. 47 of 1937); an antenuptial contract that has not been registered in terms of section 87 is only valid between the parties.

[23] J. A. Robinson, in Jacqueline Heaton (ed.), *The Law of Divorce and Dissolution of Life Partnerships in South Africa* (2014), chapter 2.

[24] Dissolution by death is automatic and does not require a court order unless spouse must be presumed dead due to a prolonged disappearance as is determined by the Dissolution of Marriage on Presumption of Death Act (No. 23 of 1979).

[25] Section 4, Marriage Act.

[26] Ibid., section 5.

[27] See *Schwartz v Schwartz* 1984 (4) SA 467; *Naidoo v Naidoo* 1985 (1) SA 366 (T).

period, acts of adultery by one party that the other party finds intolerable, and imprisonment due to the habitual criminality of a spouse.[28]

In respect of a petition for divorce on grounds of mental illness or continuous unconsciousness, the plaintiff needs to provide the court with medical proof or reports under section 5 of the Divorce Act on the irreversibility of the defendant's condition.[29] With unconsciousness, the party needs to have been unconscious for a continuous period of six months.[30] However, the plaintiff will bear the legal cost of the divorce, since the court is obliged to appoint a legal practitioner to represent the defendant where the ground of mental illness or continuous unconsciousness is relied on.

Although the court does not necessarily have the power to refuse to grant a divorce order on the ground that the marriage is irretrievably broken down, it can withhold or postpone the order under section 4(3) of the Divorce Act if this is in the best interest of the parties.[31]

Consequences of divorce

Since marriage gives rise to certain legal consequences, its dissolution equally gives rise to legal consequences for the parties. Generally, the dissolution of marriage produces personal and patrimonial consequences.

On personal consequences, the marital status of the parties will change,[32] ending *consortium omnis vitae.* There is also the possibility of an order for payment of spousal maintenance under section 7 of the Divorce Act,[33] either by

[28] Section 4(2), Marriage Act.

[29] Mental Health Care Act (No. 17 of 2002).

[30] Section 5(2), Divorce Act.

[31] See *Amar v Amar* 1999 (3) SA 604 (W), where the court withheld the order of divorce until the husband complied with his Jewish religion's matrimonial requirements for the dissolution of the marriage. In this case, the court provided a new interpretation of s5A of the Divorce Act.

[32] A spouse who married when she was a minor retains the majority status acquired through marriage.

[33] The maintenance payment could be a lump sum.

parties agreeing to do so or by the court's discretion.[34] The court will consider the welfare of the minor or dependent children in the marriage and make an order pertaining to their maintenance.[35]

On patrimonial consequences, the matrimonial property system of the marriage will be terminated, and a settlement agreement made. Where parties were married in a community of property, the court will make an order regarding the division of the joint estate, considering pension interests and forfeiture of patrimonial benefits where applicable. For a matrimonial property system that is out of the community of property, the court will either make an order of retention of a separate estate, accrual benefits claims, forfeiture of benefits, redistribution orders, and pension interest, according to the circumstances surrounding the matter.[36]

CUSTOMARY MARRIAGES IN SOUTH AFRICA

The recognition of customary marriages in South Africa brought color to legal pluralism in private law, and in particular, family law. Customary marriages are celebrated according to customary law,[37] and are in South Africa regulated by the Recognition of Customary Marriages Act (No. 120 of 1998) (RCMA). Customary law is defined as customs and usages traditionally observed by the African indigenous people of South Africa, which form part of the culture of those people.[38] However, even though customary marriages predate other marriages, they were not recognized until the RCMA came into force on 15 November 2000. This implies that before the RCMA, customary marriages did not

[34] For further details on the personal consequences of divorce see Skelton, note 8 above, chapter 9, and Sonnekus JC in Heaton, note 24 above, chapter 3.

[35] Section 6, Divorce Act; Also, section 28(2) of the 1996 Constitution of the Republic of South Africa emphasizes that in all matters affecting a child, the best interest of that child must prevail. See also the Children's Act (No. 38 2005).

[36] For further details on the patrimonial consequence of divorce see Skelton, note 8 above and Sonnekus JC in Heaton note 24 above.

[37] Section 1, Recognition of Customary Marriages Act (No. 120 of 1998) (RCMA).

[38] Ibid.

have any legal consequences,[39] even though they were active and in existence.

Recognition of customary marriages in South Africa

Customary marriages were not recognized in South Africa before the RCMA because of the socio-political climate[40] emanating from colonialism and the apartheid regime, where most indigenous laws and systems were regarded as repugnant to principles of natural justice primarily based on western law. According to Thandabantu Nhlapo,[41] until the RCMA, customary marriages were privately facilitated by families with no State intervention. However, with the adoption of the Constitution of 1996, customary law is recognized as one of the primary sources of law,[42] setting it on equal footing with common law.[43] In guaranteeing the freedom of religion, belief, and opinion, the Constitution went further in section 15(3) to encourage the enactment of a statute that would recognize marriages concluded under customary law. That is how customary marriages eventually became recognized and regulated by statute in South Africa.

In its preamble, the RCMA states that it aims to provide for the recognition of customary marriages; to specify the requirements for the validity of same; and to regulate the registration, proprietary consequence, and the dissolution

[39] However, some statutes did to some extent provide protection for customary unions (as they were labelled) even though the marriage system was not recognized itself. For instance, section 1(1) of the Law of Evidence Amendment Act (No. 45 of 1988) provided that courts should not declare unlawful the custom of *lobola* or *bogadi* or other similar customs to be repugnant to the principles of public justice or natural justice of that time. Furthermore, section 22(1) & (2) of the Matrimonial Property Amendment Act (No. 3 of 1988) provided that a spouse in a customary union was not competent to enter into a civil marriage with another party during the subsistence of the customary union.

[40] Thomas William Bennett, *Customary Law in South Africa* (2004), p. 188.

[41] Thandabantu Nhlapo, "Marriages", in Chuma Himonga and Thandabantu Nhlapo (eds.), *African Customary Law in South Africa Post-Apartheid and Living Perspectives* (2014), pp. 91-107.

[42] Section 39, 1996 Constitution of the Republic of South Africa.

[43] Ibid., section 39(3).

of customary marriages, among other functions. The RCMA has not been without its challenges, though. It has been subjected to a couple of constitutional validity tests,[44] especially pertaining to its provisions on the proprietary consequences of customary marriages entered into before its commencement. This led to major amendments in its proprietary consequence clause. Nonetheless, despite its slow start, in terms of people's confidence in its applicability, compared to the Civil Marriage Act, and the general lack of awareness about it, the RCMA is in full effect and is gaining courts' attention on marital disputes. As such, it is essential to understand its elements and prerequisites.

Requirements for valid customary marriage in South Africa

In section 2 of the RCMA two categories of customary marriages are recognized. The first category is customary marriages entered into before the commencement of the Act, both monogamous and polygamous (pre-Act marriages).[45] The second category is customary marriages entered into after its commencement in November 2000, both monogamous and polygamous (post-Act marriages).[46]

Although these marriages are entered into according to customary law, the requirements for their validity differ. The pre-Act marriages are deemed valid and recognized if they were valid at customary law and in existence at the commencement of the Act.[47] This means that a marriage which may have been valid at customary law, but is no longer in existence, either by customary dissolution or other means by 15 November 2000, will not be recognized as valid under the RCMA.[48] The requirements for the

[44] See *Gumede (born Shange) v President of the Republic of South Africa and Others* 2009 (3) SA 152 (CC) as well as *Ramuhovhi and Others v President of the Republic of South Africa and Others* 2018 (2) SA 1 (CC).

[45] Section 2(3), RCMA.

[46] Ibid., section 2(2).

[47] Ibid., section 2(1).

[48] This includes customary marriages dissolved by virtue of one spouse entering into a civil marriage with another according to the Marriage Act before December

validity of a customary marriage depend on the customary law applicable and ascertainable at the time of the marriage, together with other applicable State laws.

Requirements for valid customary marriage post-RCMA

Section 3(1) of the RCMA sets out new requirements for a valid customary marriage in South Africa. These requirements state that both spouses must be eighteen years and above and must consent to marry each other under customary law. The marriage must be negotiated and entered into or celebrated according to customary law.

The requirements of age and consent seem straightforward. They play an alignment role to ensure that customary marriages are aligned to constitutional requirements and other relevant laws of general application as required by section 211(3) of the Constitution. Yet, the requirement of negotiating the marriage in section 3(1)(b) is confusing even to the courts, especially regarding the role of customary law in establishing and validating a customary marriage. This confusion may be exacerbated by the fact that while the Act recognizes marriages entered into in accordance with its provisions in section 3(1), such marriages may significantly differ from customary marriages entered per its definition of customary marriage in section 1. This is because, in section 1, customary marriages are defined as marriages entered into according to customary law, not according to section 3(1) of the Act. The challenge here is that there are different types of marriages entered into according to customary law other than the ones on which the Act is focused. There are marriages entered into for bloodline progression and succession, such as woman-to-woman marriages,[49] and those entered into to bear a successor for a traditional leadership

1988 when the Matrimonial Property Amendment Act (No. 3 1988) came into effect; it prohibited spouses in customary marriages from entering into civil marriages during the subsistence of the former.

49 Sections 2 and 4, Reform of Customary Law of Succession and the Regulation of Related Matters Act (No. 11 of 2009).

position.[50] These are special marriages, but their status is not covered in the RCMA. Nonetheless, section 3(1) deals with the general requirements for a valid customary marriage after the commencement of the RCMA.

Customary law and the requirements for valid customary marriage

When analyzing section 3(1)(b) of the RCMA, it is useful to understand the concept and nature of customary law; there are two facets. One is the official customary law, which is customary law that is codified in books, legislation, and judicial precedents.[51] The other is living customary law, which is practiced by indigenous people and accepted as binding on them in terms of their traditions and culture.[52] It is generally accepted that the term customary law as it appears in the Constitution and various legislation primarily refers to living customary law unless otherwise stated.

Consequently, to understand the meaning and context of the requirement that a valid customary marriage must be "negotiated and entered or celebrated in accordance with customary law", it is imperative that an elaborate meaning of living customary law be given. In essence, living customary law pertains to customary law that is not written, but applied by indigenous people daily and accepted by them as their tradition and culture.[53] Some characteristics of living customary law include that it is non-static, meaning it is flexible and evolves as society evolves and changes its values.[54] Second, living customary

[50] The principal wife. *Nsati lonkulu* (Xitsonga), *Mufukadzi wa dzekiso* (Tshivenda), *Ndlovukazi* (Zulu), *Mmasechaba* (Sotho).

[51] Anthony C. Diala, "The Concept of Living Customary Law: a Critique", *Journal of Legal Pluralism and Unofficial Law*, XLIX, no. 2 (2017), p. 143; Tom Bennet, ""Official" vs "Living" Customary law: Dilemmas of Description and Recognition", in Aninka Claassens and Ben Cousins (eds.), *Land, Power & Custom: Controversies Generated by South Africa's Communal Land Rights Act* (2008).

[52] Chuma Himonga and Fatimata Diallo, "Decolonisation and Teaching Law in Africa with Special Reference to Living Customary Law", *Potchefstroom Electronic Law Journal*, XX (2017).

[53] Christa Rautenbach and Others, *Introduction to Legal Pluralism* (2014).

[54] Richman Bangilizwe Mqeke, *Customary Law in the New Millennium* (2003), pp.

law is generally passed on orally from one generation to another. Third, it is embedded in the lifestyle and beliefs of the community, where it applies through cultural practices and traditions. Last, its application may differ from one indigenous group to another, even though some principles may be similar. In the famous case of *Bhe v Khayelitsha Magistrate*[55], the Constitutional Court correctly observed that living customary law is distinguished by its flexibility to acknowledge the changes which continually take place in society. In the same breath, the Court also acknowledged that sometimes the difficulty with living customary law is in determining its content and testing it, as the Court should, against the provisions of the Bill of Rights.[56]

Against this backdrop, of the three requirements for the validity of a customary marriage, the requirement in section 3(1)(b) depends on living customary law. In other words, to determine whether a customary marriage has been negotiated and entered into or celebrated according to customary law, the demands of the living customary law of the parties must be met. Such living customs must be seen both in light of their meaning and reasonable application. This is in consideration of the fact that living customary law evolves. The flexibility of living customary law pertains to its application rather than its principles. Often the principle remains, but the application evolves with the times, adapting to the needs and values of the generation or community where it applies.

Registration of customary marriages

In the past, customary marriages could not be registered marriages. However, section 4(1) of the RCMA imposes a duty on spouses in customary marriages to ensure that their marriages are registered by a competent official at the Department of Home Affairs.[57] The registration of customary

1-25.

[55] CCT49/03, p. 87.

[56] Ibid., p. 86.

[57] Section 4, RCMA; The spouses in a customary marriage have the duty to ensure that the customary marriage is registered.

marriages is one area where it significantly differs from civil marriages. Whereas civil marriages are validated by registration of the same, customary marriages are not. For a customary marriage to be registered, it must be valid first, either under section 2 (1) or section 3(1) of the RCMA. The registration of a customary marriage only provides the couple with proof of their marriage; it does not validate the marriage. Section 4(9) of the RCMA provides that failure to register a customary marriage does not invalidate the marriage.

Although section 4(9) may sound logical in terms of the status of the marriage at customary law, it may challenge the entire institution of marriage in South Africa. Chuma Himonga and Eleena Moore[58] describe how in their research on the reform of customary marriages in South Africa, they discovered that unregistered customary marriages create landmines because spouses' marital statuses remain unchanged at the Department of Home Affairs registry. They explain that where a person is a spouse in a valid customary marriage, they could easily get away with registering and entering into a civil marriage with another party because their marital status remains as 'unmarried' even though they are married by customary law.[59] This may lead to numerous challenges. According to Monica De Souza,[60] many people, due to ignorance of the RCMA, leave their customary marriages without obtaining a divorce decree as required by section 8(1). The marriages are dissolved according to customary processes or informally under the impression that there are no legal consequences to an unregistered marriage. Nonetheless, the registration of customary marriages is required even though failure to do so does not affect its validity. Section 4(9) may be regarded as a major flaw in the Act, for it creates serious discord in the institution of customary marriages in South Africa.

[58] Chuma Himonga and Eleena Moore, *Reform of Customary Marriage, Divorce and Succession in South Africa* (2015).

[59] Ibid., chapter 4.

[60] Monica De Souza, "When Non-Registration Becomes Non-Recognition: Examining the Law and Practice of Customary Marriage Registration in South Africa", *Acta Juridica* (2013) p. 239.

Minors and equality of spouses in customary marriages

In South Africa, any person under the age of eighteen years is considered a minor[61] and generally lacks the capacity to act or enter into a contract without parental supervision and consent.[62] The same is applicable to customary marriages.[63] According to section 3(1)(a), a prospective spouse in a customary marriage must be eighteen years and older and competent to give informed consent to enter into a customary marriage. However, there is an exception; minors may be able to contract a marriage if it is in their best interest to do so. For instance, in *Allock v Allock,*[64] the court granted permission for a minor to marry because the minor was only eleven months shy of the age of majority, and it was reasonable to allow her to marry. However, in *De Greeff v De Greeff,*[65] the court sided with the parent in refusing to grant permission to a minor to marry a man who was thirteen years older than her and an alcoholic because it did not find the marriage to be in the best interest of the child. Section 25 of the Marriages Act also applies to customary marriages involving a minor and provides that a minor is required to obtain parental or guardian consent to enter into a customary marriage.[66] Where consent has not been obtained, a minor's marriage becomes voidable.[67] This provision is more important for customary marriages in curbing customary marriages involving minors, but not in the child's best interest.[68]

61 Section 17, Children's Act.

62 Sections 18(2) and (3), Marriage Act.

63 Section 5, RCMA.

64 1969 (1) SA 427 (N).

65 1982 (1) SA 882 (O).

66 Sections 3(2)-(5), RCMA.

67 However, where parental or guardian consent is obtainable or withheld unreasonably, the High Court as the upper guardian of all minors in the country may grant the consent upon application of the minor(s) concerned if the Court is satisfied that the marriage is in the best interest of the minor. See section 25(4), Marriage Act, *Allock v Allock* 1969 (1) SA 427, and *B v B* 1983 (1) SA 469.

68 In its organic nature, customary law determination of the age of majority is not according to birth age but is determined by puberty and going through the

One praiseworthy reform made by the RCMA to customary marriages is the introduction of equal capacity and rights of spouses. Section 6 of the RCMA provides that:

> A wife in a customary marriage has, on the basis of equality with her husband and subject to the matrimonial property system governing the marriage, full status, and capacity, including the capacity to acquire assets and to dispose of them, to enter into contracts and to litigate, in addition to any rights and powers that she might have at customary law.

This section plays an alignment role in ensuring that both the living and official customary law regulating customary marriages are subject to the purports and objectives of the Bill of Rights, which guarantees gender equality and human dignity, among other rights.[69] Therefore, spouses in customary marriages enjoy equal status and capacity in all things, including acquiring and disposing of assets. However, the Act acknowledges and retains rights accorded to wives in customary marriages by customary law. These rights are not as relevant in monogamous marriages as in polygamous marriages. For instance, the first wife has the right to be consulted and to give consent when her husband seeks to marry another wife. In *Mayelane v Ngwenyama*[70] the Constitutional Court confirmed that a subsequent customary marriage of a husband to another woman is invalid if he did not obtain consent from his first wife (or existing wives). However, in this case, the first wife has more rights and powers than the other wives, where there is more than one subsisting customary marriage. Another instance where additional rights and powers of a wife in customary marriage play a critical role is in royal households, where only a specific wife has the right to bear an heir among other

traditional rites of passage which marks one's transitions from being a child to being a major who is illegible for marriage amongst other things.

69 Customary law is said to be patriarchal in nature, and therefore, women were often seen as perpetual minors who were subject to male guardianship even in marriage, where their husbands would play a custodial role in overall legal transactions of the marriage to the exclusion of the wives. See Also Bennett, note 40 above, p. 248.

70 (CCT 57/12) [2013] ZACC 14; 2013 (4) SA 415,

wives by virtue of the status of her marriage. However, as mentioned before, these marriages are not given special attention in the RCMA; this was an oversight as they are significant marriages in the African indigenous communities.

Proprietary consequence of customary marriages

To stretch the implication of spousal equality, powers, and rights in customary marriages, the RCMA introduces statutorily regulated proprietary consequences to customary marriages, as opposed to the original customary law position, which was patriarchal in nature. The proprietary consequence of customary marriages differs between monogamous marriages and polygamous customary marriages. In sum, all monogamous customary marriages are by default in community of property,[71] unless an antenuptial contract excludes such a consequence.[72]

However, with regard to valid polygamous marriages entered into after the commencement of the RCMA, the husband needs to make an application to the court to approve a proprietary contract between him and his existing wife(ves) and the subsequent wife, which stipulates how the future matrimonial property of their marriage(s) will be regulated in the interest of all parties involved.[73] Where the husband was married in community of property or out of community of property with his existing wife, the court must first terminate the existing proprietary system and effect a distribution of the property, before it approves and effects the new contract in the polygamous marriage.[74]

[71] See sections 7(1) and (2), RCMA. However, this was not the position when the RCMA first came into operation. Only monogamous customary marriages entered into after the commencement of the Act was in community of property, and all pre-Act monogamous and polygamous customary marriages' proprietary consequence continued to be governed by customary law. This position was challenged in the cases of *Gumede v President of the Republic of South Africa* (CCT 50/08) [2008] ZACC 23; 2009 (3) BCLR 243; and *Ramuhovhi v President of the Republic of South Africa* 2018 (2) BCLR 217, respectively.

[72] However, the said antenuptial contract does not apply to pre-Act marriages but must be drawn and signed before the commencement of any process in terms of section 3(1)(b), RCMA (No. 120 of 1998) with regard to the post-Act marriages.

[73] Section 7(6), RCMA.

[74] Ibid., section 7 (7)-(8).

In *Ramuhovhi v President of the Republic of South Africa*, the Constitutional Court confirmed the High Court's decision[75] that pre-Act polygamous marriages will bear the proprietary consequences of a joint estate, instead of being subject to customary law. This led to the amendment of section 7(1) of the RCMA, which stipulates that spouses in pre-Act polygamous marriages enjoy joint ownership and control of family property in respect of the husband and all his wives; or joint ownership and control of house property in respect of the husband and a wife in that particular house.[76]

This proprietary system could confuse people unfamiliar with polygamous marriages. The system is based on the customary principle that when a man marries more than one wife, each wife establishes a new and separate household; she does not join a big inseparable family. This is to give the wife some autonomy in her marriage. However, because the husband is the common denominator in the polygamous relationship, there is bound to be property that belongs to him or under his care for the benefit of the entire family. However, spouses in pre-Act marriages are allowed to apply to the court for leave to change this default proprietary system and create, by contract, a more suitable one.[77] This development sounds noble, but it is yet to be seen whether it provides practical solutions to the marriages concerned.

[75] 2018 (2) BCLR 217 (CC).

[76] Section 7(1)(a), RCMA: The proprietary consequences of a customary marriage in which a person is a spouse in more than one customary marriage, and which was entered into before the commencement of this Act, are that the spouses in such a marriage have joint and equal:

(i) ownership and other rights; and

(ii) rights of management and control, over marital property.

(b) The rights contemplated in paragraph (a) must be exercised-

(i) in respect of all house property, by the husband and wife of the house concerned, jointly and in the best interests of the family unit constituted by the house concerned; and

(ii) in respect of all family property, by the husband and all the wives, jointly and in the best interests of the whole family constituted by the various houses.

(c) Each spouse retains exclusive rights over his or her personal property.

[77] Section 7(4), RCMA.

Dissolution of customary marriages

Moving to the dissolution of customary marriages, the RCMA brought reform in this aspect by introducing judicial dissolution of customary marriages. Section 8(1) of the Act stipulates that a customary marriage may only be dissolved by a judicial divorce decree on the ground that the marriage is irretrievably broken down. One main reason for the adoption of a judicial divorce for customary marriages is that the extra-judicial dissolution of customary marriages is most likely to leave women and their children without proprietary protection on dissolution of the marriages,[78] unless the court makes the order for the just distribution of property and welfare arrangements for minor children involved.

The legislative regulation of the dissolution of customary marriages through the RCMA creates many challenges. First, the failure to register a customary marriage without any consequences creates a huge loophole that often results in non-compliance with section 8(1). Spouses who did not register their marriages opt to dissolve them privately and extrajudicially. Second, there seems to be dissonance between the private nature of the formation of customary marriages in section 3(1) and the public and judicial nature of its dissolution in section 8(1). It is not surprising that research has discovered that many customary marriages are extrajudicially dissolved.[79] Customary law has processes to facilitate the dissolution of the same by asking why people would subject themselves to legal costs and judicial processes when they can privately dissolve what they privately created.

The desire for a private dissolution is encouraged by section 4(9), which provides that failure to register a customary marriage will not invalidate it. As a result, many people continue with life after their extra-judicial

[78] South African law Commission Project, *Harmonization of the Common Law and the Indigenous Law Report on Customary Marriages* (1998), p. 90.

[79] Elena Moore and Chuma Himonga, "Protection of Marital Property Rights upon Dissolution of a Customary Marriage in South Africa: A View from Inside and Outside the Courts", University of Cape Town Centre for Social Science Research Working Papers No. 350 (2015).

dissolution as though their "divorces" were valid.[80] Meanwhile, according to statute law, they are still married. This creates significant challenges when the parties enter into new marriages with other persons, especially civil marriages. These civil marriages are invalid because of the subsistence of the customary marriage, which was not dissolved according to section 8(1).

Nonetheless, there are customary marriages that comply with the requirement of obtaining a divorce decree from the court. Yet, through case law,[81] one cannot help but notice that in most cases where divorce in a customary marriage arises, the courts must first determine whether the marriage was valid or not, especially where the marriage was not registered. The court may end up declaring that there was no valid marriage.

CIVIL UNIONS

Recognition of civil unions

Since 2006, South Africa has added civil unions to its recognized unions. These are regulated by the Civil Unions Act.[82] A civil union is "the voluntary union of two persons who are both 18 years of age or older, which is solemnized and registered by way of either a marriage or a civil partnership, ... to the exclusion, while it lasts, of all others".[83] Civil unions are a clear indication of the democratic nature of South Africa. They came about as a response to the Constitutional Court decision in the case of *Minister of Home Affairs v Fourie and Another,*[84] which found the Marriage Act discriminatory as it only catered to marriages between males and females.

[80] Ibid., p. 162; Mothokoa Mamashela, "New Families, the New Law: The Practical Effects of the Recognition of Customary Marriages Act", *South African Journal on Human Rights*, XX (2004), p. 616.

[81] See *Gumede v President of the Republic of South Africa* 2009 (3) SA 152 (CC); *Motsoatsoa v Roro* [2011] 2 All SA 324 (GSJ); Southon v Maropene case no.14295/10 (SGJ).

[82] Civil Union Act (No. 17 of 2006).

[83] Ibid., section 1.

[84] *Minister of Home Affairs and Another v Fourie and Another* 2006 (1) SA 524 (CC).

As a result, civil unions were legalized. Civil unions bear a resemblance to civil marriages as they are also monogamous, and as indicated in section 13(1), they have the same legal consequences as civil marriages.

Requirements for civil unions

As mentioned, civil unions mirror civil marriages, and their requirements are similar, with minor differences. These dissimilarities include the age of the parties to the civil union. Whereas minors can contract civil marriages, only those eighteen years and above may enter into valid civil unions under the Civil Union Act[85] Because the Act does not permit minors to contract civil marriages, while other marriage laws do so permit, the Act may be considered discriminatory even though such a restriction was likely put in place to protect children. Such discrimination is considered unfair and is prohibited by the South African Constitution.[86]

The Civil Union Act requires a marriage officer to inquire from the parties to the civil union whether they want their union to be regarded as a marriage or a civil partnership.[87] This clause brings confusion to the marital legal framework. Questions such as why one would want to enter into a heterosexual civil union and not a marriage may arise, especially given that the consequences of the two are closely related. There is a fine line, if any, between heterosexual civil unions and civil marriages. Perhaps such confusion would be avoided if civil unions were only for same-sex couples. This is a result of civil marriages and civil unions having similar consequences, making the difference between civil marriages and civil unions unclear. If there is not much or no difference between the two, why are they regulated by different laws?

[85] Section 1, Civil Union Act (No. 17 of 2006).

[86] Section 9(3), Constitution of the Republic of South Africa 1996 stipulates that: The State may not unfairly discriminate directly or indirectly against anyone on one or more grounds, including race, gender, sex, pregnancy, marital status, ethnic or social origin, colour, sexual orientation, age, disability, religion, conscience, belief, culture, language and birth.

[87] Section 11, Civil Union Act (No. 17 of 2006).

Dissolution of civil unions

Just as the legal consequences of a civil union are the same as those of a civil marriage, so are the ways of dissolving civil unions. These are dissolved by divorce or upon death of one of the parties or when set aside as voidable. The dissolution of a civil union carries some personal and proprietary consequences, as those arising from the dissolution of civil marriages.

CHALLENGES POSED BY DIFFERENT MARRIAGE REGIMES IN SOUTH AFRICAN FAMILY LAW

Although the recognition of customary marriages in South Africa, as well as the enactment of the Civil Union Act, was a huge step towards inclusivity and equality, some challenges exist in South African family law. These range from legislative to operational shortcomings, as well as awareness gaps.

The disparity between the official and living customary law in customary marriages needs to be revisited. For instance, courts have heard disputes on the validity of customary marriages emanating from inconsistencies between official and living customary law. The case of *Sengadi v Tsambo*,[88] which emanated from the question of whether Sengadi and her alleged deceased husband had entered into a valid marriage, bears testimony to this.

Another issue of contestation in customary marriages is their dissolution by divorce. The legislative requirement to have customary marriages dissolved by a court on the ground of it having broken down irretrievably[89] is symptomatic of the lack of development of the legal framework regulating customary marriages. There is a high level of inconsistency between the requirements for entering into valid customary marriages and those determined for dissolving such marriages. Such irreconcilable prerequisites are the basis of much confusion and non-compliance with the law on the dissolution of customary marriages. Harmonizing the

88 *Sengadi v Tsambo* 2019 (4) SA 50.

89 Section 8(1), RCMA.

requirements for contracting and dissolving customary marriages in South Africa would be appropriate.

Judging from the given discussion and some decided case law, although civil and customary marriages should be on an equal footing, civil marriages are usually regarded as better than customary law. This perception informs the conclusion of civil marriages by multitudes of South Africans after they have contracted customary marriages. Such a perception may be cured by raising awareness about the equal status of different marriages. The rationale for many South Africans entering into customary and civil marriages when they are both recognized and equal, and with the customary union usually preceding, is probably that customary marriages were non-binding until the year 2000, when they were fully recognized. This history still informs the marriage decisions that people make. Legally, entering into both types of marriages simply converts the customary marriage into a civil marriage. The material difference between these two marriages also contributes to dual marriages. Although customary marriages are statutorily regulated, they are private, needing no State involvement in their creation, giving the impression that the process is unofficial and, therefore, not legally binding or protected. This could also explain why parties thereto usually resort to the extra-judicial dissolution of these marriages. These are some challenges brought by legal pluralism in marriages. While it affords South Africans freedom of choice in marital regimes, the perception of the status and recognition of customary marriages needs attention.

The registration of customary marriages is a subject of discord. While the RCMA places the duty to register a customary marriage on the parties,[90] it provides that non-registration of a customary marriage does not affect the validity of the marriage. This makes it difficult, if not impossible, for one's marital status to be verified. There has been a rise in cases where a person is married under customary law, but concludes other customary marriages without first dissolving the initial marriage or without the knowledge of the first and new wife. An example includes the cases of *Netshituka v*

[90] Ibid., section 4(1).

Netshituka[91] and *Mayelane v Ngwenyama*[92] where husbands to customary marriages concluded subsequent civil marriages or customary marriages without the consent or knowledge of their existing customary wives. In both instances, the courts faced a problem, which if left unattended, would have been prejudicial to the wives. Failure to register a customary marriage greatly impacts the patrimonial consequences of these marriages. Be that as it may, if registration of customary marriages was mandatory, subsequent wives would be on notice regarding the marital status of their prospective husbands and be spared unnecessary legal battles.

CONCLUSION

Some consider marriage as one of the milestones attained by many in life. It is key to have those milestones regulated in ways that unambiguously allow freedom of choice in the marriage regime. South Africa has enacted three statutes to cater to everyone's marital freedom: the Marriage Act, the Recognition of Customary Marriages Act, and the Civil Unions Act. While this is an achievement worth celebrating for a democratic nation with a legal system anchored on constitutional supremacy, the need remains to further regulate marriages in South Africa. Awareness of the diverse types of marriages must provide the end users with clarity of choice and enable them to avoid legal ambiguities. Although not a bad idea in itself, the question remains whether the proposed single Marriage Act is adequate and would provide solutions to the challenges caused by the multiple marital laws applicable in South Africa.

91 *Netshituka v Netshituka and Others* 2011 (5) SA 453.

92 *Mayelane v Ngwenyama* 2014 (4) SA 415.

eSwatini

Chapter Eleven
The Marriage Law of eSwatini

This chapter examines the types of marriages recognized in eSwatini,[1] formerly Swaziland. It considers the essentials for their validity and the requirements for dissolution and exposes the weaknesses in the laws regulating marriages, proposing specific measures to address these weaknesses. The notion of family may be understood in a wide and narrow sense.[2] It is widely understood to embrace all persons related by blood, adoption, and marriage, including functionally similar relationships such as civil unions and life partnerships.[3] In a narrow sense, the concept of family is restricted to spouses in a valid marriage and their children.[4] Conscious of the fact that family encompasses various relationships, the use of the term herein refers to those relationships established by marriage and blood.

LEGAL PLURALISM IN ESWATINI

Understanding the types of marriages recognized in eSwatini requires an understanding of the legal systems in eSwatini and the relationship between these systems. Legal pluralism in eSwatini consists of Western (Roman-Dutch)

[1] On 19 April 2018, through section 2 of the Declaration of Swaziland Name Change Notice 80 of 2018 (Declaration of Swaziland Name Change), the name of the Kingdom of Swaziland changed to the Kingdom of eSwatini. Section 3 of the Declaration of Swaziland Name Change stipulates that the name Swaziland, in any written law or international agreement or legal document, shall be read and interpreted as referring to eSwatini. The Ministry of Foreign Affairs and International Cooperation of eSwatini informed all heads of diplomatic missions, international organizations, and consular representatives, resident and non-resident in eSwatini, of the name change through Note 09/201.

[2] Jacqueline Heaton and Hanneretha Kruger, *South African Family Law* (2015), p. 3.

[3] Ibid., p. 3.

[4] Heaton and Kruger note 2 above p. 3.

and indigenous law as reinforced by the provisions of the eSwatini Constitution.[5] However, it should be noted that the application of the Roman-Dutch common law and eSwatini customary law is subject to the provisions of the 2005 Constitution, which is the supreme law of eSwatini.[6] Any law that conflicts with the Constitution shall, to the extent of the conflict, be void.[7]

It should be noted that there is no constitutional or statutory definition of eSwatini customary law. Neither have the courts defined eSwatini customary law in the cases it was found applicable. Nevertheless, Whelpton argues that eSwatini customary law originates in age-old traditions and customs that, as time went by, were categorized as "law".[8] According to Ronald Thandabantu Nhlapo, eSwatini customary law consists of the body of traditional practices and customs of the people of eSwatini which have been part of the culture of eSwatini since the establishment of the eSwatini State in the late eighteen century.[9]

Roman-Dutch law is the common law of eSwatini and applies to the extent that it is not inconsistent with the Constitution or statutory law.[10] eSwatini customary law also applies to the extent that it is not offensive to the principles of natural justice or the general principles of humanity.[11] Although the 2005 Constitution uses the expression "general principles of humanity", it does not provide guidance on its meaning. It may be assumed that in an attempt to harmonize eSwatini customary law with universal international human

5 Jan Christoffel Bekker, Christa Rautenbach, and Nazeem Muhammad Ismail, "Introduction", *Legal Pluralism in South Africa* (2014), p. 6; Section 252(1) and (2), Constitution of the Kingdom of eSwatini Act 1 of 2005 (2005 Constitution).

6 Section 2(1), 2005 Constitution.

7 Ibid.

8 F. P. van R. Whelpton "Swazi Law and Custom in the Kingdom of Swaziland", *South African Journal of Ethnology*, XX, no. 3 (1997), p. 147.

9 Ronald Thandabantu Nhlapo, "Biological and Social Parenthood in African Perspectives; The Movement of Children in Swazi Law", in John Eekelaar and Peter Sarcevic (eds.), *Parenthood in Modern Society; Legal and Social Issues for the Twenty-First Century* (1993), p. 35.

10 Section 252(1), 2005 Constitution.

11 Ibid., section 252(3).

rights norms, the framers of the Constitution intended that eSwatini customary law norms that are inconsistent with universal human rights should not be applied within the legal system of eSwatini.

In eSwatini, where couples may contract a marriage in both its customary and civil forms, real issues concerning remedies and reliefs derivable from the marriage hinge inevitably on the choices of law and forum. However, the issue of choice of law and choice of forum presents a challenge as no existing framework guides the determination of these issues. On account of the recognition of both Roman-Dutch law and eSwatini customary law in the legal system of eSwatini, the Supreme Court of eSwatini, the court of last instance, has advised other courts in the case of *Commissioner of Police and Another v Mkhondvo Aaron Maseko*[12] to make a proper choice of law in deciding cases brought before them. This means that the courts must decide on a case-by-case basis whether the applicable principles are those of Roman-Dutch law or eSwatini customary law. The Supreme Court has at least stated on one occasion that it is blatantly callous for a court to apply Roman-Dutch law principles in a case that clearly calls for the application of eSwatini customary law.[13] This attitude of deferring questions on the choice of law and choice of forum is supported by Whelpton, who suggests that the courts themselves should determine the applicable law after the litigants have properly presented all the facts and arguments.[14]

Given the existence of legal pluralism within the Kingdom of eSwatini, it is inevitable that there should be more than one recognized marital legal regime. The succeeding sections examine the types of recognized marriages.

TYPES OF RECOGNIZED MARRIAGES

Definition of marriage

Currently, two types of marriages are recognized in eSwatini. These are marriages contracted in accordance

12 (3/2011) [2011] SZSC 15 [1] - [2].

13 Ibid.

14 Whelpton, note 8 above, p. 146.

with eSwatini customary law and civil marriages. An eSwatini customary law marriage is governed by eSwatini customary law. No statute regulates an eSwatini customary law marriage. Thus, there is no statutory definition of an eSwatini customary law marriage, and no case law purports to define an eSwatini customary law marriage.

A civil marriage is governed by Roman-Dutch law and the Marriage Act of 1964. The Marriage Act does not define marriage. In the absence of a definition of marriage in the Act, the Supreme Court has stated that the term *marriage,* as used in the Marriage Act, must be understood in light of the Roman-Dutch law definition of marriage.[15] Traditionally, a civil marriage is a legally recognized life-long voluntary union between one man and one woman to the exclusion of all other persons.[16] The definition of marriage, whether contracted under the Marriage Act or eSwatini customary law, may also be discerned from the Births, Marriages and Deaths Registration Act 1983 (BMDR Act).[17] According to the BMDR Act,

> Marriage means the voluntary union between a man and a woman and intended to last for their joint lives, and any reference in this Act to a marriage means a marriage whether contracted before or after the commencement of this Act and whether contracted in Swaziland or elsewhere under any law or custom.[18]

The definition of marriage contained in the BMDR Act is consistent with the Roman-Dutch law definition of marriage in so far as it envisages a union between a man and a woman. It should be noted that the definition in the BMDR Act is also compatible with a marriage contracted under eSwatini customary marriage to the extent that it provides for a union

[15] *Dlamini v Dlamini* (33 of 2017) [2017] SZSC 58 (10 November 2017) (available online).

[16] *Seedat's Executors v The Master* (Natal) 1917 AD p. 309 ff.

[17] The BMDR Act specifically provides for the compulsory registration of all births, marriages, and deaths. The BMDR Act requires that all marriages contracted in eSwatini be registered; Sections 24-27, Births, Marriages and Deaths Registration Act 1983 (BMDR Act).

[18] Section 2, BMDR Act.

between a man and a woman. An eSwatini customary law marriage though, is a potentially polygamous union, that is, a male who is married under eSwatini customary law may marry other women during the subsistence of the customary law marriage with the first or subsequent spouses. Though the number of spouses may increase in customary marriages, the sexes of the parties do not change. Deeply embedded in these definitions is the heterosexuality of the parties. Marriages can only be contracted between men and women and not otherwise. As a result, one can safely conclude that the legal system of eSwatini, does not envisage same-sex unions.

Marriages Bill 2022

Law must adapt to the needs of the society in which it exists. Considering that some principles governing marriage in eSwatini pre-date the 2005 Constitution and some no longer address the demands of the society, the Government of eSwatini has formulated a Marriages Bill of 2022 ("Bill") to be tabled in Parliament.[19] The object of the Bill is to reform and consolidate all the laws governing marriage and to align them with the 2005 Constitution and "modern principles". The Bill does not state the modern principles with which it seeks to bring the laws governing marriage into conformity. Since the Bill seeks to regulate marriages, an inference could be made that perhaps the Bill refers to modern principles that have a bearing on the institution of marriage.

Although the Bill is not yet law, it is worthy of consideration herein because it will repeal the Marriage Act and further address some gaps in the existing marriage laws if eventually adopted. For example, the Bill expressly defines marriage as "a marriage" contracted between a female and a male or a marriage that is recognized as a marriage under the provisions of the Bill.[20] Objectionable in the Bill's definition of marriage is the use of the term marriage in the *definiens*. A better alternative would be to use the expression

19 The Bill was published in the Government Gazette on 11 March 2022.

20 Section 2, Marriages Bill 2022.

"voluntary union between a female and a male" to describe a marriage.

The Bill further defines a civil marriage as a marriage that has been solemnized before a marriage officer, a magistrate, or a regional secretary according to its provisions.[21] The Bill also defines an eSwatini customary law marriage as a potentially polygamous marriage that is concluded and celebrated under eSwatini customary law.[22] The provision of definitions of the different marital regimes in the Bill is commendable as it provides guidance on what constitutes marriage and those qualified to contract it. Also of significance is that the Bill, a single piece of legislation, seeks to regulate the different types of marriages recognized within the legal system.

Apart from recognizing civil and eSwatini customary law marriages contracted in eSwatini, the Bill recognizes as valid a marriage concluded in a foreign country if both or one of the spouses is subject to the laws of that foreign country.[23] However, a marriage concluded in a foreign country that meets the requirements referred to in section 5(2) of the Bill shall not be recognized as valid in eSwatini to the extent that it contravenes principles of morality or humanity as recognized in eSwatini or eSwatini customary law.[24] It would seem that the non-recognition of a marriage concluded in a foreign country, if it contravenes morality or humanity as recognized in eSwatini, is intended to prevent parties who ordinarily could not contract a marriage under the laws of eSwatini from concluding marriages in foreign States and then coming to seek recognition of those marriages in eSwatini.

The Bill does not provide a definition of morality or humanity. There is no evidence that the courts of eSwatini have ever pronounced on the meaning of these terms assuming that they appear in other pieces of legislation. In

[21] Ibid.

[22] Ibid.

[23] Ibid., section 5(2).

[24] Ibid., section 5(3).

determining whether same-sex marriages are permissible in the Kingdom of eSwatini, it is safely assumed that some judges may not necessarily base their determination on whether or not these marriages contravene principles of morality or humanity. They may rely on their interpretation of the law on this issue.

This assumption is based on the case of *Simelane and Others v Minister for Commerce and Industry and Others.*[25] This case involved the applicants, an LGBTI group, whose application for registration of their company had been refused by the Registrar of Companies. They approached the High Court for a review of the Registrar's decision. The Court upheld the decision of the Registrar. The majority judgment noted that LGBTIs were entitled to a catalogue of rights which included the right not to be discriminated against and the right to form a company. The Court stated that these rights were vested in LGBTIs because they were humans and not because of their sexual preferences. The enjoyment of these rights, the Court reasoned, was subject to the laws of the country. The Court took the view that the company sought to be registered intended to sell information relating to erotic matters of LGBTIs. The Court pointed out that the criminal law of eSwatini prohibited same-sex intercourse. Accordingly, it was unlawful to register a company that would directly or indirectly promote the violation of criminal law. The approach of the Court presupposes that if it were seized of a matter calling for the determination of whether same-sex marriages are allowed in eSwatini, it would not approve of same-sex marriages in light of the criminalization of same-sex intercourse.

It is worth noting that the Bill extends the types or forms of marriage that may be recognized as valid in eSwatini. This legal development will serve the increasing population in eSwatini that subscribe to religions other than Christianity or customs other than eSwatini customary law. The existing laws, apparently, do not envisage the conclusion or recognition of marriages contracted according

[25] (1897 of 2019) [2022] SZHC 66 (29 April 2022) (available online).

to other religious rites, such as Muslim rites or any other law or custom.[26]

Another major legal development is that the Bill states in unambiguous terms that all the marriages it recognizes have the same legal status.[27] There has been a mistaken impression in eSwatini that a civil marriage is superior to an eSwatini customary law marriage. This notion was evident in the so-called "double or dual marriage". A double or dual marriage arrangement exists where parties already married under eSwatini customary law contract a civil marriage with each other.[28] The mistaken idea was that the subsequent civil marriage cancels the earlier eSwatini customary law marriage. The Supreme Court has rejected this notion by stating that in a dual or double marriage set-up, the eSwatini customary law and civil marriages co-exist and have the same legal status.[29] Accordingly, a couple must register both marriages and have two marriage certificates.[30] A double or dual marriage may also result if a couple that contracted a civil marriage remarry each other under eSwatini customary law.[31]

It is difficult to determine why a couple would marry under different legal regimes since the decision to marry is a personal choice. An eSwatini customary law marriage is potentially polygamous. Thus, a husband who having contracted an eSwatini customary law marriage, subsequently concludes a civil marriage forfeits the right to marry other wives since a civil marriage is monogamous.[32] Since a civil and an eSwatini customary law marriage are different marital regimes, the incidents of the distinct marital systems differ. The formal dissolution of either of the marriages does not automatically render the other

[26] Marriage Act 1964 and eSwatini customary law.

[27] Section 5(4), Marriages Bill 2022.

[28] Section 7(1), Marriage Act 1964.

[29] *Dladla v Dlamini* [1977-1978] SLR p. 15 ff (CA).

[30] Sections 24 – 27, BMDR Act; *Dlamini,* note 15 above, para. 38.

[31] Marriage Act, s 7(2); *Dlamini,* note 15 above, paras. 21 and 37.

[32] *Dlamini,* note 15 above, para. 25.

dissolved. Put differently, the marriage in respect of which a decree of divorce has not been sought and granted remains intact.[33] A dual or double marriage presents a conflict of laws problem between eSwatini customary law and Roman-Dutch because the two legal regimes fight for dominance, requiring the court to make a proper choice of law.[34] There are no guidelines in respect of the rules that must be followed if there is a conflict arising from the different consequences of the distinct marital systems. The Supreme Court, however, has observed that the situation with respect to dual marriages is not as untidy as it seems.[35] The Court has advised that a conflict can be resolved by classifying the issues for determination as civil or customary and applying the relevant system of law.[36]

eSWATINI CUSTOMARY LAW MARRIAGE

The insistence of the eSwatini nation on its culture has seen the retention of the eSwatini customary law marriage in spite of the influence of Western culture and tradition, which introduced into the legal system a marital regime alien to eSwatini's customary law. The recognition in the 2005 Constitution of the received law, and eSwatini customary law, has seen the co-existence of two distinct marital regimes. The requirements for an eSwatini customary law marriage are as follows.

Legal requirements for an eSwatini customary law marriage

Minimum age of marriage

Before the enactment of the 2005 Constitution, parties could contract a marriage if both were above the age of

33 *Dladla,* note 29, above; *Dlamini,* note 15 above, para. 39.

34 *Dlamini,* note 15 above, para. 9.

35 Ibid., para. 30.

36 Ibid.

puberty.[37] The requirement of puberty is premised on the understanding that, traditionally, there is a link between marriageability and procreation.[38] In the absence of legislation governing eSwatini customary law marriages, the exact marriageable age of a man or woman under eSwatini customary law is unclear. It is also uncertain whether a minor or child may marry under eSwatini customary law. Even if one were to argue that it is legally permissible for a minor to contract a marriage under eSwatini customary law, the circumstances that would justify the marriage of the minor remain uncertain. It is unclear what the age of majority is under eSwatini customary law. The marriageable age of a man or woman under eSwatini customary law has not been an issue for determination in most cases submitted to the courts after the enactment of the 2005 Constitution.

The Children's Protection and Welfare Act 2012, enacted to give effect to section 29 of the 2005 Constitution, and to international human rights instruments on the protection and welfare of children, defines a child as a person below eighteen years of age.[39] Section 29 of the 2005 Constitution provides for the rights of the child. The Children's Protection and Welfare Act makes it clear that a child has a right not to undergo or uphold any custom or practice which has the potential to have a negative effect on the "child's life, health, welfare, dignity, or physical, emotional or psychological … development".[40] A possible interpretation of this provision is that a child may not enter into marriage because marriage has the potential to have an adverse effect on the emotional, physical, and psychological development of a child, considering that a child may not be able to cope with the various demands of marriage. In any case, a child is entitled to protection against, *inter alia*, any cultural practice "which

37 Ronald Thandabantu Nhlapo, *Marriage and Divorce in Swazi Law and Custom* (1992) p. 56.

38 Ibid., pp. 56-57.

39 Section 2, Children's Protection and Welfare Act 2012.

40 Ibid., section 15.

dehumanizes or is injurious to the physical, psychological, emotional and mental well-being of the child".[41]

The Bill answers the question of the marriageable age under eSwatini customary law as it fixes the minimum age of marriage at eighteen years of age, provided that the person who intends to marry is of sound mind.[42] The Bill makes clear that a person who is below the age of eighteen has no capacity to marry.[43]

Consent to marriage

The issue of consent to a marriage to be contracted in accordance with eSwatini customary law dates back to the period before the enactment of the 2005 Constitution. Thus, in *Hlawe v Seyama,*[44] Dlamini JA, writing for a unanimous court, observed that one role of a chief's representative on the day of an eSwatini customary law marriage ceremony taking place within the territorial jurisdiction of that chief is to witness whether the bride consents to the smearing with red ochre. The significance of the red ochre is discussed in (j) below under rituals or ceremonies. The smearing of the bride with red ochre is a ritual that takes place at the groom's parental home by elderly women. Some details of the ceremony have been described in the following terms:

> The anointment ceremony called '*kugcotjiswa libovu*' involves smearing the face and body of the bride with a red substance (*libovu*), a type of clay mixed with fat. This substance is commonly smeared on the face in the form of a cross across the forehead down the nose.[45]

As most eSwatini customary law is unwritten, the significance of using clay and smearing the bride's face is yet to be reliably established.

41 Ibid., section 14(1).

42 Section 8, Marriages Bill 2022.

43 Ibid.

44 (56 of 2016) [2017] SZSC 41 (08 October 2017) (available online).

45 Nhlapo, note 9 above, p. 44.

The 2005 Constitution recognizes the right of a man and a woman of marriageable age to marry and establish a family.[46] Parties intending to contract an eSwatini customary marriage must give their free and full consent before entering the marriage.[47] The Bill extends the constitutional requirement for free and full consent and requires that the consent must be informed.[48] Informed consent in the context of the Bill demands that the party or parties to the intended marriage be given information on the legal and proprietary consequences of the marriage contained in the law regulating matrimonial property.[49]

Restrictions on widow or widower

The Marriage Act forbids a widow or widower who has minor children from a previous marriage from marrying unless he or she has complied with section 89 of the Administration of Estates Act 1902. Section 89 of the Administration of Estates Act 1902 prohibits the remarriage of a surviving parent unless the minors' shares from the estate of the deceased spouse or the joint estate of the deceased spouse and the surviving spouse have been secured. This is intended to prevent a surviving spouse from unjustifiably taking what should be inherited by the minor children of the marriage for the benefit of his or her new marriage. The prohibition in the Marriage Act excludes a previous marriage contracted according to eSwatini customary law. It appears that eSwatini customary law does not insist on compliance with section 89 before a widow or widower who has minor children from a previous marriage can contract a customary law marriage. The Bill requires compliance with section 89 whether the intended marriage is a civil marriage or an eSwatini customary law marriage.[50] This provision will

[46] Section 27(1), 2005 Constitution.

[47] Ibid., section 27(2).

[48] Section 9(1), Marriages Bill 2022.

[49] Ibid., section 9(2).

[50] Section 10(1), Marriages Bill 2022.

ensure the protection of the inheritance of minor children of a previous marriage.

Notice of intention to marry

The general practice is that the chief within whose territorial jurisdiction an eSwatini customary law marriage will take place is notified of the intended ceremony.[51] The notification is necessary so that the chief can assign someone to represent him.[52] The Bill introduces a statutory obligation on a person who intends to marry, to submit to the registrar of births, marriages, and deaths, and the chief of the groom and bride, a written notice of the intention to marry.[53] The registrar will enter the notice in the register of births, marriages and deaths and further scrutinize the register to establish whether there is an existing marriage involving either party to the intended marriage.[54] The notice shall be exhibited for a period of twenty-one days in a visible place at the Regional Administration Office or offices of the chief in whose area the parties to the intended marriage reside.[55]

The requirement of notice is a positive step as it will enable persons who intend to make an objection to the intended marriage to state the grounds for the objection. This will prevent the conclusion of secret marriages. In terms of eSwatini customary law, there are certain customary rites and practices that must be performed before the intending spouses may contract a marriage. Some rites and practices may provide an opportunity for a person to object to an intended marriage. For example, before a prospective husband marries his prospective wife, he must ask for permission to marry her from her father. The practice is that a small delegation assigned by the prospective husband's

[51] *Mhlanga v Mhlanga* (16 of 2014) [2014] SZSC 51 (03 December 2014), para. 14 (available online).

[52] Ibid.

[53] Section 23(1), Marriages Bill 2022.

[54] Ibid., section 18(1).

[55] Ibid., section 23(2).

family is sent to the prospective wife's family to ask for permission to marry her.

At this meeting the prospective husband's family may learn of legal impediments, if any, to the intended marriage. If, for example, the woman is already married, it is expected that her family will inform the prospective husband's family that she cannot contract a marriage as she is already married. During this meeting, the prospective wife's family may also pose questions to the prospective husband's family to ascertain whether they should give consent to the intended marriage.

The inherent risk in this arrangement is that, since this is a meeting of families, legal impediments to the intended marriage may not be disclosed if either family is dishonest. The non-disclosure may happen if there is fear that disclosure may jeopardize the chances of either party getting married. Further, not all prospective husbands seek permission to marry their prospective wives from their fathers before they marry them. Failure to seek permission may not invalidate the marriage if the woman's family accepts the smearing of the red ochre of the woman. However, the bill would introduce a requirement that the permission of the woman's family be sought before the marriage can take place.[56] The Bill does not state what the effect of failure to comply with this requirement is, nor does it state whether it is permissible for the family of the bride to give consent tacitly. It is unclear whether the failure to comply invalidates the marriage. Since the Bill is in its preliminary stages, perhaps future consultations will help clarify the ambiguities surrounding the form and effect of any consent a man may seek from a woman's family.

Customary law marriage license

The legal position is that there is no requirement for an eSwatini customary law marriage license before parties may contract a marriage. There is a proposed change to this position as the bill requires that on the expiry of the twenty-one days of the display of the notice of intention to marry, the registrar of births, marriages, and deaths shall issue a

[56] Section 24(a), Marriages Bill 2022.

customary law marriage license.[57] The customary marriage license may only be issued if there are no objections to the intended marriage or if those objections have been cleared.[58] The requirement proposed in the bill is a positive legal development as the issuance of the customary marriage license seeks to ensure that only parties who have satisfied the provisions of the Bill may marry.

Solemnization of an eSwatini customary law marriage

The chief within whose territorial jurisdiction or chiefdom an eSwatini customary law marriage has been entered into solemnizes the marriage.[59] If the chief does not attend the marriage ceremony in person, the marriage is solemnized by an *indvuna* (governer/headman) or *umgijimi* (chief's forerunner), who is been assigned by the chief to attend the marriage.[60] *Indvuna* means "the chief's headman". He is responsible for the daily administration of the chiefdom and reports directly to the chief. In discharging his functions, he works with a committee called the chief's inner council.[61] Further, the delegation of a person to represent the chief partly provides evidence that the marriage was solemnized.[62]

It is not expressly stated anywhere whether the chief, *indvuna,* or *umgijimi* are marriage officers in respect of marriages contracted under eSwatini customary law. The Bill settles this question by explicitly designating a chief, an *indvuna,* or any other person duly assigned by the chief as marriage officers.[63]

Witnesses in eSwatini customary law marriages

The BMDR Act stipulates the required number of witnesses who must sign the marriage information form in

57 Ibid., section 27(1).

58 Section 27(2)(b), Marriages Bill 2022.

59 Section 26(1), BMDR Act.

60 Ibid.

61 *Mhlanga,* note 51 above, para. 14.

62 Ibid., paras. 14-15.

63 Section 4(4), Marriages Bill 2022.

marriages solemnized by a marriage officer appointed under the Marriage Act. The BMDR Act is silent on the required number of witnesses who must sign the marriage information form in marriages solemnized in accordance with eSwatini customary law. This omission is not addressed in the Bill. Since the Bill is not yet law, perhaps stakeholders during consultations will raise this issue and have it addressed to ensure certainty in the required number of witnesses.

Prohibited degrees of relationships

ESwatini customary law prohibits marriage between people who carry the same surname.[64] This prohibition can be traced to the clan exogamy rule, which forbids the marriage of two people if they belong to the same descent group.[65] The first schedule to the Bill contains a long list of prohibited degrees of relationships.[66]

Rituals or ceremonies

Three marriage formalities are associated with an eSwatini customary law marriage. The formalities are discussed below. First, the woman (bride) must be smeared with red ochre at the marriage ceremony.[67] The smearing of the bride with red ochre is essential to the validity of an eSwatini customary law marriage. In *Hlawe,* Dlamini JA stated that "the smearing of the woman with red ochre is the single cardinal act or element that defines a Swazi customary marriage".[68] Likewise, in *R v Fakudze and Another,*[69] Nathan CJ stated:

[64] Nhlapo, note 37 above, p. 58.

[65] Ibid., p. 58.

[66] These prohibited degrees of relationship are: one's mother, father, daughter, son, mother's daughter, father's daughter, son, any paternal or maternal grandparents, any grandchild, any siblings or their children, the parents of one's spouse, any stepchild, any maternal or paternal uncles and aunts, cousins, any spouse of one's children, other spouses of either parent.

[67] Nhlapo, note 9 above, p. 44.

[68] *Hlawe,* note 44 above, para. 17.

[69] 1970-1976 SLR 422, para. 423.

> There are a number of ceremonies performed at the wedding, but the legally significant one is the anointing of the bride with red-ochre (*libovu*). Unless and until this has been done, she is not regarded as having been married.

Similarly, Dlamini JA distinguished between the essentials of an eSwatini customary law marriage and a civil marriage as follows:

> For instance, a couple may go through a ceremony in church or elsewhere that appears on its face, [with the outward trappings], to be a marriage. But if the register has not been duly signed by the couple and their witnesses the ceremony would not be a marriage in terms of the Act, but just a ceremony, religious or other. The same would be true where *lobolo/bayeni* or *umhlambiso* ceremony is performed: the ceremony would not amount to a Swazi customary marriage if the red ochre ritual has not been performed. The signing of the marriage register and the smearing with red ochre are critical to the validity of the respective forms of marriage.[70]

The significance of smearing the women with red ochre is that it marks the exact point at which a valid eSwatini customary law marriage comes into being.[71] The Bill proposes that the bride be smeared with red ochre in the presence of two witnesses, one of which must come from the bride's family.[72] Seemingly, the requirement that one of the witnesses must come from the bride's side is intended to help in providing evidence that the bride consented to being smeared with red ochre.

The second important formality involves the full delivery or guarantee of *lobolo* cattle.[73] *Lobolo* is a form of a marriage payment delivered to the bride's family on another date, not

[70] *Dlamini*, note 15 above, para. 22; *Hlawe*, note 44 above, paras. 15 and 17.

[71] Nhlapo, note 37 above, p. 46.

[72] Section 24(c), Marriages Bill 2022.

[73] Nhlapo, note 37 above, p. 48.

necessarily on the day when the bride is smeared with red ochre. The Bill defines *lobolo* as:

> Cattle or their equivalent in money which a prospective husband, or husband, or the parent, or legal guardian of the family of that husband undertakes to give to the parent, or legal guardian of the family of the prospective bride, in consideration of a marriage in accordance with eSwatini law and custom.[74]

The third formality encompasses the transfer of beasts, known as *lugege* and *insulamnyembeti,* to the family of the bride. The *lugege* must be slaughtered.[75] In the *Mhlanga* case,[76] *lugege* was defined as "a cow or ox given to the bride's family during the *lobolo* ceremony". It should be big and fat because it is slaughtered by the "*Gozolo*"[77] during the *Lobolo* ceremony to feed the people in attendance. *Insulamnyembeti* "is a female cow given to the mother of the bride in appreciation for raising her from childhood". The cow should be young and should not have given birth. The cow is not slaughtered during the ceremony; it is kept by the bride's mother as her personal property.[78]

Registration of an eSwatini customary law marriage

A customary marriage that has taken place in eSwatini must be registered. The chief or his *indvuna* or *umgijimi,* or the person who solemnized the marriage, shall within fourteen days from the date of the marriage, submit original and duplicate copies of the marriage information to the relevant government officers of the region in which the marriage was solemnized.[79] This information is crucial for the registration of the marriage. It is an offense for a person

[74] Section 2, Marriages Bill 2022.

[75] Nhlapo, note 37 above, p. 44.

[76] *Mhlanga,* note 51 above.

[77] *Gozolo* "is the man who announces the number of cattle to the family of the bride upon their arrival at her homestead for the *lobolo* ceremony".

[78] Section 24, Marriages Bill 2022.

[79] Section 26(1), BMDR Act.

who solemnized a marriage not to submit the marriage information to the relevant government officers.[80] Likewise, this provision presupposes the physical presence of the chief, *indvuna,* or *umgijimi* at the marriage ceremony as an administrator or officer who has a specific task to execute.[81] Failure to register a marriage does not render the marriage non-existent; it only makes it difficult for litigants to prove its existence in a court of law.[82]

Dissolution of eSwatini customary law marriage

It is pertinent at the outset to briefly examine the nature of an eSwatini customary law marriage before an examination of the question of whether an eSwatini customary law is amenable to dissolution. A distinguishing feature of an eSwatini customary law marriage is durability, which reflects the fact that an eSwatini customary law marriage is a union of two families and not of the couple or spouses.[83] The direct effect of this union is that the death of one spouse does not necessarily terminate the marriage.[84] Many experts on eSwatini customary law are agreed that an eSwatini customary law marriage is difficult to dissolve.[85] Nhlapo and Alice Kavanaugh Armstrong observe that there is a theory that an eSwatini customary law marriage is not susceptible to dissolution, although this theory lacks authoritative support.[86] They argue that the position now is that an eSwatini customary law marriage may be dissolved.[87] Whereas most experts point out that divorce under eSwatini customary law marriage is hard to effect, they do concede

[80] Section 26(3), BMDR Act.

[81] *Hlawe,* note 44 above, para. 12.

[82] *Dlamini,* note 15 above, para. 5.

[83] *Hlawe,* note 44 above, p. 14.

[84] Ibid.

[85] *Hlawe,* note 44 above, paras. 16 and 17.

[86] Alice Kavanaugh Armstrong and Ronald Thandabantu Nhlapo, *Law and the Other Sex: The Legal Position of Women in Swaziland* (1986), p. 52.

[87] Ibid.

that it is possible although it rarely happens.[88] These are early authorities whose views are criticized for not being consistent with current times.[89] The basis for the criticism is that the ever-changing times have diminished traditional family values, relations, and customs such that an increase in the dissolution of eSwatini customary law marriages outside traditional courts of law should not be regarded as alarming.[90]

The Supreme Court in the *Hlawe* case brought a new dimension to the debate on whether there is divorce under eSwatini customary law. The analysis herein of the dissolution of an eSwatini customary law marriage relies principally on the *Hlawe* case. In the *Hlawe* case, the Court undertook an extensive examination of academic writings and case law to address what ought to be done to dissolve an eSwatini customary marriage. The Court hinted that the judicial excursion was needed to bring clarity to and provide guidance to other courts on the question of the dissolution of eSwatini customary marriages. The importance of the *Hlawe* case has been noted by the High Court; for example, in *Mlangeni v Mlangeni*[91] the Court emphasized that the authoritative decision in the *Hlawe* case provides guidelines and overrides any previous decisions of the High Court on the subject of dissolution of an eSwatini customary law marriage. The *Hlawe* case is significant because it is the only case that deals with the subject of dissolution and which addresses the question of the "washing off" of the red ochre, which the Court stated was critical to the dissolution of an eSwatini customary law marriage. It should be remembered that the red ochre is essential to the establishment of an eSwatini customary law marriage.

None of the academic writers and courts of the view that an eSwatini customary law marriage may be dissolved has attempted to state the exact point at which a marriage may

88 Brian Alan Marwick, *The Swazi: An Ethnographic Account of the Natives of the Swaziland Protectorate* (1940), pp. 123-134.

89 *Hlawe*, note 44 above, para 14.

90 Ibid.

91 (536 of 2018) [2019] SZHC 43 (07 March 2019) (available online).

be said to be dissolved. The *Hlawe* case deals with this issue. In analyzing the dissolution of an eSwatini customary law marriage, the Court largely relied on its understanding of eSwatini customary law because academic writers and some previous court decisions that had dealt with the subject failed to address the question of the cleansing of the red ochre which, according to the Court, is critical to a dissolution of an eSwatini customary law marriage.

In responding to Nhlapo and Amstrong's assertions, the *Hlawe* case advises that the authors need to revisit their arguments as there were no court cases that the authors cited as bases for their assertions.[92] In dealing with the subject of dissolution, the Court emphasized that:

> It should be noted that there is a difference in saying customary marriage may be dissolved and that the two families have accepted a purported dissolution of the marriage between them; there is a further difference in such 'accepted' dissolution passing muster by the standard of a Swazi court. In other words, many a purported dissolution of customary marriage would not pass muster when tested against the true (the ideal) requirement(s) for legal dissolution i.e., the final act being the cleansing or washing off the red ochre. This is so because the smearing of the woman with red ochre is the single cardinal act or element that defines a Swazi customary marriage. The Swazi pay *lobola* for a wife; not a girlfriend. Admitting that dissolution is possible, the elusive issue is at what point of the process does this event occur? Yet how often do we hear of the washing off of the 'red clay' to signify the end of a customary marriage: hardly ever.[93]

Although the Court highlighted the significance of the washing off of the red ochre in the dissolution of an eSwatini customary law marriage, it did not stipulate how this ritual is performed in practice. The approach of the Court to the dissolution of an eSwatini customary law marriage seems

[92] *Hlawe*, note 44 above, para. 17.

[93] Ibid

to have been influenced by its belief in the perpetuity marriages contracted under this type of marital regime. In other words, an eSwatini customary law marriage hardly ends. In the *Hlawe* case, the Supreme Court established that the procedure for dissolving an eSwatini customary law marriage "is by no means a clear path, without any potholes or blind rises, if there is a path at all".[94] There is no consensus even among experts on eSwatini customary law on the procedures for dissolving an eSwatini customary law marriage.[95]

The Court observed that it was extremely difficult to dissolve an eSwatini customary law marriage.[96] According to the Court, the rules regulating an eSwatini customary law marriage do not envisage or encourage its dissolution.[97] This is exemplified by the smearing of the bride with red ochre which is essential to the validity of an eSwatini customary law marriage. It is difficult to wash away the red ochre once it is smeared.[98] For this reason the red ochre may be smeared once on a woman during her lifetime.[99] The Court observed that the ultimate requirement that must be fulfilled for the legal dissolution of an eSwatini customary law marriage is the washing off or cleansing of the red ochre.[100] The Court emphasized that any dissolution proceedings must start from the premise that eSwatini customary law permits divorce as a last resort when everything else has failed to keep the marriage intact.[101]

Although the Court observed that it was difficult to terminate an eSwatini customary law marriage, the courts have upheld numerous applications to expunge the

94 Ibid., para. 7.

95 Ibid., para. 14.

96 Ibid., para. 15.

97 Ibid., para. 18.

98 Ibid., para. 15.

99 Ibid.

100 Ibid., para. 17.

101 Ibid., para. 18.

registration of certain customary law marriages. These applications are made by a party or parties to an eSwatini customary law marriage that is deemed to have been dissolved.[102]

As noted in the *Hlawe* case, there are two grounds for "divorce" under eSwatini customary law.[103] These are adultery and witchcraft; witchcraft is not tolerated by the husband's family.[104] A man married in accordance with eSwatini customary law may not be accused of having committed adultery unless he has sexual intercourse with another man's wife. The most plausible explanation for this that an eSwatini customary law marriage is a potentially polygamous marriage. Usually, a woman who has committed adultery for the first time is reprimanded orally, and the incident is not reported to her parental family.[105] Adultery is reported to the family of the woman if the woman has committed the offence repeatedly.[106] Repeated acts of adultery may not necessarily lead to a formal dissolution of the marriage.[107] The wronged husband may establish a separate home for the offending wife within the vicinity of the main homestead at which the wife may live with their children.[108] Although the husband's act may render the wife a "widow", she remains married, and no man may court her.[109] This arrangement seeks to avoid dissolution of the marriage.[110] The Court noted that even if, at some point, a woman may be regarded as separated or divorced from her husband, the woman may still be required to mourn the death of her former husband, especially where she has

102 Ibid., para. 15

103 Ibid.

104 Ibid

105 Ibid.

106 Ibid.

107 Ibid.

108 Ibid.

109 Ibid.

110 Ibid.

children with the deceased.[111] However, where no children exist between the two, the mourning requirement may be "less compelling".[112]

The proper procedure for the dissolution of an eSwatini customary law marriage involves a first meeting between the two families which seeks to foster reconciliation, not the dissolution of the marriage.[113] If the families fail to reconcile, the chief's representative is invited to the family dispute.[114] The chief or *indvuna* may appoint a representative such as *umgijimi* to hear the disputing parties and thereafter make a report to the chief.[115] The hearing takes place at the representative's home or in a place where local cases are normally heard and determined.[116] The representative acts as chairperson in the deliberations.[117] The representative plays an active role in the proceedings.[118] During the deliberations, the representative does not just accept the decision taken by the families, he listens to the parties and intervenes where necessary.[119] The chief or his representative has an interest in getting information on the cause of the breakdown of the marriage and the party responsible for it.[120] If the parties fail to reconcile their differences, the matter is referred to the chief's kraal for a full hearing and determination.[121]

If the family of the wife comes from a chiefdom other than that of the husband, the deliberations must take place at the chief's kraal and not at the husband's home or the

111 Ibid., para. 16.

112 Ibid.

113 Ibid., para. 6.

114 Ibid., para. 9.

115 Ibid.

116 Ibid.

117 Ibid.

118 Ibid.

119 Ibid.

120 Ibid., para. 11.

121 Ibid., para. 9.

home of the husband's father.[122] The reason for holding the meeting in a neutral place is to limit one's liability if a fight were to occur.[123] In the rare event that dissolution of a customary marriage is permitted, the belongings of the wife are packed and placed outside her hut in her matrimonial home and some other person is assigned to accompany the wife together with her belongings to her parental home.[124]

The Bill envisages the dissolution of an eSwatini customary law marriage on agreement by the parties to the marriage; family resolution and death of either spouse.[125] The agreement by the parties to dissolve the marriage or the family resolution must be validated by the chiefdom or a declaratory order issued by an eSwatini national court. eSwatini national courts are customary courts established in accordance with eSwatini customary law and the final authority over them resides with the King. The approach of the Bill to the dissolution of an eSwatini customary law marriage appears to be more flexible when compared to the approach of the Court in the *Hlawe* case.

CIVIL MARRIAGE

Restrictions on right to marry

Marriageable age

Generally, a male person who is below eighteen years of age and a female below sixteen years of age may not contract a civil marriage.[126] Under the Marriage Act, persons below the ages specified are minors. The Minister of Justice and Constitutional Affairs, however, may grant a special dispensation allowing a male person who is below eighteen years of age and a female below sixteen years of age to marry

[122] Ibid.

[123] Ibid.

[124] Ibid., para. 36.

[125] Section 44 (b)(i-iv), Marriages Bill 2022.

[126] Section 3(1), Marriage Act 1964.

if special circumstances exist justifying such a marriage.[127] The Marriage Act does not provide guidance on the special circumstances that can justify the marriage of persons below the marriageable age stipulated in the Act. No instances are known in which the Minister of Justice and Constitutional Affairs granted this special dispensation.

The existing practice is that the marriageable age does not differ from one sex to the other. The Marriage Act was enacted before the entry into force of the 2005 Constitution, and such laws as the Children's Protection and Welfare Act guarantee the protection of children and respect for human rights. Section 27(1) of 2005 Constitution provides that men and women of marriageable age may marry but it does not expressly state the age of marriage. It is assumed that subsequent legislation that may be enacted to address the question of the age of marriage will both clarify the provision in the Constitution and override the provisions of the Marriage Act regulating the age of marriage. It is probable that such legislation will consider the age of minority as contained in the Children's Protection and Welfare Act. Nowadays, it is usually persons who are way above the age of eighteen years that contract a civil marriage. This may partly be attributed to the recent laws enacted which sets the age of majority at eighteen years.

Consent which is required for a civil law marriage of a minor

Three categories of persons may give consent to a civil marriage involving a minor: the legal guardian of the minor, the Minister of Justice and Constitutional Affairs, and the District Commissioner.

Legal guardian

A minor who is below twenty-one years of age but above eighteen years of age in the case of a male and above the age of sixteen years in the case of a female may enter into a civil marriage if his or her legal guardian gives consent

[127] Ibid., section 3(1).

to the marriage.[128] The Marriage Act does not state whether the consent should be in writing or oral. Under the common law, consent may be given orally.[129] The Marriage Act lists the categories of persons who qualify as the legal guardian of the minor.[130] These are the father of the minor; the mother of the minor in cases where the minor does not have a father or a person who has been appointed as a guardian of the minor by a judge; or the master of the High Court if the minor does not have a father or a mother. The Marriage Act does not stipulate what qualifies the persons listed above to be designated as the guardian of the minor, but it may be assumed that on account of the duty of care that they owe to the minor, in particular, the father or mother, they are designated as legal guardian because they are expected to act in the best interests of the minor at all times. A person who has previously contracted a customary or civil marriage is not deemed to be a minor if he or she wants to enter into a marriage in accordance with the Marriage Act.[131]

The Minister of Justice and Constitutional Affairs and District Commissioner

The Minister of Justice and Constitutional Affairs may in writing authorize the marriage of a minor resident outside of eSwatini who has legal competence to marry if one of three conditions exists: first, if the minor has no legal guardian; second, if the legal guardian unreasonably withholds the consent; and last, if the consent of the legal guardian cannot be procured for a reason other than that the legal guardian is not willing to give consent.[132] If the minor is resident in eSwatini and any one of the conditions enumerated above exists, the commissioner of the district in which the minor

128 Ibid., section 3(2).

129 Heaton and Kruger note 2 above, p. 16.

130 Section 3(4), Marriage Act 1964.

131 Ibid., section 3(2).

132 Ibid., section 3(3).

resides may give the written authorization for the marriage of the minor.[133]

Persons of unsound mind

A person who, because of unsoundness of mind, lacks the capacity to manage his or her own affairs, or has been certified or adjudged by a competent authority to be of unsound mind, may not marry under the Marriage Act.[134] The restriction on the right to marry also extends to widows or widowers with minor children.

Widows or widowers with minor children

The failure to secure the inheritance of minors from a previous marriage may be a bar to an intended marriage. Thus, a widow or widower who has minor children from a previous marriage, excluding a marriage contracted in accordance with eSwatini customary law, may not marry under the Marriage Act unless there is proof that the requirements of section 89 of the Administration of Estates Act 28 of 1902 (Administration of Estates Act) have been satisfied.[135] A marriage officer or minister of religion who solemnizes a marriage involving a widow or widower before obtaining a certificate from the Master of the High Court to the effect that the minors' shares have been paid into the Guardian's Fund or otherwise secured is guilty of an offense.[136]

The Marriage Act and the Administration of Estates Act were enacted before the 2005 Constitution. In so far as both pieces of legislation seek to protect the inheritance of minors, they appear to be in line with the 2005 Constitution. Section 29(7)(a) of the 2005 Constitution mandates Parliament to adopt legislation that will entitle every child to a reasonable share out of the estate of its parents.

[133] Ibid.

[134] Ibid., section 4.

[135] Ibid., section 5.

[136] Section 89(4), Administration of Estates Act 1902.

Relationships within the prohibited degrees

The Marriage Act prohibits the marriage of persons who are related to one another within the prohibited degrees of consanguinity or affinity.[137] In respect of the prohibited degrees of consanguinity, a person is barred from marrying an ancestor;[138] two persons who are related to each other in the collateral line may not enter into a marriage if one of them is related to the common ancestor in the first degree.[139] Although the prohibited degrees of relationship by affinity are the same as the prohibited degrees of relationship by consanguinity, it is lawful for a person to enter into a marriage with the brother or sister of a former spouse or any person related to the former spouse in a more remote degree.[140] This applies whether the marriage was terminated by death or divorce.[141]

Person already married

The Marriage Act prohibits a marriage contracted by a person who is already married. A person who is lawfully married may not enter a second marriage under the provisions of the Marriage Act while the first marriage subsists.[142] This prohibition applies regardless of whether the subsisting marriage is a civil or an eSwatini customary law marriage.[143]

A person who contracts a marriage contrary to this prohibition commits the offense of bigamy.[144] In *Joseph Jabulani Dube v R*,[145] the applicant had concluded a civil

137 Section 6(1), Marriage Act 1964.

138 Ibid., section 6(2)(a).

139 Ibid., section 6(2)(b).

140 Ibid., section 6(3).

141 Ibid.

142 Ibid., section 7(1).

143 Ibid.

144 Ibid.

145 [1970-1976] SLR 93 ff.

marriage in the Republic of South Africa. This was his first marriage. Later, he purported to enter a customary marriage in eSwatini with another person other than his lawfully recognized spouse. He was charged with and convicted of bigamy. The subsequent customary marriage was not a marriage in terms of the Marriage Act. It is lawful, however, for a couple married in accordance with eSwatini customary law or other rites to remarry under the terms of the Marriage Act.[146]

Preliminaries to a civil marriage

The preliminaries to a civil marriage involve the publication of banns or the issuance of a special license.

Publication of banns

A marriage contracted in accordance with the provisions of the Marriage Act is valid if banns have been published within a period of not more than three months before the solemnization of the marriage.[147] The banns must disclose the full names of the envisioned spouses, their marital status, and the district in which they are resident.[148] The Marriage Act stipulates the places where banns should be published and the duration or period of the publication. The banns may be published in a church or other building, which is regularly used by worshipers as a place of public worship.[149] The parties intending to enter into a marriage must belong to the group of worshipers who habitually fellowship in these aforementioned building structures.[150] The publication of the banns must take place in either of these buildings during a heavenly service for three consecutive Sundays and in the district in which each envisioned spouse is resident.[151]

146 Section 7(1), Marriage Act 1964.

147 Ibid., section 8.

148 Ibid., section 9.

149 Ibid., section 10(a).

150 Ibid.

151 Ibid.

Alternatively, the banns of marriage may be published by displaying them for three consecutive Sundays in a visible place accessible to the public, at the district commissioner's office, or other local authority in the district in which each future spouse is resident.[152] The Marriage Act also empowers a marriage officer to solemnize a marriage in terms of the Act if its banns have been published in any other African country, provided that the marriage officer is satisfied the banns have been duly published in that other country in compliance with its law.[153] Written evidence, which may be on oath if the marriage officer considers it desirable, must be produced to satisfy the marriage officer that the publication of the banns complied with the law of the African country.[154] An inference could be drawn from the requirement for the publication of banns, the methods of publication, and the information that the banns must disclose that this procedure is intended to ensure that parties enter into a civil marriage in full compliance with the Marriage Act and that their marriage is not secret. In *Shongwe v Sibandze*,[155] the High Court noted that the publication of banns as a preliminary to the solemnization of the marriage was designed to give assurance that the parties had agreed to contract a civil marriage.

Special license

Persons may marry in the absence of previous publication of banns if they produce a special license issued for the purpose of joining them in matrimony and signed by a district officer.[156] The parties who are desirous of being married by a special license must present themselves before a district officer and furnish the officer with their names, submit documents and written statements which the district

152 Ibid., section 10(b).

153 Ibid., section 11.

154 Ibid.

155 (2748 of 2009) [2013] SZHC 114 (11 June 2013) (available online).

156 Section 14(1), Marriage Act 1964.

officer may require of them.[157] They must also respond to questions that the district officer may address to them for the purpose of establishing three issues. First, that a legal guardian or district commissioner or the Minister of Justice and Constitutional affairs, as the case may be, has granted consent to marriage involving a minor.[158] Second, that there has been compliance with section 89 of the Administration of Estates Act 1902 if the intended partner is a widow or widower who has minor children from a previous marriage provided that the marriage was not one contracted under eSwatini customary law.[159] Last, that the envisioned spouses are not related to each other within the prohibited degrees of consanguinity or affinity or that there are no legal obstacles to the envisaged marriage.[160]

Marriage ceremony

Marriage officers

A civil marriage is valid if solemnized by a marriage officer.[161] The Marriage Act lists persons who qualify as marriage officers.[162] A person who is not an authorized marriage officer in terms of the Marriage Act and who intentionally conducts a marriage ceremony in terms of the Marriage Act is deemed to have committed an offense.[163] By regarding it as an offense for any unauthorized person to conduct a marriage ceremony, the Marriage Act seeks to deter persons who are not authorized from solemnizing civil marriages as this renders those marriages invalid.

157 Ibid., section 15.

158 Ibid., section 15 (a).

159 Ibid., section 15 (b).

160 Ibid., section 15 (c).

161 Ibid., section 16(1).

162 Ibid., section 16(2).

163 Ibid., section 17.

Time and place of marriage ceremony

The Marriage Act prohibits the solemnization of a marriage before 08:00 and after 18:00 unless, in the opinion of the marriage officer, exceptional circumstances exist.[164] The Marriage Act does not provide guidance on what constitutes exceptional circumstances. Apparently, this may be determined on a case-by-case basis. It is mandatory that all marriages conducted in accordance with the provisions of the Marriage Act be solemnized in the designated places and in the presence of no less than two witnesses who are capable of adducing evidence in a court of law.[165] The designated places include churches, other buildings regularly used by worshipers as a place of public worship, public offices, and private residential buildings with open doors.[166] The Marriage Act stipulates how a civil and a religious marriage ceremony should be conducted.

Religious marriage ceremony

A religious marriage ceremony conducted under the Marriage Act is regarded as a civil marriage. A religious marriage ceremony is performed by a marriage officer who is also a minister of religion or a person who stands in a position of authority in any religious grouping or community in compliance with the procedure or formula applicable in the place of public worship to which he or she belongs.[167] The procedure or formula, however, must be compatible with section 20(a)(b) and (c) of the Marriage Act. Section 20 (a)(b) and (c) of the Marriage Act regulates the conduct of a civil marriage ceremony.

Civil marriage ceremony

A marriage officer who is not a minister of religion or who does not stand in a position of authority in any religious

[164] Ibid., section 18(1).

[165] Ibid., section 18(2).

[166] Ibid., section 18(2).

[167] Ibid., section 19.

grouping or community solemnizes a civil marriage in accordance with the procedure stated below.

The marriage officer poses a question separately to the bride and bridegroom by which he or she seeks to establish that they solemnly declare that they are not aware of any legal obstacle to their marriage to each other.[168] If the marriage officer receives a positive response to the question put to the bride and bridegroom, the parties shall on the instruction of the marriage officer separately repeat after the marriage officer words to the effect that they call upon all those who are present at the ceremony to be witnesses to the fact that they are taking each other to be lawful husband or wife.[169] It is normal in a civil marriage ceremony for the parties to use a ring. On the instruction of the marriage officer, the bridegroom shall place the ring on the wedding finger of the bride and the parties shall join their right hands. The marriage officer shall then declare that in accordance with civil law the parties are joined together in matrimony.[170] A civil marriage must then be registered.

Registration of a civil marriage

There is an obligation on a marriage officer who solemnized a civil marriage, the intended spouses, and two or more competent witnesses to sign a marriage information form of the marriage before they vacate the place where the marriage was conducted.[171] This information is essential to the registration of the marriage. Just as in the case of the registration of an eSwatini customary law marriage, non-registration of a civil marriage does not mean that the marriage does not exist.[172] If there is a dispute, non-registration makes it difficult for the existence of the marriage to be proved in a court of law. It is essential that the marriage register be signed.

[168] Ibid., section 20(a).

[169] Ibid., section 20(b).

[170] Ibid., section 20(c).

[171] Section 25(1), BMDR Act.

[172] *Dlamini,* note 15 above.

Signature of the bride in the marriage register

When signing the marriage information form, the bride must sign in the name she carried immediately before the marriage.[173] The signing of the marriage information form is essential to the validity of a civil marriage, unless some serious error is established.[174] In this respect, the Supreme Court stated:

> For instance, a couple may go through a ceremony in church or elsewhere that appears on its face, [with the outward trappings], to be a marriage. But if the register has not been duly signed by the couple and their witnesses the ceremony would not be a marriage in terms of the Act, but just a ceremony, religious or other.[175]

Dissolution of civil marriage

A civil marriage may be dissolved by the death of one or both spouses or by divorce. There is no legislation that governs the dissolution of a civil marriage in eSwatini. Dissolution of a civil marriage is entirely governed by Roman-Dutch law. In *Mahlalela v Mahlalela,*[176] it was stated that Roman-Dutch law recognizes only two grounds of divorce: adultery and malicious desertion. Accordingly, a party who seeks dissolution of a civil marriage must base his or her claim on either of these grounds. Roman-Dutch law is premised on the fault principle which posits that in every divorce action "there is a guilty and an innocent party".[177] The disadvantage of the conservative fault principle is that the court may not exercise its discretion and dissolve the marriage unless it is proven that one party committed either of the matrimonial offences even if after having taken into consideration all the circumstances the Court is of the

173 Section 21, Marriage Act 1964.

174 *Dlamini,* note 15 above, para. 12.

175 Ibid., para. 22.

176 (1926 of 2009) [2013] SZHC 17 (08 February 2013), para. 4 (available online).

177 Heaton and Kruger, note 2 above, p. 119.

view that the marriage has irretrievably broken down.[178] In *Sacolo v Sacolo,*[179] the High Court remarked that the divorce laws of eSwatini were outdated and completely poles apart or irreconcilable with current principles and jurisprudence on matrimonial matters. The Court noted that keeping parties to a marriage that has irretrievably broken down had the propensity to lead to domestic violence.[180] The Court emphasized that failure of the marriage rather than fault should be the determining factor in whether a decree of divorce should be granted.[181] In this respect, the Court stated that the divorce laws were in need of reform.[182]

The procedure for dissolving a civil marriage is that the plaintiff must file divorce summons commencing the divorce action and alleging that the defendant has committed either an act of malicious desertion or adultery. The plaintiff must prove that there was no condonation of these acts on his or her part. If the plaintiff bases the action for divorce on malicious desertion, the plaintiff must also apply for an order for the restoration of conjugal rights by the defendant. Upon issuing the order for the restoration of conjugal rights, the Court must instruct the defendant to restore conjugal rights on a stipulated date. In *Hlatshwayo v Hlatshwayo,*[183] the High Court emphasized that the whole purpose of granting the order for restoration of conjugal rights is to enable the defendant to remedy the fault. A messenger of court serves the court order on the person of the defendant. If the defendant fails to restore the conjugal rights, he or she must on the return date of the summons show cause in court why a final decree of divorce should not be granted. If there is a failure on the part of the defendant to restore conjugal rights on the prescribed date, the plaintiff shall file an affidavit detailing the defendant's failure. The plaintiff

[178] *Mahlalela,* note 177 above, para. 14.

[179] (4095 of 2008) [2010] SZHC 100 (01 July 2010) (available online).

[180] Ibid., para. 13.

[181] *Mahlalela,* note 177 above, para. 14.

[182] *Sacolo,* note 180 above.

[183] [1979-1981] SLR 177, 178A.

is then granted an order for a final decree on divorce on the return on account of the defendant's malicious desertion.[184]

If the defendant attempts to comply with the order for restoration of conjugal rights and is frustrated by the plaintiff, the defendant is entitled to adduce evidence on the return date and is examined by the court in order to determine whether the restoration was genuine or was a sham or farce.[185] If it is found that the plaintiff did not comply with the order of court by denying the defendant the opportunity to restore the conjugal rights, the divorce action will be dismissed. This is because the plaintiff becomes the deserter and is at fault so the law will not permit him or her to benefit from his or her own wrong.[186] If the plaintiff bases the action for divorce on adultery there will be no need for restoration of conjugal rights. The plaintiff needs only to prove this ground against the defendant.

There have been suggestions that the issue of restoration of conjugal rights should be revisited as there are various human rights that negate the ideological basis for this concept.[187] It has been argued that this practice constitutes a violation of human rights in the sense that it connotes forced sex.[188] There is merit in these observations. The 2005 Constitution, for instance, provides that the dignity of every person is inviolable.[189] An argument can be made that it would amount to a violation of the plaintiff's dignity if he or she were compelled to have sexual intercourse with the defendant who had deserted him or her. This would pose a health risk to the plaintiff to engage in sexual intercourse with a person whose sexual behavior during the period of desertion the plaintiff has no knowledge of.

[184] Ibid.

[185] *Khoza and Another v Thwala and Others* (2620 of 2009) [2009] SZHC 199 (21 August 2009), para. 29 (available online).

[186] *Sacolo,* note 180 above, para. 10

[187] Siphiwe Vilakati, *A Legal Analysis on the Validity of the Sustained Practice of the Restitution of Conjugal Rights in Swazi Divorce Law* (2017), p. 68 (LLM Thesis, Loyola University School of Law).

[188] Ibid.

[189] Section 18(1), 2005 Constitution.

RECOMMENDATIONS

In the analysis of the requirements for the dissolution of the recognized forms of marriage in eSwatini, some gaps in the law were noted. A draft Bill has been prepared to change the law and eliminate some weaknesses in the existing law. The recommendations for the improvement of the law made herein are confirmed in the Bill. Recommendations informed by certain omissions in the draft Bill will be made.

Definition of marriage

It is recommended that the proposed law should define marriage generally and then civil and eSwatini customary law marriages. This is necessary to ensure certainty in the law. The definition of marriage should be crafted in such a way that it avoids the use of the term "marriage". Terms such as "union" may be used in the definition.

Recognition of marriages contracted in foreign countries

Since marital regimes vary from one legal system to another, the legal system of eSwatini should make provision for the recognition of marriages contracted in foreign countries if the spouses meet certain requirements stipulated in the laws of eSwatini. This will enable spouses who are married under the laws of foreign jurisdictions to register their marriages in eSwatini if they so desire or have their marriages recognized as valid in eSwatini.

Recognition of equal legal status of marriages

To eliminate any doubt about the legal status of the marriages recognized in eSwatini, the proposed law should state in clear terms that the marriages it recognizes have the same legal status.

Age of marriage in eSwatini customary law

On account of the uncertainty in relation to the age of marriage under eSwatini customary law, it is necessary to enact legislation that will stipulate the marriageable age. In fixing the age of marriage, the legislation should seek to align its provisions with those of other recent pieces of legislation that protect the rights of children and women.

Consent under customary law

In compliance with the constitutional stipulation that requires spouses intending to contract marriage to give their free and full consent before entering the marriage, the proposed law must make consent mandatory for parties intending to contract an eSwatini customary law marriage.

Officers in respect of an eSwatini customary law marriage

In line with the law regulating civil marriages, it is recommended that a reform of the law of marriage in eSwatini should consider stating in clear terms those regarded as marriage officers in respect of an eSwatini customary law marriage.

Compliance with section 89 of the Administration of Estates Act

As is the case with surviving spouses of civil marriages, surviving spouses of an eSwatini customary law marriage must be prohibited from contracting another customary marriage unless it is shown that the inheritance of minors from the previous marriage has been secured for the benefit of the minors.

Notice of intention to marry under eSwatini customary law

Consistent with the law governing civil marriages, it is suggested that parties intending to marry according to eSwatini customary law must also be required to file a notice of intention to marry as a preliminary step to the marriage.

eSwatini customary law license

It must be mandatory for parties desirous of contracting an eSwatini customary law marriage to obtain a marriage license before they marry. This requirement must be satisfied in certain circumstances by parties intending to conclude a civil marriage.

Separate pieces of legislation

There should be two distinct legislative acts that regulate the types of recognized marriages in eSwatini; that is, eSwatini customary law marriage and civil marriage. This is necessary partly because the bulk of eSwatini customary law is not written. A separate piece of legislation regulating eSwatini customary law marriage will make detailed provision for various aspects of eSwatini customary law marriage. For instance, the process for dissolution of an eSwatini customary law is not covered in the Bill. The Bill also does not define certain terms such as *libovu, insulamnyembeti* and *lugege*. All these issues may be adequately dealt by a stand-alone piece of legislation.

Witnesses in an eSwatini customary law marriage

It is recommended that the number of witnesses required in an eSwatini customary law marriage should be stated. This issue has not been addressed in the Bill.

CONCLUSION

This chapter, mindful of the range of issues that may be discussed under family law, is confined to the essentials for the validity and the requirements for the dissolution of the recognized forms of marriage. A survey of the legal framework governing marriage and the gaps therein was undertaken. Attempts are in process to reform the marriage laws of eSwatini. This is exemplified by the publication of the Marriage Bill, which addresses some weaknesses in the existing law. It was beyond the scope of this work to deal with all the issues that the Bill seeks to introduce. The Bill is in its early stages, and wide consultation must take place before it is finally promulgated into law.

Further research on such issues as divorce under eSwatini customary law is in order. This will be more feasible once the Bill becomes law as it seeks, *inter alia,* to repeal aspects of the existing marriage laws with their attendant weaknesses.

Zimbabwe

Chapter Twelve
Marriages in Zimbabwe

Zimbabwe has a dual legal system with the coexistence of customary law and general law, as is the case in many African countries that experienced colonization in the nineteenth century.[1] This coexistence is recognized by the 2013 Constitution of Zimbabwe as African customary law and Roman-Dutch Law as modified by subsequent legislation.

The effect of the dual system implies that some marriages are recognized by the general law whereas others are recognized by customary law, with different norms and rights. There are three types of marriage in Zimbabwe: civil marriages, registered customary marriages, and unregistered customary law unions. The three types of marriage have different regulatory frameworks and also differ in their essential requirements, as well as the processes for their dissolution and the distribution of property.

Herein we critically assess the legal framework regulating the different forms of marriage in Zimbabwe and make recommendations for its improvement. The types of marriage, their legal effects, and the formalities for solemnization and dissolution are considered together with the strengths and weaknesses of existing marriage laws.

LEGAL FRAMEWORK OF ZIMBABWEAN MARRIAGES

The Constitution of Zimbabwe is the supreme law of the land. All laws must conform to the Constitution. Accordingly, any law, practice, custom, or conduct inconsistent with the Constitution is invalid.[2] Marriage laws must comply with the Constitution and with Zimbabwe's international obligations

[1] Agnete Weis Bentzon, et al., *Pursuing Grounded Theory in Law: South-North Experiences in Developing Women's Law* (1998), p. 34.

[2] Section 2, Constitution of Zimbabwe.

under the 1964 Convention on Consent to Marriage, Minimum Age of Marriage and Registration of Marriages; the 1966 International Covenant on Economic, Social and Cultural Rights (ICESCR); the Convention on Elimination of all forms of Discrimination Against Women (CEDAW); the 2008 SADC Protocol on Gender and Development; and the Optional Protocol to the African Charter on the Rights of Women in Africa (Maputo Protocol).

The general principles on marriage and marriage rights are provided for in sections 26 and 78, respectively, of the Constitution. Under section 26, the State must take appropriate measures to ensure that marriages are entered into with the free and full consent of the intending spouses involved and that the parties have equal rights during and at the dissolution of the marriage.[3] The Constitution offers special protection to children, indicating they cannot be pledged in marriages.[4]

In the event of dissolution of a marriage, whether through death or divorce, provision is made for the protection of children and spouses.[5] Section 26 complies with Article 16(1)(a)-(c) of CEDAW, Article 6(a), (b), (c) and (j) of the Maputo Protocol, and Article 8(1)-(2) of the SADC Protocol on Gender and Development. These international instruments state that men and women are entitled to equal rights during a marriage and upon its dissolution and must freely consent to such marriages. The Constitution stipulates in section 78 that the minimum age requirement for concluding a marriage is eighteen years. It further states that no person may be compelled to marry against their will.[6] This provision complies with Articles 6(a) and (b) and 8(2) of the SADC Protocol on Gender and Development, which provides that eighteen years is the marriageable age and prohibits forced marriages, including marriages by abduction, virgin pledging, and child marriages.

[3] Ibid., section 26(a) and (c).

[4] Ibid., section 26(b).

[5] Ibid., section 26 (d).

[6] Ibid., section 78 (2).

The laws that govern marriages in Zimbabwe included the Marriages Act (Chapter 5:11) and the Customary Marriages Act (Chapter 5:07), which two Acts have been incorporated into the Marriages Act (Chapter 5:17) of 2022, hereinafter referred to as the 2022 Marriages Act. Other legislation applicable to marriages include the Married Persons Property Act (Chapter 5:12), the Matrimonial Causes Act (Chapter 5:13), the Maintenance Act (Chapter 5:09), the Guardianship of Minors Act (Chapter 5:08), the Deceased Estates Succession Act (Chapter 6:02), the Deceased Persons Family Maintenance Act (Chapter 6:03) and the Administration of Estates Act (Chapter 6:01).

TYPES OF MARRIAGES IN ZIMBABWE

As noted, there are three types of marriage in Zimbabwe: civil marriage, registered customary marriage, and unregistered customary law union. The new Marriages Act (Chapter 5:17) governs civil and registered customary marriages, while unregistered customary marriages are governed by customary law. Of the three, only civil marriages and registered customary marriages are fully recognized in Zimbabwe law. Unregistered customary law unions are recognized for limited purposes, as will be discussed herein.

The 2022 Marriages Act: Chapter 5:17

The 2022 Marriages Act has harmonized marriage laws in Zimbabwe into a single Act, consistent with the following constitutional principles: gender equality; recognition of the rights of women, youths and children; recognition of the rights of cultural groups; preservation of cultural values and practices that enhance the dignity, wellbeing and equality of people; the general principles of marriage in Sections 26 and 78 of the Constitution as explained above; the best interests of the child; the protection of children from sexual exploitation; and the supremacy of the Constitution.[7]

[7] Memorandum of the Marriages Bill, which is now the Marriage Act, (Chapter 5:17).

The 2022 Marriages Act in section 2 defines a child as a person below the age of eighteen years. Child marriages are excluded in section 3, which prohibits the celebration of any form of marriage with a person below the age of eighteen. Child marriage was rampant and unpunished until section 78 of the Constitution stipulated the age of marriage as eighteen years. In the case of *Mudzuru and Another v Minister of Justice, Legal and Parliamentary Affairs*,[8] the Constitutional Court made a ruling declaring section 22(1) of the former Marriages Act[9] and the Customary Marriages Act,[10] which allowed children to enter marriages, unconstitutional. The 2022 Act gives effect to the common law position by criminalizing child marriages.

Section 4 provides for the free and informed consent of a party to the marriage. Such consent should be given by the parties themselves, not the guardian. Parties to the marriage have equal rights and obligations during the subsistence of the marriage and upon its dissolution.[11]

The 2022 Act further prohibits marriages of persons within certain degrees of affinity or consanguinity, and betrothals.[12] Nonetheless, section 41 introduces the concept of civil universal partnerships, which were not previously recognized in Zimbabwe. A civil partnership is defined as a relationship between a man and a woman who are at least eighteen years, have lived together without legally being married to each other, are not within the degrees of affinity or consanguinity as provided in section 7, and live together as a couple on a genuine domestic basis. On the dissolution of the relationship, the Matrimonial Causes Act

[8] Constitutional Application 79 of 2014, CC 12 of 2015) [2016] ZWCC 12 (20 January 2016) (available online).

[9] The section provided that no boy under the age of eighteen years and no girl under the age of 16 shall be capable of contracting a marriage except with the written permission of the minister.

[10] It was held to be unconstitutional in that it does not provide for a minimum age limit of eighteen years in respect of any marriage contracted under the same.

[11] Section 6, 2022 Marriages Act.

[12] Ibid., sections 7.

shall apply to the division and dissolution of assets as well as maintenance claims. Section 41(5) provides that a civil partnership exists notwithstanding that one or both persons are legally married to someone else or are in another civil partnership marriage.

Under the Act, a magistrate is the marriage officer of a district where he holds office, whereas a chief is a marriage officer for customary law marriages for the district where he holds office.[13] In section 16, every marriage contracted under customary law should be solemnized. All unregistered customary law unions that are not solemnized must be registered with the registrar within three months from the date of the union.[14] Failure to register a marriage contracted under customary law does not affect its validity with regard to status, guardianship, custody and the rights of succession of the children of such marriages.[15]

Civil marriages

A civil marriage is a monogamous marriage between a husband and a wife. As long as the marriage subsists, neither party is permitted to marry any other person. If a party to a civil marriage enters another marriage with another person during the subsistence of the first marriage, they commit the crime of bigamy, which is punishable under criminal law.[16]

Formalities of a civil marriage

A civil marriage is solemnized by a marriage officer, who may be a magistrate, a designated minister of religion, or other designated persons.[17] The marriage process is initiated either by the publication of banns, if the marriage is before a minister of religion, or the issuance of a notice of intention to marry or the granting of a marriage license, if

13 Ibid., section 8 and 9.

14 Ibid., section 17 (1) and (2).

15 Ibid., section 17(3).

16 Section 104, Criminal Law (Codification and Reform) Act (Chapter 9:23).

17 Sections 8, 10, 11 and 12, 2022 Marriages Act.

it is before a magistrate.[18] A party who intends to cause the publication of banns of marriage must apply to the minister of religion.[19] The minister of religion will thereafter publish the said banns in an audible manner or by posting the banns in a conspicuous place or in the immediate vicinity of the ordinary place of worship of the congregation concerned.[20] The reason for the publication of banns is to invite the public to lodge objections to the marriage, should there be any lawful reason for so doing.[21]

For marriages before a magistrate, the marriage is initiated by the application and publication of a notice of intention to marry or an application for a marriage license. A notice of intention to marry is applied for before a magistrate.[22] Once a magistrate is satisfied with the application, the magistrate will cause the publication of the notice by posting it in a conspicuous place or in the immediate vicinity of the magistrate court concerned for a continuous period of fifteen days and thereafter issue the parties with a certificate of publication.[23] Where a marriage is initiated by way of a marriage license, the parties desiring to get married may personally apply to a magistrate for a license to marry.[24] Marriage licenses are issued wherever the marriage is not preceded by banns or by a notice in cases of urgency. The magistrate will ask the parties relevant questions to ascertain whether there are impediments to the proposed marriage.[25] Once satisfied that there are no lawful

18 Ibid., section 18.

19 Ibid., section 19. The application should state the full particulars of the parties and be signed by both parties.

20 Ibid., section 20.

21 Ibid., section 28.

22 In terms of section 23 of the Marriages Act, the application shall bear the full names and signatures of the prospective spouses.

23 Ibid., sections 23 and 24.

24 Ibid., section 25.

25 Ibid.

impediments, he will order the parties to make a declaration to that effect and issue them a marriage license.[26]

A civil marriage can be solemnized at any time by the marriage officer in the presence of two witnesses who are aged eighteen years and above.[27] After making the marriage vows, the parties and the witnesses will sign the marriage certificates in triplicate before the marriage officer. The marriage officer will then sign the marriage certificate.[28] One original copy is issued to the parties, and another copy is transmitted to the Registrar General for registration and filing.[29]

Registered customary marriage

Unlike the civil marriage, registered customary marriages are potentially polygamous. A husband is allowed to have more than one wife. However, the reverse scenario does not apply to a woman, as the woman is restricted to one husband. A husband may register more than one customary marriage and does not need the consent of his wife to do so. Such laws favor males since men can have more than one wife. Although registration is meant to protect and secure the rights of parties to the marriage, this protection or security can be neutralized if the husband decides to marry more than one wife. Such a marriage can be converted to a civil marriage, provided the husband has only one wife. A person whose marriage is registered under customary law commits bigamy if they purport to enter into a civil marriage with someone else during the subsistence of the marriage.[30]

26 Ibid., section 23 (5).

27 Ibid., section 30 (1) and (2).

28 Ibid., section 36 (1)-(4).

29 Ibid.

30 Section 104(1)(b), Criminal Law (Codification and Reform) Act (Chapter 9:23); Should one deny the existence of the customary marriage, the onus is on the State to prove the existence of the marriage beyond reasonable doubt. See section 104(2).

Formalities of registered customary marriage

A registered customary marriage is one solemnized by a magistrate or a chief.[31] The parties to the marriage, the guardian of the woman (or a person appointed by such guardian), and one witness must be present.[32] When the customary marriage officer is satisfied that no lawful impediment exists to the proposed marriage, he will solemnize the marriage by administering the marriage vows and thereafter declaring the parties to be husband and wife.[33] The parties to the marriage, the customary marriage officer, and the witnesses present will then sign the marriage certificate, after which the customary marriage officer will give the parties a copy of the marriage certificate. A copy of the marriage certificate is retained for filing at the registry.

Unregistered customary law unions

Just as a registered customary marriage, this marriage is potentially polygamous.[34] It is predicated on the cultural practice of payment of a bride price (marriage consideration) by the man to the woman's family. It is not followed by solemnization or registration. Once the bride price process is concluded, the two parties are deemed married and can live together. An unregistered customary law union is not fully recognized in the eyes of the law. The union is only recognized for the purposes of customary law and custom relating to the status, guardianship, custody, and the rights of succession of the children of such marriage.[35]

[31] Sections 8-12, 2022 Marriages Act.

[32] Ibid., section 16(3).

[33] Ibid., section 16(6).

[34] Although an unregistered customary union is potentially polygamous, the court ruled in the case of *Karimatsenga v Tsvangirai and others* (HH 369/12) that a woman can successfully mount a legal challenge to any would-be civil marriage between their husband and some other woman.

[35] Section 17(3), 2022 Marriages Act.

Dissolution of marriages

Divorce occurs when a duly registered or solemnized marriage is brought to an end. The obligations and rights of the parties are terminated. The Constitution guarantees the equality of spouses in marriage, during the marriage, and at its dissolution.[36] Any spouse may institute an action to dissolve a marriage. Civil and registered customary marriages are dissolved by the High Court and the magistrates' courts, respectively. The High Court, a superior court of record, has jurisdiction to dissolve all marriages in Zimbabwe. A magistrate court has the power to dissolve registered customary marriages.[37] Unregistered customary marriages are excluded.

Further, the High Court has jurisdiction to determine a divorce case on several grounds. First, it may do so where the plaintiff or applicant is a female citizen of Zimbabwe who has been deserted by a husband domiciled in Zimbabwe before the desertion.[38] Second, the High Court has jurisdiction over divorce cases where the marriage was celebrated in Zimbabwe, and the woman has been resident in Zimbabwe for at least two years prior to the institution of the action, whether or not the husband was resident or domiciled and is still resident in Zimbabwe.[39] Third, a woman who is a citizen of Zimbabwe and has been resident in the country for at least two years may initiate divorce proceedings in the High Court in the same manner.[40] Moreover, the High Court has jurisdiction to entertain any counter-claims that arise from the divorce claim.[41] The Matrimonial Causes Act addresses aspects of conflict of laws with respect to marriage. Section 3(3) of the Act states that the laws of Zimbabwe shall govern matrimonial issues in which the High Court has jurisdiction, provided both parties were domiciled in the

36 Section 26(c), Constitution of Zimbabwe.

37 Section 2, Matrimonial Causes Act.

38 Ibid., section 3(a).

39 Ibid., section 3(b).

40 Ibid., section 3(c).

41 Ibid., section 3(2).

country when proceedings were initiated. Judicial oversight is guaranteed for the two recognized marriages. In contrast, no legal framework governs the dissolution of unregistered customary marriages.

Grounds of divorce for civil marriages and registered customary marriages

The law has evolved substantially concerning divorce. The common law was premised on proof of fault on the part of the defendant. It was incumbent upon the plaintiff to prove any of the grounds of divorce recognized by law, among which were cruelty, desertion, and adultery. The Matrimonial Causes Act (Chapter 5:13) revolutionized these aspects and now addresses the requirements to be fulfilled by a party seeking to dissolve a marriage. Three main grounds of divorce are irretrievable breakdown of the marriage,[42] incurable mental illness, or continuous unconsciousness of one of the parties to the marriage.[43]

Irretrievable breakdown

A competent court may grant a divorce decree once it is satisfied that the marriage between the parties has irretrievably broken down.[44] The breakdown must be such that it is no longer possible for the parties to resume a normal marriage relationship. In other words, there should be no reasonable prospect of salvaging the marriage relationship.[45] In considering whether the marriage has broken down irretrievably, the courts may consider several facts:[46]

i. The parties have not lived together as husband and wife for a period not less than one year.

[42] Ibid., section 4(a).

[43] Ibid., section 4(b).

[44] Ibid., section 5(1).

[45] Ibid.

[46] Ibid., section 5(2).

ii. The defendant commits an action which is considered by the other spouse as incompatible with a normal marriage relationship.

iii. That a court of competent jurisdiction has sentenced the defendant to a term of imprisonment of not less than fifteen years or issued a declaration that the defendant is a habitual criminal. This also applies to a defendant on whom an extended sentence has been imposed and, as a result, is incarcerated for a continuous or aggregate period of five years out of the last ten years preceding the commencement of divorce proceedings.

iv. Cruelty on the part of the defendant or habitual intoxication.

Any factor listed above, if proved, suffices.

Continuous mental illness or unconsciousness

A competent court may also grant a divorce on the ground of continuous mental illness or continuous unconsciousness of the other spouse.[47] The person must have been under medical care for five years. The treatment period can be a continuous period or an interrupted period of five years.[48] As a safeguard, an appropriate court shall not grant a divorce on the ground of continuous mental illness unless it is satisfied from the evidence of three medical practitioners that the defendant is mentally ill.[49] Two of the medical practitioners shall be qualified as psychiatrists appointed by the court.[50] A person is deemed to be under care if detained by a court order in relation to mental illness or if receiving treatment voluntarily, whilst not detained under the law, relating to mental illness in Zimbabwe or another country.[51]

47 Ibid., section 6(2).

48 Ibid., section 6(2) (a).

49 Ibid., section 6(3).

50 Ibid.

51 Ibid., section 6(4)(a) and (b).

An appropriate court may grant a divorce on proof that the defendant has been immobile because of a physical disorder or continuous unconsciousness lasting for six months.[52] Further, there must be no reasonable prospect that the spouse would be cured or regain consciousness. The evidence of medical practitioners is indispensable to prove this ground.[53] As a safeguard, therefore, the appropriate court must be guided by sound medical evidence.

Dissolution of unregistered customary law unions

Statistics show that unregistered customary law unions constitute about 84% of marriages in Zimbabwe.[54] They are not fully recognized as marriages in Zimbabwe except for the purposes of custody, guardianship, maintenance, and inheritance. By virtue of the non-recognition of these unions, parties do not approach the courts for dissolution; dissolution is conducted through the customs and traditions of the parties concerned. However, generally, a party moving for dissolution of the union hands over a rejection token (*gupuro*) to the other party. The practice is not universal and differs from tribe to tribe. It is unclear, what the divorce token should be, how it should be delivered, to whom it should be delivered, and by whom. This leads to problems in determining whether a customary law union has been terminated or subsists.

Property rights during marriage and after divorce

According to the Married Persons Property Act (Chapter 5:12), marriages in Zimbabwe are contracted out of community of property. Marriages concluded after 1 January 1929 are out of community of property save for those concluded by parties who agree to the contrary before the solemnization of the marriage.[55] Marriages concluded prior to 1 January 1929 are in community of property unless

52 Ibid., section 6 (2) (b).

53 Ibid., section 6 (3).

54 *84pc of Zim Marriages Unregistered* (2013) (available online).

55 Section 2(1), Married Persons Property Act.

the spouses entered into an anti-nuptial contract stating that the Married Persons Property Act shall not apply. Impliedly, during the subsistence of the marriage, each spouse retains sole ownership of the property registered in their name. A spouse can therefore dispose of his or her assets as is preferred, without consulting the other party. The downside is that a spouse may sell or encumber their matrimonial home without the knowledge or consent of the other party prior to the divorce.

The only property which is considered for distribution upon divorce is the properties that the parties acquired together during the subsistence of the marriage. In distributing this property, the court considers several factors, including the parties' income-earning capacity, assets and other financial resources, future financial needs, obligations, and responsibilities of each spouse. They also consider the children's best interests, the family's standard of living, the ages of the spouses and children, direct and indirect contributions made by each spouse, and the duration of the marriage.[56] In line with the Matrimonial Causes Act, the superior courts have developed guidelines to be followed in the distribution process.[57] While these efforts are commendable, there is no guarantee of fair sharing since the result will depend on what the judicial officer considers just – unlike when the parties share equally.

In contrast, unregistered customary law unions do not have established formal mechanisms for determining the distribution of property upon dissolution of the marriage.[58] Where parties are married under customary law, and the marriage is not registered, customary law will apply to a dispute arising out of the marriage or its dissolution.[59] Under unregistered customary law, a woman, upon

[56] Section 7(4)(a)-(e), Matrimonial Causes Act.

[57] See *Usayi v Usayi* 2003 (49/01) (SC 11 of 2003, Civil Appeal 149 of 2001) [2003] ZWSC 11 (23 June 2003);

Mhora v Mhora (SC 89 of 2020, Civil Appeal SC 617 of 2018) [2020] ZWSC 89 (29 June 2020) (available online).

[58] Tambudzai Gonese-Manjonjo "The Recognition of Customary Marriages in Zimbabwe and the Proposed Marriages Bill", *Southern Africa Litigation Centre Policy Brief*, V (2019), p. 4 (available online).

[59] *Chapeyama v Matende and Another* 1999 1 ZLR 534 (H) (HC).

dissolution, is entitled to only household utensils.[60] For the general law to be applied to the distribution of property, a party requesting the application of general law must convince the court that they lived their life in a manner that justifies the application of general law. Superior courts have devised two key concepts to mitigate the rigors of customary law by introducing the common law concepts of tacit universal partnership or unjust enrichment in the division of property of parties. The High Court has, in some judgments, upheld claims by women in unregistered customary law unions for equitable distribution of matrimonial property upon dissolution of the union.[61]

The principle of tacit universal partnership was clarified in the matter of *Chapeyama v Matende and Another*[62] where it was held that:

> [W]here, a husband and wife marry under customary law, and the marriage is not registered, customary law, will apply to a dispute arising out of the marriage or its dissolution. It is only possible to bring in the general law concept of a tacit universal partnership if the court lays a foundation for applying such law. Such a foundation had not been clearly articulated. Further, that the foundation for applying the concept of a tacit universal partnership was provided in s 3 of the Customary Law and Local Courts Act [Chapter 7:05], which provides that unless the justice of the case otherwise requires, customary law applies in any civil case where the parties h ave expressly agreed that it should apply, or, regard being had to the nature of the case and the surrounding circumstances, it appears that the parties have agreed that it should apply. A general law concept such as tacit universal partnership may be relied on if, in the circumstances,

60 *Mautsa v Kurebgasekwa*, HH 106/17.

61 See ibid.; *Mtuda v Ndudzo* 2000 (1) ZLR 710 (H); *Nyamakusa v Maswera* (HC 7003/13) [2016] ZWHHC 36 (14 December 2015) (available online); *Nyamukonora v Makosi* [2021] HMT 18 of 2021, HC 198 of 2019) [2021] ZWMTHC 18 (29 April 2021) (available online).

62 *Chapeyama*, note 65 above.

the application of customary law would have led to injustice. Where the elements of tacit universal partnership have been established, useful guidelines may be found in s 7 of the Matrimonial Causes Act [Chapter 5:13] in considering the division of the matrimonial property.[63]

To succeed in claiming a tacit universal partnership, the following requirements must be satisfied:[64]

i. Each of the partners must bring something into the partnership or must bind themselves to bring something into it, whether money, labor or skill,
ii. The business should be for the joint benefit of the parties,
iii. The object of the business should be to make a profit, and,
iv. The agreement should be a legitimate one.

The doctrine of unjust enrichment allows a plaintiff to recover from a defendant where the defendant has unfairly benefited from the plaintiff's efforts without compensation. In proving unjust enrichment, a spouse must satisfy the court that they contributed something which will leave the other party enriched at their expense if not equitably distributed. From the case of *Mautsa v Kurebgasekwa,*[65] the requirements of unjust enrichment were listed as follows:

i. The defendant must be enriched.
ii. The enrichment must be at the expense of another in that the plaintiff must be impoverished, and there must be a causal link between the defendant's enrichment and the plaintiff's impoverishment.
iii. The enrichment must be unjustified.

[63] Ibid., 356 F-H.

[64] *Mtuda,* note 67 above.

[65] HH 106/17.

iv. The case should not come under the scope of one of the classical enrichment actions.

v. There should be no positive rule of law that refuses an action to the impoverished person.

It should be noted that this improvisation of importing common law principles into the realm of customary law has limitations. The courts have stipulated that in a customary law union, the application of common law principles is not automatic but has to be specifically pleaded. There is no scientific formula for apportioning the property, a situation that presents challenges. This absence of clear guidelines or rules on the criteria applicable in the distribution of property leaves parties in the hands of judges who exercise discretion on how the property should be shared. Moreover, parties – mostly women – are hardly able to prove direct contribution to the acquisition of property as required in tacit universal partnerships.

The other challenge is that the principles of unjust enrichment and universal partnerships suggest that marriage is a form of a partnership or contract or a business relationship. These are not accurate conceptions of marriage. In most cases, parties find the stringent requirements difficult to prove, leading to inequitable distribution of property. In addition, women also face difficulties because they do not have access to adequate legal representation to help them navigate the complexities of the legal system.

Maintenance of spouses and children

Equality of spouses in the marriage set-up is seen in common law and the Maintenance Act (Chapter 5:09). The law on the maintenance of spouses is quite progressive because it applies to all forms of marriages contracted in Zimbabwe, whether registered or unregistered. The duty of spouses to maintain each other is reciprocal.[66] Either the wife or husband may claim maintenance under the Maintenance

[66] Welshman Ncube, *Family Law in Zimbabwe* (1989), p. 156; and *Woodhead v Woodhead* 1955 (3) SA 138 (RA).

Act. Parties to a cohabitation arrangement are, however, excluded but may claim for maintenance of the children.

Inheritance

Inheritance is regulated by the Administration of Estates Act (Chapter 6:01), the Deceased Estates Succession Act (Chapter 6:02) and the Deceased Persons Family Maintenance Act (Chapter 6:03). These statutes provide for succession under customary law and general law as well as for people married under different marriage regimes. The discriminatory customary regime that centered on the office of the male heir was abolished by the Administration of Estates Act. The male heir assumed the role of the deceased in that he would inherit everything from the deceased and was expected to look after the deceased's family. These days, the heir only inherits the name of the deceased, his walking stick (*tsvimbo*) and other traditional artefacts.[67] The heir may also benefit from the estate if recognized as a beneficiary according to the law.

The inheritance laws are generally progressive in favor of the surviving spouses and children. Succession for persons married under the Marriage Act recognizes the centrality of the surviving spouse. Succession can be by will,[68] or intestate, where one dies without leaving a will. Where the deceased has left a valid will, the estate is distributed according to the will or wishes of the testator. This applies to all marriages and extends to cohabitants. For those in registered customary marriages and those in unregistered customary unions, the amendment to the Administration of Estates Act has brought relief to spouses because they are recognized for the purposes of sharing of property. In the event of competition for the office of executor, the surviving spouse is preferred to any other person.[69] Beneficiaries of deceased estates under customary law are primarily

[67] Section 68C, Administration of Estates Act.

[68] Wills Act [Chapter 6:06].

[69] Section 26, Administration of Estates Act.

the surviving spouses and children of the deceased.[70] An unregistered customary marriage is regarded as valid under the Act.[71]

It should be noted, however, that despite the recognition of unregistered customary law unions for the purposes of inheritance, some complications still exist for parties in these unions. In unregistered customary law unions, a surviving spouse needs confirmation of the union in the form of affidavits from the deceased's relatives before they can inherit from the estate.[72] The verification of the customary marriage from the relatives of the deceased spouse is an uphill task, especially where the surviving spouse has a bad relationship with the relatives or where the relatives, out of greed and to benefit from the estate, refuse to confirm the marriage.[73]

The Administration of Estates Act seeks to protect the proprietary rights of the surviving spouse and children, regardless of the type of marriage. It provides the surviving spouse and children with the right to occupy the matrimonial home pending the final winding up of the estate. This is a response to the incidence of property grabbing that saw widows and children being evicted from their homes.[74]

Section 10 of the Deceased Person Family Maintenance Act also protects a deceased person's family and property:

> Notwithstanding any law, including customary law, to the contrary, when any person dies, any surviving spouse or child of such person shall, subject to section eleven, have the following rights - (a) the right to occupy any immovable property which the deceased had the right to occupy and which such surviving

[70] Ibid, section 68(1)(a).

[71] Ibid, section 68 (3).

[72] Centre for Conflict Management and Transformation, *Cultures in Conflict: Challenges of Marriage and Divorce under Zimbabwe's Dual Legal System* (2016), p. 9 (available online).

[73] Human Rights Watch, *You Will Get Nothing: Violations of Property and Inheritance Rights of Widows in Zimbabwe* (2017), p. 21 (available online).

[74] Ibid.

spouse or child was ordinarily occupying immediately before the death of the deceased; (b) the right to use any household goods and effects, implements, tools, vehicles or other things which immediately before the death of the deceased the surviving spouse or child was using in relation to such immovable property; (c) the right to use and employ any animals which immediately before the death of the deceased were depastured or kept on such immovable property; (d) to an extent that is reasonable for the support of such surviving spouse or child, the right to any crops which immediately before the death of the deceased were growing or being produced on such immovable property.[75]

Claims for adultery damages

Under the general law, an outsider who unlawfully has sexual intercourse with a man or woman who is married under the Marriages Act commits a *delict* (tort) against the other spouse. Accordingly, damages for adultery may be claimed by either spouse. The claim is predicated on the premise that the third party, by being intimate with a married person, causes a loss of consortium.[76]

In contrast, a woman in a registered customary marriage or an unregistered customary law union cannot claim damages against a woman who has committed adultery with her spouse.[77] The reason is that customary marriages, whether registered or unregistered, are potentially polygamous, unlike civil marriages, which are monogamous. However, a husband in a registered customary marriage or an unregistered customary law union has a legal right to sue for adultery committed with his spouse. This is discriminatory against women. Cohabitants cannot claim damages for adultery from the lover of a partner since their

[75] Section 10(1)(a) – (d), Deceased Person Family Maintenance Act.

[76] Ncube, note 72 above, p. 154.

[77] *Mukono v Gwenzi* 1999 (1) ZLR 117 (S).

marriage is not recognized under the general or customary law.

Guardianship and custody of children

Following traditional rites, the custody of children during the colonial era was governed by tradition and customary law.[78] Upon divorce, a father who had paid the full bride price was entitled to the custody of all children above seven years old.[79] The wife had to relinquish their custody and return to her parents.[80] This position was first altered by the African Law and Tribal Courts Act of 1969 (Chapter 237).[81] Now, however, both parents have equal rights concerning the custody of their minor children. A court has to determine which of the two parents is better suited to obtain custody of the child, considering the "best interest of the child".[82] The Constitution recognizes equal parental responsibility for all children born to married parties, irrespective of the form of marriage contracted by the child's parents.[83]

Children born to unmarried parents

Common law regarded the father's right to custody and guardianship of a child born out of wedlock as analogous to that of any other third party.[84] The child was regarded as fatherless. In *Sadiqi v Muteswa*[85] the court rightly approached the matter according to the equality and non-discrimination provisions in the Constitution.[86] The common law was

[78] Ncube, note 72 above, p. 126.

[79] Ibid., where the author cites *Chiwaka v Machinga* 1979 CAACC 16 and *Jokonia v Simanga* 1967 AAC 34.

[80] Ibid.

[81] Section 3(5), African Law and Tribal Courts Act.

[82] Section 81(2), Constitution of Zimbabwe.

[83] Ibid., section 80(2).

[84] *Sadiqi v Muteiswa* (HH 249 of 2020, HC 3971 of 2019) [2020] ZWHHC 249 (18 March 2020) (available online).

[85] Ibid.

[86] Section 81(1)(a), Constitution of Zimbabwe.

declared unconstitutional. The Guardianship of Minors Act (Amendment) Act 2022 effectively changes the position by acknowledging the biological father of the child born out of wedlock as part of the child's rights.[87]

STRENGTHS AND WEAKNESSES OF MARRIAGE RIGHTS IN ZIMBABWE

There seems to be a hierarchy of marriages in Zimbabwe. The laws seem to favor civil marriages and offer parties to such marriages more protection during the marriage, upon divorce, and on inheritance matters following the death of the other spouse. Registered customary law unions are afforded some protection by the law, although their protection is inferior to that afforded to civil marriages. In contrast, the law does not recognize unregistered customary law unions as valid except for the purposes of maintenance, inheritance, guardianship, and custody. It has been shown how parties in unregistered customary law unions face difficulties in getting a fair distribution of property upon divorce. Whereas the 2022 Marriages Act stipulates when a marriage comes into existence and the requirements for its validity, there is no legal standard for when an unregistered customary law union comes into being and when it ends. Parties in unregistered customary law unions also face problems in inheritance matters where there is a need to confirm their customary law marriages to access benefits from the deceased partner's estate or obtain pension benefits. The problems highlighted above mostly affect women.

In the case of *Karimatsenga v Tsvangirai and others,*[88] the judge, while conceding that many marriages in Zimbabwe are unregistered, lamented the lack of harmony in the marriage laws and the consequence of applying customary law and general law simultaneously.[89] The court recommended urgent legislative intervention to review the marriage laws.[90]

87 Section 3, Guardianship of Minors Amendment Act 2022.

88 HH 369/12.

89 Ibid.

90 Ibid.

It can be surmised that the current laws on marriages in Zimbabwe do not comply with international legal standards, given that elements of inequality and discrimination abound. Although the Constitution has provisions on marriage rights, the marriage laws do not align with the Constitution.

Strengths and weaknesses of 2022 Marriages Act

The 2022 Marriages Act is a positive step towards aligning the marriage laws with the Constitution and other international standards. It recognizes gender equality, protection of the child's best interests, consent to marriage, the right to participate in one's culture, and civil partnerships or cohabitation arrangements. The non-recognition of civil partnerships places parties in a disadvantaged position in the event of death or separation. The inclusion of such a family set-up in the Act protects the property rights of parties if they decide to end the relationship.

Although the Act has been applauded as progressive, it has shortcomings. It only recognizes registered customary law marriages and maintains the non-recognition of unregistered customary law marriages unless and until they are registered. According to the Act, unregistered customary law unions are only recognized for the purposes of guardianship, custody, maintenance, and inheritance. By conferring different rights on unregistered customary law unions from those conferred on registered customary law unions and civil marriages, the Act vitiates the principle of equality and non-discrimination in section 56 of the Constitution.

The Act fails to directly address the problems faced by women in unregistered customary law unions regarding property sharing upon dissolution of the marriage since unregistered customary law unions are not recognized as marriages for this purpose. Section 41 of the Act affords protection to parties in a civil partnership. This cannot be construed to include parties in unregistered customary law unions, since it specifically singles out parties in a civil partnership. The Act fails to protect the property rights of parties to an unregistered customary law union upon divorce.

It is inconvenient to refer to various pieces of legislation when dealing with issues on inheritance, property rights, guardianship, and maintenance of spouses to a marriage. The Marriages Act is, however, silent on the aforementioned issues and resorts to the relevant legislation in dealing with the consequences of marriages regarding the highlighted aspects.

RECOMMENDATIONS AND CONCLUSIONS

Recommendations

To address the gaps and challenges in the Zimbabwean marriage system the following measures are recommended:

First, the 2022 Marriages Act consolidates the old laws on civil and customary marriages, it does not go far enough. The 2022 Marriages Act should have covered all the relevant provisions relating to the distribution of property, guardianship, custody, maintenance and inheritance upon death or divorce of spouses. This would have prevented references to various pieces of legislation in determining the consequences of marriage. The 2022 Marriages Act should be amended at the appropriate time to reflect this suggestion.

Second, the 2022 Marriage Act must be amended to give unregistered customary marriages full recognition. This will ensure fairness and equity and remove barriers that spouses in these marriages face in registering inheriting property, or sharing property upon divorce.

Conclusion

The types and systems of marriage in Zimbabwe, which has a pluralist legal system, have been identified. As regards civil marriages, the various modes of contracting such marriages, the steps pertaining to the publication of banns or an intention to marry, the application for a special license, and the solemnization of civil marriages were explored. The processes for the celebration of registered customary marriages have also been discussed.

There are limited grounds on which a civil marriage or a registered customary marriage may be dissolved, though the law on divorce has moved from a fault-based approach to a more neutral approach. Thus, a civil marriage or registered customary marriage in Zimbabwe may be dissolved where it is proved that the marriage has irretrievably broken down or there is some mental illness or continuous unconsciousness which makes the future viability of the marriage impossible.

The robust legal and regulatory framework available to civil and registered customary law marriage is unavailable to unregistered customary unions. At best, the law adopts a minimalist approach which affords guarded protection in matters of guardianship, inheritance, and the distribution of property obtained jointly by the parties during the existence of the union. In respect of the distribution of joint property, upon the dissolution of the unregistered customary union, note was taken of the discriminatory customary law practice which entitles the woman to the household utensils and nothing more. The courts have employed concepts like "tacit universal partnerships" and "unjust enrichment" to rebalance women's property rights in unregistered customary law unions. Nonetheless, these concepts are limiting because they wrongly assume that marriage is similar to a business contract.

Although the Constitution provides for equality in marriages, some inequalities exist regarding the rights of parties in customary marriages, especially unregistered ones, whereas parties to civil marriages enjoy the full protection of the law. Although the courts have tried to interpret marriage laws to ensure equality between spouses in all types of marriages, there are no standard guidelines for judges to apply, and they must exercise discretion in dealing with marriage rights.

Although the 2022 Marriages Act clarifies the age of marriageability, consent, and civil partnerships, it fails to address the validity of unregistered customary law unions other than stating that they have limited validity in respect of status, guardianship, custody, and succession. These concerns need to be dealt with in order to ensure that the matrimonial regime sufficiently protects rights and privileges irrespective of the legal regime under which marriage is contracted.

Mauritius

Chapter Thirteen
The Mauritian Law of Marriage and Divorce

Despite being a small island of 2,000 km^2 with 1.3 million inhabitants, the Republic of Mauritius has a long history in culture and traditions. Its legal system is based on a strong institutional and legal framework borrowed from various foreign sources of law, mainly France (1715-1810) and England (1810-1968).

Slavery was abolished in Mauritius in 1833. After the abolition of slavery, indentured Indian laborers arrived in Mauritius in the mid-nineteenth century to satisfy Britain's demand for labor on local sugarcane plantations. Many indentured laborers remained to form a significant part of the Mauritian population. The island is cosmopolitan in religion, culture, tradition, and languages, with people of African, Asian, and Indian origin.[1] Mauritians contract civil, religious, and customary marriages, although the sole legally recognized form of marriage is the civil marriage.

It is important to understand Mauritius law on marriages and divorces within the context of the Mauritius hybrid legal system as influenced by legal developments in other jurisdictions.[2]

GROWTH OF MAURITIAN FAMILY LAW IN A HYBRID SYSTEM

The civil law of Mauritius is inspired by the 1804 French Code Napoléon. When the British took over the control and administration of the island through the Capitulation Act

1 67% Indo-Mauritians, 28% Mauritian Creoles, 3% Sino-Mauritians, and 2% Franco-Mauritians.

2 The Mauritian Company Act 2001 is borrowed directly from The New Zealand Act 1995, and its Prevention of Corruption Act 2002, and Prevention of Terrorism Act 2002 are borrowed directly from the laws of Singapore and Hong-Kong respectively.

of 1810, the body of civil law emanating from the French code was retained. The Capitulation Act stipulated that the inhabitants of the island, then known as Isle de France, could maintain their religions and customs.[3] The 1807 French Code de Commerce and the 1883 French Code Pénal remain in force in Mauritius, albeit with amendments.

The French Penal Code plays an important role in family law, including cases of larceny between spouses, bigamy, or the right of the married spouse to trade. However, as regards marriage, the Code Civil Mauricien (CCM) or the Mauritian Civil Code is the most important surviving French code applicable in Mauritius.[4] The Mauritian Civil Code covers more than marriage and divorce; it regulates such spheres of private law as contracts, torts, succession, and property law.

British legal influence on Mauritius commenced with the Capitulation of 1810. Since then, English law has heavily influenced the Mauritius public law structure. The same influence appears to exist in such areas of Mauritanian commercial law as banking.[5] This mixture of two systems – the French and English – persists today. Angelo describes the legal system of Mauritius as "basically that of Napoleonic France with a strong overlay of English law".[6]

However, the Mauritius legislature has not aggressively pursued reforms in either the English or French systems of law. Although substantive principles of Mauritian family law can be found in the French-inspired civil code, Mauritian judicial institutions and procedures are based on English legal and political systems. Injunctions, for example, are a recognizable form of judicial remedy, whereas the "plaint

[3] Article 8, Capitulation Treaty 1810, stipulates that: "... the inhabitants will preserve their religions, laws and customs ...".

[4] Hereinafter: the "Mauritian Civil Code".

[5] A. H. Angelo, "French and English Legal Cultures Meet – Aspects of Recent Mauritanian Legislation", *The Comparative and International Law Journal of Southern Africa*, IX, no. 3 (1976), p. 372.

[6] Angelo, "Mauritius: The Basis of the Legal System", *The Comparative and International Law Journal of Southern Africa*, III, no. 2 (1970), p. 228.

with summons" is an appropriate mode of initiating an action in a court of law.

Since 1804, the French Code Napoléon (replaced by the Mauritian Civil Code) has remained applicable in all civil and religious marriages for all Mauritians, irrespective of caste, color, or religion. There is no room for exemptions or accommodations on religious or cultural grounds. This is unsatisfactory because Mauritius is a country where customary law is strong among the various communities.[7] Mauritius is home to diverse religions, churches, temples, pagodas, and *kovils*.

SOURCES OF MAURITIAN FAMILY LAW

Constitution

To deal with marriage and divorce cases, the Mauritian legislature has constituted a regulatory framework of colonial law with an overlay of amendments and innovations crafted to protect all Mauritians. The principal source of family law remains sections 8 and 9 of the Constitution, which allow all individuals to enjoy their right to property and privacy, respectively. Section 11 of the Constitution provides for freedom of conscience.

Homosexual marriage is non-existent compared to France or England, from which Mauritius borrowed its laws and legislation. Though the Constitution does not expressly prohibit same-sex marriages, it is taboo in Mauritius to contract a same-sex marriage.

Statutes

These constitutional provisions are coupled with the following pieces of legislation.

a) The Civil Status Act 1981 (Act 23/1981);

b) The Divorce and Judicial Separation Act (Act 20/1981);

[7] Its population of 1.3 million inhabitants comprises communities of Indians, Tamils, Chinese, Muslims, and Africans who live harmoniously in Mauritius.

c) The Divorce and Judicial Separation (Miscellaneous Provisions) Act 2011 (Act no. 2 of 2011);
d) The Children's Act 2020 (Act 13/2020);
e) The Child Sex Offender Register Act 2020;
f) The Protection from Domestic Violence Act 1997.

In addition, French and local doctrines, judicial precedents, and relevant ratified international covenants[8] have contributed to the evolution of Mauritian family law.[9]

Mauritian civil law as influenced by French civil law

Title V of the Mauritian Civil Code provides for, *inter alia*, the substantive law of marriage and obligations. It covers a wide spectrum, including nullity of marriage,[10] divorce, filiation, parental authority, and adoption. However, fraud to mislead the other spouse is not a ground to nullify a marriage under French and Mauritian marriage law.

In addition, the Mauritian legislature innovated by converting past religious marriages into civil marriages through registration.[11] In the past, parties to these religious marriages remained concubines under the law. Their offspring were not legitimate, but natural, children. There was a gap in the law of religious marriages. As a result, the Mauritian Civil Code was amended to confer on past religious marriages civil effects under certain conditions

[8] For example, the Convention on the Elimination of All Forms of Discrimination against Women.

[9] The Republic of Mauritius has ratified and implemented most international and African regional covenants to protect all individuals in Mauritius. The island is active in the African region as a member of regional economic blocs (SADC, COMESA or the Indian Ocean Rim Association-IORA) and Regional Economic Partnership Agreements (REPAs).

[10] Based on the French civil law on nullity (*la nullité relative*), where only the parties to the marriage are concerned, and *une nullité absolue* (any person including the Public Minister may object to the celebration of the civil marriage).

[11] Articles 228(1) – 228(10), Mauritian Civil Code, provides for the registration of past religious marriages with civil effects.

so that individuals who had previously been married religiously may register their marriage.[12] The Mauritian legislature also introduced a form of adoption known as *la légitimation par adoption* (adoption by legitimation), which allows one parent to adopt their own child in cases of adultery.

Mauritian penal law as influenced by French penal law

Sections of the Mauritian Penal Code deal with adultery,[13] abortion,[14] rape and sodomy,[15] prostitution,[16] family abandonment,[17] alimony,[18] change of domicile,[19] child trafficking,[20] or abandonment of child.[21]

English rules of interpretation

The Mauritian judiciary relies on English rules of interpretation, various maxims, and internal and external aids to construction to determine the precise intention of the Mauritian legislature. In certain circumstances, an aid to interpreting a law, such as the *travaux préparatoires* would

12 Ibid., Articles 228(1) – 228(10).

13 Section 242, Mauritian Penal Code provides: "Manslaughter committed by any person on his spouse, as well as on his accomplice, at the very moment he finds them in the act of adultery is excusable".

14 Ibid., section 235.

15 Ibid., sections 249, 250.

16 Ibid., section 253.

17 Ibid., section 260.

18 Ibid., section 261.

19 Ibid., section 262 provides: "Any person who, having the custody of a minor, fails to notify to any person who, by virtue of a judgment, has a right of visit or lodging in respect of the said minor any change of his domicile or of the residence of the minor, shall commit an offence and shall, on conviction, be liable to imprisonment for a term not exceeding 6 months and to a fine not exceeding 5000 rupees".

20 Ibid., section 262(a).

21 Ibid., section 263.

be useful, as explained in the leading Mauritian case of *Francoeur v Francoeur.*[22]

Rules of private international law

As regards divorce cases between foreigners and Mauritian nationals, the applicable law in Mauritius remains French private international law, following the case of *Austin v Bailey.*[23] In this case, the Mauritian Supreme Court held that marriages and divorces of an international nature are governed by French private international law.

CAPACITY OF MINORS TO CONTRACT MARRIAGES

Based on Asian and Indian traditions, customary rules are strong and palpable among the population. Traditionally, parents of Asian and Indian origins often "arrange" marriages for their daughters with future spouses they have never known or seen.

This type of "arrangement" in family affairs has been deplored consistently but in vain. For a long time, minors under eighteen but above sixteen could marry, with their parents' consent. If there was no parent, a Judge in Chambers could authorize the solemnization of the marriage, provided it was in the interest of the minor(s).[24] In *De Chazal v De Chazal and Ors,*[25] De Chazal married a minor in the United States, and the plaintiff prayed for a judgment decreeing the nullity of the marriage contracted by his son because the latter had not secured the consent of his parents according to the law of his domicile.[26] This was the practice before the Children Act 2020. Since the Children Act 2020 came into force, parties to a civil marriage must be eighteen years of age. With this major change in Mauritius family law, the

22 1989 MR 31.

23 1962 MR 113.

24 *Ex parte Vuillemein and ors* 1992 MR 93, and the case of *Gowry v Gowry and Ministère Public* 1986 MR 144

25 1961 MR 5.

26 *Nullité relative* in the case of *Choppy v Choppy* 1960 MR 81/1966 MR 1.

Mauritian legislature prevents minors from being married off hastily by their parents[27] once these parents give their consent or a Judge in Chambers authorizes the marriage.[28]

Various reforms on the marriage of minors have been implemented to replace obsolete articles in the Code Civil Mauricien to provide better protection to minors. In addition to the Children's Act 2020, notable legislation includes the Children's Court Act 2020[29] and the Child Sex Offender Register Act 2020.

CIVIL MARRIAGES: NATURE AND PROCESS

Based on French civil law, a civil marriage in the Mauritian context is a contract and an institution. As a solemn act, there are various preliminary conditions that the parties must meet before celebrating the marriage. These include the age, health, and sex of the parties to the marriage.

Based on French civil law, consent of the spouses to a civil marriage is imperative. In the case of *Mayput v Bheenick,*[30] the Supreme Court refused to annul a marriage that the plaintiff contracted with the defendant. The plaintiff complained that he was drugged during the ceremony. The plaintiff failed to prove, on a balance of probabilities, that he gave his consent under the influence of drugs.

Although Mauritians normally celebrate a religious marriage before a local priest as per the Civil Status Act 1981, it is now required that a civil marriage must be celebrated first.[31] The celebration of a civil marriage in Mauritius is a matter of public policy (*d'ordre public*)[32]. A marriage may be cancelled or declared null and void if it is celebrated

[27] Under customary law some religions in Mauritius prefer to marry their offspring as early as age fourteen.

[28] *X v Y* 1984 SCJ 39.

[29] (Act 14/2020).

[30] 1986 MR 121/SCJ 197.

[31] Article 150, Mauritian Civil Code provides: "A second marriage cannot be contracted previously to the dissolution of the first".

[32] Based on French civil law, all civil marriages are celebrated openly in the presence of the Registrar of the Civil status.

clandestinely. The Civil Status Act 1981 provides that parties who wish to contract a civil marriage, together with their two witnesses, must appear before the Registrar of Civil Status. The parties must present all the relevant official documents, including their birth certificates and national identity cards to the Registrar. After this, the intention of marriage is published for ten days, during which any person residing in Mauritius may object to the intended civil marriage. Once the civil marriage is celebrated, the parties often proceed with a religious marriage before a priest, depending on their religion, faith, and customs.

A "waiting period" is observed before a new civil marriage is celebrated, if a previous civil marriage has been dissolved by a decree *nisi* or permanent divorce. The divorced wife must not marry within three hundred days after a permanent divorce because the divorced spouse might be pregnant from her previous marriage. Instead of waiting, she may produce a medical certificate showing that she was not pregnant at the time of the dissolution of the marriage.

DISSOLUTION OF MARRIAGE

A marriage may be declared a nullity based on various vitiating factors affecting the marriage, such as error or violence.[33] In contrast, a divorce petition is based on the French notion of *faute* (fault) or *injures graves* (serious insults). The Supreme Court may pronounce *un divorce aux torts partagés* (divorce of shared-fault)[34] provided both petitioner and respondent are guilty. In the case of *Dhayam v Dhayam*,[35] a provisional decree of divorce *aux torts partagés* was pronounced, although it was rescinded because the time for reconciliation had not been exhausted.

[33] Based on nullity of marriage (violence, error, and fraud), whereas for divorces cases, the petitioner must prove *faute* or *injures graves* to succeed before the Supreme Court (Family Division); Error and fraud/*manoeuvres dolosives* are vitiating factors but, exceptionally, they are not vitiating factors in French and Mauritian family law.

[34] A divorce of shared fault.

[35] 1996 SCJ 39.

The Mauritian legal system had no divorce by mutual consent, as confirmed in the case of *Nundoosing v Nundoosing,*[36] until the Mauritian legislature amended the Civil Code.

Grounds for divorce

Mauritian law provides that a divorce may be pronounced based on *faute, injure grave,* or *rupture de la vie commune* (irretrievable breakdown of the marriage).[37] Consequently, it is left to the Supreme Court (Family Division) to interpret these three grounds from judgments inspired by the French *Cour de cassation.* The Supreme Court will examine whether there has been *faute, injure grave,* or *rupture de la vie commune*[38] to validate a divorce petition.

There is no exact definition of the term *faute,* but the Supreme Court will decide on a case-by-case basis, and the onus is on the petitioner to prove *faute.*[39] In *Minverve v Minerve,*[40] both parties were intolerant of each other's religion and faith and were equally to blame for the breakdown of the marriage.

Injure graves covers different situations. For example, section 231 of the Mauritian Civil Code provides that penal servitude for at least five years may constitute *injure graves.* In *H v H,*[41] it was held that a sentence of two years for embezzlement was, in the circumstances of the case, an *injure grave* justifying the court in granting a divorce to the other spouse. Similarly, in the case of *Adolphe v Adolphe,*[42] it was held that a sentence of imprisonment, which carries

36 1972 MR 188.

37 Based on French Civil Law, once the petitioner has proved *fautes* or *injures graves* on a balance of probabilities, the court may pronounce the divorce.

38 *Ramsamy v Ramsamy* 1990 MR 58/SCJ 78.

39 Facts which may suffice to prove *faute* include adultery (*Ng Kwai Fat v Ng Kwai Fat* 1966 MR 96), and sexual abuses (*Mackdaoonmaccus v Mackdoombaccus* 1990 MR 181).

40 1987 MR 45/SCJ 121.

41 1937 MR 192.

42 1955 MR 297.

with it a stigma of shame affecting the other spouse, justified the grant of a decree of divorce for *injure grave*. However, in the case of *P v P*,[43] Justice Shand CJ and Justice Colin took a different position and held that a conviction against one spouse for larceny with a term of imprisonment without hard labor for six years did not amount to a *peine infamante* (shameful punishment), entitling the other party to sue for divorce. In the case of *C v C*,[44] the Supreme Court found that ante nuptial unchastity of the wife concealed by her from her husband at the time of the marriage, did not constitute an *injure grave* affording a ground for divorce. Failure to maintain one's wife and children may constitute *une violation grave ou renouvelée des devoirs du mariage* (a violation of one's marital obligations), and the Supreme Court may pronounce a divorce for *injures graves*. In the case of *Poussin v Poussin*,[45] the failure of the husband to make adequate provision for his wife and children when he was able to do so, constituted an *injure grave* justifying the grant of a decree of divorce.

After the Family Division of the Supreme Court has pronounced the divorce, the former spouses owe obligations to the children.[46] In the leading authority of *Jagatsingh v Jagatsingh*,[47] it was held that the obligation of a parent to pay alimony for his offspring does not cease at the latter's coming of age. The other parent,[48] if he or she has custody and is responsible for attending to the child's maintenance, may apply for alimony.

In addition to the Mauritian Civil Code, relevant legislation provides for the procedures to be followed. In a case of divorce, the procedure is by way of a petition before

[43] 1870 MR 137.

[44] 1917 MR 63.

[45] 1955 MR 282.

[46] Articles 254-258, Mauritian Civil Code.

[47] (1984) MR 141.

[48] Even if the children are not minors, the Supreme Court may grant alimony if they are in need, as held in *Jagatsing v Jagatsingh* 1984 MR 141.

a Judge in Chambers according to the provisions of the Divorce and Judicial Separation Act 1981.

Jurisdiction of Mauritian courts in divorce cases

Under the Divorce and Judicial Separation Act 1981, the first step in divorce petitions begins with the Judge in Chambers, who will try to reconcile the parties. All relevant documents, petitions, and cross petitions are sent to the Master and Registrar of the Supreme Court, who will fix a date and time for the parties to the divorce petition to appear before the Judge in Chambers to hear the dispute. With the recent introduction of divorce by mutual consent, divorce petitions are on the rise in Mauritius.

Consequently, it is deplored that foreigners married to Mauritian nationals often leave the country when their visas have not been extended by the Home Office while their petitions or cross petition are pending before the Mauritian Supreme Court (Family Division). Alternatively, foreigners might be expelled from Mauritius on national security and public policy grounds. Despite the Deportation Act 1968 and the Extradition Act 1070, there is no existing law to protect the deportation and extradition of foreigners once the Home Office in Mauritius so decides, despite an injunction from a Judge in Chambers. The Mauritius Ombudsperson has witnessed cases where children are left with their mothers or their grandparents as their only custodian.

As per the relevant jurisdictions, all preliminary hearings are before a Judge in Chambers. He is fully empowered to reconcile the parties to a dispute, and/or to take temporary measures. Only the Supreme Court (Family Division) has inherent jurisdiction to pronounce a permanent decree, confirm, or set aside the decision which emanates from the Judge in Chambers. The Supreme Court (Family Division) has unlimited jurisdiction in all civil and criminal proceedings with considerable powers to give alimony to one party provided they are in need and to their children. Based on the best interests of the child, the Supreme Court can give custody of the child to one parent, with a right to visit to the other parent. Grandparents may be given custody of the child provided this is in the child's interests.

A District Magistrate, a Judge in Chambers, and the Supreme Court have jurisdiction in alimony cases. In divorce cases, alimony is an amount of money awarded to the spouse in need, provided they can prove on a balance of probabilities that they are in need, following what has been said in the case of *Ramsaha v Dwarka*.[49] However, no alimony will be awarded to any party responsible for the breakdown of the marriage, as explained in the case of *Leelodharry v Leelodhary*.[50]

RECOMMENDATIONS

Prohibiting addicts and social deviants from marrying

It would be desirable that the Mauritian legislature introduce a prenuptial certificate (*certificat prenuptial*), which exists in France, to ensure that any individual who wishes to marry is drug-free and in good health to avoid unnecessary breakdown of marriage among drug addicts in Mauritius.

Clarifying the position on Islamic personal law

In the absence of any Muslim personal law, bigamy is a criminal offence under section 257(1) of the Criminal Code.[51] Mauritians of the Muslim faith have expressed in Parliament that their personal, constitutional, and religious rights have been infringed, as section 11 of the Constitution provides that all individuals shall fully enjoy their freedom of conscience. In various cases, the Mauritian Supreme Court has maintained its position in the leading case of *Nayeck v Nayeck*.[52] In that case, the jurisdiction of the judge was in issue. The petitioner, party to a Muslim religious marriage, sought a divorce. It was argued that the judge had jurisdiction to grant the decree under Article 228-9

[49] 1976 MR 6.

[50] 1977 MR 77.

[51] Section 257(1), Mauritian Penal Code provides: "Any person who, being married, marries another person before the dissolution of the first marriage shall be punished by penal servitude for a term not exceeding ten years".

[52] 1987 MR 61.

of the Civil Code. The court held that Article 228-9 of the Mauritian Civil Code does not give a Judge in Chambers the power to decide on the dissolution of a marriage which has been celebrated according to Muslim customary rules.

Offering better protections against human rights violations

Perpetrators of human rights violations are left unpunished. In Mauritian law, there is no larceny between husband and wife under section 301(2) of the Criminal Code.[53] Rape and sodomy between husband and wife are not offences, although there have been regular complaints of rape and sodomy leading to the breakdown and dissolution of the marriage. The Mauritian legislature should introduce relevant penalties for rape and sodomy within marriage and larceny among spouses to eradicate gender-based violence. However, these issues remain the subject of vigorous debate in the Mauritian Parliament.

Making the law more understandable

Creole, a French *patois*, is a national language. It is important to have an English version of the Mauritian Civil Code, which was drafted in French, as pleadings are mainly in English. There is demand for the Civil Code to be translated into Creole, the local language on the island, so that everybody may have access to it.

Making courts more accessible

Only the Supreme Court (Family Division) may hear divorce cases and pronounce a permanent divorce; this has resulted in a heavy caseload. This function should be decentralized to allow inferior courts to enjoy similar jurisdiction, remove divorce bottlenecks, and expedite all family issues.

53 Section 301(2), Mauritian Penal Code, provides: "The abstraction of property by the husband to the prejudice of the wife, or by the wife to the prejudice of the husband, shall not give rise to a prosecution".

CONCLUSION

The Mauritius legal system is influenced by two major western legal systems, the French and English. The substantive law on marriage in Mauritius is based on French law, but the procedure governing matrimonial matters is influenced by English law. The form of marriage recognized by Mauritian law is the civil marriage. However, the law does not adequately protect spouses from acts of larceny, sodomy, or rape committed by the other spouse. Islamic law is not provided for.

The substantive law is not easily accessible because it has not been translated into the *lingua franca* of Mauritius: Creole. The substantive marital laws should be translated into the most-widely spoken and understood language of the State so that citizens can ascertain the law and align their lives accordingly. It is recommended that the law be amended to protect spouses against gender-based violence and to recognize Islamic law.

Côte d'Ivoire

Chapter Fourteen
A Look at Marriage in Ivorian Law

> (...) that we must be sober about novelty in matters of legislation, because if it is possible, in a new institution, to calculate the advantages that theory offers us, it is not possible to know all the disadvantages that practice alone can discover; that we must leave the good, if we are doubtful about the best; that in correcting an abuse, we must still see the dangers of the correction itself, that it would be absurd to indulge in absolute ideas of perfection, in things that are only susceptible to relative goodness; that instead of changing laws, it is almost always more useful to present citizens with new reasons to love them.[1]

In June 2019, Côte d'Ivoire adopted a new law on marriage. From the outset, and to remove any ambiguity in the forms of marriage that are legally valid in Ivorian law, it should be noted that, under Article 14 of the Ivorian law on marriage, "only marriages celebrated by a civil registrar have legal effect". This means that marriages celebrated in a religious form or those celebrated according to customary rules have no legal validity in Côte d'Ivoire. This situation leads, in fact, to spouses wishing to comply with the customary, religious and civil requirements of marriage to indulge in what may be called a matrimonial *triathlon,* "marrying three times"[2], in most cases.

It is important to understand the historical evolution of Ivorian personal and family law from the colonial period. Côte d'Ivoire has more than sixty dialects or ethnic groups whose customs, cultures, institutions, or social structures differ, depending on the region of the country. During the

[1] Jean-Etienne-Marie de Portalis, *Discourses, Reports and Unpublished Works on the Civil Code* (1844), p. 12.

[2] Abbé Landry Gbaka-Brede, "Why Do We Get Married Three Times?", *Revue Actualités Juridiques*, LXX (2011).

colonial era, the colonial administration, for various reasons, respected all customs and traditions. Most of the population was governed by customary law; a minority was governed by French civil statutes. Cases concerning personal law were adjudicated before the customary courts, and judgments were rendered according to customary law.

When Côte d'Ivoire gained independence as a State, it adopted a constitution, established institutions, and enacted a law on persons and the family. First, with regard to the status of persons, the Ivorian legislature was faced with a delicate situation: the customs of the various communities were too different to be unified. Early efforts at codification were in vain. Maintaining these customs was incompatible with the unity of the country and its modernization plans. Some customs ran counter to the principles of equality and non-discrimination affirmed by the Constitution.

Second, the introduction of the market economy, especially in agriculture, introduced the notion of personal profit, traditionally unknown at custom. Individual appropriation of land, in particular, was a break from the old traditional order where land belonged to the community. Thus, the fragmentation of the old lineage society began with agricultural production. Finally, the process of economic development in Côte d'Ivoire was more advanced than elsewhere in West Africa. This was the context in which Côte d'Ivoire found itself when it gained independence on 7 August 1960.

In the interregnum between independence and the adoption of laws on the family, the laws applicable from 1960 to 1964 were solely French texts which exemplified "the principle of the speciality of legislation".[3] This principle meant that laws and regulations enacted for the French metropolis were not automatically applicable to the colonies unless Ivorian legislature so provided. As a result, the 1960 Ivorian Constitution stated in Article 76 that "the legislation currently in force in Côte d'Ivoire remains applicable, except for the intervention of new texts, insofar as it is not contrary to the present Constitution".

[3] Pierre-François Gonidec, *Overseas Law* (1959).

In 1964, Côte d'Ivoire adopted a unified civil law based on the French Civil Code. The laws that comprised the unified civil law dealt closely with the organization of the family. These ten or so constitutive laws were adopted by the National Assembly on 7 October 1964. Adopting these laws was particularly revolutionary because this led to the abandonment of almost all customary law. The then President, Félix Houphouët-Boigny (1905-1993), on the occasion of the sixth anniversary of Côte d'Ivoire's independence in August 1966, gave the following reasons for the reforms:

> When it appeared to us that the survival of certain traditions constituted an obstacle or a limitation to the harmonious development of our country, we did not hesitate to make the necessary changes. Thus, after a long campaign of explanation undertaken by our activists and our political and administrative leaders to the populations concerned, essential texts have been produced. A renovated Civil Code enshrines the abolition of polygamy and reforms the dowry; a modern civil registry is in place.[4]

In so doing, the Ivorian State claimed to be the only one with authority to confer legitimacy on marital relationships.[5]

The law relating to marriage (*Law No. 64-375 of 7th October 1964, relating to marriage*) gave an essential place to the legal status of women in the family institution. Indeed, for those familiar with the matrimonial customs in the different regions of Côte d'Ivoire, the marriage instituted by the Ivorian law in 1964 appeared to contradict the customs of most inhabitants, who are generally polygamous, both in rural and urban areas. Describing the relationship between polygamy and the sustenance of the family, one author indicates that:

> Through polygamy, the man seeks helpers for his daily work... the man marries several wives in the

[4] Félix Houphouet-Boigny, *Anthology of Speeches 1946-1978* (1978), pp. 742-743. Quoted by Chantal Vlei-Yoroba, "Family Law and Family Realities: The Case of Côte d'Ivoire Since Independence", *Open Edition Journals* (1997) (available online).

[5] Anne-Marie Hortense Assi-Esso, *Civil Law, The Family* (2008), p. 5.

> hope of having many children... The more wives there are, the less tiring the work in the fields is... It is the performance of the work in the fields that mainly imposes polygamy.[6]

The fact, however, remains that in the big cities, the possession of material goods most often overrides a man's aspiration to have several wives.

Thus, by opting for monogamy in 1964, Côte d'Ivoire intended to ensure the equality of sexes enshrined in its Constitution. It consciously broke away from the sometimes immemorial customs of the populace. However, by ruling out polygamy, the legislature intended to enhance women's status:

> [in 1964], the Ivorian legislature wanted the young girl to be able to choose for herself, to have a certain maturity to ensure her choice and above all to prevent the situation where a girl who had begun her studies would be forced to interrupt it. [...]On the other hand, in order not to raise the age of marriage of young men excessively, it was necessary to prevent older men from taking several wives: this is what article 2 allows. It is quite clear that this article is the summit and the crucial point of the whole edifice of laws elaborated by the Ivorian legislature.[7]

In essence, the 1964 law sought to implement the break from the lineage-based marriage in which the levirate system predominated in various local customs in Côte d'Ivoire. Since then, the basic family unit has been constituted by monogamous marriages.

The effects of monogamous marriages are numerous. This marriage creates alegitimate family, and the spouses are obliged to live together, owing each other fidelity, help and assistance.[8] However, the legislature did not want spouses to cease assisting their parents. Thus, under Article

[6] Henri Raulin, *The Law of Persons and the Family in Ivory Coast* (1989), p. 230.

[7] Ibid., p. 227.

[8] Article 51, Law No. 64-381 of 7 October 1964 on marriage.

55 of the 1964 law, spouses owe maintenance to their parents and other needy ascendants. The husband is the head of the family and must exercise this function in the interests of the children and household. The wife is required under Article 58 to help the husband ensure the family's moral direction, provide for its maintenance, raise the children, and prepare for their establishment. The choice of family residence belongs to the husband; the wife is obliged to live with him, and he is obliged to receive her.[9]

Two decades later, the family model introduced by the 1964 law was reformed by Law No. 83-800 of 2 August 1983, relating to marriage. The reforms were not substantial insofar as they did not disrupt the paradigm of monogamous marriage accepted in 1964. The 1983 reforms were important for the legal status of women because they reinforced their autonomy within the household. Moreover, the 1983 law revolutionized the financial effects of marriage by making it possible for each spouse to hold property separately. Thus, contrary to the past, and in relation to the effects of marriage, each spouse could open any bank account in their name without the consent of the other. The spouse who deposits the funds is deemed to have control over such. Moreover, a wife may exercise a profession separate from her husband, unless it is judicially established that the profession is contrary to the family's interests.[10] Also, unlike in the past, spouses may dispose of their earnings freely after paying marital expenses.[11]

By a law of 2013, the marriage law was revised to eliminate discrimination between spouses. The reference to the husband as "head of the family" was removed from the law because the household was supposed to be managed "jointly" by the spouses. The latest legislative marriage reforms took place in 2019, giving rise to Law No. 2019-570 of 26 June 2019. The explanatory memorandum accompanying this law is quoted extensively to show the purpose of the Ivorian marriage laws.

[9] Article 60, ibid.

[10] Article 67, ibid., as amended by Law No. 64-375 of 2 August 1960.

[11] Article 68, ibid., as amended by Law No. 64-375 of 2 August 1960.

As soon as it gained independence, Côte d'Ivoire adopted a law to govern matrimonial relations established by persons on its soil. This law has been revised twice: first by law No. 83-800 of 2nd August 1983, then by law No. 33 of 25th January 2013. The main effect of these various amendments was to translate into action the principles of non-discrimination and equality of rights and responsibilities of spouses in marriage, principles supported by the international conventions ratified by Côte d'Ivoire and taken up by the constitution.

However, these various reforms of the law relating to marriage have not succeeded in completely eliminating inequalities between men and women in marriage and in ensuring the full protection of the family, contrary to the principles proclaimed by the Constitution of 8th November 2016. It is therefore to balance and improve the relationship between spouses that the Government has undertaken a more comprehensive reform of the marriage law, which is part of the reform of the judicial system.

This revision, which led to the drafting of the present bill on marriage, enshrines the innovations in form and substance of the current system. In terms of form, the bill contains 104 articles. In addition, this text reformulates certain provisions to simplify their understanding. These include Articles 2, 14 and 25 of the current law relating respectively to the conditions required to enter into marriage, oppositions to marriage and the celebration of marriage. In terms of substance, the major innovations of the draft law relate to:

1. the strengthening of equality between men and women in marriage;

2. the effective consideration of the best interests of the family;

3. strengthening the protection of public order.

With regard to strengthening the equality of men and women in the matrimonial bond, marriage is defined as the union of a man and a woman (Article 1 of the bill). In addition, the marriageable age is set at eighteen years and is the same for men and women (Article 2 of the bill). In other words, any marriage of a minor is prohibited. To reinforce this prohibition, the age exemption for men and women for marriage is also abolished.

Equality between men and women has been reinforced with regard to the property effects of marriage. Indeed, the bill provides for the joint management of household property, without distinguishing between areas reserved for the administration of a particular spouse (Article 82 paragraph 1 of the bill). Even if, as a general rule, each spouse commits the other by his or her acts of household administration, the authorization of the other is nevertheless required for the performance of certain important acts (Articles 53, 82 paragraph 2 of the draft law). The spouses may also jointly regulate the effects of their union by notarial agreement (Article 58 of the draft law) (...)'.

Various international human rights conventions influence national legislation, including marriage-related ones, sometimes upsetting certain traditional legal paradigms. Integrating these international conventions into the internal legal order often leads to amending national legislation to ensure harmonization with international instruments.

The 2019 marriage reforms took place in an international context in which the political and legal debate on the notion of family, both in the so-called Northern and Southern countries, was largely dominated by two inconsistent conceptions of the family. The first is the notion of family as the "basic unit of society", requiring the State to establish an archetypal family, which it promotes and protects. The second and more liberal conception postulates that the State should legitimize other forms of family life, whatever they may be, including de facto family ties.[12]

12 Eva Maria Belser and Andrea Egbuna-Joss, "Protection and Promotion of the

As a result, the concept of family appears to be a reality with a "variable content", in view of the many sociological changes in the world. The concept of family may first refer to the nuclear family composed of parents and their children. The traditional African legal conception of the family refers to the grouping that brings together all those descended from a common ancestor (lineage) or mythical ancestor (clan or tribe).[13] It may also refer to single-parent families or reconstituted families.[14] Finally, the spotlight on same-sex unions compounds the uncertainty of the meaning of the word "family".

Under Ivorian family law, certain expressions of marriage are only understood as "free unions" or de facto marriages and are left to court discretion in the event of litigation. A de jure marriage refers exclusively to a union celebrated by the civil registrar.

DE FACTO MARRIAGE IN CÔTE D'IVOIRE

The independence of Côte d'Ivoire in 1960 gave rise to intense legislative activity, the most striking being the abrogation in 1964 of almost all customary rules relating to marriage[15]. This was the product of the conscious will of the national leaders to build Ivorian society on a renewed family basis. This conception of marriage law has not disappeared with the 2019 reform, insofar as certain expressions of marriage continue to be understood as mere de facto unions.

Engagement

The Ivorian legislature has not defined the term "engagement". Nevertheless, an allusion to "engagement" is found in Article 24-2 of the 2019 law on filiation, referring to engagement as a case in which a person may initiate an action to seek paternity. Understanding engagement as a

Family: The Influence of Human Rights and Fundamental Freedoms on Family Law", CSDH, (2014), p. 2 (available online).

13 Assi-Esso, note 5 above, p. 5.

14 Judith Rochfield, *The Main Notions of Private Law* (2011), p. 110.

15 Marc Dumetz, *Marriage Law in Côte d'Ivoire* (1975), p. III.

legal fact is well established in Ivorian law;it is not a contract but a legal fact that does not give rise to an obligation to enter into marriage.[16] This is a doctrinal position that confirms the principle of freedom of marriage.

Usually, an engagement does not pose problems when it leads to marriage. However, when the engagement breaks down problems arise, particularly with regard to the fate of gifts given or the damage suffered in the event of improper termination. In principle, the engagement can be broken off freely by the engaged couples without incurring any liability towards each other. However, the rule is not absolute: an improper termination may give rise to the payment of damages based on tortious liability. Thus, according to Ivorian case law, breaking off an engagement is justified when the reason given is serious. This is the case for the fiancée, who breaks off the engagement because she suffers physical abuse from her fiancé due to her inability to procreate. She does not commit a fault that could give rise to compensation.[17] The fact remains that breaking off the engagement may be improper. For example, jilting the other party hours before a marriage ceremony could lead to material and moral loss. Such conduct may ground an action for damages.

With regard to the fate of gifts, Ivorian jurisprudence distinguishes between gifts of value and gifts of use. While the former must be returned,[18] the latter need not be if the parties do not marry. It is generally accepted that social morality demands the return of the engagement ring if the engagement ends by mutual disagreement, or by the fault of the fiancée, or death. Conversely, the abandoned fiancée who has done nothing wrong may keep the ring; she may also keep it if the fiancé dies'.[19] In practice, however, the Ivorian courts often declare as void actions for improper

16 Assi-Esso, note 5 above, p. 45; Mathurin Kouakou Brou, *Civil Law, Persons -The Family* (2021), p. 292.

17 See Tribunal de Première Instance de Daloa, Judgement No. 09 of 4 February 2005.

18 Abidjan Court of Appeal, judgment of 16 June 1972.

19 Brou, note 16 above, p. 298.

termination because such actions are "based on the termination of a cohabitation arrangement, contrary to the established social order".[20]

In any event, engagement and cohabitation are often inextricably linked with custom, and the courts sometimes have to disentangle the different systems of law involved in a dispute. This decision of the Abidjan Court of Appeal gives an illustration:

> ... But,considering that the civil laws of October 1964 have abolished customs concerning civil status, that no legal effect can be given to the ceremony of 'attachment of colas', the first judge rightly decided that F. having not entered into a regular marriage with D., was free to break off what he 'rightly' called the cohabitation and which D. called 'an engagement'. Considering that the first judge was also right to decide that the expenses incurred by D. for his "fiancée", from whom, moreover, he had a child, could not give rise to reimbursement, even though she had lived with him for two years (....).[21]

Cohabitation

The term "concubinage" comes from the Latin *cum cubare,* which means sleeping with. It is a free union in the sense of a union formed without formality. Cohabitation is a de facto union whose conditions of formation or effects are not legally organized. Although cohabitation has no recognized legal value, it is a de facto union that is difficult to ignore. Judges faced with the difficulties raised by such de facto unions are therefore led to consider certain issues arising from cohabitation. These include the question of liability for the breakdown of the cohabitation or issues of custody and maintenance of children.

Certainly, since the freedom to consent to marriage must be preserved, the non-performance of a promise to marry

[20] Supreme Court, Invalidity Chamber, Judgment no. 10 of 4 April 1969 (RID 1970), p. 30.

[21] Court of Appeal of Abidjan, Hearing of 17 April 1970.

cannot be legally sanctioned. However, the termination of cohabitation may probably be accompanied by fault, including fraudulent seduction, giving rise to a right to compensation. One author observes:

> Such seduction is constituted when a promise of marriage, prior or subsequent to the cohabitation, is not respected. The fault, like the damage, results from the break-up of the cohabitation which coincides simultaneously with the break-up of the promise. It is rather curious to note that the combined breach of the promise to marry and the cohabitation is the cause whereas neither the breach of the promise alone, nor that of cohabitation alone constitutes a fault.[22]

Ivorian case law tends to avoid conflating the effects of marriage with those of concubinage, so judges sometimes refuse to compensate the concubine in the absence of proof of the other party's fault in the breakdown of the concubinage. Nevertheless, the case law seems to favor the concubine, particularly in being able to claim certain indemnities. In one case: Mrs. W. had effectively lived as a cohabitant with the deceased and had participated in the acquisition of common property in the de facto household. The court held that although the relationship was not regularly formalized before a civil registrar, the fact remained that de facto community confers rights on the claimant.[23]

Furthermore, the case law seems to be more favorable to the concubine in recognizing her right to oppose the sale of a property carried out without her consent and knowledge, when the disputed property is the fruit of the joint efforts of the two. The courts have explained in one case that:

> (...) Whereas it is not disputed that Mr Harold and N. Julienne have, for fifteen years, lived in a notorious cohabitation from which two children were born; that the disputed villa was acquired during this common life; whereas Mrs N. Julienne maintains

22 Henri Temple, "Civil Law, Personal Law and Family Law", *Ivorian Law Review*, L, no. 1- 4 (1982-1983).

23 Tribunal de Première Instance de Daloa, Judgment No. 72 of 26 January 1982. Dame W v X, Y, Z, p. 47.

> that the acquisition, refurbishment and modification of the disputed building were made possible by her contribution of money from her commercial activities; whereas this assertion is not in any way contested; whereas the cohabitants necessarily behaved as partners, without even always being fully aware of it, each making at least one contribution in kind; whereas this is sufficient to recognize the existence of the de facto partnership created between Mr. Harold and Mrs. N. Julienne, and the fact that they had a common interest in the property. This is sufficient to recognize the existence of the de facto partnership created between Mr Harold and Mrs N. Julienne, and consequently, of a right of ownership of the latter over the disputed property and justifying the annulment of the sale of the said property, which was carried out without her knowledge and consent.[24]

The field of application of the concept of de facto partnership remains so broad that "it can be considered a panacea, given the disparate illustrations of this concept. A privileged field of choice where the concept flourishes is the field of family".[25] However, in terms of its form, concubinage does not necessarily follow all the contours of customary marriage.

Customary marriages

A customary marriage is a union celebrated in accordance with customary law. Because of the diversity in local customs, it is difficult to describe the practical modalities for concluding such unions. In Côte d'Ivoire, the validity of customary marriages before 1964 (when the first national civil laws were adopted) was subject to conditional civil recognition. Their formal validity was made dependent on compliance with the formalities of marriages contracted at

[24] Supreme Court, Judicial Chamber, Judgment No. 277/2000 of 4 May 2000, in *Actualités Juridiques*, XXII (2022).

[25] Temple, note 22 above, p. 46.

the civil registry or judicial recognition of such marriages.[26] With regard to their substantive validity, marriages celebrated according to custom had to be assessed according to the custom of the spouses in force at the time of the celebration.[27] From 1976 onwards the marriages which failed to comply with the said formalities for contracting marriages at the civil registry, or were not recognized by the courts, were characterized by case law as concubinage.[28] Post-1964 customary marriages did not benefit from this conditional recognition as did marriages celebrated according to tradition before 1964. This means that customary marriages celebrated after 1964 are considered simple concubinage and do not have the same effects as marriage in civil form.

Among the customary marriage arrangements, the dowry appeared impossible to maintain in the context of the 1964 legislative reform. However, it is always difficult to regulate by authority[29] traditional or modern institutions that affect people so closely. The example of the dowry,30 whose "force of inertia" remains considerable in traditional and modern society, bears witness to this. [31]

In many African societies, a dowry generally consists of benefits from a young man or his family to the person who has authority over the prospective spouse. Two fundamental differences separate the conception of the dowry in Africa from those of certain European societies. First, in Europe, the dowry is given by the parents and friends of the bride, whereas in Africa, it is given by the young man or his family. As for the beneficiaries of the dowry, it is not the future spouses who benefit from it in Africa, but only the future wife's family. Under these conditions, as one author points out, "a European mind is inclined to believe that the

[26] Article 10, Law No. 64-381 of 7 October 1964 on marriage.

[27] Ibid.

[28] Assi-Esso, note 5 above, p. 199.

[29] Emilienne Abitbol, "The Conjugal Family and the New Marriage Law in Côte d'Ivoire", *Penant*, DCCXII (1966), p. 305. Quoted by Vlei-Yoroba, note 4 above, p. 5.

[30] Dumetz, note 15 above, p. 69.

[31] Ibid., p. 25.

dowry [in Africa] is in reality only a purchase price for the young girl".[32] Indeed, seen from the outside, the dowry is rather the source of alienation[33] of the woman, an attack on her freedom.[34] In addition, there are dowry-related forms of abuse.[35] Nevertheless, in reality, the traditional dowry has a "probationary" character in addition to unquestionably providing stability to the traditional marriage:

> When the marriage is broken by the fault of the wife, her family must return the dowry to the husband's family. This will have the consequence that the woman's family will temper any eagerness she may have to leave her husband. […] On the contrary, if the divorce is pronounced at the request of the wife fora serious fault on the part of the husband, he will not be able to claim the restitution of the dowry.[36]

Several combined factors,[37] including the emergence of women's social and political role, led to the prohibition of the dowry. The 1964 law on marriage stipulated a term of imprisonment for persons who violated the dowry prohibition.

32 Ibid., p. 69.

33 Ibid., p. 71.

34 At the Brazzaville Conference, it was decided that "if the family of the Black man represents an element of stability in the social order, which it would be imprudent to undermine, it seems possible or desirable, however, to introduce from now on the notion of freedom of marriage, which is, strictly speaking, the freedom of the woman". Ibid., p. 24.

35 It must be admitted that under the influence of social and economic changes following colonization, the traditional nature of this institution will be altered.

36 Dumetz, note 15 above, pp. 71-72.

37 Noel Gbaguidi, *Conference on Family Law in Black Africa at the Beginning of the 21st Century: West African Trends* (2009) Unpublished: "[...] customary rights have been criticised for being an obstacle to the development of Africa. Roland Mousnier, in his book "l'histoire des civilisations" argued that 'the reasons for the advance of European man over all others lies in his conception of the family, based on the liberation of the individual from the groups, of the families from the communities of the village, from the constraints exerted by the animist tribe (...)". These elements that Mousnier criticizes are precisely the African conception of the family. Moreover, some great African jurists, such as Keba M'baye, have even affirmed that the African conception of the family is the cause of its economic and technological backwardness.

But given the ineffectiveness of the dowry prohibition, this issue was not considered by the 2019 marriage law reform. While dowry and polygamous unions are not unknown to customary law, the fact remains that, like dowry, polygamy is rejected by Ivorian civil law.

Polygamous unions

Originally, polygamous marriages were, by nature, customary marriages. In this regard, polygamy is a customary practice that allows an individual to marry and live with more than one spouse. Unlike monogamy, polygamy takes two forms: polygyny and polyandry. Polygyny is the union of a man with several women, and polyandry is the union of a woman with several men. Polyandry is an unknown institution under Ivorian customs. Various reasons are usually advanced in support of polygamy.

A natural argument is usually put forward. In fact, in many ethnic groups, it is considered that a man should no longer have sexual relations with his wife as soon as she becomes pregnant, until the end of the breastfeeding period, which may continue for two years after birth. For example, among certain peoples in Côte d'Ivoire, it is believed that sexual relations with a pregnant or breastfeeding woman are harmful to the child's health. At other times, an economic argument is made. In the traditional economy, which was essentially agrarian, the main source of wealth was land, and its development was essential. In most cases, women and children were actively involved in the exploitation of the farm. More women meant more children cultivating a larger area of land. From this point of view, wealth seemed dependent on the number of women available to a man. A recent study sheds light on the proliferation of polygamous unions.

> The perpetuation of this ancestral custom feeds into and affects the organization of African societies in general,and marriage relationships are not immune to its influence. From an early age, boys are prepared to exercise a profession in order to bring income to their families. In contrast, girls are educated to marry. As a result, women are not put in a position to be

> active. However, the financialautonomy that would result from this would be a condition for true marital freedom. [...] Indeed, when she is not working, her priority is to marry, even to a polygamous man, if he can provide for her primary needs. Moreover, the patriarchal conception of resource appropriation in African societies does not allow women who have reached puberty to survive on their own. Women opting to enter into polygamous unions can therefore be explained by the woman's concern to avoid marginalization, as it is better for her to be the wife of a polygamist than to be single. These social constraints are imposed on the woman seeking a first marriage, as much as on thewoman wishing to remarry. Thus, limiting access to resources is at the heart of the problem.[38]

Nevertheless, the fact remains that polygamy favors men and is widely tolerated in many African States. For its part, the Ivorian State opted for monogamous marriages, as opposed to polygamous marriages, in the 1964 and 1983 laws. This situation has been maintained with the 2019 reform.

But in practice, "the prohibition of polygamy is in most cases circumvented by maintaining one or more mistresses outside the marital home".[39] In other cases, the violation of the prohibition is direct. In the absence of any mention in the husband's civil status record of the existence of a first marriage, he enters into one or more legal unions, taking care to change the place of celebration. But generally, these polygamous unions only come to light after the husband's death when several widows appear, each with an authentic marriage certificate. In other cases, the person concerned enters into a single legal union and one or more customary unions; the legal wife and the "customary wives" may all live in the matrimonial home.[40] This circumvention of

[38] Aïssata Dabo, "The Equality of Men and Women in Marriage in French-speaking Black Africa. Comparative Study of the Rights of Benin, Burkina-Faso and Mali", *U-Bordeaux* (2017), p. 284.

[39] Raulin, note 6 above, p. 235.

[40] Assi-Esso, note 5 above, p. 45.

legislative provisions, while highlighting the problem of the appropriate methods of regulating family realities, shows that urbanization, and legislative action have not overcome polygamy. Nonetheless, the positive law must be capable of evolving along with emerging ways of life. For, if the law must find its inspiration in the context to which it is to be applied, "it does not imply that it must coincide with this context at the time it is enacted, for then, as evolution is continuous, it would quickly become outdated. It must, therefore, necessarily anticipate and be an important driving force in the evolution".[41]

What about the lack of civil recognition of monogamous religious marriage in Ivorian law?

Monogamous religious marriage

A religious marriage is a marriage celebrated by a religious authority (priest, imam, pastor). Just as civil marriages, religious marriages follow a ritual, after which a marriage certificate is issued. In some cases, a family record book[42] is issued to the spouses as in the civil ceremony. Thus, the formalities for celebrating a civil marriage, as defined by the legal provisions, are essentially the same as those for celebrating a religious marriage. However, Ivorian civil law does not recognize a religious marriage as having the same legal value as a civil marriage.

Prior to the 2019 reform, despite its secular nature, the Ivorian State could be said not to have totally ignored religious marriages, even if it preferred civil marriages. This preference resulted in the chronological order of celebrating the two marriages: the civil marriage had to be celebrated before the religious marriage. This solution was provided by Article 20 of the marriage law of 1964, which prohibited ministers of religion from performing religious ceremonies unless the future spouses had a certificate from the civil celebration. The minister of religion had to demand the

[41] Extract from the explanatory memorandum of the 1964 law on marriage.

[42] The "family record book" is a small notebook that the wedding celebrant gives to the newlyweds after the exchange of their consent has taken place. It usually contains various information about marital status, and the like.

certificate before proceeding with the religious celebration. The lack of legal value of religious marriage meant that the religious union had only spiritual value for the spouses. However, the marriage law no longer refers to ministers of religion in the celebration of marriage, as if to express a certain adherence of the legislature to the radical distinction between the spiritual and temporal orders.

Such an excessively watertight separation between the State and religion in the regulation of monogamous religious marriages seems to have the sole interest of increasing the financial burdens of citizens who wish to "render to Caesar what is Caesar's and to God what is God's". However, in this case, could the State not draw inspiration from the Church by facilitating the marriage celebration of citizens claiming to be of the "two Cities"[43]? Indeed, as one author observes:

> The Church recognizes the validity of natural marriage. Therefore, when people who have contracted a marriage (customary or civil) become faithful through the reception of baptism, they no longer marry 'in the Church'; and this for the simple reason that they are already married. In this case, these newly baptized brides receive a nuptial blessing which, as the expression itself indicates, presupposes the prior existence of a matrimonial bond.[44]

In any case, Ivorian civil family law is clear that a religious marriage celebrated in Côted'Ivoire, even if monogamous, has no legal effect. There is a sense of the French revolutionary law of 20 September 1792, which instituted civil marriages in a republican regime. This law then comprised part of the 1804 French Civil Code and was finally received by the former French colonies, including Côte d'Ivoire, through various legal mechanisms. However, the original context of this law, which originated in the French Revolution, does not reflect the contemporary relationship between Church and State in Côte d'Ivoire, or, more generally, between religion and State. There is some common ground between

[43] This metaphor refers to the present temporal world, on one hand, and the spiritual world religious people believe they will join in the afterlife.

[44] Gbaka-Brede, note 2 above, p. 19.

monogamous religious marriages and civil marriages so that they can co-exist.

DE JURE MARRIAGE IN CÔTE D'IVOIRE

The institution of marriage in Côte d'Ivoire is the basis of the family as a basic unit of society.[45] To conduct a holistic discussion of the formation of the matrimonial bond, the substantive conditions for the formation of marriage, the formal conditions for the formation of marriage, the conditions for the nullity of marriage, and the conditions for the dissolution of marriage will be examined.

Basic conditions for formation of marriage

The examination of these conditions relates to the heterosexuality of the future spouses, the matrimonial age of the future spouses, the personal consent of the future spouses, the observance of the waiting period in the event of a previous marriage, and impediments to marriage.

Heterosexuality of future spouses

There is no "marriage for all persons" in Ivorian law. If the Ivorian legislature had stated no legal definition of marriage on the occasion of the 1964 and 1983 marriage laws, it was certainly because it had seemed sufficient to limit itself to stating the purpose of marriage: "marriage creates the legitimate family".[46] However, with the reform of the law of marriage, in addition to the continuous affirmation of the purpose of marriage,[47] the Ivorian legislature brings a major innovation to the law of marriage, by affirming, in Article 1 of the said law, that "marriage is the union of a man and a woman celebrated before the civil registrar". In so doing, the heterosexuality of the spouses is unequivocally established as a necessary precondition for the existence of

[45] Gérard Neyrand, "Contemporary Conjugality, a New Way of Thinking about the Bond", *Open Edition Journals* (2016), p. 25 (available online).

[46] Article 50, Law No. 64-381 of 7 October 1964 on marriage.

[47] Article 44, Law No. 2019-570 of 26 June 2019 on marriage.

civil marriage in Ivorian law. Thus, while it is opposed[48] elsewhere, the exclusive character of the family archetype, which is based on the heterosexuality of the spouses, is, on the other hand, endorsed by the Ivorian State. It may be considered that the Ivorian legislature conceives of marriage as a natural institution[49] that "ensures the renewal of the social body".[50] The legislature sees marriage as the site of procreation, and for which reason it gives its blessing to heterosexual marriage. The refusal of Ivorian law to recognize non-heterosexual marriages attests to the relativity of law, particularly family law.[51] The family constitutes the basic cell of society, which requires the State's protection.

However, insofar as reactions tending to recognize the legal status of homosexual unions are echoed in various parts of the world, this raises questions about the Ivorian legal system. Let us assume, for example, that a homosexual couple, resident in Côte d'Ivoire, brings an action before the Ivorian courts for the dissolution of their union celebrated in a country that has legalized such unions. What decision will an Ivorian judge render? It must be considered that the attachment expressed by the Ivorian State to heterosexual marriage reflects this State's adherence to certain specific values, values which the State intends to safeguard and from which individual aspirations cannot derogate. A judge is most likely to hold the view that a public authority cannot take part in violating the legal order or the law that instituted it. Thus, he will take the position that the recognition of homosexual marriage is incompatible with Ivorian public policy and block the admissibility of the action insofar as it

[48] See in particular, speech presenting the bill to legalise same-sex marriages in France delivered by Christiane Taubira on 29 January 2013, in Wanda Mastor, et al., *The Speeches of Legal Culture* (2017), p. 665. It was afterwards that the right to same-sex marriage came into existence in France.

[49] "We are convinced that marriage, which existed before the establishment of Christianity, which preceded all positive law, and which derives from the very constitution of our being, is neither a civil nor a religious act, but a natural act which has attracted the attention of legislators, and which religion has sanctified (...)". Jean Etienne Marie Portalis, "Preliminary Speech on the Draft Civil Code, 1er Pluviôse an IX", in Mastor, note 49 above.

[50] Gbaguidi, note 37 above.

[51] Jean-Louis Bergel, *General Theory of Law* (2012), p. 150.

would undermine the values of the forum. From this point of view, the judge's reaction would then have the effect of paralyzing the foreign law under which the same-sex union received its legal recognition.

In short, from the standpoint of Ivorian positive law, the legislature did not intend the civil law of marriage to conform to dominant or competing social practices. Such a law reveals that the Ivorian State seems to place a premium on family matters such as the love between spouses, natural procreation, and the interests of children and family. From this point of view, Ivorian family law seems to admit that: "the duration and good order of general society depend essentially on the stability of families, which are the first of all societies, the seed and foundation of empires".[52]

Matrimonial age of future spouses

The non-existence of "marriage for all persons" under Ivorian law is also explained by the requirement of a minimum marital age. According to Article 2 of the law on marriage, the minimum age of marriage is eighteen years for men and women. This means there is no longer an age distinction as in the past when the legal minimum age for marriage was twenty-one for men and eighteen for women. The matrimonial age or puberty, therefore, presumes the physiological aptitude for marriage. Marriage of minors is prohibited. It follows that the dispensation given by the public prosecutor, who previously could allow minors to marry, has ended.[53]

Personal consent of the future spouses

There can be no marriage without the consent of the future spouses. Article 5 of the law reaffirms the requirement of the future spouses' personal consent. While this provision would seem to exclude the consent of the parents, the situation is different in practice, where the influence exercised by the parents usually remains preponderant:

[52] Portalis, note 49 above, p. 695.

[53] Brou, note 16 above, p. 347.

> Before the celebration of the marriage, the family of the future husband meets with the family of the future wife to officially propose the marriage. Thereafter, the future husband's family, despite the legal prohibition, proceeds, in most cases, to pay the dowry to the future wife's family. The dowry payment marks the agreement of both families to the marriage. The intervention of the families is still evident during the preparation of the civil and religious marriage ceremonies. During these meetings, the family members of the future spouses, if they have not done so beforehand, express their approval or disapproval of the planned union. While their disagreement may not affect the celebration of the marriage, it definitely impacts the duration of the marriage.[54]

As for the characteristics of consent, it should be noted that "consent is not valid if it was extorted by violence or if it was given only as a result of a mistake as to the physical or civil identity of the person. Consent is also invalid if before the marriage, the person who gave it was unaware of the physical incapacity of the other party to consummate the marriage or their inability to procreate".[55]

Observance of waiting period after dissolution of previous marriage

A widow, a divorced woman, or a woman whose marriage has been annulled by the courts must wait for three hundred days from the dissolution or annulment of the marriage before getting married. It is enshrined in Article 6 of the revised law: "the woman may not remarry until the expiry of the waiting period of three hundred (300) days from the dissolution of the previous marriage (...)".

The waiting period was formerly invoked for reasons of convenience.[56] The purpose was to give the widow time to mourn her husband. This argument is not convincing, since

[54] Assi-Esso, note 5 above, p. 33.

[55] Brou, note 16 above, p. 324.

[56] Ibid.

it is unclear why the husband is exempted from mourning his wife, nor why the period is also required of a divorced woman or a woman whose marriage has been annuled. Therefore, the real reason for the institution of the waiting period is to avoid confusion about the paternity of a child born shortly after the dissolution of the first marriage and after the conclusion of the second marriage[57]. Such a child is covered by the presumption of paternity, meaning that the ex-husband is presumed to be the father of a child born within three hundred days of the dissolution of the marriage.[58]

However, if the woman gives birth within this period, it is no longer necessary to respectthe waiting period; she can immediately remarry, if she so wishes. In any case, if it is medically established that she has not cohabited with her previous husband for three hundred days, the waiting period may be shortened by the President of the court of the woman's domicile or residence, under Article 6 of the 2019 law relating to marriage. However, the decision of the court is subject to appeal.

Prohibitions on marriage

In addition to the waiting period, which temporarily prevents marriage, there are two facts that may constitute definitive prohibitions on marriage. The first is the existence of a previous marriage that has not been dissolved (the offence of bigamy), and the second is kinship or alliance. Both moral and eugenic reasons justify the prohibition of incestuous unions. Thus, Article 7 of the revised law lists seven cases of incest. However, for some of these prohibitions, the law allows the public prosecutor, under Article 7 of the revised law, to "lift the prohibitions for serious reasons between relatives in the direct line and in the collateral line to the degree of brother-in-law and sister-in-law, when the person who created the alliance is deceased". However, as one author explains,

[57] Ibid.

[58] Ibid.

> The result is that, as in the past, impediments do not have the same character. Indeed, there are cases of absolute impediment and cases of relative impediment:
>
> In the first case of absolute impediment, the impediment cannot be lifted by any dispensation. This is the case for marriages between ascendants and descendants and between brothers and sisters. Any marriage celebrated between these persons is nulland void. Thus, the prohibition applies to the marriage of a man with the daughter of his consanguineous sister, since the law does not distinguish according to whetherthe uncle and the niece are the offspring of one or both of the common progenitor (...).
>
> As for the second case of relative impediment, a dispensation may be granted by the public prosecutor on serious grounds (under French law, the President of theRepublic is competent to do so - Article 164 of the Civil Code). Thus, dispensationsmay be granted between relatives in the direct line when the person who created the alliance is deceased, between uncle and niece, aunt and nephew and between relatives in the degree of brother-in-law and sister-in-law, when the person who created the alliance is deceased (Article 7 paragraph 2).[59]

Formal requirements for formation of marriage

These conditions are not only related to the actual celebration on the day of the wedding, but also include the formalities before the wedding.

Pre-marriage formalities

Essentially, these formalities enable the civil registrar to ensure that future spouses meet the conditions required by law to get married. They consist of compiling the marriage file and submitting it to the civil registrar. Before the

[59] Brou, note 16 above, p. 324.

celebration of the marriage, each future spouse must hand in the following documents to the civil registrar:[60]

- A birth certificate or a supplementary judgment dated less than three months ago, or failing that, a deed of notoriety in accordance with the provisions relating to civil status;
- A certificate of residence in the place where the marriage is to be celebrated. In addition to these documents required by law, in practice, the identity documents of the future spouses as well as those of their respective witnesses are also presented to the civil registrar.

It may happen that the particular situation of one future spouse obliges him or her to submit other documents to the civil registrar. For example, a future spouse previously married will provide either a death certificate of the previous spouse or a court decision definitively confirming their divorce. However, this document is not necessary if their divorced status is mentioned in the margin of their birth certificate. A future military spouse must also provide a certificate of presence in the corps and an authorization to marry dated less than six months and issued by the Minister of Defense or the Chief of Staff. The future spouses who are relatives or allies must enclose the dispensation from the public prosecutor with their application.

As for future foreign spouses who wish to marry in Côte d'Ivoire, they must provide their residence permit (this residence permit requirement no longer applies to ECOWAS nationals since an order issued by the Head of State of Côte d'Ivoire on 8 November 2007) and a certificate of matrimonial capacity issued by their embassy or consul. If the latter document cannot be obtained, it is replaced by a certificate of matrimonial capacity issued by the registrarof the place of celebration.

It has been observed that the requirement of a certificate of matrimonial capacity is the result of practice and is explained by the difficulties of implementing the rules of

[60] See François Komoin, *Civil Marriage in Côte d'Ivoire* (2008), pp. 13-14.

private international law.[61] According to these rules, the assessment of the substantive conditions of the marriage of future foreign spouses is a matter for their respective national laws and not for the law of the place where the marriage is celebrated. This obliges the civil registrar to consult the different national laws of the future foreign spouses in order to verify that the substantive conditions of marriage are respected by these laws. To avoid this potentially difficult task for the civil registrar, in practice, future foreign spouses are required to produce this certificate of matrimonial capacity or, failing that, an attestation of matrimonial capacity.

This marriage file must be submitted to the civil registrar for the celebration of the marriage, as well as the information relating to the choice of the matrimonial regime of the future spouses. The spouses must choose between the community of property regime or the separation of property regime or agree on the rules governing their matrimonial regime.

Formalities specific to wedding day

Although a civil registrar must celebrate marriage, it is not celebrated by just any civil registrar. The one who can do so is the civil registrar of the place where one of the future spouses has his or her domicile or residence. The marriage ceremony must be publicized. The Ivorian legislature has provided for the marriage to be celebrated publicly at the headquarters of the district or civil status center of the domicile or residence of either spouse.[62] This means the marriage is celebrated either at the town hall or the subprefecture. The basic idea is that future spouses marry where they are deemed to be known, although the marriage may, for exceptional reasons, be celebrated in some other place following authorization by the public prosecutor for good reason.[63] Furthermore, in the event of a serious impediment, the public prosecutor may request the civil registrar to go to the home or residence of one of the parties to celebrate the marriage.

[61] Assi-Esso, note 5 above, p. 59.

[62] Article 20(1), Law No. 2019-570 of 26 June 2019 on marriage.

[63] Ibid., Article 20(3).

The public nature of marriage remains a legal requirement, even when the marriage is celebrated at home. The same applies to the solemn nature of marriage, which has been reaffirmed by the legislature through a certain number of rules. These rules include the compulsory presence of the future spouses, so that one cannot marry by proxy in Côte d'Ivoire,[64] and the compulsory and exclusive intervention of the civil registrar under Article 13 of the new law: "marriage is compulsorily celebrated by a civil registrar".

It is generally accepted that the marriage is sealed after the civil registrar makes a declaratory statement to that effect. Subsequently, the marriage certificate is signed by the civil registrar, the parties, and the witnesses. Finally, the spouses are issued with a family record book and a certificate of civil celebration, established in accordance with the regulatory provisions in force.

CONDITIONS FOR NULLITY OF MARRIAGE

A distinction is made in Ivorian law between cases in which a marriage may be annulled and those in which it is necessarily annulled. The cases of optional annulment of marriage envisaged by the legislature highlight the existence of a defect in consent.

Consent

First, consent is vitiated due to a mistake made in respect of the physical or civil identity of the spouse. In order to vitiate consent, the mistake as to identity, that is, civil identity, nationality, or name and family affiliation, must have been decisive, such that without it, the other party would not have consented to the marriage. A mistake as to a party's physical identity or civil identity may relate to that party's civil status. In one case, the Court of First Instance of Abidjan refused the error regarding the wife's age. According to the court, "the alleged error, according to the court, not relating to the complete person of the wife, but only on one of the elements, that of the age which composes her, does not

[64] Ibid., Article 3(1).

constitute a true question of identity".[65] The application was dismissed because the husband could not prove that the error as to age was critical to the consent he gave.[66]

Second, consent is vitiated as a result of violence suffered by the spouse. In any case, whether the consent is vitiated by error or violence, the spouse concerned is no longer entitled, after the spouses have cohabited continuously for six months after the discovery of the defect, to request the annulment of the marriage.[67] It should be noted that in matters of marriage, fraud, which is an error caused by maneuvers, tricks, or silence, has no effect on the validity of the marriage.

Error as to essential qualities

Finally, the law envisages errors of essential qualities. Prior to the 2019 reform of Ivorian marriage law, the legislature did not envisage the nullity of marriage based on essential qualities. However, by virtue of Article 4(3) of the 2019 law relating to marriage: "Consent is not valid either, if the person who gave it was unaware of the physical incapacity of the other party to consummate the marriage or their inability to procreate, though the other party knew". In short, the sanction for the above-mentioned defects in consent is the relative nullity of the marriage. Thus, under Article 30 of the 2019 law on marriage, only the victim can sue, and the action for nullity is time-barred after thirty years.

Other grounds of annulment

Furthermore, there are cases in which the marriage is necessarily annulled at the request of the spouses, their parents, any interested party, or the public prosecutor on grounds of legal immaturity or lack of matrimonial age; lack of consent of the spouses; and bigamy.

65 Tribunal de Première Instance d'Abidjan, 7 November 1986.

66 Assi-Esso, note 5 above, p. 262.

67 Article 32 (1), Law No. 2019-570 of 26 June 2019 on marriage.

It remains that in matters of bigamy, an action for the nullity of marriage will only be admissible if it is brought against the person who commits bigamy.[68]

By reference to Articles 2 and 5 of the 2019 law on marriage, the marriage of homosexuals and transsexuals is prohibited and, therefore, impossible in Côte d'Ivoire. Also prohibited are marriages celebrated by a person other than the civil registrar and marriages celebrated abroad in breach of the laws of the place of celebration.

Ultimately, a distinction must be made between the conditions for the nullity of a marriage, which concern irregularities in the formation of the marriage, as examined, and the dissolution of a marriage, which will now be examined.

CONDITIONS FOR DISSOLUTION OF MARRIAGE

According to Article 103 of the law on marriage, five conditions are likely to lead to the dissolution of a marriage under Ivorian law. These are: the death of one of the spouses; divorce; the judicially declared absence of one of the spouses; the judicial declaration of death in case of disappearance; and the annulment of the marriage.

Death of one spouse

A spouse's death dissolves the marriage. The surviving spouse may remarry, provided the woman respects the waiting period. However, death leaves certain effects of the marriage intact, such as the name of the widow, who retains the use of her deceased husband's name, according to custom.

[68] Thus, according to the Ivorian Supreme Court, "The law on marriage only has meaning in relation to the spouse who contracts a second marriage and is thus in a situation of bigamy, and that the action for annulment having not been brought against the offending spouse, the Court of Appeal has misinterpreted the text referred to in the plea, which is therefore well-founded, that the contested judgment should be quashed and annulled". Judgment No. 158 of 10 March 2011; *B. Léontine v. H. Béatrice* (AJ 2011) p. 74.

Divorce of spouses

Unlike the dissolution of the matrimonial bond by death, divorce is the break-up of the marriage during the lifetime of the spouses. Therefore, unlike nullity, the causes of which are in principle prior to the celebration of the marriage, the causes of divorce relate to facts after the marriage. Divorce is not a repudiation, which generally results from the unilateral will of the spouse and is not recognized in Ivorian law as a condition for breaking the matrimonial bond. Divorce seriously undermines the stability of the family, which is considered the basic unit of society. Admittedly, the Ivorian legislature opted in 1964 for the concept of "divorce-sanction" to the detriment of "divorce by mutual consent", to ensure the family's stability. However, subsequent reforms will enshrine the two divorce modalities. Divorce-sanction is the divorce requested by a spouse based on the other party's failure to fulfil one or more marital obligations. According to Article 1 of the law on divorce, the causes of divorce-sanction are as follows.

Adultery by one spouse

Adultery is understood as a spouse having sexual relations with a third party during the marriage. Adultery can be proven by any means. However, Ivorian jurisprudence considers that the minutes of the hearing of witnesses produced cannot constitute proof of adultery when the wife denies the facts of adultery.[69] Similarly, according to the jurisprudence,"adultery being defined as the maintenance of extramarital relations, the mere presence of Mrs K. Lydie in the building where her alleged lover lives, even at six o'clock in the morning, is insufficient to establish it".[70] On the other hand, adultery will be established by the mere fact that the husband "has had seven adulterous children, for whom he also produces birth certificates" or by the fact that the husband "maintains a second woman in the marital

[69] Supreme Court, Judicial Chamber, Judgment No. 65 of 11 February 2010.

[70] Supreme Court, Judicial Chamber, Judgment No. 352 of 7 June 2001.

home"[71] in the absence of the wife. In doing so, case law has sometimes relied on "statements by the domestic employee living in the marital home"[72] to establish proof of adultery.

Other facts used to prove adultery include excesses, abuse, or serious insults by one spouse towards the other; the criminal conviction of a spouse for acts prejudicial to honor and reputation; and abandonment of the family or the marital home.

As regards divorce by mutual consent, this is, a divorce granted by the judge based on the sole common will of the spouses to end their marriage.

Judicially declared absence

In addition to the death of one spouse or their divorce, "the judicially declared absence of one of the spouses" may constitute a cause for dissolution of the marriage. According to the provisions of Ivorian law relating to civil status,[73] when a spouse has disappeared in Côte d'Ivoire or outside Côte d'Ivoire and has ceased to appear under life-threatening circumstances and their body has not been found within one year, the death of such a spouse may be judicially declared at the request of the public prosecutor or the interested parties[74]. In such a case, the marriage is dissolved by the judgment declaring the death. However, if the spouse whose death has been declared reappears after the declaratory judgment, the judgment may be annulled.

Judicially declared death in event of spouse's disappearance

In addition, another cause of dissolution of marriage is "death declared by the court in case of disappearance". According to Article 70 of the 2019 Civil Status Act, a spouse who has ceased to appear at his or her domicile or residence

71 Supreme Court, Judicial Chamber, Judgment No. 596 of 13 November 2003.

72 Supreme Court, Judicial Chamber, Judgment No. 361 of 15 June 2000.

73 Article 64, Law on civil status 2019.

74 Ibid.

without being heard from for ten years may be judicially declared dead, and such a presumption is deemed to have occurred on the day the decision was handed down. In any event, a marriage which has ended with the declaration of death, after ten years without news of the spouse, remains final.

SOME RECOMMENDATIONS

Legal pluralism expressed in terms of the State attempt to accommodate the customs and practices of different ethnic groups or regions of the State is alien to the Ivorian State. Ivorian law has always been concerned with the formal equality of persons before the law. From 1964 to 2019, the date of the last legislative reform relating to marriage, Cote d'Ivoire legally recognizes only the civil marriage. Thus, the Ivorian legal system does not accept other forms of partnerships generally accepted by society as valid.

Careful observation of the Ivorian legal system shows that Ivorian law is still sensitive to local matrimonial customs. This can be seen in the extent to which Ivorian courts adjudicate disputes arising from de facto unions.

It is recommended that the prohibition against polygamous marriages since independence be revisited. The Ivorian State could also integrate the celebration of marriage in its customary, religious, and civil forms into a single ceremony. This simplification of the celebration of monogamous marriages would help couples save money so that they do not have to marry multiple times.

In the celebration of a marriage in civil form, it appears that only the consent of the spouses remains decisive. The Ivorian legislature appears to have ruled out forced marriages, in which the young girl has not consented. However, marriages in Africa are not exclusive unions of the spouses; the adhesion of the families is indispensable. Although the consent of the parents of the spouses should not affect the validity of a marriage, such consent is desirable in that it signifies the approval of the family. It is appropriate to provide for such consent.

The Ivorian State should remove gender-based restrictions on marriage, particularly regarding the waiting period imposed on women, as modern medical developments can now achieve the same purpose served by the waiting period.

The fate of same-sex unions is only implicitly addressed by Ivorian marriage law. According to Article 1 of the 2019 law, marriage is the union of a man and a woman, celebrated by the civil registrar. It follows that same-sex unions do not fall within the scope of legal marriage under Ivorian law. Such unions do not even appear to qualify as de facto unions, since de facto unions, according to Ivorian jurisprudence, require heterosexuality. From this point of view, has the Ivorian legislature left it to case law to provide an answer to the fate of homosexual unions? In any case, explicit guidelines should be provided on this matter.

Finally, though "engagement" as a term is often referred to by both the legislature and the courts, it is not a term legally regulated by Ivorian law. This raises uncertainties: what is an engagement? What is its legal nature and status within the legal regime? These are all questions that the legislature should have clarified.

CONCLUSION

At the outset, the determination of the family model promoted by the reform of Ivorian marriage law held our attention, followed by a consideration of the evolution of Cote d'Ivoire family law. A general observation is made between 1964 and 2023: the evolution of morals has not affected Ivorian civil family law because the conditions for contracting a marriage have not fundamentally changed. The only marriage legally recognized in Côte d'Ivoire is a monogamous marriage celebrated in civil form. Nevertheless, customary marriages are celebrated though they are regarded as concubinage. Ultimately, the Ivorian State has not adopted legal pluralism in marriage law. A single form of marriage has been imposed throughout the country for almost sixty years. An attempt has been made over the years to offer greater legal protection to married women. While this is commendable, the State should consider legalizing other unions that reflect the Ivorian people's lived realities.

Index of Names

www.ingramcontent.com/pod-product-compliance
Lightning Source LLC
LaVergne TN
LVHW091342101126
852199LV00002B/33
* 9 7 8 1 6 1 6 1 9 6 8 4 4 *